HANDBOOK OF WORLD PHILOSOPHY

HANDBOOK OF WORLD PHILOSOPHY

Contemporary Developments Since 1945

Edited by John R. Burr

GREENWOOD PRESS
WESTPORT, CONNECTICUT

Library of Congress Cataloging in Publication Data
Main entry under title:

Handbook of world philosophy.

    Bibliography: p.
    Includes indexes.
    1. Philosophy, Modern—20th century—Addresses,
essays, lectures. I. Burr, John Roy, 1933-
B804. A1H36   190'.904   80-539
ISBN 0-313-22381-5 (lib. bdg.)

Library of Congress Catalog Card Number: 80-539
ISBN: 0-313-22381-5

First published in 1980

Greenwood Press
A division of Congressional Information Service, Inc.
88 Post Road West, Westport, Connecticut 06881

Printed in the United States of America

10 9 8 7 6 5 4 3 2 1

Contents

Preface

This book represents a beginning rather than a summation; as such, it is exploratory, not definitive. Anyone even vaguely aware of the complexity of the subject matter will be realistic enough to expect only what is possible now. As editor, I feel this work will be a success if it casts into intelligible form what appears to us to be a bewildering profusion of ideas. Accordingly, this work seeks to point beyond itself to further paths of exploration and to guide the reader along these paths.

It is my hope that this book will do more than merely enable the reader to move on from section to section with unflagging interest. I intend it to serve as a kind of compass by means of which those consulting it can get and keep their bearings in a subject matter that opens out indefinitely in all directions.

Now there remain only happy tasks. Here I want to express my appreciation to the distinguished contributors and translators who have so skillfully fashioned the parts of this compass. Their forbearance in the face of unforeseen, yet unavoidable, delays (whether illness, postal strikes, death, natural disasters, revolution, or the harsh vagaries of international politics) has been admirable and sustaining. The book has benefited greatly from their suggestions. I regret that limitations of space and time and the rigorous requirements of stylistic consistency have prevented me from implementing all of them.

I wish to express my gratitude to Marilyn Brownstein of Greenwood Press for her inexhaustible patience, wise advice, and practical assistance.

Nathalie Moore, secretary of the University of Wisconsin-Oshkosh Department of Philosophy, assisted by Steve Grinnell, Virginia Marcoe, Alice Persons, Darlene Schliewe, and Sally Wilke, carried out what must have seemed to them the unending task of typing the manuscript and its revisions. The personnel of the University of Wisconsin-Oshkosh Library provided invaluable help in verifying bibliographic references to works published in so many different parts of the world.

My wife, Marjorie Bakirakis Burr, a mathematician by training and a meticulous individual by nature, relentlessly scrutinized the typescript for typographical errors and consistency of format.

Having labored on this book so long, I more than anyone else realize how short this volume falls of perfection. What virtues it possesses are due to so many; its defects are those of the editor alone.

J.R.B.

Introduction

That portion of the great, worldwide public that is not only literate but also interested in abstract ideas holds two inconsistent views of the character of contemporary philosophy. It sees philosophy today as senescent and as renascent.

The alleged dying of contemporary philosophy could be symbolized by an incident briefly reported in the press in October 1976. "Plato's tree," a fifteen-foot olive tree under which the son of Apollo is said to have taught, judged by scientists to be 3,000 years old and standing alongside the "Sacred Way" highway between Athens and the port of Piraeus, was hit by a bus, completely uprooted, and split into four parts. Portions of the tree were replanted in the original location and surrounded by a protective steel fence in an effort to save it. "Plato's tree" stands for contemporary philosophy, and the destructive bus represents our industrial, technological society relentlessly smashing the remnants of the past. Attempts to preserve and revive any still remaining bits and pieces of what was planted long ago and cultivated up to the present are diligently carried out. Yet, this restoration seems more commemorative than resuscitative.

Opposed to this pessimistic view is the optimistic conviction that contemporary philosophy is in revival, that the period from 1945 to the present has been one of assimilation and incubation of some new broader and more complex synthesis. In a late 1967 interview, the physicist Gerald Holton spoke encouragingly.

It seems to me that philosophy may be now in a position similar to that of physics in the 1920's when quantum mechanics were emerging—full of interesting things, and ready for a very large synthetic advance. Now that logic, linguistic analysis, philosophy of science, aesthetic criticism, cognitive psychology, the new theology and other modern fields have each of them made some impact on more classical styles of philosophy, the ground has been prepared for a more interesting synthesis. I speak here only as an outsider myself, but I do feel that philosophy now may be one of the most exciting of all subjects. You catch that feeling from those who want to help to create the revolution, to help sweep out old styles. Perhaps they are wrong; but such is what young people ought to be in favor of, to be in there fighting their own new battles.[1]

Those who remember with some dismay the attempts of pious physicists to reconcile religion and science may look with a dubious eye on any likening of philosophy to physics by a genial physicist who appears to be a kind of fan of philosophers. Still, not only the pessimistic but also the optimistic lay judgments echo in contemporary philosophy with its calls for "reconstruction in philosophy,'' its criticisms of philosophers for wasting their time on pseudoproblems of their own unintentional creation, its summonses to philosophers to return to the search for Being from which they have strayed for over a thousand years, its proclamations of a "revolution" in philosophy that will, if not solve all the problems, at least reveal them in their true lineaments. None of this is unfamiliar to the philosophical historian of philosophy who discerns in the moving shadows of the spreading and intertwining branches of "Plato's tree" that ever-recurring pattern or "Idea" of struggle, testing, *agon,* and new conception to which the intellectual life of mankind approximates to one degree or another again and again. It is a classic story that is old yet always new, familiar yet ever original.

Today we suffer from no poverty of generalizations. What is needed is a more detailed and comprehensive knowledge of facts on which to base our generalizations. We need to know more, much more of the "form and pressure" of contemporary philosophizing on a world scale. What actually have been the recent courses of philosophy internationally?

The general aim of this book is an empirical one: it is to progress beyond easy generalizations and oversimplified labels to particular philosophic tendencies and cross-currents, to individual philosophers and the distinctive styles and content of their philosophizing. In summary, the comprehensive object of this book is to provide an internationally representative sample since 1945 of the characters, directions, wealth, and varieties of the reflections and activities called "philosophic" as described, interpreted, and evaluated by philosophers particularly knowledgeable about the region or country being discussed; to exhibit the increasingly international development of philosophy; and to point to future possibilities.

Obviously, an encyclopedia of many volumes could be devoted to the subject of this book. Hence, in organizing materials for this book and in selecting countries or regions and authors, the emphasis has been on achieving the most internationally representative sample possible. The limitations of a single volume of finite length prevent the inclusion of every country or region and the discussion, and even notice, of every philosopher professionally active since 1945. Omission from this book does not mean a philosopher or area is unworthy of attention and consideration. The editor left to each contributor the decision as to what to include from 1945 to the present. Since no philosopher any longer claims omniscience or exhaustive philosophic interests and universal sympathies, other authors well might have reached different conclusions as to what to include and what to exclude. Whether or not their decisions would have been better than those of the present authors must be left to debate since "better" in the sense of "more philosophically important" is a judgment influenced by one's philosophical persuasion and a judgment which may change in the course of time. Anyone expecting complete agreement on what is more philosophically important by a phenomenologist, linguistic empiricist, and a Vedantist would be naive.

Universal agreement is also made impossible by the fact that foreign philosophical influences exert a considerable effect on the philosophical development of various countries and regions, although those influences are scarcely the same for every country and region. Professor L. Jonathan Cohen of Great Britain sees the emergence of "a kind of continuum of North Atlantic philosophical culture"; no one makes a similar claim concerning the relation of the European continent to the United States. Anglophone Canadian philosophy differs markedly in its assessment of philosophic significance from that of Francophone Canadian philosophy. The influence of continental European philosophy clearly dominates in Latin America. Native language and the cultural traditions bound up with it play a major role in determining which foreign philosophical influences predominate in a country. Colonialism continues to affect the philosophic complexion of various countries and regions, e.g., the weight carried by Victorian English philosophy in India, the impact of Cartesian philosophy and Comtean positivism in Persia, and the authority of English and French philosophy in Egypt. The major foreign philosophic influence on a country can change relatively rapidly; Sweden has become "Anglo-Americanized" only in the last fifty years. The communists' assumption of power in various countries after World War II has brought with it the doctrine that philosophy's chief task is to serve socialist society. Communist control of the government, however, is not always necessary for this doctrine to be applied. Today in Denmark, for example, as the result of certain legal changes, universities and philosophy departments are reported to be dominated by those who hold that Karl Marx offers the ultimate truth.

Yet, no matter how powerful and prolonged foreign philosophical influences may be (and perhaps because of them), every country resists total intellectual domination from outside and remains unshakably convinced it can make a unique, continuing contribution deeply rooted in its life and history to the character and development of philosophy generally. The enterprise of philosophy is considered to be, not wholly, perhaps, but, at least partly, ineradicably indigenous. Contact with foreign philosophies may be welcomed and even actively sought out by a country. Yet, the motive never seems to be one of simply adopting some exotic philosophy lock, stock, and barrel so much as finding worthy opponents to refute or, at best, enriching and strengthening one's native philosophizing. The unambiguous implication in all of this is that philosophy is not, and should not be, the same everywhere.

Deciding what is "more philosophically important" is further complicated by the immense proliferation since the end of World War II in the number of professional philosophers, departments of philosophy, schools of philosophy, books of philosophy, journals of philosophy, philosophical associations, and philosophical congresses and other meetings for professional purposes. The essays in this book call attention to this rapid expansion. One consequence of this philosophic boom is that no one philosopher or even trio of philosophers can reasonably be expected to possess an exhaustive knowledge of every development and turn of dialectic in their own country over the last thirty-five years—any more than they can be expected to have read and digested every book and every journal article in every field of philosophy, attended every conference, and heard every paper. The growth in philosophy and philosophical specialization has been accompanied by a reciprocal growth in philosophic modesty.

Indeed, one problem for the editor was to persuade some of the contributors to this volume to shed their excessive modesty over their having to write at least partially autobiographical essays. They have been intimately and extensively involved in the recent philosophical affairs about which they are writing, as a result of which the "objectivity" presumably possessed by the outsider is lost. This loss may well be more than compensated for by the supple, though detailed, understanding of the active participant. Every contributor was left free to discuss his or her own ideas and to criticize those of others. Honesty and frankness are preferable to an anonymous blandness. The final decision as to what to include and exclude from their essays, the style of composition to be employed, and the degree of emphasis to be given to the various aspects of the subjects treated was left to the contributors. The decision as to whether to cover all of the familiar divisions of philosophy such as metaphysics, epistemology, ethics, logic, philosophy of science, aesthetics, philosophy of religion, and history of philosophy, or only some of them was also left to the discretion of the contributors.

For the purposes of this book, "contemporary" refers to the period stretching from 1945 to the present. Why 1945? That year, of course, marks the end of World War II. That struggle does not have the same meaning for all countries and regions because it did not affect them all in the same way. To some, World War II meant devastation, occupation, the torture and slaughter of relatives, friends, and professional colleagues. The war differed radically from the conventional military conflict not only in geographical extent and amount of death and destruction but also in that it was waged consciously and deliberately by all combatants as a culture war in which one way of life fought for the eradication of its opponents' way and the latter's replacement by its own. In a full-blown culture war, intellectuals, teachers, and scholars become instant fighters, for they advance, preserve, and transmit their culture. Therefore, they are marked by their enemies for unemployment or reeducation, or even physical extermination.

To others, World War II meant adventure, the extension of one's own empire as old ones disintegrated, the possibility of freedom from colonial oppression, a new division of the global power and pelf, or some confused struggle not one's own and sedulously to be avoided. Nevertheless, beyond these different meanings, World War II was generally accompanied by a temporary caesura in the development of world philosophy. Major energy had to be devoted to fighting, to survival, to making propaganda, or at least to maintaining neutrality rather than to increasing philosophic progress. This break was followed by three benefits: (1) greater perspective on the prewar past; (2) release from cultural isolation imposed by wartime conditions; and (3) increased energy and resources devoted to philosophic activity compared to that utilized in the prewar period.

The interruption of World War II loosened the grip of prewar interests and controversies on the minds of many philosophers, thus freeing them to direct their attention to new philosophic problems and fresh formulations of old problems. Much could simply be dismissed as out of date, as irrelevant because it belonged to a past era now gone forever. The philosophic decks had been cleared for action, so to speak. This did not mean that prewar philosophizing was to be totally forgotten or rejected. Rather, it could now be seen more clearly and dispassionately in its true dimensions, undistorted by partisan loyalties. In 1945 and in the years immediately following, it was easier to admit having been mistaken in one's prewar views. For one thing, one could be sure of having lots of company. For another, although immediate conservative attempts were made to blame the entire catastrophe into which civilization had fallen on a few war criminals, the uneasy feeling that something fundamental was wrong remained and grew in the postwar period, to erupt in the 1960s. Socrates' daimon spoke to him only when he was about to do something wrong. Nothing seems to stimulate philosophic activity more than a sense that something is seriously out of joint in one's conceptual structure. Thus, the period after 1945 has proved to be not an absolute break with the past but rather a sober reassessment of it. After 1945, not a few philosophers who had gained professional prominence prior to World War II sharply criticized their earlier views and struck out in new directions. They wrote critical rather than purely laudatory studies of earlier philosophers who once had been major influences on their own philosophizing. Some even undertook thoroughgoing critiques of their entire philosophic inheritance.

Wartime isolation meant a separation not only from one's recent past but also from philosophic activity elsewhere in the world. The end of World War II released an unprecedented effort to make contact with philosophizing in other parts of the world as well as to reestablish connections with prewar philosophizing in one's own country or region. Translations increased; international philosophic congresses multiplied. Leading philosophers traveled about the world and engaged in discussions with their counterparts. The cold war may have temporarily slowed this process of internationalization, but it did not halt it.

Philosophic activity and production expanded beyond anything known in prewar days. The faculties of existing departments of philosophy burgeoned, and curricula expanded and diversified. New departments of philosophy were founded at existing institutions. Of particular significance is the fact that many new institutions of higher education were established around the world. Correspondingly, the number of philosophical books, journals, and meetings bulged. Some philosophers, fondly recalling a past that had seemed on a smaller scale, more leisurely, and more intimate, spoke acerbically of philosophic "inflation." Whatever the ultimate judgment as to the true value of this growth in philosophic activity and production may turn out to be, there can be no denying that governments and private individuals invested heavily in the development of philosophy after 1945, in terms of both human resources and money. What returns were expected on this investment by the investors remains less clear. To some extent, of course, the growth of philosophy was simply a byproduct of the overall expansion of academe. Nevertheless, no departments of phrenology were established. Philosophy was no longer the queen of the intellectual realm, but neither had she been abandoned. Doubtless, some investors wanted philosophical bodyguards for their cultural souls.

Marxism-Leninism has always attached great importance to philosophy. Could opponents seeking to refute Marxism-Leninism value philosophy any less? A careful reading of the essays in this volume shows that it would be a gross misrepresentation to impugn all postwar support of philosophy as dishonest, self-serving, and cynical. The conviction that the advancement of civilization in the honorific sense of the refinement of knowledge, manners, and taste necessitates the cultivation of philosophy pervades these essays, even though it may be tacitly assumed rather than expressly stated. What is explicitly asserted in essay after essay is that each country or region is making a unique contribution to the future progress of philosophy, regardless of the nature of past contributions. Perhaps this claim applies most emphatically to those countries and regions in which the professional, academic development of philosophy is in an early stage. While the postwar burst of philosophic activity and production initially meant many more teaching positions in philosophy, these essays do not view the enterprise of philosophy merely as a job, a career among others, but as an activity as natural and necessary as breathing.

If philosophy really had become senescent after 1945, it was not petering out but going out in style. Indeed, if there is a problem about the present and future existence of philosophy, that problem is not one of too little philosophy but one of too rich a philosophic diet. Descent through sweeping generalizations and oversimplified labels to a clearer view of the detailed terrain below provided by the essays in this book reveals an immense wealth and variety. The danger for any inquirer into the state of world philosophy today is not the possibility of intellectual starvation but rather of intellectual indigestion. The appropriate tactic today is not to stimulate more philosophizing everywhere but to avoid bewilderment by all the philosophizing everywhere. The initial problem for the investigator of contemporary world philosophy is to escape being overwhelmed by its wealth and variety as Faust was by the vision of the cataract of the totality of human experience. Complaints about a dearth of contemporary philosophizing are confessions of provincialism. This book attempts to resolve this initial problem of the investigator, not by telling everything anyone conceivably would want to know about contemporary philosophy (which would be impossible in a single volume) but by giving a sense of the individuality of the trees and a grasp of the configuration of the forest of contemporary world philosophy which has grown up around "Plato's tree." The essays and the select bibliographies provide the coordinates which will enable each inquirer to cut his own path.

An examination of the essays in this book reveals certain common and particularly salient themes or currents. Contemporary world philosophy is characterized by a pronounced devotion to localism and a desire for universal sophistication on several levels. The term "localism" is used instead of "provincialism" in order to avoid any suggestion of the crude, the ignorant, or a lack of exposure to cultural and intellectual activities. These essays reject clannish devotion to and promotion of any particular locality, country, region, culture, philosophic movement, or field of philosophy. Elaborate sophistication is quite possible within a very limited compass and is consequently compatible with localism, though incompatible with provincialism. The term "cosmopolitan" has been avoided because it suggests rootlessness. By "sophistication" is meant a character not only sensitive to but also actively seeking contact with all ideas, tastes, or ways of life everywhere in the world. George Santayana's dictum crisply captures the essence of this truly internationalized sophistication: "A man's feet must be planted in his country, but his eyes should survey the world." It was what was best in the best of the ancient Sophists. It is an analogue, not of absolute skepticism, but of that scientific skepticism which would have us hold all beliefs tentatively, to test them diligently and repeatedly, and yet be able to act on them resolutely.

The contemporary problem of consistently combining a receptivity to extra-local philosophic doctrines and methods with a loyalty to local philosophic doctrines and methods in such a way as to avoid an unstable eclecticism recurs in essay after essay. It marks the United States, Japan, Korea, and West Germany as well as the Islamic, Marxist-Leninist, and African nations. We are told that since 1945 American philosophy has been instinct with "openness, pluralism, and change." According to Andrew J. Reck, traditional American philosophic tendencies "have been transformed," while transplanted foreign philosophical tendencies "have flourished, with differing measures of yield, on American soil." The Japanese equivalent for the Western term "philosophy" *(Tetsugaku)* was coined as recently as 1874. The one hundred-year history of philosophy in this sense in Japan is described as a period of efforts to master the tradition of European philosophy without becoming European in mind but remaining Japanese in philosophy as an expression of *wakon* (Japanese mind). Korean thought, as Min-Hong Choi notes, has been stimulated by "conflict between native Korean conservative ideas and the very different, progressive ideas introduced from the West," with the result that "today Korean philosophy has a new value system, a new view of truth and the world." Scholars have been reexamining Korea's past "in an effort to find a truly Korean, and at the same time, flexible, developing mode of thinking." Since 1945, West Germany has passed through several stages, according to Hans M. Baumgartner, including a renewal of relations with the philosophies of the 1920s and older traditions, an internationalization of philosophical research, and a "confrontation between analytic-scientistic and traditional philosophy," and is now undergoing the emergence of a period of "critical co-existence" and the exploration of new possibilities. In nearly all Islamic countries, Seyyed H. Nasr finds that "a revival of interest in all aspects of the Islamic tradition" has occurred along with a struggle against an intellectual and cultural domination by foreign philosophies ranging from positivism to Marxism. Most recently and for the future, according to Nasr, the "most notable feature of philosophical activity in the Islamic world" is the emergence of "a few Muslim intellectuals who are at once profoundly Islamic and possess a truly intellectual perspective and who are seeking to provide an Islamic answer for the challenges posed by modern philosophy and science." A detailed, thorough Marxist critique of non-Marxist philosophies steadily supplants the old tactic of lumping together all of the latter as "idealisms" and summarily rejecting them. The contribution of Romanian philosophy includes, as Alexandru Tānase and Octavian Cheṭan emphasize, "a comprehensive approach to non-Marxist philosophy today, receptivity to all new trends and problems, openness to the assimilation of valuable contributions, replacement of simplistic and vulgarizing name-calling by serious, well-founded criticism" as unmistakably characterizing the history of the philosophical thought of that country. While it is true that Western-style philosophy is taught at African universities, it is also the case that serious efforts are being made to show the relevance of indigenous world-views and myths for philosophy. Anna-Louize Conradie, the author of the essay on Africa, approvingly states that "Western philosophy has given birth to a type of philosophizing which is no longer specifically Western but global in the true sense of the term."

A decline of localism in another sense has taken place within countries and regions. Contemporary philosophizing has been carried on largely by individuals on university and college faculties. Until after 1945, the number of these institutions in any country or region remained small, and the most influential ones tended to be concentrated in the larger cities and areas of greatest population density. Furthermore, access to these institutions stayed limited to a very small minority of the population. This has been changing since 1945; more and more universities and colleges have been founded in regions which earlier had none. Larger numbers of the university-age population have begun attending them. What is more, those going on to higher education increasingly come from socioeconomic strata of the population which supplied far fewer or no students before 1945.

Even in supposedly advanced "democratic" countries like the United States, many institutions of higher education, some of which only yesterday were institutions primarily for the training of elementary and secondary school teachers, enroll a steadily growing number of students whose parents never attended a college or university. What effect, if any, this diffusion of higher education through the population will have on philosophizing is not clear at present. The evidence is conflicting. Will these changes mean an increasing emphasis on career and vocational education to the detriment of philosophy which traditionally "bakes no bread"? Or will it mean a growing application of philosophy to other fields, including professional and management ones? Or will it mean an immense increase in philosophic criticism directed at throwing off traditional beliefs, values, and customs still gripping the previous nonuniversity-educated population? Will it bring about a concentration on ethics and social and political philosophy, on the application of philosophy to daily life? Will it radicalize philosophy? Or will it exert a powerfully conservative influence, turning philosophy into a rationalization of traditional religious, social, and moral beliefs? Will it mean a simpler, more "democratic" sort of philosophizing that can be understood and carried on by people without vast learning in the sciences, humanities, and mathematics? Or will it mean an even more refined and learned philosophizing in defense against populist pressures? Will philosophy in the schools be forced into, in effect, recapitulating the history of philosophy from the pre-Socratics to Aristotle or, say, from the Vedas to Shankara? Will it mean intellectual revolution, evolution, or stagnation? To some extent, it will doubtless mean all of these things, and, perhaps, something quite unimaginable at present. In any event, the ingredients now exist for an intellectually potent, even explosive, mixture.

At present, a lessening of localism also may be seen in the fact that no single, special field of philosophy monopolizes the attention of contemporary world philosophy. Of course, in the skeptical ambience of contemporary world philosophizing, the problem of the nature of proof looms large. However, problems in metaphysics, ethics, aesthetics, philosophy of history, ontology, and other specializations interest able thinkers. As the result of historic circumstance, local philosophic development, the presence of some distinguished philosopher, the reign of an official philosophy, or subtle undercurrents of national temperament, a particular set of problems may absorb philosophic energies in one region and be ignored in a neighboring territory. Yet, pluralism rules the world stage. Even in one country or region, the dominance of one sort of problem seems temporary, almost evanescent, destined to change abruptly at any time. Contemporary world philosophy is much like a conglomerate army always on maneuvers. There is a curious fluidity about everything. Once sharply drawn lines blur and become indistinct and then rapidly reform in new configurations.

Philosophic fervor and partisanship have subsided markedly and have been replaced with a kind of enlightened matter of factness, an empirical particularity. The philosophers discussed in the following essays do not vanish into some philosophic movement or school but retain a distinctive individuality. Along with this lesser intensity of commitment has gone a greater thoroughness. Anyone now claiming to have solved all of the important philosophic problems would at best be met with a patronizing smile. Philosophic movements such as linguistic analysis, existentialism, Marxism, and phenomenology no longer generate the blanket enthusiasm they once did. Fresher, subtler exploration and evaluation of their philosophic potentialities have replaced a single-minded refutation of opponents. They no longer have to fight for philosophic respectability, having stepped back into familiar niches in the general philosophic background. Many of the most prominent international philosophic figures of the postwar period such as Ludwig Wittgenstein, Martin Heidegger, Bertrand Russell and Jean-Paul Sartre, have died, and others apparently have ceased major philosophic production. Wittgensteinianism and ordinary language philosophy are reported to have died out in Great Britain in the 1960s. Bertrand Russell declared that it was not an altogether pleasant experience to find one's self out of fashion in one's own lifetime. Already Heidegger has been placed in an earlier period extending from the end of World War II to the middle 1950s. Although there are new philosophic movements reported aborning, none as yet has achieved the broad, commanding influence of the earlier ones. No new individual philosophers have moved to the center of the international philosophic stage. The recent is now the old; it continues but inspires less and less.

Pluralism is Janus-faced; its opposite visage is skepticism, a characteristic equally distinctive of contemporary world philosophy. The spirit of philosophy today is a critical one, not a consolatory or contemplative one. To call a philosopher a special pleader or an apologist would be to insult him. Dogmatism is the cardinal philosophic sin. Accepted premises, however fundamental, should be scrutinized critically. Our categorical maps should be redrawn in unfamiliar and more intriguing and fruitful ways. There is a pervasive conviction that we don't know enough about nature, about man, about society, about anything. Indeed, we don't know *how* to come to know all we need to know and would like to know. The degree of skepticism varies from country to country, from region to region, but nowhere is it completely absent. If there is an official philosophy, then philosophers attempt to interpret the spirit rather than merely the outward letter of that philosophy. If a particular philosophy is held to be sounder than all others, it is emphatically deemed insufficient simply to assert its superiority. Any such assertion must be supported—negatively by an argued refutation of opposing views, and positively by an argued case that the claim is confirmed by a preponderance of the evidence. Abusive rhetoric no longer suffices. Ultimate truth may be said to be in the keeping of some particular philosophy or philosopher. Yet, in the next breath it is said that we also do not fully understand that philosophy or philosopher. Skepticism also has a toehold in subjects that are only partially covered or not treated at all by the official philosophy. It must not be forgotten that official philosophies that not only survive but also retain their authority for any length of time are never completely rigid. They make a place for change and may include a "superstructure" where alteration may take place, even though it may be described as merely a realm of conjecture, of mere opinion, of pseudoproblems.

On the basis of the essays in this book, the form of skepticism which contemporary world philosophy would like to think it embodies is not absolute skepticism but a skepticism of autonomy. Perhaps this is in part due to a lingering memory of the murderous absolutes culminating in the catastrophe of World War II, as well as to growing scientific knowledge and the huge variety of ideas, beliefs, and customs percolating throughout the world. Contemporary world philosophy does not seriously doubt certain propositions—for example, the advance of philosophy is essential to the advance of human civilization; one's own country or region has a unique, valuable contribution to make to the progress of philosophy; it is better to know than not to know; critical reflection is preferable to unthinking faith; some philosophic problems are real; and some truth can be known. The skepticism of autonomy is the rejection of merely a "handmaiden," branch, or logical corollary status for philosophy. Philosophy is viewed as a separate discipline in its own right and worth pursuing for its own sake. Philosophy has its own distinctive problems and methods of analysis. It is a discipline. It is honest inquiry, not subservient rationalization. Philosophy is not the appanage of psychology, advanced physics, or mathematical logic any more than it is of theology. A philosopher may advocate some social policy or political ideology, but, if his philosophic conscience is not to be violated, such an advocacy must not ignore relevant philosophic analyses proffered by supporters and critics. Any and all doctrines may and perhaps should be brought to philosophic judgment. The old individualistic ideal of philosophy as a total vocation, rather than an avocation or a "job" done only in the classroom or while seated at the office desk, remains dominant in contemporary world philosophy. Philosophers still lose their jobs or go into exile or go into prison or go to their deaths rather than cease following the argument wherever it may lead. They are not yet mere functionaries; they are not yet wholly ignored by the police.

Yet, in the midst of this immense philosophic activity, production, and dedication, there is a sense of a pause, a lull, an expectant waiting. Philosophical movements such as phenomenology, existentialism, linguistic empiricism, and Marxism have lost their earlier charisma. They are now philosophic resources to be used rather than causes to be championed. There are and probably will continue to be highly skilled philosophers elaborating ever more sophisticated variations on these older themes and thereby gradually transforming them into something scarcely recognizable to their originators. However, there is a widespread conviction that the important implications of these and other philosophic movements have been worked out and now we must move on to something different. All known philosophic alternatives seem to become less and less what William James called "living options." At the moment, contemporary world philosophy seems transfixed. Nijinsky allegedly explained his magnificent leaps by saying that one simply leaps into the air and pauses a moment. Contemporary world philosophy has leaped but so far has not come down firmly anywhere. Yet, everywhere there is an expectancy tinged with apprehension that the descent is about to begin. Nijinsky went insane. Pluralism could degenerate into chaos. Outside the study window today mobs scream in the streets. Rifle shots pop in the distance. A tang of blood hangs in the air. The Iranian revolution should not be viewed as a unique, isolated affair, as a mere "palace revolution" resulting in the change of a few political leaders with everything else remaining as it was. The glare of publicity and diplomatic bustle this dramatic event has produced for domestic and international political and economic reasons, particularly in the United States, should not blind us to the deeper truth this revolution reveals. Such phrases as "pluralistic world" and "world order" are euphemisms masking an immense variety of cultures, traditions, philosophies, religions, and political and economic systems not only different from one another but often implacably hostile to one another and driven by a fierce passion for triumph over all opponents. The division of the spoils made after World War II by the victors has held up remarkably well, certainly far better than the one reached at Versailles after World War I. However, those mindful of human history realize that any division of the spoils, no matter how durable it may seem, can only be temporary. But how temporary? This question haunts the world and compels it to catch its breath at each new incident.

Is contemporary world philosophy now in a period of stability or a period of stagnation fringed with disintegration? On the whole, the essays in this book espouse the optimistic view that the period since 1945 has been one of recovery followed by a prolonged preparation, a slow but steady gathering of strength, a progressive organization of new forces that eventually will transform the international philosophic landscape. No detailed predictions as to what might emerge in the future are hazarded in these essays. There are references to ''new tendencies,'' ''new possibilities,'' ''universal philosophy,'' ''global philosophy.'' The essays suggest that important changes are imminent and that contemporary world philosophy will not remain transfixed for long in its current state. Where will contemporary world philosophy alight, say, a decade from now? Will it come down decisively anywhere at all, at any single place, or at many different places at the same time? Will there emerge a world philosophy and philosophizing distinguishable from the more localized past and present forms? Will the adjectives ''British'' or ''Japanese'' before ''philosophy'' become just as incidental as they now are when modifying ''physics?''

The intent of the essays in this book is description, not prognostication. As this introduction has emphasized, although significant progress in creating a worldwide grasp of the detailed condition of contemporary world philosophy has been achieved since 1945, much more empirical work, of which this book is a part, needs to be done. To make precise predictions now would be premature because they would be based on insufficient evidence, to say nothing of the controversy about the existence of any laws of cultural development. Yet, it is difficult to withstand the temptation to speculate on the future on the basis of a realistic assessment of the present. If anywhere, an introduction would seem to be the most excusable place to succumb to that temptation. Since it does not have to maintain the full dignity and gravity incumbent on the main body of a work, an introduction may be more rash. Besides, the editor can always be blamed when the predictions prove erroneous.

As the essays make clear, at present there is no world philosophy in the sense of an agreed-upon set of doctrines, methods of analysis, or even terminology. Nor is there any evidence that such a world philosophy will emerge in the foreseeable future in the absence of a common worldwide language and culture.

Different languages and different cultures will continue to produce different philosophies. Nor is there universal agreement as to the nature of philosophy itself. A number of essays warn against any identification of philosophy in general with Western philosophy. Each country or region feels it has something unique to contribute to philosophy. The rate of the internationalization of philosophy can easily be exaggerated. Karl Popper's *Logik der Forschung* was originally published in Vienna in 1934. An English translation by the author first appeared in 1959, a quarter of a century later. Furthermore, Popper's translation of his own work into English could not guarantee an insightful understanding of it by English-speaking philosophers. The diversity of languages and problems of translation alone present formidable obstacles, to say nothing of obtaining a grasp of philosophic works growing out of an unfamiliar philosophic tradition and general culture.

As indicated earlier, one of the salient characteristics of the development of contemporary world philosophy has been the growth of new departments of philosophy resulting from the founding of new universities and colleges. It is likely that the faculties of these departments will be increasingly staffed with graduates from other home institutions. In the future, fewer and fewer departments of philosophy will presumably have faculties composed of philosophers trained in other countries and cultures. Declining enrollments and tightening budgets in higher education will encourage hiring native philosophers rather than foreigners. Home departments of philosophy will be reluctant to admit their graduates are inferior to those trained at foreign institutions. A philosopher who has received his advanced professional education in Great Britain or on the European continent is likely to be more knowledgeable about British or European philosophical developments than a philosopher totally educated at home. There are and, no doubt, will continue to be exceptions, but here we are concerned with the general pattern. Thus, in the long run the great increase in the number of universities and colleges and departments of philosophy all over the world since 1945 may well retard the development of an enlarged international philosophic consciousness. Overshadowing all is the possibility of profound political, religious, and social changes, now unforeseen, which could transform the international intellectual scene.

In view of these somber possibilities, it would seem that the most realistic ideal prospect would be the gradual growth of a combined local-international philosophy, ineradicably indigenous yet carried on in the light of a full and up-to-date knowledge of and sympathetic, yet critical, understanding of relevant philosophical developments everywhere in the world. Obviously, at present such a combined local-internationalized philosophizing remains more an ideal than a fact. We are now closer to the rude beginning, the earliest stage of the emergence of such a truly world philosophizing. Nonetheless, it is always a solid achievement to recognize who and where we are. This book will have justified its existence if it contributes to that recognition. If the reader of this book comes to realize how much he does not know about contemporary world philosophy, he will have been freed from what Socrates called the worst ignorance.

NOTE

1. "On Science, Scientists, and Education," An interview with Gerald Holton, *Harvard Today,* Autumn 1967, p. 9.

BIBLIOGRAPHICAL NOTE

Bibliographies of philosophy have become so numerous, diverse, and specialized that bibliographies of international philosophical bibliographies are now indispensable instruments for the inquirer. Some recent, widely available guides to international philosophical bibliographies are:

De George, R. T. *A Guide to Philosophical Bibliography and Research* (Englewood Cliffs, N. J.: Prentice-Hall, 1971).

Gerber, W. "Philosophical Bibliographies," in *The Encyclopedia of Philosophy,* VI, ed. P. Edwards (New York: Macmillan, 1967).

Guerry, H. (ed.). *A Bibliography of Philosophical Bibliographies* (Westport, Conn.: Greenwood Press, 1977).

Part I: Western Europe, Australia, and Israel

Denmark

JUSTUS HARTNACK

The year 1945—the year the world saw the end of the war that had threatened to destroy Western civilization—was the year in which the academic spirit again could unfold freely. The threat of being suffocated was over, and the owl of Minerva could begin its flight. In Denmark, however, the end of the war and of the German occupation did not occasion any noticeable or radical change in the philosophic climate. It remained much as it had been before the war.

Having a powerful and influential philosopher occupying a chair at a country's one and only university has both a positive and a negative effect. Its positive effect is the enrichment and growth of the philosophic spirit; the intellectual climate receives a philosophic inspiration. On the negative side are the difficulties in bringing about renewal, i.e., the difficulties in freeing the philosophic spirit from the controlling and dominating philosophic teaching. This was precisely the situation in Denmark. The powerful philosopher was Harald Høffding (1843–1931), and it was his students and disciples who occupied the philosophic chairs in Denmark in 1945—three chairs at Copenhagen University and one chair at the rather new university in Aarhus (established in 1928).

Høffding's philosophy can be characterized as empirical, utilitarian, and positivistic. Its influence was beneficial insofar as it marked a needed break with a dominant Hegelianism. The defects of Høffding's philosophy were his tendency to blur the distinction between a philosophic problem and certain empirical, primarily psychological, problems. Epistemological problems were treated not as purely epistemological problems but as problems of the psychology of knowledge. Likewise, problems within ethics, religion, and metaphysics were treated without distinguishing the philosophic aspects of the problem from the psychological aspects. The result, of course, was that a philosophical examination became open to psychological falsification. The validity of the philosopher's treatment of a problem thus became dependent on psychological research. The final arbiter of philosophy was external to philosophy. Obviously, to view philosophy as being indistinct in its inner nature from one or more of the empirical sciences is to endanger its autonomy. Throughout its history, philosophy has displayed a tendency to let the *salva veritate* test be something distinct from philosophy. After philosophy had liberated itself from theology, it threw itself in the arms of either the empirical or the deductive sciences. In recent times, G. E. Moore elevated common sense to the *salva veritate*. Although it was a step in the right direction of recognizing the full autonomy of philosophy, of philosophy gaining self-consciousness of its own nature, Moore did not do much more than to emphasize common sense as the ultimate basis for justification.

In Denmark, however, until the mid-1950s philosophy was in danger of losing its autonomy to psychology and, to a lesser degree, to advanced physics or mathematical logic. In other words, Danish philosophy could be characterized as an intellectual discipline suffering from schizophrenia. On the one hand, it wanted to maintain itself as an autonomous discipline; on the other hand, it tended to conceive of itself as heteronomous by recognizing its *salva veritate* as something distinct from itself.

The most independent and internationally best known of the postwar Danish philosophers was Jørgen Jørgensen (1894–1969). Nevertheless, Jørgensen is a typical representative of the dual or schizophrenic view of the nature of philosophy. In his writing, both the autonomy and the heteronomy of philosophy are displayed. In his younger years, he published a work on the philosophy of Paul Natorp, a work in which he shared the nonpsychological interpretation of Kant's philosophy with the neo-Kantians. In his later years, however, he accepted a psychological interpretation of Kant.[1] In other words, the necessity and universality Kant claims for his categories hold only for beings that have the same psychological structure as human beings. For angels or Martians the categories may have no validity. Thus interpreted, Kant's epistemology is really not an epistemology but an essay on the psychology of knowledge.

In Jørgensen's well-known three-volume work *A Treatise of Formal Logic,* he revealed an extensive knowledge of and a great insight into modern logic and its philosophic aspects and problems. But again psychology got the last word. In his later writings,[2] he conceived of the necessity of logic and its principles as rooted in the structure of the human mind. If we were structured differently, the law of contradiction might not be a necessity!

Jørgensen began his career as a professor by offering, besides graduate seminars, a one-year introductory course in philosophy published as *Philosophic Lectures.* The course was an introduction, first, to logical-deductive thought and principles, and second, to some of the fundamental problems of physics, biology, and psychology. At the same time, it displayed Jørgensen's acceptance, though not uncritical and dogmatic, of logical positivism. Later, he changed his introductory course to a one-year course in psychology published as *Psykologia paa biologisk grundlag* (''Psychology Based on Biology''). In a sense, this change was a logical one, for with Jørgensen's view of psychology as being basic to philosophy, it follows that psychology (and not philosophy) is the fundamental science. Psychology (and not philosophy) was regarded as the queen of all sciences.

The three other professors who occupied chairs at Copenhagen University and Aarhus University were even more treacherous to philosophy than was Jørgensen. Victor Kuhr (1882–1948) wrote a couple of books on some aspects of psychology, and a book on art *Aesthetisk opleven og runstnerisk skaben* ("Aesthetic Experience and Artistic Creation"). Kuhr's view on the history of philosophy was close to, if not identical with, Høffding's view. Nevertheless, he did write a small book on Heraclitus in which he ignored (what a follower of Høffding was neither expected nor supposed to ignore) the psychological working of the human mind in the opposed views of Heraclitus and Parmenides. Instead, he gave an almost Hegelian description of the dialectical logic connecting concepts such as being, nonbeing, and becoming.

Kuhr's introductory course in philosophy (until recently, all students in Denmark were required to take a two-semester course in philosophy) was very popular, and his lectures were extremely well attended. First-year students always found his lectures interesting and often inspiring. His lectures were so popular and so well attended not so much because of their philosophic content but because of their nonphilosophical aspects. The lectures were on the history of ideas and on the literary and artistic expressions of the different cultural epochs. His graduate seminars were usually on Greek philosophy, a field in which his great knowledge of the Greek language increased the scholarly aspect of the seminars. But in these seminars Kuhr also tended to emphasize the cultural aspects of the Greek mind instead of the logic of arguments and concepts used in, for example, Plato's different dialogues.

The third professor at the University of Cophenhagen was Frithiof Brandt (1892–1968). His book *Thomas Hobbes' Mechanical Concept of Nature* made him famous as a Hobbes scholar; it is almost universally referred to or mentioned in later works on Hobbes. Brandt possessed extensive knowledge and an excellent understanding of the history of philosophy and of ethics. Consequently, the students who attended his seminars received a solid education within these two areas, though the areas covered were somewhat limited. Within the history of philosophy, philosophers such as Spinoza and Kant dominated, if not monopolized, his selection. In ethics, Brandt seldom went beyond Sidgwick and Westermarck. Nevertheless, his great pedagogical abilities made his seminars a rewarding experience to all the participants. Brandt, who wrote only in Danish, was famous for the style of his writings. He is exceeded by few, if any, with respect to the clarity and the aesthetic simplicity of language. Many of his followers had looked forward to a book on either the history of philosophy (or at least some chapters of the history of philosophy) or a book on ethics, but such expectations were unfulfilled. However, besides the above-mentioned book on Hobbes, Brandt did publish a book on Kierkegaard *Den Unge Søren Kierkegaard* ("The Young Kierkegaard"). But since the book was written long before the vogue of existentialism (that is, long before Sartre's *L'Etre et le Néant* and before Heidegger's *Sein und Zeit* was known as a major work), it is not an examination of Kierkegaard as the father of existentialism, nor is it a study of Kierkegaard's relation to modern Protestantism. Rather, it is an examination of Kierkegaard's historical development and, at least partly, a psychological explanation of it. In fact, more Danish theologians than philosophers have expounded on Kiergekaard as a forerunner of existentialism and modern existential-Protestantism.

In his introductory course, Brandt lectured on the history of modern philosophy—unfortunately, not on the book he never wrote but on Høffding's *Kort oversigt over den nyere filosofie historie* ("A Short Survey of the Modern History of Philosophy"). That he used Høffding's book instead of writing his own (a book that would surely have been better than Høffding's none too clearly written book) was the result not of any laziness on Brandt's part but of his devotion to and admiration for Høffding. In his view, no book on the history of philosophy could possibly be better than Høffding's book. For the introductory course, Brandt did write a clear but very short book on logic. It dealt only with the principles of classical logic and contained nothing on symbolic logic. *Principia Mathematica* was totally ignored in Brandt's logic. He also wrote a two-volume work on psychology. This work did not quite satisfy the professional psychologists. It was a sound and clear exposition of what today may be termed classical, though experimental, psychology.

As mentioned above, a book on the history of philosophy and a book on the problems of ethics never appeared. If they had, they would have done more justice to Brandt's talents and knowledge than his work on psychology. But the psychological demon of Danish philosophy destroyed this possibility.

At Aarhus University, Svend Ranulf (1894–1953) specialized in sociology. Consequently, his graduate seminars were more on sociology than on philosophy. A professor of philosophy could offer seminars on sociology instead of philosophy proper, at least in part because of Høffding's positive attitude to August Comte's enthusiasm for sociology, a science he introduced and defined as a description of society. This positive attitude lent a philosophic prestige (a prestige it no longer enjoys) to sociology.

Although Høffding's influence is not directly felt in Denmark today, his spirit has not quite died out, at least not at Copenhagen University. Whereas Kuhr and Brandt cannot be said to have any followers, not to say disciples, Jørgensen has both. As we have seen, despite his interest in and abilities as an epistemologist and a logician, Jørgensen kept alive the psychological demon and thereby prevented philosophy from gaining its autonomy. As a consequence, the new generation at Copenhagen University has not been cured of its schizophrenia. What characterized the philosophic spirit at that university between Jørgensen's retirement in 1964 and 1969 or 1970 is an epistemology which is close to, if not identical with, logical positivism (and therefore a philosophy which is antimetaphysical and submissive, or almost submissive to the empirical and deductive sciences). At the same time, this epistemology accepts psychological concepts as the ultimate epistemological concepts—or, rather, accepts the categories as being psychological concepts.[3]

Svend Ranulf at Aarhus University died in 1953, and in 1954 Justus Hartnack (1912–   ) was appointed his successor. Hartnack had the good fortune to come to Aarhus University after having taught for eight years in the United

States. He therefore came to his new job influenced more by Anglo-American philosophy than by the philosophy he was taught at his alma mater Copenhagen University. At Aarhus University, his introductory course as well as his graduate seminars were in the spirit of conceptual analysis. Russell, Moore, Wittgenstein, Ryle, and others—all of whom, at that time were either unknown in Denmark or at least not studied or taught—and philosophies such as ordinary language philosophy, or Oxford philosophy, which were hitherto unpracticed and unknown, now occupied appropriate places in the curriculum of the philosophy department at Aarhus University. The goal of Hartnack's teaching was to exorcise the psychological demon and to emphasize, actualize, and vitalize the autonomy of philosophy—an autonomy which had been enjoyed as little at Aarhus University as at Copenhagen University. With no little justification, it may be maintained that the goal was reached,[4] but it was reached only at Aarhus University. Hartnack's influence on philosophy at Copenhagen University was more limited among the professors at the university than among its students.

Peter Zinkernagel (1921–   ), an independent and original philosopher, received his Ph.D. (Dr. phil.) from Copenhagen University in 1957. His dissertation, published in Danish, was later (in 1962) published by Routledge and Kegan Paul under the title *Conditions for Description*. In the book (which reveals that its author is influenced much more by Oxford philosophy than by the philosophy prevalent at his alma mater), Zinkernagel attempts to discover the fundamental rules constituting the condition for all descriptions of reality. According to Zinkernagel there are three such rules. Zinkernagel, whose originality and independence as a thinker is undisputed, has never applied for a teaching position at any of Denmark's universities. He rejected an offer from Aarhus University to join the staff of its philosophy department on the ground that he wanted to devote all his time to philosophic research. At present, he is the recipient of a long-term research grant.

Denmark's third university, Odense University, was established in 1964. A young philosopher, David Favrholdt (1931–   ), educated at Copenhagen University, was appointed as its first, and so far, only full professor. Even though Favrholdt was educated at Copenhagen University and took a degree in psychology before his graduate work in philosophy, he has a full understanding of the autonomous nature of philosophy. That he has acquired this understanding is, of course, first of all attributable to his own philosophic abilities—he is probably Denmark's most talented philosopher today. It may also be due to an influence from Aarhus philosophy, from *Philosophia Arhusiensis*. In fact, while a student at Copenhagen University he won first prize (the so-called gold medal) from Aarhus University for an essay on the concept of mind (including, of course, an analysis of G. Ryle's *Concept of Mind*). Shortly before his appointment to the chair at Odense University, he wrote a book (his doctoral dissertation) on Wittgenstein's *Tractatus (An Interpretation and Critique of Wittgenstein's Tractatus)*. The book has been well received all over the world and has made its author an internationally known philosopher. In the preface, Favrholdt states that his interest in Wittgenstein's ideas stemmed from a book on Wittgenstein written by the professor at Aarhus University. In his book, Favrholdt criticizes such central ideas in the *Tractatus* as the thesis of extensionality and the picture theory.

During the latter part of the 1960s, there were signs that philosophy in Denmark was about to be cured of its schizophrenia. More and more, the understanding spread that the *salva veritate* test for a philosophic argument and position was to be found not in another discipline different from philosophy, but in the inherent logic of the relevant concepts. At Aarhus University, Niels Egmont Christensen (1927–   ) received his Ph.D. with a work entitled *On the Nature of Meaning*. The book gives a good summary of the findings of semantic philosophy. Furthermore, it advances and defends the thesis that

the meaning of an expression pertains to the capacity of that expression of being rightly produced when and where, and only when and where, something specific of a non-linguistic kind is present, be it an object, property, relation, situation, or whatever it may be. The abstract entity defined by this capacity is, we maintain, the meaning of at least a large class of expressions and accordingly the "thing" sought by analytic philosophers when raising the general question above (op. cit., p. 14).

What is more, quite a few students have graduated in philosophy from Aarhus University; by and large, they have viewed the nature of philosophy as conceptual analysis. At Odense University, under the direction of Favrholdt, philosophy was taught with the emphasis on analytic philosophy, and at Copenhagen University, an improved way of philosophizing was on its way. This improvement was at least partly due to Zinkernagel who, although he did not have a teaching position, influenced many of the students. Favrholdt, who taught at Copenhagen University before he came to Odense, also helped improve the philosophic atmosphere.

This progress has been seriously jeopardized in recent years. Student unrest in Demark started at Copenhagen University in 1968–1969 and soon spread to the other universities. It finally resulted in the Danish government passing a new law concerning the governing and organization of the universities. The law, which became effective in 1970, essentially states that in all committees, staffs, councils, boards, and the like, student representatives (with voting rights) account for 33⅓ percent of the total. Exempt are the curriculum committees in which student representatives constitute 50 percent of the total. By passing this law, the government thought it would increase the democratic spirit within the universities and thereby create better working conditions and ultimately heighten the standard and worth of higher education.

If the students get one-third of the votes, it would seem that the faculty would get the remaining two-thirds and therefore always be certain of a majority. But this is not the way it has turned out, and for the following reason. According to the law, students who have received their M.A. and have received a university stipend to enable them to continue their studies and to undertake research are regarded as faculty members. Hence, members of the university community, who in terms of age, attitude, views, and interests are like students, can be counted on to vote with the students against the regular faculty. In practice, therefore, this means an increase of student votes and a decrease of faculty votes. An analysis of why it is so will not be given here. Let it suffice to state that within a short time the result has been that the universities and their departments are now dominated by or are in the hands of members of the university community who generally accept the views of the more or less radical left (usually of a revolutionary kind).

Inasmuch as the new spirit has permeated the different philosophy departments, it is endangering the autonomy of philosophy. The tendency among the new generation of philosophers, that is, those who began their philosophy careers under the new law, is to regard the ultimate truth as resting with Karl Marx. At the same time, they have only a slight inclination to undertake an objective study of Marx. One argument usually met with is that there are no such things as objective studies, an argument which, of course, is in danger of defeating itself.

That this situation would create a schism within the universities was unavoidable. Some professors took advantage of a new law which gave them the right to retire (with a reduced pension to be sure) at the age of sixty. Among the philosophers, Justus Hartnack made use of that law and is now occupying a chair at the State University of New York. Other professors who were sixty or slightly older thought they could not afford to retire, and thus they had to remain until the mandatory age for retirement (which in Denmark is seventy). The Danish professors' former great interest in and devotion to teaching, research, and the university they served are now in danger of being lost. On the other hand, a new generation of professors has arisen which is inspired by the truth they feel certain they possess and by the idea of the new order and structure of the world which they believe is the inevitable outcome of the march of time. The alleged truth gives them not only interest in but also enthusiasm for working toward an implementation of the program implied by the truth in which they believe.

The tendency in Denmark to move toward the radical left is especially evident at Roskilde University, Denmark's fourth and newest university, established in 1971. Some newspapers and some members of Parliament described conditions at that university as nothing less than a scandal and a gross misuse of the taxpayers' money. To a considerable extent, the development of conditions at that university, as well as at the other three universities, was indeed conducive to initiating efforts to revise the law concerning the governing and organization of the universities. In all likelihood these efforts will meet with some, though rather limited, success. It will not be a radical revision, for the aim is to take away the worst absurdities. The revision seeks to depoliticize what according to its very nature and idea is nonpolitical, and it may inspire independent research.

The development of Danish philosophy from 1945 to the present may be divided for the purpose of simplification into three periods. During the first period, Danish philosophy had not yet attained self-consciousness, and psychology and advanced physics (quantum mechanics and theory of relativity) were recognized as the ultimate authority. Jørgen Jørgensen's extensive work on psychology *Psyckologia paa biologisk grundlag* ("Psychology Based on Biology"), the *opus major* of Danish philosophy of that period, is written in Danish and has not been translated.

During the second period, Danish philosophy was gaining its self-consciousness and moved from a heteronomous to an autonomous state. A work which expresses (and to a certain degree created) the philosophic climate of the second period is Justus Hartnack's *Filosofiske problemer og filosofiske argumentationes* ("Philosophical Problems and Philosophical Arguments"). The book is written in Danish and has been translated into Swedish and Finnish but not into English. His book *Taenkning og virkelighed* ("Thinking and Reality") has been read by a larger public; it has been translated into English under the title *Philosophical Problems: A Modern Introduction.* Among his other books are the following (all in English): *Wittgenstein and Modern Philosophy* (English edition by Doubleday and New York University Press, 1965), published also in German, Japanese, Italian, and Spanish; *Language and Philosophy; History of Philosophy; Kant's Theory of Knowledge;* and *Kant, An Explanation of His Theory of Knowledge and Moral Philosophy.* Among other works from this period are Favrholdt's *An Interpretation and Critique of Wittgenstein's Tractatus,* Zinkernagel's *Conditions for Description,* and Niels Egmont Christensen's *On the Nature of Meaning.*

The third period, dominated by the influence of Marxism, especially Marx's dictum that for too long philosophers have tried to understand the world instead of trying to change it, has not been very productive. One book from the period worth mentioning, however, is *Videnskabsteorie* ("Theory of Science"), a two-volume work by Uffe Juul Jensen (1944–   ) from Aarhus University. The book views such relations as those between science and ideology, theory and praxis, and sickness, mind, and society from a Marxist-Leninist point of view. (Juul Jensen declares himself a Leninist.) The work is of high scholarly quality and is no doubt the most authoritative Danish examination and defense of a Marxist-Leninist interpretation of science and its role in and dependence on the structure of society. So far, the book is available only in Danish, but there are plans to translate it into other languages.

A division of the time from 1945 to the present into three periods is a simplification, though indeed not a falsification. In all three periods, there have been philosophers who did not fall within the special period or any of the periods. One such person is Johannes Sløk (1916–   ). Sløk, who has his doctorate in theology from Copenhagen University, has written extensively on the history of philosophy, especially Greek philosophy, and on individual philosophers as different as Plato, Nicholas of Cusa, and Kierkegaard. (He is *the* Danish specialist on Kierkegaard.) He is also the author of books on existentialism and on the history of ideas, including a book comparing Kierkegaard and Shakespeare. Before assuming his present chair in the history of ideas at Aarhus University, Sløk occupied a chair as a professor of theology, also at Aarhus University.

Another philosopher who has shown his independence is Alf Ross (1899–   ). Ross, who was a professor of jurisprudence at Copenhagen University until 1969, has achieved international fame through his works on the philosophy of law. He has been influenced by Axel Hägerström, the founder of the Uppsala school of philosophy, by the logical positivists, and by ordinary language philosophy. Although influenced by these different philosophies, he is not a follower, at least not a dogmatic follower, of any of them. Among his latest works are *Directives and Norms* and *Culpability, Responsibility, and Punishment.*

Independent of the eventual change of the law for the organization and governing of the Danish universities—a change which can only be an improvement—are signs that the strong politicization of education at the Danish universities will decrease. The radical left in Denmark, of course, receives impulses and inspiration from corresponding movements in other countries. For example, it is noteworthy that in France intellectuals within the radial left are at present warning and arguing against what they term a vulgarized politicization.[5] Let it also be noted that the so-called Frankfurt school, which to a considerable degree has influenced Danish philosophy in the last eight years, no longer exists as a school. One of its leaders, Jürgen Habermas, has repudiated the views of the once existing school.

Thus there are some reasons why this essay may end on an optimistic note. The alleged myth that philosophy cannot be separated from the political system may one day be seen to be itself a myth. When this happens, the queen of the sciences may regain its proper place in Denmark.

NOTES

1. In a letter to me in the early 1960s Jørgensen told me that he thought Kant could be interpreted only from a psychological point of view.

2. See, for example, his paper "Some Remarks Concerning Languages, Calculuses, and Logic," in *Logic and Languages, Studies Dedicated to Professor Rudolf Carnap on the Occasion of his 70th Birthday,* eds. Y. Bar-Hillel, et al.

3. A famous American philosopher once told me (while visiting me at Aarhus) that in the mid-1960s, when he was reading a paper at Copenhagen University on "Memory," it was almost impossible to have any discussion of the paper. Whereas he was trying to solve some puzzles connected with the logic of the concept of memory, his audience was constantly arguing in terms of the psychological phenomena of memory.

4. Compare R. E. Olson and A. M. Paul (eds.), *Contemporary Philosophy in Scandinavia,* p. 8.

5. Compare, for example, D. Grisoni, F. Chatelet, and M. Foucault (eds.), *Politiques de la Philosophie.*

SELECT BIBLIOGRAPHY

BOOKS AND ARTICLES

Brandt, F. *Den Unge Søren Kierkegaard* ("The Young Kierkegaard") (Copenhagen: Levin and Munksgaard, 1929).

————. *Thomas Hobbes' Mechanical Concept of Nature* (Copenhagen: Levin and Munksgaard, 1928).

Christensen, N. E. *On the Nature of Meaning*, 2d ed. (Copenhagen: Munksgaard, 1965).

Favrholdt, D. *An Interpretation and Critique of Wittgenstein's Tractatus*, 2d ed. (Copenhagen: Munksgaard, 1965).

Grisoni, D., Chatelet, F., and Foucault, M. (eds.). *Politiques de la Philosophie* (Paris: Grasset, 1976).

Hartnack, J. *Filosofiske problemer og filosofiske argumentationer* ("Philosophical Problems and Philosophical Arguments"), 1st ed. (Copenhagen: Gyldendal, 1956).

————. *History of Philosophy* (Atlantic Highlands, N. J.: Humanities Press, 1973).

————. *Kant, An Explanation of His Theory of Knowledge and Moral Philosophy* (Atlantic Highlands, N. J.: Humanities Press, 1974).

————. *Kant's Theory of Knowledge* (New York: Harcourt, Brace, and World, 1967).

————. *Language and Philosophy* (The Hague: Mouton, 1972).

————. "Performative Utterances," in *The Encyclopedia of Philosophy*, VI, ed. P. Edwards (New York: Macmillan, 1967).

————. *Philosophical Problems: A Modern Introduction* (New York: Humanities Press, 1971). Based on the author's *Taenkning og virkelighed*.

————. "Scandinavian Philosophy," in *The Encyclopedia of Philosophy*, VII, ed. P. Edwards, (New York: Macmillan, 1967).

————. *Taenkning og virkelighed* ("Thinking and Reality") (Copenhagen: Berlingski, 1959).

————. *Wittgenstein og den moderne filosofi* ("Wittgenstein and Modern Philosophy") (Copenhagen: Gyldendal, 1960).

————. *Wittgenstein and Modern Philosophy*, trans. M. Cranston (New York: New York University Press, 1965).

Heidegger, M. *Sein und Zeit* (Tübingen: M. Niemeyer, 1957).

Høffding, H. *A Brief History of Modern Philosophy*, trans. C. F. Sanders (New York: Macmillan, 1931).

————. *Kort oversigt over den nyere filosofie historie* ("A Short Survey of the Modern History of Philosophy") (Copenhagen: Gyldendal, 1946).

Jensen, U. J. *Videnskabsteorie* ("Theory of Science") (Copenhagen: Berlingske, 1973).

Jørgenson, J. *A Treatise of Formal Logic* (Copenhagen: Levin and Munksgaard, and London: Humphrey Milford, 1931); rpt. (New York: Russell and Russell, 1962).

————. *Psykologia paa biologisk grundlag* ("Psychology Based on Biology") (Copenhagen: Munksgaard, 1963).

————. "Some Remarks Concerning Languages, Calculuses and Logic," in *Logic and Languages, Studies Dedicated to Professor Rudolf Carnap on the Occasion of his 70th Birthday*, eds. Y. Bar-Hillel, et al. (Dordrecht: Reidel, 1962).

Kuhr, V. *Aesthetis opleven og kunstnerisk skaben* ("Aesthetic Experience and Artistic Creation") (Copenhagen: Gyldendal, 1927).

Olson, R. E. and Paul, A. M. (eds.). *Contemporary Philosophy in Scandinavia* (Baltimore: Johns Hopkins Press, 1972).

Ross, A. *Culpability, Responsibility, and Punishment* (Berkeley, Calif.: University of California Press, 1975).

————. *Directives and Norms* (London: Routledge and Kegan Paul, and New York: Humanities Press, 1968).

Ryle, G. *Concept of Mind* (London: Hutchinson, 1960).

Sartre, J.-P. *L'Être et le Néant* (Paris: Gallimard, 1943).

Zinkernagel, P. *Conditions for Description* (London: Routledge and Kegan Paul, 1962).

JOURNALS

Danish Yearbook of Philosophy
Kierkegaardiana
Philosophia Arhusiensis

Finland

J A A K K O   H I N T I K K A

The cultivation of a field like philosophy in a country of the population of Finland is not without built-in dangers. The smallness of the nation as a whole entails a relatively small community of scholars working in any one field—a condition that easily fosters jealousies and sectarianism.

One possible solution to these difficulties would be to integrate the national group of scholars into a wider international community. In Finland, one of the most striking characteristics of philosophy since 1945 has in fact been the active participation of a number of leading philosophers both in international scholarly efforts and in the work of international, scholarly organizations in the field. Of Finnish philosophers of this period, G. H. von Wright served as professor of philosophy in Cambridge (1948–1951). Since 1965 he has been Andrew D. White Professor-at-Large at Cornell University, in both cases while simultaneously holding an appointment in his home country. Jaakko Hintikka has had a permanent connection with Stanford University since 1965. Von Wright is a former president of the Institut International de Philosophie, and Hintikka has been president of the American Philosophical Association (Pacific Division). Both von Wright and Hintikka have served as president of the International Union of History and Philosophy of Science, Division of Logic, Methodology, and Philosophy of Science. Larger or smaller international philosophical meetings have been held almost annually in Finland in the last decade and half. Indeed, large segments of post-World War II philosophy in Finland have been so much part and parcel of the international philosophical scene that they can scarcely be discussed in isolation from what has happened in England, the United States, and Scandinavia. For instance, no overall history of theories of inductive generalization, of deontic logic or epistemic logic, can be written in which the philosophers discussed below do not play a major part.

This internationalization of philosophical efforts is in contrast to the prewar situation. Here we find a marked difference in degree, if not in kind. In spite of frequent trips and other contacts abroad, before 1945 there was not nearly the same degree of integration of actual scholarly efforts and exchange of working information. J. E. Salomaa's prewar book on idealism and realism in contemporary British philosophy could not make its subjects look any more alive had they been contemporaries of Locke or Berkeley. In his intellectual autobiography, G. H. von Wright tells of arriving in Cambridge in 1939 without knowing that Wittgenstein was teaching there.

One consequence of this change is a somewhat new yardstick in evaluating professional philosophical efforts. In the 1920s and 1930s, Eino Kaila performed an impressive service not only for the general intellectual life in Finland but also for its professional philosophers by making known there such novelties as logical empiricism and Gestalt psychology. However, in the 1960s and 1970s, a claim of introducing into Finland some more or less new movement—be it hermeneutics or neo-Marxism—did not impress active professional philosophers. These philosophers have inevitably come across any number of representatives of such movements on the international scene and have had a chance of weighing the merits and demerits of their claims. Such pursuits of the latest intellectual fashion typically seem to deteriorate into purely journalistic criteria of scholarly achievement.

In spite of the international character of their efforts, the leading Finnish philosophers of recent decades have exhibited a great deal of independence and originality. Although he was one of Wittgenstein's closest associates and although he has repeatedly acknowledged Wittgenstein's influence on him, G. H. von Wright is freer than any other neo-Wittgensteinian philosopher of the master's mannerisms and of all superficial signs of influence. Sometimes this independence has led to a weaker international influence than a Finnish philosopher might have exerted had he been part of an English or American group or school. For instance, such carefully argued and suggestive works as Stenius' book on Wittgenstein's *Tractatus* and von Wright's *The Varieties of Goodness* have scarcely received the recognition they deserve. Likewise, the development of an explicit semantics for modal logics is frequently attributed to Saul Kripke, even though it was first pioneered by Stig Kanger (1957) and (independently but a little later) by Jaakko Hintikka (1957, 1961).

Since the number of chairs in philosophy in Finland is rather small, a list of their occupants affords a quick overview of the main personalities as well as the expansion of the field (Table 1). This expansion started quite late. In the early 1960s, a new teaching slot in Helsinki could still be motivated by pointing out that, except for the duplication of chairs necessitated by the bilingual character of the country, the new position meant the first increase in the number of full-time philosophers at the university since it was founded in Turku in 1640. Of the philosophers listed, Kanger and Segerberg are Swedes by nationality and largely also by training, and hence fall outside the scope of this essay.

The dominant figure in Finnish philosophy in the 1930s and 1940s was Eino Kaila (1890–1958). The life and work of this fascinating, impressive man remain

TABLE 1. **OCCUPANTS OF CHAIRS OF PHILOSOPHY IN FINLAND'S UNIVERSITIES**

Academy of Finland (ad hominem appointments)

Eino Kaila	(academician 1948–1958)
G. H. von Wright	(academician 1961–)
Jaakko Hintikka	(research professor 1970–)

University of Helsinki
* "Theoretical" philosophy
    Eino Kaila   1930–1948
    Oiva Ketonen   1951–
* "Practical" philosophy
    Rafael Karsten   1922–1948
    Erik Ahlman   1948–1952
    Jaakko Hintikka   1959–1970
    Jussi Tenkku   1973–
* Swedish language chair
    G. H. von Wright   1946–1961
    Erik Stenius   1963–1974
Methodology of social sciences
    Raimo Tuomela   1970–
Foundations of mathematics
    Ilkka Niiniluoto   1975–

University of Turku
* Undivided chair (divided in 1964)
    J. E. Salomaa   1931–1958
    Sven Krohn   1960–1970
** "Theoretical" philosophy
    Risto Hilpinen   1972–
*** "Practical" philosophy
    Jussi Tenkku   1969–1973
    Juhani Pietarinen   1976–

Åbo Akademi (Swedish University of Turku)
* Philosophy
    Erik Stenius   1954–1963
    Stig Kanger   1968–1969
    Krister Segerberg   1972–

University (earlier, Teacher's College) *of Jyväskylä*
Philosophy (earlier, philosophy and educational theory)
    Erik Ahlman   1935–1948
    Jussi Tenkku   1965–1968
    Risto Hilpinen   1970–1972
    Reijo Wolenius   1973

University of Tampere
    Raili Kauppi   1969–

University of Oulu
History of Ideas
    Juha Manninen   1977–

---

* Existed on a regular basis in 1945.
** "Theoretical" philosophy means roughly epistemology, metaphysics, and logic.
*** "Practical" philosophy covers ethics, value theory, and social and political philosophy.

to be studied, even though there can scarcely be more interesting tasks for an intellectual historian or a biographer. The only extensive description of Kaila's philosophical thought is found in von Wright's introduction to an English translation of some of Kaila's work entitled *Reality and Experience: Four Philosophical Essays* in the Vienna Circle Collection series.

In the late 1920s and 1930s, Kaila had been working, broadly speaking, in the tradition of logical positivism or logical empiricism. (Kaila seems to have been the first philosopher anywhere to use the term logical empiricism.) This is connected with Kaila's strong emphasis on the scientific character of philosophy. His own deepest philosophical impulses were primarily in the direction of *Naturphilosophie*, however. He was intensely interested in the most recent scientific developments in physics, biology, and psychology. As von Wright aptly emphasizes, Kaila was to a large extent concerned with an attempted reconciliation of two visions: a monistic vision of the fundamental unity of all reality and an antireductionistic vision of the quantitative uniqueness of several different kinds of phenomena.

The period of Kaila's activity which falls within the scope of this article is characterized by a bold attempt to synthesize these two diverging tendencies by means of the concept of a new kind of causality which Kaila called terminal causality *(Terminalkausalität)*. He contrasted this causality to the usual mechanistic causality, which Kaila labeled initial causality *(Initialkausalität)*. Unfortunately, Kaila never explained the contrast in sufficient logical, mathematical, or physical detail. He seems to have had in mind laws in which initial conditions or stage-by-stage transitions do not play a crucial role but which turn essentially on the structure of a whole extensive "field." In nature, terminal causality is supposed to play a role mostly in subatomic phenomena governed by quantum-theoretical laws. These determine to a large extent the most characteristic biological phenomena. Kaila thought that field theories relying on terminal causality "also gave the clue to the problem how quality is related to structure, the 'phenomenal' to the 'physical'. It is not a coincidence that Kaila's turn to microphysics happened simultaneously in his epistemology and in his theoretical psychology." Both of the important problems which von Wright mentions in this quote had repeatedly occupied Kaila through the preceding two decades.

In his last years, Kaila was trying to carry out this ambitious synthesis in the form of two works: a three-volume treatise characteristically entitled *Terminalkausalität als die Grundlage eines unitarischen Naturbegriffs: Eine naturphilosophische Untersuchung*, and a more popular and more epistemological book in Finnish which he called *Hahmottava maailma* (an approximate translation might be "World into Gestalt"). Of these, only the first volume of the treatise, subtitled *Terminalkausalität in der Atomdynamik* (1965), and a long chapter of the second, entitled (in English translation) *The Perceptual and Conceptual Components of Everyday Experience* (published posthumously in Finnish in 1960), reached completion.

Kaila's impressive project was unsuccessful, but not just because of his unexpected death. Nor was it bound to remain less than a complete success because

Kaila had not mastered fully the difficult physical and mathematical problems involved. From the very beginning, there was more than a little *hubris* in the very scope of Kaila's attempted synthesis. This proud man was imposing a truly Promethean task on himself. His vision was grander than any man's discursive and argumentative capacities. This superhuman effort cast something of a tragic spell over Kaila's last years. He was much more isolated in 1945–1958 as far as his philosophical work was concerned than he was in 1928–1939 when he had been carrying on conversations, correspondence, and sometimes public scholarly exchanges with many internationally known philosophers.

The same can be said *mutatis mutandis* of Kaila's influence. His semipopular writings were a tremendous source of inspiration for most younger philosophers in Finland; for several of them, they were a major influence in turning them to the subject in the first place. His own synthetic vision was too ambitious and too sketchy to afford starting points for ordinary piecemeal research, however. (Needless to say, the few attempts that have been made to discuss Kaila's ideas critically have been pathetically inadequate; see Jaakko Borg in *Ajatus* [1962] and Kari Lagerspetz in *Ajatus* [1968].) It is in fact characteristic that all those successful Finnish philosophers of the next generation who were inspired by Kaila nevertheless had a firm foothold in some other intellectual tradition. In the case of Oiva Ketonen (1913–   ) and Erik Stenius (1911–   ), this other tradition was primarily that of symbolic logic and foundational studies, and in the case of G. H. von Wright (1916–   ), Wittgenstein and the British analytical tradition.

Erik Stenius wrote his dissertation on paradoxes in logic and set theory *(Das Problem der logischen Antinomien)*. In his monograph *Das Interpretationsproblem der formalisierten Zahlentheorien und ihre formale Widerspruchsfreiheit*, Stenius struck out in a direction which later logical and foundational studies have found rewarding but which Stenius himself did not pursue further. The focal point of his philosophical interests has been the picture theory of Wittgenstein's *Tractatus Logico-Philosophicus*, whose precise import and implications Stenius has studied in a long sequence of interesting and lucid papers. His overall interpretation of Wittgenstein's *Tractatus* is summed up in Stenius' book on this subject of 1960, subtitled *An Exposition of Its Main Lines of Thought*, and partly also in the stimulating paper of the same year on "Wittgenstein's 'Critique of Pure Language'." Stenius' clarification of the close relation of Wittgenstein's picture idea to the logical concept of isomorphism (isomorphic representation) is a considerable philosophical achievement.

The retrospective collection of Stenius' *Critical Essays* illustrates the variety of his philosophical interests. Of this variety, Stenius' interesting and lucid essay on the pragmatics of intensional logics ("Mood and Language-Game") perhaps deserves special mention.

Oiva Ketonen made important early contributions to the so-called Gentzen methods in mathematical logic. His main influence on philosophy in Finland has been through his teaching and through a large number of excellent textbooks and surveys.

If Eino Kaila was the preeminent influence in Finnish philosophy in the 1930s and 1940s, G. H. von Wright has been its towering figure since World War II. The scope of his interests is exceptionally wide, which makes his achievement difficult to summarize. Fortunately, evaluations and discussions of his *oeuvre* will soon be easily available in English in the form of the Library of Living Philosophers volume on G. H. von Wright. (See also *Essays on Explanation and Understanding,* edited by Juha Manninen and Raimo Tuomela, 1976.) Hence, we can perhaps dispense with attempts to reach any kind of exhaustiveness here. It is worth mentioning, however, that von Wright's interests extend further than English-speaking philosophers may realize. To the Swedish- and Finnish-speaking reading public, he is as well known through the half-literary, half-philosophical essays on Tolstoy, Dostoevsky, Toynbee, Spengler, Jaeger's *Paideia,* and "The Tree of Knowledge" collected in *Tanke och förkunnelse* ("Thinking and Announcing") as through his more technical books. Finnish and Scandinavian readers are also familiar with von Wright's excellent book-length surveys of recent philosophy entitled *Den logiska empirismen* ("Logical Empiricism") and *Logik, filosofi och språk.* ("Logic, Philosophy and Language").

Much of von Wright's early work focused on the problem of induction. His first book, *The Logical Problem of Induction,* summarized this early work. Even before the end of World War II, his book was discussed at length by C. D. Broad in a three-part article in *Mind* (1944). Von Wright deepened his analysis of inductive logic in *A Treatise on Induction and Probability,* in which the influence of Keynes and Broad is more clearly visible than in the earlier book. In later studies, von Wright discusses among other topics the so-called paradoxes of confirmation and subjective probability. The latter investigation, presented at the 1960 Stanford Congress, also helped to kindle von Wright's interest in preference theory (compare below).

One of the most striking characteristics of von Wright's work in this area is the multiplicity of his interests and contributions. The title of his first book refers to the epistemological problem of the justification of induction. Elsewhere, von Wright emphasizes the role of the epistemic element in concepts like randomness and equiprobability. He has likewise studied the axiomatics of probability calculus and the role of probabilistic considerations in induction, especially the role of the famous Bayes' theorem. However, he has also been deeply interested in the qualitative and eliminative aspects of induction, such as the role of sufficient and necessary conditions. Moreover, the interrelations of the probabilistic and the eliminative aspects of induction have held a special fascination for him. (The challenge von Wright has issued to correlate the increase in probability of a hypothesis on evidence with the power of this evidence to eliminate competing hypotheses was in effect taken up later by Hintikka in his 1966 paper on induction by elimination and induction by enumeration, thus providing one of the many instances of continuity in recent philosophy in Finland.)

An early insight into an analogy between the logical behavior of quantifiers and of modal operators ("necessarily," "possibly," and so on) prompted von Wright to investigate modal logics. His work in this direction is characterized by a systematic use of the technique of distributive normal forms and, more importantly, by a keen eye on the uses of modal logic for the purposes of conceptual analysis. In *An Essay on Modal Logic* and in "Deontic Logic" in *Mind* (see also *An Essay in Deontic Logic and the General Theory of Action*), he pioneered several new "logics" of this sort. Later, in the same spirit he discussed the logic of preference *(The Logic of Preference)* and tense-logic *(And Next; And Then)*. Many of his ideas and suggestions in these different directions have proved extraordinarily fruitful in the hands of logicians and philosophers as well as his own hands. Other ideas, such as the concept of a "dyadic" modality, have provoked interesting, though perhaps less spectacular, developments. One of von Wright's most important ideas has been the general theory of modality, that is, the idea that there is a common part in the logics of the different modal or intensional concepts.

Von Wright's study of deontic logic led him to the logic and semantics of norms and their relations to human action. This study in turn served to direct his interest in the vast field of value theory and ethics. An invitation to give the Gifford Lectures in 1959–1960 crystallized von Wright's thoughts on these subjects into the pair of important books *Norm and Action* and *The Varieties of Goodness*.

The links between von Wright's different lines of work are not without historical interest. In his early work on deontic logic, he dealt with norms as if they could be true or false. Nevertheless, the Nordic countries had a strong tradition emphasizing the noncognitive status of norms. How could deontic logic be defended in the teeth of this tradition? This led von Wright to study the "ontology" of norms, for instance, questions concerning the norm-authority, norm-subjects, and sanction.

There are also connections between norms and value concepts, of which the most important is often thought to be the overall concept of goodness. More important than von Wright's remarks on these connections is his work on different kinds of goodness and on their interrelations. *The Varieties of Goodness* is one of his most independent and original books. His main vision, which puts moral values squarely into a wider framework of such values as welfare, health, and happiness, is more reminiscent of Aristotle than of recent moral philosophy. Subsequently, von Wright has himself raised the question of whether the individualistic vantage point adopted in *Varieties* does justice to the societal aspects of value theory. In his intellectual autobiography in the Schilpp volume, von Wright uses a Wittgensteinian analogy to express his suspicion that "private action" is as hopeless a concept as the "private languages" Wittgenstein criticizes.

If *The Varieties of Goodness* lies somewhat outside the most recent fashions in philosophy, von Wright's recent interest in the analysis of human action—another outgrowth of the work that went into *Norm and Action*—is in a direction which has attracted a large number of other philosophers. His approach is rather different from that of many others, with the important exception of G.E.M. Anscombe whose work *Intention* influenced von Wright and whose interest in practical reasoning along the lines of the Aristotelian "practical syllogisms" is shared by von Wright.

This work has led von Wright to the related problems of understanding, historical explanation, determinism, causation, and so on. His work on these subjects is so much an on-going venture, however, as to allow no brief summary, or even a prediction concerning its eventual outcome. Interim results are recorded in *Explanation and Understanding* and *Causality and Determinism*, and interim evaluations (with von Wright's replies) in *Essays on Explanation and Understanding*, eds. J. Manninen and R. Tuomela.

G. H. von Wright sees the task of philosophy—certainly the task of his own philosophy—as the clarification of our conceptual intuitions. This can be considered the greatest common denominator of most of his professional philosophical work. From this vision on the nature of the philosophical enterprise, it seems to follow that the most general problems of philosophical logic—logical paradoxes, the nature of logical truth, of logical consequence, and of conditional statements, and so on—are likely to be the most central ones. They have been studied by von Wright over the years, and a number of his contributions were collected in 1957 in the volume entitled *Logical Studies*. Although many of his works in this direction have been influential and otherwise successful, one can scarcely avoid the impression that von Wright's best gifts do not come to play in them as fully as in those works in which logical techniques are applied to the analysis of concepts with a substantial, nonformal content. It is in the latter enterprise that von Wright's vast reading, finely attuned perception, and wide sweep of his intellectual sympathies are perhaps seen most clearly.

G. H. von Wright's influence is amply in evidence in the work of the next age group of Finnish philosophers. This group includes Jaakko Hintikka (1929–   ) who studied under von Wright in 1947–1948 and 1949–1952. Since his philosophy, too, will soon be examined in a separate book (in one of the first volumes in the Reidel *Profiles* series), this survey will mainly be restricted to mentioning those aspects of his philosophical activities which are relevant to the continuity of Finnish philosophy.

Hintikka adopted from von Wright the idea of distributive normal forms, developed it further, and turned it into a tool for dealing with different problems in mathematical and philosophical logic and in philosophy. (See his monograph *Distributive Normal Forms*, the last chapter of *Logic, Language-Games, and Information*, and his essay "G. H. von Wright on Logical Truth," in the forthcoming Schilpp volume on von Wright.) In one direction, distributive normal forms led Hintikka to the idea of deductive information which can be increased by nontrivial logical inferences (which are therefore shown not to be "tautological" in the sense of the logical positivists). This idea and its philosophical implications are elaborated in several chapters of *Logic, Language-Games, and Information*. Its model-theoretical basis was nevertheless secured only later by Hintikka's and Veikko Rantala's discovery of so-called urn models, models with a varying population; see their respective papers in *Journal of Philosophical Logic* (1975).

In another direction, Hintikka generalizes the semantical basis of normal forms in his technique of model sets (in Smullyan's term "Hintikka sets"). They have in turn enabled Hintikka to study the semantics of modal logics, especially deontic and epistemic logics, together with their philosophical applications and their generalization into a "possible-worlds semantics." (See *Quantifiers in Deontic Logic*, "Modality and Quantification," *Knowledge and Belief*, and *Models for Modalities*.) Perhaps the most intriguing application has been to the logic of perceptual concepts, in the context of which two different individuation (cross-identification) methods are used *apud* Hintikka. They yield a new perspective on such classical problems as sense data and knowledge by acquaintance in general. The problems of perception turn out to be partly analogous to the basic problems of intentional logic. Furthermore, Hintikka's two-quantifier analysis can be extended to other intentional concepts. So extended, it yields an interesting semantics of the direct-object constructions with such verbs as "sees," "remembers," and "knows." Most of Hintikka's work in this general direction is collected in *Models for Modalities* and *The Intentions of Intentionality*.

In another direction, distributive normal forms enable us to define measures of probability which, unlike those defined in Carnap's classical work, yield nonzero probabilities *a priori* also to unrestricted generalizations. Thus, it makes possible a probabilistic treatment of inductive generalization, a task sometimes claimed to be impossible. (The axiomatic basis of Hintikka's probability distributions has recently been studied jointly by Ilkka Niiniluoto and Jaakko Hintikka who show how they can be obtained by slightly loosening Carnap's general assumptions.) As the mirror images of these probability measures, we obtain interesting measures of semantical information.

These observations turned Hintikka's attention to several central topics in the philosophy of science in the early 1960s. It also aroused the interest of several younger Finnish philosophers. Some of the work of Hintikka and of his associates in this field has been collected in the two volumes *Aspects of Inductive Logic* and *Information and Inference*, both edited by Hintikka and Suppes. Of Hintikka's collaborators, Raimo Tuomela (1940–   ) first examined the problem of theoretical concepts in empirical theories and their possible definability in terms of observables. (See his monograph *Theoretical Concepts*.) Together with Ilkka Niiniluoto (1946–   ), he has studied the interaction of this theoreticity problem with the problem of induction *(Theoretical Concepts and Hypothetico-Inductive Inference)*. The underlying logical problems of definability (identifiability) have been studied by Veikko Rantala (1933–   ).

Tuomela has also written extensively on several topics in the philosophy of science, including the deductive explanation of scientific laws, the explanation of action, psychological concepts and functionalism, and other problems in the philosophy of psychology.

Risto Hilpinen (1943–   ) likewise began his work under Hintikka's inspiration. The direction of his early work is shown by the 1968 monograph *Rules of Acceptance and Inductive Logic* which shows that Hintikka's inductive logic enables us to formulate satisfactory rules for the inductive acceptance ("detachment"). Hilpinen has since worked on other aspects of inductive logic, including decision-theoretical and informational-theoretical methods of induction, on deontic logic and other modal logics (where he offers highly interesting ideas about relativized modalities), on epistemology, and on the philosophy of language.

Another problem on which the new inductive logics have thrown light is studied by Juhani Pietarinen (1938–   ) in *Lawlikeness, Analogy, and Inductive Logic*. Pietarinen's other philosophical interests include decision theory, formal theories of justice, and David Hume. Earlier, Hintikka and Pietarinen reached one of the most striking observations in recent theorizing about inductive inference, viz., the observation that inductive inference can naturally be thought of as maximization of expected (semantic) information, at least in some representative cases.

In the mid-1970s, Hintikka turned his attention more to the no man's land between logic, linguistics, and the philosophy of language. Together with his associates Esa Saarinen (1953–   ) and Lauri Carlson (1952–   ), he has developed a new approach to logical and linguistic semantics, tentatively called game-theoretical semantics. In it, the semantics of existential and universal quantifiers is examined in terms of certain games of verification, played against a malicious nature. The possibility of varying the rules of these games is especially interesting philosophically in that it yields a fully realistic pragmatic model of how certain nonclassical logics could actually be used in real communication. These philosophical implications of possible-worlds semantics are enhanced by the connections which Hintikka has argued there are between his semantical games and Wittgenstein's so-called language-games.

A marriage of game-theoretical semantics with epistemic logic has produced a new theory of the logic and semantics of questions (see Hintikka, *The Semantics of Questions and the Questions of Semantics*), which in turn is leading via question-and-answer sequences to fresh possibilities of analyzing the logic and semantics of dialogues.

All this work by several members of the younger generation of Finnish philosophers illustrates another way in which they have compensated for the handicaps of working in a small-population country. More cooperation and teamwork has occurred among the philosophers just mentioned—Hintikka, Hilpinen, Tuomela, Pietarinen, Niiniluoto, Rantala, Saarinen, and Carlson—than among the members of earlier generations of scholars in Finland and probably also more than among the members of any comparable contemporary group anywhere. In some ways, this spirit of cooperation and continuity goes back at least to G. H. von Wright who considered his early work to be an outgrowth of Kaila's work on induction and probability and whose normal form technique inspired Hintikka. This spirit of teamwork stands in especially sharp contrast to the traditional isolation in which most Finnish scholars used to work in humanistic fields—and often still work. However, the cooperation among Finland's younger philosophers goes far beyond mere continuity of themes and interests or general inspiration. It has led to an unusual degree of collaboration and co-authorship.

The influence of the von Wright-Stenius generation is not limited to the philosophers just mentioned. Their former students include Ingmar Pörn (1935–   ) who has been teaching in England for a long time. His philosophical work has been directed to such topics as *The Logic of Power* and the *Elements of Social Analysis*. Another name relevant here is Lars Hertzberg (1943–   ) who has been working in the neo-Wittgensteinian tradition. His interests include the theory of action, the philosophy of psychology, and induction. He belongs to the international tradition commented on earlier: he received his doctorate at Cornell, and he taught for a while elsewhere in the United States.

For historians relying on crude conventional classifications, there might be a temptation to label all the philosophers so far mentioned analytic or in some cases even positivistic. Although we have seen that there are genetic connections that might seem to excuse the use of such terms, those particular labels are, systematically speaking, highly misleading. Eino Kaila called his own philosophy synthetic rather than analytic, and the similarities between his thought and the most general ideas of romantic philosophy of nature are obvious enough. Much of von Wright's latest work represents an attempt to do justice to the seminal idea of a special way of understanding human action which has played an important role in several different types of antiscientistic and antipositivistic philosophies. The focal point of his work in this direction has been the concepts of practical inference and practical syllogism. It is indicative of von Wright's independence that this particular paradigm is not at all fashionable at the present moment on the continent because of its "teleological" ends-means separation (be this apparent or real). The interim statement of his position in *Explanation and Understanding* no longer fully satisfies von Wright. However, the seriousness of the attempt to incorporate in his thought some of the most important elements of a tradition which was originally foreign to him is most impressive.

Along entirely different lines, Hintikka has emphasized the promise of a sufficiently undogmatic Kantianism which maintains the special significance of human activity and its constructions in all human knowledge. He has also sought (in the title essay of *The Intentions of Intentionality*) to interpret some of the central notions of Husserlian phenomenology in the light of possible-worlds semantics, prominently including the central concept of intentionality.

Whatever one can say of the details of these developments, they belie every attempt to fit the main figures of Finnish philosophy since 1945 into any simplistic category. They are likewise apt to expose the hollowness of the claims of several *soi-disant* antipositivistic philosophers to represent alone in Finland ''continental'' philosophy as distinguished from ''Anglo-American'' philosophy (as if logical empiricism had not been a continental movement) or to defend a ''humanistic'' philosophy contrasted to a ''scientistic'' one. Such claims are typically among the most unfortunate consequences of the jealousies and sectarianisms alluded to earlier.

One of the early samples of such antipositivism was Sven Krohn's (1903–   ) two-volume polemical work *Der logische Empirismus.* However unhappy one is with the kind of logical neopositivism Krohn criticizes there, his work can scarcely be considered a success. For instance, to logical empiricists he attributes an attempt to reduce every proposition to immediate experience, while he himself holds that such a reduction can be achieved only concept by concept. Yet, the latter reduction, not the former, is what, for example, Eino Kaila was in so many words advocating in 1933 (*Ajatus,* pp. 119–138). Krohn's argumentation is sloppy in other respects, too.

Krohn's later work, exemplified by *Definitionsfrage und Wirklichkeitsfrage* and *Die normative Wertethik,* is of a somewhat better quality, and the positions he defends (for example, Platonism in the philosophy of mathematics) are often interesting and important. Yet, one cannot help being wary of a group of philosophers who, like Krohn and a number of philosophers who have obtained their doctorates under him, profess a reliance on phenomenological methods but nevertheless often exhibit ignorance and misunderstanding of Husserl's methodological doctrines. Such misunderstanding occurs, for instance, in the writings of Unto Tähtinen (1927–   ) and Lauri Rauhala (1914–   ) and unfortunately reduces the value of their otherwise interesting work. Rauhala has sought to integrate his psychotherapeutic theory and practice with phenomenological philosophy, while Tähtinen has written on moral philosophy, often against the background of his extensive acquaintance with Indian philosophy.

Some younger philosophers with a continental orientation exhibit much greater promise of real philosophical insight and achievement. Lauri Routila (1934–   ) deserves special mention here. He has written on the concept of meaning from a hermeneutical vantage point as well as on the nature of truth, Husserl, and Heidegger. It is distinctly premature, however, to speak of a new hermeneutical ''current,'' ''trend,'' or ''school,'' as has sometimes been done, unless one is prepared to include nonexistence as a serious systematic enterprise among its predicates. As yet, this alleged school has not produced enough serious nonderivative systematic work even to begin to define its doctrines or methods or other characteristics.

Of the older philosophers who remained outside Kaila's orbit, one can mention J. E. Salomaa (1891–1960), Erik Ahlman (1892–1952), and Urpo Harva (1910–   ). Salomaa's main period of philosophical activity falls outside of this survey. His late work includes books on such philosophers as Schopenhauer (1944), Kant (1959), and the great Finnish nineteenth-century philosopher-statesman J. W. Snellman (1945). These are summaries of available information rather than new interpretations, however. Salomaa's most important book is undoubtedly *Die Philosophie der Geschichte*.

Ahlman also belongs more to the 1930s and early 1940s than to the postwar period. Of his late work, only the posthumously published, unfinished book *Ihmisen probleemi* belongs squarely to the period under discussion. Ahlman was a perceptive and dedicated philosopher whose work would ordinarily deserve closer discussion, but his influence on active younger philosophers was so minimal that he can justifiably be given a brief mention here.

One characteristic feature of the cultivation of philosophy in Finland has long been a vivid sense of history and a great respect for studies in the history of philosophy and in intellectual history more generally. Eino Kaila's unpublished lectures on the history of philosophy were famous in the 1930s and 1940s, and his influential book *Inhimillinen tieto* ("Human Knowledge") contains a bold and suggestive sketch of the development of scientific and philosophical thinking. This sketch, based partly on Ernst Cassirer's interpretations, culminates in a contrast between "Aristotelian" and "Galilean" conceptions of knowledge. This contrast has unfortunately been forced to bear more traffic both in Kaila's own work and in the subsequent discussion in Finland than it can bear, especially as a stepping stone for a criticism of one of the two "traditions."

Of the other philosophers mentioned earlier, G. H. von Wright has written on Descartes and his place in the history of scientific thought (1950), on Lichtenberg, and on the history of the probability theory. Erik Stenius has written a general book on pre-Socratic philosophy *Tankens gryning* ("The *Dawn of Thought*") and essays on Kant and Leibniz.

Jaakko Hintikka has written extensively on Aristotle (see especially *Time and Necessity*) and Kant and less extensively on Plato, Descartes, and Leibniz. He has also studied the long-range history of several important philosophical ideas or assumptions, particularly the idea A. O. Lovejoy called the principle of plenitude and the ancient geometrical method of analysis and synthesis. On this last topic, he co-authored a book *The Method of Analysis* in 1974 together with Unto Remes (1940–1975). Several of Hintikka's historical essays are collected in *Knowledge and the Known: Historical Perspectives in Epistemology* (1974).

In connection with Aristotle, Hintikka has emphasized his characteristic assumptions concerning time, truth, and modality (necessity, possibility, and impossibility). These assumptions include what might be called a statistical model of modality. Recently, Simo Knuuttila (1946–   ) charted the role of the same assumptions in medieval philosophy, especially in the Aristotelians of the thirteenth century. His studies, of which the dissertation abstract *Time and Necessity in Aristotelian Scholasticism* (1976) offers a brief glimpse, document the role of the Aristotelian assumptions in much of the most central medieval thought and hence open an interesting new perspective on it.

The so-called principle of plenitude (asserting the eventual realization of each genuine possibility) belongs to this same complex of ideas. Its rejection by

Leibniz has been studied by Hintikka (1969) and its role in Kant, jointly by Hintikka and Kannisto (1976). (See also Hintikka's American Philosophical Association Presidential Address, "Gaps in the Great Chain of Being," 1976.)

Most of Hintikka's work on Kant is collected in *Logic, Language-Games, and Information* and in *Knowledge and the Known*. It is largely an outgrowth of his systematic work on deductive information. According to this interpretation of Kant, analytic judgments are—at least in the field of mathematics and logic—those that do not increase this deductive information. This insight can be extended into a general perspective on much of Kant's ideas on space, time, mathematics, and things-in-themselves whose unknowability from this perspective becomes a corollary of the impossibility of separating deductive information and ordinary empirical information.

As far as the study of ancient philosophy is concerned, both professional philosophers and professional classicists have made contributions to it. The professional philosophers include, besides Hintikka and Remes, Jussi Tenkku (1917–   ), whose dissertation dealt with Plato's views on pleasure (1955), and Mårten Ringbom (1934–   ). Moreover, Lauri Routila has *inter alia* authored a highly interesting monograph on Aristotle's metaphysics (1969). The most prominent classicists are Rolf Westman (1927–   ) and Holger Thesleff (1924–   ). Westman has written, among other topics, on Plutarch as a source for the history of philosophy (1955), and Thesleff, on Plato's style (1967) as well as on ancient Pythagoreanism.

Raili Kauppi (1920–   ) has combined an interest in Leibniz's logic (1960) with her own work on intentional logics. (It is curious that her intentional logic studies have remained totally outside the mainstream of recent work on modal and intentional logics in Finland.)

Several of the works mentioned above illustrate the interplay of historical and systematical studies, which is characteristic of much of recent Finnish philosophy. The same interaction is seen from the historical awareness which permeates many primarily nonhistorical works, for instance, von Wright's *Logical Problem of Induction* and Hintikka's *Logic, Language-Games, and Information*. The work on the history of modal concepts has likewise been connected with contemporary systematic studies in modal logics and their semantics. Nevertheless, the scholars in question have taken great care against the dangers of anachronism. On the contrary, the emphasis often has been on differences between the conceptions of earlier and our own philosophers rather than on projections of recent techniques backwards. Cases in point are Hintikka's essays on time, truth, and knowledge in ancient Greek philosophy (reprinted in *Time and Necessity*) and on knowledge and its objects in Plato (reprinted in *Knowledge and the Known*).

An extensively cultivated field of philosophical studies in Finland in recent years has been the history of moral, political, and social philosophy. Jussi Tenkku has written at length on early modern natural law theorists as well as on Adam Smith and, more briefly, on David Hume, Kant, Hegel, and Marx.

Reijo Wilenius's (1930–   ) choice of Suarez as his dissertation topic (1963) was motivated by a clever observation. Suarez represents a collectivistic variant of theories of natural law which differs from the more familiar individualistic versions of these theories and which has certain affinities with Karl Marx's thought. These affinities have delighted neither the Marxists nor Roman Catholic theorists; nonetheless they are worth serious attention. Wilenius exaggerates these affinities somewhat but corrects his statements partly in a subsequent work on Marx's early thought *Marx ennen Marxia* ("Marx before Marx"). In a semipopular survey, *Filosofia ja politiikka* ("Philosophy and Politics"), Wilenius outlines an overall view on the development of the epistemological bases of social and political thought. The view is stimulating but too sketchy to be useful for actual research. Unfortunately, Wilenius has not filled in this sketch in his subsequent work, nor has he refuted the criticisms that Juha Manninen (1945–   ) has leveled at his interpretations of Hegel and Marx.

Manninen's own work moves on a much higher scholarly level and has more philosophical insight than most of the other work on the history of political and social philosophy in Finland. His shorter essays on Hegel, Marx, Engels, Feuerbach, and Bolin are extremely interesting and insightful, and his forthcoming monograph *Subjectivity and the Ascent to the Absolute: The Dialectics of Education and Ethical Life in J. W. Snellman's (1806–1881) Philosophy* is a masterful exposition and evaluation of the philosophy of the most important Finnish statesman of the nineteenth century. In it, Finnish philosophy is returning to its own past.

Finally, a few more or less isolated names have to be recorded here. Some of them, for instance, Veli Valpola (1922–   ), Eljas Siro (1917–   ), and Veikko Salonen (1919–   ), have made their careers outside philosophy, even though they obtained their doctorates in philosophy. Valpola's dissertation was on negationless logics (1955), Siro's (1969) on the philosophical implications of the so-called phi-phenomenon in the psychology of perception, and Salonen's (1951) on the theory of reduction of empirical concepts. Similarly, Kalle Sorainen (Sandelin, 1893–   ) successfully defended a dissertation on Kierkegaard, on whom he has also written several smaller papers, but he has not been otherwise active as a professional philosopher.

Yrjö Reenpää (1894–1976) was a long-time professor of physiology at the University of Helsinki. He wrote extensively, not only on the philosophical problems arising out of his own specialty, sense physiology, but also on straight philosophy: Heidegger, Kant, the concepts of time and of understanding, and so on.

Some other scholars, for instance, Rolf Lagerborg (1874–1958), belong to an earlier period in the history of philosophy in Finland. Lagerborg was an associate and biographer of Edward Westermarck (1862–1939), and hence the last link in an important earlier tradition which nevertheless has had practically no influence in the last thirty years.

Other writers, among them Urpo Harva (1910–   ) and Matti Luoma (1925–   ), are more important as popularizers and expositors than as contributors to actual philosophical research.

SELECT BIBLIOGRAPHY

BOOKS AND ARTICLES

Ahlman, E. *Ihmisen probleemi* ("The Problem of Man") (Helsingfors: Söderström, 1953).
Anscombe, G.E.M. *Intention* (Oxford: Blackwell, and Ithaca, N. Y.: Cornell University Press, 1957).
Hilpinen, R. *Rules of Acceptance and Inductive Logic* (Amsterdam: North-Holland, 1969).
Hintikka, J. *Distributive Normal Forms in the Calculus of Predicates* (Helsinki: Societas Philosophica Fennica, 1953).
————. "G. H. von Wright on Logical Truth," in *The Philosophy of Georg Henrik von Wright*, ed. P. Schilpp (forthcoming).
————. *Knowledge and the Known: Historical Perspectives in Epistemology* (Boston: Reidel, 1974).
————. *Logic, Language-Games, and Information* (Oxford: Clarendon Press, 1973).
————. "Modality and Quantification," *Theoria* 27 (1961).
————. *Models for Modalities* (Dordrecht: Reidel, 1969).
————. *Quantifiers in Deontic Logic. Selected Essays* (Copenhagen: Munksgard, 1958).
————. *The Intentions of Intentionality and Other New Models for Modalities* (Dordrecht: Reidel, 1975).
————. *The Semantics of Questions and the Questions of Semantics* (Amsterdam: North-Holland, 1976).
————. *Time and Necessity* (Oxford: Clarendon Press, 1973).
———— and Remes, U. *The Method of Analysis, Its Geometrical Origin and Its General Significance* (Boston: Reidel, 1974).
———— and Suppes, P. (eds.). *Aspects of Inductive Logic* (Amsterdam: North-Holland, and New York: Humanities Press, 1967).
———— (eds.). *Information and Inference* (Dordrecht: Reidel, 1970).
Kaila, E. *Die perzeptuellen und konzeptuellen Komponenten der alltagserfahrung* (Helsinki: Societas Philosophica Fennica, 1962).
————. *Inhimillinen tieto* ("Human Knowledge") (Helsinki: Otava, 1939).
————. *Reality and Experience. Four Philosophical Essays*, ed. R. S. Cohen and trans. P. Kirschenmann and A. Kirschenmann (Dordrecht and Boston: Reidel, 1978).
————. *Terminalkausalität als die Grundlage eines unitarischen Naturbegriffs; eine naturphilosophische Untersuchung*. I: *Terminalkausalität in der Atomdynamik* (Helsinki: Societas Philosophica Fennica, 1956–   ).
Krohn, S. *Definitionsfrage und Wirklichkeitsfrage* (Helsinki: Akateeminen Kirjakauppa, 1953).
————. *Der logische Empirismus; Eine kritische Untersuchung* (Turku: Turun Yliopiston Kustantama, 1949).
————. *Die normative Wertethik in ihrer Beziehung zur Erkenntnis und zur Idee der Menschkeit* (Turku: Turun Yliopiston Kustantama, 1958).
Manninen, J. *Subjectivity and the Ascent to the Absolute: The Dialectics of Education and Ethical Life in J. W. Snellman's (1806–1881) Philosophy* (forthcoming).
———— and Tuomela, R. (eds.). *Essays on Explanation and Understanding* (Dordrecht: Reidel, 1976).
Pietarinen, J. *Lawlikeness, Analogy, and Inductive Logic* (Amsterdam: North-Holland, 1972).
Pörn, I. *Elements of Social Analysis* (Uppsala: Filosofiska föreningen och Filosofiska institutionen vid Uppsala universitet, 1971).

————. *The Logic of Power* (Oxford: Blackwell, 1970).

Salomaa, J. E. *Die Philosophie der Geschichte* (Turku: n.p., 1935–1936).

Schilpp, P. (ed.). *The Philosophy of Georg Henrik von Wright* (forthcoming).

Stenius, E. *Critical Essays* (Amsterdam: North-Holland, 1972).

————. *Das Interpretationsproblem der formalisierten Zahlentheorien und ihre formale Widerspruchsfreiheit* (Turku: Abo akademi, 1951).

————. *Das Problem der logischen Antinomien* (Helsingfors: Finska v vetenskaps-societeten, 1949).

————. "Mood and Language-Game," *Synthese* 17 (1967).

————. *Tankens gryning* ("The Dawn of Thought") (Stockholm: Almqvist and Wiksell, 1953).

————. "Wittgenstein's 'Kritik av det rena språket'," *Societas Scientiarum Fennica Årsbok-Vuosikirja* 38B, No. 5 (1960).

————. *Wittgenstein's "Tractatus": An Exposition of Its Main Lines of Thought* (Oxford: Blackwell, and Ithaca, N. Y.: Cornell University Press, 1960).

Tuomela, R. *Human Action and Its Explanation: A Study on the Philosophical Foundations of Psychology* (Dordrecht: Reidel, 1977).

————. *Theoretical Concepts* (New York: Springer, 1973).

———— and Niiniluoto, I. *Theoretical Concepts and Hypothetico-Inductive Inference* (Dordrecht: Reidel, 1973).

von Wright, G. H. *A Treatise on Induction and Probability* (London: Routledge and Kegan Paul, and New York: Harcourt-Brace, 1951).

————. *An Essay in Deontic Logic and the General Theory of Action* (Amsterdam: North-Holland, 1968).

————. *An Essay on Modal Logic* (Amsterdam: North-Holland, 1951).

————. *And Next,* Acta Philosophica Fennica Series 18 (Helsinki: Societas Philosophica Fennica, 1965).

————. *And Then,* Suomen Tiedeseura Commentationes Physico-Mathematicae Series 32, 7 (Helsinki: Societas Scientiarum Fennica, 1966).

————. *Causality and Determinism* (New York: Columbia University Press, 1974).

————. *Den logiska empirismen En huvudriktning i modern filosofi* ("Logical Empiricism. A Main Direction in Modern Philosophy") (Helsingfors: Söderström, 1943).

————. "Deontic Logic," *Mind* 60 (1951).

————. *Explanation and Understanding* (Ithaca, N. Y.: Cornell University Press, 1971).

————. *Logical Studies* (London: Routledge and Kegan Paul, and New York: Humanities Press, 1957).

————. *Logik, filosofi och språk* ("Logic, Philosophy, and Language") (Stockholm: Bonniar, 1957).

————. *Norm and Action: A Logical Enquiry* (London: Routledge and Kegan Paul, and New York: Humanities Press, 1963).

————. *Tanke och förkunnelse* ("Thinking and Announcing") (Helsingfors: Söderström, and Lund: Gleerup, 1955).

————. *The Logic of Preference* (Edinburgh: University Press, 1963).

————. *The Logical Problem of Induction* 2d rev. ed. (New York: Barnes and Noble, 1966).

————. *The Varieties of Goodness* (London: Routledge and Kegan Paul, and New York: Humanities Press, 1963).

Wilenius, R. *Filosofia ja politiikka* ("Philosophy and Politics") (Helsinki: Tammi, 1967).

————. *Marx ennen Marxia* ("Marx before Marx") (Helsinki: Wellin and Göös, 1966).

Wittgenstein, L. *Tractatus Logico-Philosophicus* (London: Routledge and Kegan Paul, and New York: Humanities Press, 1961).

JOURNALS

Acta Philosophica Fennica
Ajatus

Annales Academiae Scientiarum Fennicae
Commentationes Physico-Mathematicae
Commentationes Scientiarum Socialium
Synthese

France

ROBERT B. ROSTHAL

Limitations of space render a certain selectivity in the choice of authors inevitable; the present selection exhibits the preferences of the writer and may dissatisfy readers who have discovered the omission of a deserving author. I have made a partial attempt to remedy this deficiency by providing in the Notes a short list of studies and anthologies on contemporary French philosophy to which the reader may repair.

In connection with the postwar philosophers of existence, I have confined myself to a brief mention of principal themes and have stressed more recent orientations of thought disclosed in later writings where these are present; I have not wished to labor over familiar ground. I have in the same vein included some newer names among the authors established after midcentury where I have thought their work was of interest. Finally, I have provided an account of the present generation of structuralists, limiting my attention to Derrida and to those structuralists who are sometimes referred to as "les quatre grands."

I am grateful to Professor Colin Smith of the University of Reading for his kind encouragement and to Professor Francis Jacques of the University of Rennes for his hospitality and for enlightened discussion on contemporary French philosophy. I should also like to express my appreciation to James Edie, editor of the Northwestern University Studies in Phenomenology and Existential Philosophy, and to Richard de George and Roland Blum for their prompt response to my queries.

POSTWAR PHILOSOPHIES OF EXISTENCE AND PHENOMENOLOGY

GABRIEL MARCEL (1887–1973). Professor at the lyceés of Vendôme, 1911–1912, Condorcet, 1915–1918, de Sens, 1919–1922; publisher's reader, Grasset, 1923–1935 and at Plon since 1923; editor of the Plon series, *Feux croisés;* drama critic of the *Nouvelles littéraires* since 1945; member of the Institute (the Academy of Moral and Political Sciences); Knight of the Legion of Honor; Grand Cross of the National Order of Merit; Commander of Arts and Letters with Academic Palms; Grand Prize in Literature of the French Academy, 1948; National Prize for Letters, 1958; Peace Prize of the Booksellers Association of the Federal Republic of Germany, 1964; Literary Grand Prize of the

City of Paris, 1968; The Erasmus Prize, 1969. Selected Works (See Select Bibliography).

INCARNATE BEING AND THE ONTOLOGICAL MYSTERY

There is a discernible kinship between Marcel's views on the limitations of conceptual thought and its relation to experience and F. H. Bradley's dialectic of immediacy and thought.[1] For both, (1) conceptual thought is too abstract and systematic to describe a reality which does not possess the unity of a system; (2) the inadequacy of discursive thought to its object is grounded in the separation of thought from a reality of which it is essentially a part and of which we are dimly aware in our unreflective experience; (3) we may discover in our immediate experience what emerges at a higher level in being—hence, immediate experience provides the model for a suprarelational experience of the Absolute. Despite these similarities, the early *Metaphysical Journal* represents a reaction against Bradley's monism and seeks to replace the idealist dialectic between thought and experience and their inclusion in a higher reality, with a philosophy of individual "participation." Thus, in his belief in the inefficacy of thought to achieve a reconciliation with being by dialectical means; in the primacy of the act with which we respond to the "exigence" of being; and finally, in his theistic conception of being as an Absolute Thou rather than the whole of reality or being in general, Marcel is opposed to an idealism he had earlier espoused.

According to Marcel, thought must be "within" experience if it is to follow the contours of that experience with all its singularities and deficiencies without losing what is essential in it. The withdrawal of thought from experience (objectivity) constitutes a "betrayal," and its continued practice inspires Marcel's "concrete approaches," i.e., the translation of the familiar categories of philosophical thought into experiential terms: space and time are "paired modes of absence," the object "what does not take us into account," conceptualization, an "exorcism." Marcel's theater is an example of such an approach, and it has a crucial role to play. For the ordinarily separate Marcellian themes of existence, objectivity and being exhibit a certain continuity, and being may be illuminated "from below," i.e., by way of an analysis of human-being or experience. Thus, existence is revealed as a state of being characterized by vague and indeterminate aspirations; objectivity exhibits an effort to discover a rational solution to one's problems and to recreate the affective unity I had with the world by thought alone; finally, the restitution of existence on a higher level of being implies a degree of self-awareness lacking on the lower level of intelligibility.[2]

Each of the above themes, (1) existence, (2) objectivity, and (3) being, is the object of a negative critique demonstrating the inadequacy of traditional philosophical solutions. (1) "Incarnate being" refers to the unique relation which I bear to my body and is the central datum of existence.[3] Marcel refers to the nonrelational unity of myself and my body, of which I possess direct knowledge, as a "participation" and expresses it in terms of what appears to be an identity statement, "I am my body." The conceptual links between self and body, however, can be expressed neither in terms of a materialist identification of the self with a physical body or observable thing, nor in terms of a contingent relation between the body and a Cartesian ego, mind, or "epistemological subject," with "thought in general" or with "whatever thinks." For Marcel, I am not identified with this particular body nor am I distinguished from it; I possess both an observable and nonobservable knowledge of my body, a consciousness both distinct from and identical with its object. Marcel's "sensualist metaphysics" embodies an attempt to clarify this "mystery" which is not directly amenable to conceptual analysis, in terms of a critique of causal or "instrumentalist" theories of the body associated with materialism and dualism. The instrumental view of the body as an ensemble of sense organs which transmits or receives "messages" and whose sensations are identified with physical stimulations of the sense organs which must somehow be "interpreted" in order to permit transcendental inferences to physical objects, is replaced by an intentional analysis of sensation involving a "centrifugal" tendency towards the world. For the analysis of sensation discloses that the direct knowledge I have of my body, my sense of embodiment or of existence, so to speak, is fused with an awareness of myself as in the world, as being there for others. The transformation of sensation into (a) a *"disponibilité"* openness or availability to the world and to others, and (b) the continuity of sensation with the "higher affectivities" such as love and fidelity, based on an "exclamatory" or "manifestory" awareness of my body as *in the world,* leads to the conclusion that being manifests itself in interpersonal communion: *Esse is Co-Esse.*[4]

(2) Objectivity or objective thought satisfies the following descriptions: (a) an exercise of conceptual thought which abstracts from a reality that has been shown to be essentially nonrelational, hence incapable of being grasped by concepts; (b) scientific generalization in which the individual possesses significance only as an instance of a universal law, the general application of scientific standards and procedures, the method of successive approximations to a truth that is eternally elusive, the concept of the standard observer and the intersubstitutability of observers, and the requirement of normal conditions of observation and of public criteria of evidence; and (c) an attitude one may adopt towards oneself or others which is either motivated by or inspires the above exercises of thought, e.g., a posture of detachment towards the world or a spectator view of reality. It should be noted that what Marcel condemns are the pernicious consequences of this attitude with respect to the individual and society. He does not intend to impugn the criteria of scientific inquiry themselves so much as their inappropriate extension to interpersonal rapports which may result in the destruction of human relationships or which may lead to dehumanization.[5]

(3) Finally, the role of "secondary reflection" is to join what objective thought has disjoined. The nature of this reflection is ambiguous. A meditation on one's personal experience which rejects any concessions to the requirements of abstract

thought, it sometimes suggests a Bergsonian act of recollection which restores continuity to our experience, sometimes obedience to the injunction *il faut pas juger*. What it seeks to illuminate is a being which is indefinable and access to which is only to be gained through the mutuality or reciprocity of those personal relationships which exhibit our capacity for commitment and fidelity. Such relationships are for Marcel "metaproblematic"; like incarnate being, what is metaproblematic cannot be "solved" in accordance with some rule or technical procedure. It cannot be identified with a pseudoproblem whose "solution" lies in the clarification of the logical difficulty which would exhibit the senselessness of the "problem," nor is it an as yet unsolved problem due to lack of knowledge and resolvable in principle by further scientific inquiry. The metaproblematic involves a response to an invocation or appeal which lies outside our unaided efforts, and it depends on such intentional attitudes as hope and faith. For Marcel, faith may be viewed as the shadow of a more absolute fidelity to the Thou.

JEAN-PAUL SARTRE (1905–1980). Professor at the lycées of Laôn and le Havre, 1929–1934; resident at the French House in Berlin, 1934; professor of philosophy at the Lycée Pasteur, Neuilly-sur-Seine, 1935–1939 and 1941 and at the Lycée Condorcet prior to his resignation in 1944 to devote himself to writing; founder and editor of *Les Temps modernes,* 1946–1980; foreign member of the American Academy of Arts and Sciences; vice-president of the European Society of Writers, 1965–1980; president of the International Tribunal on War Crimes of the Russell Foundation, 1966–1980; interim editor of *La Cause du peuple,* a leftist newspaper, 1920–1980; editor of the Maoist weekly publication, *Tout,* 1970–1974; editor of the leftist organ, *Révolution,* 1971–1974; founder with Maurice Clavel in 1971 of the news agency *Libération* and editor of the daily *Libération,* 1973–1974; editor of the Gallimard series, La France sauvage, 1973–1980; Nobel Prize for Literature (rejected), 1964. Selected Works (See Select Bibliography).

EXISTENTIALISM AND MARXISM

The development of Sartre's views from the publication of *L'Etre et le néant* (1943) to the *Critique de la raison dialectique* (1980) may be conveniently considered under the following heads: (1) the distinction between two ontologically primitive or irreducible types of being, conscious beings, or beings-for-themselves (the *pour-soi*), and the objects of consciousness existing independently of the latter (the *en-soi*);[6] (2) the subsequent identification of the *pour-soi* with freedom and the restrictions on that freedom with respect to our relations with objects and other persons, e.g., the limitations imposed on our freedom by our situation or our "facticity" and by the existence of other agents; (3) the "conversion" (already announced in *L'Etre et le néant*) to a dialectic of freedom and constraint which attempts to reconcile existentialist assumptions concerning freedom with Marxism.

(1) Sartre's "radicalized" interpretation of intentionality entails the realist conclusion that consciousness logically presupposes something independent of itself which the subject is constrained to regard as a real thing: "transcendence is the constitutive structure of consciousness; that is, . . . consciousness is born supported by a being which is not itself."[7] One argument bases the truth of the proposition that what we perceive are not ideas or appearances but real objects on the premise that its denial would render phenomenological knowledge, i.e., the determination of what things are in themselves, impossible. Thus, Sartre's refutation of the existence of a transcendental ego is based on the idealist implications of the latter, viz., that what is experienced is inseparable from the experience of it. For such an ego, the object of experience *cannot* exist independently of our experience of it, for the intentional meaning-products or contents of the transcendental ego are necessarily subjective, i.e., dependent on its activity.[8] The analysis of intentionality, however, entails not only the realist conclusion that the objects of consciousness exist independently of consciousness, but also the idea that the "I" or subject of experience which is assumed to provide the unifying structure of consciousness is itself such an object existing in the world. For if all awareness is of something other than itself; if, further, the awareness of a mental state or act such as the perception of x is logically indistinguishable in prereflective consciousness from the perception of x, as Sartre claims, then the self or referent of the "I" disappears. There is no subject necessarily entailed by every act of consciousness, and the unifying role of the subject is assumed by the object. Accordingly, there is no ego or self standing outside of any possible experience, and *everything* relegated to consciousness, including the ego, exists as an object "out there" in the phenomenal field.

The foregoing conclusions are based on the assumption that a realist analysis of intentionality is the correct one. But Sartre attempts to support this conclusion by (a) an "ontological proof" for the transcendence of the object,[9] and (b) an argument relating to the cognitive dimensions of intentional acts such as perception. Thus, to believe in the reality of x is to believe that x has aspects or can present appearances of which one is not now aware. Hence, the appearance or presentation of a thing is believed to belong to something whose aspects are not exhausted by the momentary appearance. Since it is self-contradictory to maintain that an appearance itself can possess aspects that are not given, it follows that x is not identical with any given appearance.[10] Again, Sartre's allusion to the fact that "not all consciousness is knowledge . . . but all knowing consciousness can be knowledge only of its object"[11] suggests that if perceptual acts possess a cognitive dimension, then if I see or otherwise perceive x, x must be really there to see. (Equivalently, sentences employing cognitive verbs may be said to imply the existence of the objects of these verbs.) It is evident that the above arguments are inconclusive either because they assume that the realist conditions of intentionality are satisfied, or because they restrict themselves to *what* it is we believe when we believe x to be a real object, without determining whether that belief is true or whether the perceptual claim to make direct contact with reality is valid. Hence, we may conclude that Sartre has not succeeded in resolving the question whether appearances are of existing things or not, nor has he wholly eluded the suspension of judgment characteristic of phenomenological reduction. It has not been shown that the object transcends any of its appearances and that every appearance presupposes a transphenomenal foundation or belongs to something independent of consciousness. Whatever their value, however, it should be observed that the foregoing arguments tend to place the whole weight of being on the *en-soi* and to reduce consciousness to a pure intentionality, to a "revealing intuition of things" or "openness" to the world to which it contributes nothing. We seem, therefore, to be left with a consciousness which is a transcendentally necessary condition for the appearance of things but which possesses no qualities of its own.

(2) The above conclusion with respect to the *pour-soi* or consciousness is placed in doubt when we observe that Sartre endows consciousness with a specifiable activity—with what has been termed a "transitive nihility."[12] Thus, the *pour-soi* is said to be responsible for the "gap" in being, for the insertion of "nothingness" into the world of things, or for the "generation of nonbeing." What Sartre seems to mean is that the structure of human consciousness involves an apprehension of things in the mode of possibility. The *pour-soi* is identified with an act of "nihilation" or negation *(néantisation)* which is primarily an imaginative capacity to consider things as other than they are or to conceive of what is not the case. It is this ability to confirm or deny what it chooses which in turn allows us to "identify" the *pour-soi* with freedom. For the transformation of the world into a set of possibilities is a necessary condition for the existence of a world which I can control through my choices and actions. "Free action stems from the gap which constitutes consciousness and which separates a man from the world in which he is, enabling him to imagine and envisage what is not the case."[13] That "distance" or "emptiness" is filled by the "project," for such consciousness of the world implies a praxis or point of view of a potential agent who is prepared to act responsively on the world as something to be changed. Now if the self's engagement in the world implies that I structure the world into a set of possibilities from my own vantage point or perspective, and that it is always up to me which possibility is to be realized, the praxis or system of relationships established in virtue of my intervention into things which interprets them in accordance with my ends or aims nevertheless encounters certain limitations: (a) my freedom is limited by the given, external conditions of my "facticity," i.e., the material conditions of my existence which are inescapable, despite the repudiating structures of nihilation and the distance established between the world and the self;[14] (b) the freedom possessed by the *pour-soi* is an attribute of other selves like my own, and the exercise of their freedom imposes limits on my own. For the other escapes my effort to control him by reducing him to an object, while he is at the same time responsible for the consciousness I have of myself as a being-for-the-other *(être-pour-autrui)*, i.e., as an object which he in turns seeks to possess. Hence, for Sartre, "conflict is the original meaning of being-for-others."[15]

(3) *Being and Nothingness* contains a hint of a later solution to the problem of the limitations imposed by the material conditions of existence and the hopeless condition of our freedom. In this work Sartre suggests that these structures "do not exclude the possibility of an ethics of deliverance and salvation achievable only after a radical conversion."[16] This new vision of a possible life with other human beings takes more fully into account the fact that material necessity must share responsibility for the conflict which had largely been ascribed to the structure of consciousness and is presented in the *Critique of Dialectical Reason.*

The *Critique* embodies a dialectic of freedom and necessity which seeks to complement Sartre's existentialism with a Marxism which will protect the "authentic Marx" against modern Marxists. An outline of Sartre's views is provided in the essay preceding the *Critique, Search for a Method.*[17]

The conversion to Marxism announced by the *Critique* makes certain concessions to Marxism while reaffirming the reality of freedom and the necessary limitations of historical knowledge. (a) "Dialectical rationalism" advocates a concept of social violence or revolution which is no longer grounded in the ontology of freedom of *Being and Nothingness* but in a material scarcity regarded as a purely contingent and therefore eliminable feature of the world. (b) Violence is justified in terms of its aim to achieve a better society and is realizable through the cooperative revolutionary action of the "group," identified by its community of interests and aims. Identity of will must emerge from the egoistic condition of "seriality" characteristic of the collective. The history of struggle and conflict can only be consummated when men are no longer separated and history possesses a single meaning corresponding to the intentions of those who make it. (c) Any effort however, at *complete* "totalization," i.e., the unification of a multiplicity of projects in a single historical direction, is futile. History is forever an unachieved "totality," and the succession of historical events is dependent not only on human intervention (praxis) but also on the "pratico-inert," i.e., the material conditions of action and other forms of necessity such as existing social structures or the chain of physical events unleashed by human action, all of which possess an independent reality and impose constraints on future actions. (d) The view that men's activities are not wholly determined or predictable in accordance with any laws implies that economic forces are "mediated" by the actions of individuals who have unique ways of surpassing (dépasser) the material conditions of their lives. (Flaubert, the central figure in Sartre's latest work, *L'Idiot de la famille,* is a leading example.)[18] Hence, human actions are not reducible to causally determined events, or if they do involve causal relations these do not instantiate lawful regularities.

It is clear that Sartre's "progressive-regressive" method, i.e., his explanatory model of human behavior which enables us to understand Engels' view that man is at once an agent and a product of historical forces, involves both praxis or voluntary action and an element of causal determination. The model closely resembles a familiar pattern of explanation connecting motives and intentions: an action may be explained in terms of an unwanted state of affairs preceding the action, i.e., backward-looking reasons or motives, or by reference to a wanted state of affairs to be brought about by the action or intentions, or both.[19] For Sartre, behavioral explanation ordinarily implies both together. But while each of the above explanations applies only to voluntary actions, for Sartre it is clear that the "starting conditions" impose causal constraints on our actions and are therefore not to be identified with "reasons" or "motives." If we regard such conditions as instrumentalities of purpose or intention, however, that is, if the situation is articulated in terms of my needs or desires (conditions, for example, are "unbearable"), we have the prescription for avoiding bad faith of *Being and Nothingness:* intentions themselves must be explained by motives and reasons, not by external causes. We may conclude that Sartre's dialectic of "negation of negation" (the "interiorization" of the material situation) implies an unwillingness to provide a causal account of behavior or to interpret needs or desires in causal terms, even though his aim is to show that patterns of justification of an action are not necessarily incompatible with causal accounts of behavior.

MAURICE MERLEAU-PONTY (1908–1961). Professor at the lycée, 1931–1945; professor of philosophy at the University of Lyon, 1945–1949; University of Paris, 1949; named to the chair of philosophy at the Collège de France, 1952; co-founder with Sartre and Simone de Beauvoir of *Les Temps modernes;* contributor to the *Express.* Selected Works (See Select Bibliography).

THE PRIMACY OF PERCEPTION

Merleau-Ponty's most influential doctrines relate to the primacy of perception[20] and the concept of incarnate consciousness *(le corps vécu).*[21] Adopting Husserl's life-world *(Lebenswelt)* as the intentional object of consciousness, he attempts to show that perception is the privileged conscious activity in which this object appears and that perception is presupposed in all other objectivities, including thought and language. His task is therefore twofold: first, to reduce consciousness to a level of primary perceptual experience in which the world is given prior to any scientific interpretation: science is construed as a second-order expression of a lived world of experience which is *déjà-là* prior to the constituted world of science; second, to show how scientific activity develops out of this primary perceptual experience: a genetic phenomenology must be elaborated which traces the genesis of scientific concepts, judgments, and meanings from those more elementary meanings present in the "prepredicative," prescientific life of consciousness.

The primacy of perception is established on the basis of a phenomenological analysis of the body, the latter entailing the development of a "new *cogito*" or concept of subjectivity as *être-au-monde.* Thus, our presence or "inherence" in the world implies that the phenomenal field is structured or prereflectively synthesized by our body; the lived-body in its sensorimotor behavior distinguishes and objectifies the realities around us, bestowing a meaning on our surrounding world. The role of the body in perception is variously described in terms of a "primitive spatiality" where the body is "of" space rather than "in" it; of "bodily purpose" where the body is "polarized" by its tasks; of being in an "oriented space" of "situation" rather than of "position," and so forth. These descriptions, which are intended to show that my relations to my body are not assimilable to my relationship to other objects of knowledge, imply, first, that my body is "co-present" with my perception of things, in the sense that objects are normally perceived in the context of an activity of the body. Those aspects of the object that are not given or presented are actualized by my realizing bodily movements of various kinds. Second, since a property of my sensory field is that *I* am in the center of it and my *body* is also *perceived* to be in the center of the sensory field (Armstrong), I am necessarily situated in the same place as my body (I cannot be identified with a consciousness existing independently of the body), for if this were false, no account could be provided of the necessarily perspectival knowledge we possess of objects (the perceptual reference to objects depends on a point of origin identical with my body).

The analysis of the role of the body in perception liberates phenomenology from Cartesianism, for the above account of being-in-the-world entails (1) the inseparability of subject and object: the body as subject of perception is a condition for there being objects, and as such cannot also be an object (the body nevertheless cannot be absent from the perceptual field).[22] (2) The opacity of consciousness: the open reference of the act of perception implies that consciousness has a transcendent character. The world is given in perception as an indefinite series of perspectival views. Since the nonvisible sides of the object are indeterminately given together with the visible sides or aspects, the object is never fully present or exhaustively given. Perceptual objects "always recede beyond their immediately given aspects,"[23] and there is always more than what is actually given to consciousness. This "presence requiring absence," which Merleau-Ponty also terms "the paradox of immanence and transcendence,"[24] implies an unreflective reference to something that must always remain opaque to consciousness.

Signes (1960) and the posthumously published *Le Visible et l'invisible* (1964) exhibit Merleau-Ponty's growing interest in language and in the development of a phenomenological ontology.[25] The latter work, which involves a generalization of certain themes of the *Phenomenology of Perception,* is too fragmentary to permit any definitive conclusions. We can only single out two themes: first, perception shares the differential structure of language; second, the body as at once seer and seen, as sensible and sentient, is (as for Marcel) paradigmatic of being.[26] The earlier work embodies the author's reflections on Husserl's view concerning the possibility of an eidetic description of language and of a universal grammar which would fix the meaning structures indispensable to any natural language; and on Saussure's diacritical or differential view of meaning and the distinction between a diachronic and synchronic linguistics. Merleau-Ponty concludes that a phenomenology of language must reconcile the autonomous status of linguistic phenomena with the experience we have in using language; he proposes a "dialectical" study of language which would include both the speech-act *(parole)* that incorporates contingent linguistic facts where equivocation of meaning is never wholly eliminable and an objective science of language *(langue)* which can never be completely realized. This view of language as an "equilibrium in movement," or *"logique dans la contingence,"* is a development of his earlier conclusions on perception in "The Body as Expression and Speech" of the *Phenomenology of Perception*. Thus, language is itself said to be an example of corporeal intentionality and has its origin in the body, the gesture or bodily sign being the most elementary or natural form of expression on which the meaning of our vocal utterances continue to depend.[27] Expression, he concludes, is "closer" to its meaning or referent than other uses of language, and is indeed but an extension of spatialized body perception. The alleged primacy of expressive meaning, where speech is understood on the model of the bodily gesture, resembles Wittgenstein's view that language is a learned replacement of preverbal behavior. According to such an "avowal theory" of language, first-person psychological utterances are learned bits of behavior expressive of inner states, or are the effects of inner causes and are not used to report or describe anything. Merleau-Ponty does not provide us, however, with a clear description of the "primary" meaning relation, "x expresses y," although his various affirmations to the effect that the vehicle of expression is effaced or that the meaning "swallows up" the sign is consistent with Husserl's distinction between indicative and expressive signs. In the latter case, meaning is directly present without the benefit of a physical token. Merleau-Ponty's view of aesthetic objects as exhibiting the nonmediated presence of meaning similarly suggests a "one-term" theory of aesthetic expression. If we assume that the expressive properties of the work, that is, those ordinarily designated by emotion or feeling predicates as these are applied to persons, are "embodied" in, or "fused with," its other visible properties, then expressive predicates are nonrelational or noninferential and designate constituent properties of the object. The absence of any distinction between the expressive thing and what is expressed (meaning) presumably applies to the bodily sign, vocal utterance, and the object of art alike.

GASTON BACHELARD (1884–1962). Postal employee in Remiremont and Paris, 1903–1913; professor of physics and chemistry at the Collège de Bar-sur-Aube, 1919–1930; professor of philosophy at the University of Dijon, 1930–1940; named to the chair of the history and philosophy of science at the University of Paris, 1940–1954; officer of the Légion d'Honneur, 1951; director of the Institute of the History of Science and member of the Institut (Académie des Sciences Morales et Politiques), 1955; National Grand Prix in Letters, 1961; doctor, *honoris causa,* University of Brussels; co-director of *Dialectica.* Selected Works (See Select Bibliography).

SCIENCE AND IMAGINATION

A distinguished philosopher of science has remarked that a reader ignorant of the identity of the author could hardly guess that the writer of *Le Nouvel esprit scientifique* and other works on the history and philosophy of science was one and the same as the author of such works on the imagination as *L'Eau et les rêves* and *L'Air et les songes*.[28] Bachelard belonged to two worlds, that of science and that of poetry. His academic career was devoted to the elaboration of a scientific epistemology in a dozen works written between 1927 *(La Connaissance approchée)* and 1953 *(Le Matérialisme rationel)* and to a parallel series of studies on the creative imagination from 1938 *(La Psychanalyse du feu)* to 1960 *(La Poetique de la rêverie).* Despite the opposed nature of scientific thought and the poetic imagination, there is an underlying unity between the two already suggested in Bachelard's popular *La Formation de l'esprit scientifique* written in the same year as the *Psychanalyse du feu.* Subtitled "Contribution à une psychanalyse de la connaissance objective," *La Formation* poses the problem of scientific knowledge in terms of the obstacles to its development, i.e., the images and analogies based on our direct perceptual experience. But the "images simplistes" which presented what Bachelard termed "obstacles epistemologiques" or barriers to the development of scientific thought were clearly rooted in the same reality as scientific curiosity. Both science and imagination were creative, both were independent of immediate experience, and the relation between the two would later prove to be complementary rather than opposed.

In common with a number of philosophers who were inclined to view philosophical problems (especially those relating to human knowledge) from the perspective of elementary particle theory and microphysics, Bachelard's "modified rationalism" or "rationalisme ouvert" reflected the astonishing scientific developments of his time: quanta theory, wave mechanics, the uncertainty principle, relativity, the development of non-Euclidian geometries, axiomatization, and the role of mathematics in physical thought. These developments required a revision of LaPlacian certitudes about science as well as the rejection of philosophical platitudes deriving from the traditional confrontation of empiricists and rationalists. For science proceeded in terms of a mutual adjustment or "rectification" of theory and experience, and scientific verification involved an "uneliminable dualism" or "mobile synthesis" which issued in continual "compromise."[29] Philosophical perplexities arose because of "the conceptual tensions generated between the polar coordinates of pure mathematics and raw sense experience."[30] In a measure, these implications of scientific method had already been noted by Bachelard's older contemporaries, Duhem and Brunschvicg, in their challenge to empirical reductionism. In *La Théorie physique,* Duhem had demonstrated that scientific observation was a "theory-laden" activity and that we are not merely passive "data-receptors."[31] Brunschvicg in his *L'Expérience humaine et la causalité physique* was similarly critical of empiricist theories of pure experience and confronted the myth of the given with the conceptual elaborations of experience characteristic of scientific thought. "La science," Bachelard affirmed in one of his many lapidary formulations, "ne correspond pas à une monde à décrire, elle correspond à une monde à construire." Science was not a mere "pleonasm of experience,"; it was *"réalisante"* not *"empiriste."*[32]

To Bachelard belongs the distinction of having discriminated at an early date a number of themes discussed in contemporary philosophy of science, including the operational character of scientific concepts; the nature of the scientific revolution; the role of mathematics and of axiomatization in physical theory; the importance of theoretical constructs, ideal properties, and pure cases ("noumenal" or "thought objects") to the understanding of actual phenomena; the limitations of reductive explanation with respect to microphenomena; and the relation of instrumentation and measurement to theory. A few brief remarks may be made about Bachelard's views on some of the above issues.

(1) Like Kuhn for whom scientific development depends on "non-cumulative developmental episodes in which an older paradigm is replaced in whole or in part by an incompatible new one,"[33] Bachelard maintained that science progresses by *"saccades,"* by mutation and leaps involving ruptures in the continuity of its evolution requiring the radical reorganization of its conceptual schema.[34] The failure to assimilate new phenomena or account for novel "effects" (themselves products of scientific experiment) was a sign of malfunction with respect to the accepted paradigms. Scientific progress was born of such crises shaking the edifice of rational knowledge which required the rebuilding of its foundations. This discontinuity in the history of scientific thought involved two further consequences. First, the typical focus of scientific interest was a particular problem, i.e., an unresolved difficulty or inconsistency insoluble under the conditions in which it had previously been posed. Second, the history of science (and its pedagogy which continued to claim Bachelard's attention) required a normative interpretation. A badly explained fact remained a fact for the historian but for the epistemologist it was an obstacle or "counterthought" which need not be retained since it had not contributed to the solution.[35] In the history of science, Bachelard claimed, it was not as essential to revive the past as it was to judge it.

(2) The view that science was *"réalisante"* or creative of reality received support from Bachelard's (and Duhem's) recognition that instrumentation is not a docile intermediary between theory and the data of experience. Instruments are themselves *"théories materialisées,"* and the *"déformations"* inseparable from our instruments and techniques of measurement are fundamental to our understanding of phenomena.[36] In short, science was a "phenomenotechnique," its observations carried on "with the aid of specially devised instruments the nature and limitations of which must be known and whose readings must be interpreted and corrected in the light of a comprehensive theoretical system."

In order to deduce certain conclusions from a theoretical hypothesis H, therefore, "a number of other assumptions, K, must be made about the instruments of measurement. Hence H and K are being put to the test and not H alone."[37] "L'instrument de mesure," Bachelard affirms, "finit toujours par être une théorie et il faut comprendre que le microscope est un prolongement de l'esprit plutôt que de l'oeil."[38] The role of instrumentation leads Bachelard to conclude that physical science is not a science of "facts" at all but a technique for producing effects, an art of manipulating matter. His objections to Poincaré's conventionalism are based on the role of instrumentation. For Poincaré, the Euclidian theorem that the angle sum of a physical triangle was equal to two right angles which Gauss tested by optical methods, i.e., by interpreting physical straight lines as paths of light rays, could always be defended even if Gauss had encountered an experimental deviation from this value. For we can always preserve the Euclidian postulate by introducing new hypotheses concerning deforming or deflecting forces (light rays are bent, and so on). For Poincaré, wherever experience conflicts with the Euclidian interpretation of physical space, we can modify our physical theory rather than the geometry. However, if we include the physical theory of the instruments of measurement and observation, we must reject this conclusion. For the total physical theory may require a non-Euclidian geometry as a part: relativity physics requires an interpretation of a straight line as a great circle on a sphere.[39]

(3) Bachelard recognized the dominant role of mathematics as the language of science and the axiomatization of theory that it permitted. He did not, however, accept the conclusion that the usefulness of mathematics was restricted to providing a means for the precise expression of empirical hypotheses and methods for the job of eliciting their consequences.[40] A scientific theory is axiomatized when the analysis of an uninterpreted system has established a minimal axiom set which is accepted without demonstration, which is logically consistent, and which allows us to deduce together with logical principles of inference all the theorems belonging to the theory. As Hempel has pointed out, once the postulates for a theory have been laid down, every further proposition or theorem of the theory must be proved exclusively by logical deduction without appeal to our experience, the feeling of self-evidence, and so forth.[41] Bachelard recognized the advantages of formalization: the establishment of theorems without any reference to empirical data, i.e., the fact that mathematics does not assert the truth of any set of geometrical postulates; that in an uninterpreted system we need assign no meaning to the undefined primitive terms and can treat them as logical variables or abstract sets of objects. But geometry is also an empirical science, i.e., a theory of the structure of physical space, and Bachelard is clearly interested in the relation between pure and physical geometry, i.e., in the physical interpretations or meanings assigned to the originally uninterpreted primitives of the theory. Thus, axiomatization must be handled "intelligently and not mechanically," and the *"délire systématique"* (Brunschvicg), attentive only to the deductive consequences of a given set of postulates, must be supplemented

by an appropriate choice of axioms and of the physical interpretations of the primitive terms figuring in the postulates.[42] Nevertheless, there is evidence that Bachelard's allusion to the mathematical "realization" of the phenomena implies a coherentist view which, unlike the above, rejects any sharp distinction between scientific and mathematical statements commonly made in terms of the methods used to demonstrate their truth or falsity. The acceptability of the former kind of statement, like that of the latter, depends on the fact that it implies or is implied by other already accepted statements of the theory.[43]

(4) It is plausible to hold that the root of Bachelard's principal *"obstacle epistémologique,"* which he terms the "substantialist obstacle,"[44] is a disregard of the difference between the behavior of macrophenomena and microphenomena. Although substantialism may be variously viewed as the substitution of things or concrete particulars and their observed or "hidden" properties for the events and their relations with which science must deal, the ascription to objects of properties derived from immediate sense experience, the reification of such properties, or even the resort to easily imagined mechanical processes to explain phenomena, substantialism may be better described in terms of microreductive explanation of the properties of the whole in terms of the same properties possessed by its parts[45]—appeals to coagulation or fermentation as explanatory principles, to the "sponginess" or porosity of the air, or to the fluidity or "gelatinous" properties of electrical phenomena,—which are vacuous and postpone rather than provide an adequate explanation of the phenomena. (Bachelard is equally opposed to Cartesian reductionism, i.e., reduction to simple ideas that purport to be intuitively clear and to the hierarchical organization of the sciences in terms of the complexity of their objects, those dealing with the least complex such as physics being the more basic.)[46]

Two comments may be made on all of the above. First, Bachelard's rationalism, his insistence that the "epistemological vector" goes from the rational to the real, leads him to underestimate the importance of the hard stubborn facts which constitute the significant observations for a theory and which are capable of modifying a theory. We may also have to amend the so-called definitions of a theory to accommodate the findings that conflict with the theory. Second, it is a moot question, as a recent writer has shown,[47] whether Bachelard's (and Duhem's) contrast between the logical and imaginative kind of mind is parallelled by two kinds of physical theory, the abstract and systematic which Duhem advocated, and the familiar, mechanical type which both found incoherent and which "distracted the mind from the search for logical order" or from the construction of "an ideal physical theory," viz., a mathematical system with deductive structure . . . unencumbered by extraneous analogies or imaginative representations." For if it is true that explanation implies an account of the new and unfamiliar in terms of the familiar and intelligible, then analogy with familiar objects and events may be essential to theory and "model-thinking in science [will] imply positive analogies between the properties of models and reality."

Although Bachelard would have rejected such a view, he turned from the task of purifying objective knowledge of images to an exploration of the subjective structure of the imagination.

Imagination is a necessary ingredient in perception or in perceptual recognition, i.e., in the reidentification of objects as of a certain kind.[48] But it is not restricted to reproducing impressions or to thinking about things in their absence. It is also creative, can construct what it likes out of the elements at its disposal, and has a crucial role to play in the context of creative art, its production and appreciation.[49] Bachelard set out to establish a science of the creative or "dynamic" imagination viewed as a capacity for transforming the images provided by perception, i.e., liberating us from perceptual imitation and enabling us to create new images. The productive as distinct from the reproductive imagination is possessed of a certain structure, fulfills an essential role in the psychic economy, and responds to basic human needs.[50]

(1) Imagination operates in accordance with Jungian-like archetypes or paradigms of human experience rooted in the unconscious, each individual imaginative faculty exhibiting a preference for some material type of image which "polarizes" the particular images constituting our experience. Hence, individual images are associated with what Bachelard refers to as the "hormones of the imagination,"[51] viz., the archaic material elements, earth, air, fire, and water. The "law of the four elements"[52] is appealed to in order to explain central poetic fixations and to provide us with a typology of "oneiric dispositions." (Bachelard's work on the material imagination has been used by literary critics interested in the archetypal imagery of writers and has led to a classification of poets according to their favorite substance.)[53] Care, however, must be exercised in interpreting the law linking the archetypes with particular images. The relation of image to archetype is not a causal one, i.e., no law-like generalizations relating to the imagination can be inferred from the facts, there is an isomorphism of images which cuts across the different elements, i.e., the image is rather of the polyvalent properties of matter such as its varying motions or states. Finally, there may be images based on plant or animal life, snow, the night, and so forth, which are apparently irreducible to the four material elements.[54] The archetypal structures may best be viewed as the outcome of a transcendental argument, that is, they express the necessary conditions for the possibility of an imaginative experience, while their application or empirical exemplification is contingent. The analysis shares two other features with that of Jung. First, it involves a rejection of Freud's reductive view of images as effects or symptoms of concealed or repressed desires: sexual motivations do not exhaust the meaning of an image. Thus, Bachelard's *"psychologie directe"* of the imagination purports to deal with an "oneiric reality" which preserves the autonomy of the imagination and the primitive or underived character of the symbolic transformation of nature. Second, Bachelard insists on the unconditional spontaneity of the archetype: the imagination is construed as a causal agent, form of energy, or force responsible

for the transformation of experience into images of a certain type[55] (a view of causal efficacy he had earlier congratulated science for dispensing with in favor of "formal" concepts such as frequency and periodicity).

(2) The imaginative representation of objects is always accompanied by emotion and involves what Bachelard terms a "valorization" or evaluation of the object, an ascription of evaluative and expressive properties to the object.[56] Such "projections" or "humanizations" by the subject suggest a species of pathetic fallacy wherein we endow objects with the felt qualities which in fact qualify our emotional responses to objects. Bachelard is not altogether clear on the status of expressive or tertiary properties and their relation to the sensory qualities of the object, and there is a certain tension between the material and dynamic characteristics of the imagination. Thus, he maintains that our sense impressions are already expressive of various second-order properties which render the former fit for symbolization. Elsewhere he refers to the "intentional resistance" of matter to the imagination and characterizes matter as an "energetic mirror" which focuses our powers or "provokes" the imagination. Like Spinoza's *natura naturans* and *natura naturata*, matter is at once inert and an immanent force.[57]

(3) Finally, Bachelard's metaphysics of the imagination involves a generalization of the role assigned to the imagination as "function of the unreal." Thus, in his later work, *The Poetics of Reverie*, the active imagination is identified with the waking dream or creative daydream, its products phenomena not of "psychic detente" but of the will, designed to preserve the self from an alien not-self. By abolishing the distinction between subject and object so that "the dreamer diffuses into the world," imaginative reverie, like Schopenhauer's aesthetic contemplation, guards consciousness from the brutalities of a hostile world, "vitalizes the beauty of the mute world," and thereby reconciles us to an unresponsive external reality. Formerly held to be obstacles to scientific progress, image and metaphor now compensate for the deficiencies of conceptual thought. Like Jung's "androgynous" human psyche which has a harmonized double nature involving both "anima" and "animus," both poetic and critical powers,[58] poetic expression possesses an integrative function, responding to the need of human consciousness to "create" reality.

PHILOSOPHY AFTER MID-CENTURY

EMMANUEL LEVINAS (1905–   ). Director of the École Normale Orientale, 1946-1963; professor of philosophy, University of Poitiers, 1964; professor of philosophy, Paris-Nanterre, 1967; Paris-Sorbonne, 1973–   ; doctor, *honoris causa*, Loyola University, Chicago, and of the universities of Leyden and Louvain; recipient of the Albert Schweitzer International Prize for Philosophy, 1971. Selected Works (See Select Bibliography).

METAPHYSICAL PLURALISM

Levinas' early reflections on Husserl's and Heidegger's analyses of intentionality[59] anticipate his philosophy of "otherness" of *Totality and Infinity*. For Husserl, intentionality implies a tension or consciousness towards something other, but this does not imply a relationship to an independently existing being. For Husserl's signifying acts intend universals that do not exist in space and time and that depend on the act itself. Moreover, the *cogito* provides its own evidential criteria for the immanent meanings which are its objects, and the intentional relation is primarily a cognitive one which, like the Cartesian *cogito*, apprehends the necessary properties of phenomena and their relations. Heidegger, on the other hand, rejects the *res cogitans* or purely epistemological subject: the self *(Dasein)* is given as already being-in-the-world; to exist is just to find oneself in a world to which one is related by his practical preoccupations and personal involvements; the subject's awareness of his mode of existing in the world, moreover, his concern for his *own* existence, entails a comprehension of being as such. Finally, the existential relation, while still intentional and indeed implying a *"sortie de soi-même"* or transcendence towards the world, is not a cognitive relation of judging or perceiving but a prereflective or preconceptual relation to the world disclosed in feeling or mood.

For Levinas, neither the Husserlian egology which construes the self as a conceptual consciousness or thinking reality for whom nothing is external, nor Heidegger's existential relation to a contingent future and ultimately to the event of nonbeing or death, is satisfactory. In his summary of the two doctrines,[60] Levinas hints at a philosophy of absolute "alterity" discoverable in Descartes' *Third Meditation,* which would provide for both exteriority and infinitude. Descartes reconciles the finitude of the subject with the infinite in which it participates, a view which Levinas elaborates in his major work, *Totality and Infinity*.

The preface of *Totality and Infinity* declares that its aim is "to distinguish between the idea of totality and the idea of infinity and affirm the philosophical primacy of the idea of infinity."[61] The concept of infinity entails the absolute separation of the Other *(Autrui)* from the subject and derives from Descartes' causal argument in the *Third Meditation*. But though Levinas admits that his concept of the Other "resembles God," "there can be no knowledge of God separated from the relationship with men."[62] The Other, then, is to be identified with the other self or person in his intransigent individuality. My relatedness to the Other, which Levinas refers to as the "metaphysical relation" or as "transcendence," preserves the separate identity of the Other: "Transcendence designates a relation with a reality infinitely distant from my own reality, yet without this distance destroying this relation and without this relation destroying this distance."[63] What is this analogy between the "face" or the *"face à face,"* as Levinas terms the I-Other relation, and Descartes' argument?

In the *Third Meditation,* Descartes argues that he could not recognize his own imperfection or finitude, as he in fact does, unless he had an idea of perfection, and since he finds no perfection in his experience, the idea must originate in some kind of encounter with what is itself actually perfect.[64] There are several features of this argument which illuminate Levinas' metaphysical relation: (1) the primacy of the Other in the establishment of the relation; (2) the necessary character of the separation of subject and Other; and (3) the ultimate unintelligibility of the Other and the ambiguity of the evidence establishing the existence of the Other. Thus, with respect to this last, Levinas refers to the logical circularity involved in the principle that clear and distinct ideas are true is to be proved by an appeal to the veracity of God, while the principle is itself used in proving the existence of the veracious God. According to Levinas, however, the fact that "The I and God are revealed as distinct moments of evidence mutually founding one another"[65] does not constitute a basis for dismissing the argument. For such circularity is a necessary property of separation.

Primacy, on the other hand, implies that the absolutely Other is not derivable from the I: No analogical inference from my own case, no *Sinngebung* or Husserlian apperception, no construction or constitution of the Other, is possible. "To receive from the Other beyond the capacity of the I, is the meaning of the infinite."[66] The Other is nevertheless unintelligible, for the ideatum is infinitely removed from its idea. Infinity is the preeminently inadequate idea entailing separation from its object since God surpasses his idea in us. (In Cartesian terms, the reality discoverable objectively or by representation in the idea must be formally in its cause in comparison with which the idea necessarily falls short.)

The analogy between the I-Other relation and Descartes' concept of infinity involves Levinas in an uncritical acceptance of the argument in the *Third Meditation.* There are two serious objections to those features of the argument relevant to the analogy. (1) The alterity of the Other is for Levinas an actuality and not merely an idea. But concepts such as infinity or perfection need not have nonideal archetypes. We may identify the best possible thing with God, but imperfection in the finite creature does not entail the existence or actuality of the best possible thing. (2) Descartes assumes that I could not know that I was imperfect if I did not already have the idea of a more perfect being, i.e., the positive is always prior to the negative, and, therefore, God's perfection cannot be the mere negation of my own imperfection. But as Kenny points out, the ability to use a predicate is not prior to but identical with the ability to use its negation.[67]

Although Levinas labors to provide a conceptual account of the metaphysical relation, like Marcel he is compelled to clarify the relation by an appeal to "concrete approaches," i.e., to experiences such as love, enjoyment, "dwelling" in the world, and "fecundity,"[68] or by negative qualification. Thus, the subject as a term in the metaphysical relation is not to be identified as a member of a class, it does not exemplify any set of properties, nor is its identity to be construed in terms of mere logical self-identity. Nevertheless, Levinas attempts to clarify the metaphysical relation (1) in ethical terms and (2) as embodying a "metaphysical desire." The first resembles Kant's effort to vindicate the unconditional regard we owe to other persons as ends in themselves in his *Foundations of the Metaphysics of Morals*. The second is indebted to Hegel's dialectic of desire in the section on self-consciousness in the *Phenomenology of Mind*. Some brief comments may be made on both of these antecedents.

"Metaphysics," Levinas claims, "is ethics."[69] Elsewhere he maintains that "Morality is not a branch of philosophy but first philosophy."[70] In this context alterity implies the calling into question of my autonomy, the imposition of limits on the exercise of my will, the submission of my freedom to the judgment of the Other. The most serious difficulty, however, is that of establishing the primacy of the Other (what Levinas elsewhere terms "height"). For if, as seems to be the case, the indubitability of my own moral experience is limited to my person,[71] that experience can only assure me of *my own* responsibility and therefore of *my own* dignity and worth. Yet, it is the dignity of others that is in question if I am to limit my own freedom out of respect for theirs.[72] But is it possible to base the dignity of others on my own sense of responsibility or voluntary self-limitation if I reject all appeal to a rational awareness common to all men or to a will universally determined by reason which could provide a proof of the dignity of all men? The absence of any commitment to rationality or to the symmetry of reasons indeed suggests that I can *choose* on whom to confer dignity.[73] This conclusion is reinforced by the admitted asymmetry of the metaphysical relation: if the relation is not to be transformed into an objective one known by a third person, I cannot be interchanged with the Other and the relation can only be known by the I who originates it. I can remain separated or can welcome the appeal, but the moral initiative is my own. The same may be said for the Other, for the Other, too, is endowed with the power to choose for or against me, to take the moral initiative or not as he chooses. And this can hardly compel my respect for the Other. Yet, for Levinas the vision, revelation, or "epiphany of the face" clearly implies self-limitation.

In the section on self-consciousness in the *Phenomenology of Mind*,[74] Hegel's interest shifts from knowledge to desire and its fulfillment. Desire has as its aim integral expression in which the external reality of the other person is fully expressive of the subject and contains nothing alien. This aspiration for total integration with the Other Hegel terms "infinity"; it is the very antithesis of the Cartesian concept, and Levinas baptizes it "totality." At an early stage of the dialectic of desire, the Other is regarded as a limit imposed on the self which the self must abolish or "negate" in order to feel integrity. Now Levinas shares Hegel's view on (1) the inadequacy or illusoriness of the measures the subject takes to overcome his ontological dependence on an alien reality. Neither the strategy of retreat into oneself as "inner spiritual being" or pure interiority, nor the possession of the other to cancel his otherness is possible. (2) The subject is nevertheless a being "who returns to himself *through the other*"; hence, the bipolarity of self and other is, for Levinas as for Hegel, inescapable. Levinas, however, rejects "totality," i.e., the Hegelian attempt to overcome separation and to negate finitude by the thought of the universal. According to Hegel, the self can only find itself in the universal, in the drama of mutual recognition in which other men recognize him as a human being. The I for Hegel is free only in the thought of the universal where it is no longer in another because the subject now sees himself as reflected in the world as a universal, as a thinking being.

But the I cannot be sublimated in the universal. History of the Hegelian sort, Levinas claims, cannot integrate myself and the Other within an impersonal spirit. It cannot ignore the position of the I before the Other in which the Other remains transcendent with respect to me. In short, the I and the Other are not parts of a wider totality or whole, i.e., merely members of the same class, exemplifying the same set of attributes. Totality is in fact "totalitarian."[75] Political theory or universal history, which conceive of individuals as exemplifying social forces, apprehend the individual in his generality, but ontologies which affirm the priority of being over the existent are instruments of "conceptual totalitarianism," "ontological imperialism," "exploitation," "domination," or "surrender," and inaugurate the reign of the impersonal.[76]

Language and discourse also exhibit this universality of thought and reflect the passage from the individual to the general.[77] To speak is "to make the world common." All the same, there exists for Levinas a speech or mode of discourse which is not a "mere modification of thought" but "an original relation with an exterior being." Levinas endows the verbal utterance where the speaker "is present" with a certain superiority. Such discourse is "a concrete expression of the idea of infinity," "is revelatory of the other," and has an expressive rather than a cognitive function. Unlike language which is used as an instrument of an "ontology of power," reducing the Other to the "same," it is a mode of discourse which recognizes that the Other cannot be divested of his alterity and that he escapes my grasp. But what this mode of discourse is is not altogether clear.

PAUL RICOEUR (1913–   ). Professor at lycée St.-Brieuc, 1933–1934; Colmar, 1935–1936; Lorient, 1937–1939; research, National Center for Scientific Research, 1945–1948; professor of history of philosophy, University of Strasbourg, 1948–1956; professor of philosophy, University of Paris, 1956–   ; John Nuveen Professor, Divinity School, Department of Philosophy, University of Chicago, 1976–   ; dean of the Faculty of Letters, Paris-Nanterre, 1969; member of the editorial board of *Esprit*, 1947–   ; editor of *Revue de Métaphysique et de Morale*. Selected Works (See Select Bibliography).

PHENOMENOLOGY OF THE WILL AND HERMENEUTICS

The first volume of Ricoeur's *Philosophie de la volonté, Le Volontaire et l'involontaire (Freedom and Nature)*, dedicated to Gabriel Marcel, appeared in

1950. The second volume was published in two parts a decade later,[78] followed by the *De l'Interpretation. Essai sur Freud* (1965). The development of ideas in Volume 2 was unforseen, for what had begun in *Freedom and Nature* as a phenomenological or structural analysis of the experience of willing or of choice ended with a psychopathology of the will concerned with uncovering latent meanings in the symbolic expression of experience.[79] It may be doubted whether such a hermeneutics or theory of interpretation preserves the features we ordinarily associate with phenomenology or whether the new development may be accurately represented as a "phenomenology of language." The move from description to interpretation involved in the decoding or exegesis of texts, and the resulting dissociation of meanings from the testimony of immediate consciousness, are alien to the principles of phenomenology.[80] Ricoeur has admitted that the concept of the unconscious with which he had to come to grips in his essay on Freud was antiphenomenological.[81] A projected *Poetics of the Will* promises to dispense with the *cogito* altogether in favor of the text.

Ricoeur shares with the post-Husserlian phenomenologies of bodily existence a sense of the limitations of transcendental phenomenology. If by transcendental phenomenology we understand the view that the world can have its meaning as existing reality only as the intentional meaning-product of a transcendental ego, i.e., an ego to which everything in the world is relative but which is itself removed from the world, then the self becomes isolated from its body and loses contact, as Merleau-Ponty points out, with whatever is not thought.[82] The subject-body or body-for-me, of which I possess direct knowledge as distinct from the body-for-others or object-body, however, is not an idea or representation. Ricoeur, in common with other existential phenomenologists, finds encouragement for his project of transforming the *cogito* and "breaking the circle the subject forms with itself," in Husserl's last philosophy. Husserl's concept of the *Lebenswelt*, Ricoeur remarks, encourages us "to extend intentionality beyond theoretical and even practical representation and to include in consciousness its own relation to the body."[83]

If, however, the person is not what Marcel termed a pure epistemological subject restricted to the knowledge of ideal meanings, the extension of our intendings to "lived meanings" or to "bodily significations" poses a fresh set of problems. In this connection, Ricoeur observes that phenomenology must "go beyond an eidetics which is all too clear," in order to elaborate "the indices of the mystery of incarnation."[84] For as Marcel had claimed, the relation of consciousness to its body could not be "thematized" or "problematized" without falsifying our experience or altering the very terms of the "problem." Nevertheless, Ricoeur proceeds with an analysis of the subject-body as an opaque or obscure datum lacking conceptual clarity. Eidetic description, though inexact, is possible. The focus of his attention, like that of Biran, is the willed act. It is the polar structure of the I and its body, the "reciprocity" of the voluntary and the involuntary, implying both the initiation of activity and the reception of limits, that best expresses the intuition we have of the *cogito* as that of "a body conjoined to a willing which both submits to it and governs it."[85]

Ricoeur's analysis is similar to Brian's in a number of respects. (1) Like Biran, Ricoeur regards the *"dualité originaire"* or experience of an act inseparable from the experience of organic or bodily resistance, as the paradigmatic act constitutive of the self. Ricoeur's "bodily significations," which preserve an active element of intentionality, resemble Biran's analysis of the complex relation between the active and passive life, between the things that happen to us (sensations) and the things we do.[86] (2) Like Biran, Ricoeur seeks to preserve the unity of experience of the subject-body, resisting both its polarization by thought into subject and object (dualism) and its identification with the object-body (reductionism). (3) Both appeal to neurophysiological descriptions of willed acts (motor determinations, muscular contractions) as of "diagnostic" value in locating experiences of which we are only obscurely aware. (Biran called such descriptions "symbolic.") But while Ricoeur ostensibly employs the diagnostic as symptomatic of intentional structures or as a "rough translation" helping us to bridge two universes of discourse ("functional dualism"), its significance extends far beyond Biran's own methodological use of physical descriptions. The concept of the diagnostic is for Ricoeur a "latent hermeneutics" or interpretation *of* experience, not a description. Indeed, the application of the diagnostic to the analysis of intentional structures of the body issued in a transformed notion of "structure." Structure now represented both possibilities and limits, and implied both a "border of indefiniteness" and an "ideality." Hence, like Jaspers' boundary situations, it designates not abstract but existential possibilities reflecting man's mode of being in the world. A still further transformation of the phenomenological concept of structure is first clearly in evidence in *Fallible Man*. The existence of two incommensurate universes of discourse and the dualism of perspectives suggested by the diagnostic now warrant the conclusion that "man is a faulted creature" and that "dualism is invincible."[87] A final transformation of "structure" made it capable of *mythic* expansion: the "upper" limits of ideality and obscurity were represented as "dreams of innocence" or the perfect freedom of effortless action, and the lower as "consent to necessity." Both limits were amenable to symbolic expressions of experience whose latent meanings had now to be uncovered by a hermeneutic. The analysis of the structure of willed action anticipates these later developments.

The principles of reciprocity and the diagnostic are first applied by Ricoeur to the analysis of the willed act and the bodily movement which depends on its performance. The task is "to clarify the experience of the corporeal involuntary within the limits of eidetic analysis of motivation and intention with objective, empirical treatment of the body."[88] The task presents a certain ambiguity, however, for it is not clear whether an intentional analysis can be provided of bodily states and processes which are involuntary and which do not seem to share the intentional character of consciously willed acts. In "reintroducing the body into the *cogito*,'' however, we are committed to an analysis of bodily significations and intentionalities which, while retaining an uncoercible quality, must still be partly assimilable to the will. The analysis of ''active affects'' or of affective experiences which are also intentional, therefore, imposes a certain strategy. In order to show how ''the *cogito* becomes actual in the world,'' an analysis is required of the underlying intentional structures of the body, i.e., that directedness of the body towards the world which shares the intentional structure of consciousness (''adherence'').

The following propositions embody Ricoeur's theory of the will:

(1) For any willed act (choice, decision) performed by the agent, the agent has a motive which has its ''source'' in the body.

(2) No bodily movement realized by the agent in virtue of his willed act is a ''terminus'' of that act. That is, when a person does something like raising an arm, it is not usually required that he first perform some other act like making a neuron fire or making a muscle move. There is no other act he must do first, only proceeding afterwards to the bodily performance.

(3) For any willed act, there is a further act by the agent of consent or acquiescence to ''necessity,'' i.e., to certain facts about the agent's body believed to be beyond his control.[89]

We may justify the liberties we have taken in our formulation of the foregoing on the grounds that the diagnostic allows us to view voluntary acts in a linguistic context and that Ricoeur's own description of ''active affects'' relies on the distinction of reasons and causes on which recent analytical discussion of motivation has centered.[90] It should be noted, however, that for Ricoeur any description of these three ''cycles'' of the will bars any causal explanation of our actions except as these may be ''symptomatic'' of the structure of our experience. Nevertheless, while the requirements of phenomenological reduction do not permit a physicalist identification of human actions with bodily movements or the movements of bodily parts, Ricoeur's functional dualism invites us to discover correlations suggesting that these are two different names for, or descriptions of, the same event.[91]

Some further explanation is required of our three propositions. With respect to (1), the act of will is also said to imply imputability, i.e., the agent's belief that the action projected is within his power. The willed act is further described as intentional in the sense that it implies the ''project'' of a practical possibility of action. Finally, the ''bodily'' or ''organic'' motive determining the willed act is identified as need, or as need conjoined with imagination, i.e., desire. (2) The ''pragma'' or action that is realized is described in terms of the ''traversing'' of the intention ''across'' the body and towards the world. From the perspective of our immediate experience of our actions, what this comes to is that we are ordinarily unaware of our body as mediating our actions, i.e., as an organ or tool. ''I can be so engaged in what I do that I do not think of my moved body.''[92] (3) The facts referred to as the objects of consent are my birth, including my heredity, filiation, and "beginning" as well as my character and my unconsicous and biological existence.

Doubts may be registered with respect to each of the three propositions. We may wish to deny (1) that all willed acts are both intentional and "motivated" and that needs are motives; (2) that the agent in performing an action did not move his body or "make it happen" that his body moved; (3) that there are subjective, experienced equivalents for such facts as my birth or "beginning." Thus, (1) it does not seem to be the case that all acts are to be explained in terms of both purposes and motives (I can, to be sure, have a motive for an intentional act, though not conversely), nor does the absence of a motive disqualify an intentional choice as a freely willed act. Nevertheless, Ricoeur claims that "there are no decisions without motives."[93] Again, need is said to *be* a motive, to be the *material* of a motive, and *to lend itself* to motivation.[94] Similarly, desire, as an "intentionality of the body," may be described in causal terms. But it is not clear that desire, which like intention *may* explain an act by mentioning something future, can at the same time be described in terms of something that affects me, i.e., as a need, craving (such as hunger); it is not both a psychological predicate ascribing a mental property to an individual and a physiological predicate. (2) Does the relation between decision and bodily motion exemplify a principle of agent causality? It is tempting to think so. But the various "cycles" of the will are apparently independent, and causal explanations are unacceptable. (The relation between decision and bodily motion is one of meaning and intentionality.) Now if we restrict ourselves to our experience of our actions, it is true that we are not aware of the changes we cause or "make happen" in the body, nor do we ordinarily do something for the purpose of causing ourselves to perform an action. But it may be claimed that a theory of agent causality which explains bodily movements in terms of "making something happen" has neither of these undesirable consequences.[95] Finally, (3) consent to necessity or to the involuntary is an anomaly in Ricoeur's analysis of willing, both because it is a presupposition rather than a consequence of the analysis and because consent itself is a willed or intended act. A more serious difficulty, however, is the identification of subjective equivalents for my birth or beginning, or for my biological inheritance (I do not "feel" my genes). That we possess an "umbilical consciousness" or Freudian desire to return to the womb that is reflected in consciousness is dubious. Nor is there any testimony of consciousness to my birth. We have no memory of the event, and as Ricoeur admits, the absence of memory is not equivalent to the memory of a beginning.[96] Finally, if the fact of my birth entails a "sense of limits," this does not seem to be a datum of immediate experience.

Space does not permit an adequate account of the subsequent development of Ricoeur's thought, in particular his investigation of the symbols and myths of Western culture and their interpretation as expressions of human evil and suffering.[97] We can only note that his latest study on Freud extends the interrogation of symbolic meaning to the unconscious construed as one of the structures of necessity, and the problem of symbolism becomes the problem of language: psychoanalysis must provide the interpretive rules of the unconscious conceived of as the language of desire. The study on Freud thus completes a development involving a linguistic turn. The unconscious has become a latent theory of language, albeit a difficult and metaphorical one, and a ''hermeneutics of suspicion'' in which symbolic meaning is other than what consciousness may intend has replaced descriptive phenomenology.

MICHEL HENRY (1922–   ). Professor at the lycée de Casablanca, 1946; Alger, 1950; Angers, 1958; associated with the Centre National de la Recherche Scientifique à Paris, 1946–1950 and 1956–1957; lecturer and professor at the Université Paul Valéry de Montpellier, 1960–   ; recipient of the Renaudot Prize for the novel *L'Amour les yeux fermés,* 1976. Selected Works (See Select Bibliography).

PHENOMENOLOGICAL ONTOLOGY

Henry's massive and complex work, *L'Essence de la manifestation,*[98] shares with Heidegger the following assumptions: (1) Phenomenology is the method of ontology. Thus, if phenomenology is the science of essences and ontology is concerned with the being of those essences, then a phenomenological ontology will have as its aim a description of the manner in which being appears or manifests itself. (2) Essence or meaning cannot be found in things independently of any reference to human consciousness or subjectivity. (3) The being which is the object of a universal phenomenological ontology is disclosed through affectivity *(le sentir).* Henry develops each of these themes in an original way. However, his attempt to widen the scope of phenomenology to include not merely the constitution of the noematic world but also the essence of the real world gives rise to familiar difficulties.

(1) The *ontologie régionale* of phenomenology may be compared to Wittgenstein's conception of language or modes of discourse as forms of life, each with its own logic or norm of rationality, intelligibility, and coherence. Regional ontology similarly implies an inquiry into a plurality of regions, each with its own distinctive properties, types of evidence, and modes of intuition. Such an ontology, however, presupposes an *ontologie fondamentale* concerned with the meaning of being in general, i.e., the conditions which any kind of object must satisfy in order to appear to consciousness. It follows that a phenomenological ontology is reflexive, i.e., phenomenology becomes its own object of inquiry. The analysis of the structure of phenomenality or meaning of ''presence'' itself implies the application of phenomenological method to the problem of the meaning of phenomena and therefore to the elucidation of its own grounds.[99]

The above inquiry immediately encounters two conflicting interpretations of the ''phenomenon,'' one idealist, the other realist. A source of the difficulty dividing existential phenomenologists on the one hand and those who have remained faithful to Husserl's view of phenomenology as a transcendental idealism on the other was precisely the incompatible aims that Husserl himself had with respect to the nature of the phenomena. For Husserl was concerned both with a phenomenology which would bring us "to the things themselves as they are *given* in immediate experience" and with a *"rationalization"* of that experience. If philosophy was to be a rational science, consciousness had to be conceived of as a constitutive source of its objects. The phenomenon or object of the intentional act had to be a wholly ideal reality or essence, "immanent in consciousness and thereby *detached* from the real world" of the subject's actual experience, an essence whose necessity depended on its *a priority*. On this view of the phenomenon, the ideal essence is actualized and constituted within "the immanent sphere of subjectivity." Immanence is required if the essence which is intuited is to possess the necessary and universal validity of a rational science.[100]

It should be observed, however, that with respect to the essence of the real world Husserl claimed that it, too, was relative to transcendental subjectivity and therefore involved the correlates of acts which were immanent contents or *cogitata*. The real world has its meaning as existing reality only as the intentional meaning-product of transcendental subjectivity.[101] Now the notion of mental acts as conferring meaning *(Sinngebung)* presupposes a consciousness which can achieve a complete awareness of its acts and their objects. But if we attend to what is in effect given, "the progressive clarification of the phenomenon may in principle be unending." For neither the ego nor the world is known with full rational clarity; reflection cannot achieve total clarification. Each phenomenon is embedded in a milieu or "horizon" of indeterminacy or indefiniteness; each phenomenon has an implicit context which implies an "exteriority," separation, or "epistemic distance" of the object from the subject with respect to what is intuitively given. Here, Henry observes, transcendence does not show or manifest itself,[102] and the rationalization of experience is no longer possible. The perception of physical objects, where the varying aspects of the object presented to consciousness are surrounded by or given with, a ground of interrelated horizons, is the most obvious example of this sort. For perception, as Merleau-Ponty had pointed out, resists a Husserlian-type reduction and fails to satisfy the requirements of rationalization because of its indefiniteness. Nor can the perceptual act be separated, as is required, from the evidence to which it is directed, since it "transcends" towards the world in the sense that we cannot suspend the existential belief-component as reduction requires.[103] We may sum up Henry's objection to Husserl's intuitionism as follows: the deficiency of intuitionism is its treatment of the horizon in which all intuited presences "bathe," as a contingent rather than necessary feature of consciousness.[104] The horizon which surrounds all effective presence implies, as we have seen, an indeterminacy with respect to the evidence. The differing acts of intending are never intuitively realized or fulfilled, and intuitionism can only regard such indeterminacy as indicative of the path our intendings must follow if they are to be converted into intuitive realization. Thus, it is only concerned with those modifications of the datum necessary to relate what is *"simplement visé"* to what is *"originaire,"* i.e., to the datum which would provide a fully adequate intuition.[105] But if essences are thereby defined in terms of intuitive realization or presence, i.e., determinate content, intuitionism cannot provide a coherent account of that indeterminacy which surrounds every presence.

The dilemma confronting a phenomenological ontology is clear. If the phenomenality of being is indeterminate, then it cannot be shown, i.e., it is not *rationalizable*. And if it is determinate, i.e., the object is *constituted* by the act, and the act provides the *a priori* conditions for the possibility of the object, then the object is not *given*. Hence, being is either not rationalizable or not given (does not manifest itself or appear). Henry attempts to seize the second horn of the dilemma, which, however, is resolved into the form of the following antinomy. If phenomenology is the method of ontology, then it follows that "being must show itself," i.e., being must become a phenomenon. Now being is the condition for the possibility of all manifestations or appearances in general. *But the conditions for the possibility of an experience, i.e., what makes of a phenomenon something that is capable of appearing, is not itself a real experience.* Hence, being cannot become a phenomenon or determinate manifestation.[106] Henry's attempted resolution of this antinomy bristles with difficulties; the second volume of *L'Essence de la manifestation* is largely devoted to argument showing how the essence of manifestation can manifest itself. But it is in his work on Biran's ontology and in his new analysis of subjectivity, opposed to both the Cartesian *cogito* and to Kant's transcendental ego and the deduction of the categories,[107] that we shall find the proposed solution based on a denial of the italicized premise above.

(2) Like Heidegger, Henry maintains that "l'être de la réalité humaine doit d'abord faire le thème de la problématique qui vise à élucider le sens de l'être en général."[108] As we have seen however, the problematic entails a view of the self as *conscience confuse* rather than knowing subject. Hence, we must first of all reject the privileged status of the *cogito* which imposes a certain conception of evidence on the given, i.e., one which satisfies the criteria of rational certitude. There is no unique, ideal type of evidence of which the *cogito* can furnish the prototype. Ontology cannot be subordinate to egology, i.e., it cannot accept an ideal type of evidence in which an intentional act must be completely fulfilled by a corresponding intuition or by the *"présence vivante"* of the thing itself. Second, the requirement that the essence appear must be accompanied by the rejection of any interpretation of the *condition of the appearance of being* in terms of ideas, concepts, or abstract possibilities. Hence, Henry rejects both the Cartesian view of consciousness as a "Je pense" in which "toutes les modifications de la vie de la conscience ne sont que des déterminations de la pensée, c'est à dire des idées";[109] and Kant's view of the subject as thinker rather than experiencer, who can know nothing about the world as it is in itself. We cannot deduce the *a priori* conditions for the possibility of an experience since the

categories must be "facts," not possibilities. To deduce a category can only be to *reduce* it to an original datum of experience, for the categories established by a transcendental deduction constitute the *a priori* conditions for the possibility not of being but of the knowledge of being for a judging consciousness, i.e., of a subject that thinks the world in fully reflexive intellectual judgments and does not experience it.[110]

According to Henry, the above requirements can be satisfied only by a clarification of the transcendental field of experience as a *Lebenswelt* or object of immediate experience prior to any thought *about* experience. The *Lebenswelt* must be the point of departure for subsequent research, i.e., for any conceptual elaboration of the data.[111] Hence, the reduction of ideas to a datum of experience must show that ideas have a more basic mode of existence anterior to that by which they appeared under the form of ideas. Phenomenological ontology implies a genetic constitution or derivation of concepts from the data, disclosing the historicity of essence and providing an account of the genesis of meaning. For Henry, "l'existence est déjà une science,"[112] a claim the truth of which must depend on the success of the reduction or "archaeology" of consciousness which purportedly uncovers the primary structures of prepredicative experience. But if the "hidden achievements" of intentional consciousness, as Edie, following Husserl, has aptly noted are the origin of all derived constructions of thought,[113] we must show how this is so, and our account must be unprejudiced by any interpretation of experience antecedent to experience itself. It is not at all clear, however, that we can provide a description of experience independent of our thought about experience.[114]

(3) What light does Biran's analysis of the self *(le moi)* throw on affectivity or "auto-affection," which Henry regards as the mode in which being manifests itself? First, what Biran referred to as *le fait primitif* is an immediate datum of experience which "carries its own criterion of evidence," i.e., is self-evident, and therefore satisfies the requirement of apodicity. Second, the distinction between being and appearance was, as we have seen, a consequence of "distancing." That is, the world as a transcendental condition of something appearing implies the deployment of a thing *(étant)* against a horizon of indeterminacy, i.e., a nonpresence. But the knowledge I possess of myself as incarnate being, the "ownership" relation I have with my body *(appartenance)*, implies an absence of distance, of exteriority or separation of the subject from its intended object or content. In the sensation of motor effort, the subject both acts and is aware of the resistance of the body, i.e., it simultaneously experiences itself and is affected by itself.[115] "Auto-affection," therefore, provides the self-knowledge which is also a revelation of being. Finally, the analysis of subjectivity discloses a reflective system of ideas such as identity, substance, cause, and self, which express the phenomenal structure of the ego and are not deduced. For all such categories are reducible to an originating sphere of certainty, a self-evident datum, which is logically prior. That is, they can be shown to have a mode of existence anterior to the mode in which they appear as concepts and are but different expressions of the same fact of consciousness.

FRANÇOIS DAGOGNET (1924–   ). Doctor of medicine; professor at the lycées in Thionville, 1947–1948, Langres, 1948–1949, Aix-en-Provence, 1949–1950, Dijon, 1950–1954; at the Lycée Ampère, Lyon, 1954–1959; professor, University of Lyon, 1959–   . Selected Works (See Select Bibliography).

SCIENCE AND DIALECTIC

Dagognet is a psychiatrist as well as a philosopher and historian of science whose primary interest is in the foundations of biology and medicine. He is a foremost disciple of Bachelard, and his work *La Raison et les remèdes,* (which is dedicated to Bachelard), like Bachelard's writings, makes a cumulative impact on the reader through its ample documentation of cases. Like Bachelard, Dagognet is impressed with the radical discontinuities and revolutions in scientific thought and with its conceptual inventiveness, totally remote from the mere reproduction of reality.[116] The scientific rationalization of experience is a *"rationalisme ouvert"* or *"dialectique"* involving a continuous interaction between thought and experience. Hence, scientific practice is incompatible with analytic procedures which seek to reduce the data to simple, observably identifiable entities. The "substantialist fallacy"[117] reflects this empirically naive view of reality which assumes that scientific concepts are the product of abstraction from experience. On the other hand, science has little in common with *"le savoir clos,"* the formal deductive systems that are sometimes presented as models of scientific thought. There is another aspect of Bachelard's thought, however, which is more controversial and whose relation to scientific theory is more tenuous. For Bachelard has also provided a theory of creative imagination which allegedly "reproduces the life of things." Active, intrusive, occupied with the mixing and combining of properties, the exercise of creative imagination implies a transformation of matter which is nevertheless rooted in the ambivalence of matter itself. Imagination does not merely reproduce our perceptual experiences, but rather it displays the *"antinomies matérielles"* which reflect the existence of the contrary forces and properties exemplified in natural phenomena. Dagognet adopts this *"coincidentia oppositorum,"* or coalescence of opposing forces, as a methodological principle, which he also assumes is embodied in physical reality. Illness is definable as a "compenetration" of microbe and organism,[118] and so understood, it is a presupposition of modern pharmacology and is confirmed by therapeutic practice.

The aim of *La Raison et les remèdes* is the same as that of Canguilhem's essay on the *Normal and the Pathological* and Foucault's *The Birth of the Clinic:* to subject the therapeutic practices of medicine to philosophical analysis.[119] Curative strategies have historically entailed certain views with respect to what constitutes health in the organism.[120] Thus, we have the following views of illness: the "manichean" theme which assumes that the body is possessed by the bad, which accordingly must be expelled or removed to the periphery where it can be dislodged; an inverse or "rehabilitative" strategy where illness is regarded as the result of weakness or debility rather than some harmful intromission; "relativism" which assumes that the same physical substance can be the source of good or bad depending on the circumstances (nature has blessed both the ailment and its antidote); the ancient doctrine of "harmonia": health is a balance of contraries, cold/warm, bitter/sweet, wet/dry, and the therapeutic goal is to reestablish the harmony between the hostile elements of the body; the homeopathic view which seeks to assure the progress and consummation of the illness since the illness is regarded as an unsuccessful effort on the part of the organism to rid itself of what is harmful, compensate for some deficiency, neutralize some secretion, and the like; the therapeutic aim is to "attiser le mal pour en délivrer" (stir up the ailment to get rid of it). These views of illness and cure are initially presented without commentary, and for the most part they appear to represent a "mythical pharmacology," although it is clear that some of them are consistent with Dagognet's own dialectical strategy. This strategy, which he characterizes as a "pharmaco-dynamism," is based on the ambivalent nature of drugs which can have opposite effects, alternatively stimulant and sedative, toxic and beneficial effects; and on the relation of habit and sensitivization to curative effects, which suggests a "debate" between patient and drug modifying both. These and similar phenomena suggest to Dagognet the appropriateness of his method, a (non-Marxist) dialectical materialism which rejects the separation of the normative question concerning the nature of health from the empirical question as to whether a certain substance can effect a cure, the practical from the theoretical: in medicine, practice and theory are inseparable, and one only knows what one tries to change.[121]

These conclusions can be illuminated further if we consider the following propositions in detail. (1) Remedies are in part social or cultural products. (2) The "substantialist fallacy" is the principal obstacle to a dynamical pharmacology. (3) A dynamical pharmacology implies a dialectical view of illness which imposes a revised conception of cure; therapy must seek to establish an optimum rather than a maximum state in the organism and to circumscribe the illness, not suppress it.

(1) In the obvious sense, what is accepted as a remedy in a society is determined not only by its material efficacy but also by beliefs, social aims, fears, and the like. Drugs energize a number of psychological forces;[122] the therapeutic nature of a particular substance may rest on its capacity to remove a potential social threat, e.g., to permit a "supervised equilibrium" in the patient who cannot otherwise assume his social responsibilities. Illness itself entails notions of social rejection. Through habitual use, remedies become institutionalized, although they have lost their efficacy because psychological factors such as surprise (which may on occasion be a necessary condition of cure) are absent. The "conventional" nature of the remedy suggests that the remedy is more properly the subject of a sociology of belief or of the latest psychology in fashion and that its historically relativized definition requires a reference to social norms.

(2) The substantialist fallacy, or failure to recognize that conceptual elaboration in science is not based on sense observations or on what is immediately

given, may lead to the hypostatization of certain abstracted properties of the phenomenon which are assumed to constitute its essential nature. Abstraction of certain properties as essential, and their hypostatization may lead to any of the following: (a) a *"modèle chosiste"* of the curative agent which, like Berkeley's *Siris*, assumes that there exists a panacea, an archetypal cure, or "philtre which can alter our destiny";[123] (b) the belief in an invariant causal relation between the chemical composition of a substance and its physiological properties; since we cannot regard a substance as a remedy apart from its effects, and the "reality" of x lies in its biological effects, it may be wrongly assumed that we can distinguish the biological from, say, the psychological effects of x, i.e., we can liberate *"la matière médicale"* from all contingent factors; (c) a semantic confusion between "x has such and such chemical properties," and "x is a medicament." In a chapter in which he attempts to define the term "remedy," Dagognet claims that we cannot isolate the variable y in the following equation: a (total effect) $= x$ (real effect) $+ y$ (effects due to suggestion, or psychological effects). Hence, we cannot solve the equation x (the remedy) $= a - y$, and we cannot determine *"le remède lui-même."* But this inability may stem from the fact that the curative value of a remedy depends on the kind of beliefs which, for example, placebo therapy dramatically exhibits,[124] that is, remedies are always overdetermined. It is not at all clear, however, whether Dagognet wishes to maintain that the "cannot" is a logical "cannot," or whether it represents an empirical difficulty in specifying the various conditions that figure in the explanans of a scientific explanation where the explanation is construed as deductive subsumption under general laws. (3) Finally, the foregoing entails for Dagognet a certain view about correct therapeutic practice and the nature of cure. If there are neither universal nor topical remedies, either because there cannot logically be any and the expectation that they exist is based on a falsifying "ontological imagination"; or we have been empirically unable to discover one; or else, we find it methodologically impossible to isolate "real" properties from purely conventional factors, then the hope for a *restitutiones ad integrum*[125] is impossible of fulfillment. Modern pharmacology must seek the more modest goals of establishing optimum rather than maximum states, inhibiting the illness rather than eliminating it, and circumscribing it, not suppressing it. It must try to reestablish an equilibrium of forces or provide the patient with a sufficient mastery of himself which will enable him to function in a social context.

Dagognet's dialectical materialism is consistent with the facts, although its successful use as a methodological or theoretical model does not entail that physical processes are themselves dialectical or that matter is "antinomic" in nature. The method implies a *"ruse des médiations"* or a strategy of *"détours"*[126] which unites drugs with opposing effects, employs substances which act indirectly, or deliberately creates difficulties in order to avoid others. Thus, we must inhibit inhibiters like enzymes to affect heartbeat; we administer antibiotics which do not eliminate the microbe directly but suppress whatever is essential to its growth. For Dagognet, vaccination is the most illuminating example of this strategy, and a paradigm: we augment or amplify what we desire to correct or avoid. The "contradictory" nature of the method on occasion leads Dagognet to make certain affirmations which suggest that pharmacology cannot be a science. Thus, he claims that "Il n'existe donc pas de réel curatif entièrement débarrassé de sa magie ou de nuances individuelles," and he maintains that there is no *"objectivité curative."*[127] But these are overstatements which he is himself at pains to caution us against. He concedes that drugs do cure and that they can be perfected, and he warns us not to fall into the trap of justifying the irrational. There is no absolute remedy for all or even any illness, but there is a "curative dynamism."[128] What exactly is implied by such dynamism, however, other than the continual need to adjust therapeutic practices to the progress of medicine is not clear.

The absence of invariant relations between the chemical composition of a substance and its physiological effects, owing to such factors as individual differences, cultural factors, feedback, the effect of the patient's beliefs, the ambiguity of experimental results, and the unreliability of animal experimentation, suggests that the laws expressing the relation between chemical substances and the state of the organism are not deterministic but statistical. If such laws are generalizations yielding only high statistical probablities, then cure is not always predictable, nor can we always obtain a measurable degree of precision in the evaluation of effects. In explanations resting on statistical laws, the explanandum is not a logical consequence of the explanans as is the case when the laws are of universal form. The "commonplaces of secular medicine," viz., faith-healing, the potency of the "bedside manner," the "placebo effect," and suggestibility phenomena, where the success of a cure "does not depend on the truth of the patient's conviction but merely on its existence," cannot support dialectical conclusions. What it suggests rather is the need to extend the domain of laws regulating psychosomatic or psychogenic effects.[129] Finally, it is plausible to assume that the confusion of statistical correlations indicative of underlying causal relations, with the causal relations themselves, i.e., of symptoms with their causes,[130] is the source of Dagognet's "illusions of pharmacology."

STRUCTURALISM: STRUCTURAL LINGUISTICS

Structuralism may be defined as the transfer of a linguistic model, which has had a measure of success since Saussure, to other domains of human experience.[131] The application of an explanatory model to social phenomena assumes the existence of some analogy between the two, i.e., between the various aspects of the linguistic phenomena abstracted in the model and the wider range of experience to which it is applied. In the present case, the data to which the model is applied are to be construed as a system of signs.

Saussure's linguistic model embodies the following principles: (1) The distinction between language as a system of signs or meanings *(la langue)* and as actual speech *(la parole);* (2) the distinction between the synchronic state of a language which makes no reference to time or to historical development, and diachronic processes, the evolution or development in time of a language; (3) a differential view of meaning and of the sign function: linguistic units possess a purely relational identity, hence, the identity of a sign is wholly a function of differences, i.e., oppositions and contrasts between signs within the system. In connection with (1) (similar to Chomsky's distinction between linguistic knowledge or competence, and performance or the actual use of the language),[132] attention is focused on the system of linguistic rules the knowledge of which is presupposed by any actual use of the code or by any particular speech act. Thus, phonology is interested not in the actual sounds uttered by the speaker, which may vary on different occasions of use, but in the functional distinctions between, say, vowels, which differentiate units at a higher level of structure. With respect to (2), Saussure insisted on the priority of synchronic descriptions of language. Diachronic statements of historical filiation, i.e., the relation between an element from one state of a linguistic system to an element from a later state, are in fact derived from synchronic identities. The interchangeability of elements or the displacement of synchronic forms is nonfunctional, and the system adjusts to those changes which are the consequences of evolutionary processes.[133] Finally, (3) the sign which is a unity of vocal utterance or an "acoustic image" (signifier) and concept (signified) is "arbitrary" and possesses a purely relational identity. The relative or differential opposition between signs is an essential property of the sign. It should be observed that the differential nature of the sign, the fact that linguistic elements have only contrastive and combinatorial properties, applies to each of the two components of the sign. There is no natural link (with some exceptions) between the two components, sound and concept, no sound sequence is better suited to its referent than any other, and both the articulation of the sound continuum and the conceptual organization of the world are arbitrary or conventional.

Some brief comments may be made with respect to each of the above points to set structuralism within the framework of contemporary philosophical discussion. First, it may be objected that meaning is after all a correlate of our experience. What is essential is what sounds are taken by the subject to mean, and the distinctions that are made within a given range of sounds require willed meaning-intentions or mental acts which are events in time and which invest thoughts and sounds with meaning.[134] Hence, the view that the subject is "decentered" because meanings are wholly explicable in terms of conventional systems of rules of which the subject is unaware or which escape his conscious grasp, is untenable. Second, the distinction between synchronic and diachonric states is not an exclusive one. The notion of a synchronic cross-section of time unexposed to change is an abstraction, and one can adopt a position which accepts both, e.g., a series of structural phases or transitions subject to historical discontinuities or "revolutions."[135] Finally, it is more difficult to distinguish between the synchronic and the diachronic in the case of semantic as distinct from sound change, since the semantic is more dependent on human intentions, purposes, and historical processes than the sound change. However, it is characteristic of a differential view of meaning to focus on the syntactical aspects of language and to ignore the semantical aspects. These criticisms, directed against certain alleged deficiencies of the model, may be interpreted as a defense of subjectivity and historicity.[136]

JACQUES DERRIDA (1930–   ). Lecturer in philosophy, University of Paris, 1962-1967; senior lecturer, École Normale Supérieure, 1967–   Selected Works (See Select Bibliography).

LANGUAGE AND METAPHYSICS

Derrida's main concern is with the Western tradition of philosophical thought which grounds meaning in "presence," that is, in some self-presenting or self-authenticating experience which can serve as the foundation of the meaning of signs. Phenomenology and the phenomenological concept of evidence represent the completion or final working out *(clôture)* of that tradition, since they provide a foundationalist theory of meaning in terms of what is self-presenting or directly known.[137] A "deconstruction" or dismantling of the traditional "metaphysics of presence" will lay bare the presuppositions of the latter, revealing the contradictions and conceptual oppositions within the system whose source is *"différence."* For signs, according to Derrida, have a purely differential character: linguistic meaning is not the product of an explicit meaning-intention whose object or content can be directly known, but of an arbitrary configuration of differences between signs. Every sign system is constituted by a representation or reference to what is *not* present or absent. Deconstruction must in this respect encompass the various dimensions of the metaphysics of presence: (1) the presence or givenness of the object of sensible intuition (the sensible object); (2) the presence of objectivities given to thought (meaning-contents, propositions); (3) self-awareness or the presence of the subject to itself in the immediacy of a conscious act.[138] The privileged mode of access to this metaphysics, Derrida claims, is writing. The whole nature of our experience is prescribed by a certain interpretation of writing[139] and by a "logocentrism" or doctrine of the primacy of the spoken word associated with that interpretation.

The philosophy of presence is based on the view that the written inscription is purely derivative. It merely represents a speech-act or vocal utterance which is primary in the sense of directly signifying a meaning or rendering the self present to itself. In his *Grammatology,* which is devoted for the most part to Rousseau's *Essai sur l'origine des langues* and is focused on the role Rousseau assigns to writing and on his notion of an "originative" language, Derrida attempts (1) to provide a description of the mediate character of writing as a visible sign or representation of the "absent" utterance; (2) to describe the ethical and social implications of a writing which "resists" presence or "does violence" to speech and thereby serves as an instrument of exploitation; [140] (3) finally, to exhibit the "traces" of an "archi-ecriture," an originative or archetypal writing which he regards as essential to language, and which speech or the verbal utterance actually presupposes. This primacy of writing, and therefore of an original nonpresence, is reflected in what Derrida refers to as the "movement of difference" (with an "a"). The traditional conceptual oppositions between presence and absence, as well as the attempt to reduce difference, are themselves rooted in difference. Of the latter, however, we can have only "traces" or can perceive only the historical effects. Nietzsche's view of the impossibility of self-knowledge and Freud's view of the primacy of the unconscious represent such historical traces. (In his early *Speech and Phenomena*, a critique of Husserl's distinction between two modes of signification, indication and expression, Derrida similarly attempts to demonstrate the impossibility of presence as a criterion of meaningfulness.)

The metaphysics of presence and the primacy of the vocal utterance have been historically exemplified in various guises since Plato. Thus, in the *Phaedrus* Plato eulogizes speech and condemns writing because it cannot respond to the questioner. Biran observed that only speech preserved the unity of the sign, i.e., the identity of the vocal sound and the expressed meaning, since in the vocal expression I am simultaneously aware of both my act and its thought-content. Saussure had maintained that while speech and writing are two distinct sign systems, the purpose of writing is to represent speech. Husserl similarly assigned a privileged status to the expressive sign.[141] The expression of meaning is exemplified in silent speech of soliloquy where the signifier is reduced to its signified content; hence, meaningful language is limited to expression since it alone carries a signified content which is present. It is in Rousseau, however, that the ambiguities of a "phonocentrism," which views writing as a mediate representation of a thought directly conveyed in speech, are fully manifest. For if language for Rousseau first occurred in connection with feeling, giving natural expression to feeling through cries and gestures, this was due to the fact that feeling is an experience whose unmediated presence provides the foundation of what we mean when we speak. Writing then seems exterior to speech, providing a conventional supplement for the natural sign of feeling and thereby deferring our immediate experience of feeling. But Rousseau recognizes that this conventional substitute for the natural sign having no essential link with its meaning is nevertheless a *"supplement originaire."* The immediacy of speech is illusory, the vocal utterance (the phoneme) as well as the graphic inscription is conventionally articulated, and a conception of speech in which the self is fully present to itself is an idealization. Distance (*"arrachement"*) from oneself is necessary, for the coincidence of speaker and subject, i.e., total presence, would stop thought. The *cogito* cannot know itself directly, and all reflection implies distance or difference. Hence, the self-avowals of the *Confessions* required writing.

That writing "resists" presence, does "violence" to speech, or "deforms" meaning implies an evaluation of writing as contrary to life. Writing is antithetical to the customs and oral traditions of a society, it is claimed, and spells the rupture of interpersonal bonds and the disappearance of natural presence.

According to Rousseau, the use of the sensible sign leads to the neglect of things, and natural or expressive language is thereby transformed into discourse which is capable of greater pecision but destructive of personal presence. A special case of such violence is the replacement of proper names by class names which Lévi-Strauss attributes to the practice of writing. The absence of writing on the other hand is coextensive with the innocent and nonviolent character of the political order, and implies a recognition of the Other in his otherness. Hence, for Lévi-Strauss, "the primary function of writing as a means of communication, is to facilitate the enslavement of other human beings."[142] A careful reading of Rousseau, however, suggests that the spoken language does not have logical priority, the written language being secondary or derived. On the contrary, presence presupposes the sign function, and the sign function does not merely supervene on presence. Writing resists reduction and does not constitute the trace of an absent present but rather of the nonpresential structure of experience itself, i.e., of what can never be present. Thus, the principle of writing is itself the condition of language, a *"supplement originaire"*: there is no presence behind the sign which is the foundation of meaning.

"Differ*a*nce" possesses at least two related meanings. Thus, "differer" may mean to distinguish, i.e., it implies the nonidentity of x and y or difference proper; or it can mean the interposition of delay, postponement, putting off until later, or deferring, in the temporal sense of the term. It is neither name nor concept, neither event, process, nor thing. Nevertheless, it shares the features of Saussure's semiological difference construed as the *a priori* condition for the existence of a system of functional relations; and of Heidegger's ontological difference as the condition for all appearances to appear which cannot itself appear.[143] Yet, its "activity" is revealed in the play of "traces" which are themselves like signs without symptoms of what can never present themselves. The transposition of difference into the register of time is already suggested by Husserl who held two inconsistent views on the subject: a philosophy of presence (both of the self and of ideal meanings) on the one hand; and a view of the present as essentially related to past retentions and future protensions, on the other. In the latter case, the present moment is analyzed in terms of a synthesis of traces and entails the denial of the possibility of a temporally isolated instant. As an activity "originating" differences, however, differ*a*nce may be viewed in a more dramatic modality. If we think of "deferral" as the suspension or delay until later of what is already present but only as a trace, i.e., that of the absolute loss of presence (as distinct from pure presence without loss), we are confronted with an analysis similar to the Heideggerian analysis of being-towards-death of the second part of *Being and Time*.[144] That is, differ*a*nce implies the finitude of my life as essentially linked with my death, and it is this relation, conditioning all thought and experience, which produces the distancing that marks the impossibility of presence or that renders presence enigmatic.

CLAUDE LÉVI-STRAUSS (1908–   ). Professor at the lycées of Mont-de-Marsan, 1931–1932, and Laôn, 1932–1933; professor of sociology at the University of São Paulo, 1934–1938; leader of a number of ethnological expeditions into central Brazil, 1935–1939; professor at the New School for Social Research, New York, 1942–1945; cultural attaché, French Embassy in the United States, 1946–1947; director of studies at the École Pratique des Hautes Études, 1950–1974, named to the chair of comparative religions; secretary general of the International Council of the Social Sciences, 1953–1960; professor, named to the chair of anthropology at the Collège de France, 1959; elected member of the Academie Française (occupying the seat of Montherlant), 1973; member of the Royal Academy of Holland, the Academy of Sciences and Letters of Norway, the American Academy of Arts and Sciences and the National Academy of Sciences, the British Academy and Royal Anthropological Institute of Great Britain and Ireland, the American Philosophical Society, the London School of African and Oriental Studies, and the American Museum of Natural History; commander of the Legion d'Honneur, of the Ordre National du Mérite with Palmes Académiques; officer des Arts et des Lettres; recipient of the Gold Medal for Scientific Research of the Centre National de la Recherche Scientifique, 1967; doctor, *honoris causa* at the universities of Brussels, Oxford, Yale, Chicago, Columbia, Stirling, and the National University of Zaïre; recipient of the Erasmus Prize, 1973. Selected Works (See Select Bibliography).

STRUCTURAL ANTHROPOLOGY

Lévi-Strauss's investigations in the areas of kinship theory, the logic of myth, and the theory of primitive classification are paradigms of the structuralist approach. They fulfill Saussure's expectations with respect to the applicability of a more generalized science of signs. Thus, social anthropology may be regarded as a branch of semiology. Social interaction embodies a "language," and social conventions may be treated as systems of signs. The ascription of meaning to things adheres to structuralist principles: (a) the principle of antihistoricism according to which structural similarity precedes the question of origins or of historical relationships; (b) the distinction between the system of conventions constituting a language (the "code") and its actual exercise (the "message")—for Lévi-Strauss this also implies a distinction between surface events and implicit or deep structure; (c) a differential view of meaning: the meaning of a term is definable in terms of its syntactical relations to the other words in the language. Just as sounds, for example, are conveniently associated with particular meanings, although the same sounds occur elsewhere in different combinations, so mythical symbols involve invariant relationships despite their differing contents.

Lévi-Strauss's analysis of cooking is an exemplary case of the application to anthropology of Jacobson's method and that of the Prague school of structural linguistics. For Jacobson, the phonological oppositions and contrasts characteristic of the great variety of phonemes of a language are reducible to a system of twelve oppositions embodying such distinctive features as vocalic/nonvocalic and tense/lax. The primary phoneme distinctions are schematized in Jacobson's vowel-consonant triangles representing the binary opposites, compact/diffuse and grave/acute.[145] Similarly, cooking can be shown to be based on an underlying system of distinctive features schematized in a "culinary triangle."[146] The latter constitutes a "semantic field" whose three points correspond to the categories of the raw, the cooked, and the rotted, involving a double opposition which differentiates these along two axes, culture/nature and normal/transformed. (Cooking, for example, is a cultural transformation of the raw, the rotted, a natural transformation.) The model is capable of further extension in terms of the modes of cooking. Thus, roasting, smoking, and broiling form another structured set involving either natural processes or cultural mediation. A still further complication of the model relates the kind of food eaten to social occasions, establishing a relation between food categories and levels of social prestige.

An earlier application of structuralist principles to kinship systems exhibits the binarism and conventionalism characteristic of phonology.[147] Thus, kinship systems, like language, are not established at the level of single terms but of ordered couples, husband/wife, father/son, maternal uncle/sister's son (the avunculate). They are systems of communication based on a conventional system of representations or signs founded not on biological facts such as consanguinity but on alliances. Thus, the rules of marriage exemplify a system of exchange or "rule of the gift" which enjoins the giving of the mother, sister, or daughter to the other. Such exchange is a language insuring communication between individuals and groups; the "message" is constituted by the circulation of women between clans and families, the convention of gift-giving constituting a "code" or symbolic expression for something more abstract, viz., the network of relationships that link together members of the society. The principle of reciprocity or exchange which proscribes exogamy has as its converse the incest taboo which Lévi-Strauss regards as the cornerstone of human society, since it insures giving womenfolk away to create political alliances, and thus effects the transition from nature to culture.[148]

Finally, the same logic is manifest in Lévi-Strauss's more recent work in primitive mythology. Myths from unrelated contexts may be construed as variants or transformations of an underlying logical structure common to all, the differing versions or permutations being related by inversion or homology. If, for example, the Indians of the two Americas attribute the same actions to different animals, these may be regarded as different permutations of the same relationship, the meaning of which is dependent upon our awareness of the invariant relationship underlying the differing contexts. If, to take a simple illustration,[149] the eagle appears during the day and the owl at night, and both have the same function, we can conclude that the eagle is a diurnal owl, the owl a nocturnal eagle, and the opposition that is germane is that of night and day. Similarly, in the analysis of the Oedipus myth, the structural law that is disclosed implies the operation of basic oppositions (opposed theories of man's origin). This law thereby exhibits the universe of the tale as one of differently combined oppositions analogous to Jacobson's phoneme considered as a bundle of differential elements.

Some observations may be made about the implications of the method illustrated in the foregoing examples. First, the social discourse constituted by mythical language as well as by the other sign systems renders the individual speaker irrelevant since the understanding of the system as such *(la langue)* is not dependent on who said what. Second, Lévi-Strauss's pervasive interest in the dichotomy of nature and culture implies a kind of Rousseauism. It is in savage thought which is rebellious to change and dedicated to order and to fixity that we may discover that mediation between nature and culture which allows us to understand the relation of man and the world and the continuity between primitive society and our own.[150] We have seen further how natural relations can generate cultural products embodying the same relations, how nature is transformed into culture. Cooking categories can be appropriated for use as symbols in social differentiation, and totemism implies a like classification of social phenomena by means of categories derived from the natural world of animal species.[151] Finally, there is a suggestion that the polar oppositions involved require an intermediate position or a dialectical resolution. Thus, a code based on the principle of exogamy or the incest taboo is viewed as a prototype of social organization because it reconciles the opposed demands of nature and culture. That is, it mediates natural desire or the sexual or appropriative instincts on the one hand, and the social and political desire to forge an instrument of alliance on the other. Like the myth, however, which expresses unconscious wishes inconsistent with our conscious experience and which can only provide a notional resolution of conflict by equating contradictory relations, so the proscription of incest for Lévi-Strauss is a hidden message concerned with the resolution of unwelcome contradictions.[152]

We may ask whether binary discriminations or bipolar oppositions derived from Jacobson's distinctive-feature analysis is an adequate characterization of thought or whether the dichotomizing of possibilities is the only mental operation on which primitive culture relies. Perhaps it is only one component of any communicative process.[153] Again, it is not clear that Lévi-Strauss applies these oppositions with the proper discrimination, or even that systems such as that embodied in the set of kinship arrangements constitutes a language properly speaking. The focus on a restricted set of alternatives among the various sets of behaviors and attitudes considered appropriate to, or inappropriate between, related individuals is not warranted by our observations, but is based on a preconception that binary oppositions are at play.[154] Nor is exchange in the case of kinship relations identical with a language; what I give I no longer possess, while a message transmitted by a speech act does not entail deprivation. In short, the kinship community is not quite the same as a speech community, reciprocity is not mutuality or the sharing of a common resource, and there is nothing in the kinship relation to correspond to the sentence in language. Nor, it may be objected, is the constituting of such arrangements an activity comparable to linguistic competence.[155]

Lévi-Strauss's studies of kinship structure, primitive classification, and myth form the bases of hypotheses about the nature of the human mind. These implications are particularly in evidence in *The Savage Mind* [156] in which the concern is to establish true facts about *"l'esprit humain."* Myth reflects the mind that engendered it, and the logic of myth is rooted in a psychology common to all men, as kinship systems are variations or "syntagms" of a single system reflecting the universal attributes of mind. The "categories" of this "Kantianism without a subject" (Ricoeur) are not discoverable by a transcendental deduction but by anthropological investigation. A further conclusion, related to the universals of mind, may be elicited from Lévi-Strauss's reference to his "three mistresses," geology, Marx, and Freud. [157] If geology can exhibit abstract relationships by a juxtaposition of ages remote from one another in time, Marx and Freud have also brought order to a seemingly incoherent collection of facts, the one by an appeal to underlying causes and the distinction between infra- and superstructure, and the other by the use of the unconscious as a structural organizing principle underlying conscious reality. Hence, the mind which articulates experience through the mediation of concepts is not the transparent individual or *ego cogitans* of Descartes. For the structuring of social life is unconscious, and the various systems are constructed by the mind on the level of unconscious thought. All forms of social life consist of systems of behavior representing the projection of universal laws regulating the unconscious activity of mind. In this respect, they are analogous to linguistic behavior, since the native speaker is not aware of using syntactic constructions or phonemes to convey meanings. As the linguistic system used by all speakers involves rules that are internalized in the speaker's mind and of which he is unconscious, so the unconscious logical faculty of the mind organizes collective life.

MICHEL FOUCAULT (1926–   ). Senior lecturer and professor of philosophy, Clermont-Ferrand, 1960–1962, 1964–1968; professor, University of Paris-Vincennes, 1968–1970; professor, named to the chair of the history of thought, Collège de France, 1970–   ; director of the monthly *Zone des tempêtes,* 1973–   . Selected Works (See Select Bibliography).

THE ARCHAEOLOGY OF THE HUMAN SCIENCES

Foucault's epistemological theory is not a theory of scientific method but rather an "archaeology" of thought, i.e., a history of the *a priori* principles or conceptual schema that constitute the necessary conditions for the development of the sciences at a particular period. [158] Therefore, the "archive" does not consist of the historical documents or texts that have been preserved from the past, but of the epistemes, categories, or "transcendentals" determining the knowledge of the period. Foucault generally restricts his investigation to the human sciences of biology, economics, and language. In his influential work, *The Order of Things,* the conceptual archetype dominating the epistemological field in the classical period beginning in the seventeenth century is representation. Linked with a naming theory of meaning, representation, like the *a priori* concept of similitude which it supplanted (things are linked by resemblances among themselves), is tied to language and first acquires its scientific status in discourse. Thus, things are arranged in a serial order of increasing complexity. The task of analysis is to discriminate or to provide a distinct representation of things, and the conventional system of signs, i.e., language is called upon to perform this function.[159]

It has been observed that the ancestry of the *episteme* includes the *Weltan-schauung* of German philosophy of history and the cultural unities of American anthropology.[160] (Lovejoy's elaboration of the "great chain of being" as the presupposition of Western thought is perhaps a more familiar example of a similar, though less localized, enterprise drawn from the history of ideas). A closer parallel is the Kantian system of categories which constitute the *a priori* conditions for the possibility of knowledge. It should be noted, however, that Foucault's *epistemes* do not form a system of Kantian categories since they are neither logically necessary nor permanent. Although a necessary condition of knowledge, the *episteme* is applicable for only a limited period, that is, it is an "*historical* a priori."

The archaeology of thought shares with Nietzsche's genealogical method and Marx's notion of the infrastructure the aim of exploring the hidden, necessary conditions of the visible phenomena. But despite the suggestiveness of the results and the brilliance and erudition with which Foucault's archaeological exploration is carried out, the latter is exposed to a number of serious difficulties. (1) No criteria are provided for determining when a new *episteme* is in force or whether an alternative interpretation of the history of science is invalid; (2) the classical *episteme* is reduced to taxonomies, classifications ignore the growing interdisciplinary relations between the sciences, and the other human sciences are denied the title because they do not fit Foucault's schema or table of the sciences; and (3) the transformations undergone by reason have no rationale and are the outcome of fortuitous mutations—hence, we cannot conceive of any progress in our knowledge. This challenge to an historical explanation of the development of knowledge may also be criticized on the grounds that it ignores the interpenetration of concepts as well as their continued survival, the fact that acquired knowledge is not wholly superseded.[161]

Foucault's primary interest,[162] the history of medicine and especially of pathology, offers an early example of his archaeological method. Western culture, Foucault affirms, has adopted a negative attitude towards madness. For the Renaissance, madness still possessed a tragic and eschatological aspect. But in the seventeenth century it was regarded as an illusion of the mind against which reason must protect itself. Its exclusion from reason is institutionally embodied in confinement: the madman must be interned, for there is no place for him in a free and rational society. Madness is interpreted as the sign of a perverse will, and confinement has a correspondingly moral rather than medical significance. It is an exorcism for the inmate and source of edification for the sane. The madman, in choosing unreason and the animal nature in man, must be displayed to deter man from the same fate. The house of confinement is a place of correction and redemption, but more significantly, it is a social and economic fact, "ratified" by psychiatry, rather than a chapter in the history of medicine. For Foucault, madness thus has its origin in the contact with the aspiration to truth of the seventeenth century, and is not allowed to speak of itself in the first person until the nineteenth century. When it does, it points to certain truths about man which were both silent and threatening.[163] Foucault's sympathy for madness is founded on a truth about man, a hidden "secret" associated more with the dream world than with rational discourse. It is to be sought at a point prior to the modern "partition" between reason and unreason. It suggests a Neitzschean vision of an inchoate universe and a nostalgia for a primordial unity of the self to which madness is a witness.

More recently, Foucault has turned his attention to an allied subject—penal justice and the origin of the prison.[164] He traces the development of criminal justice from a concern with corporeal punishment to that of the treatment and cure of the criminal, from punishment to rehabilitation, from expiation to amelioration. The *"pénalité incorporelle"* and the new *"âge de la sobriété punitive,"* however, do not indicate a progress in humanity so much as a change in the object of control: the soul, heart, will, and disposition of the subject rather than the body. The penal process mirrors that change, substituting for the simple judgment of guilt accompanied with sanctions, a complex scientific-juridical judgment which is both diagnostic and evaluative, and which includes technical prescriptions for "normalization." This metamorphosis of punitive methods and practices is less a consequence of judicial theories than a chapter in "political anatomy." It reveals a technique of power, a "political technology" of the body disguised by a technology of the soul.[165] Foucault claims that this technology still seeks control of the body, but as a productive force possessing economic utility. Subjugation, he affirms, is to be explained by the system of production and the needs of a free labor market, just as earlier on in his study of madness, confinement had economic significance, providing cheap manpower and social protection.[166]

It is clear that the *"discontinuité anonyme"* of the *episteme* implies what Dufrenne has described as a "dehistoricized history."[167] The mutation of events in the field of knowledge are both impersonal and unpredictable and do not arise from individual choice. The very being of language and of the discourse on which science is based implies the disappearance of the subject, since language is a structural reality with no concern for the speaking subject. Moreover, the *episteme* of the classical period is associated with the representational properties of the sign system and not with the empirical subject. If to these observations we add the fact that Kant and a later positivism have destined man to an ephemeral existence consequent on the discovery of his finite nature, and if we recognize the inhuman nature of life confirmed by man's alienation and the significance of the unconscious, we may wonder whether Piaget's harsh judgment that "Foucault has it in for man"[168] is not after all justified.

LOUIS ALTHUSSER (1918–   ). Lecturer and secretary of the École Normale Supérieure, 1948–   ; director of the series *Théorie* published by Maspero, 1965–   . Selected Works (See Select Bibliography).

STRUCTURAL MARXISM

According to Althusser, a "symptomatic" reading of Marx will disclose an "epistemological break" between the scientific structure of Marxism and a Marxist ideology inspired by an earlier liberal humanism.[169] More particularly, a comparison of *Capital* with the 1844 Manuscripts reveals a discontinuity of thought at the time of the *German Ideology* when Marx, rejecting the concept of a fixed human nature and such nonscientific concepts as alienation in favor of wage labor, established historical materialism on a scientific basis. The break between ideology and science was accomplished by a new Marxist philosophy, dialectical materialism, a meta-theory of social practice whose task it was to integrate the knowledge established by historical materialism and to provide a theoretical expression for a solution already exhibited in practice.[170] Hence, in *Capital* we have a scientific theory of the economic mode of capitalist production based on historical materialism. But such a *theoretical* activity or practice is distinct on the one hand from other social practices such as the economic, the political, and the ideological, and on the other from a scientific epistemology or general theory of practice which represents an attempt to establish the necessary conditions for something to be an object of science at all.[171] If we confine our attention to the autonomy of theoretical practice from other practices and from empirical reality generally, we may observe that the thoughts or concepts which are its characteristic "products" are radically different from the real objects or events that are *represented by* theoretical models and structures. The scientific investigation of a system consists in discovering the hidden structures beneath the visible functions or concrete social relationships. Thus, the structure underlying economic reality, e.g., that profit actually represents unpaid labor, explains the hidden logic of visible relationships and cannot be identified with them.[172]

The structuralist view of scientific autonomy seeks to overcome a fundamental problem in Marxist theory, namely, the requirement that historical determinism provide a theory of the production of knowledge which is not identifiable with the blindly caused productions of ideology (reflecting the economic class position of the thinker).[173] But Althusser's effort to specify the relation between theory and practice encounters a number of difficulties. We may assume, for example, that Marx's break between ideology and science was based on a purely theoretical revolution in the concepts employed rather than on political events, i.e., the break was not itself socially determined. Hence, Althusser rejects the claim of a Lukács that "correct" knowledge can only be achieved through a proletarian standpoint, for theory is unrelated to class-consciousness. We must not confuse theoretical and ideological practice, the historicist view of the determination of consciousness by class position is untenable, and there are a number of contradictions internal to the particular practices or levels and between the various levels, not merely one principal contradiction between bourgeoisie and proletariat. But how then shall we characterize that consciousness of objective contradictions which converge on a revolutionary situation where active struggle occurs? Here Althusser merely seems to replace economic with political "monism." For the integration of the varying levels and the "fusion of contradictions" in the revolutionary situation is ultimately attributed to conscious political activity or choice.[174]

The object of dialectical materialism is the set of distinctive practices which constitute the social whole. Each of the practices in this complex unity is determinate and autonomous, although autonomy is relative and each level or practice is related to the others and to the whole in various relations of determination and interdependence. These relationships may be described in the following terms. First, in view of the relative autonomy of each practice, the history of the practice and of its internal elements may be articulated independently of any other. In economic practice, for example, the differing modes of production which Althusser analyzes in terms of five elements that may be differently related are not thought of as evolving through stages but as discontinuous, for each element of the combination, such as free worker and capital, has its own history or genealogy. Hence, the various levels or practices do not develop in a continuous or homogeneous ("Hegelian") time. Second, the variety of possible relationships cannot be reduced to the simple dialectic of essence (economic base) and phenomena (superstructure). The social formation may be dominated by any one of its elements which Althusser terms a "structure in domination" *(structure à dominante)*. Third, although noneconomic dominance is possible at a particular time and in a particular social formation, economic practice is nevertheless determinant of the social whole "in the last instance," i.e., economic causality is of a different order than that of the others. Fourth, such causality must be rendered consistent with pluralism, i.e., with the fact that noneconomic structures are independent variables, that they cannot grow out of economic relationships, and that the causality of the economic factor cannot be interpreted as the genesis of the superstructure from within one infrastructure. Noneconomic structures are not simply phenomena which accompany economic activity having only a passive role to play in social life, leaving the economic relationships alone with an active causality whose effects are automatic.[175] "The social formation is determined by the economy in the last instance, but the economy is never active in a pure state and the last instance may never come."[176] Finally, the autonomy, yet interdependence, of the various levels implies the absence of any single, main "contradiction" between the forces of production (labor and capital) as we find in historicist versions of Marxism. Hence, the evolution of the social system and the existence of a revolutionary situation cannot be attributed to economic determinism but rather to a multiplicity of contradictions within and between practices.[177] Althusser refers to the complexity of contradiction as "overdetermination" which involves (a) a displacement of contradiction from the economic forces of production to a multiplicity of contradictions between different levels of practice whose differential effects can be specified, and (b) a theory of revolutionary rupture as a situation which is dependent on a "convergence" of contradictions.[178]

It is clear that Althusser's epistemology hinges in large part on the notions of relative autonomy and overdetermination. Althusser regards the relation between determinant and dominant as two aspects of contradiction. Economic causality, which exhibits both of these features, is a "structural" or "metonymic" causality, which, like Spinoza's substance, is said to be "immanent" in its effects; an "absent presence," the role of the economy is not itself observable except in the effects produced on other levels. The concept of overdetermination is attributable to Freud who introduced the term to denote how an effect such as a single dream image expresses several unconscious desires. But it may be asked whether either the notion of immanence or that of a plurality of causes is sufficient to explain the manner in which external relationships between practices are consistent with "internal correspondances,"[179] i.e., how these differing causal roles are to be construed.

Althusserian Marxism is explicitly antihistoricist and antihumanist, opposing "a philosophy of the concept to a philosophy of the subject."[180] Discontinuity and differential temporality prevail. The unit of analysis is the social formation as a whole and not the individual, for the concept of man is not held to be capable of scientific elaboration and history must be explained without resort to human agents. Consequently, all doctrines of praxis are called into question. Synchronic study has precedence over the diachronic: the study of the genesis of a structure presupposes a knowledge of the structure, and economic history depends on a prior identification of structural elements and their relations.

JACQUES LACAN (1901–   ). Psychiatrist; director of the Clinic of the Faculty of Medicine of Paris, 1932; doctor at the Psychiatric Hospitals, 1936; professor at Sainte-Anne Hospital, 1953; specialist in children's neuropsychiatry and psychoanalysis; lecturer at the École Pratique des Hautes Études, 1963–   ; editor at Du Seuil, 1963–   ; founder of the École Freudienne de Paris, 1963. Selected Works (See Select Bibliography).

LANGUAGE AND THE UNCONSCIOUS

Psychoanalysis is a therapeutic practice as well as a science, and cure is dependent on what the patient tells the analyst: "The analyst operates on what the subject says to him. He considers him in the discourses which he holds with him and examines him in his locutory or 'fabulatory' behavior, and through the patient's discourses another discourse slowly takes shape for the analyst, one which he will endeavor to explain: that of the complex buried in the unconscious."[181] Freud's analyses of jokes, slips of the tongue, and the like, in his

Psychopathology of Everyday Life, and of dreams in the *Interpretation of Dreams*, suggest that speech is a manifestation of, and symbolic substitute for, the unconscious self or "Other." The stronger, Lacanian thesis assumes that the unconscious exhibits the structure of language[182] and that psychic reality is identical with a purely symbolic order. Lacan's main effort then has been directed to interpreting Freud as a linguist who may be viewed from a Saussurian perspective. The distinctions supplied by modern structural linguistics and by the rules of the traditional rhetoric, its tropes, euphemisms, and allusions, may be applied to our understanding of the unconscious as the "Discourse of the Other."[183] This conclusion may be supported by the following. First, the analyst's regression to an alleged biographical experience, or "cause" of the subject's symptoms, is dependent on the affirmations of the subject which have their entire reality in his discourse without regard to their historical reality. Hence, from an epistemological point of view, the analyst's concern must be with the articulation of "signifiers," and the unconscious may accordingly be construed as a system of syntactical rules of combination, conversion, displacement, and so forth, without relation to an external reality. Second, the dictum that "the being of language is the non-being of objects"[184] suggests an explanation as to why the imaginary material with which the analyst deals is indifferent to the truth and why biological need is not a sufficient causal condition of psychic reality.[185] For first, the desire of the subject and the varying demands that he makes for its satisfaction, as distinct from organic need, is generated by the lack of an object or by an absent or lost object (the mother is the first representative of the Other as desired object). Second, speech is a substitute for what is necessarily an imaginary or fantasy relation to such absence: the significans replaces the real object which is lacking. Although it is difficult to follow Lacan here, it is possible to reconstruct his logic of desire and to explain how the Other or object becomes part of the symbolic order of language. Thus, if we consider Lacan's "phallocentrism,"[186] i.e., the view that all speech acts ultimately revolve around the phallus and that the analyst's regression along the chain of signifiers will accordingly disclose this as the first signifier, it is clear that the phallus itself is but a symbol or "paternal metaphor" irreducible to any real object and a substitute for the absence of the mother. Now if, as Lacan maintains, the dialectic of desire is endless and there can be no "ultimate" signifier (the phallus itself being replaced by a multiplicity of object-demands with an infinite regress in the order of signifiers), this is because desire must be recognized as seeking the impossible annihilation of all difference. Where, for example, the child's desire is to be the mother's sole object of desire, the subject seeks the annihilation of the Other as an independent subject, but the desire for unity or completeness is impossible of satisfaction and represents a disavowal of reality. Thus, the phallus must be construed as being without a real object or significatum, as a *manque à être* signifying desire itself; and demand which mediates desire will maintain the lack of real objects by the indefinite substitution and displacement of words.

Two further consequences follow from the above. First, where the analyst's regression along the chain of signifiers discloses an "absent center" at the very beginning, psychoanalytic interpretation is in principle infinite, for the analyst cannot arrive at any meaning or significatum in the unconscious which anchors the signifier in reality. The coherence of the signifier depends on its relation to the entire system of signifiers, the significatum or "meaning" being merely a signifier that has been replaced. The discourse of the Other involves an endless displacement or substitution of symbols representing the imaginary and grounded in the gap *(béance)* between desire and its object. Second, contrary to Saussure's view, signifier or speech-act and signified and meaning are not on the same level and any movement from one to the other is barred, for structure exists only on the level of signifiers, not on that of concepts. Lacan illustrates this conclusion with Poe's story "The Purloined Letter" whose contents are unknown and cannot be communicated but whose existence and that of the various letters substituted for it determine the actions and roles of those who come into its possession.[187]

The accession to language and entry into the symbolic order has curative value, for it serves to reveal to the subject his unconscious desires and permits him to recognize his true relation to the other, releasing him from an alienating image of himself.[188] The appropriation of language is exemplified in Freud's analysis of the logic of the signifiers "Fort! Da!" (gone-here) in *Beyond the Pleasure Principle*. These terms are uttered by the child in order to protect himself against the mother's absences by imitating her departures and returns, and they constitute a substitute for a fantasy relationship to a lack of object. The example illustrates (a) the structural alternation or binary opposition of phonemes articulating the presence and absence of the desired object, characteristic of the language of the unconscious, and (b) the mastery of one's privation through the expression of his desire. The paradigm of the imaginary relationship (the later phase of which is identical to the early Oedipal stage), however, is the "mirror-stage" of infancy *(stade de miroir)*.[189] This specular relation is derived from Wallon's essay on the development of the child's notion of his own body, and it is an extension of Freud's own views on narcissism and object-choice. Briefly, the mirror phase exhibits the child's quest for the self in the Other. The child identifies himself with a double or alter ego, the mirror image, which enables him to recognize himself, i.e., discover a corporeal or visible unity lacking to him at an earlier stage of development when he was unable to distinguish his body from the world around him. The identification of the *moi* with its image, however, is alienating, for the self is confused with the Other as alter ego which acts as mirror for the self. For Lacan this identification with the Other is based on the subject's desire to be the phallus, i.e., the entire object of desire of the mother, but internalization of the Other can only lead to conflict and rivalry and the self-alienation of the subject. Liberating access to the symbolic order is related to the Oedipal relation and to sexual differentiation. The intervention of the father (the father's law) deprives the child of his identification with the Other (symbolic castration), and the subsequent identification with the father in a symbolic act which assumes the father's function "normalizes" the Oedipus complex. Distinguished from the phallus and separated from the mother, the *moi* now becomes *sujet,* a distinct subject rather than image of the other, hitherto the object of an unconscious discourse conducted in the register of a hopeless unification. He is now able to recognize the unconscious desire on which his relation to the other depended.[190]

Among the grammatical and rhetorical forms which enable Lacan to assimilate unconscious formations to language are (a) metaphor and metonymy and (b) indexical terms or "switchers" such as the personal pronoun "I."[191] The first two tropes (which Lacan borrows from Jacobson's studies on aphasia) embody, through the combination and substitution of signifiers, the same structural laws of condensation and displacement which govern the unconscious. Metaphorical substitutions, based on similarity, involve the repression of a particular signifier, while the return of the repressed meaning or of what is not said, distorted by censorship, is what gives metaphor its singular evocative power. The displacement characteristic of metonymy and synecdoche entails a concealment of or escape from the displaced meaning or real object of desire; hence, it exhibits the *manque à être* of its object. The two tropes are related respectively to the paradigmatic and syntagmatic modes of language. Similarly, the discourse of the unconscious involves the use of indexical terms or shifters such as the personal pronoun "I" which both represents the subject and masks him. Thus, the referent of the indexical sign or token-reflexive word is relative to the speaker (i.e., knowledge of who spoke and the context of utterance is essential in determining the reference of the word), and the reference may change from one occasion of utterance to another. Each utterance, however, means the same thing. In view of the distinction between meaning and reference, the subject can communicate a message in order to convey an "intended" meaning without being "present" in the message. That is, the message may be attributed to the grammatical subject rather than to the speaker or referent (the report of a rumor, e.g.). Shifters which raise the question "Who is speaking?" exhibit the characteristic ambiguity of the unconscious.

NOTES

1. See "The Questioning of Being," in *Tragic Wisdom and Beyond Including Conversations Between Paul Ricoeur and Gabriel Marcel,* pp. 61–62.

2. For a more detailed account, see my introduction to my translation of G. Marcel's *Creative Fidelity*, pp. ix–xxvi. For other comprehensive views of Marcel's philosophy, see K. T. Gallagher, *The Philosophy of Gabriel Marcel*, and S. Cain, *Gabriel Marcel*.

3. "Incarnate Being as the Central Datum of Metaphysical Reflection," in *Creative Fidelity*, pp. 11–37; *Metaphysical Journal*, trans. B. Wall, especially Part II, p. 129 passim. See also the continuation of the *Metaphysical Journal* for the years 1928–1933 in *Being and Having: An Existential Diary*, trans. K. Farrer, especially the Appendix, "Existence and Objectivity," pp. 319–339, Ch. VI; "Feeling as a Mode of Participation," in *The Mystery of Being*, I: *Reflection and Mystery*, trans. G. S. Fraser, pp. 127–153.

4. See "A Broken World," in *The Mystery of Being*, I, pp. 22–47; *Metaphysical Journal*, passim; *Homo Viator*, trans. E. Craufurd, pp. 13–28.

5. Chs. VII–VIII in *Creative Fidelity*, pp. 147–174; "On the Ontological Mystery," in *The Philosophy of Existence*, trans. M. Harari; "Positions et approches concrètes du mystère ontologique"; *Homo Viator*, pp. 29–67; *The Mystery of Being*, II.

6. J.-P. Sartre, *Being and Nothingness*, trans. H. Barnes, Part I. Accounts of the grounds of this distinction are to be found in Chs. I–III in W. Desan, *The Tragic Finale*, pp. 3–60; M. Warnock, *Existentialist Ethics*, pp. 19–29; and Chs. II–III in A. Danto, *Jean-Paul Sartre*, pp. 38–106.

7. *Being and Nothingness*, pp. xlv–lxvii, lxi.

8. See *The Transcendence of the Ego*, trans. F. Williams and R. Kirkpatrick. The translators' introduction provides a good account of Sartre's argument, pp. 11–27. See also M. Natanson, "Phenomenology and Existentialism: Husserl and Sartre on Intentionality," in *Philosophy Today*, No. 3, ed. J. Hill, pp. 61–71.

9. *Being and Nothingness*, pp. xlv–lxvii.

10. See *Jean-Paul Sartre*, pp. 46-50, for Danto's reconstruction of this argument.

11. *Being and Nothingness*, p. lii.

12. *Jean-Paul Sartre*, pp. 68-69.

13. *Existentialist Ethics*, p. 23. See passim for this account of the relation between imagination and freedom.

14. *Jean-Paul Sartre*, p. 91.

15. *Being and Nothingness*, p. 364.

16. Ibid., p. 412n. See *Existentialist Ethics*, pp. 50–52.

17. Translated by H. Barnes. A discussion of this essay and of the *Critique de la raison dialectique* is provided by W. Desan, *The Marxism of Jean-Paul Sartre*. The *Critique* has been translated for Humanities Press by A. Sheridan-Smith (1976). See also Chs. 5, 6, and 7 in M. Grene, *Sartre*, pp. 184–262; M. Poster, *Existential Marxism in Postwar France*, pp. 264–305, and R. D. Laing and D. G. Cooper, *Realism and Violence*.

18. See *Search for a Method*, pp. 106–107 and 140–150; and Sartre's discussion with an interlocutor on the significance of his work on Flaubert *(L'Idiot de la famille)* in "The Itinerary of a Thought," in *Between Existentialism and Marxism*, trans. J. Mathews, pp. 33–64.

19. See Ch. 4 in A. Kenny, *Action, Emotion and Will*, pp. 86–89.

20. Ch. 2, "The Primacy of Perception," in M. Merleau-Ponty, *The Primacy of Perception and Other Essays*, ed. and trans. J. M. Edie, pp. 12–42.

21. Chs. I–II in M. Merleau-Ponty, *Phenomenology of Perception*, trans. C. Smith. The following essays may also be cited: F. A. Olafson, "A Central Theme of Merleau-Ponty's Philosophy," in *Phenomenology and Existentialism*, eds. E. N. Lee and M. Mandelbaum, pp. 179–205; D. Carr, "Incarnate Consciousness," in *Existential Philosophers: Kierkegaard to Merleau-Ponty*, ed. G. A. Schrader, pp. 370–429; H. Spiegelberg, *The Phenomenological Movement*, II, pp. 516–562.

22. See Ch. 2, "The Body and Perception," in J. Bannan, *The Philosophy of Merleau-Ponty*, pp. 59–75. See also Ch. I, "Persons and Their Situation," in S. Hampshire, *Thought and Action*, pp. 11–89, for an analytical account of this theme.

23. *The Primacy of Perception and Other Essays*, pp. 14–15.

24. Ibid., p. 16.

25. Ch. 2, "On the Phenomenology of Language," in M. Merleau-Ponty, *Signs*, trans. R. C. McCleary, pp. 84–97. For Merleau-Ponty's later phenomenology of language, see *The Visible and the Invisible*, ed. C. Lafort and trans. A. Lingis; P. E. Lewis, "Merleau-Ponty and the Phenomenology of Language," in *Structuralism*, ed. J. Ehrmann, pp. 9–31; J. M. Edie, *Speaking and Meaning*. Ch. III, "Merleau-Ponty's Structuralism," in *The Phenomenology of Language*, pp. 72–123; R. L. Lanigan, *Speaking and Semiology. Merleau-Ponty's Phenomenological Theory of Existential Communication*. Northwestern University Press has translated and published the posthumous works of 1968 and 1969 cited in the biographical data (*Themes from the Lectures*, 1970, and *The Prose of the World*, 1973), together with Merleau-Ponty's article, "Consciousness and the Acquisition of Language" (1973).

26. "Innate Consciousness," in *Existential Philosophers: Kierkegaard to Merleau-Ponty*, p. 423. See "The Intertwining—The Chiasm," in *The Visible and the Invisible*, pp. 130–155.

27. See Ch. 2, "The Body and Perception," in *The Philosophy of Merleau-Ponty*, pp. 155–159.

28. G. Canguilhem, "Sur une épistémologie concordataire," in *Hommage à Gaston Bachelard*, eds. G. Bouligand, et al., p. 3.

29. For an account of the dialectical relation between observation and theory, see Bachelard's introductory chapters in *Le Nouvel esprit scientifique* and *La Philosophie du "non."* See also Chs. I–II in P. Quillet, *Bachelard*, pp. 5–72; F. Dagognet, *Gaston Bachelard*, pp. 9–33; also Ch. I in J. Gagey, *Gaston Bachelard ou la conversion à l'imaginaire*, pp. 19–42. Gagey's work also contains helpful references to articles by R. Martin, G. Canguilhem, and others.

30. N. R. Hanson, *Observation and Explanation*, p. 1. There is a resemblance between Hanson and Bachelard in both content and style.

31. The terms are Hanson's. *Observation and Explanation*, pp. 5 and 15.

32. *Le Nouvel esprit scientifique*, p. 5.

33. T. S. Kuhn, *The Structure of Scientific Revolutions*, 5th printing, p. 91.

34. *Gaston Bachelard*, pp. 9–12. Bachelard's views on this subject are to be found in his *Essai sur la connaissance approchée*, p. 270, and *L'Activité rationaliste de la physique contemporaine*, p. 25.

35. *La Formation de l'esprit scientifique*, p. 17.

36. *Le Nouvel esprit scientifique*, p. 13. *La Formation de l'esprit scientifique*, p. 61. See also D. Lecourt, *L'Epistémologie historique de Gaston Bachelard*, p. 66ff.

37. Quoted from M. Cohen and E. Nagel, *An Introduction to Logic and Scientific Method*, pp. 217–221. The authors as well as Hanson and Bachelard all refer to Duhem's well-known illustration in *La Théorie physique*, p. 218, to support the absence of any sharp distinction between experimental fact and theory.

38. *La Formation de l'esprit scientifique*, p. 242.

39. See Ch. I, "Les Dilemmes de la philosophie géométrique," in *Le Nouvel esprit scientifique*, pp. 35–40. Hempel makes the same point in his well-known article "Geometry and Empirical Science," reprinted in *Readings in Philosophical Analysis*, eds. H. Feigl and W. Sellars, pp. 238–249. See especially the last pages of section 6, "On Poincaré's Conventionalism Concerning Geometry."

40. A good account of the nonformalist approach to the role of mathematics in science which is applicable to Bachelard may be found in Ch. II, "The Nature of Mathematics," in K. Lambert and G. G. Brittan, Jr., *An Introduction to the Philosophy of Science*, pp. 4–23.

41. "Geometry and Empirical Science," p. 239.

42. *Bachelard*, pp. 62–64; *Le Nouvel esprit scientifique*, p. 7.

43. See the introductory chapter of *La Philosophie du "non,"* especially p. 4.

44. Ch. VI, "L'Obstacle substantialiste," in *La Formation de l'esprit scientifique*, pp. 97–129.

45. *An Introduction to the Philosophy of Science*, pp. 60–65.

46. Ch. VI, "L'Epistémologie non-Cartésienne," in *Le Nouvel esprit scientifique*, p. 138 ff.

47. M. Hesse, *Models and Analogies in Science*, pp. 3 ff. Hesse's discussion of such topics as the explanatory function of metaphor in science and the nature of material analogy implicitly provides an interesting perspective on Bachelard's views with respect to substantialism.

48. See P. Strawson, "Imagination and Perception," in *Experience and Theory*, eds. L. Foster and J. W. Swanson, pp. 31–54.

49. M. Warnock, *Imagination*, pp. 15–16 and 35.

50. Two studies in English on Bachelard's poetic imagination may be mentioned: M. A. Caws, *Surrealism and the Literary Imagination: A Study of Breton and Bachelard*, and the "Introduction" by C. Gaudin to *On Poetic Imagination and Reverie*, selections from the works of Bachelard. See also E. K. Kaplan's article, "Gaston Bachelard's Philosophy of Imagination," *Philosophy and Phenomenological Research* 33 (1972–1973):1–24. Beacon Press has translated three of Bachelard's works on the imagination: *The Psychoanalysis of Fire*, *The Poetics of Space*, and *The Poetics of Reverie*.

51. *L'Aire et les songes*, p. 19.

52. *L'Eau et les rêves*, p. 4.

53. "Gaston Bachelard's Philosophy of Imagination," p. 2.

54. For a careful analysis of the "law of the elements" and the reservations that may be expressed in its regard, see F. Pire, *De l'Imagination poetique dans l'oeuvre de Gaston Bachelard*, pp. 58 ff., 79–80, 116–117, passim.

55. *De l'Imagination poétique dans l'oeuvre de Gaston Bachelard*, pp. 15–53.

56. For a characteristic formulation of this theme, see *La Terre et les rêveries de la volonté*, p. 165.

57. See "Gaston Bachelard's Philosophy of Imagination," pp. 9–19, for an account of Bachelard's metaphysics of the imagination together with appropriate references.

58. See the *Poetics of Reverie*. Jung's original text is his essay "The Relation Between the Ego and the Unconscious" in the *Two Essays on Analytic Psychology*, especially Part II, "Anima and Animus." A helpful edition containing the *Two Essays* is *The Basic Writings of C. G. Jung*, ed. with Introduction by V. S. de Laszlo, pp. 158–182.

59. E. Levinas, *En Découvrant l'existence avec Husserl et Heidegger*. See C. Schrag, "Phenomenology, Ontology, and History in the Philosophy of Heidegger," in *Phenomenology. The Philosophy of Edmund Husserl and Its Interpretation*, ed. J. J. Kockelmans, pp. 277–293.

60. *En Découvrant l'existence avec Husserl et Heidegger*, pp. 91–107.

61. E. Levinas, *Totality and Infinity: An Essay on Exteriority*, trans. A. Lingis.

62. Ibid., p. 78.

63. Ibid., p. 41.

64. *The Philosophical Works of Descartes*, trans. Haldane and Ross, I, pp. 157–171.

65. *Totality and Infinity: An Essay on Exteriority*, p. 48.

66. Ibid., p. 51.

67. For these criticisms, see A. Kenny, *The Five Ways*, p. 81, and *Descartes. A Study of His Philosophy*, pp. 136–137.

68. Thus, enjoyment is characterized as being *"chez-soi,"* i.e., being at home in itself but dwelling in what is not itself; fecundity or parenthood gives birth to what is both itself and not itself, and so on. These analyses of "sufficiency in non-sufficiency" resemble Marcel's concrete approaches, and they challenge the Heideggerian analysis of *Dasein* as care or concern and finitude as a fall. See also E. Levinas, "Le Temps et l'autre," in *Le Choix, le monde, l'existence*, pp. 125–196, for Levinas' critique of the "solitude" of *Dasein*.

69. *Totality and Infinity: An Essay on Exteriority*, pp. 43 and 210.

70. Ibid., p. 304.

71. Thus, Levinas affirms that "relatedness to the other starts from me" and that "the other is visible only from an I," and so forth. See "Martin Buber and the Theory of Knowledge," trans. R. B. Rosthal in *The Philosophy of Martin Buber*, eds. Paul A. Schilpp and M. Freidman, pp.

133–150. In Part VIII, "Some Objections," Levinas attempts to deal with Buber's view on the reciprocity of the I-Thou relation and insists on the absence of interchangeability between the two terms or on the difference of level or "height." The distinction between the I and the Thou, i.e., otherness, is established by the relational act or moral initiative of the I.

72. See P. Haezrahi, "The Concept of Man as End in Himself," in *Kant, Foundations of the Metaphysics of Ethics with Critical Essays*, eds. L. W. Beck and R. P. Wolff, pp. 292–318.

73. Ibid., p. 300.

74. "Self-Consciousness," in G.W.F. Hegel, *The Phenomenology of Mind*, trans. J. B. Baillie, pp. 217–240. A good account of this section of the *Phenomenology* is provided by C. Taylor, *Hegel*, pp. 148–157. The influence of Hegel in France was in large part the result of A. Kojève's lectures on the *Phenomenology* published in his *Introduction à la lecture de Hegel*. An English translation edited by A. Bloom and translated by J. H. Nichols, Jr., has been published by Basic Books (1969).

75. *Totality and Infinity: An Essay on Exteriority*, p. 302.

76. Ibid., pp. 44–47. See J. Derrida's essay on Levinas, "Violence et métaphysique," in *L'Ecriture et la différence*, pp. 117–228.

77. *Totality and Infinity: An Essay on Exteriority*, pp. 66–69, 73, 96, passim. On occasion Levinas compares such discourse to the Kierkegaardian teaching where the truths elicited in discourse are not, like the Socratic maieutic, derived from the self. See "The God as Teacher and Savior," in S. Kierkegaard, *Philosophical Fragments*, trans. D.F. Swenson and H.V. Hong, pp. 12–45. See also E. Wyschogrod, *Emmanuel Levinas. The Problem of Ethical Metaphysics*, especially Ch. VI, pp: 128–158 and 135–137.

78. *Finitude et culpabilité*, I: *L'Homme fallible*, II: *La Symbolique du mal*.

79. See D. Ihde, *Hermeneutic Phenomenology. The Philosophy of Paul Ricoeur*. The author of this excellent, though noncritical, exposition of Ricoeur's work stresses the continuity of Ricoeur's development from a structural phenomenology to a phenomenology of language and hermeneutic. See also K. Hartmann, "Phenomenology, Ontology and Metaphysics," *Review of Metaphysics* 22, No. 1 (1968):85–112, and the translator's introduction to *Freedom and Nature*, pp. xi–xxxviii.

80. For the contrary opinion, see *Hermeneutic Phenomenology. The Philosophy of Paul Ricoeur*, pp. 143–155, and "Existence and Hermeneutics," in Ricoeur's *The Conflict of Interpretations, Essays in Hermeneutics*, pp. 3–24.

81. Ricoeur, "Philosophy of Will and Action," in *Phenomenology of Will and Action*, eds. E. W. Straus and R. M. Griffith, pp. 7–33. This essay provides a good synoptic account by the author of his own development.

82. M. Merleau-Ponty, *L'Union de l'âme et du corps chez Malebranche, Biran et Bergson: Notes prises au cours de Maurice Merleau-Ponty à L'École Normale Supérieure, 1947–1948*, p. 62. These early notes defend Biran against Brunschvicg and exhibit the affinities of the existential phenomenology of the body with Biran's analysis of *le moi*.

83. *Freedom and Nature*, p. 219.

84. Ibid. See also his Marcellian pronouncement in *Freedom and Nature*, p. 14: "The bond which in fact joins willing to its body requires a type of attention other than an intellectual attention to structures. It requires that I participate actively in my incarnation as a mystery. I need to pass from objectivity to existence."

85. *Freedom and Nature*, p. 10.

86. See *L'Union de l'âme et du corps chez Malebranche, Biran et Bergson*, pp. 70–78, "Biran et les philosophes du cogito." The source of this distinction between the active and the passive life and their relations is Biran's *Essai sur les fondements de la psychologie et sur ses rapports avec l'étude de la nature, Oeuvres de Maine de Biran*, VII, ed. P. Tisserand. For a description of the distinction as a methodological principle, see F.C.T. Moore, *The Psychology of Maine de Biran*, p. 107 ff., and the review of this book by R. B. Rosthal, *Journal of Philosophy* 69, No. 2 (1972):29–37.

87. *Hermeneutic Phenomenology. The Philosophy of Paul Ricoeur*, p. 55.

88. *Freedom and Nature*, p. 88.

89. Ibid., pp. 37–84, 201–230, 341–354.

90. See R. S. Peters, *The Concept of Motivation*.

91. See the discussion between Thomson, Strawson, and G. J. Warnock on this issue in "Determinism," in *Freedom and the Will*, ed. D. F. Pears, pp. 48–68.

92. *Freedom and Nature*, p. 216.

93. Ibid., p. 66.

94. Ibid., pp. 89–93.

95. R. M. Chisholm, "Human Freedom and the Self," in *Reason and Responsibility*, ed. J. Feinberg, pp. 391–397.

96. *Freedom and Nature*, p. 442.

97. See *Hermeneutic Phenomenology. The Philosophy of Paul Ricoeur*, p. 59 ff., for a fuller account of the transition to Ricoeur's theory of interpretation, elaborated in *The Symbolism of Evil* and *Freud and Philosophy: An Essay on Interpretation*.

98. *L'Essence de la manifestation*, 2 vols.

99. Ibid., I, p. 69.

100. Ibid., I, p. 21ff. My account of the ambiguity with respect to the "phenomenon" in Husserl's work is indebted to J. Edie's essay, "Transcendental Phenomenology and Existentialism," *Philosophy and Phenomenological Research* 25 (1964):52–63. The essay is reprinted in *Phenomenology: The Philosophy of Edmund Husserl and Its Interpretations*, ed. J. J. Kockelman, pp. 237–251. See also A. Lewit, "D'Où vient l'ambiguité de la phénoménologie?," *Bulletin de la Société Francaise de Philosophie* (1971):33–68. There is a corresponding ambiguity with respect to the meaning of the term "transcendent." The term has the narrower sense of an inadequately fulfilled intuition as well as a wider sense of the independence of the object of knowledge from the intentional act. See D. Levin, "Induction and Husserl's Theory of Eidetic Variation," *Philosophy and Phenomenological Research* 29 (1968):7–8.

101. For a reconstruction of Husserl's idealist argument, see the "Introduction," in *Realism and the Background of Phenomenology*, ed. R. Chisholm, p. 21.

102. *L'Essence de la manifestation*, p. 24. Also *Phenomenology: The Philosophy of Edmund Husserl and Its Interpretations*, p. 57.

103. See D. Levin, "Husserl's Notion of Self-Evidence," in *Phenomenology and Philosophical Understanding*, ed. E. Pivcevic, footnote p. 59, and D. Carr, "Intentionality," in the same volume, p. 26.

104. *L'Essence de la manifestation*, p. 21.

105. Ibid., p. 22.

106. Ibid., pp. 48–51.

107. M. Henry, *Philosophie et phénoménologie du corps*.

108. *L'Essence de la manifestation*, pp. 40–41.

109. *Philosophie et phénoménologie du corps*, p. 71.

110. Ibid., p. 16ff. See also *Phenomenology: The Philosophy of Edmund Husserl and Its Interpretations*, pp. 53–54.

111. Ibid., p. 58.

112. *Philosophie et phénoménologie du corps*, p. 36.

113. *Phenomenology: The Philosophy of Edmund Husserl and Its Interpretations*, p. 61.

114. See R. Harrison, "The Concept of Prepredicative Experience," in *Phenomenology and Philosophical Understanding*, pp. 93–107.

115. *Philosophie et phénoménologie du corps*, p. 15ff., *L'Essence de la manifestation*, p. 573ff.

116. F. Dagognet, *Gaston Bachelard*, p. 10ff.

117. Ibid., pp. 15–31. See G. Bachelard, *La Formation de l'esprit scientifique*, "L'Obstacle substantialiste," pp. 97–129.

118. Ch. IV in F. Dagognet, *La Raison et les remèdes*, pp. 186–187.

119. See J. Lacroix, *Panorama de la philosophie française contemporaine*, p. 215.

120. *La Raison et les remèdes*, pp. 1–21.

121. Ibid., p. 330.

122. Ch. I, "Le Problème de la définition du remède," in *La Raison et les remèdes*, p. 30ff.

123. La Raison et les remèdes, p. 330.

124. Ibid., p. 32ff.

125. Ibid., p. 328.

126. See Ch. VI in *La Raison et les remèdes*, pp. 266–313. For a more detailed example of the antinomic properties of matter, see Dagognet's discussion of the early nineteenth-century debate in chemistry on the properties of two salts, tartrate and paratartrate of soda (sodium ammonium tartrate), which possessed the same crystalline properties but different optical properties. Explanations were provided in terms of the theory of dimorphism ("identity with difference") and the isomeric view ("difference despite identity"). Pasteur's explanation of the differing properties of the two isomers of sodium ammonium tartrate in terms of the neutralizing effects of microorganisms is a typical example of the application of the dialectical method. Ch. II, "La Logique de la découverte," in F. Dagognet, *Méthodes et doctrine dans l'oeuvre de Pasteur*, pp. 37–84.

127. *La Raison et les remèdes*, p. 280.

128. Ibid., p. 43.

129. See M. Scriven, *Primary Philosophy*, p. 139.

130. W. Salmon, "Determinism and Indeterminism in Modern Science," in *Reason and Responsibility*, ed. J. Feinberg, pp. 364–365.

131. See P. Aubenque, "Language, structures, société," *Archives de philosophie* 34 (1971):353–371.

132. Ch. 1 in N. Chomsky, *Aspects of the Theory of Syntax*.

133. See Ch. 2 in J. Culler, *Ferdinand de Saussure*, ed. F. Kermode. Saussure's *Course in General Linguistics*, trans. W. Baskin, is the basic text. A number of books on the history of linguistics, which provide brief accounts of Saussure's work, may be cited: Ch. 4 in D. Crystal, *Linguistics and Phonology*, p. 158 ff.; R. H. Robins, *A Short History of Linguistics;* and J. Lyons, *An Introduction to Theoretical Linguistics*.

134. J. M. Edie, *Speaking and Meaning. The Phenomenology of Language*, p. 32.

135. P. Aubenque, "Language, structures, société," pp. 361–362. See note 131.

136. See P. Ricoeur, "Structure and Hermeneutics," and "Structure, Word, Event," in *The Conflict of Interpretations*, pp. 27–61; 79–96. Ricoeur stresses such factors as the uniqueness of the mental act as a psychical event, the intent to communicate which involves addressing oneself to another, and the relation of signifying intentions to the world. See also M. Dufrenne, *Pour l'homme*. For the opposing view, see Lévi-Strauss's polemic with Sartre in Ch. 9, "History and Dialectic," in *The Savage Mind*, pp. 245–269. The following books containing extensive bibliographies on structuralism may be cited: J. Viet, *Les Méthodes structuralistes dans les sciences sociales;* Y. Simonis, *Claude Lévi-Strauss ou la 'passion de l'inceste';* G. Schiwy, *Der Französische Strukturalismus;* J. Ehrmann (ed.), *Structuralism;* M. Lane (ed.), *Structuralism: A Reader*.

137. See Introduction by D. Allison in J. Derrida, *Speech and Phenomena*, trans. D. Allison, Preface by N. Garver, pp. xxxi–xlii.

138. *Speech and Phenomena*.

139. J. Derrida, *Of Grammatology*, ed. G. C. Spivak.

140. See especially "The Violence of the Letter: From Lévi-Strauss to Rousseau," in *Of Grammatology*, pp. 101–140. See also the essay on Levinas, "Violence et Métaphysique," in *L'Ecriture et la différence*, pp. 117–228.

141. *Investigation I:* "Expression and Meaning," in E. Husserl, *Logical Investigations*, trans. J. N. Findlay, pp. 269–333. Derrida's critique of the First Investigation is to be found in *Speech and Phenomena*. See also Derrida's Introduction to Husserl's *Origin of Geometry*. A translation of and preface to this work by J. P. Leavey, Jr., has been published by Nicholas Hays and Humanities Press, (1978).

142. *Of Grammatology*, pp. 110, 130.

143. See Spivak's Preface to *Of Grammatology* on the influence of Heidegger, Nietzsche, and Freud on Derrida, pp. ix–xc.

144. M. Heidegger, *Being and Time*, p. 274 ff.

145. See R. Jacobson and M. Halle, *Fundamentals of Language*.

146. C. Lévi-Strauss, "Le Triangle culinaire," *L'Arc* 26 (1965):19–29. An English version of this essay is to be found in *New Society* (December 1966):937–940. See also Lévi-Strauss, *The Raw and the Cooked: Introduction to a Science of Mythology*, I, trans. J. Weightman and D. Weightman. There are a number of expositions of this essay and its relation to the primary phoneme triangle: Ch. 2 in E. Leach, *Claude Lévi-Strauss*, ed. F. Kermode, pp. 15–32; and M. Glucksmann, *Structuralist Analysis in Contemporary Social Thought*, pp. 73–75. Both books contain good bibliographies.

147. See especially Ch. XXIX, "The Principles of Kinship," in C. Lévi-Strauss, *The Elementary Structures of Kinship*, pp. 478–497. See also "Structural Analysis in Linguistics and Anthropology," in C. Lévi-Strauss, *Structural Anthropology*, pp. 29–53.

148. See Y. Simonis, *Claude Lévi-Strauss ou la 'passion de l'inceste'*.

149. The example is owed to J. Lacroix, *Panorama de la philosophie française contemporaine*, pp. 234–235. [My translation.]

150. Ibid., p. 237.

151. C. Lévi-Strauss, *Le Totémisme aujourd'hui*.

152. *Claude Lévi-Strauss*, pp. 57–58.

153. *Structuralist Analysis in Contemporary Social Thought*, p. 76.

154. See P. Pettit, *The Concept of Structuralism: A Critical Analysis*, pp. 87–88. This book also contains a good bibliography on structuralism.

155. *The Concept of Structuralism: A Critical Analysis*, pp. 70–71; *Claude Lévi-Strauss*, pp. 118–119.

156. C. Lévi-Strauss, *The Savage Mind*.

157. In C. Lévi-Strauss, *Tristes Tropiques*, p. 61. See also Introduction in R. and F. de George (eds.), *The Structuralists from Marx to Lévi-Strauss*, pp. xi–xxix. De George emphasizes the distinction between surface events and deep structure as the element uniting Saussure, Marx, Freud, and the structuralists.

158. See M. Dufrenne, *Pour l'homme*, pp. 37–47. A volume of Foucault's selected essays entitled *Language, Counter-Memory Practice* has recently been translated and published by Cornell University Press.

159. Ch. 3, "Representing," in M. Foucault, *The Order of Things*, pp. 46–77.

160. *Pour l'homme*, pp. 39–40.

161. See Ch. VII, "Structuralism Without Structures," in J. Piaget, *Structuralism*, trans. C. Maschler, pp. 128–135, for some of the above criticisms. See also Ch. II in M. Corvez, *Les Structuralistes*, pp. 35–76.

162. M. Foucault, *Madness and Civilization. A History of Insanity in the Age of Reason*.

163. Ibid., especially Ch. II, pp. 38–64.

164. Ch. I in M. Foucault, *Surveiller et punir: Naissance de la prison*, pp. 6–35. A translation by A. Sheridan has just been published by Pantheon.

165. *Surveiller et punir. Naissance de la prison*, pp. 33–34.

166. *Madness and Civilization. A History of Insanity in the Age of Reason*, pp. 46–50.

167. *Pour l'homme*, p. 43.

168. *Structuralism*, p. 129. Two further essays on the subject may be cited: M. de Certeau, "Les Sciences humaines et la mort de l'homme," *Etudes* (March 1967) and G. Canguilhem, "Mort de l'homme ou épuisement du cogito?," *Critique* (July 1967):599–618.

169. L. Althusser, *For Marx*, trans. B. Brewster. Althusser's view of the epistemological break *(coupure)* bears a close similarity to Kuhn's paradigm theory of scientific revolution. See T. Kuhn, *The Structure of Scientific Revolutions*, p. 91.

170. *For Marx*, "On the Materialist Dialectic," pp. 161–218.

171. For an account of these relations, see Ch. 4 in M. Glucksmann, *Structuralist Analysis in Contemporary Social Thought*, pp. 94–138.

172. See M. Godelier, "System, Structure, and Contradiction in *Das Capital*," in *The Socialist Register*, eds. J. Saville and R. Miliband. A good resume of Althusser's views is to be found in another article by the same author, "Remarques sur les concepts de structure et de contradiction," *Aletheia* 4 (1966):228–236. Althusser's view of the autonomy of conceptual schema, their independence of empirical reality, owes much to Bachelard.

173. *Structuralist Analysis in Contemporary Social Thought*, pp. 137–138. See also Lucian Sebag, *Marxisme et structuralisme*.

174. *Structuralist Analysis in Contemporary Social Thought*, p. 131ff.

175. See L. Althusser, Ch. 9, "Marx's Immense Theoretical Revolution," in *Reading Capital*, trans. B. Brewster, pp. 182–193. "System, Structure, and Contradiction in *Das Capital*," pp. 354–355.

176. M. Glucksmann, "The Structuralism of Lévi-Strauss and Althusser," in *Approaches to Sociology*, ed. J. Rex, p. 238.

177. Ibid., pp. 236–237.

178. "Contradiction and Overdetermination," in *For Marx*, pp. 88–128.

179. "System, Structure, and Contradiction in *Das Capital*," p. 356. Godelier illustrates this relationship in terms of the kinship systems of primitive societies which function as economic relationships of production as well as political relationships. But how kinship relationships are both infrastructure and superstructure and why the determining role of the economy does not contradict the dominant role of kinship but "expresses itself through it" is not clear.

180. M. Poster, *Existential Marxism in Postwar France. From Sartre to Althusser*, p. 345. See the footnotes in Chs. 7 and 8 for an excellent bibliography on the controversy between Marxian existentialism and structuralism, pp. 264–360. Althusser's view of Sartre and existential Marxism may be found in his *Réponse à John Lewis*.

181. Ch. 7, "Remarks on the Function of Language in Freudian Theory," in E. Benveniste, *Problems in General Linguistics*, trans. M. Meek, p. 65. See "Fonction et Champ de la parole et du langage" (more familiarly known as the *Discours de Rome*), in J. Lacan, *Écrits*, pp. 237–322. This essay has been translated by A. Wilden in *The Language of the Self*, ed. A. Wilden, pp. 3–87. The editor also provides an extended commentary on Lacan's thought ("Lacan and the Discourse of the Other," pp. 159–311). A selection of essays from *Ecrits*, translated by A. Sheridan, has recently been published by W. W. Norton, 1977.

182. "La Direction de la cure," in *Écrits*, p. 594.

183. See "L'Instance de la lettre dans l'inconscient ou la raison depuis Freud," in *Écrits*, pp. 493–528. This essay has been translated by J. Miel as "The Insistence of the Letter in the Unconscious" and published in *Structuralism*, ed. J. Ehrmann, pp. 101–137. It is preceded by Miel's short introductory essay, "Jacques Lacan and the Structure of the Unconscious," pp. 94–101. (The volume originally appeared as a special issue of *Yale French Studies*, 1966.) Other good accounts of the role of grammatical forms and tropes may be found in *The Language of the Self*, pp. 183–185, 238–249, and in J. B. Fages, *Comprendre Jacques Lacan*, pp. 36–66. This volume also contains a lexicon of Lacanian terms.

184. *Écrits*, p. 627.

185. This issue is discussed in "L'Instance de la lettre," and "Propos sur la causalité psychique," in *Écrits*, pp. 151–193; "Position de l'inconscient," in *Écrits*, pp. 829–850. See also J. Laplanche and S. Leclaire, "L'Inconscient." *Les Temps modernes* 183 (1961):81–129. The debate between Lacan and his two disciples focuses on the issue of whether language is the condition of the unconscious (Lacan), or conversely. See also S. Leclaire, "A la recherche des principes d'une psychothérapie des psychoses," *l'Evolution psychiatrique* (April–June 1958): 377–419, for a description of the psychoses in terms of symbolic functions.

186. "La Signification du phallus," in *Écrits*, pp. 685–695; *Comprendre Jacques Lacan*, pp. 27–28. A helpful account of the logic of desire which shows its relationship to Hegel's *Phenomenology* is to be found in A. Wilden (ed.), *The Language of the Self*, pp. 185–196.

187. "Le Séminaire sur 'la lettre volée'," in *Écrits*, pp. 11–61.

188. For a description of the dialectic of identification, see Y. Bertherat, "Freud avec Lacan ou la science avec le psychanalyste," *Esprit* 366 (1967):979–1003.

189. "Le Stade du miroir comme formateur de la fonction du Je," in *Écrits*, pp. 93–100. See also *Comprendre Jacques Lacan*, pp. 14–15; *The Language of the Self*, pp. 167–177.

190. *Écrits*, pp. 685–695.

191. "Remarque sur le rapport de Daniel Lagache," in *Écrits*, p. 664. See also "Indexical Signs, Egocentric Particulars, and Token-Reflexive Words," in *Encyclopedia of Philosophy*, IV, pp. 151–152.

SELECT BIBLIOGRAPHY

BOOKS AND ARTICLES

Althusser, L. *Eléménts d'autocritique* (Paris: Hachette, 1974).

———. *For Marx*, trans. B. Brewster (New York: Pantheon, 1969).

———. *Lenine et la philosophie* (Paris: Maspero, 1969).

——— (trans.). *Manifestes philosophiques de Feuerbach Textes choisis 1839–1845* (Paris: Presses Universitaires de France, 1960).

———. *Montesquieu, la politique et l'histoire* (Paris: Presses Universitaires de France, 1959).

———. *Philosophie et philosophie spontanée des savants, 1967* (Paris: Maspero, 1974).

———. *Positions* (Paris: Sociales, 1976).

———. *Pour Marx* (Paris: Maspero, 1965).

———. *Reading Capital*, trans. B. Brewster (New York: Pantheon Press, 1970).

———. *Réponse à John Lewis* (Paris: Maspero, 1973).

———, et al. *Lire le Capital*, 3d ed., 2 vols. (Paris: Maspero, 1970).

Aubenque, P. "Language, structures, société," *Archives de philosophie* 34 (1971).

Bachelard, G. *Essai sur la connaissance approchée* (Paris: Vrin, 1927).

———. *Etude sur l'évolution d'un problème de physique: la propagation thermique dans les solides* (Paris: Vrin, 1927).

———. *L'Activité rationaliste de la physique contemporaine* (Paris: Presses Universitaires de France, 1951).

———. *La Dialectique de la durée* (Paris: Boivin and Cie, 1936).

———. *La Flamme d'une chandelle* (Paris: Presses Universitaires de France, 1961).

———. *La Formation de l'esprit scientifique*, 5th ed. (Paris: Vrin, 1969).

———. *L'Air et les songes: essai sur l'imagination du mouvement* (Paris: Corti, 1943).

———. *La Philosophie du "non"* (Paris: Presses Universitaires de France, 1940).

———. *La Poétique de la rêverie* (Paris: Presses Universitaires de France, 1960).

———. *La Poétique de l'espace* (Paris: Presses Universitaires de France, 1957).

———. *La Psychanalyse du feu* (Paris: Gallimard, 1938).

———. *La Terre et les rêveries de la volonté: essai sur l'imagination des forces* (Paris: Corti, 1947).

———. *La Terre et les rêveries du repos: essai sur les images de l'intimité* (Paris: Corti, 1948).

———. *Lautréamont* (Paris: Corti, 1939).

———. *La Valeur inductive de la relativité* (Paris: Vrin, 1929).

———. *L'Eau et les rêves: essai sur l'imagination de la matière* (Paris: Corti, 1942).

———. *Le Materialisme rationnel* (Paris: Presses Universitaires de France, 1953).

———. *Le Nouvel esprit scientifique* (Paris: Alcan, 1934).

———. *Le Pluralisme cohérent de la chimie moderne* (Paris: Vrin, 1932).

———. *Le Rationalisme appliqué* (Paris: Presses Universitaires de France, 1949).

———. *Les Intuitions atomistiques* (Paris: Boivin and Cie, 1933).

———. *L'Expérience de l'espace dans la physique contemporaine* (Paris: Alcan, 1937).

———. *L'Intuition de l'instant, étude sur le Siloë de Gaston Roupnel* (Paris: Stock, Delamain and Boutelleau, 1932).

———. *Psychoanalysis of Fire,* trans. A. C. Ross (Boston: Beacon Press, 1964).

———. *The Poetics of Reverie: Childhood, Language and the Cosmos* (Boston: Beacon Press, 1971).

———. *The Poetics of Space,* trans. M. Joles (Boston: Beacon Press, 1969).

Bannan, J. *The Philosophy of Merleau-Ponty* (New York: Harcourt, Brace and World, 1967).

Benveniste, E. *Problems in General Linguistics,* trans. M. Meek (Coral Gables, Fla.: University of Miami Press, 1971).

Bertherat, Y. "Freud avec Lacan ou la science avec le psychanalyste," *Esprit,* No. 366 (1967).

Cain, S. *Gabriel Marcel,* eds. E. Heller and A. Thorlby, Studies in Modern European Literature and Thought (New York: Hillary House, 1963).

Canguilhem, G. "Mort de l'homme ou épuisement du cogito?," *Critique* 242 (1967).

———. "Sur une épistémologie concordataire," in *Hommage à Gaston Bachelard,* ed. G. Bouligand, et al. (Paris: Presses Universitaires de France, 1957).

Carr, D. "Incarnate Consciousness," in *Existential Philosophers: Kierkegaard to Merleau-Ponty,* ed. G. A. Schrader (New York: McGraw-Hill, 1967).

———. "Intentionality," in *Phenomenology and Philosophic Understanding,* ed. E. Pivcevic (New York: Cambridge University Press, 1975).

Caws, M. A. *Surrealism and the Literary Imagination: A Study of Breton and Bachelard* (The Hague: Mouton, 1966).

Chisholm, R. "Human Freedom and the Self," in *Reason and Responsibility,* 3d ed., ed. J. Feinberg (Belmont, Calif.: Dickenson, 1975).

——— (ed.). *Realism and the Background of Phenomenology* (Glencoe, Ill.: Free Press, 1960).

Chomsky, N. *Aspects of the Theory of Syntax* (Cambridge: MIT Press, 1970).

Cohen, M. and Nagel, E. *An Introduction to Logic and Scientific Method* (New York: Harcourt, Brace, 1934).

Contat, M. and Rybalka, M. (eds.) *Les Ecrits de Sartre* (Paris: Gallimard, 1970).

——— (eds.) *The Writings of Jean-Paul Sartre* 2 vols., trans. R. C. McCleary (Evanston, Ill.: Northwestern University Press, 1974).

Corvez, M. *Les Structuralistes* (Paris: Aubier-Montaigne, 1969).

Crystal, D. *Linguistics and Phonology* (Harmondsworth: Penguin, 1971).

Culler, J. *Ferdinand de Saussure,* ed. F. Kermode, Penguin Modern Masters (New York: Penguin, 1977).

Cuvillier, A. *Anthologie des philosophes français contemporain,* 2d ed. (Paris: Presses Universitaires de France, 1965). (Especially recommended as offering a more extended treatment of French philosophy in the postwar period.)

Dagognet, F. *Ecriture et iconographie* (Paris: Vrin, 1973).

———. *Gaston Bachelard* (Paris: Presses Universitaires de France, 1972).

──────. *L'Agronomie les Révolutions vertes* (Paris: Hermann, 1973).

──────. *La Raison et les remèdes* (Paris: Presses Universitaires de France, 1964).

──────. *Le Catalogue de la vie* (Paris: Presses Universitaires de France, 1970).

──────. *Méthodes et doctrine dans l'oeuvre de Pasteur* (Paris: Presses Universitaires de France, 1967).

──────. *Philosophie biologique* (Paris: Presses Universitaires de France, 1955).

──────. *Pour une théorie générale des formes* (Paris: Vrin, 1975).

──────. *Sciences de la vie et de la culture* (Paris: Hachette, 1953).

──────. *Tableaux et langages de la chimie* (Paris: Seuil, 1969).

Danto, A. *Jean-Paul Sartre,* ed. F. Kermode, Modern Masters Series (New York: Viking Press, 1975).

de Biran, M. *Essai sur les fondements de la psychologie et sur ses rapports avec l'étude de la nature,* in *Oeuvres de Maine de Biran,* VII, ed. P. Tisserand (Paris: Alcan, 1932).

de Certeau, M. "Les Sciences humaines et la mort de l'homme," *Etudes* 326 (1967).

de George, R. and de George, F. (eds.). *The Structuralists from Marx to Lévi-Strauss* (New York: Doubleday, 1972).

Derrida, J. *De la Grammatologie* (Paris: Minuit, 1967). (A complete bibliography of Derrida's works together with critical commentary is provided in *Research in Phenomenology* 8 [1978].)

──────. *Edmund Husserl's "Origin of Geometry"; An Introduction,* trans. J. P. Leavey (Stony Brook, N.Y.: Nicholas Hays, 1978).

──────. *Eperons: Les styles de Nietzsche* (Venice: Corbo e Fiore, 1976).

──────. *Glas* (Paris: Galilée, 1974).

──────. *Introduction à la géométrie de Husserl* (Paris: Presses Universitaires de France, 1962).

──────. *La Dissémination* (Paris: Seuil, 1972).

──────. *L'Archéologie du frivole: Lire Condillac* (Paris: Gonthier, 1976).

──────. *La Voix et le phénomène* (Paris: Presses Universitaires de France, 1967).

──────. *L'Ecriture et la différence* (Paris: Seuil, 1967).

──────. *Marges* (Paris: Minuit, 1972).

──────. *Of Grammatology,* trans. G. C. Spivak (Baltimore: Johns Hopkins Press, 1976).

──────. *Positions* (Paris: Minuit, 1972).

──────. *Speech and Pheomena,* trans. D. Allison (Evanston, Ill.: Northwestern University Press, 1973).

──────. "Violence et métaphysique," in *L'Ecriture et la différence* (Paris: Seuil, 1967).

──────. *Writing and Difference,* trans. A. Bass (Chicago: University of Chicago Press, 1978).

Desan, W. *The Marxism of Jean-Paul Sartre* (New York: Doubleday, 1965).

──────. *The Tragic Finale* (New York: Harper Torchbooks, 1960).

de Saussure, F. *Course in General Linguistics,* trans. W. Baskin (New York: McGraw-Hill, 1966).

Descartes, R. *The Philosophical Works of Descartes,* trans. E. S. Haldane and G.R.T. Ross (London: Cambridge University Press, 1967).

Dufrenne, M. *Pour l'homme* (Paris: Seuil, 1968).

Edie, J. M. *Speaking and Meaning. The Phenomenology of Language* (Bloomington, Ind.: Indiana University Press, 1976).

──────. "Transcendental Phenomenology and Existentialism," *Philosophy and Phenomenological Research* 25 (1964–1965).

Ehrmann, J. (ed.). *Structuralism* (New York: Doubleday, 1970).

Fages, J. B. *Comprendre Jacques Lacan* (Toulouse: Privat, 1971).

Fisher, A. (ed.). *The Essential Writings of Merleau-Ponty* (New York: Harcourt, Brace and World, 1969).

Foucault, M. *Birth of the Clinic* (New York: Pantheon, 1973).

──────. *Ceci n'est pas une pipe, Moi, Pierre Rivière, ayant égoré ma mère, ma soeur et mon frère* (Paris: Fata Morgana, 1973).

———. *Discipline and Punishment: The Birth of the Prison*, trans. A. Sheridan (New York: Pantheon, 1978).

———. *Histoire de la folie* (Paris: Gallimard, 1972).

———. *Histoire de la sexualité*, 2 vols. (Paris: Gallimard, 1976), (Vols. III to VI forthcoming).

———. *La Leçon inaugurale* (Paris: Gallimard, 1970).

———. *Language, Counter-Memory, Practice*, ed. and trans. D. F. Bouchard (Ithaca, N.Y.: Cornell University Press, 1977).

———. *L'Archéologie du savoir* (Paris: Gallimard, 1969).

———. *Les Mots et les choses* (Paris: Gallimard, 1966).

———. *L'Histoire de la folie à l'âge classique* (Paris: Plon, 1961).

———. *Madness and Civilization. A History of Insanity in the Age of Reason* (New York: New American Library, 1965).

———. *Maladie mentale et personnalité* (Paris: Presses Universitaires de France, 1954).

———. *Naissance de la clinique* (Paris: Presses Universitaires de France, 1963).

———. *Raymond Roussel* (Paris: Gallimard, 1963).

———. *Surveiller et punir: Naissance de la prison* (Paris: Gallimard, 1975).

———. *The Archaeology of Knowledge* (New York: Harper and Row, 1976).

———. *The History of Sexuality*, trans. R. Hurley (New York: Pantheon, 1978).

———. *The Order of Things* (New York: Pantheon, 1970).

Gagey, J. *Gaston Bachelard ou la conversion à l'imaginaire* (Paris: Marcel Rivière, 1969).

Gale, R. M. "Indexical Signs, Egocentric Particulars, and Token-Reflexive Words," in *Encyclopedia of Philosophy*, IV, ed. P. Edwards (New York: Macmillan, 1967).

Gallagher, K. T. *The Philosophy of Gabriel Marcel* (New York: Fordham University Press, 1962).

Gaudin, C. (ed.). "Introduction," in *On Poetic Imagination and Reverie: Selections from the Works of Gaston Bachelard* (Indianapolis, Ind.: Bobbs-Merrill, 1971).

Glucksmann, M. *Structuralist Analysis in Contemporary Social Thought* (London: Routledge and Kegan Paul, 1974).

———. "The Structuralism of Lévi-Strauss and Althusser," in *Approaches to Sociology*, ed. J. Rex (London: Routledge and Kegan Paul, 1974).

Godelier, M. "Remarques sur les concepts de structure et de contradiction," *Aletheia*, No. 4 (1966).

———. "System, Structure, and Contradiction in *Das Capital*," in *The Socialist Register*, eds. J. Saville and R. Miliband (London: Merlin Press, 1967).

Grene, M. *Sartre* (New York: Viewpoints, 1973).

Haezrahi, P. "The Concept of Man as End in Himself," in *Kant, Foundations of the Metaphysics of Ethics with Critical Essays*, eds. L. W. Beck and R. P. Wolff (Indianpolis, Ind.: Bobbs-Merrill, 1969).

Hampshire, S. *Thought and Action* (London: Chatto and Windus, 1959).

Hanson, N. R. *Observation and Explanation* (New York: Harper, 1971).

Harrison, R. "The Concept of Prepredicative Experience," in *Phenomenology and Philosophical Understanding*, ed. E. Pivcevic (New York: Cambridge University Press, 1975).

Hartmann, K. "Phenomenology, Ontology and Metaphysics," *Review of Metaphysics* 22, No. 1 (1968).

Hegel, G.W.F. *The Phenomenology of Mind*, trans. J. B. Baillie (London: Allen and Unwin, 1931).

Heidegger, M. *Being and Time*, trans. J. Macquarrie and E. Robinson (New York: Harper and Row, 1962).

Hempel, C. "Geometry and Empirical Science," in *Readings in Philosophical Analysis*, eds. H. Feigl and W. Sellars (New York: Appleton-Century-Crofts, 1949).

Henry, M. *L'Essence de la manifestation*, 2 vols. (Paris: Presses Universitaires de France, 1963).

———. *Marx*, 2 vols. (Paris: Gallimard, 1976).

———. *Philosophie et phénoménologie du corps* (Paris: Presses Universitaires de France, 1965).

Hesse, M. *Models and Analogies in Science* (Notre Dame, Ind.: University of Notre Dame Press, 1966).

Husserl, E. *Logical Investigations,* trans. J. N. Findlay, 2 vols. (London: Routledge and Kegan Paul, and New York: Humanities Press, 1970).

———. *Origin of Geometry,* trans. J. P. Leavey, Jr. (New York: Nicholas Hays, and Humanities Press, 1978).

Ihde, D. *Hermeneutic Phenomenology. The Philosophy of Paul Ricoeur* (Evanston, Ill.: Northwestern University Press, 1971).

Jacobson, R. and Halle, M. *Fundamentals of Language* (The Hague: Mouton, 1956).

Jung, C. G. *The Basic Writings of C. G. Jung,* ed. V. S. de Laszlo (New York: Modern Library, 1959).

Kaplan, E. K. "Gaston Bachelard's Philosophy of Imagination," *Philosophy and Phenomenological Research* 33 (1972–1973).

Kenny, A. *Action, Emotion and Will* (London: Routledge and Kegan Paul, 1964).

———. *Descartes. A Study of His Philosophy* (New York: Random House, 1968).

———. *The Five Ways* (London: Routledge and Kegan Paul, 1969).

Kierkegaard, S. *Philosophical Fragments,* 2d ed., trans. D. F. Swenson and H. V. Hong (Princeton, N.J.: Princeton University Press, 1962).

Kohak, E. V. *Freedom and Nature* (Evanson, Ill.: Northwestern University Press, 1966).

Kojève, A. *Introduction à la lecture de Hegel* (Paris: Gallimard, 1947).

———. *Introduction to the Reading of Hegel,* ed. A. Bloom and trans. J. H. Nichols, Jr. (New York: Basic Books, 1969).

Kuhn, T. S. *The Structure of Scientific Revolutions* (Chicago: University of Chicago Press, 1967).

Lacan, J. *De la Psychose paranoïaque dans ses rapports avec la personnalité* (Paris: Libraire E. Le François, 1932).

———. *Écrits* (Paris: Seuil, 1966).

———. *Ecrits,* trans. A. Sheridan (New York: W.W. Norton, 1977).

———. *La Télévision* (Paris: Seuil, 1974).

———. *Le séminaire I. Les écrits techniques de Freud* (Paris: Seuil, 1975).

———. *Le séminaire XI. Les quatre concepts fondamentaux de la psychanalyse* (Paris: Seuil, 1973).

———. *Le séminaire XX. Encore.* (Paris: Seuil, 1975).

———. *Scilicet* (Paris: Seuil, 1968).

———. "The Function of Language in Psychoanalysis," in *The Language of the Self,* ed. A. Wilden (Baltimore: Johns Hopkins Press, 1968).

———. "The Insistence of the Letter in the Unconscious," in *Structuralism,* ed. J. Ehrmann (New York: Doubleday, 1970).

Lacroix, J. *Panorama de la philosophie française contemporaine* (Paris: Presses Universitaires de France, 1968). (Especially recommended as offering a more extended treatment of French philosophy in the postwar period.)

Laing, R. D. and Cooper, D. G. *Reason and Violence* (New York: Pantheon, 1971).

Lambert, K. and Brittain, Jr., G. G. *An Introduction to the Philosophy of Science* (Englewood Cliffs, N. J.: Prentice-Hall, 1970).

Lane, M. (ed.). *Structuralism: A Reader* (London: Cape, 1970).

Lanigan, R. L. *Speaking and Semiology. Merleau-Ponty's Phenomenological Theory of Existential Communication* (The Hague: Mouton, 1972).

Laplanche, J. and Leclaire, S. "L'Inconscient," *Les Temps modernes.* No. 183 (1961).

Leach, E. *Claude Lévi-Strauss,* ed. F. Kermode, Modern Masters Series (New York: Viking, 1970).

Leclaire, S. "A la recherche des principes d'une psychothérapie des psychoses," *l'Evolution psychiatrique* (April–June 1958).

Lecourt, D. *L'Epistémologie historique de Gaston Bachelard* (Paris: Vrin, 1974).

Levin, D. "Husserl's Notion of Self-Evidence," in *Phenomenology and Philosophical Understanding,* ed. E. Pivcevic (New York: Cambridge University Press, 1975).

———. "Induction and Husserl's Theory of Eidetic Variation," *Philosophy and Phenomenological Research* 29 (1968–1969).

Levinas, E. *Autrement qu'être* (The Hague: Nijhoff, 1974).

————. *Difficile liberté* (Paris: Albin Michel, 1963).

————. *En Decouvrant l'existence avec Husserl et Heidegger* (Paris: Vrin, 1949).

————. *La Théorie de l'intuition dans la phénoménologie de Husserl* (Paris: Alcan, 1930).

————. *L'Humanisme de l'autre homme* (Montpellier: Fata Morgana, 1972).

————. "Le Temps et l'autre," in *Le Choix, le monde, l'existence*, eds. J. Wahl et al. (Grenoble: Arthaud, 1948).

————. "Martin Buber and the Theory of Knowledge," trans. R. B. Rosthal in *The Philosophy of Martin Buber*, eds. P. Schillp and M. Friedman, Library of Living Philosophers (La Salle, Ill.: Open Court, 1967).

————. *Quatre lectures talmudiques* (Paris: Minuit, 1968).

————. *The Theory of Intuition in Husserl's Phenomenology*, trans. O. Orianne (Evanston, Ill.: Northwestern University Press, 1973).

————. *Totalité et infini* (The Hague: Nijhoff, 1961).

————. *Totality and Infinity: An Essay on Exteriority*, trans. A Lingis (Pittsburgh: Duquesne University Press, 1969).

Lévi-Strauss, C. *Anthropologie structurale* (Paris: Plon, 1958).

————. *Anthropologie structurale deux* (Paris: Plon, 1973).

————. *From Honey to Ashes*, trans. J. Weightman and D. Weightman (New York: Harper and Row, 1973).

————. *La Pensée sauvage* (Paris: Plon, 1962).

————. *La Voie des masques*, 2 vols. (Paris: Skira, 1975).

————. *Les Structures élémentaires de la parenté* (The Hague: Mouton, 1949).

————. *Le Totémisme aujourd'hui* (Boston: Beacon Press, 1962, and Paris: Presses Universitaires de France, 1974).

————. "Le Triangle culinaire," *L'Arc*, No. 26 (1965).

————. *Mythologiques*, 4 vols. (Paris: Plon, 1964).

————. *Structural Anthropology*, 2 vols. (New York: Doubleday, 1967).

————. "The Culinary Triangle," trans. P. Brooks *New Society* 8, No. 221 (1966).

————. *The Elementary Structures of Kinship* (Boston: Beacon Press, 1969).

————. *The Origin of Table Manners*, trans. J. Weightman and D. Weightman (New York: Harper and Row, 1978).

————. *The Raw and the Cooked: Introduction to a Science of Mythology* I, trans. J. Weightman and D. Weightman (New York: Harper and Row, 1969).

————. *The Savage Mind* (Chicago: University of Chicago Press, 1970).

————. *Tristes Tropiques* (Paris: Plon, 1955, and New York: Atheneum, 1974).

Lewis, F. E. "Merleau-Ponty and the Phenomenology of Language," in *Structuralism*, ed. J. Ehrmann (New York: Doubleday, 1970).

Lewit, A. "D'Où vient l'ambiguité de la phénoménologie?," *Bulletin de la Société Française de Philosophie* 65 (1971).

Lyons, J. *An Introduction to Theoretical Linguistics* (New York: Cambridge University Press, 1968).

Marcel, G. *Being and Having: An Existential Diary*, trans. K. Farrar (New York: Harper Torchbooks, 1965).

————. *Creative Fidelity*, trans. R. B. Rosthal (New York: Farrar Straus and Giroux, 1964).

————. *Du Refus à l'invocation* (Paris: Gallimard, 1940).

————. *Être et avoir*, 2 vols. (Paris: Aubier-Montaigne, 1968).

————. *Homo viator* (Paris: Aubier-Montaigne, 1965).

————. *Homo viator*, trans. E. Craufurd (New York: Harper Torchbooks, 1962).

————. *Journal Métaphysique* (Paris: Gallimard, 1928).

————. *La Métaphysique de Royce* (Paris: Aubier-Montaigne, 1945).

————. *Le mystère de l'être*, 2 vols. (Paris: Aubier-Montaigne, 1951).

————. *Metaphysical Journal*, trans. B. Wall (Chicago: Regnery, 1952).

————. "On the Ontological Mystery," in *The Philosophy of Existence*, trans. M. Harari (New York: Philosophical Library, 1949).

————. *Positions et approches concrètes du mystère ontologique* (Louvain: Nauwelaerts, 1949).

————. *The Mystery of Being*, 2 vols., trans. G. S. Fraser and R. Hague (Chicago: Regnery, 1960).

————. *Tragic Wisdom and Beyond Including Conversations Between Paul Ricoeur and Gabriel Marcel*, trans. S. Jolin and P. McCormick (Evanston, Ill.: Northwestern University Press, 1973).

Merleau-Ponty, M. *Adventures of the Dialectic*, trans. J. J. Bien (Evanston, Ill.: Northwestern University Press, 1973).

————. *Consciousness and the Acquisition of Language*, trans. H. J. Silverman (Evanston, Ill.: Northwestern University Press, 1973).

————. *Eloge de la philosophie* (Paris: Gallimard, 1953).

————. *Humanism and Terror* (Boston: Beacon Press, 1969).

————. *Humanisme et terreur* (Paris: Gallimard, 1947).

————. *In Praise of Philosophy*, trans. J. E. Edie and J. Wild (Evanston, Ill.: Northwestern University Press, 1963).

————. *La Phénoménologie de la perception* (Paris: Gallimard, 1945).

————. *La Prose du monde* (Paris: Gallimard, 1969).

————. *La Structure du comportement* (Paris: Presses Universitaires de France, 1942).

————. *Les Aventures de la dialectique* (Paris: Gallimard, 1955).

————. *Le Visible et l'invisible* (Paris: Gallimard, 1964).

————. *L'Union de l'âme et du corps chez Malebranche, Biran et Bergson: Notes prises au cours de Maurice Merleau-Ponty à L'École Normale Supérieure, 1947–1948* (Paris: Vrin, 1968).

————. *Phenomenology of Perception*, 4th ed., trans. C. Smith (London: Routledge and Kegan Paul, 1962).

————. *Résumés de cours, Collège de France, 1952–60* (Paris: Gallimard, 1968).

————. *Sens et nonsens* (Paris: Nagel, 1948).

————. *Sense and Non-Sense*, trans. H. L. Dreyfus and P. A. Dreyfus (Evanston, Ill.: Northwestern University Press, 1964).

————. *Signes* (Paris: Gallimard, 1960).

————. *Signs*, trans. R. C. McCleary (Evanston, Ill.: Northwestern University Press, 1964).

————. *Structure of Behavior* (Boston: Beacon Press, 1963).

————. *Themes from the Lectures at the College de France, 1952–1960*, trans. J. O'Neill (Evanston, Ill.: Northwestern University Press, 1970).

————. *The Primacy of Perception and Other Essays*, ed. J. M. Edie (Evanston, Ill. Northwestern University Press, 1964).

————. *The Prose of the World*, ed. C. LeFort and trans. J. O'Neill (Evanston, Ill.: Northwestern University Press, 1968).

————. *The Visible and the Invisible*, ed. C. LeFort and trans. A. Lingis (Evanston, Ill.: Northwestern University Press, 1968).

Moore, F.C.T. *The Psychology of Maine de Biran* (Oxford: Clarendon Press, 1970).

Natanson, M. "Phenomenology and Existentialism: Husserl and Sartre on Intentionality," in *Philosophy Today*, No. 3, ed. J. Gill (New York: Macmillan, 1970).

Olafson, F. A. "A Central Theme of Merleau-Ponty's Philosophy," in *Phenomenology and Existentialism*, eds. E. N. Lee and M. Mandelbaum (Baltimore: Johns Hopkins Press, 1967).

Pears, D. F. (ed.). *Freedom and Will* (London: Macmillan, 1964).

Peters, R. S. *The Concept of Motivation* (London: Routledge and Kegan Paul, 1958).

Pettit, P. *The Concept of Structuralism: A Critical Analysis* (Berkeley, Calif.: University of California Press, 1975).

Piaget, J. *Structuralism*, trans. C. Maschler (New York: Harper Torchbooks, 1970).

Pire, F. *De l'Imagination poétique dans l'oeuvre de Gaston Bachelard* (Paris: Corti, 1967).

Poster, M. *Existential Marxism in Postwar France. From Sartre to Althusser* (Princeton, N.J.: Princeton University Press, 1975).

Quillet, P. *Bachelard* (Paris: Seghers, 1964).

Ricoeur, P. *De l'Interprétation. Essai sur Freud* (Paris: Seuil, 1965).

———. *Finitude et culpabilité*, 2 vols. (Paris: Aubier, 1960).

———. *Freud and Philosophy: An Essay on Interpretation* (New Haven, Conn.: Yale University Press, 1970).

———. *Historie et vérité* (Paris: Seuil, 1955).

———. *History and Truth*, trans. C. A. Kelbley (Evanston, Ill.: Northwestern University Press, 1965).

———. *La Métaphore vive* (Paris: Seuil, 1975).

———. *Le Conflit des interprétations* (Paris: Seuil, 1969).

———. *Philosophie de la volonté*, 3 vols. (Paris: Aubier, 1950–1961).

———. "Philosophy of Will and Action," in *Phenomenology of Will and Action*, eds. E. W. Straus and R. M. Griffith (Pittsburgh: Duquesne University Press, 1967).

———. *Platon et Aristote* (Paris: Centre de Documentation Universitaire, 1960).

———. *The Conflict of Interpretations: Essays on Hermeneutics* (Evanston, Ill.: Northwestern University Press, 1974).

———. *The Symbolism of Evil*, trans. E. Buchanan (Boston: Beacon Press, 1967).

Robins, R. H. *A Short History of Linguistics* (Bloomington, Ind.: University of Indiana Press, 1968).

Rosthal, R. B. "F. C. T. Moore: *The Psychology of Maine de Biran*," *Journal of Philosophy* 69, No. 2 (1972).

Salmon, W. "Determinism and Indeterminism in Modern Science," in *Reason and Responsibility*, 3d ed., ed. J. Feinberg (Belmont, Calif.: Dickenson, 1975).

Sartre, J.-P. *Being and Nothingness*, trans. H. Barnes (New York: Philosophical Library, 1956).

———. *Between Existentialism and Marxism*, trans. J. Mathews (New York: Pantheon, 1974).

———. *Critique de la raison dialectique, précédé de Question de methode* (Paris: Gallimard, 1960).

———. *Critique of Dialectical Reason, Theory of Practical Ensembles*, ed. J. Rée and trans. A. Sheridan-Smith (London: NLB, and Atlantic Highlands, N. J.: Humanities Press, 1976).

———. *Esquisse d'une théorie des émotions* (Paris: Hermann, 1939).

———. "La transcendance de l'ego: Esquisse d'une description phénoménologique," *Recherches Philosophiques* 6 (1936).

———. *L'être et le néant: Essai d'ontologie phénoménologique* (Paris: Gallimard, 1943).

———. *L'Existentialisme est un humanisme* (Paris: Nagel, 1946).

———. *L'Idiot de la famille*, 3 vols. (Paris: Gallimard, 1971–1972).

———. *L'Imaginaire: Psychologie phénoménologique* (Paris: Gallimard, 1940).

———. *L'Imagination* (Paris: Alcan, 1936).

———. *The Transcendance of the Ego*, trans. F. Williams and R. Kirkpatrick (New York: Noonday, 1957).

Schiwy, G. *Der Französische Struckturalismus* (Hamburg: Rowohlt, 1969).

Schrag, C. "Phenomenology, Ontology, and History in the Philosophy of Heidegger," in *Phenomenology. The Philosophy of Edmund Husserl and Its Interpretation*, ed. J. J. Kockelmans (New York: Doubleday, 1967).

Scriven, M. *Primary Philosophy* (New York: McGraw-Hill, 1966).

Sebag, L. *Marxisme et structuralisme* (Paris: Payot, 1964).

Simonis, Y. *Claude Lévi-Strauss ou la 'passion de l'inceste'* (Paris: Aubier-Montaigne, 1968).

Smith, C. *Contemporary French Philosophy* (London: Methuen, 1964). (Especially recommended as offering a more extended treatment of French philosophy in the postwar period.)

Spiegelberg, H. *The Phenomenological Movement*, 2 vols. (The Hague: Nijhoff, 1965).

Strawson, P. "Imagination and Perception," in *Experience and Theory*, eds. L. Foster and J. W. Swanson (Amherst, Mass.: University of Massachusetts Press, 1970).

Taylor, C. *Hegel* (New York: Cambridge University Press, 1975).

Troisfontaines, R. *De l'Existence à l'être. La Philosophie de Gabriel Marcel*, 2 vols. (Louvain Nauwelaerts, 1953).

Viet, J. *Les Méthodes structuralistes dans les sciences sociales* (The Hague: Mouton, 1965).

Warnock, M. *Existentialist Ethics* (London: St. Martin's, 1967).

———. *Imagination* (Berkeley, Calif.: University of California Press, 1976).

Wyschogrod, E. *Emmanuel Levinas. The Problem of Ethical Metaphysics* (The Hague: Nijhoff, 1974).

JOURNALS

Archives de Philosophie
Bibliographie de la Philosophie
Bulletin de la Société Française de Philosophie
Critiques
Diogenes
Esprit
Etudes
Etudes Philosophiques
Monde
Recherches de Philosophie
Recherches Philosophiques
Revue d'Esthétique
Revue de Métaphysique et Morale
Temps Modernes

Great Britain

L. JONATHAN COHEN

I

The six long years of World War II represent a major divide in the history of modern British philosophy. With all available human and economic resources devoted to the war effort, little philosophical activity of any interest or importance took place. As a result, there was time for the dust to settle on old disputes. The earlier part of the century had been dominated by controversy between Hegelian idealists, like F. H. Bradley and J. McTaggart, and commonsensical or empirical realists, like G. E. Moore and Bertrand Russell. By 1945, Moore had retired, Russell had almost made his last contribution to academic philosophy, and Hegelianism was represented mainly by a few rather secondary figures in Scotland. R. G. Collingwood, whose most direct influence was Croce rather than Hegel, died in 1943, leaving no intellectual posterity, and after 1948, H. H. Price was the only British philosopher who continued to publish important work (such as *Thinking and Experience* and *Belief*) in the style of the older realists.

The way was now clear for certain new tendencies, which had been developing in the 1930s, to come into the forefront of discussion. A. J. Ayer's exposition of logical positivism *(Language, Truth and Logic)* was first published in 1936, but it had scarcely had time to provoke wide attention before the war broke out in 1939. The publication of a second edition in 1946 revived discussion of its highly controversial theses. According to logical positivism, all cognitively meaningful statements are either empirically verifiable or mere tautologies. Consequently, metaphysical issues, such as whether God exists or the human soul is immortal, are incapable of meaningful formulation. Utterances of moral praise or blame, or imputations of ethical obligation, have to be regarded not as statements, which may be true or false, but as expressions or evocations of emotion, which may be effective or ineffective but cannot be either true or false.

Ayer's views were criticized from two very different points of view. On the one hand, there were those, like A. C. Ewing,[1] who sought to defend the orthodoxies Ayer had attacked. In order to vindicate the possibility of metaphysical truth, these critics needed to refute Ayer's fundamental doctrine that every cognitively meaningful statement was either tautologous or empirically verifiable. For that purpose, they often argued that Ayer's doctrine was itself neither tautologous nor empirically verifiable, and that it looked suspiciously like an example of the metaphysics that Ayer claimed to be impossible. But this argument was not as strong as its proponents thought, since Ayer was content to have his fundamental doctrine regarded as a recommendation about how to classify people's utterances rather than as a description of what is in fact the case.

More serious were the criticisms that came from Ayer's own generation. These criticisms were founded on ideas that had originated in the 1930s in a general movement of dissatisfaction among the avant-garde with the logical positivist program of the Vienna Circle. For example, a philosophy that regarded physics, not theology, as queen of the sciences might reasonably be expected to give a more convincing account of fundamental scientific theories, and their validation, than Ayer's verificationist principle seemed to permit. To some extent, this defect was supplied by R. B. Braithwaite's 1946 Tarner Lectures at Cambridge University, subsequently published as *Scientific Explanation: A Study of the Function of Theory, Probability and Law in Science.* Braithwaite sought to exhibit the logical structure of a scientific theory in terms of an underlying formal calculus. The axioms of the calculus corresponded to fundamental laws about the behavior of theoretical, unobserved entities like, say, electrons and protons, but the actual interpretation of the calculus is achieved only via its more derivative theorems, which are assigned observational meanings. Braithwaite followed E. P. Ramsey *(The Foundations of Mathematics)* in rejecting Russell's view (which the Vienna Circle had taken up) that the theoretical terms of fundamental science are just logical constructions out of observational ones. He also faced up to the problem posed to verificationists by the fact that many scientific hypotheses are statements of probability (e.g., of the probability that a radium atom will disintegrate within twenty-four hours) and so are not subject either to verification or to falsification by single observation statements. To deal with the problem, he examined in detail certain possible strategies for making rational decisions between rival statistical hypotheses.

We shall return to some related issues in the philosophy of science later, but we must now turn to yet another flaw in the logical positivist program—its excessively schematic philosophy of language.

II

Wittgenstein returned to Cambridge in 1929, and his new ideas about philosophy and language began to influence a number of friends and disciples in the 1930s. Wittgenstein himself did not publish any account of these ideas, but after the war they became fairly familiar to professional philosophers through the wider and wider circulation of two privately duplicated sets of dictations known, from the colors of their wrappings, as the Blue Book and the Brown Book. These had originally been dictated in 1933–1934 and 1934–1935, respectively, but were not officially published until 1958 as *Preliminary Studies for "The Philosophical Investigations."* In fact, Wittgenstein's death in 1951 was followed by the publication, at intervals, of quite a number of volumes, representing the development of his thought over a considerable period. The most important of these were *Remarks on the Foundations of Mathematics* (written in the years 1937–1944 and published in 1956) and *Philosophical Investigations* (Part I, completed by 1945 and Part II, written between 1947 and 1949, published in 1953).[2]

In this later work, Wittgenstein repudiated the rather schematic conception of language that he had formulated much earlier in his *Tractatus Logico-Philosophicus* and that had strongly influenced the Vienna Circle. He no longer believed that propositions were essentially pictures of facts or that the structure of language could be best understood in terms of the logical relations borne by complex propositions to atomic ones. Instead, he insisted on the variety of uses to which language is put: giving orders, describing, reporting, making a joke, asking, thanking, cursing, greeting, praying, and so forth. Philosophical error arose, he thought, through the temptations that language generates to draw erroneous analogies. Meaning, for example, is not to be understood as a form of naming whereby every word is coordinated with its appropriate object or objects. The cure for such "bewitchment of the intelligence by means of language" *(Philosophical Investigations)* is a painstakingly detailed examination of the innumerable similarities and differences that exist between different word uses. Similarly, terms in our psychological vocabulary, like "know" or "understand," are not to be regarded as naming private experiences to which he who knows or understands has sole access. To suppose this is to suppose that each person speaks a private language, the words of which have incommunicable meanings. Nor does the notion of using a word correctly or incorrectly make sense unless one can specify how to detect whether or not the rule governing its use has been obeyed. Correspondingly, the function of such sentences as "I am in pain" cannot be to describe a private state that I discover in myself. If sentences like "I know I am in pain" made sense, we could contrast their use with that of sentences like "I rather believe I am in pain," which is obviously absurd.

Wittgenstein's magnetic personality and deeply original thinking exerted a powerful influence on a number of younger philosophers who attended his lectures or became his friends. Some of these, like A. Ambrose and N. Malcolm, entered academic life in the United States and helped to promote discussion of Wittgenstein's ideas in North America. Others, like G.E.M. Anscombe, R. Rhees, and A.J.T. Wisdom, pursued most of their philosophical careers in Britain and developed attitudes broadly in keeping with Wittgenstein's own position. For example, Anscombe published a study of the concept of intention *(Intention)* in which she examined the various ways in which intentions are expressed, the kinds of questions that can be answered by statements of intention, the differences between wants, motives, causes, and intentions, and so on. Intending, she argued, is not to be regarded as a performance of the mind or act—not even as an interior act. In *Other Minds* and *Philosophy and Psycho-*

analysis, Wisdom was particularly concerned with those patterns of language use, in metaphysical theorizing, aesthetic judgment, and elsewhere, that the logical positivists held to be cognitively meaningless.[3] He pointed out that even our statements about other people's minds cannot be verified in the same way as statements about familiar physical objects like tables and chairs. He, too, like Wittgenstein, preferred to avoid the formulation of general theses and to treat his own writings rather as an "assembly of reminders" (as Wittgenstein once put it) for the dissolution of particular puzzlements. He compared these puzzlements, induced by muddles about language, to neuroses that were rooted in the subconscious; he compared the philosophical therapy that was needed for their elimination to the talking-out procedures of psychoanalysis.

III

As far as the first half of the twentieth century is concerned, the major innovative influences on British philosophy originated in the University of Cambridge. Moore, Russell, and Wittgenstein were all closely connected with that university for considerable periods of time, and so was Ramsey. But after Wittgenstein's retirement from his professorship in 1947, it soon became clear that the main scene of creative ferment had moved to Oxford University. Cambridge remained active principally in the more specialized area of the philosophy of science, as evidenced by Braithwaite's work (already mentioned) and by the later contributions of M. Hesse (*Forces and Fields* and *The Structure of Scientific Inference*), I. Hacking *(Logic of Statistical Inference),* and H. Mellor *(The Matter of Chance).* The undergraduate curriculum at Oxford had long helped to maintain a substantially larger number of teaching posts in philosophy than at Cambridge, and this in turn made possible the creation of a much larger graduate school when graduate studies in philosophy came to be systematically organized at Oxford in 1947. The graduate school attracted many able students from all over the English-speaking world. These students generally carried back with them to their own universities, whether in Britain or elsewhere, a lively interest in the approach to philosophical problems that they had encountered at Oxford.

At first, the most influential figure at Oxford was G. Ryle. Ryle succeeded to R. G. Collingwood's university professorship in 1945 and to G. E. Moore's editorship of *Mind,* the leading British philosophical periodical, in 1948. As early as 1931, Ryle had announced his conversion, albeit a reluctant one, to the view that the characteristic task of philosophy was "the detection of the sources in linguistic idioms of recurrent misconstructions and absurd theories."[4] At that time, Ryle thought this task could best be accomplished by reformulating misleading locutions in a logically purified idiom. Russell's theory of descriptions was the paradigm for his conception of philosophical analysis. But Ryle gradually came to prefer a more informal pattern of analysis and in particular to think of his objective as the job of assigning to their correct categories those linguistic expressions that other philosophers had misclassified. His major work, *The Concept of Mind*, sought to deal in this way with what he sometimes called "Descartes' myth" and sometimes "the dogma of the Ghost in the Machine." According to the dogma, said Ryle, the terms "mind" and "body" are coordinate names for the two entities that are combined in a typical living person: the term "mind" denotes a secret inner studio in which events are linked in some puzzlingly inscrutable fashion with the behavioral activity denoted by the term "body." Similarly, expressions like "thinking," "imagining," "trying," or "being angry" are supposed to denote certain kinds of episodes in this inner drama. Ryle proposed a systematic recategorization of all such mental terms whereby they would cease to be classified as object- or event-names and would coordinate with the object- or event-names of the physical world. Instead, he argued, many of them belonged alongside public, dispositional terms like "fragile" and "brittle." To describe a man as being angry, for example, is to say that, if provoked, he is likely to do such things as shout, slam doors, or throw things across the room. And to say "I intend" or "I feel hungry" is not to describe one's own inner state. Indeed, it is not to use language descriptively at all but to make an avowal.

There were obvious similarities between Ryle's mature views and those of the later Wittgenstein. Both thought of themselves as attacking philosophical errors that could be attributed to misinterpretations of linguistic use. Both found a particular target in the widespread philosophical tendency to suppose that the world of mind is a private and unobservable one. But there were also important differences. Although Ryle's style is so epigrammatic and staccato that the exact structure of his reasoning is not always immediately apparent to those unfamiliar with his writings, he nevertheless advances positive philosophical theses, of some generality, and supports them with arguments designed to establish their correctness. For Ryle, the "logical geography" of our concepts is a branch of human knowledge. Wittgenstein, on the other hand, conceived of his philosophy as an activity that would, hopefully, effect the dissolution of his hearers' or readers' puzzlement, but would only create new problems if it were construed as propounding and defending general principles. When the mathematician A. M. Turing once asked him, in the course of a discussion, "Is your thesis that . . .?," Wittgenstein replied, "I have no thesis."

Wittgenstein and Ryle forced a whole generation of English-speaking philosophers to reconsider their views about the body-mind problem. But both philosophers are open to at least two criticisms. First, in their anxiety to attack the view that everything mental was essentially private, they tended to overlook the possibility that some mental events, such as the occurrence of mental imagery, might be both private and describable. Second, in their determination to trace all philosophical error to muddles about language, they overlooked the influence of certain nonlinguistic factors, such as religious beliefs about the separability of body and soul.

IV

In the period 1945–1960, a number of other Oxford philosophers developed approaches to philosophy that were sufficiently similar to Ryle's for Ryle and them to be known collectively to the outside world as the Oxford school of ordinary language philosophy. They shared an interest in the study of existing patterns of word use and found these patterns far too complex and heterogeneous to admit of useful representation within any logico-mathematical system. In their respect for what people ordinarily say, there were echoes of an older Oxford generation's Aristotelianism, as evidenced in the work of J. Cook Wilson and W. D. Ross. There was undoubtedly also some influence from Wittgenstein's later work at Cambridge and, perhaps to a lesser extent, from the rather parallel development of F. Waismann's philosophy of language, (*The Principles of Linguistic Philosophy,* published posthumously), which became better known at Oxford when he taught there after the war. As is often the case in philosophical schools, however, the Oxford ordinary language philosophers were at least as conscious of their disagreements with one another as of their communities of interest and methodology.

Russell's theory of definite descriptions, which was a paradigm of philosophical analysis to the Vienna Circle and its British sympathizers, was published in an article entitled "On Denoting" in *Mind* in 1905 (pp. 479–493). In 1950, also in *Mind* (pp. 320–344), P. F. Strawson published a powerful criticism of it in an article entitled "On Referring." The main issue at stake was what to say about sentences like "The king of France is bald" which seem to refer to a nonexistent entity. In Russell's view, the assertion of such a sentence was false: in Strawson's, it had no truth-value because what it presupposed, viz., the existence of a king of France, was false. Russell's account of such uniquely identifying descriptions as "the king of France" was closely integrated with his logical analysis of numerical expressions and so with his plan to exhibit the whole of mathematics as a part of logic. His account also involved making the economical assumption that every assertion was either true or false. Strawson's account, however, was much more faithful to our ordinary assignments of truth-values, and on this basis he asserted that Russell's analysis was incorrect.

In 1952, in *Introduction to Logical Theory,* Strawson went on to publish an introduction to logic in which this kind of critique is applied more generally. The proper task of logic is to reveal the general types of inconsistency, validity, and invalidity that occur "in our ordinary use of ordinary language." Modern formal logicians are diverted from this task, Strawson suggests, by the intellectual charm of deductive systems. In order to achieve a comprehensive and elegant system of logical laws, with an ordered arrangement of their derivations from one another, logicians distort the representation of actual usage.

The main objection to Strawson's view of logic is that it ignores the primary intellectual value of axiomatic systematization. By being combined into a single deductive system, different laws—whether they be laws of logic, science, mathematics, or ethics—come to corroborate one another. To achieve such powerful combinations, however, often requires some tradeoff of representational fidelity. No one ever supposed it a major demerit of Euclidean geometry that something with length and no breadth exists nowhere in nature. Euclidean lines are idealizations; so too, it may be objected to Strawson, are formal, logically defined relations.

In the same year Strawson's book on logic appeared, R. M. Hare published a book which he described as an introduction to ethics but which was more appropriately entitled *The Language of Morals*. Ethics, as Hare understood it, was not concerned at first hand with principles of human conduct but rather with the logical structure of the sentences in which such principles are formulated and applied. Hare agreed with the logical positivists, like Ayer, that moral judgments were not a statement-making form of discourse. But he did not agree that their typical function was to express or evoke emotion or that they could not constitute the premises or conclusions of rationally valid arguments. In every indicative or imperative sentence, like "You are shutting the door" or "Shut the door!," he distinguished between a phrastic and a neustic, as he called them. The phrastic, which can be paraphrased as "Your shutting the door," could be common to both types of sentences. What distinguished them was the neustic, paraphrased as "Yes" and "Please," respectively. Since the phrastic alone determined logical entailments, it was quite possible to have a logic of imperatives. Hare thought of a moral principle as a universal imperative (e.g., "Everyone is to tell the truth"), to the acceptance of which anyone committed himself who uttered a particular moral prescription instantiating it (e.g., "You ought to tell the truth about your past life to her now").

Hare's moral philosophy was, of course, open to the objection that it did not provide any guidance for choice between conflicting principles, in the way that Kant's categorical imperative or Mill's principle of utility might do. But Hare did not profess to be providing moral guidance, and he could at least claim to have clarified the way in which people might think about such dilemmas.

H.L.A. Hart adopted a somewhat analogous attitude to the philosophy of law. In his inaugural lecture *(Definition and Theory in Jurisprudence)* as university professor of jurisprudence, Hart argued that it was possible to elucidate the meanings of fundamental legal terms like "right," "duty," or "corporation" without assuming any "incubus of theory." The actual use of such terms in a legal system could be quite satisfactorily described without any recourse to the theory, say, that "right" denotes an objective reality, or that it denotes a fictitious or imaginary power, or that it is a term by which we describe the prophecies we make of the probable behavior of courts or officials. Similarly, we should not try to analyze statements about corporations into equivalent statements about the behavior of individuals, but simply to determine the conditions under which a statement about a corporation is true and the legal consequences of its being so. Thus, Hart was applying to the particular case of legal terminology a general principle that both Wittgenstein and Ryle were active in propagating—the principle that one should not confuse meaning with naming. In his attempt to provide theory-free definitions of legal terms, however, Hart overlooked the fact that requests for definitions of legal terms are rarely made in order to satisfy a bare curiosity about the flat facts of existing linguistic usage. They spring instead from a desire for guidance in borderline cases where the exact interpretation or application of a legal rule seems not to be settled by the legal system itself. Hart's definitions supply no such guidance.

Later, in 1961, in *The Concept of Law,* Hart put forward his own account of the nature of a legal system. He drew a fundamental distinction between two different kinds of rules: the primary, which imposes obligations or duties, and the secondary, which confers powers. He criticized the nineteenth-century English jurist John Austin for making the mistake of supposing that laws were essentially primary rules imposed by a sovereign. In Hart's view, law can instead best be understood as a union of primary and secondary rules. Although the criminal law consists largely of primary rules, the laws that confer jurisdiction, or legislative powers, are secondary rules, as are the laws regulating such private transactions as marriages, contracts, and will-making. But now the difficulty with his philosophy of law is an opposite one. In the inaugural lecture, he stuck so close to a bare description of ordinary legal usage that his analyses were too superficially linguistic to meet the needs for which practicing judges and lawyers resort to the study of jurisprudence. But in his theory of primary and secondary rules, he moved so far away from existing legal usage that a considerable hiatus appeared between his overall thesis, on the one side, and his ordinary language methodology, on the other. A principal purpose of his theory was to elucidate "the specifically legal concepts with which the lawyer is professionally concerned." Yet, he spoke of powers to marry or make wills, where English law speaks only of capacities, and of duties to abstain from robbing or murdering, where English law speaks only of the crime or felony involved in doing such things. Whereas Hare was content to deal with those problems within his field that were amenable to fruitful treatment by ordinary language analysis, Hart was rather more ambitious and his philosophy was correspondingly more incoherent.

During the 1950s, most of ordinary language philosophy at Oxford came to be dominated by J. L. Austin. He had been the leading spirit of a small discussion group of avant-gardist younger philosophers in the years 1936–1939. During the 1950s, he organized a discussion group on Saturday mornings to which he invited a number of his colleagues. Austin's keen wit and quick penetrating intelligence made him the master of most oral discussions in which he participated. Unfortunately, although he published a number of influential articles in his lifetime, he died in 1960 at a relatively early age, and his only published full-length philosophical studies were two lecture series that were edited posthumously and appeared in 1962.

The first of these two volumes, *Sense and Sensibilia,* contained criticisms of sense datum philosophy, particularly Ayer's *The Foundations of Empirical*

Knowledge. The general pattern of Austin's criticisms, which he had been developing in his lectures since 1947, was to argue that sense datum philosophers had not properly understood the various ways in which words like "real," "looks," and "seems," function, and had founded erroneous theories on the basis of these misunderstandings. One such error was Ayer's theory that words like "see" and "perceive" have a variety of senses, and in particular one sense in which it may be true that a man looking at the night sky sees a star and another sense in which it may be true at the same time that he sees a silvery speck.

Austin had a finer eye for the nuances of ordinary usage than most of his contemporaries, but as he pursued his researches into them in greater detail his critics began to accuse him of trivializing philosophy. To this criticism he had two main replies. One was that, while he did not think importance was important, he was sure that truth was. The other reply was to argue[5] that the distinctions present in the English vocabulary of some nontechnical activity, like that of making excuses, deserved study in their own right because ordinary English embodies the inherited experience and acumen of many generations of men. Thus, he applied a rather naive, eighteenth-century notion of enlightened progress to the particular case of ordinary language. He assumed, without argument, that ordinary language has moved, is moving, and presumably will move (without any need for critical philosophical analysis) in a desirable direction.

The second published volume of Austin's lectures, dating originally from 1952–1954, is entitled *How to Do Things with Words*. Austin began by pointing out that certain verbs like "promise" are used in the first person present indicative to perform the very action that, in other uses, they describe. The utterance of "I promise" so as to *make* a promise could therefore be termed a performative, as distinct from a statement-making, one. But what then was to be said of utterances like "I state that it is raining" which seem to be both performative and statement-making? Austin was prompted by this kind of difficulty to replace the distinction between performative and statement-making kinds of utterances by a distinction between different aspects of the same utterance. Every normal utterance, he said, embodied three distinguishable acts: the locutionary act—the utterance of a proposition, with a sense and reference; the illocutionary act—roughly what the speaker achieved in saying what he did (e.g., asking a question, making a promise); and the perlocutionary act—the result produced by his saying what he did (e.g., persuading, puzzling, or frightening his audience). Austin's theory of speech acts has attracted some attention from grammarians, and his term "illocutionary force" now sometimes occurrs in the literature of linguistics as if its meaning and scope are well understood and need no further clarification. Unfortunately, however, Austin did not have the opportunity to revise his lectures before publication, and his theory of speech acts is not altogether coherent. His definitions of the term "illocutionary force" are conflicting, and it appears that his trichotomous classification is oversimplified and inadequate.[6] His work on speech acts, however, had the merit of emphasizing the differences between different dimensions of semantic inquiry, which Wittgenstein and his disciples seemed sometimes to ignore.

Further progress in this direction was made by H. P. Grice[7] in his theory about the implications (or "implicatures" as he called them) attaching to human utterances in virtue of the presumption that speakers will conform to certain standard principles of conversational activity, such as maxims of rationality and relevance. Grice's exposition of this idea would have been improved if he had distinguished between those conversational maxims, if any, that are intrinsic to all intelligent communication and those that embody the preferences and attitudes of particular cultures. There is a trace here of the kind of insularity that in Austin's case tended to reduce the study of ordinary language to the study of ordinary English and in Hart's case tended to reduce analysis of the nature of a legal system to a study of how English lawyers handle their technical terms.

V

The ordinary language philosophy of the 1945–1960 period was often called Oxford philosophy. This description was scarcely fair to the considerable number of able and active Oxford philosophers whose conceptions of their subject were rather different. In *Thought and Action,* S. Hampshire wrote about the philosophy of mind in a way that defied Ryle's arguments against the doctrine of mental privacy. P. Foot[8] argued that principles of moral value were objectively constrained in a way that Hare's imperativism did not allow. When B. Williams argued in his article "Personal Identity and Individuation" that bodily identity is always a necessary condition of personal identity, he did not base his arguments on the facts of ordinary usage. Again, those who had a deeper knowledge of mathematical logic or of the theory of probability were naturally disinclined to accept ordinary language solutions for problems about the nature of deductive or inductive reasoning. This is evident from the work of M. Dummett and E. J. Lemmon[9] in the deductive field and of W. Kneale (in *Probability and Induction*) in the inductive.

An earlier criticism of linguistic philosophy in general had come from H. H. Price under the title "Clarity Is Not Enough." Direct attacks on ordinary language methodology came mainly from outside Oxford, especially from a trio of Oxford-educated philosophers, all of whom held posts at Edinburgh University at the same time in the late 1940s, though they subsequently dispersed elsewhere. In "The Appeal to Ordinary Language," P. L. Heath argued that "the casual and irregular speech-habits of everyday intercourse" are intrinsically unable "to furnish unique and authoritative criteria for the interpretation of terms in common use among philosophers." E. Gellner (in *Words and Things*) attacked Wittgensteinians and ordinary language philosophers alike, in a way that tended to confound many important differences. For example, he attributed to them all the view that "the holding of positions is the prime philosophic error"—a characterization that had some relevance to Wittgenstein and his disciples but was a travesty of Oxford ordinary language methodology. But Gellner's book attracted considerable public interest because it attacked people as well as ideas. According to Gellner, the trouble with linguistic philosophy was not just that its intellectual pretensions were unfounded but also that it was sociologically categorizable as a form of secularized religion. Echoing Veblen, Gellner attributed to linguistic philosophy a kind of "conspicuous triviality": it was an activity in which gentlemen could conspicuously waste time and talent.

There was a certain absurdity in the frequency with which linguistic philosophers claimed to be occupied solely with problems created by the mistakes of other philosophers, as if their professional function was "to treat a disease which they catch from each other and impart to their pupils," as C. D. Broad had put it. Unfortunately, however, Gellner did not offer any rival theory of language, so his criticisms lacked the intellectual power to displace the doctrines he attacked. L. J. Cohen proposed such a theory in a book that found fault with Wittgenstein, Ryle, and others for adopting a static rather than a dynamic conception of human language. Talk about the logical geography of human concepts implies, according to Cohen, that these concepts have uniquely correct analyses that are as timelessly true as the laws of logic, whereas in fact the history of ideas reveals a continuous flux from which, at any one time, philosophers may argue the superiority of some appropriate selection.

Whether through the efforts of these and other critics or because of Wittgenstein's death in 1951, Waismann's in 1959, and Austin's in 1960, or because the movement just ran out of steam, both Wittgensteinianism and ordinary language philosophy tended to die out in Britain in the 1960s. Occasional books and articles were still published in the old style, but interest in Wittgenstein's methodology became more and more scholarly and historical (rather than creative and philosophical), as a substantial quantity of his surviving manuscripts became available for study. New contributions to ordinary language philosophy tended to come from outside Oxford, like A. R. White's *Modal Thinking*. In Oxford itself, interest began to shift towards a treatment of problems about language and reasoning which had a higher regard for the advantages of formalization. However, formal systematization was now considered a technique appropriate to the solution of particular problems rather than as itself the goal of all philosophy like a Russellian ideal language of the pre-1939 era. Examples (though very diverse ones) of this new trend were A. N. Prior's work[10] on tense-logic; J. R. Lucas's reconstruction of probability as a generalization of truth and falsehood *(The Concept of Probability);* R. Harré's critique of the positivist philosophy of science *(The Principle of Scientific Thinking);* L. J. Cohen's analysis of inductive reasoning in terms of a generalized modal logic rather than the familiar calculus of probabilities *(The Implications of Induction);* J. L. Mackie's study of problems about truth, conditional propositions, dispositions, probabilities, and the logical paradoxes *(Truth, Probability and Paradox);* M. Dummett's critical examination and development of Frege's views about sense and reference *(Frege: Philosophy of Language);* and the considerable amount of discussion[11] devoted to questions about the scope and value of truth-conditional semantics. At the same time, there were traces of a revived interest in transcendental arguments. Strawson pioneered this trend in 1959 with a book, *Individuals,* about personal identity and individuation in which he was content to derive the conclusion that material bodies are the basic particulars in human thought from the premise that identification rests ultimately on location in a unitary spatio-temporal framework of four dimensions. Strawson boldly subtitled his book *An Essay in Descriptive Metaphysics.* P.M.S. Hacker later took up the theme in a book *(Insight and Illusion)* that reads a "metaphysics of experience" into Wittgenstein's texts and stresses their Kantian affinities.

In retrospect, it is natural to view these developments at Oxford during the 1959–1977 period as a healthy reaction to the earlier predominance of "linguistic" philosophy. I have not written about the later developments at such length because these new fashions were part of a rather larger current of opinion. The rapid growth of bigger philosophy departments in the universities of the United States in the years after 1945 brought about a kind of continuum of North Atlantic philosophical culture by the late 1950s. Frequent intervisiting by faculty members and migrations for graduate study ensured a degree of mutual understanding that made fruitful controversy possible. Consequently, at least the new logical interests at Oxford may be seen no less as a contribution to trans-Atlantic debates than as a reaction to the native "linguistic" philosophy of an earlier period.

VI

In this description of major trends in British philosophy during the period 1945–1977, large numbers of individual contributions have inevitably had to be disregarded. For example, it is difficult to relate S. Körner's analysis[12] of scientific reasoning to any of the above trends, even though his systematic contrasting of observation statements with theoretical ones, as being concerned with inexact, rather than exact, classes, had considerable usefulness and originality. In addition, other individuals at other universities who contributed in one way or another to the trends discussed have also been omitted here. But any survey would be grossly incomplete if it did not mention four other lines of philosophical activity that distinguished this period, even though they never involved the activities of so many people or such a large quantity of published material.

First, amid the usual welter of books, in which each generation of philosophers reinterprets its predecessors and rewrites the history of its subject, one new development was of particular interest. The immense advances that formal logic had achieved could now be exploited to achieve a better understanding of the logical theories of previous philosophers. J. Łukasiewicz, who had migrated from Poland to Ireland, published a study of Aristotle's syllogistic in these terms in 1951 *(Aristotle's Syllogistic from the Standpoint of Modern Formal Logic)*. Some work on the rediscovery of Leibniz's philosophy of logic and language had already been done long since by Couturat and by Russell. In 1972, in Leibniz's *Philosophy of Logic and Language,* H. Ishiguro was able to correct errors in their interpretations and reveal hitherto unsuspected subtleties of logical insight in Leibniz's thoughts. And in a work of monumental scholarship *(The Development of Logic)*, W. and M. Kneale rewrote the whole history of logic and at last supplanted the undeservedly long reign of Prantl's *Geschichte Der Logik in Abendlande,* which was published in 1855–1870.

Second, the early 1970s saw a growing interest in Marxism among younger philosophers. A new journal, *Radical Philosophy,* was founded to further this interest. The specifically Marxist contributions to this journal tend to be rather humdrum critiques of non-Marxist ideas, institutions, and publications; as yet, no important novel twist in the Marxist tradition seems to have originated.

Third, dissatisfaction with the purely meta-ethical approach of linguistic moral philosophy led in the 1960s to a renewed interest in more concrete problems. A typical product of this interest was R. Atkinson's *Sexual Morality.* The 1960s also witnessed a sharply renewed debate on the merits of utilitarianism.[13] Körner introduced a new level of sophistication into the discussion by attempting (in *Experience and Conduct*) to develop a framework for the systematic comparison of different kinds of ethics. He was particularly concerned with problems about the relative priorities to be assigned to different principles, where these might conflict with one another.

Finally, the work of K. R. Popper and his associates has to be mentioned. Popper was born in Vienna and came to England from New Zealand in early 1946. He taught at the London School of Economics and Political Science (part of London University) from 1946 until his retirement in 1969. He himself had always adopted "the principle of never arguing about words and their meanings,"[14] and his attitude naturally led him into a position of contempt for logical positivism, Wittgensteinianism, and ordinary language philosophy. At the same time, Popper's somewhat relaxed attitude towards questions of scholarship about the philosophers he criticized and the rather wide-ranging claims he made on behalf of the originality and importance of his own ideas combined to promote a reciprocal contempt for Popper's philosophy among some of his contemporaries at Oxford and elsewhere. The result was that little or no cross-fertilization occurred between the dominant schools of linguistic philosophy, on the one hand, and Popper's small group in London, on the other. Neither was willing (at any rate, as a collective act) to appreciate the quite substantial merits and achievements of the other.

Popper's seminal work, *Logik der Forschung,* was originally published in Vienna in 1934, but it did not become as well known in Britain as it deserved to be until an English translation, *The Logic of Scientific Discovery* (by Popper himself), appeared in 1959. Popper introduced several new appendices into this edition and continued to develop his philosophy of science in further works (for example, *Conjectures and Refutations* and *Objective Knowledge*). Science progressed, he claimed, by the proposal of hypotheses to solve problems and by the rigorous testing of these hypotheses. The merit of a hypothesis lay not only in its actual resistance to falsification, when rigorously tested, but also in the degree to which it was logically exposed to falsification. Bold hypotheses were better than more timid ones. Popper denied any scientific value to inductive reasoning, for two main reasons. First, he insisted that hypothesis construction occurred before, and not after, the execution of experimental tests: the occurrence of such a test presupposes the existence of a hypothesis to be tested. Second, he argued against the logical positivist emphasis on verification. Scientists characteristically seek to falsify a hypothesis, he urged, not to verify it. Therefore, they have no need of an inductive logic to assess the extent to which the truth of the hypothesis has been established.

Popper was able to maintain plausibility for this doctrine only by concentrating on the progress of science as a purely theoretical inquiry. After all, engineers and other technologists need inductive criteria on the basis of which they can compare the reliability of one hypothesis with another, and reliability does not necessarily correlate with unfalsified boldness. Nevertheless, Popper's philosophy of science enjoyed substantial esteem among leading scientists. He also achieved wide popularity among liberal intellectuals for his defense (in *The Open Society and Its Enemies*) of an open society against various forms of totalitarian doctrine, such as those whose origins are traceable to the ideas of Plato, Hegel, or Marx.

Popper's views exercised a considerable influence on the philosophical development of I. Lakatos, who was born in Hungary in 1922 and taught at the London School of Economics and Political Science from 1960 until his death in 1974. Lakatos' initial work (see "Proofs and Refutations," pp. 1–25, 120–139, 221–245, 296–342) was in the philosophy of mathematics. Here he presented an account of the subject that was entirely different from the normal modern concern (typified by Russell, Hilbert, and Brouwer) with foundations and the study of constructions thereon. According to Lakatos, the progress of mathematics does not consist in the gradual accumulation of conclusively established truths but rather in a process of conjecture, attempts to "prove" the conjecture by reducing it to other conjectures, and criticism by counterexample. Lakatos illustrated his theory with a brilliantly rationalized reconstruction of the later history of the Descartes-Euler conjecture about polyhedra. It is not entirely clear, however, that all other parts of the history of mathematics would lend themselves quite as well to reconstruction in terms of Lakatos' idealized heuristic.

Lakatos turned later to the philosophy of natural science. He saw two main weaknesses in Popper's account. First, it was wrong to suggest—as he thought Popper sometimes did—that falsified theories were standardly rejected. Instead, he emphasized that if a more powerful hypothesis is not available to replace it, a theory is often not eliminated by the discovery of anomalies. Second, he thought it important to apply criteria of evaluation not just to single hypotheses, as Popper had done, but also to sequences of them, or "problem-shifts" as he called them. A progressive (i.e., scientific) problem-shift, in Lakatos' view is a sequence of hypotheses in which each successive hypothesis explains all the evidence that its predecessor can explain, and some evidence that its predecessor cannot explain, and also predicts successfully some hitherto unknown facts. A degenerating (i.e., pseudoscientific) problem-shift is a sequence of hypotheses that have replaced one another without all those conditions being satisfied. Lakatos found numerous illustrations, for the importance of this distinction, in the history of physics and chemistry. He did not see that he was now implicitly endorsing the evaluation of scientific hypotheses by criteria identical with those originally proposed by Bacon's inductive logic, as L. J. Cohen later pointed out in *The Probable and the Provable*. Lakatos was as convinced as Popper that the value of a scientific hypothesis could not be measured in degrees of probability. He did not see that the arguments against such an assessment did not necessarily apply to non-Pascalian probabilities—probabilities that were different in structure from those conforming to the mathematical calculus of chance.

Popper's associates and disciples performed much other work, both in Britain and elsewhere. While almost all of it was concerned with the philosophy of science, this concern covered a considerable variety of interests. For example, it enabled Popperians to argue against the logical positivist thesis that metaphysical statements are intellectually valueless because they are cognitively meaningless as well as against the Wittgensteinian thesis that such statements arise through some pathological misunderstanding of the way in which language actually functions. Thus, in 1958 in "Confirmable and Influential Metaphysics," J.W.N. Watkins emphasized the regulative and influential role of metaphysical principles in the history of science. This attitude to metaphysics was very different from that which Strawson had arrived at, by approximately the same year (see above). Both attitudes rejected the intellectual excommunication of metaphysics, which logical positivists and Wittgensteinians had promoted. Whereas Strawson saw a task for metaphysics in uncovering the most general features of our ordinary, nonscientific ways of thinking about the world, Watkins viewed metaphysicians as being concerned rather with the proper direction of scientific inquiry. Both conceptions have a precursor, which their exponents acknowledge, in Kant's critical philosophy.

NOTES

1. *The Fundamental Questions of Philosophy*. Ewing, an Oxford graduate, taught at Cambridge.
2. Both books were published by Blackwell, with German and English texts on opposite pages. The original text was the German one, and the translation was by G.E.M. Anscombe.
3. Wisdom's later book, *Logical Constructions*, reprints some papers originally published in 1931-1933 that were still under the influence of Russell and of Wittgenstein's *Tractatus Logico-Philosophicus*.
4. "Systematically Misleading Expressions," *Proceedings of the Aristotelian Society* 32 (1932):130–170.

5. In "A Plea for Excuses," *Proceedings of the Aristotelian Society* 57 (1957):1–30.

6. Cf. L. Jonathan Cohen, "Speech Acts," in *Current Trends in Linguistics*, XII, ed. T. A. Sebeok, pp. 173–208.

7. Grice's theory was developed in his William James Lectures at Harvard University in 1968. Thus far, only the second lecture has been published, under the title "Logic and Conversation," in *The Logic of Grammar*, eds. D. Davidson and G. Harman, pp. 64–75.

8. E.g., "Moral Beliefs," *Proceedings of the Aristotelian Society* 59 (1959):83–104.

9. E.g., "Truth," *Proceedings of the Aristotelian Society* 59 (1959):141–162; and "Quantifiers and Modal Operators," *Proceedings of the Aristotelian Society* 58 (1958):245–268.

10. *Past, Present and Future*. Prior's earlier book on this subject *(Time and Modality)* contained his 1955–1956 John Locke lectures at Oxford, but his permanent post then was still in New Zealand.

11. Cf. especially G. Evans and J. McDowell (eds.), *Truth and Meaning: Essays in Semantics*.

12. *Experience and Theory: An Essay in the Philosophy of Science*. Körner took his Ph.D. at Cambridge and taught at Bristol.

13. Cf., e.g., J.J.C. Smart and B. Williams, *Utilitarianism, For and Against*.

14. Cf. his "Intellectual Autobiography," in *The Philosophy of Karl Popper*, I, ed. P. A. Schilpp.

SELECT BIBLIOGRAPHY

BOOKS AND ARTICLES

Anscombe, G.E.M. *Intention* (Oxford: Blackwell, 1957).

Atkinson, R. *Sexual Morality* (London: Hutchinson, 1965).

Austin, J. L. "A Plea for Excuses," *Proceedings of the Aristotelian Society* 57 (1957).

———. *How to Do Things with Words* (London: Oxford University Press, 1962).

———. *Sense and Sensibilia* (London: Oxford University Press, 1962).

Ayer, A. J. *Language, Truth and Logic*, 1st ed. (London: Gollancz, 1936).

———. *Language, Truth and Logic*, 2d ed. (London: Gollancz, 1946).

———. *The Foundations of Empirical Knowledge* (London: Macmillan, 1940).

Braithwaite, R. B. *Scientific Explanation: A Study of the Function of Theory, Probability and Law in Science* (London: Cambridge University Press, 1953).

Cohen, L. J. "Speech Acts," in *Current Trends in Linguistics*, XII, ed. T.A. Sebeok (The Hague: Mouton, 1974).

———. *The Diversity of Meaning*, 2d ed. (London: Methuen, 1962).

———. *The Implications of Induction* (London: Methuen, 1972).

———. *The Principles of World Citizenship* (Oxford: Blackwell, 1954).

———. *The Probable and the Provable* (London: Oxford University Press, 1977).

Dummett, M. *Frege: Philosophy of Language* (London: Duckworth, 1973, and New York: Harper and Row, 1974).

———. "Truth," *Proceedings of the Aristotelian Society* 59 (1959).

Evans, G. and McDowell, J. (eds.). *Truth and Meaning: Essays in Semantics* (London: Oxford University Press, 1976).

Ewing, A. C. *The Fundamental Questions of Philosophy* (London: Routledge and Kegan Paul, 1951).

Foot, P. "Moral Beliefs," *Proceedings of the Aristotelian Society* 59 (1959).

Gellner, E. *Words and Things* (London: Gollancz, 1959).

Grice, H. P. "Logic and Conversation," in *The Logic of Grammar*, eds. D. Davidson and G. Harman (Encino, Calif.: Dickenson, 1975).

Hacker, P.M.S. *Insight and Illusion: Wittgenstein on Philosophy and the Metaphysics of Experience* (London: Oxford University Press, 1972).

Hacking, I. *Logic of Statistical Inference* (London: Cambridge University Press, 1965).

Hampshire, S. *Thought and Action* (London: Chatto and Windus, 1959).

Hare, R. M. *The Language of Morals* (London: Oxford University Press, 1952).

Harré, R. *The Principles of Scientific Thinking* (London: Macmillan, 1970).

Hart, H.L.A. *Definition and Theory in Jurisprudence* (London: Oxford University Press, 1953).

———. *The Concept of Law* (London: Oxford University Press, 1961).

Heath, P. L. "The Appeal to Ordinary Language," *Philosophical Quarterly* 2 (1952).

Hesse, M. *Forces and Fields* (London: Nelson, 1961).

———. *The Structure of Scientific Inference* (London: Macmillan, 1974).

Ishiguro, H. *Leibniz's Philosophy of Logic and Language* (London: Duckworth, 1972).

Kneale, W. *Probability and Induction* (London: Oxford University Press, 1949).

——— and Kneale, M. *The Development of Logic* (London: Oxford University Press, 1962).

Körner, S. *Experience and Conduct: A Philosophical Enquiry into Practical Thinking* (London: Cambridge University Press, 1976).

———. *Experience and Theory: An Essay in the Philosophy of Science* (London: Routledge and Kegan Paul, 1966).

Lakatos, I. "Proofs and Refutations," *British Journal for Philosophy of Science* 14 (1963–1964).

Lemmon, E. J. "Quantifiers and Modal Operators," *Proceedings of the Aristotelian Society* 59 (1959).

Lucas, J. R. *The Concept of Probability* (London: Oxford University Press, 1970).

Lukasiewicz, J. *Aristotle's Syllogistic from the Standpoint of Modern Formal Logic* (London: Oxford University Press, 1951).

Mackie, J. L. *Truth, Probability and Paradox* (London: Oxford University Press, 1973).

Mellor, H. *The Matter of Chance* (London: Cambridge University Press, 1971).

Popper, K. R. *Conjectures and Refutations: The Growth of Scientific Knowledge* (London: Routledge and Kegan Paul, 1963).

———. "Intellectual Autobiography," in *The Philosophy of Karl Popper*, I, ed. P. A. Schilpp (LaSalle, Ill.: Open Court, 1974).

———. *Logik der Forschung* (Vienna: Springer, 1934).

———. *Objective Knowledge: An Evolutionary Approach* (London: Oxford University Press, 1972).

———. *The Logic of Scientific Discovery*, trans. K. Popper (London: Hutchinson, 1959).

———. *The Open Society and Its Enemies* (London: Routledge and Kegan Paul, 1945).

Price, H. H. *Belief* (London: Allen and Unwin, and New York: Humanities Press, 1969).

———. "Clarity Is Not Enough," *Proceedings of the Aristotelian Society*, Supplementary Vol. 19 (1945).

———. *Thinking and Experience* (London: Hutchinson, 1953).

Prior, A. N. *Past, Present and Future* (London: Oxford University Press, 1967).

———. *Time and Modality* (London: Oxford University Press, 1957).

Ramsey, F. P. *The Foundations of Mathematics* (London: Routledge and Kegan Paul, 1931).

Russell, B. "On Denoting," *Mind* 14 (1905).

Ryle, G. "Systematically Misleading Expressions," *Proceedings of the Aristotelian Society* 32 (1932).

———. *The Concept of Mind* (London: Hutchinson, 1949).

Smart, J.J.C. and Williams, B. *Utilitarianism, For and Against* (London: Cambridge University Press, 1973).

Strawson, P. F. *Individuals* (London: Methuen, 1959).

———. *Introduction to Logical Theory* (London: Methuen, and New York: John Wiley, 1952).

———. "On Referring," *Mind* 59 (1950).

Waismann, F. *The Principles of Linguistic Philosophy* (London: Macmillan, and New York: St. Martin's Press, 1965).

Watkins, J.W.N. "Confirmable and Influential Metaphysics," *Mind* 68 (1958).

White, A. R. *Modal Thinking* (Oxford: Blackwell, 1975).

Williams, B. "Personal Identity and Individuation," *Proceedings of the Aristotelian Society* 57 (1957).

Wisdom, A.J.T. *Logical Constructions* (New York: Random House, 1969).
———. *Other Minds* (Oxford: Blackwell, 1952).
———. *Philosophy and Psychoanalysis* (Oxford: Blackwell, 1953).
Wittgenstein, L. *Philosophical Investigations* (Oxford: Blackwell, 1953).
———. *Preliminary Studies for "The Philosophical Investigations," generally known as the Blue and Brown Books* (Oxford: Blackwell, 1958).
———. *Remarks on the Foundations of Mathematics* (Oxford: Blackwell, 1956).
———. *Tractatus Logico-Philosophicus* (London: Routledge and Kegan Paul, 1922).

JOURNALS

Analysis
Aristotelian Society. Supplementary Volume
British Journal for Philosophy of Science
British Journal of Aesthetics
History and Philosophy of Logic
Journal for the Theory of Social Behaviour
Journal of the British Society for Phenomenology
Mind
Philosophical Books
Philosophical Journal
Philosophical Quarterly
Philosophy
Proceedings of the Aristotelian Society
Question
Radical Philosophy
Ratio

Greece

EVANGHELOS MOUTSOPOULOS

The Roots and the Present Dimensions of Contemporary Greek Philosophy

During the Middle Ages, ancient Greek philosophy survived in Byzantium primarily in a Platonic or Neoplatonic, or in an Aristotelian form. Christian thought assimilated many Neoplatonic trends and felt a particularly strong Stoic influence. As Stoicism was Eastern in its origins, it fitted particularly well into the Judeo-Christian tradition. The Platonic and Aristotelian traditions, on the other hand, served as the bulwarks of pagan resistance to Christian thought for many centuries. It was not until the eleventh century that Michael Psellos, Ramon Lull's predecessor in logic, was able to bring all the persisting currents of ancient philosophy into Christianity in a synthesis.

Although the predominant flavor of Byzantine philosophy was Platonic, Platonism alternated with Aristotelianism as the most prominent philosophical influence. As a rough generalization, one may say that periods of liberalism coincide with the flourishing of Platonism and that Aristotelianism prevailed during periods of conservatism. For instance, Platonism prevailed during the ninth century, with Photius and Arethas, and during the fifteenth century, with Pletho. But immediately after the fall of Constantinople, a new period of Aristotelianism began under the leadership of Scholarios, as a result of the new wave of conservatism in the Eastern Orthodox church. At this same time, many Byzantine Platonists fled to Italy where as expatriates they made significant contributions to the revival of classical learning.

The fact remains that during the centuries of Ottoman occupation Greek philosophical thought remained basically Aristotelian. The brilliant tradition of Aristotelian commentators continued in the seventeenth century with Corydaleus, whose work became known throughout Southeastern Europe. The work of a scholar famous for his writings in the same area, Eugenius Bulgaris, a disciple of Christian Wolff, marked the transition from Aristotelianism to the so-called philosophy of the Enlightenment. Strictly speaking, there was no real philosophy of Enlightenment in Greece during the eighteenth and nineteenth centuries, but rather a decline in the philosophical tradition. The ideal of the French Encyclopedists influenced in no small measure the attempt to achieve widespread educational improvements which were necessary in the Greek struggle for freedom. The philosophy of the Enlightenment covers a rather wide area of intellectual activity, from radicalism, with Codricas as its most ardent representative, to liberalism, led by the outstanding scholars Coraes and Bambas. Aristotelian conservatism was steadily declining by this time.

In about the middle of the nineteenth century, Petros Brailas, who might be labeled a liberal of the right wing, effected a conciliation between the liberal aspect of the philosophy of the Enlightenment and the Platonic and Aristotelian tradition. This he was able to achieve through the Cartesian tradition of French eclecticism. Brailas' philosophical synthesis prevailed until the end of the nineteenth century.[1] Since then, and with a considerable delay, all of the main currents of European thought have had some influence in Greece.

Since the first decades of the twentieth century, Greece has had a profusion of philosophers as well as philosophical publications. These manifestations of the vitality and dynamism of contemporary Greek thought developed in ways that enable us now to distinguish certain general tendencies in the evolving process of each thinker. The most important of these tendencies are discussed in the following sections.

THE RENEWAL OF GREEK PHILOSOPHICAL THOUGHT AND TRADITION

The most eminent representatives of this renewal have been Greek university professors who have tried to show that ancient Greek thought was still alive in their writings. Alexander Cotzias, a disciple of Schelling, published the monumental *History of Philosophy* in the latter part of the nineteenth century. Christos Androutsos wrote *A Critical Survey of the Fundamental Doctrines of Stoic Philosophy* and edited a *Dictionary of Philosophy*. Constantine Logothetes began publishing in 1905 with *Petros Brailas' Philosophical System*, which shows how Brailas, although open to European influences, remained a typically Greek philosopher. In his books *The Philosophy of the Church Fathers, The Philosophy of Hegel*, and *The Philosophy of the Renaissance*, he demonstrates how medieval philosophy as well as the philosophy of the sixteenth century and that of German romanticism are indebted to ancient Greek thought. Margarites Evanghelides translated Zeller's *History of the Philosophy of the Greeks*, and in his commentaries, Zeller stressed the importance of ancient Greek thought for contemporary thought. Nicolaos Louvares, a deep admirer of the German spirit, wrote a *History of Philosophy* in which he emphasized the perennial character of Greek philosophy. Charalampos Theodorides, aside from his *Introduction to Philosophy*, wrote a book with a strong materialistic bent, under the suggestive title *Epicurus: The True Aspects of the Ancient World*, and was criticized for his strongly stated theses. In the same spirit, Demetrios Glenos wrote a commentary on Plato's *Sophist*. Basil Tatakes' writings, on the other hand, gave more prominence to the late ancient and medieval Greek thought. Among his numerous publications should be mentioned his books (written in French) *Panaetius of Rhodes* and especially his *Byzantine Philosophy* (published in 1977 as a separate volume of Bréhier's *History of Philosophy*), which is regarded as the best introduction and perhaps the most complete history of Greek medieval thought to date. Tatakes has also written (in Greek) two other important books, one on the philosophical thought of the great Cappadocians (Basil, Chrysostom, and Gregory of Nazianzus) and one on *Socrates*. Constantine Georgoulis published a number of books, among them a *History of Greek Philosophy*, which goes from ancient times to the twentieth century, and *Aristotle of Stagira*, which is regarded as the most complete monograph in Greek on this area. Georgoulis points out the extent to which medieval Greek thought anticipated the main theses of the existentialist movement.

THE IDEALISTIC CONSIDERATION OF HELLENISM

In the last decades of the nineteenth century, a general tendency emerged, under the auspices of liberty movements, which sought to underline the importance of the specific character of Greek culture and to distinguish it from non-Greek thought. The representatives of this tendency flourished between the years 1897 and 1922, the dates of two particularly grave defeats for Greece in her struggle against Turkey. The twenty-five-year period between these dates was marked by wars that characterized the dynamic expansion of Greece. The most important figures of this movement were Pericles Yannopoulos, who in his book *The Greek Line* proposed a kind of aesthetic cult of Hellenism, and Ion Dragoumēs, who expressed the same romantic and nationalistic views in numerous writings by exploring the political aspect of the issue. This tendency, which has its roots in literary aspirations, has had an immense influence on the poetry of that period, especially the poets Costis Palamas and Anghelos Sikelianos. Palamas' parnassianism did not impede him from assimilating it to his own commitment to the doctrine of Hellenism. Sikelianos, following a somewhat different road, tended to give primacy to the mythical elements of Greek nature. Both poets, however, were predominantly pantheists, though in a particularly Greek way. In spite of the diverging existentialist and hellenocentric poetry of Constantine Cavafy (1869–1933), whose work has become a major influence on most young poets, other leading poets who are still living were directly inspired by the works of Palamas and Sikelianos. A whole paraphilosophical literature came out of the message of Yannopoulos and Dragoumēs.

THE ACADEMIC APPROACH TO PHILOSOPHY

Two different currents may be distinguished within this main tendency. The first trend has a thoroughly didactic character. Its representative par excellence is Theophilos Boreas, professor of philosophy at the University of Athens (d. 1954) and a disciple of W. Wundt. Boreas published four volumes under the general title *Academeica: Logic, Psychology, Ethics,* and *Introduction to Philosophy.* His method is strictly objective. His *Introduction to Philosophy,* in particular, reminds one of the similar book by O. Külpe. Boreas' most important contribution to contemporary Greek philosophy lies in his systematic effort to refurbish the philosophical vocabulary upon which contemporary Greek thought is based by rendering in Greek the philosophical terminology in European languages up to the mid-1930s. The second academic trend is represented by Evanghelos Papanoutsos, who is the direct spokesman for the philosophical ideas of the eighteenth-century Enlightenment thinkers. He has reached a very wide audience and still enjoys the admiration of progressive thinkers today. Aside from his publications on Plato and Aristotle, he provided a rather complete philosophical system, expounded in separate but related volumes: *Epistemology, Aesthetics,* and *Ethics.* In these books, Papanontsos discusses various theories that have been proposed before proceeding with his own critical solutions.

THE CHRISTIAN APPROACH TO PHILOSOPHY

A large number of the philosophers mentioned above were also theologians or at least had studied theology. Furthermore, a great number of thinkers, philosophers as well as scientists, have expressed interest from a Christian viewpoint in solving the philosophical problems of today. In one way, the doctrine of the revivial of Hellenism in the early part of the twentieth century was a reaction to the Christian philosophical tradition of the Middle Ages and postmedieval times in Greece. In 1946, under the leadership of Professor A. N. Tsirintanēs, a teacher of law at the University of Athens, a strong movement towards the philosophy of Christian faith was launched with an ambitious declaration signed by hundreds of scientists. This movement failed to produce any important new philosophical ideas, for two interrelated reasons: first, the great majority of modern Greek thinkers have also been Christian thinkers; second, even deeply religious minds showed no willingness to join a movement that seemed to them to encourage (even if Christian) indoctrination. Nevertheless, this approach to philosophical thought, through the social efforts of the movement, gained an impressive number of partisans and considerable success.

THE "HEIDELBERG GROUP"

During the late 1920s, the so-called Heidelberg group tried to introduce Rickert's neo-Kantianism in Greece. Soon this neo-Kantianism switched to Platonism and retained this form from the late 1930s to the late 1950s. Following separate paths, John Theodorakopoulos, Constantine Tsatsos, and Panayotes Canellopoulos evolved in similar ways. From 1929 to 1940, the Heidelberg group published an important periodical entitled *Archives of Philosophy and the Theory of Sciences.* Theodorakopoulos reintroduced Plato in the universities by bringing that ancient philosopher close to the interests of contemporary youth. He saw Plato as an initiator of knowledge and beauty and at the same time as a teacher. Theodorakopoulos' *Introduction to Plato,* and *Plato's Phaedrus* have been widely read and reprinted in many editions. His *System of Philosophical Ethics* is a far-reaching synthesis of ancient and modern ethical positions within a strongly idealistic framework. As a university teacher, Theodorakopoulos has for many decades influenced almost every student of philosophy in Greek universities. Tsatsos has been interested mainly in the philosophy of law, but he has also done work in aesthetic values. Canellopoulos, while a holder of a chair in sociology at the University of Athens, has also been interested in the philosophy of culture. His *History of European Mind,* an impressive synthesis, reflects his broad learning and scholarship.

PRESENT TRENDS

The present generation of philosophers in Greece has a wide spectrum of interests, all of which have their roots in previous developments. Ancient Greek philosophy is the main preoccupation of George Bozonis, August Bayonas, and Anastasios Zoumpos whose original investigations on Heraclitus have been widely praised. George Antonopoulos' chief interest is the special nature of neo-Hellenic values. Existentialism is the main concern in the works of Demetrios Koutsoyannopoulos-Theraios, John Aravantinos, and Gregory Costaras. Philosophical analysis is reflected in the publications of Demetrios Nianias and Constantine Boudoures. Bergsonism is reflected in the writings of George Mourelos. Religious concerns are dominant in the works of Spyridon Kyriazopoulos. A historian of philosophy and a structuralist philosopher, Evanghelos Moutsopoulos is interested chiefly in ontology, aesthetics, and the philosophy of history.

Although all of the recent European philosophical currents have been transported to Greece, Platonism is so profoundly enmeshed in contemporary Greek thought that even the recent tendencies described above have acquired a Platonic character. One may safely predict that the renewed Platonic tradition will continue to influence Greek philosophy for some time to come.[2]

NOTES

1. The Foundation for Research and Editions of Neohellenic Philosophy, under the direction of the author of this article, is editing published, unpublished, and even recently discovered manuscripts of Greek philosophical texts from 1400 up to 1900.

2. Two primarily philosophical periodicals are now being published in Greece: *Philosophia,* under the auspices of the Academy of Athens; and *Diotima,* by the Hellenic Society for Philosophical Studies. In addition, philosophical articles are usually published in literary and educational periodicals, such as *Nea Hestia, Euthyne, Epopteia,* and *Philosophikoi Dromoi.*

SELECT BIBLIOGRAPHY

BOOKS AND ARTICLES

Androutsos, C. *A Critical Survey of the Fundamental Doctrines of Stoic Philosophy* (Athens, 1909).

Antonopoulos, G. *From the World of Phenomena to the Metaphysical World of Mind* (Athens, 1966).

———. *Introduction to Philosophy*, new edition (Athens, 1976).

———. *The Metaphysical Dimensions of Existence in the Platonic Myth* (Athens, 1973).

Bayonas, A. *The Political Philosophy of Cynics* (Athens, 1970).

Boreas, T. *Academeica*, 4 vols. (Athens, 1932–1935).

Boudouves, C. *Philosophy of Education* (Athens, 1976).

———. *Soul and Republic* (Athens, 1970).

———. *The Theory of Knowledge* (Athens, 1977).

———. *The Theory of Meaning in the Philosophy of L. Wittgenstein* (Athens, 1972).

Bozonis, G. *"Atopa" in the Philosophy of Empedocles. A Logical and Psychological Analysis* (Athens, 1974).

———. *The Essence of the Greek Civilization* (Athens, 1964).

———. *The Procedure of the Greek Thought* (Athens, 1972).

Brehier, E. *Histoire de la philosophie* (Paris: Presses Universitaires de France, 1951).

Canellopoulos, P. *History of European Mind*, 8 vols. (Athens, 1966–1974).

Costaras, G. *Kierkegaard's Dialectic as a Repetition of the Socratic Midwifery* (Athens, 1971).

———. *Martin Heidegger: The Philosopher of Care* (Athens, 1973).

Cotzias, A. *History of Philosophy* (Athens, 1878).

Georgoulis, C. *Aristotle of Stagira* (Thessaloniki: Historical and Popular Society of Halkidiki, 1962).

———. *History of Greek Philosophy* (Athens: Papademas, 1975).

Koutsoyannopoulos-Theraios, D. *Contribution to the System of the Greek Philosophy* (Athens, 1968).

———. *Elements of Philosophy* (Athens: Gregory, 1966).

———. *Historical Introduction to Philosophy* (Athens, 1971).

———. *Substance. The Union of Greek Metaphysics* (Athens, 1967).

Kyriazopoulos, S. *Freedom and Self-Transcendence* (Athens, 1962).

———. *Logos and Ethos* (Ioannina, 1976).

———. *Socialistic Realism* (Athens: Tropes, 1977).

———. *The Political Causes of Aristotle's Ethics* (Ioannina, 1971).

———. *The Political Religion of Greece* (Ioannina, 1970).

Logothetes, C. *Petros Brailas' Philosophical System, Xenophanes* (Athens, 1905).

———. *The Philosophy of Hegel* (Scientific Proceedings of the Philosophical School of the University of Athens, 1935–1936).

———. *The Philosophy of the Church Fathers* (Athens: I. D. Kollaros, 1930).

———. *The Philosophy of the Renaissance* (Athens, 1955).

Louvares, N. *History of Philosophy* (Athens: Ekdotikos Oikos Elehtheroudakes, 1933).

Mourelos, G. *Subjects of Aesthetics and Philosophy of Arts* (Thessaloniki, 1974).

Moutsopoulos, E. *Aesthetic Categories. An Axiology of the Aesthetical Object* (Athens, 1970).

———. *Cognition and Error* (in Greek), 2d ed. (Athens, 1975).

———. *Form and Subjectivity in Kant's Aesthetics* (in French) (Aix: Ophrys, 1964).

———. *Knowledge and Science* (Athens: University Press, 1972).

———. *Music in Plato's Work* (in French) (Paris: Presses Universitaires de France, 1959).

———. *P. Brailas Armenis Philosophical Works*, 5 vols. (Athens, 1969–1977).

———. *Philosophical Inquiries* I (Athens, 1971).

———. *Pleasures, A Phenomenological Study* (in Greek) (Athens, 1977).

———. *Presocratic Thought* (in Greek) Athens: Hermes, 1978).

————. *The Consciousness of Space* (in French) (Aix: Ophrys, 1969).

————. *The Criticism of Platonism According to Bergson*,2d ed. (in Greek) (Thessaloniki, 1969).

————. *The Procedure of Spirit*, 3 vols. (in Greek) (Athens, 1974–1977).

Papanoutsos, E. *Aesthetics* (Athens: Ikaros, 1956).

————. *Epistemology* (Athens: Ikaros, 1962).

————. *Ethics* (Athens: Ikaros, 1949).

Tatakes, B. *Byzantine Philosophy* (Athens: Moraites School, 1977).

————. *Socrates* (Athens, 1975).

Theodorakopoulos, J. *Introduction to Plato*, 5th ed. (Athens, 1970).

————. *Plato's Phaedrus*, 2d ed. (Athens, 1968).

————. *System of Philosophical Ethics* (Athens, 1960).

Theodorides, C. *Epicurus: The True Aspects of the Ancient World*, 2d ed. (Athens: Garden, 1966).

————. *Introduction to Philosophy*, 2d ed. (Thessaloniki, 1955).

Yannopoulos, P. *The Greek Line* (Athens: Galaxias, 1961).

Zeller, E. *History of the Philosophy of the Greeks* trans. M. Evanghelides (Athens, 1904).

Zoumpos, A. *Interpretation of the Pythagorean Symbol* (Athens, 1948).

————. *Problems of Philosophy* (Athens, 1964).

COMMENTARY

Glenos, D. *On Plato's Sophist*, 2d ed. (Athens: Greek-European Movement of Youth, 1971).

JOURNALS

Archives of Philosophy and the Theory of Sciences
Diotima
Epopteia
Euthyne
Nea Hestia
Philosophia
Philosophical Inquiry
Philosophikoi Dromoi

Italy

EUGENIO GARIN

For Italy, the year 1945 meant not only the end of a disastrous and tragic war, but also the end of a dictatorship that had lasted more than twenty years. It was the beginning of a new period of its history, accompanied by radical transformations.

In Italy, especially in recent years, there has been much discussion about the extent to which fascism influenced its culture, including philosophy. Some, like Benedetto Croce, contend that fascism and culture are incompatible terms and that fascism was like a barbaric invasion from without (the invasion of the Hyksos) that withdrew in the end without leaving a trace. Others maintain that fascism only expressed motives already present in the culture, intertwining itself with Italian intellectual development in every field. However the dispute may be resolved, it is certain that the twenty years from 1925 to 1945 had special importance for the field of ideas, while the dictatorship sought to impose its ideology. Censorship and condemnations struck not only at political dissent but also at particular doctrines and trends, to the point, especially after 1938, where the reading of even the works of the great thinkers in schools was forbidden or rendered difficult.

In 1945, with the definitive collapse of the dictatorial regime in Italy, perceptible alterations occurred even in philosophical debate. New interests appeared, while doctrines and personalities that were formerly eminent either were disappearing entirely or were assuming a position of secondary importance. But while the year 1945 apparently represents a clean break in philosophy, in fact a profound turnabout had already begun to occur much earlier, even though its consequences did not become clear until the conclusion of World War II.

Idealistic trends, which had predominated and characterized the first decades of the twentieth century in Italy, had experienced a number of challenges at the end of the 1920s as a result of a series of momentous political events. The accords between the Roman Catholic church and the fascist state (the Lateran Pacts of February 11, 1929) had struck a heavy blow to the hegemony of "actualism," the idealistic philosophy of Giovanni Gentile. This philosophy had become increasingly widespread after World War I, above all because of its pedagogic charge and its nationalistic inspiration. Although he professed

English translation by Ronald A. Cordero, associate professor of philosophy, University of Wisconsin-Oshkosh.

indebtedness to Hegel, Gentile was in reality inspired by Fichte and Gioberti, again taking up their themes of the national mission and the educational function of philosophy, both of which were particularly lively at the time of the 1915–1918 conflict.

Other practical factors had contributed to the predominance of actualism: the reform of the educational system, from elementary schools to the university, completed by Gentile after he became minister in Mussolini's first government in 1922; the circulation of school books inspired by his ideas; and the increasingly massive presence of Gentilian instructors in secondary schools, teachers' colleges, and university schools of education, that is, schools that prepared future instructors. Fascism, at its birth, had appropriated Gentile's renovation program, characterized by a strong spirit of activism and a profound sentiment of nationalism.

All of these factors contributed to the rapid spread of Gentile's philosophy between 1920 and 1930. At the same time, Benedetto Croce, for political reasons, was breaking off his long-standing friendship with Gentile and, in 1925, was moving into open opposition to fascism and a constant philosophic polemic against Gentile and his school. Croce's influence had already been diminishing on the eve of World War I, after having been dominant during the first decade of the century, when the so-called rebirth of idealism had supplanted the various positivistic movements that had characterized Italian culture in the first decades of national unity. Without doubt, the rebirth of idealism, proclaimed loudly at the beginning of the twentieth century, had not been monolithic. Irrationalists and mystics, pragmatists and idealists, were not in agreement with each other, but they were all united against the scientific method of the positivists, their evaluation of science, and their naturalistic and deterministic conceptions of the world. Croce and Gentile, who differed radically from each other in their theories, even though both claimed kinship to German idealism and undertook to "reform" Hegel, were the most prominent figures in a vast cultural movement that especially affected the historical and moral disciplines, linguistics, and aesthetics. Their influence on many sectors of intellectual life in Italy, though frequently underground and not acknowledged, was profound and was felt everywhere well beyond the end of World War II. It cannot be said to have waned even today, although it has now been transformed and must be sought outside the groups that explicitly claim descent from either Croce or Gentile and generally only repeat either one or the other with little originality.

This "idealism," which was starting afresh from Hegel and which presented itself as "absolute historicism," because of its immanentism, its concept of the state, and its laicism, proclaimed itself heir to the national revivial that had found in the Catholic church, with which fascism was allied, the greatest obstacle to the realization of political unity. The result in the field of philosophy was the contrast between secular thought (it matters little whether positivist or Hegelian) and the Catholic movements, especially neo-Scholasticism, which continued to adhere to Thomism. The center for these movements was the Catholic University of Milan, founded in 1919 by the Franciscan Agostino Gemelli (1878–1959), a psychologist and philosopher who until his death was harshly polemical against idealists and positivists, in the name of a traditional Catholic restoration, and who called for a return to the substance of the medieval sources.

Mussolini's agreement with the Church of Rome, reached in 1929, was decisive in accelerating the crisis of idealism and in fragmenting the philosophical panorama in Italy. Not a few Gentilians, endowed with the strong religious inspiration of actualism, became converts to spiritualistic positions. Some went to swell the ranks of a Catholic philosophy which was open to demands put forward especially in France, for example, by Blondel. Those spiritualists who were most pugnacious even after 1945 and who distinguished themselves most in polemics sometimes had Gentilian origins, most notably Michele Federico Sciacca (1908–1974). However, it was precisely in the decade of the Concordat at the beginning of the war that from the splintering of the idealists' ranks there issued not a few of the theoretical thrusts and personalities that were active even after 1945. While Benedetto Croce, together with his faithful followers, remained the exponent of a resistance that was not only theoretical but also political, Gentile witnessed the disperson of his school. What we could call the right wing went from experiment to experiment, from catholicizing spiritualism to a religious existentialism. The so-to-speak left wing of the school radicalized certain of its goals (Guido Calogero, Ugo Spirito) to the point of overturning its premises.

As the debate became bitter, rendered more difficult by political pressures, younger elements, many of whom had grown up under fascism, tried new solutions, even taking up old theories again. The years of torment between the conquest of Ethiopia and the Spanish Civil War saw the demands of positivism reemerge in endeavors of a neopositivistic tone, while vague professions of realism sought alliances among the neo-Scholastics for a common anti-idealistic front. The constant interweaving of the philosophical discussion with a political battle fought in quiet often rendered the debate of those years confused and difficult to understand. It was then, in the torment of daily tragedy, that many, especially the youngest, passed through a confused ''existentialism,'' lived as an attitude and an experiment rather than defined in precise theoretical formulations. It was precisely in this experiment, however, that many of them achieved detachment from their initial conceptions and came, from 1945 on, to adopt independent theories. It was just then that an increasingly vigorous effort was made to be open to that European and worldwide debate from which the dictatorship had tried to isolate Italy. If one does not take into account the climate of isolation and suspicion created by fascism, one risks not understanding, in the philosophic panorama of postwar Italy, the obsessive need to bring the national culture up to date with the latest foreign achievements, even at the cost of a lack of original developments. One can add that fascism had become established immediately after World War I, during which a peaceful circulation of ideas did not prevail. On top of those nationalistic intolerances and closures, fascism introduced a long period of censorship and ideological pressure, in which open debate and the clash of ideas were not possible—some ideas, in fact, being prohibited.

As a result, it is impossible to understand the spread and peculiarities of the new Italian Marxism, with its enthusiasm and its ingenuousness, without remembering first the important beginning made by Antonio Labriola (1843–1904) and Rodolfo Mondolfo (1877–1976), and then the absolute silence imposed by the dictatorship. It is often forgotten that the ingenious theoretical work of Antonio Gramsci (1891–1937), which has been so influential in present-day thought, even outside the Marxist camp, goes back to the prison period; and that the *Quaderni* ("Notebooks"), completed well before his death, have come to be known little by little from 1948 on and have been available in complete, rigorous form only since 1975. From this there follows an inevitable distortion, because of the difficulty of recapturing the sense of controversies tied to different times and situations.

Thus, even the very strong tendency in many young Italian philosophers of the postwar period to discuss and experiment with the great theories of others, perhaps also striving to combine them into fragile syntheses, indicates not so much an innate speculative incapacity as a real need to fill in the empty spaces of several decades. Phenomenology, epistemology, logic, the philosophy of science, psychoanalysis, to give only a few examples, had remained cut off from a great part of the national culture. Marx as well as Freud, Russell as well as Dewey, Husserl as well as Heidegger, and Lukács as well as Sartre found only belatedly an echo that was adequate and, in the end, perhaps excessive. This does not, of course, mean that they were unknown names. Husserl had been taken up early on by Antonio Banfi (1886–1957), who, from a rethinking of Kantianism and of Simmel, arrived at his own vision of Marxism during the postwar period. Frederico Enriques (1871–1946) had made important contributions to the philosophy of science, and so too, moving from positivistic theories, had Ludovico Geymonat (1908–   ). Annibale Pastore (1868–1956) had also worked on the philosophy of science and logic. Nicola Abbagnano (1901–   ) had lucidly discussed, distinguished, and surpassed the various theories of existentialism in *La struttura dell'esistenza*. And yet, before 1945, these were always isolated voices or small groups without successors.

The dominant feature of the postwar period was therefore a reaction to isolation. This statement may give the impression that for thirty years nothing has been done in Italy but translation, exposition, dissemination, repetition, imitation, or, at most, the introduction of a few variations or combinations in more or less original forms of different, and not always compatible theories. Thus, Giulio Preti (1911-1972), a member of the school of Antonio Banfi, began immediately in 1945 to attempt to combine Dewey and Marx, that is, pragmatism and the philosophy of praxis. In 1957, in *Praxis e empirismo*, a book which provoked a great deal of discussion, he compared logical empiricism, pragmatism, and Marxism. Analogously, Enzo Paci (1911–1976), after experience with existentialism, proceeded to develop a philosophy of relation, stressing his interest in what Hegel called the constitution of intersubjectivity. In this work, Paci sought to reinterpret Marx's theory of alienation in light of Husserl's critique of science, allying himself in the end with American neopositivism in *Funzione delle scienze e significato dell'uomo*.

In summary, it can be said that reaction to the cultural autarchy desired by fascism, as well as weariness with the great abstract systems dear to idealists, helped produce certain characteristics of the new philosophical situation in Italy: (1) dread of any "provincial" narrowmindedness and therefore an exaggerated attention to even passing fashions, with the double risk of an indiscriminate rejection of national tradition and a passive acceptance of doctrines as soon as they become prevalent; (2) distrust of general conceptions of the world and, on the contrary, commitment to precise, definite research and differentiated analysis, even though since then such commitment has often been reduced to programmatic declarations and rhetorical exhortations; and (3) reaction to the privilege accorded "history" by idealism and glorification of a frequently mythologized "science"—a glorification which, in Italy, has exacerbated the controversy over the "two cultures," in many cases even transforming the formerly dominant "historicism" into "scientism."

One other legacy of the fascist dictatorship can be added: the knowledge of how easily political powers can influence philosophical activity, degrading it into ideology. Hence, many have felt the urgency (rendered increasingly acute in the postwar period by the confrontation between the Church of Rome and a Communist party of great strength among intellectuals) of facing up to the problem of ideologies, intellectuals, the relation between practical and theoretical activity, and the relation between politics and philosophy. Another consequence has been the connection, stronger than in other countries, between sociopolitical divisions and philosophical disputes: "secular" philosophers against "Catholic" philosophers, and neo-Enlightenment thinkers, rationalists, and neo-empiricists against theologizing metaphysicians. Even the age-old opposition between north and south (the "Southern question") seems to be reflected in the contrast between an industrialized northern Italy, the heir to a tradition of enlightenment, positivism, and "scientism," and a backward, agrarian southern world, the cradle of a humanistic and rhetorical idealism.

Only in the perspective which this article has been delineating are the Italian philosophical movements after 1945 fully intelligible. In fact, in their most original aspects, they only develop—often even the persons are the same—theories previously held, reversing them occasionally. In what is new in them, they are not generally original, and they limit themselves to repeating, albeit with a few variations, that which they borrow elsewhere, contrasting it with coarse vigor to preceding theories which they dismiss as "provincial." In this way, the aspects of continuity and discontinuity seem to intertwine continuously.

Without doubt, the disappearance of some of the protagonists of the preceding period contributed to the sense of hiatus. Giovanni Gentile disappeared in 1944, and in 1952, Benedetto Croce died, after he himself had reopened debate on his own relation to Hegel and his own interpretation of the dialectic in *Indagini su Hegel e schiarimenti filosofici*. But a considerable part of postwar Italian scholarship, even though sharply critical of them, continued to deal with Croce and Gentile. It was from Croce that Carlo Antoni (1896–1959) took his inspiration, giving an historical analysis and theoretical defense of Croce's historicism in *Commento a Croce*. In contrast, Guido de Ruggiero (1888–1948) reproached the value relativism of Croce's theories in the name of a reason capable of assuring the foundation of values beyond historical becoming in *Il ritorno della ragione*. To Gentile's "actualism," Gudio Calogero (1904–   ) had long been opposing the autonomous development of a "moral" philosophy capable of rediscovering the locus of human duty that was contrary to every abstract logical and epistemological system, in the conscious willing of a "dialogue" capable of constituting us as persons together with others. ("Other people are not, because I am the one who must make them be.") The "dialogue rule," which is the model for every rule, "expresses the moral will to understand others and to make oneself comprehensible to others." Its foundation is not the knowledge of a polycentric reality; it is a decision of the will, a supreme ethical imperative in *Logo e dialogo* and *Filosofia del dialogo*.

The *enfant terrible* of actualism, Ugo Spirito (1896–   ), has progressively radicalized Gentile's anti-intellectualism, defining philosophy as life, search, love, art, recognition of its own contradictoriness, and problem in *Il problematicismo* and as renewed victory of science over myth in *Dal mito alla scienza* and *Storia della mia ricerca*. Similarly, Franco Lombardi (1906–   ) has examined independently and at great length the theories of Croce and Gentile, turning toward a humanism that would give full value to all the concreteness of human dialogue. As can be seen, a common feature of all those Italian thinkers who in the postwar period discussed and criticized the great idealistic movements of the first half of the century is a sort of primacy of practical reason—a strong demand for morality and social feeling, which in recognizing historical becoming does not overturn values and in demanding unity does not efface the rights of the majority. This emphasis has often drawn philosophers favoring independent forms of Christian spiritualism closer to the thinkers just mentioned. One such philosopher is Augusto Guzzo (1894–   ), who independently organized the most complex, architectonically arranged system of our contemporary philosophical literature, pervaded by an intense moral demand culminating in religion. Even Gustavo Bontadini (1903–   ), a typical defender of neo-Scholasticism and an ardent proponent of classical metaphysics, has constantly felt the need to contend with the objections of idealism as it developed in Italy, introducing his own speculative objections into its problematics.

As can be seen, the postwar thinkers able at last to be in contact with the thinkers of other nations, managed to maintain their contact with their own cultural traditions while incorporating their own criticisms into it and thereby perfecting it and going beyond it without rejecting it. The very work that had been under way was often opposed to the dominant ideas and forces, but it seemed to permit innovation without excluding continuity. Even the extensive success of Antonio Gramsci's "open" Marxism which developed through an intense exchange with the theses of Croce (and Gentile) can be placed in this perspective.

Others stressed breaking with the past and rejecting national tradition, which they dismissed as "provincial," "humanistic," and "rhetorical." Scholars of differing views, who had for the most part tried existentialism as the solution to the radical crisis of traditional philosophies, ended up questioning the very meaning and function of philosophy. They began asking themselves whether new developments in logic, and in the philosophy of science in general, together with the growth of the humanities, still left any free space for the traditional figure of the philosopher. *A quoi bon les philsophes?* is a question that rings out often in Italy, too.

When an international philosophical conference was organized in Rome in 1946 with the aim of putting the national situation into focus at the end of the war, the themes chosen were existentialism, historical materialism, principles of science, and linguistic analysis. The conference precisely documented the problematic nature of the very existence of philosophy. For many at the meeting, the choice that seemed imperative was between reducing all philosophy to a discourse on philosophy and resolving it into a moment of concrete research in specific fields of particular disciplines—so long as the *old* theologizing metaphysics was not to be restored. In fact, the most active scholars of the new generation, who have not wanted to reduce themselves to propagandizing for this or that "philosophical" fad, have devoted themselves in recent years to investigations into the history of scientific and philosophic thought, into logic, anthropology, psychology, linguistics, and so on, assigning to philosophy a critical, methodological role within the bounds of their research itself. The positive existentialism of Nicola Abbagnano, no less than the empiricist and enlightenmentalist demands advanced by him and by Norberto Bobbio, were concretized into specific research in sociology, anthropology, juridical science, and philosophy of culture.

The spread of phenomenology, begun by Antonio Banfi and later sustained by Enzo Paci with *Aut Aut* has had some effect in certain sectors. Structuralism has found its place in linguistics. At a general theoretical level, this interest has produced little but rhetoric and "propaganda" disguised as serious doctrinal development. Anyone who wanted to could categorize the activity of many "young" Italian philosophers after 1945 according to the names in fashion: Lukács, Sartre, Husserl, Adorno, Lévi-Strauss, Althusser. In general, as has already been indicated, the greatest attention has been given by many to combining or comparing them, especially with Marxism. The debate over Marxism, in fact, has been perhaps the liveliest, most original aspect of philosophical discussion in Italy since 1945 and, for various reasons, has involved everyone from idealists to neo-Scholastics. Even a summary account would be a lengthy matter.

Begun by Antonio Labriola, the in-depth philosophical study of Marxism had, in the 1900s, seen above all the contributions of Benedetto Croce, Giovanni Gentile, and Rudolfo Mondolfo. Antonio Gramsci, in the *Quaderni*, written in the 1930s, left a lasting legacy that continues to be criticized. After 1945, contributions to the development of Marxism came from thinkers of varied origins who brought with them diverse interests and experiences. If Antonio Banfi constitutes a special case, with his neo-Kantian origins, his Hegelian sympathies, and his critical rationalism of which Marxism is the liberating conclusion, not a few came to Marx from actualism and existentialism. Thus, for example, Cesare Luporini (1909–   ), after having tried idealism, existentialism, and historicism, came to reject historicism completely by accepting certain suggestions derived from Althusser. Galvano Della Volpe (1895–1968), of actualistic descent, after having rejected the Hegel-Marx connection, stressed, in his anti-idealistic arguments, a methodology of an empiricist, neopositivistic tenor. Associated with him at the start, although in an independent manner, was the pugnacious Luigi Colletti (1924–   ), whereas the influence of Antonio Gramsci has been felt in the theories of Nicola Badaloni (1924–   ).

Gramsci's critical review of the whole cultural tradition of Italy gave his work a special character. Its intense controversy with the philosophy of the first half of the century made it a useful reference point for a contemporary fresh start with what had been the characteristic themes of the land of Machiavelli, Galileo, and Vico: politics, history, and science.

SELECT BIBLIOGRAPHY

BOOKS AND ARTICLES

Abbagnano, N. *Esistenzialismo positivo* (Turin: Taylor, 1948).
———. *La struttura dell'esistenza* (Turin: Paravia, 1939).
———. *Per o contro l'uomo* (Milan: Rizzoli, 1968).
———. *Possibilità e libertà* (Turin: Taylor, 1956).
Antoni, C. *Commento a Croce* (Venice: Neri Pozza, 1955).
Badaloni, N. *IL marxismo degli anni sessanta* (Rome: Riuniti, 1971).
———. "La philosophie italienne," in *Histoire de la philosophie* III, ed. Y. Belaval Encyclopédie de la Pléiade (Paris: Gallimard, 1974).
———. *Marxismo come stoicismo* (Milan: Feltrinelli, 1962).
Banfi, A. *L'uomo copernicano* (Milan: Mondadori, 1950).
Bobbio, N. *Politica e cultura* (Turin: Einaudi, 1955).
Bontadidi, G. *Conversazioni di metafisica*, 2 vols. (Milan: Vita e Pensiero, 1971).
Calogero, G. *Filosofia del dialogo* (Milan: Comunità, 1962).
———. *Logo e dialogo* (Milan: Communità, 1950).
Center for Philosophical Studies of Gallarate. *Dizionario dei filosofi* (Florence: Sansoni, 1976).
Colletti, L. *Ideologia e società* (Bari: Laterza, 1969).

――――. *Il marxismo e Hegel* (Bari: Laterza, 1969).

――――. *Intervista politico-filosofica* (Bari: Laterza, 1974).

Croce, B. *Indagini su Hegel e schiarimenti filosofici* (Bari: Laterza, 1952).

Della Volpe, G. *Critica del gusto* (Milan: Feltrinelli, 1960).

――――. *Logica come scienza positiva* (Messina: D'Anna, 1950).

de Ruggiero, G. *Il ritorno della ragione* (Bari: Laterza, 1946).

Garin, E. *Cronache di filosofia italiana,* 2d ed., 2 vols. (Bari: Laterza, 1966).

Geymonat, L. *Filosofia e filosofia della scienza* (Milan: Feltrinelli, 1960).

Gramsci, A. *Quaderni del carcere,* 4 vols., ed. V. Gerratana, Critical edition of the Gramsci Institute (Turin: Einaudi, 1975).

Guzzo, A. "La moralita," *Filosofia* (1950).

――――. "La scienza," *Filosofia* (1955).

Lombardi, F. *Dopo lo storicismo* (Asti: Arethusa, 1955).

――――. *Nascita del mondo moderno* (Asti: Arethusa, 1953).

Luporini, C. *Dialettica e materialismo* (Rome: Riuniti, 1974).

Paci, E. *Funzione delle scienze e significato dell'uomo* (Milan: Il Saggiatore, 1963).

Preti, G. *Praxis ed empirismo* (Turin: Einaudi, 1957).

――――. *Retorica e logica: Le due culture* (Turin: Einaudi, 1968).

Santucci, A. *Esistenzialismo e filosofia italiana,* 2d ed. (Bologna: Il Mulino, 1967).

Sciacca, M. F. *Atto ed essere* (Rome: Bocca, 1956).

――――. *Dall'attualismo allo spiritualismo critico (1931–1938)* (Milan: Marzorati, 1961).

Spirito, U. *Dal mito alla scienza* (Florence: Sansoni, 1966).

――――. *Il problematicismo* (Florence: Sansoni, 1948).

――――. *Storia della mia ricerca* (Florence: Sansoni, 1971).

Verra, V. (ed.). *La filosofia dal '45 a oggi* (Turin: Eri, 1976).

JOURNALS

Aut Aut
Bibliografia Filosofica Italiana
Filosofia
Giornale Critico Della Filosofia Italiana
Gironale Di Metafisica
Rivista Di Estetica
Rivista Di Filosofica
Studi Internazionali Di Filosofia

English translation by Ronald A. Cordero, associate professor of philosophy, University of Wisconsin-Oshkosh.

The Netherlands

CORNELIS A. VAN PEURSEN

The Netherlands is a small country at the crossing of the international roads of commerce, tourism, and . . . philosophy. This was the case long before 1945. In the seventeenth and eighteenth centuries, many people from abroad came to the Netherlands. Among them was Descartes who stayed more than twenty years and wrote his main works there. Locke lived six years in the Netherlands. Leibniz came to Holland in order to meet Spinoza. La Mettrie worked with the famous physician Boerhaave at Leiden where he published his *L'homme machine*. All of these philosophers did important work in the sciences as well.

This tradition was intensified after World War II. The isolation was broken, the windows were opened, and the winds from divergent countries brought philosophical flavors into a spiritual atmosphere that before the war had already been influenced by Anglo-American, French, and German trends of thought. The traditional interaction between philosophy and the scientific disciplines was also continued from a fresh approach. Such an intersection of ideas, styles, and methods does not mean, however, that philosophy in the Netherlands is only an amalgam of foreign ideas, lacking any character of its own. On the contrary, it is precisely by such an encounter of divergent philosophies that, as in the times of a Descartes or a Spinoza, a more profiled philosophical life could flourish.

The primary philosophical trends in the Netherlands, apart from those of more traditional schools like neo-Thomism and neo-idealism, are existentialism, phenomenology, analytical philosophy, neo-Marxism, structuralism, and others that belong mainly to the postwar period. Scientific disciplines, including the humanities, that have had an impact on philosophy are mathematics, logic, the natural sciences (especially biology) psychology, history, and theology. Despite this broad spectrum of trends and disciplines, a main line in this postwar period can be traced. There was a kind of convergence, closely related to the traditions mentioned before. It was not a convergence in opinion or in the solution of the dilemmas of philosophy, but rather towards one problematic issue: the relationship between the validity of rules and the contingency of facts. This issue is, of course, an old one. Kant's distinction between the logical status (*quaestio iuris*) and the factual condition (*quaestio facti*), as well as the fight against psychologism in philosophy by people like Frege, Husserl, Meinong, and Moore in the beginning of this century, are milestones in the history of philosophy.

After 1945, this issue received a new impulse in Dutch philosophy from the varied information brought in by many scientific disciplines and from an increased sensitivity to such divergent climates of thought as those of French, British, American, and German philosophies. But perhaps there is more behind this awareness of a tension between information about facts and decisions about valid rules. Many new factual situations disturbed the minds of men, in the Netherlands as well as in other countries. Traces of the war remained visible in particular types of neuroses that, even thirty years after the war, were made public through television and reports protesting against a so-called sane society. Factual changes were brought about by a rapid industrialization, the overwhelming impact of methods of organizing society, and the psychological influence of advertising and the news media. The validity of traditional structures became a problem. New movements in education and religion, new contacts with countercultures and with a freshly discovered Third World, and new tensions between scientific neutrality and social responsibility provoked a widespread effort towards renewal and a restless reflection on factual changes and new rules to be found.

In the years after 1945, various successive waves of new philosophies reached the country. First, there was existentialism, especially the French form of this philosophy (espoused by Sartre, Merleau-Ponty, Marcel, Jankélévitch, Wahl), as the prewar writings of German philosophers like Heidegger and Jaspers were already known. The publication, after the war, of the posthumous works of Husserl by a Dutch publisher gave a strong impulse for the elaboration of phenomenology in the Netherlands. Although there is a close relationship between existentialism and phenomenology, one might say that the first trend of thought puts factual existence at the center, whereas the second one brackets factual existence in order to discover the validity of the structures that are grasped by phenomenological "intuiting." Against the background of the tradition of previous ages, it is understandable that Dutch philosophers have always been historiographers as well, not least contemporary Dutch philosophers. Thus, various authors have written surveys of existentialism and phenomenology since 1945: R. Bakker, R. F. Beerling, B. Delfgaauw, T. A. Kockelmans, R. Kwant, W. Luijpen, C. A. van Peursen, H. Robbers, J. Sperna-Weiland, and S. Strasser. Several of these names will turn up again later in this article when the systematic parts of philosophy are discussed.

A second wave in postwar Dutch philosophy has been the increasing influence of analytic philosophy. During at least fifteen years after World War II, Dutch philosophical life was dominated by existential-phenomenological tendencies. Was not this approach often too descriptive and too emotional? Was it not necessary to come closer to a logical analysis of rules and validity or, at any rate, to analyze the use made of certain words and certain types of language? The British type of ordinary language philosophy has been introduced, and good surveys have appeared on the Dutch scene since then by Dutch authors like G. Nuchelmans, C. Schoonbrood, and F. Staal.

The slogan "clarity is not enough" was also heard in the Netherlands after

World War II. In particular, the discussions around the "neutrality" or "objectivity" of the sciences and of the universities brought neo-Marxist arguments into the field. Is our scientific language value-free? Are there not, in our culture and society, hidden structures of power and of ideology that frequently control out seemingly neutral behavior and language systems? These questions did not exclusively arise in the neo-Marxist philosophy but were also formulated from a religious viewpoint. Quite another influence, that of French structuralism (Lévi-Strauss, Foucault, Derrida, Barthes), combined the search for objective and valid structures with the conception of a constitution of patterns of culture, rules of language, and systems of sciences by those structures, those "depth-grammars." Moreover, Chomsky, who related the structures of language to those of society, as well as Althusser, the French Marxist who gave a structuralistic analysis of Marx, influenced Dutch thinkers. However different those conceptions may be, they converge toward the analysis of structures that give account of apparently neutral facts and theories. Neo-Marxism (as represented by Bloch, Adorno, Habermas, Kolakowski, and Garaudy) has been described by various authors (among them philosophers as well as sociologists) such as R. F. Beerling, A. Brand, J. Klapwijk, H. Hoefnagels, and B. C. van Houten. Structuralism has been surveyed by R. Bakker, J. M. Broekman, and A. Peperzak.

More characteristic of Dutch philosophy situated at the crossroads of contemporary philosophy are studies that offer a comparison of the above-mentioned trends of thought. Not all thinkers listed before as describing one particular school of philosophy would confess themselves adherents of such a philosophy. By drawing a comparison between two rather antagonistic philosophies, one tries to overcome onesidedness and to delineate systematically new themes for the further development of philosophy. These comparisons, written by some of these Dutch philosophers, are mainly the following: existentialism and Marxism; phenomenology and analytical philosophy; and structuralism and modern French phenomenological approaches (like those of Ricoeur and Levinas). These studies also are more characteristic than the comprehensive surveys from the angle of the central theme, mentioned before. They all have something to do, systematically, with the tension between the contingency of facts and the validity of rules; between factual existential freedom and the dialectical laws of history; between analysis of concretely given meaning and analysis of the grammars defining such a meaning; between the never finished clarification of the plus-value of human symbols and the delimited structures interpreting those symbols.

ANCIENT PHILOSOPHY AND COMPARATIVE PHILOSOPHY

Studies in both contemporary philosophy and past philosophy form another trend in Netherlands philosophy. Perhaps here both aspects described before—descriptive survey and more interpretative comparison—are intertwined more closely. This section, the history of philosophy, includes two categories: interpretation of philosophers and their schools; and special subjects (non-Western philosophy and history of specific themes and of specific sciences).

Many studies have appeared in the field of Greek philosophy, notably studies on Plato by J. Mansfeld and G. J. de Vries that often combine good interpretation with conclusions related to more modern philosophical problems. The scholarly studies of Mrs. C. J. de Vogel discuss at length the transformations of Plato's thought through which a more dynamic and less dualistic image of his philosophy is achieved. There is already a kind of "movement" in Plato's world of Forms. In his later work in particular, this world is knowable directly, and not just indirectly or vaguely. Plato anticipates various ideas of Aristotle. Within a wider framework, Mrs. de Vogel traces lines from early Greek philosophy to the Middle Ages and concludes there is a closer relationship between the God of Christianity and the God of the Greek philosophers, especially Plato. The stress on the growth and change of a philosophy is also found in the study of Nuyens (a prewar study that was translated after 1945) on the variations in Aristotle's view of the soul, variations that enable a better chronology of his writings to be devised. This chronology is also one of the topics in other studies on Aristotle, among which we may mention studies on the "Politica" by P. A. Meyer, on "De Caelo" by L. Elders in 1966, and another on "De Caelo" by A. P. Bos in 1973. Some authors (C. J. de Vogel, J. H. Waszink, C. Mohrmann, A. Sizoo, M. van Straaten, J. C. M. van Winden, and C. W. Wolfskeel) not only interpret dynamic tendencies in the philosophies of Plato and Aristotle but also trace lines of development to Neoplatonism and even lines of comparison with the early Christian thought of Augustine and other church fathers. For lines of comparison, there are also important studies of the Gnosis (G. Quispel) and of the Arab translation of Aristotle (H. J. Drossaart Lulofs). These studies frequently combine scholarship with the clarification of problems that still have an impact on contemporary thought. One such study is a comparison between Greek and Christian thought (H. Robbers). Others investigate the rise of scientific problems within the context of ancient philosophy: the history of mathematics (B. L. van Waerden, E. W. Beth), of medicine (G. A. Lindeboom), and of physical problems (A.G.M. van Melsen).

The same tendencies can be seen in the more restricted number of studies of philosophical and theological thought in the Arab tradition (D. C. Mulder, W. R. van Brakell Buys, J.D.J. Waardenburg) and in Indian philosophy (J. Gonda, J.A.B. van Buitenen, T. E. Vetter, J. J. Poortman). Comparative studies in this field are by S. L. Kwee and F. J. Staal. The philosophy of the Middle Ages has found good interpreters in H. Braakhuis and in L. M. de Rijk. De Rijk makes use of the insights of modern logic, especially those of the logicians of the late Middle Ages, in his publications. The sharpest convergence of historical research and systematic philosophical investigation is to be found in G. Nuchelmans, *Theories of the Proposition,* which covers the periods of ancient and medieval philosophy. The work analyzes linguistic forms of propositions and the ways in which they can act as bearers of truth and falsity. This study, to be followed by a similar analysis of the history of "proposition" in modern philosophy, is characteristic of the aforementioned interrelationship between problems of validity and those of factual historical formation.

HISTORY OF MODERN PHILOSOPHY

There are so many investigations in the field of modern philosophy that they can be referred to here only in passing. At any rate, aspects of the comparison of thinkers and their importance for actual discussions also have to be mentioned here. It is obvious that Descartes and Spinoza, both of whom lived and worked on Dutch soil, also drew the attention of the historians of philosophy after 1945. In addition to many articles (articles on Spinoza are published every year by the Spinoza Society), books were written on Descartes' conception of physics by P. van der Hoeven, who also wrote an introduction to Descartes (the same was done by F.L.R. Sassen), while Mrs. C. L. Thijssen-Schoute published a voluminous study of Descartes' influence, *The Netherlands Cartesianism*, in 1954. Studies were published on Spinoza's methodology by H. G. Hubbeling and on his first kind of knowledge by C. de Deugd. Another study, by T. H. Zweerman, uses tools of analysis partly derived from the French structuralist thinkers. Other philosophers who received extensive studies were Kant (K. Kuypers, J. Plat, and H. de Vos) and Hegel (J.H.A. Hollak, W. van Dooren, J. A. Oosterbaan, A. Peperzak, S. Griffioen, and G. Sarlemijn). The authors of the Hegelian studies, in their other studies and articles, connected Hegel's dialectics with the interpretation of Marx or with problems arising out of the neo-Marxist analysis of contemporary society. The voluminous study of Rousseau by R. F. Beerling is a good example of historical investigation and analysis of critical questions concerning contemporary society. With regard to more recent philosophers, many introductions were written that gave only short surveys (on Marx, Bergson, Jaspers, Heidegger, Husserl, Wittgenstein, Sartre, Merleau-Ponty), as was also done with regard to the more classical philosophers (such as Berkeley, Hume, Leibniz, Descartes, and Spinoza). More important are the extensive studies on Poincaré (J.J.A. Mooij), K. Marx (J. van der Hoevan), Bakunin (A. Lehning), Bolzano (B. van Rootselaar), Husserl (T. de Boer, J. M. Broekman), Merleau-Ponty (R. C. Kwant), M. Scheler (J. H. Nota), and E. Bloch (G. van Asperen, M. Plattel). It is, of course, impossible to offer even succinct abstracts from these works here. Suffice it to say that the most important aspect is that almost all these studies combine good investigation with the effort to make explicit directives that open new paths in the fields of systematic philosophy. It is significant that many of these authors are referred to again in the subsequent paragraphs on systematic philosophy. A more purely historical approach is to be found in the many works of F.L.R. Sassen (d. 1971), the Netherlands' most fruitful historiographer of the history of philosophy and teaching in philosophy, covering the time from the Middle Ages up until 1960. Sassen also wrote a general history of Western philosophy (five volumes).

As a transition to systematic philosophy, two types of historical studies can be mentioned. One type is illustrated in E. J. Dijksterhuis who wrote on the mechanization of the picture of the world, a history of the natural sciences, particularly mechanics, covering the time from the early Greek thinkers up to and including Newtonian mechanics. His work, translated into many languages, explained that a real break is to be found between the conception of the Middle Ages and that of the new times. Galileo, Torricelli, Huygens, Newton, and others gradually accomplished the mathematicization of movement. This change is more decisive than what today would be called a "paradigm-switch." Dijksterhuis believes that the contemporary natural sciences still show a continuity with the period of that renewal: a "functional thinking with its essential mathematical form of expression." This work (1950) paves the way for further investigations into the breakthrough of a system of scientific validity in the factual course of history and of cultural change.

A second type is found in the works of R. Hooykaas. His interest in the background of theological questions, an interest that is typical of many Dutch philosophical studies, gives his investigations in the field of the history of the natural sciences a wider setting. A new vision of the idea of the world as creation, as a given object for scientific research, makes understandable why, in the time of Newton, Puritanism is largely represented among physicians. This leads to a further disclosure of certain rules or standards like the principle of uniformity in geology or biology.

The philosophical history of science in the nineteenth century is the subject of the work of H.A.M. Sneldess. The history of psychology and its philosophical background have been investigated by C. Sanders and by his collaborators L.K.A. Eisenga and J.F.H. van Rappard; other studies are by W. van Hoorn.

SYSTEMATIC PHILOSOPHY

Systematic philosophy can be divided into two categories: philosophy of the sciences, including the social sciences, and systematic philosophy in a stricter sense (epistemology, metaphysics, philosophy of culture, and so forth). The characteristic features of philosophy in the Netherlands, mentioned in the beginning of this chapter, imply a close relationship between these two categories and even with more historical investigations.

The philosophy of the sciences poses problems about the validity of scientific theories, the contingent aspect (reference to reality), the impact of a more metaphysical context (influence of religious outlook, social and ethical values) and the changeability of validity (integration into historical and cultural structures). Do the sciences deal with reality or do they provide only autonomous systems for deduction? Or are they halfway between full reality and the empty rules of formal systems? And in which way do they point to reality, or even more poignantly, how far do they affect the responsible or irresponsible praxis of daily life? The first part of this essay shows how various philosophical trends, like analytical philosophy, phenomenology, and neo-Marxism, have influenced Dutch philosophers. It seems clear that this leads to divergent approaches to these problems, and even to different answers. Nevertheless, a certain convergence is visible. A sensitivity to concreteness needing clarification by rules and formal validity must be made explicit in the contingencies of events, in the laboratory situation as well as in daily life.

These tendencies touch various fields of pure philosophy: metaphysics and ontology, philosophical anthropology and philosophical ethics. Some philosophical trends try to evoke, within philosophy itself, the concrete contact or encounter with fellow men and with God. Such a philosophy tries to disclose, ontologically, the ethical and divine dimensions of reality. This is not a scientific approach; even the inexpressible becomes a perspective. There is a strong impact of the "factual," not in the sense of the pure facts of the sciences, but more as evaluative and inexhaustible facticity. It becomes evident, however, that such a philosophy needs a certain control by practical situations and rules for communication: the urge for a universe of discourse, theoretically and practically. Other trends put at the center of philosophical endeavor the necessity of formal validity and the use of scientific prediction and control. Although a theoretical position, its importance for daily life, even in its political aspects, is clear: it eliminates the dangers of irrationalism in thought and action. But in the course of further philosophical development, it is precisely a more logical analysis that turns out to be a kind of a funnel towards the more contingent problems of the meanings of words, linguistic behavior, skillful action, personal attitudes, cultural conventions, and the relevancy of certain facts and events. Hence, a kind of convergence is also visible in these fields of divergent philosophical trends.

PHILOSOPHY OF THE FORMAL SCIENCES

A first illustration of these tendencies is offered by the philosophy of the formal sciences. If logic can be classified in this field, then it gives one of the best illustrations, as its starting point is precisely the formal validity of rules. Long before the last war, a native Dutch logical school existed. This was the "Significa," which grew into an international association. Its leader was G. Mannoury (1867–1956) who after the war published an extensive manual on "analytic significa." The purpose was the logical clarification of language. It is understandable that in the 1930s it came into contact with representatives of logical positivism. This logical clarification, this defining the meaning of terms, was closely interrelated with a kind of psychological analysis and differed, by this more factual analysis, from a purely logical approach. In the Netherlands, this school had contacts with thinkers who developed their own systems, notably, the mathematician Brouwer and the logician Beth.

E. W. Beth (1908–1966) has been the Netherlands' most influential logician and has proceeded along strict logical lines. While he does not adhere to logical positivism, he agrees with its thesis that the fight against irrationalism is essential for the progress of our culture. Logical analysis, in the strict sense and in an applied form within the various disciplines, is indispensable in this struggle. In Beth's development, however, a rapprochement to factual data takes place. This becomes clear in his studies on logical semantics; his use of semantic tableaus has been partly inspired by Tarski, as was also the case with Carnap's semantics. Nevertheless, Beth's method remained a purely logical analysis. He took a further step when he modified his original sharp rejection of any psychological—too factual—interpretation of logical thought. Through his contacts with J. Piaget, he accepted a more genetical interpretation of logic: that is, every logical system is characterized by a continuous development. It is inherent in any logic that its possibilities of formalizing language are inexhaustible, and this leads to increasing improvements of given logical systems. D. Nauta, partly influenced by Beth, focuses on the relevance of logical structures in modern information-theory and in the use of models in the sciences. His conclusion is that the symbolic systems of logic are one of the products of the interaction of man with his factual world; they are formal maps of the environment.

L.E.J. Brouwer (1881–1966) developed intuitionism in mathematics before World War II. Some of his works were published after 1945, and they have great importance for the philosophy of mathematics both within and outside the Netherlands. Brouwer rejects the formalism of, for instance, Hilbert, as well as the logicism of Russell. Mathematics, particularly the construction of natural numbers, is related to the actual given intuition of time—more or less in the sense in which Kant judged time-consciousness to be indispensable for the sequence of natural numbers. Brouwer's intuitionism has a number of implications, namely, that logic is not truth-functional, as actual construction is needed to prove truth or falsity, and that the principle of the excluded middle is not valid. Could we draw the philosophical conclusion that there are alternative mathematics (and logics)? Or even that every "mathematical theory is an idealization of empirical discourse" (S. Körner)? Or, in even more general terms, in the wider context of contemporary discussions about the disputed uniqueness of existing scientific theories: do different ways of logical argumentation and of scientific validation result from differences in world-view and cultural contexts? Brouwer views mathematics as a system of rules resulting in validity because they hypnotize, as it were, those who enter their playground. Brouwer had already developed this idea in a lecture at Vienna in 1928. (This lecture was a decisive turning point for one of his auditors, L. Wittgenstein.) Brouwer recognizes an analogy between the language of mathematics and the language of command.

The most important representative of mathematical intuitionism in the Netherlands today is A. Heyting who has elaborated on the ideas of Brouwer. In different ways, the mathematicians D. van Dantzig (1900–1959) and J. F. Koksma (1904–1964) both related mathematics to empirical reality. H. Freudenthal describes mathematics as the science of structures and has developed a "cosmic language" as these structures have a universal rationality that must be understandable in principle for any factual, reasonable being in the universe. D. van Dalen has dealt with mathematics and logic.

PHILOSOPHY OF THE NATURAL SCIENCES AND BIOLOGY

In the field of the philosophy of natural sciences, one encounters similar problems of the relationship between validity and contingencies. Primarily, the coherence between theory and fact is discussed by authors like J.P.M. Guerts, H. J. Groenwold, A. Kockelmans (now in the United States), H. Koningsveld, and J. B. Ubbink. In some cases, the concept of "model" in physics is also analyzed. A more metaphysical approach is found in the work of J. M. Burgers (now also in the United States) who relates physical conceptualization to a dynamic view of reality, inspired by A. N. Whitehead and by A.G.M. van Melsen who tried to make explicit what had been implicit in the physical conception of "matter." A kind of disclosure of "matter," more or less in the Aristotelian sense, is possible, by which the horizons of "life" and of "spirit" become visible. Some of these notions are also found in *Philosophy of Science,* the ample study by P. H. van Laer, which is very important for the neo-Thomist tradition.

The philosophy of biology has a special position in the Netherlands. Its main tendency is the evaluation of the validity of biological laws and structures, resulting in the discovery of the interaction of these laws with the changing environment. Partly inspired by Kant's conception of a regulative finality, C. J. van der Klaauw (1893–1972) developed a functional morphology. He states that the coherence of form and function make possible the use of new and exact methods and at the same time he advocates the avoidance of a restricted, purely causal approach. Van der Klaauw's school produced numerous studies of philosophical biology. P. Dullemeyer and M. Jeuken stressed the necessity of a special methodology for the phenomena of life. Modern concepts like "model" and "system" are very suitable for such a methodology. C. P. Raven has also made important contributions in this area. Raven's investigations into the role of "information" in biology resulted in a philosophically valuable concept of a multidimensional method. A still wider context is given in the work of J. Lever who points to the interaction between different world-views (Christian, Marxist, and so forth) and biology. A philosophical analysis shows that a world-view has a regulative function with regard to a scientific discipline, but it must not act in order to fill gaps in scientific knowledge. One of Lever's collaborators, W. J. van der Steen, has written an introduction to the philosophy of biology. The convergence is greater in this whole field than, for instance, in the field of the philosophy of mathematics. With regard to the philosophy of mathematics, there were common problems, but some authors tried to integrate the facts into the sovereignty of the rules; others saw the rules as idealizations of empirical reality. In the field of biology, the philosophical approach to the friction between facts and validity points in the same direction of gradually refined methodological approaches to reality, in a biological as well as in a more cultural sense.

PHILOSOPHY OF THE SOCIAL SCIENCES

In the field of the social sciences, the divergence is increasingly coming to the fore. On the one hand, a more phenomenological approach, especially in the fields of psychology and psychiatry, has been important. The school of Utrecht, with its leading figure, F.J.J. Buytendijk (d. 1974), produced many interesting studies that greatly inspired other writers, notably, J. H. van den Berg, M. J. Langeveld, J. van Lennep, J. Linschoten, H. Rümke, and S. Strasser. Many of these studies are philosophical. (Their significance is dealt with later in this essay in the section on philosophical anthropology.) As was stated at the beginning of this article, a subsequent influence on philosophy in the Netherlands has been logical positivism. This quite different tendency has been increasingly influential in philosophical psychology. Linschoten (?–1964) turned away from a merely phenomenological approach. The more positivistic methodology of A. D. de Groot acquired an influential place of its own. This approach has come mainly from the Anglo-Saxon countries. On the other hand, the phenomenological approach has exerted an increasing influence outside the Netherlands, mainly in the United States.

There is an intensive interaction between the social sciences, especially sociology and the study of history. The wider cultural and "spiritual" (worldview) context that came to the fore in the fields mentioned above plays a traditional role here, not only becuase the Dutch thinkers willy-nilly often have theological issues to discuss, but also because of the impact of a philosophical reflection on culture. Before 1945, the famous Dutch historian, J. Huizinga (1872–1945), localized historical periods within the structures of a changing culture and even developed a philosophy of culture which he called "*homo ludens.*" All philosophical studies on history and society that reflect upon the status of scientific method point to such a context of culture, even though they may take quite different starting points. J. Romein (1893–1962) gives a Marxist, dialectical interpretation of the course of history, and T.J.G. Locher discusses the problem of European centrism in historiography. Both studied under Huizinga. P. Geyl criticizes the speculative approach of A. Toynbee. H. Berkhof and M. C. Smit treat theological themes in relation to the meaning of history. The problem of the delineation of historical periods is treated by J.H.J. van de Pot, who also wrote on general problems of the philosophy of history. A close relationship with the analysis of social and economic situations is given in a pioneering work on the philosophy of history, *Between Structure and Event* by C. Bertels. Structuralistic and neo-Marxist analyses are used to prove the importance of a heuristic method of discovery instead of a context of justification. Along these lines, only deeper demographic and cultural contexts are discovered, in many aspects using the conceptions of Braudel, Febvre, Dumézil, and Lévi-Strauss. In a less methodological and philosophical way, another author, P. J. Bouman (1902–1977), years before had shown how history is not made by an elite of great men but how macrohistory is constituted by many microhistories.

Divergency is the primary aspect of the philosophy of language, although here again a tendency towards wider contexts can be seen. As in the field of psychology, the chief difference is attributable to antagonistic philosophical influences. Discussion around the ideas of N. Chomsky takes place mainly within the confines of general linguistics. G. Nuchelmans presents a general philosophy of language, inspired by analytical philosophy, and investigates a variety of linguistic tools. Mrs. E. M. Barth analyzes a special topic: the logic of articles. J. M. Verhaar offers a more general philosophical approach to language. "Language" acquires a quite different, more ontological meaning in the studies of R. C. Kwant who follows the philosophical insights of Merleau-Ponty. Inspired by H. Bergson, H. Oldewelt offers subtle reflections on language. These discussions on the problem of language result in two approaches: one inspired primarily by analytical philosophy, the other treating the more metaphysical dimensions of language. H. G. Hubbeling and W. A. de Pater analyze, along different lines, language about God; Hubbeling is working in the wider field of logic, especially deontic logic. The word "God" cannot be excluded from language considered from the standpoint of "non-positivistic logical empiricism." W. A. de Pater, influenced partly by Ian Ramsey, also discusses language pertaining to the phenomena of culture. Both Pater and Ramsey attempt to enlarge the logically meaningful field of language in order to do justice to the claims of reality with its religious, ethical, and cultural dimensions. In other fields, such as the language of jurisdiction, other dimensions of language are investigated—for instance, the persuasive and rhetorical aspects, which are probed by H. P. Visser't Hooft (working in the line of the Belgian philosopher C. Perelman) and S. Ijsseling (in the line of Heidegger and the French structuralists).

The above surveys of the philosophies of the various disciplines elucidate important philosophical issues which are acquiring increasing importance on the international philosophical scene. The first issue is the restriction in methodological approach to questions of validity, eliminating too haphazard and spontaneous insights. The result is a closed system of knowledge that leads to a deadlock if such a system is not integrated into the praxis of the process of culture. This integration implies, however, that the confines of such a system open into a wider playground—wider not only in a spatial sense but also in the sense of a wider modification. Here the kernel of many contemporary philosophical problems can be found. It has two aspects. First, the restricted rules afford clarification and valid analysis, but at the same time, they must point beyond those limits. This means that they have to be regarded as maps related to a reality outside those maps. Therefore, keywords like "model," "information," "paradigm," and "structure" play a central role in every methodology. At the same time, these scientific and methodological issues exert a direct impact on philosophy itself. In this sense, the philosophies of scientific disciplines play an indispensable role in Dutch philosophy. Second, these rules delineate the clear ground of theoretical communication. However, they touch other fields that are so vast and different that often words like "inexhaustible," "appeal," "command," and "contingent," are used. These words indicate that even within the confines of scientific disciplines some sensitivity for fields outside their universes of discourse is present. Or to put it in more metaphysical terms, a modification takes place when the realm of finiteness (a surveyable system of rules) is being opened under pressure of infinity. The important feature within the realm of the above-mentioned philosophies of the sciences is that such a sensitivity has to be translated within the language systems of scientific intercourse, or at least within the convincing ("rational") categories of methodological reflection.

METAPHYSICS AND EPISTEMOLOGY

What has been indicated as "infinity"—breaking through any given system of delimitations—is dealt with more directly in those regions of philosophy that are labeled metaphysics (including ontology); epistemology (theory of knowledge); philosophical anthropology; philosophical ethics (including social philosophy); and philosophy of culture.

Metaphysics in the traditional sense is hardly found; contacts with the rough ground of the modern sciences, epistemological problems, and value systems in society are too close. A study of metaphysics by J. Peters in the line of neo-Thomism incorporates insights from existentialism. A.G.M. van Melsen describes the disclosure of reality as a result of his studies on the natural sciences and on evolution. Various theologians who are also qualified in philosophy, such as G.D.J. Dingemans and J. M. de Jong) approach the problem of the relationship between the belief in God and the modern sciences. Around the 1930s, a school of Calvinistic philosophy was founded by H. Dooyeweerd (1894–1977) and D.H.T. Vollenhoven. The school attempted to reveal the hidden religious presuppositions in philosophy—one Christian foundation over and against the other non-Christian ones—and to integrate the structures of the sciences in an ontological construction of reality. After the war, Dooyeweerd and various thinkers of his school published works on philosophy. These works were partly polemic, opposing non-Christian tendencies in modern philosophy and even in the works of Christian thinkers like the theologian Karl Barth. For another part, they dealt with systematic problems; e.g., the relationship between technics, civilization, and faith. Authors in these fields included S. U. Zuidema, K. J. Popma, H. van Riessen, H. J. Hommes, E. Schuurman, A. Troost, and J.P.A. Mekkes.

A few studies were published after World War II by two opposite thinkers, H. J. Pos (1898–1955) and A. J. de Sopper (1875–1960). Both started with forms of neo-Kantianism, and both later turned to some kind of metaphysics. Pos intended to come to an attitude of praxis based on a purely rational insight into reality, rejecting, at that time, modern philosophical trends (logical positivism and existentialism). De Sopper developed a Christian type of philosophy, describing metaphysics as the total response of human existence on the claims of reality. The work of A. E. Loen also has a strong emphasis on Christian faith as a radical possibility to reveal the dynamic, ontological structures of reality. He was influenced by existential philosophy. In his view, making manifest the religious dimension of reality also implies an investigation into the presuppositions of the sciences. Similar ideas, but more from the viewpoint of phenomenology, can be found in the work of W. Luijpen. His metaphysics remains in contact with the language about empirical reality and asks for the meaning, not for being. Instead of speculating, it points, through the intentionality of language, indirectly to divine Reality.

The theory of knowledge sustains close relationships with the philosophies of the sciences. Problems like theory and fact, form and function, and the structures in historical change all have epistemological aspects. Closer to a pure theory of knowledge are studies of the sciences in general and of the interaction between theoretical thought and reality. H. Meyer (1893–1959), who turned to philosophy as an elderly man, pleads for a pure scientific knowledge. The modern sciences, he states, make metaphysics impossible; knowledge relates only to the things as they are for us. But the concept of a "thing," constituted by our knowledge, nevertheless touches a given perceptual ingredient.

C. A. van Peursen relates the sciences and reality more closely. The laws of physics are a limited network within the more complex network, with more parameters, of biology; the laws of biology are more restricted structures within the wider methodology of psychology. This means that the scientific disciplines, from the most formal ones like mathematics to the scientific investigations of more concrete, factual data, like the social sciences, constitute a series of methodological networks with an increasing number of dimensions (greater "density"). This can be interpreted as a structural urge towards the concrete ("full") reality beyond scientific theory: the daily events with their practical, political, ethical, and religious dimensions. Scientific explanation and description ("rules," "facts," "is") are curtailments of human policy and evaluation ("values," "ought").

A sharp demarcation between epistemology and ontology or metaphysics is impossible in the works of all the previously mentioned authors. This is clear in the work of O. D. Duintjer who analyzes the rules defining the scope of epistemology, that is, the validity of knowledge; rules defining the structures of the sciences (methodology); and rules defining the meaning of human behavior. Epistemology has a transcendental approach, which means that the presupposition of the rules has to be made explicit. However, such a reflection implies a critical attitude, the discovery of social criteria and of alternatives. This second level of critical reflection opens to a third metaphysical level: the hidden openness around all standardized possibilities, a kind of suprarational contact with Reality beyond rules.

Other efforts have been made to relate an epistemology based on the modern sciences to more ontological problems. Some of them are present in the works on the philosophy of the natural sciences discussed before. The older work of J. M. Burgers and the recent work of J.P.M. Geurts point, to some extent, in that direction. Within the restricted field of the problems of finiteness and infinity in mathematics, E. van de Velde attempts to disclose a more ethical and ontological dimension. Those problems are also found in other aspects of science and culture, and they indicate the impact of "otherness" (the ethical implications of the existence of fellow-men, for instance) on our closed systems. More related to the philosophy of culture are the investigations in the field of "meta-science" by S. L. Kwee, who does not offer a logical analysis but relates reflection on scientific method to human practical attitudes in technical and social organization. The astronomer H. Zanstra describes modern physics as only a glimpse of a much wider metaphysical reality, of which paranormal faculties of knowledge provide some hints.

PHILOSOPHICAL ANTHROPOLOGY, ETHICS, AND SOCIAL PHILOSOPHY

Philosophical anthropology is an important part of systematic philosophy, especially in continental Europe. It is wider than the philosophy of mind in the Anglo-Saxon tradition since it discusses problems like body and soul, man and fellow man, human and animal behavior. Various thinkers have been productive in this field. F.J.J. Buytendijk gives many phenomenological descriptions of human phenomena, by which he makes acceptable the idea that there is no strict separation between an inner world and a world outside man. The human world, in its social and cultural structures, reveals human "inner life" in its outwards-directed "intentionality." Thus, the difference between man and animal becomes visible, although in animal behavior there are anticipations of human life. In practical physiological research, it can be proven that human physiology needs the context of an interpretation simulated by philosophical anthropology. The same physiological processes, like walking in a museum or receiving an equal quantity of food, can have quite different results. The one who likes the exhibition is less tired, and the children of parents who prefer fat boys will become heavier. Hence, even in fundamental physiological processes, the body acts as a human body. The human body is never mere object; it is also subject in a certain world of culture and social traditions. The separation between body and mind is impossible.

Other scholars who probe the relationship between body and soul may differ in approach, but they agree, first, on the unity of body and soul, both of which they see as one-sided models, and, second, on the dimension of "subjectivity." Human beings can never completely be objectified, and this dimension has to be taken into account in every human science. Philosophers like S. Strasser and C. A. van Peursen have elaborated these ideas. They discuss various philosophical views (Aristotle, Descartes, and so forth, but also existentialism and analytical philosophy) in terms of this theme. The notion of "person" has been analyzed by A. de Wilde. Another theme in this field is the relationship between man and fellow man. Does the subject discover his fellow man after long and difficult epistemological investigations ("the problem of other minds")? No, the "encounter" is primordial and constitutes even the human subject in its self-consciousness. F.J.J. Buytendijk, J. H. van den Berg, A. L. Janse de Jonge, R. C. Kwant, and others defend this thesis. S. Strasser has given a wider elaboration to this theme, relating it to human freedom. This last theme is also central in the studies by W. A. Luijpen and A. Peperzak. Peperzak extends his field of anthropological investigation by studying similar themes in the field of ethics, whereas T. de Boer does the same thing but in the direction of the relationship between a philosophy of man and the methods of the human sciences. A special theme in these fields is that of self-alienation, a key term in the philosophies of Hegel and the young Marx. C.E.M. Struyker Boudier investigates its anthropological implications. An important contribution in the field of anthropobiology has been given to discussions in the field of epistemology as well as in that of philosophical anthropology by A. de Froe. Man is said to transform his vital world; he creates an environment of symbols. In this way, he proceeds from perception, which is already symbolic interpretation, to scientific judgments and cultural activities.

The philosophy of ethics and social philosophy have close ties with philosophical anthropology—as well as with the social sciences. Meta-ethics is, of course, related to logic (deontic logic, of which there are a few studies in the Netherlands, among them those by H. G. Hubbeling and Mrs. A. M. Bos). Besides more general, historical, or systematic surveys (R. Bakker, J. de Graaf, and H. de Vos), the trend in the Netherlands since 1945 has been to relate philosophical ethics directly to concrete problems. These problems partly concern the ways in which values and norms can be discussed, especially as to questions of law (J. F. Glastra van Loon, R.A.V. van Haersolte, H. J. Hommes, and G. E. Langemeijer), and partly social situations, often growing into a critical social philosophy (L. Nauta, M. G. Plattel, and H. Hoefnagels). A fundamental problem, especially in the confrontation with abstract utopian thinking, is the problem of evil. H. J. Heering wrote on this subject, and in another study, he gives a statement of the morals appropriate for a provisional situation. This idea of provisional ethics is obvious in a time of transition. The idea is not new; during his stay in the Netherlands, Descartes developed a similar program. The Netherlands, open to divergent influences from abroad, has in recent years acquired a sharpened awareness of the changing structures in religious, ethical, and cultural life. It is important to note that the scientific disciplines are sending out signals for a new, concrete ethical program. In particular, the medical profession has formulated questions that are also discussed by philosophers and theologians (J. H. van den Berg, G. A. Lindeboom, M.F.J. Marlet, W. Metz, P. J. Roscam Abbing, and Mrs. H. Terborgh-Dupuis).

From the above it is clear that social philosophy supplies a framework for many philosophical investigations. Some studies (G. J. Harmsen) have a Marxist orientation and deal with specific questions. A typical trend in the Netherlands is personalism in philosophy and theology, which was developed before 1945 by the physicist P. A. Kohnstamm (1875–1951) in a broad ontological setting. According to Kohnstamm, the truth behind the endeavor at objective knowledge in the sciences is a personal truth. His ideas, which show affinity with, for instance, the philosophy of the late M. Polanyi in Britain, also had consequences for social life. W. Banning (1888–1971) presents a personalistic social philosophy, taking a socialistic standpoint in political life and a Christian standpoint in religious life. From a different viewpoint, R.A.V. van Haersolte shows that personification is a kind of social mechanism that nevertheless has an indispensable role in the constitution of norms and the integration of the social order.

R.J.A. van Dijk gives a more systematic reflection on social philosophy and its possibilities. His thought also touches on the philosophy of the social sciences but has a more independent philosophical signification. He asserts that social reality is characterized by its "subjectivity," which means that reflection on its own status is inherent in any society. This reflection is much more than theoretical reflection; it is also a kind of facticity that incorporates the self-construction of society through language and labor. The social sciences can produce only objectified models or paradigms of this fundamental process of self-constitution. A much vaster fundamental philosophical reflection is found in the works of R. F. Beerling. Indirectly through studies on Rousseau, Weber, Simmel, Schuetz, and Wittgenstein and directly through studies on intersubjectivity, symbols, power, and self-alienation, a social philosophy is being developed with roots in ontological conceptions that have a partly phenomenological and partly neo-Marxist root but are framed in a mild skepticism. Philosophy itself and the social sciences have lost their contact with the historical and social perspectives in which they exist as social and cultural enterprises. Reflection demands a certain distance from the object, even a kind of phenomenological reduction of reality. But this must not lead to an absolute standpoint, which would be identical with isolation and the loss of identity. Social philosophy has to function as the risky way back to the relativity of social perspectives.

PHILOSOPHY OF CULTURE: A POSTSCRIPT

The philosophy of culture has taken on a new and concrete shape in the Netherlands in recent years. The philosophy of Beerling implies such a philosophy that goes back into the more concrete situations of historical relativity, social perspectives, and, notwithstanding all this finiteness, ethical responsibility. It is more than mere cultural anthropology or a branch of another social science as it also reveals the underlying epistemological and ontological problems of a genuinely cultural dimension of reality. Reflection on history, not merely on history as a scientific discipline, provides one of the entries to the modern philosophy of culture. Beerling wrote studies on the possibilities and limitations of historical knowledge. J. H. Nota has a phenomenological approach to these problems. Historical studies on aesthetic consciousness also highlight some aspects of cultural development (J.M.M. Aler and C. de Deugd). Another entry is given by philosophical anthropology. Subtle studies on human feelings, cultural habits, and the like are offered in refined literary form by H. Oldewelt and C. Verhoeven. A third entry is found in the studies of the impact of technology on civilization written by C. J. Dippel, S. L. Kwee, E. Schuurman, and F. A. Tellegen.

A first program for a philosophy of culture is the idea of "synthesis" developed by J.H.M.M. Loenen (1919–1978). It is not the necessary synthesis of the Hegelian conception of culture but rather a process with open possibilities and impossibilities through which conflicts can result in qualitatively new policies. Behind this idea is a philosophy of values and norms. The structure of human existence implies an urge towards self-realization, which entails intrinsic values—with a dimension of infinity—that can be made manifest within the relativity and variety of the many possible value systems. C. A. van Peursen has developed a philosophy of culture based on the idea of a policy to be formulated in concrete terms. Here the fundamental idea is that "culture" is not a noun but a verb, or, in other words, a strategy in the interaction between human society and the often overwhelming aspects of the environmental reality. In a model, some of these strategies are sketched, in particular a contemporary "functional" strategy in which values, norms, as well as scientific theories act only in relationship with actually given human situations.

All of these conceptions have ontological implications: there is no purely objective reality; there exists no autonomous human reason (also, "reason" has a specific function according to the framework of a culture); finite systems have to map out the demands of "infinity"; and evaluations precede factual descriptions. Influenced partly by Marxism, partly by Teilhard de Chardin, and partly by a modern neo-Thomist tradition, B. Delfgaauw has formulated a philosophy which comprehends ontological, metaphysical, and anthropological aspects resulting in a conception of history and culture. As an existentialist, Delfgaauw describes the human being as a process, as "becoming-human." Individual freedom and social freedom are realizations in the course of history. He explains the evolution of the cosmos—matter, life, consciousness, human culture—"micro-ontologically": the coming into existence of a worldwide human society. But this explanation does not imply a finite ontology. In the history of culture, transcendence becomes manifest, and the task of metaphysics to clarify this dimension. H.M.M. Fortmann, in a more psychological vein, points to a divine dimension of culture.

T. Lemaire recently wrote about a philosophy of culture with a less spiritualistic outlook than that of Delfgaauw or Fortmann. Referring, among others, to Marx and to Lévi-Strauss, Lemaire stresses the indispensable material content of culture. He states that cultural anthropology has given a wider meaning to "culture," including all human activities such as the technical economic ones. Furthermore, this contribution has destroyed the "Europe-centric" way of analyzing culture. A certain cultural relativism resulting from it can have therapeutic functions. One has to discover the aspect of self-alienation in culture in order to reconquer man as subject. This conquest has to lead to a new culture with a new experience of nature, overcoming modern self-alienation.

In all these studies, culture becomes the dynamic story of tasks to be realized. Earlier in this article, it is shown that scholars in the field of metaphysics, and even in the philosophy of sciences, interpret the respective reflections in those fields as a disclosure of reality itself. An example is van Melsen who holds that matter, via evolution, acquires a new dimension in human responsibility. Before the war, the historian Huizinga and, shortly after 1945, the theologian G. van der Leeuw (1890–1950) described culture as a game, a dance, a finite order with infinite dimensions. It is understandable that many studies mentioned previously have significance for a cultural strategy for the future. In his "metabletics," J. H. van den Berg describes how reality itself changes within the changing pattern of human culture. C. Bertels analyzes deeply hidden structural changes. The philosophy of the sciences discusses the possibility of alternative theories and even, epistemologically, the possibility of alternative meanings of terms like "explanation" and "rationality."

Two aspects of the Netherlands' recent work in philosophy become manifest. First, the old tension between rules of validity and contingent historical and factual situations is not one of mutual exclusion. The interaction between both implies the denial of an enforced choice between absolutism and relativism. Second, even metaphysical problems entail some consequences for a philosophy of culture and the other way round—no transcendence without justification in daily, social life and no empirical reality without transempirical criteria.

The Netherlands is aware of the diverse world cultures and activities, especially with regard to the Third World; this awareness has shaped the political and spiritual climate there more intensively than in many other countries. Philosophical activities are not completely outside these perspectives. They indirectly reflect the human effort to find and invent valid rules for newly arising factual situations. Some tendencies towards a closer interaction between philosophy and daily life might be traceable and might indicate how philosophy can become functional in a given historical situation. In that sense, a national survey could have some significance outside geographical and linguistic boundaries.

SELECT BIBLIOGRAPHY

BOOKS AND ARTICLES

Bakker, R. and Hubbeling, H. G. *History of the Philosophy of Ethics of the XXth Century* (The Hague: Nijhoff, forthcoming).

Banning, W. *De mens in sociale en geestelijke verhoudingen* (Haarlem: De Erven F. Bohn, 1963).

Beekman, G. *Filosofie, filosofen, filosoferen* (Ambo: Biethoven, 1973).

Beerling, R. F. *Het cultuurprotest van J. J. Rousseau* (Deventer: Van Loghum Slaterus, 1977).

————. *Sociologie en wetenschapscrisis* (Meppel: Boom, 1973).

————. *Wijsgerig-sociologische verkenningen*, 2 vols. (Arnhem: de Haan Zeist, 1964–1965).

Bender, F. *George Berkeley's Philosophy Re-examined* (Amsterdam: Paris, 1945).

Bertels, C. P. *Geschiedenis tussen structuur en evenement* (Amsterdam: Wetenschappelijke Uitgeverij, 1973).

Beth, E. W. *La crise de la raison et la logique* (Paris and Louvain: Gauthier-Villars, 1957).

———— and Piaget, J. *Epistémologie mathématique et psychologie* (Paris: Presses Universitaires de France, 1962).

Bos, A. P. *On the Elements. Aristotle's Early Cosmology* (Assen: Van Gorcum, 1973).

Bots, J. *Tussen Descartes en Darwin. Geloof en natuurwetenschap in de 18e eeuw in Nederland* (Assen: Van Gorcum, 1972).

Boudier, K. S. *Vervreemding en Bevrijding* (Baarn: Ambo, 1972).

Bouman, P. J. *Wetenschap en wekelijkheid* (Assen: Van Gorcum, 1967).

Broekman, J. M. *Phänomenologie und Egologie* (The Hague: Nijhoff, 1963).

————. *Structuralism: Moscow, Prague, Paris*, trans. J. F. Beekman and B. Helm, Synthese Library 67 (Dordrecht and Boston: Reidel, 1974).

Brouwer, L.E.J. "Consciousness, Philosophy and Mathematics," in *Proceedings of the 10th International Congress of Philosophy* (Amsterdam: North-Holland, 1948).

Burgers, J. M. *Experience and Conceptual Activity* (Cambridge, Mass.: MIT Press, 1965).

Buytendijk, F.J.J. *Das Menschliche. Wege zu seinem Verständnis* (Stuttgart: Koehler, 1958).

————. *Mensch und Tier*, 2d ed. (Hamburg: Rowohlt, 1961).

————. *Pain: Modes and Functions* (Chicago: University of Chicago Press, 1962).

————. *Prolegomena van een antropologische fysiologie* (Utrecht and Antwerp: Het Spectrum, 1965).

————. *Recontre/Encounter/Begegnung. Contributions Dedicated to F.J.J. Buytendijk* (Utrecht and Antwerp: Aula-Boeken, 1957).

————, Christian, P., and Plugge, H. *Ueber die menschiche Bewegung* (Schondorf: Hofmann, 1963).

de Boer, T. *De ontwikkelingsgang in het denken van Husserl* (Assen: Van Gorcum, 1966).

————. *The Development of Husserl's Thought*, trans. T. Plantinga (The Hague: Nijhoff, 1978).

————. *Tussen filosofie en profetie: de wijsbegeerte van E. Levinas* (Baarn: Ambo, 1977).

de Deugd, C. *From Religion to Criticism. The Growth of Aesthetic Consciousness in Greece* (Amsterdam: Athenaeum-Polak and Van Gennep, 1971).

————. *The Significance of Spinoza's First Kind of Knowledge* (Assen: Van Gorcum, 1966).

de Groot, A. D. *Methodology. Foundations of Inference and Research in the Behavioral Sciences* (The Hague: Mouton, 1969).

————. *Wat is Existentialisme?* (Baarn: Het Wereldvenster, 1969).

de Pater, W. *Reden von Gott. Reflexionen zur analytischen Philosophie der religiösen Sprache* (Bonn: Linguista Biblica, 1974).

————. *Theologische Sprachlogik* (Munich: Kösel, 1971).

de Rijk, L. M. *Logica Modernorum. A Contribution to the History of Early Terministic Logic*, 2 vols. (Assen: Van Gorcum, 1962–1967).

154   Western Europe, Australia, and Israel

de Swart, H.C.M. and Hubbeling, H. G. *Inleiding tot de symbolische logica* (Assen: Van Gorcum, 1976).

de Vogel, C. J. *Antike Seinsphilosophie und Christentum im Wandel der Jahrhunderte* (Baden-Baden: Grimm, 1958).

——. *Greek Philosophy*, 4th ed. (Leiden: Brill, 1969).

Delfgaauw, B.M.I. *A Concise History of Philosophy* (Dublin and Sidney: Gill, 1968).

——. *Evolution. The Theory of Teilhard de Chardin* (London and New York: Collins, 1969).

——. *Geschichte als Fortschritt*, 3 vols. (Cologne: Bachem, 1964–1966).

——. *Philosophy of the XX Century* (Dublin and Sidney: Gill and Macmillan, 1969).

——. *The Young Marx* (London: Sheed and Ward, 1967).

Dijksterhuis, E. J. *The Mechanisation of the World Picture* (Oxford: Oxford University Press, 1955).

Dooyeweerd, H. *A New Critique of Theoretical Thought*, 4 vols. (Amsterdam: Paris, 1953–1958).

——. *In the Twilight of Western Thought* (Philadelphia: Presbyterian and Reformed, 1960).

——. *Transcendental Problems of Philosophic Thought, an Inquiry into the Transcendental Conditions of Philosophy* (Grand Rapids, Mich.: Eerdmans, 1948).

Duintjer, O. D. *Rondom Regels* (Meppel: Boom, 1977).

Elders, L. *Aristotle's Cosmology. A Commentary on the De Caelo* (Assen: Van Gorcum, 1966).

Fortmann, H.M.M. *Als ziende de Onzienlijke*, 3 vols. (Hilversum: Paul Brand, 1964–1968).

Freudenthal, H. *Lincos. Design for Cosmic Intercourse* (Amsterdam: North-Holland, 1960).

——. *Mathematics Observed* (New York: McGraw-Hill, 1967).

——. *The Language of Logic* (Amsterdam: Elsevier, 1966).

Geurts, J.P.M. *Feit en theorie* (Assen: Van Gorcum, 1975).

Geyl, P. *Debates with Historians* (Groningen: Walters, 1955).

Gonda, J. *Change and Continuity in Indian Religion* (The Hague: Mouton, 1965).

Griffioen, S. *De roos en het kruis: Hegel* (Assen and Amsterdam: Van Gorcum, 1976).

Heering, H. J. *Ethiek der voorlopigheid* (Nijkerk: Callenbach, 1969).

——. *Inleiding tot de godsdienstwijsbegeerte* (Meppel: Boom, 1966).

Heyting, A. *Intuitionism: An Introduction*, 2d ed. (Amsterdam: North-Holland, 1966).

Hofstee, H. *Het Bijbels Personalisme van Ph. A. Kohnstamm* (Assen: Van Gorcum, 1973).

Hollak, J. *Van Causa sui tot automatic* (Hilversum: Paul Brand, 1966).

Hooykaas, R. *Religion and the Rise of Modern Science*, 2d ed. (Edinburgh and London: Scottish Academic Press, 1973).

——. *The Principle of Uniformity in Geology, Biology and Theology*, 2d ed. (Leiden: Brill, 1963).

Hubbeling, H. G. *Denkend geloven* (Assen: Van Gorcum, 1966).

——. *Language, Logic and Criterion* (Amsterdam: Born, 1971).

——. *Spinoza's Methodology* (Assen: Van Gorcum, 1964).

Ijsseling, S. I. *Rhetoric and Philosophy in Conflict* (The Hague: Nijhoff, 1976).

Klapwijk, J. *Dialektek der Verlichtung* (Assen: Van Gorcum, 1976).

——. *Tussen Historisme en Relativisme: Ernst Troeltsche* (Assen: Van Gorcum, 1970).

Koningsveld, H. *Het verschijnsel wetenschap* (Meppel: Boom, 1976).

Kuypers, K. *Immanuel Kant* (Baarn: Wereldvenster, 1966).

——. *Verspreide geschriften* (Assen: Van Gorcum, 1958).

Kwant, R. C. *Phenomenology of Expression* (Pittsburgh: Duquesne University Press, 1967).

——. *Phenomenology of Social Existence* (Pittsburgh: Duquesne University Press, 1965).

——. *Philosophy of Labor* (Pittsburgh: Duquesne University Press, 1960).

——. *The Phenomenological Philosophy of Merleau-Ponty* (Pittsburgh: Duquesne University Press, 1966).

Kwee, S. L. *De mens tussen mythe en machine* (Amsterdam: Wetenschappelijke Uitgeverij, 1974).

——. *Denken met de rechterhand* (Amsterdam: Elsevier, 1966).

Langeveld, M. J. *Studien zur Anthropologie des Kindes* (Tübingen: Niemeyer, 1956).

Lemaire, T. *Over de waarde van Kulturen* (Baarn: Wereldvenster, 1976).

Lever, J. *Where Are We Headed? A Christian Perspective on Evolution* (Grand Rapids, Mich.: Eerdmans, 1970).

Linschoten, J. *Auf dem Wege zu einer phänomenologischen Psychologie: W. James.* (Berlin: de Gruyter, 1961).

──. *Idolen van de psycholoog* (Utrecht: Bijleveld, 1965).

Locher, T.J.G. *Die Ueberwindung des europazentrischen Geschichtsbildes* (Wiesbaden: Steiner, 1954).

Loen, A. E. *Säkularisation* (Munich: Kaiser, 1965).

Luijpen, W. A. *Existential Phenomenology,* rev. ed. (Pittsburgh: Duquesne University Press, 1969).

──. *Myth and Metaphysics* (The Hague: Nijhoff, 1976).

──. *Phenomenology and Metaphysics* (Pittsburgh: Duquesne University Press, 1965).

──. *Theology as Anthropology* (Pittsburgh: Duquesne University Press, 1974).

Mannoury, G. *Handboek der Analytische significa,* 2 vols. (Bussum: Kroonder, 1947–1948).

Meyer, H. *Le role médiateur de la logique* (Assen: Van Gorcum, 1956).

Mooij, J.J.A. *La philosophie des mathématique de Henri Poincare* (Paris and Louvain: Nauwelaerts, 1966).

Nauta, D. *The Meaning of Information* (The Hague: Mouton, 1970).

Nota, J. H. *Phenomenology and History* (Chicago: Loyola University Press, 1967).

Nuchelmans, G. *Overzicht van analytische wijsbegeerte* (Utrecht and Antwerp: Het Spectrum, 1969).

──. *Theories of the Proposition. Ancient and Medieval Conceptions of the Bearers of Truth and Falsity* (Amsterdam and London: North-Holland, 1973).

──. *Wijsbegeerte en taal: twaalf studies* (Meppel: Boom, 1976).

Nuyens, F. *L'Evolution de la Psychologie d'Aristote,* 2d ed. (The Hague: Nijhoff, 1973).

Peperzak, A. *Le jeune Hegel et la vision morale du monde,* 2d ed. (Paris: Nijhoff, 1969).

──. *Vrijheid* (Utrecht: Ambo, 1972).

──. *Weefsels* (Baarn: Ambo, 1974).

Peters, J. *Metaphysics. A Systematic Study* (Pittsburgh: Duquesne University Press, 1964).

Plattel, M. G. *Utopian and Critical Thinking* (Pittsburgh: Duquesne University Press, 1972).

Poortman, J. J. *Ochema. De zin van het Hylisch pluralisme,* 5 vols. (Assen: Van Gorcum, 1954–1967).

──. *Philosophy, Theosophy, Parapsychology* (Leiden: Sijthoff, 1964).

Pranger, M. B. *Consequent Theology. Anselm of Canterbury* (Assen: Van Gorcum, 1975).

Quispel, G. *Gnosis als Weltreligion* (Zurich: Origo, 1951).

Raven, C. P. *Oogenesis. The Storage of Developmental Information* (Oxford: Pergamon, 1961).

Reitsma, G. W. E. *Troeltsch als godsdienstwijsgeer* (Assen: Van Gorcum, 1974).

Révész, G. (ed.). *Thinking and Speaking* (Amsterdam: North-Holland, 1954).

Robbers, H. *Neo-Thomisme en moderne wijsbegeerte* (Utrecht and Brussels: Het Spectrum, 1951).

Romein, H. *Theoretische geschiedenis* (Groningen: Wolters, 1946).

Sanders, C. *De behavioristische revolutie in de psychologie* (Deventer: Van Loghum Slateras, 1972).

Sarlemijn, A. *Hegelsche Dialektik* (Berlin and New York: de Gruyter, 1971).

Sassen, F.L.R. "Dutch Philosophy," in *The Encyclopedia of Philosophy,* III, ed. P. Edwards (New York: Macmillan and the Free Press, 1967).

──. *Geschiedenis der Wijsbegeerte,* 5 vols. (Amsterdam: North-Holland, 1945–1957).

──. *Geschiedenis van de wijsbegeerte in Nederland tot het einde van de 19e eeuw* (Amsterdam and Brussels: Elsevier, 1959).

──. *Wijsgerig leven in Nederland in de twintigste eeuw,* 3d ed. (Amsterdam: North-Holland, 1960).

Schuurman, E. *Techniek en toekomst* (Assen: Van Gorcum, 1972).

Sperna-Weiland, J. *Philosophy of Existence and Christianity. Kierkegaard, Jaspers* (Assen: Van Gorcum, 1951).

Springer, J. L. *Waar, wat en wie is God?* (Wageningen: Veenman, 1969).

Staal, J. F. *Advaita and Neo-Platonism* (Madras: University of Madras, 1961).

Strasser, S. *Phenomenology and the Social Sciences* (Pittsburgh: Duquesne University Press, 1963).

──. *The Idea of Dialogical Phenomenology* (Pittsburgh: Duquesne University Press, 1970).

156   Western Europe, Australia, and Israel

————. *The Soul in Metaphysical and Empirical Psychology* (Pittsburgh: Duquesne University Press, 1957).

Tennekes, J. *Anthropology. Relativism and Method* (Assen: Van Gorcum, 1971).

Thijssen-Schoute, C. L. *Nederlands Cartesianisme* (Amsterdam: North-Holland, 1954).

van Asperen, G. M. *Hope and History: A Critical Inquiry into the Philosophy of Ernst Bloch* (Thesis, University of Utrecht, 1973).

van Buitenen, J.A.B. *Ramanuja on the Bhagavadgita* (The Hague: Mouton, 1953).

van Dalen, D. *Formele logica* (Utrecht: Oosthoek, 1971).

van Dijk, R.J.A. *Gesellschaft und Gesellschaftswissenshaft* (Leiden: Sijthoff, 1973).

van Dooren, W. *Vragenderwijs* (Assen: Van Gorcum, 1975).

van Haersolte, R.A.V. *Personifactie van sociale systemen* (Deventer: Kluwer, 1971).

van Laer, P. H. *Philosophy of Science*, 2 vols. (Pittsburgh: Duquesne University Press, 1956–1962).

van Melsen, A.G.M. *Evolution and Philosophy* (Pittsburgh: Duquesne University Press, 1965).

————. *From Atomos to Atom* (New York: Harper, 1960).

————. *Physical Science and Ethics* (Pittsburgh: Duquesne University Press, 1967).

————. *Science and Responsibility* (Pittsburgh: Duquesne University Press, 1970).

————. *Science and Technology* (Pittsburgh: Duquesne University Press, 1961).

————. *The Philosophy of Nature*, 5th ed. (Pittsburgh: Duquesne University Press, 1961).

van Peursen, C. A. *Body, Soul, Spirit* (London: Oxford University Press, 1966).

————. *Orientación filosófica* (Barcelona: Herder, 1975).

————. *Phenomenology and History* (Chicago: Loyola University Press, 1967).

————. *Phenomenology and Reality* (Pittsburgh: Duquesne University Press, 1972).

————. *Une stratégie de la culture* (Paris and Brussels: Elsevier-Sequoia, 1976).

————. *Wirklichkeit als Ereignis* (Freiburg and Munich: Alber, 1971).

van Riessen, H. *The University and its Basis* (Ontario: Reformed Publications, 1963).

————. *Wijsbegeerte* (Kampen: Kok, 1970).

van Waerden, B. L. *Science Awakening. Egyptian, Babylonian and Greek Mathematics* (New York: Science Editions, 1963).

van Winden, J.C.M. *Calcidius on Matter*, 2d ed. (Leiden: Brill, 1965).

van den Berg, J. H. *A Different Existence: Principles of Phenomenological Psychopathology* (Pittsburgh: Duquesne University Press, 1972).

————. *Divided Existence and Complex Society* (Pittsburgh: Duquesne University Press, 1974).

————. *The Changing Nature of Man* (New York: Dell, 1964).

————. *Things: Four Metabletic Reflections* (Pittsburgh: Duquesne University Press, 1970).

van der Hoeven, J. *Karl Marx, the Roots of His Thought* (Assen and Amsterdam: Van Gorcum, 1976).

van der Klaauw, C. J. "Biology and Philosophy," in *Philosophy in the Mid-Century*, ed. R. Klibansky (Firenze: Nuova Italia, 1958).

van der Leeuw, G. *Religion in Its Essence and Manifestations*, 2d ed. (London: Allen and Unwin, 1962).

Verhaar, J. M. *Some Relations Between Perception, Speech and Thought* (Assen: Van Gorcum, 1963).

Verhoeven, C.W.M. *Het grote gebeuren* (Utrecht: Ambo, 1966).

————. *Rondom de legeete*, 5th ed. (Utrecht: Ambo, 1967).

Waardenburg, J.D.J. *L'Islam dans le miroir de l'occident*, 2d ed. (The Hague: Mouton, 1963).

Zanstra, H. *The Construction of Reality* (Oxford: Pergamon, 1962).

Züricher, E. and Vos, F. *Spel zonder snaren* (Deventer: Kluwer, 1964).

Zwart, P. J. *Het mysterie tijd* (Assen: Van Gorcum, 1971).

SPECIAL BIBLIOGRAPHICAL NOTE

A complete bibliography of philosophical studies by Netherlands philosophers can be found in:
Poortman, J. J. *Repertorium der Nederlandse Wijsbegeerte* (Amsterdam and Assen: Wereldbibliotheek, 1948).

————. *Repertorium, Supplement I* (Amsterdam and Assen: Wereldbibliotheek, 1958).

Klever, W.N.A. *Repertorium, Part III. (1958–1967)* (Amsterdam and Assen: Wereldbibliotheek, 1968).

A description of the contents of the works of the chief Dutch philosophers of the twentieth century can be found in:
Sassen, F.L.R. *Wijsgerig leven in Nederland in de twintigste eeuw*, 3d ed. (Amsterdam: North-Holland, 1960).

JOURNALS

Algemeen Nederlands Lijdschrift Voor Wijsbegeerte
Amersfoortse Stemmen
Beweging
Bijdragen
Bulletin International d'Esthétique
Erkenntnis
Handelingen Van Het Nederlands Filosofisch Genootschap
International Humanism
Kennis en Methode
Lier en Boog
Phronesis
Poznań Studies in the Philosophy of the Sciences and the Humanities
Rechtsphilosophie en Rechtstheorie
Scripta Recenter Edita

Norway

ARNE NAESS AND JON HELLESNES

I

"This is WAR! Go home!" When airborne troops invaded Norway on April 9, 1940, children and teenagers rushed out to see what was happening. The invading soldiers had to shout warnings when the young and curious stood in their way of advance. Norway was mentally quite unprepared for war, but the stern realities could not long be ignored. Later, beginning in about 1943, "illegal" newspapers contained detailed, horrifying descriptions of death camps and of torture. In a building only three hundred yards from the main university complex in Oslo, torture was applied to people some of us knew very well. Many young philosophers lost their lives or underwent hellish experiences before the guns were silenced. Then came the disgusting persecutions of people who had been on the "wrong" side, and, in 1947, the cold war got started.

These awesome events made most of the "academic philosophers" feel obliged to take up problems closely related to social issues. This situation encouraged cooperation with the new sociological and other social science researchers, many of whom were refugees from Germany and Austria, and were now operating from superbly endowed institutions in the United States. Generous grants from that country made it easy to establish contacts of lasting value. Whereas philosophy in Norway had been influenced largely by Germany, Austria, and France, intimate Anglo-American contacts strengthened the influence of Anglo-American trends of thought.

The most conspicuous trend in Norwegian philosophy during the first fifteen years after the war was the so-called Oslo school of empirical semantics[1] which regarded central formulations in the history of philosophical ideas as sources of thinking, deliberation, and action rather than expressing definite doctrines. Thus, the formulations "the will is free," "spirit is more real than matter," "democracy is the best form of government," and "freedom is not opposed to necessity" are considered point of departure formulations capable of indefinitely many interpretations in indefinitely many directions. Terms isolated from sentences are considered still more liable to diverse interpretations. If a formulation expressing an interpretation of a point of departure formulation excludes some of its other interpretations and admits no new ones, it is called "precisation." Since communication goes on in an ever changing world amidst changing cir-

Part I is written by Arne Naess, Part II by Jon Hellesnes.

cumstances and social settings, precisations are not permanent. What for some persons in some situations is a "precisation" is a "deprecisation" for others.

Accordingly, for every person or group there is a limited depth or definiteness of intention. Thus, if a philosopher or anybody else is asked persistently about what he or she meant by "people" or "rule" in the sentence "the rule of the people is (is not) the best form of rule," there will, if honesty prevails, sooner or later be answers of the *"nescio* class," that is, admitting that a certain discrimination between two slightly different precisations is relevant but was not made. The intention did not reach the depth which is presupposed in that particular discrimination.

Philosophical research, as opposed to philosophizing, consists mainly in the explication and exploration of points of view or general perspectives by making them maximally precise in a maximally wide context and the assessment of the validity of the ensuing philosophical or other systems. "Or other" is an important addition because making them precise in certain ways will result in views belonging to old or new sciences. Thus, a subgroup of precisations of "x is infinite" leads into old branches of mathematics, and a subgroup of precisations of "x has greater freedom of decision than y" leads into social science. The main work of Harald Ofstad consisted in tracing precisations of just this sentence.

Precisation of philosophical point of departure formulations has led to new scientific disciplines, for instance, psychophysics. The philosophic researcher should be task-minded, not discipline-minded, and should follow his questions wherever they lead.

According to this school of thought, it is to be expected that the flow of questions from philosophy to the sciences will continue indefinitely. But the direction may well be reversed as has happened in modern physics, where formulations believed to be definitively established in a closed and secure science reverted to the extremely open field of philosophical reflection.

The Oslo school of semantics elicited widespread interest, but also a good deal of perplexity.[1] In stressing empirical research, it sometimes deliberately provoked the serious philosopher and logician through the use of the most depreciated research instrument—questionnaires—inside the most holy domains, such as those of the eternal questions concerning truth, certainty, contradiction, and *tertium non datur.*

On the other hand, empirical semantics did not in any way hold that philosophy or metaphysics could and should be reduced to, or made into, science. In these matters, it firmly rejected logical empiricist, early Wittgensteinian, as well as Oxford ordinary language views. It found itself free to make use of any research instruments of old or new sciences without discarding traditional central philosophical or metaphysical formulations. They were considered more or less inexhaustible as sources of thought, deliberation, and action. In ethics and politics, the job of the philosopher is mainly to make explicit and to announce norms, not to remain on the metalevel of analysis. This goes against the tenets of most analytical trends.

Considering the relation of philosophy to social and political questions to be intimate, Arne Naess accepted the job as a leader of the UNESCO project on the controversies between East and West. Starting just before the cold war began, Naess and Stein Rokkan made this project into an instrument of contact between more than four hundred researchers and politicians in the various ideological camps. The history of the usages of the term "democracy" was stressed, including the precisations from the time of Plato and Aristotle in both a Western and a Soviet direction. This and other themes were taken up in an effort to show that both belonged to old, wide European traditions.

The value of this research for the "third point of view" was discovered by the administration, and continuation of the project was forbidden. UNESCO had to be very cautious because of the cold war, and "hot" issues had to be avoided. If not, certain nations would threaten to leave the institution. The volume *Democracy in a World of Tension* rapidly sold out and was not reprinted. In Christian circles, it was found unpardonable to speak about the "precisation of 'God' "; communists objected to expressions such as "the slogans 'Communism' and 'Fascism'."

This brings us to the vivid interest of the Oslo school in performative uses of language. Under the influence of Carl Bühler, Bronislaw Malinowski and others in anthropology, the scientific cognitive use was seen not only as extremely important culturally but also as a very special case of the use of language. The school tried to introduce opposition to the very considerable influence of Frege and symbolic logic in attacking problems of language. For example, the school found an abysmal contrast between the level of definiteness of intention in Tarski's treatise on the definition of truth and his formulations about the relation of his findings to the ordinary use of the term "true."

Intense interest in empirical semantic research and in the ethics of precise unbiased communication made publication in the more or less metaphysical fields of philosophy difficult but not impracticable. This was shown notably by Peter Wessel Zapffe (1899–   ) who published a dramaturgy with stress both on metaphysical and empirico-semantical aspects. He looked for increased testability of aesthetical merit through operational definitions. This effort alienated him from the strong Christian, neoplatonic, and *geisteswissenschaftliche* traditions in Norway. His cooperation with Arne Naess found its point of departure formulation in Zapffe's combined mythical and philosophical sentence to the effect that once long ago man awakened and saw the human self and experienced the brotherhood of pain between all living beings.

Naess has elaborated this theme stressing identification with all living beings, an ethics of nonviolence in conflict, and the unlimited source of joy (Spinoza's *hilaritas*) and of human understanding (Spinoza's *cognitio tertium genris*) made possible through the brotherhood of pain and joy. Zapffe, on the other hand, has found that for the first time in the history of man the capacity of the human brain has revealed the atrocity and lack of justice in the universe. Human nature is such that humans either must refuse to live in a universe without a moral order or must distract themselves from conscious experience of injustice through entertainment and other activities that have narrow perspectives.

According to Zapffe, *homo sapiens* is overdeveloped in relation to the limited possibilities of existence. The adequate population policy is a lenient, long-term reduction to zero. Zapffe's philosophy of life, nature, and culture is written in an exquisite language with both poetical and scientific undertones. It may be said to represent an original Scandinavian form of existentialism, if we permit ourselves to use vague current isms.

The main work of Zapffe, *The Essence of Tragedy* (1941), introduces a "qualified" sense of the term "tragedy" as a sort of life history: the destruction of the perfect exactly because of its perfection, or the catastrophe of the most qualified being because of its quality. The human species crowns the evolution of life but at the same time involves its rejection. The tragic figures of human history are those who because of their higher merit are destroyed by fate and their fellow men. The category of tragedy as developed by Zapffe is thus clearly separated from the mere sorrowful or melancholy, and is made into a philosophical, not a dramaturgical, concept.

After ceasing to believe in the possibility of establishing a consistent kind of empirical theory of knowledge, Naess came to hold that any theory of knowledge presupposes, at least on the metalevel, all major philosophical disciplines, including methodological rules and an entire ontology. No decisive arguments seem to be at hand which can separate valid from invalid consistent general systems—if they ever were elaborated. Naess accordingly embraced a skepticism in the sense of Sextus, that is, not denying the possibility of verified knowledge but finding no decisive kinds of arguments. Among Norwegian philosophers only Gullvåg and Hannay reached similar conclusions.

Thus, in the last years of the 1950s no general tendencies were apparent in Norway. Publications in empirical semantics were reduced to a mere trickle, and these were mostly by Swedish authors. Social science got more professional than ever just when an effort was made through the institution of the journal *Inquiry* to revive the cooperation between social science and philosophy.

In the ensuing vacuum, Hans Skjervheim introduced German social and transcendental philosophy into Norway. He objected to the "objectivist" and "positivist" character of Norwegian social science. Indeed, there was a kind of "positivistic" stress on the collection of data in harmony with the latest and most refined statistical and other techniques. Politically and socially relevant subjects (nearly always in favor of peace or "the underdog") were covered, but the problems of "operationalization" inevitably narrowed the scope as well as the number of participants in the research process. The rest of us were mere consumers!

The criticism by Skjervheim did not change the research methodology, but it did open a rich field of philosophical and social subjects where an intensive resource collection of new data was either of secondary importance or impracticable. Thus, social as well as political philosophy could engage a much wider circle of active participants. They concentrated on reflection and discussion rather than on research requiring testability through empirical procedures.

The international ecological movement revitalized the philosophy of nature. Through a number of small but beautiful and belligerent articles, Zapffe anticipated the general moral and philosophical condemnation of the destruction of life and of technical-industrial civilization. The latter's attack upon the dignity and intrinsic value of nonhuman nature revealed basic attitudes that would have to change, or else a radical human self-destruction would ensue. Naess developed an "ecosophy," a philosophy inspired by the attitude of field ecologists adhering in principle to the equal right of living beings to live and flourish. From this point of view, the crisis is a value crisis as much as one of political economy. It is one of eco-sophy rather than of eco-logy and eco-nomy.

Whereas the Oslo semantical school and Zapffe's philosophy of tragedy most clearly dominated Norwegian philosophy in the 1940s and 1950s, valuable philosophical work was carried out in a variety of fields in those years and later that was not part of a national or Scandinavian trend. Unfortunately, the work of these scholars is not adaptable to a short survey: hence, this article must somewhat arbitrarily be limited to a discussion of a small number of contributions.

Professor Knut Erik Tranøy at the University of Bergen has long defended the rationality of normative ethical activity.[2] More specifically, he has worked in the ethics of science, stressing the normative presuppositions and implications of scientific activity which is understood as organized norm- and value-governed social action.[3] In numerous lectures and in articles in newspapers, Professor Tranøy has discussed normative ethical questions in a broad public setting. Norwegian philosophers profit from the smallness of the country. Its many newspapers are less centralized and are dominated by more professional journalists than those in large countries like the United States. The voices of philosophers are heard (but, of course, are rarely taken seriously at the top political level).

Professor Egil A. Wyller, who has also been very active in a broad social setting, has worked out a Platonic form of Christian philosophy of unity called "henology."[4] As a holder of a chair in the History of Ideas within Antiquity, Professor Wyller has published works (mainly in German) on Plato, especially on the *Parmenides* and the later period of Platonic thought, and on Platonism, especially Nicholas of Cusa. He is now working on a systematic and personal exposition (in Norwegian) of henological thought, based on the tradition of Plato, Nicholas of Cusa, and Kant. He refers extensively to today's thinkers Heidegger and Adorno.

Since the early 1950s, Professor Dagfinn Stigen has worked within the Aristotelian tradition, not only as a scholar, but also as a participant in contemporary pedagogical and general social debate. He maintains that the Aristotelian view of man set forth in Aristotle's psychological and biological writings (with consequences for his ethics) is of importance and relevance for life-styles in our big technical-industrial societies. Basing his theories upon Aristotle, he sees man in close relation to the rest of nature. These relations define the conditions under which man can achieve happiness. Man is a biological being who needs the rest of nature. In the pedagogical and social debate, Stigen thus maintains a "green political philosophy" on his own philosophical premises.

Dagfinn Føllesdal, professor at Oslo and Stanford universities, has concentrated for many years on the phenomenon of consciousness, approaching it via a study of intentionality and meaning. Frege, Husserl, and Quine are among the philosophers he often refers to in his argumentations.[5] Taking for granted that we do not experience "bodies" but "persons," not "movements" but "actions," he asks: When we have these experiences, exactly what do we experience? How far can we get through an empirical approach to this kind of problem? What can be found out about intentionality and meaning, about understanding others in communication, on the basis of evidence gathered by the senses? Turning the tables, he also asks: What can this realm of phenomena teach us about empiricism?

II

In surveys of contemporary philosophy, Scandinavian philosophy is sometimes referred to by the term "analytical philosophy" and it is suggested that the philosophical orientation is roughly of the same kind as in the Anglo-American world. It is true that Scandinavian philosophy normally has an "analytical" rather than a "continental" orientation; it is also true that Norwegian philosophy has the characteristics of "normal" Scandinavian philosophy. Scholarly studies in the field of logical theory, the analytical philosophy of science, ethics, the history of philosophy, and so forth have been made. Norwegian philosophy, however, includes a trend that is rather atypical for Scandinavian philosophy. This atypical trend is treated here at length.

The starting point of the atypical trend was 1959, the publication date of *Objectivism and the Study of Man* by Hans Skjervheim. "Objectivism" stands for something to be criticized. It does not denote one philosophical position, but rather a family of philosophical and metascientific positions, including certain interpretations of naturalism, logical empiricism, pragmatism, behaviorism, and so forth. The "objectivism" of such positions was said to consist in the methodological transformation of "subjective" and "intersubjective" phenomena (e.g., meaning, reason, intention, action) into "objective" phenomena (e.g., data, cause, behavior) and in the methodological reduction of intentional to extentional sentences.

The critique of "objectivism" was carried out partly by elaborating some elementary distinctions that were presented as epistemologically and ontologically important. These were the distinctions between, for instance, vocal noises and verbal statements, behavioral movements and intentional acts, causal explanations and justifications by reasons, predictions of behavioral reactions and first person statements of intention, participant and observational attitudes. (Here we will refer to Skjervheim and his followers as "anti-objectivists.")

When arguing for the fundamental status of distinctions of this kind, the anti-objectivist very often turned to continental schools such as phenomenology, existentialism, and the *Verstehen* tradition in sociology (Dilthey, Weber, and Schütz). In the early 1960s, Dag Österberg and Audun Öfsti, in addition to Hans Skjervheim, were the main figures in this anti-objectivist school. Later, especially as the school turned more neo-Marxist, there were a number of others (including one of the authors of this article).

The continental orientation of the anti-objectivists also inspired scholarly studies of continental thinkers. Such studies can be said to have had a feedback influence on the anti-objectivist group. Studies of the philosophy of Heidegger were carried out by G. Flöistad, A. Naess, and G. Skirbekk. E. A. Wyller's studies of Plato's dialectics also seem to have influenced the milieu.

The anti-objectivsts shared some ideas with the post-Wittgensteinians. In the early 1960s, there was a group studying the philosophy of the later Wittgenstein (including J. Melöe, W. Rossvaer, K. S. Johannessen, H. Johannessen, and E. Dalseth). But the interaction between anti-objectivism and Wittgensteinian philosophy did not come until the middle and late 1960s. The anti-objectivists seem to have developed their ideas independently of Wittgensteinian or post-Wittgensteinian philosophy. In trying to present anti-objectivist thinking, however, we shall find it useful to compare these two kinds of philosophy.

Quite a few studies in the philosophy of mind are inquiries into the use of terms like "intention," "reason," and "wish"; that is, everyday terms for everyday behavior. Both the post-Wittgensteinians and the anti-objectivists agree that any methodological elimination of such terms blurs the essential characteristics of human behavior.

The following position can be maintained. The language of physics is radically different from ordinary language. This position cannot, however, be turned into an argument against physics. Why should it be an argument against behavioral and social scientists that their language is radically different from ordinary language? The post-Wittgensteinians, at least some of them, would answer that human behavior and ordinary language have a noncontingent relation to each other. (See Charles Taylor, "Explaining Action," *Inquiry.*) The anti-objectivists would give a similar answer. They would say that there is a constitutive or internal relation between ordinary (intentional) language and human behavior, and that actions are different from natural processes because they are mediated by concepts. In the case of the apple falling to the ground, either we have a concept of gravitation or not, i.e., the natural phenomenon gravitation is not conceptually mediated. The social phenomenon *making a promise,* on the other hand, would exist only if the social agents themselves had a concept of "promise" and a set of rules governing "promise-behavior," the relation between the performative act of making a promise and the concept of promise being noncontingent. It would be odd to say that people in the *x*-society are making and keeping promises, but that they neither know what they are doing nor have any ideas of what making and keeping promises mean. The post-Wittgensteinians as well as the anti-objectivists view the oddity of such a statement as important. They refer to it in arguing that the concept of promise is "present" in the "promise-behavior" and that the concept therefore cannot be conceived of as a construct in theoretical explanations of "promise-behavior." One of the main theses in Peter Winch, *The Idea of a Social Science,* is that the notion of society involves a scheme of concepts that is logically incompatible with the kinds of explanation offered in the natural sciences. The anti-objectivists gradually "discovered" this book.

In comparing post-Wittgensteinian and anti-objectivist philosophy, we find the term "family resemblance" more adequate than "similarity." The two schools were not simply formulating the same ideas in different philosophical idioms. There is clearly a difference of opinion. While the post-Wittgensteinians, or at least some of them, were analyzing social institutions in terms of language games—"leaving everything as it is"—the anti-objectivists tried to criticize institutions. The critique of value neutrality in social science is a fundamental anti-objectivist project. The identification of this project is probably also the identification of one of the fundamental differences between post-Wittgensteinian and anti-objectivist philosophy.

Here we will try to show that the critique of institutions was conceived of as analogous to the critique of theories. Whether the sociological theory *T* is valid or not valid is not dependent upon what people think of its validity. It is not a question of public opinion. The validity of *T* cannot be checked by inquiries into the number of citizens believing that *T* is true. The social scientist claiming that *T* is true will, of course, defend his claim by reference to his empirical findings, but the (eventual) fact that the majority believe that *T* is true is irrelevant. In order to defend his truth-claim, the social scientist has to argue as a participant in the "community of investigators." He cannot defend his own truth-claim through neutral observational statements about what is accepted or not accepted by public opinion. He has to participate in scientific discourse. The question of the validity of empirical theories is in this sense not an empirical question. Instead of merely mentioning arguments, the social scientist has to use arguments; that is, he has to argue. Empirical arguments are arguments when performatively used in the attitude of a participant. To say this is to stress the importance of intersubjective discourse in scientific research.

Very few, however, would deny the difference between using an argument and mentioning generally accepted arguments. Pointing out the difference, therefore, seems to be nothing more than a trivial identification of a generally accepted distinction. But the anti-objectivists tried to do more than this. One of their questions was the following: What is the relation between the intersubjective discourse of science and everyday communication? In answering this question, they tried to show (as transcendental philosophers) that the conditions of the possibility of scientific communication are also the conditions of the possibility of interaction and communication more generally. Since the intersubjective communication of scientific investigators is embedded in the intersubjective communication of the lived-world *(Lebenswelt)*, scientists are committed to the lived-world in the sense that they have to legitimate themselves vis-à-vis the community of the lived-world. The "objectivist" reduction of the lived-world or the social community to a mere field of research was considered as the elimination of the context in which the normative problems of social science could be intersubjectively formulated.

When stressing the difference between use and mention, between the participant and observational attitude, the anti-objectivists also tried to make people aware of a whole "family" of distinctions referring to intersubjectivity, "the forgotten theme" as Skjervheim called it. To this "family" of distinctions belongs the distinction between showing that a political system is legitimate and showing that it is accepted as legitimate by public opinion. The awareness of this distinction seems to be a necessary condition of the critique of ideology.

If general acceptance were the criterion of a legitimate political system, it would be absurd to talk about general acceptance and public opinion in terms of false consciousness and ideology. The independent status of legitimacy is a necessary condition for the meaningfulness of this kind of talk. Does this mean that the critique of ideology presupposes an elitarian and privileged position from which "legitimate" and "illegitimate" are predicated of political systems? The anti-objectivists would answer certainly not! We will try to show what is meant by this answer, first by discussing two statements (1) "The government fought a cause accepted as just by the people"; (2) "The government fought a just cause." The difference between them stands out when we add "but it fought an unjust cause." Statement (1) will not turn into a contradiction by this addition. It will, however, turn into a statement about the error and the illusion of the people, about false consciousness. On the other hand, by this addition statement (2) will turn into a contradiction, being a statement in which the contradictory terms "just" and "unjust" are predicated of the same subject.

Now, the question is this: Is a statement about widespread false consciousness necessarily an elitarian judgment? If the answer were yes, the implication seems to be that such a statement could not, and necessarily could not, be intersubjectively argued for. But such a necessity does not seem to exist. It is possible, but not necessary, that the statement is made from an elitarian position, i.e., that it is made by an observer who does not see any point in discussing his statement with people. But if the statement is made to people, it "pragmatically" implies a truth-claim which has to be defended by arguments vis-à-vis the people. Because it has to be defended, it is possible that the statement might turn out to be wrong and unjustifiable. In other words, the statement about false consciousness can be presented in a way that is similar to statements about errors made by scientists to their colleagues.

The questions of whether a theory is true or whether a political system is legitimate cannot be fully answered simply by observing what most people think about the theory or the political system. In order to find the answers, we ourselves have to assess the reasons being presented as reasons for accepting the theory or the political system. We have to decide whether they are good reasons or not; we have to defend a position in the current discussion. At least this is the opinion of the anti-objectivists.

"Truth," "justice," and other such concepts are said to involve a claim for acceptance, and such a claim we have to assess. The participant attitude is the attitude of assessment of the claims being made. The anti-objectivists have also argued that the value-neutral abstinence from assessment of, for instance, claims for legitimacy is indirectly an acceptance of the status quo and thus a conservative attitude.

The possibility of experimental observation, for example, the possibility of keeping one variable constant while varying another, refers to a special kind of relationship between the experimenting observer and the phenomena observed. The anti-objectivists describe this relationship as a subject-object relation wherein the subject is controlling the object and its conditions of behavior.

In order to explicate the point of the anti-objectivists, we will refer to the object of explanation as "historically resting" and to the explaining subject as "historically moving." What we suggest by this terminology, is that, for instance, Galileo Galilei and modern scientists are facing the same nature. According to this terminology, the universe of physical phenomena has been "resting" from the time of Galileo Galilei to our time. The scientific approach to this same nature has indeed changed very much; science has been "historically moving." When we say that modern science has better explanations of the behavior of natural phenomena than Galileo Galilei had, we presuppose the unchangeability of nature. If Galileo Galilei and modern scientists were facing different natures, we could hardly talk about scientific progress. The comparison between different levels of scientific development seems to presuppose something constant that constitutes the standard of comparison. The comparison is relatively easy if the object of research can be said to be constant over time.

The "unchangeability of nature" is also the precondition for establishing experimental techniques giving the same results at time t_1 as at t_n. The repeatability of experiments is a precondition for establishing natural laws. On the basis of established natural laws, we are able to predict and control. The control is facilitated by our ability to predict what happens under such and such conditions, conditions that we are technically able to produce. According to this scientific paradigm, established theoretical knowledge facilitates technology. A technologist is able to take advantage systematically of predictable regularities in nature. He talks about ends and means. To know the means to an end E is to know the causal factors of E. Ends and means, effects and causes, are correlative distinctions.

If nature "made up her mind" to behave in a radically different way, if she "made up her mind" to get "historically moving," our experiments would not be repeatable as experiments giving the same results at different moments of time. The concept of experiment and the concept of technological control would at the same time have been very problematic indeed (as they are in the social sciences). We would have to suppress nature in order to make her react according to the established laws of nature. The technological control would thereby change into a kind of authoritarian and technocratic manipulation. Accordingly, to transfer the subject-object relation to the social field seems to be a political act, the consequences of which are technocratic control and manipulation.

This kind of talk is conceptually too poor to say very much about natural science. But to say much about natural science was not the intention of the anti-objectivists. What they intended to say something about was the epistemological and ontological constitution of objects, or rather "the constitution of the meaning of possible objects of experience," to use a phrase of transcendental philosophy. They tried to say something about the constitutional difference between natural and social phenomena.

According to the anti-objectivists, the relationship between the social scientist and his field of inquiry cannot be conceived as a subject-object relation. There is a kind of reciprocity in the relationship that is overlooked in this kind of conception. It is theoretically and practically important that the social scientist belongs to the same "ontological order" as his theme of inquiry and that sociological research is a process going on in society. By reducing his field of inquiry to another order than that to which he himself belongs, i.e., when the social scientist tries to transform the subject-subject relation into a subject-object relation, he produces a relation of technocratic control and manipulation. According to the anti-objectivists, there is not only a political commitment in discussions of the "aims of social engineering." The definition of applied social science as social technology and engineering antecedently is politically committed to technocracy.

The anti-objectivists anticipated many ideas that later became well known as the ideas of "critical theory." Concepts like "one-dimensional thinking" and "control-knowledge" (*Herrschaftswissen*) were used before anybody knew about Herbert Marcuse or Jürgen Habermas. Later, the anti-objectivists developed their ideas explicitly through discussions of the "critical theory" of Jürgen Habermas and the "transcendental pragmatics" of Karl Otto Apel. Such discussions have sometimes resulted in a kind of "self-criticism" among the anti-objectivists.

"Ethics of science" is a field of inquiry that represents a challenge to the anti-objectivists. In Norway, the analytical philosopher Knut Erik Tranøy has done interesting work in this field. There seems to be a growing interest in his work among the anti-objectivists. The ecological problems and the "eco-sophy" of Naess are also a challenge. To some extent, this challenge has been taken up by Gunnar Skirbekk.

Representative texts have been collected and edited by Rune Slagstad (*Positivisme, dialektikk, materialisme* ["Positivism, Dialectic, Materialism"]). The *fetschrift* to Skjervheim (*Refleksjon og handling* ["Reflection and Action"]) is also representative of the anti-objectivists.

NOTES

1. *Literature. Oslo School of Empirical Semantics and related works.* Because of the scarcity of resources just after the war, some of the most interesting studies were only mimeographed. In the bibliography, studies written in English are given priority of mention.

2. This was already the main theme of his doctoral dissertation in 1953, *On the Logic of Normative Systems*. Also see his article "Ought Implies Can: A Bridge from Fact to Norm?" published in two parts in *Ratio*.

3. See his article in *Contemporary Aspects of Philosophy*, edited by Gilbert Ryle.

4. Conference article "Henologie," in *Historisches Wörterbuch der Philosophie.*

5. The second volume of W. Stegmüller's *Hauptströmungen der Gegenwartsphilosophie* places the philosophy of Føllesdal in a larger setting.

SELECT BIBLIOGRAPHY

BOOKS AND ARTICLES*

Christopherson, J. A. *The Meaning of "Democracy" as Used in European Ideologies from the French to the Russian Revolution* (Oslo: Universitetsforlaget, 1967).

Gullvåg, I. "Criteria of Meaning and Analysis of Usage," *Synthese* 9 (1954).

————. *Definiteness of Intention* (Oslo: Universitetsforlaget, 1951).

Hellesnes, J. *Sjølvkunnskapen og det framande* ("Self-knowledge and Other Minds") (Oslo: Tanum, 1968).

————. *Sosialiserung og teknokrati* ("Socialization and Technocracy") (Oslo: Gyldendal, 1975).

McKeon, R. and Rokkan, S. (eds.). *Democracy in a World of Tensions* (Chicago: University of Chicago Press, 1951).

Naess, A. *Communication and Argument. Elements of Applied Semantics,* trans. A. Hannay (Oslo: Universitetsforlaget, London: Allen and Unwin, and Totowa, N. J.: Bedminster Press, 1966).

————. *Four Modern Philosophers. Carnap, Wittgenstein, Heidegger, Sartre,* trans. A. Hannay (Chicago: University of Chicago Press, 1965).

————. *Gandhi and Group Conflict* (Oslo: Universitetsforlaget, 1974).

————. *Interpretation and Preciseness. A Contribution to the Theory of Communication,* Det Norske videnskabsakademi i Oslo (Oslo: I kommisjon hos J. Dybwad, 1953).

————. "Logical Equivalence, Intentional Isomorphism and Synonymity as Studied by Questionnaires. Sacred to the Memory of Gerrit Mannoury," *Synthese* 10 (1956–1958).

————. "Synonymity as Revealed by Intuition," *Philosophical Review* 66 (1957).

————. "Toward a Theory of Interpretation and Preciseness," *Theoria* 15 (1949); rpt. in *Semantics and the Philosophy of Language,* ed. L. Linsky (Urbana, Ill.: University of Illinois Press, 1952).

————. "What Does 'Testability' Mean? An Account of a Procedure Developed by Ludvig Løvestad," *Methodos* 9 (1957).

————, Christophersen, J. A., and Kvalø, K. *Democracy, Ideology and Objectivity. Studies in the Semantics and Cognitive Analysis of Ideological Controversy* (Oslo: Oslo University Press, and Oxford: Blackwell, 1956).

*The title in Norwegian where given is followed by the English translation within parentheses.

Ofstad, H. *An Inquiry into the Freedom of Decision* (Oslo: Norwegian Universities Press, 1961).

———. "The Descriptive Definition of the Concept 'Legal Norm' as Proposed by Hans Kelsen," *Theoria* 16 (1950).

———. *Refleksjon og handling: festskrift til Hans Skjervheim på 50-årsdagen 9. oktober, 1976,* ("Reflection and Action: Festschrift for Hans Skjervheim on his 50th Birthday October 9, 1976") red. komité A. Haga, H. Høibraaten, and A. Måseide (Oslo: Gyldendal, 1976).

Ryle, G. (ed.). *Contemporary Aspects of Philosophy* (London and Boston: Routledge and Kegan Paul, 1977).

Simonsson, T. *Logical and Semantic Structures in Christian Discourses* (Oslo: Universitetsforlaget, 1971).

Skjervheim, H. *Objectivism and the Study of Man* (Oslo: Universitetsforlaget, 1959); rpt. in *Inquiry* 17 (1975).

Slagstad, R. *Positivisme, dialektikk, materialisme* ("Positivism, Dialectic, Materialism") (Oslo: Universitetsforlaget, 1976).

Stegmüller, W. *Hauptströmunger der Gegenwartsphilosophie,* 2 vols. (Stuttgart: Kröner, 1975).

Taylor, C. "Explaining Action," *Inquiry* 13 (1970).

Tennessen, H. (also Tønnesen, H.). *Holdninger til rettsoppgjøret 1945-1948* ("Attitudes Toward Legal Settlement 1945-1948") (Oslo: Universitetsforlaget, 1950).

———. *Language Analysis and Empirical Semantics, Eighteen Papers* (Edmonton, Alberta: University of Alberta, 1964).

———. "Ordinary Language in Memoriam," *Inquiry* 8 (1965).

———. *Typebegreper, I, II* ("Type Concepts, I, II") (Oslo: Universitetsforlaget, 1949).

Tranøy, K. E. *On the Logic of Normative Systems* (Thesis, Cambridge University, 1953).

———. "Ought Implies Can: A Bridge from Fact to Norm?" Part I, *Ratio* 14 (1972); and Part II, *Ratio* 17 (1975).

Winch, P. *The Idea of a Social Science* (London: Routledge and Kegan Paul, and New York: Humanities Press, 1958).

Wyller, E. A. "Henologie," in *Historisches Wörterbuch der Philosophie,* 2 vols., ed. J. Ritter (Basel and Stuttgart: Schwabe, 1971-1972).

Zapffe, P. W. *Indføring i litteraer dramaturgie* ("Introduction to Literary Dramaturgy") (Oslo: Universitetsforlaget, 1961).

JOURNALS

Inquiry

Norsk Filosofisk Tidsskrift

Sweden

The Academic Background

During the entire postwar period, each of Sweden's two old universities, Lund and Uppsala, has had two full professors of philosophy, one of "theoretical philosophy" (roughly logic, epistemology, the philosophy of science and of language) and one of "practical philosophy" (roughly ethics, the philosophy of law and religion, and aesthetics). During this period, the university of Gothenburg has had a professor of theoretical philosophy, while instruction in practical philosophy has been headed there by a "docent." Practical philosophy has been represented by a professorship at Stockholm University since the 1930s, and in 1949 a professorship of theoretical philosophy was created there. The "theory of science" (roughly the philosophy, organization, history, and sociology of science), also introduced as a separate discipline, now has two professorships, one in Gothenburg and one in Umeå. There is a separate institute of aesthetics in Uppsala. Special chairs of the philosophy of religion and of ethics have been created within the theological faculties of Lund and of Uppsala. The "general theory of law," which is close to the philosophy of law, has also become a separate discipline within the faculties of law in Lund, Stockholm, and Uppsala. Mathematical logic is studied within theoretical philosophy and at least in Stockholm, in the Department of Mathematics, as well.

In addition to full professors, the Swedish academic system includes "docents" (the German *Privatdozenten* which has no equivalent in the United States), "lectors" (literally lecturers), and "assistants," as well as other types of teachers and researchers. A docent may receive a salary but only for a maximum of seven years. A lector has a lifetime appointment with a salary. The lower academic ranks perform much research. As is readily apparent, the Swedish university system is too complex to be explained in detail here.

Although the lower ranks are as important in Swedish philosophy as the *ordinarii*, reasons of space prevent more than a listing for the postwar period. (The names of those who are active today are italicized.) The *ordinarii* of theoretical philosophy and their periods of active service have been as follows: in Gothenburg, Gunnar Aspelin (1936–1949) and *Ivar Segelberg* (1949–   ); in Lund, Alf Nyman (1929–1949), Gunnar Aspelin (1949–1964), and *Sören Halldén* (1964–   ); in Stockholm, Anders Wedberg (1949–1975) and *Dag*

Prawitz (1976–   ); in Uppsala, Anders Karitz (1934–1946), Konrad Marc-Wogau (1946–1968), and *Stig Kanger* (1968–   ). The full professors of practical philosophy and their periods of active service have been, in Lund, Åke Petzäll (1939–1957), Manfred Moritz (1959–1975), and Göran Hermerén (1975–   ); in Stockholm, Einar Tegen (1937–1951) and *Harald Ofstad* (1954–   ); and in Uppsala, Torgny Segerstedt (1938–1947), Ingemar Hedenius (1947–1973), and *Lars Bergström* (1973–   ). *Ordinarii* of the theory of science and their periods of active service have been, in Gothenburg, *Håkan Torneböhm* (1963–   ); and in Umeå, Göran Hermerén (1970–1975). The philosophy of religion chair in Lund has been held by Harald Eklund (1949–1960) and *Hampus Lyttkens* (1961–   ); and in Uppsala by *Hans Hof* (1969–   ). *Ordinarii* of the general theory of law and their periods of active service have been, in Lund, *Tore Strömberg* (1962–   ); in Stockholm, Ivar Agge (1958–1970) and *Jacob Sundberg* (1970–   ); and in Uppsala, Lars Hjerner (1963–1969) and *Stig Stromholm* (1969–   ).

Philosophy is a required subject in several lines of study in the Swedish high school. In addition to the philosophers of the universities, of course, a fairly large number of philosophical writers (in a broad sense of "philosophical") have no university affiliation.

Older generations of Swedish philosophers usually had a thorough knowledge of German, English, and French, as well as Latin and Greek, and in writing they often used German. In the last fifty years, however, Swedish philosophy, like Swedish culture in general, has become very Anglo-Americanized. Today, university students rarely have a knowledge of German or French, most textbooks are in English, and increasingly the tendency is to publish in English. Much has been gained and much lost in this process. In some people the habits of analytical philosophy have created a fear that their philosophizing may not be scientific enough: philosophy must be a "science," as "hard" as possible! Since logic seems to be about the hardest thing available, there has arisen a tendency to dwell on logic, formalization, and formal models, even in fields of philosophy where these techniques are of doubtful value. The dominant view of philosophy as a "hard science" is also threatening to narrow its field as far as humanistic studies are concerned.

THE HERITAGE FROM THE UPPSALA SCHOOL

The Uppsala professors Axel Hägerström (1868–1939) and Adolf Phalén (1884–1931) were the founders of the so-called Uppsala school of philosophy which flourished during the second, third, and fourth decades of this century. Phalén was foremost an epistemologist, and he approached the problems of epistemology from an act-psychological point of view. He also formulated the program of the school according to which philosophy ought primarily to be "the analysis of concepts." One of his most characteristic views (probably inspired by Hegel) was that common sense notions are to a large extent "dialectical" (inconsistent) and that the history of philosophy is largely the "dialectical movement" of such notions, i.e., a process where alternately the one and the other side of the contradictions come to the surface. Hägerström had much wider interests, including epistemology, value theory, the philosophy and history of law, and the philosophy of religion and of science. Hägerström and Phalén left their imprint on subsequent development through six doctrines: (1) stress on the importance of conceptual analysis; (2) condemnation of metaphysics (in Hägerström combined with an outspoken atheism and anticlericalism); (3) the critique of epistemological idealism ("subjectivism"); (4) Hägerström's emotive theory of value statements and his denial that they possess truth-value; (5) his similar view of normative statements; and (6) Hägerström's critique of traditional jurisprudence where he condemned such fundamental legal notions as "right" and "obligation" as metaphysical or even magical.

The first doctrine is one of the factors that has placed Swedish philosophy squarely within the analytical camp. Together, (1), (2), and (3) have had the effect that one has to seek long to find ideas that would traditionally be called metaphysical or idealistic. The emotive theory (4) has been an important theme in Sweden's postwar philosophy, and so has Hägerström's view (5) of normative statements. The critique of theology and jurisprudence has helped to awaken a rather lively interest in philosophy among Swedish theologians and jurists.

Unfortunately, the programmatic tenets (1), (2), and (3) have been more or less generally accepted without much explicit discussion. The most vigorous philosophical policy statement has come from Harald Ofstad who, in *The Functions of Moral Philosophy,* argues for a combination of analytical, empirical, and normative elements in moral philosophy. The continuing discussion of the Uppsala views (4), (5), and (6) will be mentioned under the proper headings in the survey by disciplines that follows.

A large number of Hägerström's and Phalén's manuscripts, deposited in the library of Uppsala University, are still unpublished—which is the more deplorable for the historian as their published writings are exceedingly difficult reading. In the postwar period, about twelve volumes of Hägerström's posthumous work have been published, ranging from an engaged "character analysis" of Jesus, a history of socialist ideas, and a learned study of ancient Roman law to essays in the philosophy of science. Available in English is C. D. Broad's translation *Inquiries into the Nature of Law and Morals* and R. T. Sandin's translation *Philosophy and Religion.* A series of Phalén's lectures on epistemology and its history is being published; thus far, seven volumes have appeared.

In *Studies in Axel Hägerström's Philosophy,* Marc-Wogau has put together a number of penetrating essays on various aspects of Hägerström's thought. A biography, *Axel Hägerström, The Man Known by Few,* which explains much of his development from a psychological viewpoint, was written by his daughter, Margit Waller.

One may well ask why the Uppsala school exerted such a strong influence. Several factors should be taken into account here. The Uppsala school was the first unequivocally naturalistic academic school of philosophy: all previous philosophy had been epistemologically and/or metaphysically idealistic. (The Uppsala school itself claimed, in moments of hybris, to be a revolution, not only in Swedish philosophy but also in world philosophy.) Sweden is a small country, and so new, original ideas did not appear very frequently; hence, for some time, there was simply a lack of competent competition. Before World War II, Sweden was rather isolated from what went on in the philosophical world at large.

ONTOLOGY

Ivar Segelberg, perhaps Sweden's most original postwar philosopher, has devoted himself to constructing what might almost be characterized as a system of ontology and phenomenology, inspired somewhat by Adolf Phalén but above all by Edmund Husserl and C. D. Broad. One of Segelberg's fundamental notions is that of one entity containing another as a part. This relation obtains, e.g., between an object and its qualities, a set and its elements, a spatial complex and its spatial parts, a fact and its constituents. Complex entities, that is, entities with parts, may be either collections or complex units. A collection is uniquely determined by its parts, and it ultimately must be made up of parts that are not collections. A complex unit differs in both respects from a collection: it is not determined by its parts, and it does not require ultimate parts that are not complex units. (An example of a collection might be *red + circle,* and example of a complex unit *red circle.*) Reality is a complex unit built up from two kinds of building blocks, quality moments and elementary relations. When two objects show exactly the same shade of blue, each of them nevertheless possesses its own unique moment of this shade. (Segelberg's quality moments have a strong kinship with Nelson Goodman's famous qualia in *The Structure of Appearance.*) By subtle intuitive considerations and his choice of sense data as his sample of reality, Segelberg tries to show in detail how units of various orders of complexity are built from their parts. These ideas are presented in *The Paradoxes of Zeno;* and *The Notion of Property.* In his third published volume, *Studies in Consciousness and the Idea of the Ego,* Segelberg closely studies the notion of the intentional act, first introduced by Husserl, and argues for its importance in philosophical psychology and epistemology.

Considerations that may be classified as ontological are also found in Marc-Wogau (e.g., the distinction between qualitative and abstractive difference), in Halldén's work on nonsensical propositions, in Regnéll, in Kanger (an extreme extensionalism), and in Prawitz (in his work on propositions). But none is an ontologist like Segelberg.

EPISTEMOLOGY

The classical Uppsala school showed a tendency to embrace views of a somewhat naive-realist type. It was often argued that physical objects must be conceived as literally being (sensibly) colored. In *Die Theorie der Sinnesdaten,* Marc-Wogau presented an extensive review of the British literature on the role of sense data in perception and elaborated a theory of his own which, to the present writer, appears as a sophisticated version of a sort of naive realism. According to Marc-Wogau, most sense data theorists have assumed that perception involves three essential components: the sensible awareness a, the sense datum d, and a material object m. (See Moore's "I see a penny.") The theorists in question argue that (1) d is always immediately apprehended in a, (2) m is never so, and, hence, (3) always $d \neq m$, with all the well-known epistemological consequences that this position entails. Using the results of Gestalt psychology, Marc-Wogau thinks that (2) is a mistake, in large part because of an oversimplified psychological theory concerning a and d. The datum d may itself be a material object, although one that is abstractively but not qualitatively distinct from m. There is a good sense in which objects that are merely abstractively distinct can be called identical, and there is also a good sense in which d, in certain privileged cases, can be called an existing material object. The question of sense data has been discussed by other Swedish philosophers, for example, by Lennart Åqvist in his characteristically formalist style.

The act psychology met with in Phalén has been further developed, not only by Segelberg, but also by Phalén's pupil Andries MacLeod and by Segelberg's pupils Helge Malmgren and Thomas Wetterström.

PHILOSOPHY OF LANGUAGE

On the whole, Swedish philosophers have been untouched by the intense worldwide interest in the philosophy of language. Two early works are Hans Regnéll's *Symbolization and Fictional Reference,* where he argues that fictions are at the heart of the use of symbols, and Torgny Segerstedt's *The Power of Words.* As an indirect contribution to the philosophy of language, one may consider Sören Halldén's *The Logic of Nonsense.* Literally, it deals with nonsensical propositions (Frege's *Gedanken* without truth-value), but obviously a particular class of nonsensical sentences will correspond to them. Another work by Halldén is *True Love, True Humour and True Religion. A Semantic Study.* Among Swedish philosophers, Mats Furberg perhaps has the strongest interest in the philosophy of language, especially in its Oxford form. In *Saying and Meaning,* he carefully studies the distinction between locutionary and illocutionary acts made by the Oxford philosopher J. L. Austin. He has also published a number of semipopular works, treating of various subjects influenced by language (morals, death, the history of philosophy) from predominantly semantic points of view.

The notion of a performative, likewise introduced by Austin, has attracted the interest of a large number of Swedish philosophers, namely, Jan S. Andersson, Sven Danielsson, Mats Furberg, Bengt Hansson, Ingemar Hedenius, Manfred Moritz, Karl Olivecrona, Thomas Wetterström, and Lennart Åqvist.

It may be mentioned that Axel Hägerström anticipated this Austinian notion in his discussion (included in C. D. Broad's translation) of the legal concept of a so-called declaration of intention.

On the whole, it seems unnatural to include logical semantics and similar logical studies in the philosophy of language. If they were included, here we would have to discuss much of the work mentioned later under the title of logic. However, I would like to report here that, in connection with their studies of specific logical themes, the logicians Dag Prawitz and Per Martin-Löf have both become inclined toward theories of meaning that are reminiscent of later Wittgensteinian views. In "Meaning and Proofs: On the Conflict Between Classical and Intuitionistic Logic," Prawitz sees the meaning of statements in the manner in which they are justified or proved. Martin-Löf finds, for example, that the meaning of natural numbers coincides with their role in the recursion process. In addition, the logician Sören Stenlund has shown a strong inclination toward the Wittgensteinian theory of meaning.

PHILOSOPHY OF SCIENCE

In Sweden, a distinction is made today between the "philosophy of science," which traditionally is considered to be a part of theoretical philosophy, and the "theory of science," which since 1963 has been a separate academic discipline. Perhaps the essential dividing mark is that, whereas the philosophy of science studies scientific theories and arguments merely from semantical, logical, and methodological points of view, the theory of science applies a wider perspective and also studies the processes of which theories and arguments are the result and the long-range development of scientific endeavors. Most of the actual postwar research, however, has been done within the confines of the philosophy of science, as defined above, and the distinction between the two approaches, however important in itself, may here be taken lightly.

Håkan Törnebohm, the founder of the Swedish theory of science, has devoted a fairly large number of books and papers to a philosophical analysis of Newtonian mechanics, and the special theory of relativity, and the transition from the one to the other, beginning with *A Logical Analysis of the Theory of Relativity*. He has also tried to develop "models over how theories are formed and over how the theoretical work is connected with the experimental work." His ideas in this respect are still on the whole tentative.

A group of younger theorists of science has gathered around Törnebohm; this group has been extraordinarily productive of mimeographed research plans and work reports. The most spectacular publication from the group so far is no doubt Gerhard Radnitzky's dissertation *Contemporary Schools of Meta-Science*. The first volume is a temperamental attack on "Anglo-Saxon" logical empiricism, especially Hempel's theory of explanation. The second volume advocates certain "continental" views, especially views pertaining to the German dialectical and hermeneutic traditions.

Several scholars have investigated the logic of explanation. Explanation in history has attracted the attention of Konrad Marc-Wogau and Erik Ryding, both of whom have introduced interesting new points of view. In *Explanation of Human Actions*, Lennart Nordenfelt rejects Hempel's nomological model of such explanation but keeps a generally deductive model. The place of Hempel's general law may be taken by a nonlaw, say a statement asserting the existence of an individual habit. Even more un-Hempelian is Bengt Hansson in a paper in which he takes explanations as answers to why-questions. In such a question, say "Why did Richard catch influenza?," there are one or more terms that, so to speak, are in the focus of the questioning. Say that we understand our question as "Why did *Richard* catch influenza?" With the sentence "Richard caught influenza," are associated a number of possible alternatives such as "John caught influenza," "Allen caught . . . ," and so forth. Hansson takes the why-question as a quest for a reason why "Richard caught influenza" is more probable than its possible alternatives. The idea is interesting but hardly convincing.

Objectivity was once a generally accepted (even if not clearly defined) ideal of science, but it has now been questioned, both as to its feasibility and desirability, by modern Marxists and their sympathizers. Lars Bergström, in *Objectivity*, and Göran Hermerén, in *Valuation and Objectivity*, have both endeavored to clarify the issue by introducing relevant conceptual distinctions.

Ingvar Johansson's *Critique of the Popperian Methodology* is a very thorough and detailed scrutiny of Popper's many methodological suggestions.

VALUE THEORY AND MORAL PHILOSOPHY

The emotive theory of value and normative statements, and the problem as to whether they have truth-values, which was introduced by Hägerström, have been much discussed and from many different points of view. Essential tenets in Hägerström's original position have been retained by an older generation of thinkers like Hedenius, Marc-Wogau, Moritz, and Wedberg. The original theory is well analyzed by Bo Pettersson in *The Value Theory of Axel Hägerström*. In *Introduction to Value Theory*, Manfred Moritz surveys what he takes to be the possible theories in the field.

In *On Law and Morals*, Hedenius restated Hägerström's view in a simplified and more sober form, thereby much facilitating later debate. Unlike Hägerström, he put more stress on semantics than on the psychology of emotion in formulating the theory that evaluative and normative statements lack truth-value.

Developing further an idea suggested by Einar Tegen, Sören Halldén tried, in *Emotive Propositions*, to show that acceptance of an emotive theory of value does not force us to deny truth-value to value statements. Halldén accepted an emotive theory but nevertheless took value statements to be true or false. According to Halldén, emotive qualities, apprehended in emotional experiences, figure as predicates in value statements whose truth-conditions are no different from those of nonevaluative statements.

In *New Foundations for Ethical Theory*, the logician Stig Kanger maintained a somewhat similar view with respect to deontic statements. He was prepared to accept some kind of emotive theory with respect to them, but he maintained that he could define an adequate schema of a definition of truth for them. This he did by applying a semantical system, which he had developed primarily to fit classical modal logics, to a language incorporating the deontic modality "It ought to be the case that. . . ."

Hägerström sometimes thought that his emotive theory implied the impossibility of a logic for value and normative statements. In a number of writings, Manfred Moritz has vigorously argued for this impossibility, and he has directed his critique particularly against modern versions of deontic logic. But here Moritz stands rather alone among present-day Swedish philosophers, many of whom (for example, Dánielsson, Hansson, Kanger, and Åqvist) have shown a lively interest in developing deontic logic.

Ingemar Hedenius, through several publications, has made himself the spokesman of a utilitarian ethics. In contrast, Harald Ofstad has claimed that utilitarianism runs counter to deep-seated ethical intuitions. This divergence in morals between Uppsala and Stockholm has given rise to a rather technical discussion concerning the logical structure of utilitarian, or teleological, ethical systems. This debate was opened by Lars Bergström's dissertation *The Alternatives and Consequences of Actions*, and, later, several authors (Bergström himself, Sven Danielsson, Dag Prawitz, and Lennart Åqvist) helped sharpen the issues.

The ancient question of man's freedom is treated in a very thorough and original manner by the Norwegian-born Harald Ofstad in *An Inquiry into the Freedom of Decision*, a work that belongs at least as much to Norwegian as to Swedish philosophy. Ofstad, who received his original schooling under Arne Naess in Oslo, here applies the method, introduced by Naess, of successively replacing a rough statement: "*P* decided freely in the situation *S*," by more and more specific and more and more precise statements. According to Ofstad, the most relevant sense of freedom from an ethical standpoint is found in a "power to decide in alternative ways," which does not involve any of the classical indeterminisms. Ofstad's work is the most circumspect that has been written on its subject.

The problem of freedom and responsibility has also been studied by Hedenius and Moritz. In contrast to the anti-utilitarian Ofstad, Hedenius maintains that the notion of a responsible action should be replaced by the notion of an action of such a kind that the frequency of actions of that kind can be changed by praising or blaming, punishing or rewarding the agents. Moritz thinks that an agent is free if, and only if, he is responsible, and responsible if, and only if, he may be morally judged for his action. Thus, whether we think someone is free (responsible) or not will depend on our moral convictions.

Hägerström proclaimed that there can be a science *about* morals but no science

Sweden   181

in morals, thereby meaning that a discourse in which evaluative and normative statements are made cannot claim scientific status, since the statements in question lack truth-value. This view may seem highly out of date today when the most respectable sciences so often deal with only vaguely interpreted "models" and even with quite uninterpreted axiomatic systems. The Swedish economist and Nobel laureate Gunnar Myrdal, at one time strongly influenced by Hägerström, has argued that objectivity and valuation can be scientifically reconciled if an author initially lists the value premises he intends to utilize. Myrdal is thinking primarily of such social sciences as sociology and economics. In the field of philosophical ethics, it is above all Hedenius and Ofstad who have reintroduced the evaluative and normative element, banished by Hägerström. Ofstad has inspired a group of younger people to treat normative questions with the tools of analytical philosophy and empirical research, coupled with doses of "ethical intuition." Two examples of such studies are Giuliano Pontara's *Does the End Justify the Means?* and Lars O. Ericsson's *Justice in the Distribution of Economic Resources.*

Lars Bergström and, after him, Torbjörn Tännsjö in *The Relevance of Meta-ethics to Ethics,* have argued that meta-ethical inquiries (such as Hägerström's) into the meaning of ethical terms have no relevance for ethical discourse. This standpoint may be an overstrong reaction to prior trends in Swedish moral philosophy.

PHILOSOPHY OF LAW

Hägerström was as much the father of a school of jurisprudence as of a school of general philosophy. His closest juridical pupils were Vilhelm Lundstedt and Karl Olivecrona. Also strongly influenced by Hägerström were the Danish legal scientist and philosopher Alf Ross and the Swedish jurist Per Olof Ekelöf. Paradoxically, it is not at all easy to state what Hägerström thought on jurisprudence, and this presentation will not satisfy demands for greater clarity. As basic to his legal philosophy, Hägerström considered his critique of that once fashionable "legal positivism" according to what the legal norms express some supreme will present in society. There is no such will, he pointed out; what there is is a "legal machinery" by which the norms are maintained. To posterity this critique may seem to express little more than a preference for a mechanical over a psychological metaphor. Sometimes society may resemble an organism with a will and sometimes an inexorable machine.

Of greater consequence were Hägerström's views on the notions of a right and an obligation. In his interpretation—which he supported by extensive studies in ancient Roman law—a subjective right, e.g., ownership, means a power over the thing owned, which the owner may be unable to assert (through theft and the like) but which still exists in the realm of magic. To buy potatoes is to acquire a magical force over the potatoes. Hägerström claims that an obligatory sentence, for instance, "It is my duty to pay two dollars," when used seriously, expresses a "simultaneous association" between a compulsion of the will and the idea of my paying two dollars. To this association is added the error that the very word "duty" inheres as a property in the object of the idea. Thus, the belief in the existence of legal obligations and legal rights is magic and error. Nevertheless, when the jurist asserts that an obligation or a right exists, his obscure conceptual apparatus points to certain existing social facts. A man with a right enjoys a certain socially protected position, and one with an obligation runs the risk of incurring sanctions if he fails to fulfill it. Thus, Hägerström at least implicitly distinguished between the meaning of these juristic terms and the facts to which they point. A modernized version of a Hägerströmian legal philosophy is Karl Olivecrona's *Law as Fact.*

In *On Law and Morals,* a work that gave rise to a very heated discussion, Ingemar Hedenius questioned this rather obscure semantic distinction of Hägerström's and advocated the introduction of another. Hedenius assumes that all legal norms can be reduced to legal ought statements. When such a norm *N* is genuine, or is used in a genuine manner, an emotive theory à la Hägerström is true of *N*, and *N* lacks truth-value. However, *N* can also be nongenuine, or used in a nongenuine manner. It is then used as a synonym for (1) "*N* is part of the legal order (of an understood society)," and when so used, *N* is true or false. In turn, (1) can be construed as a hypothetical statement about the workings of society, especially of its legal authorities. In legal science, Hedenius suggests that normative statements are largely used in this nongenuine manner. Hedenius' way of talking about norms seems definitely easier to handle than his teacher's. This discussion has been continued by many authors, and the terminological inventiveness has been great.

The notion of a right, which was originally more or less ruled out by the Hägerströmians, has been studied in a more positive spirit. An example of a right is ownership. A legal order contains norms of the type: (a) "If F_i, then p owns o at t" ($i = 1, \ldots , m$), and of the type: (b) "If p owns o at t, then C_j" ($j = 1, \ldots , n$), where "F_i" stands for some "fact," and "C_j" stands for some legal consequence. In the search for an explanation or definition of ownership, the idea readily presents itself to use either the statements (a) or the statements (b); i.e., we may consider the phrase "*p* owns *o* at *t*" as defined either by the disjunction "F_1 or F_2 or. . .or F_m" or by the conjunction "C_1 and C_2 and. . .and C_n." (To avoid vicious circles in the definitions, certain logical precautions must, of course, be taken.) One could also take the phrase to be undefined, and even without semantic meaning, it would serve only as a means to infer statements of the type: (c) "If F_i then C_j" from those of types (a) and (b). The discussion, in which Björn Ahlander, Per Olof Ekelöf, Ingemar Hedenius, Karl Olivecrona, Alf Ross, and Anders Wedberg have taken part, seems to Wedberg to have moved essentially within the frame of ideas hinted at here. It is of some interest to note that the well-known Swedish social-democratic politician Östen Undén, for many years Sweden's foreign minister, saw in an idea of this sort a decisive reason why the right of property must be considered relative to the legal order, decided on by the politicians, and, hence, adaptable to socialism.

A related theme is how best to understand the American jurist W. N. Hohfeld's famous set of eight "fundamental legal conceptions." The question has been discussed by Manfred Moritz and, with more complex logical technique, by Stig Kanger. The most thorough treatment of the question so far is Lars Lindahl's Kanger-inspired work *Position and Change. A Study in Law and Logic.*

As the reader will have noticed, modern Swedish legal philosophy often wears a formal logical costume. In Lennart Åqvist's *Causality and Culpability Within a Logically Reconstructed Law of Damages,* the formal costume has become very heavy. Game theory, preference theory, probability theory, and the like are mobilized in formalized versions, and the distance to actual legal reasoning appears almost unbridgeable.

Of greater interest are the studies in the evaluation of proofs undertaken by Per Olof Ekelöf, Sören Halldén, and Anders Stening. A byproduct of these studies is Halldén's elegant *Logic of Probability.*

Finally, Harald Ofstad has published a series of excellent critical studies on definitions of the notion of a "legal norm" put forward by a number of legal philosophers.

PHILOSOPHY OF RELIGION

The philosophy of religion was one of Hägerström's deepest interests. Once he rejected all "metaphysics," the truth of religious ideas was no longer a problem for him. What interested him primarily was the psychological mechanisms of religion. Here he made frequent and complex use of his peculiar theory of emotion: in emotional experiences, we apprehend emotive qualities as not localized in either time or space, or we experience them, as Hägerström sometimes suggests, in a double way—as both unlocalized and localized, either in our own bodies or in external objects. Such experiences easily make us believe in spiritual powers and beings that also lack localization. Here we have one of the main sources of primitive magic and spiritual religion. After Hägerström, Ingemar Hedenius is the philosopher who has devoted the greatest interest to religion. In *Faith and Knowledge,* Hedenius directed a scathing attack against Christianity and contemporary Swedish theology. Whereas the psychology of religion was at the center of Hägerström's interest, Hedenius has above all been interested in the truth of religious beliefs. There are no logical proofs in support of Christian beliefs, and the ethics of belief, accepted by Hedenius, forbids acceptance of Christian beliefs. Even worse, the central corpus of Christian beliefs is, according to Hedenius, logically inconsistent and, hence, as a whole false. Clearly, the philosophy of religion of the Uppsala philosophers has been anti-Christian and antireligious.

In contrast, the religious philosophy of the theologians has more often than not had a subtle, apologetic errand. In part as a reaction against Hägerström, the internationally known so-called Lund theology evolved. Its father was the theologian Anders Nygren. In an early work, *Religious Apriori,* he advocated the use of a "transcendental" method in religious philosophy. To do so is to ask the question: "What must be valid in order that any statement be valid?" Assuming that all statements can profitably be rewritten as what is today known as "eternal statements," he finds the sought-for condition in the category of eternity, which is of the very essence of religion. Thus, in Nygren's view, religion is at the base of all intellectual activity. In later works, among them *Meaning and Method. Prolegomena to a Scientific Philosophy of Religion and a Scientific Theology,* he argues that each statement gets its meaning in and through the "context of meaning" to which it belongs. Such a context is determined by a basic question. Whereas the theoretical context is governed by the quest for facts, the religious is determined by the quest for something else. According to Nygren's collaborator, Ragnar Bring, this is salvation.

Among the younger theological philosophers of religion should be mentioned Lars Bejerholm, Urban Forell, Anders Jeffner, Jarl Hemberg, and Tord Simonsson. They have all been influenced by modern analytical philosophy, as is evident in *Wort und Handlung. Untersuchungen zur analytischen Religionsphilosophie* by Lars Bejerholm and Gottfried Hornig; *Wunderbegriffe und Logische Analyse* by Urban Forell; *The Study of Religious Language* by Anders Jeffner; and *Logical and Semantical Structures in Christian Discourses* by Tord Simonsson.

AESTHETICS

The line between aesthetics as a philosophical discipline and aesthetics as an integral part of the analysis and history of art is not easily drawn. The selections of works mentioned here are admittedly quite subjective.

In *Representation and Meaning in the Visual Arts,* Göran Hermerén distinguishes and tries to make precise a number of "semantic" functions that a work of art may fulfill, such as "depicting," "representing," "symbolizing," "illustrating," and "expressing." He also discusses the reasons that may be adduced for attributing a specific function to a given piece of art. In another work, *Influence in Art and Literature,* Hermerén first distinguishes a number of distinct concepts of influence, then formulates a set of five necessary conditions for the existence of influence, and finally addresses the question of how to measure degrees of influence. His *Aesthetic Qualities* is an attempt to determine the "logical status" of adjectives such as "gracious," "melancholic," "dynamic," and "harmonic" as used to characterize works of art. Hermerén's above-mentioned works have perhaps been the most substantial contributions to aesthetics by a philosopher in the postwar period.

Tryggve Emond pursues a similar analytic aim in his *On Art and Unity:* where, with little success, he seeks to define the term "work of art" when used as an evaluative predicate.

A number of aestheticians have published collections of essays that are only weakly held together by a common theme but contain stimulating ideas. Examples are Erik Götlind (*The Enormous Words)* and Hans Ruin *(The Transformations of the Beautiful).* In addition, Gunnar Berefelt, Teddy Brunius, Rolf Ekman, and Göran Sörbom have written books designed to introduce students to the problems of aesthetics.

An important work is Göran Sörbom's *Mimesis and Art* which presents a very thorough discussion of the ideas on art expressed by the word "mimesis" and its cognates in ancient Greek philosophy, particularly in Plato and Aristotle.

FORMAL LOGIC

Sweden's first doctoral thesis in modern formal logic was Sören Halldén's *Some Results in Modal Logic.* But Swedish formal logic did not come of age until 1957 when Stig Kanger's *Provability in Logic* appeared. In the first part of this compact work, Kanger, utilizing Gerhard Gentzen's *Sekventkalkül,* developed a mechanical proof procedure for quantification theory and simultaneously obtained a number of classical metalogical theorems like Gödel's completeness theorem, Löwenheim-Skolem's theorem, and Gentzen's *Hauptsatz.* Perhaps even more interesting is the second part of the book in which a semantical characterization is given of a series of modal logics. Here Kanger makes ingenious use of a binary denotation function, "the denotation of the symbol *A* relative to the universe *U,*" and a ternary truth function, "the truth-value of the sentence *A* relative to the denotation function *V* and the universe *U.*" The truth-value of sentence *A* relative to *V* and *U* is constructed so that it may depend on *A*'s truth-values relative to other functions *V'* and *U'.* Kanger's work was thus the first publication of the idea that has become known as "possible world semantics."

Kanger's mechanical procedure—akin to procedures devised independently by E. W. Beth and Karl Schütte—has been improved by Kanger himself and by Dag Prawitz.

In "The Morning Star Paradox" in *Theoria,* Kanger applied his modal semantics to obtain a solution to this Fregean paradox as it seems to arise within ordinary language. The result is open to further discussion.

Gentzen's *Hauptsatz* for a logical system of the Gentzen type states, broadly speaking, that any proof of a theorem within the system can be transformed into a "normal proof" of the same theorem. The structure of a normal proof is so simple that obviously no contradiction can result from it. The *Hauptsatz* is thus of central interest in the attempt to prove the consistency of various logico-mathematical theories. Kanger's interest in the *Hauptsatz* heralded intensive work on this subject. In his dissertation *Natural Deduction. A Proof-Theoretical Study,* Dag Prawitz was the first to prove the *Hauptsatz* directly for certain systems of so-called natural deduction in Gentzen's sense. Prawitz has extended these results. He has also proved the *Hauptsatz* for the classical second-order logic, for the classical simple type theory, and for the second-order intuitionistic logic. Per Martin-Löf's interests overlap those of Prawitz. Beyond Prawitz, he has proved the *Hauptsatz* for a number of strong intuitionistic theories; i.e., for an intuitionistic type theory which he has devised. Sören Stenlund's *Combinators, λ-terms, and Proof Theory*, although largely concerned with other matters, gives a new and elegant proof of the *Hauptsatz* for second-order intuitionistic logic. Lars Svenonius (originally in Uppsala and now in Maryland in the United States) has also done work on the *Hauptsatz*.

With his dissertation *Some Problems in Model Theory*, Svenonius was the first Swedish logician to work with model theory. The foremost representative of this logical discipline in Sweden today is Per Lindström. One of Lindström's major contributions has been his characterization of elementary logic in abstract model-theoretic terms. An interesting attempt to develop the philosophical consequences of this result is Dag Westerståhl's *Some Philosophical Aspects of Abstract Model Theory*.

The logical topics which have traditionally been considered to be closer to philosophy have been much debated by Swedish logicians. Modal logic in general has been studied, from various points of view, by Bengt Hansson, Sören Halldén, Stig Kanger, Dag Prawitz, and Krister Segerberg (formerly in Uppsala, now in Turku, Finland). Deontic logic has been treated by Kanger in *New Foundations of Ethical Theory*, by Lennart Åqvist, and by Bengt Hansson. In his work *A New Approach to the Logical Theory of Interrogatives*, Lennart Åqvist approaches the logic of questions as a special case of deontic logic combined with a Hintikka-type epistemic logic. (The question "Is it Monday?" is construed as the exhortation "Let it be the case that either I know that it is Monday or I know that is isn't Monday!")

Preference logic (with the basic notions "that *p* is better than /just as good as/ that *q*") was first considered in Sören Halldén's pioneer work *On the Logic of 'Better'*. Bengt Hansson has continued this line of research. Sven Danielsson's dissertation, *Preference and Obligation*, is an attempt to create an intimate union between deontic logic and preference logic. The American economist Kenneth Arrow, through his famous impossibility theorem concerning "social choice and individual values," has done much to stimulate interest in preference theory in general, without the restriction to propositions. Contributions to the clarification of this topic have been made by Bengt Hansson, who has made preference theory the subject of a profound study, and by Sven Danielsson. Jan Berg (formerly of Stockholm and now of Munich) in *Bolzano's Logic* makes an exemplary presentation of the logical ideas of this early precursor of modern logic.

HISTORY OF PHILOSOPHY

If one were to single out the one book which has had the largest influence on philosophical interest in Sweden in recent times, one would probably mention the Christian idealist Alf Ahlberg's popular history of philosophy, first published in the 1920s. It has introduced many generations of young people to philosophy. In the tradition of broad humanistic learning, Gunnar Aspelin has written another history of philosophy, *The Ways of Thought* as well as a more general history of ideas, *World Views and Ideals of Life*. Anders Wedberg's *History of Philosophy* is conceived from a narrower analytical point of view. He tries to present ideas of the past in a more precise way than they were described by their originators, he analyzes the arguments, and he does not abstain from criticism. Konrad Marc-Wogau's *Philosophy Through the Ages* is primarily an anthology, but the editor's comments also make it an excellent concise history of philosophy. Mats Furberg's *Vision and Doubt* treats themes from ancient philosophy from an essentially semantical perspective.

Hans Regnéll has written two studies on pre-Socratic philosophy. But Plato and Aristotle have received the greatest scholarly attention in Sweden. Nils Almberg, Ingemar Hedenius, Konrad Marc-Wogau, Harald Morin, and Anders Wedberg have all studied various aspects of Plato's thought. Wedberg's monograph *Plato's Philosophy of Mathematics* attempts to give a "likely account" of Plato's views concerning the subject matter and the methodology of mathematics, as well as to trace the trains of thought that may have led him to adopt them. The philologist Ingemar Düring has written on Aristotle.

The theologico-philosophical thinking of the Middle Ages has, of course, engaged the interest of theologians. Hampus Lyttkens has analyzed Aquinas' notion of analogy; Hans Hof has written on Eckhart's notion of *scintilla animae;* and Olle Herrlin has tried to unravel the mysteries of the ontological proof (a subject which other philosophers such as Jan Berg, Halldén, MacLeod, and Marc-Wogau have pondered).

The philosophy of Descartes has been discussed by Rolf Lindborg, Marc-Wogau, and particularly Hjalmar Wennerberg in his *The Cartesian Circle*. Anders Jeffner has compared the religious philosophies of Butler and Hume, and Teddy Brunius has explored Hume's aesthetic views. Erik Ryding's *The Notions of Utility and Truth in French Philosophy of the Enlightenment* revises the traditional view of the Enlightenment's cult of reason. Many of the ideas presented in this work are actually reminiscent of Freud's psychoanalysis and Vaihinger's and others' biological epistemologies. Lennart Åqvist has written a penetrating study, *The Moral Philosophy of Richard Price*.

There are two Kant specialists in Sweden, Konrad Marc-Wogau and Manfred Moritz. Marc-Wogau's great Kant studies belong to the prewar era, but Moritz published two studies of Kant's moral philosophy after the war. Sven Eric Liedman investigates the post-Kantian romantic German philosophy of nature in *The Organic Life In German Debate 1795–1845*. In *A World to Win. Aspects of the Young Karl Marx*, Liedman presents the humanistic Marx. Representative of the recent upsurge of interest in Marxism in Sweden are Gunnar Aspelin's two books on Marx as a social scientist and a number of essays by Marc-Wogau.

SELECT BIBLIOGRAPHY

BOOKS AND ARTICLES*

Åqvist, L. *A New Approach to the Logical Theory of Interrogatives* (Uppsala: University of Uppsala, 1965) E.

———. *The Moral Philosophy of Richard Price* (Lund: Gleerup, 1960) E.

Aspelin, G. *Tankens vägar* ("The Ways of Thought") (Stockholm: Almqvist and Wiksell, 1958) S.

———. *Varldsbilder och Livsideal* ("World Views and Ideals of Life") (Lund: Gleerup, 1968) S.

Bejerholm, L. and Hornig, G. *Wort und Handlung. Untersuchungen zur analytischen Religionsphilosophie* (Gütersloh: Guterslohen Verlagshaus G. Mohn, 1966) G.

Berg, J. *Bolzano's Logic* (Stockholm: Almqvist and Wiksell, 1962) E.

Bergström, L. *Objectivet* ("Objectivity") (Stockholm: Prisma, and Solna: Seelig, 1972) S.

———. *The Alternatives and Consequences of Actions* (Stockholm: Almqvist and Wiksell, 1966) E.

Danielsson, S. *Preference and Obligation* (Uppsala: Filosofiska föreningen, 1968) E.

Emond, T. *On Art and Unity* (Lund: Gleerup, 1964) E.

Ericsson, L. *Justice in the Distribution of Economic Resources: A Critical and Normative Study* (Stockholm: Almqvist and Wiksell, 1976) E.

Forell, U. *Wunderbegriffe und Logische Analyse* (Göttingen: Vandenhoeck and Ruprecht, 1967) G.

Furberg, M. *Saying and Meaning* (Totowa, N. J.: Rowman and Littlefield, 1971) E.

———. *Vision och skepsis. Från Thales till skeptikerna* ("Vision and Doubt") (Stockholm: Bonnier, 1969) S.

Goodman, N. *The Structure of Appearance* (Cambridge, Mass.: Harvard University Press, 1951) E.

Götlind, E. *Der Oerhörder Orden* ("The Enormous Words") (Stockholm: Svenska bokförlaget, 1961) S.

Hägerström, A. *Inquiries into the Nature of Law and Morals*, trans. C. D. Broad (Uppsala: Almqvist and Wiksell, 1953) E.

———. *Philosophy and Religion*, trans. R. T. Sandin (London: Allen and Unwin, and New York: Humanities Press, 1964) E.

Halldén, S. *Emotive Propositions* (Stockholm: Almqvist and Wiksell, 1954) E.

———. *Några resultat i modal logik* ("Some Results in Modal Logic") (Uppsala: Almqvist and Wiksell, 1950) S.

———. *On the Logic of 'Better'* (Lund: Gleerup, 1957) E.

———. *Sannolikhetens logik* ("Logic of Probability") (Lund: Gleerup, 1973) S.

———. *The Logic of Nonsense* (Uppsala: Lundequistka bukhandeln, 1949) E.

———. *True Love, True Humour and True Religion. A Semantic Study* (Lund: Gleerup, 1960) E.

Hedenius, I. *Om rätt och moral* ("On Law and Morals") (Stockholm: Wahlström a Widstrand, 1963) S.

———. *Tro och Vetande* ("Faith and Knowledge") (Stockholm: Bonnier, 1949) S.

Hermerén, G. *Influence in Art and Literature* (Princeton, N. J.: Princeton University Press, 1975) E.

———. *Representation and Meaning in the Visual Arts* (Stockholm: Läromedelsforlaget, 1969) E.

———. *Värdering och objektivitet* ("Valuation and Objectivity") (Lund: Studentlitteratur, 1972) S.

Jeffner, A. *The Study of Religious Language* (London: S.C.M. Press, 1972) E.

*The title in Swedish where given is followed by the English translation within parentheses. A capital "S" means that the book is available in Swedish; a capital "E," that the book is available in English; and a capital "G," that the book is available in German.

Johansson, I. *Kritik av den popperianska metodologin* ("Critique of the Popperian Methodology") (Göteborg: Göteborg University, 1973) S.

Kanger, S. *New Foundations for Ethical Theory* (Stockholm: Almqvist and Wiksell, 1957) E.

———. *Provability in Logic* (Stockholm: Almqvist and Wiksell, 1957) E.

———. "The Morning Star Paradox," *Theoria* 23 :1957) E.

Liedman, S. E. *Det organiska livet i tysk debatt 1795–1845* ("The Organic Life in German Debate 1795–1845") (Göteborg: Göteborg University, 1966) S.

———. *En värld att vinna. Aspekter pa den unge Karl Marx* ("A World to Win. Aspects of the Young Karl Marx") (Stockholm: Bonnier, 1968) S.

Lindahl, L. *Position and Change. A Study in Law and Logic* (Dordrecht and Boston: Reidel, 1977) E.

Marc-Wogau, K. *Die Theorie der Sinnesdaten* (Leipzig: O. Harrassowitz, 1945) G.

———. *Filosofiska diskussioner* ("Philosophy Through the Ages") (Stockholm: Ulbildningsförd, 1964–1970) S.

———. *Studier till Axel Hägerström's filosofi* ("Studies in Axel Hägerström's Philosophy") (Stockholm: Prisma Uppsala: Föreningen Verdandi, and Solna: Seelig, 1968) S.

Moritz, M. *Inledning i värdeteori* ("Introduction to Value Theory") (Lund: Studentlitteratur, 1967) S.

Nordenfelt, L. *Explanation of Human Actions* (Uppsala: Filosofiska föreningen og Filosofiska institutionen vid Uppsala universitet, 1974) E.

Nygren, A. *Meaning and Method. Prolegomena to a Scientific Philosophy of Religion and a Scientific Theology* (London: Epworth Press, 1972) E.

———. *Religiöst apriori* ("Religious apriori") (Lund: Gleerup, 1921) S.

Ofstad, H. *An Inquiry into the Freedom of Decision* (Oslo: Norwegian University Press, 1961) E.

———. *The Functions of Moral Philosophy* (Oslo: Oslo University Press, 1958) E.

Olivecrona, K. H. *Law as Fact* (London: Stevens, 1971) E.

Pettersson, B. *Axel Hägerströms värdeteori* ("The Value Theory of Axel Hägerström") (Uppsala: Akad. avh. Uppsala University, 1973) S.

Pontara, G. *Does the End Justify the Means?* (Stockholm: Filosofiska institutionen vid Stockholms universitet, 1967) E.

Prawitz, D. "Meaning and Proofs: On the Conflict Between Classical and Intuitionistic Logic," *Theoria* 43 (1977) E.

———. *Natural Deduction. A Proof-Theoretical Study,* Stockholm Studies in Philosophy 3 (Stockholm: Almqvist and Wiksell, 1965) E.

Radnitzky, G. *Contemporary Schools of Meta-Science,* 2d rev. ed. (Göteborg: Läromedelsförlaget, and New York: Humanities Press, 1970) E.

Regnéll, H. *Symbolization and Fictional Reference: A Study in Epistemology* (Lund: Gleerup, 1949) E.

Ruin, H. *Det skönas förwandlingar* ("The Transformations of the Beautiful") (Stockholm: Wohlström and Widstrand, 1962) S.

Ryding, E. *Begreppen nyrta och sanning inom fransk upplysningsfilosofi* ("The Notions of Utility and Truth in French Philosophy of the Enlightenment") (Lund: Gleerup, 1951) S.

Segelberg, I. *Begreppet egenskap* ("The Notion of Property") (Stockholm: Svenska tryckeriaktiebolaget, 1947) S.

———. *Studier over medvetandet och jagidén* ("Studies in Consciousness and the Idea of the Ego") (Stockholm: Svenska tryckeriaktiebolaget, 1953) S.

———. *Zenons paradoxer* ("The Paradoxes of Zeno") (Stockholm: Natur och Kultur, 1947) S.

Segerstedt, T. *Ordens makt* ("The Power of Words"), 2d ed. (Uppsala: Argos, 1968) S.

Simonsson, T. *Logical and Semantical Structures in Christian Discourses* (Oslo: Universitetsforlaget, 1971) E.

Sörbom, G. *Mimesis and Art* (Stockholm: Svenskabokförlaget, 1966). E.

Stening, A. *Beviswärde* ("The Value of Proofs") (Stockholm: Almqvist and Wiksell, 1975) S.

Stenlund, S. *Combinators, λ-terms, and Proof Theory* (Dordrecht: Reidel, 1972) E.

Svenonius, L. *Some Problems in Logical Model Theory* (Lund: Gleerup, 1960) E.

Tännsjö, T. *The Relevance of Meta-ethics to Ethics* (Stockholm: Almqvist and Wiksell, 1974) E.

Törnebohm, H. *A Logical Analysis of the Theory of Relativity* (Stockholm: Almqvist and Wiksell, 1952) E.

Waller, M. *Axel Hägerström människan som fa kände* ("Axel Hägerström, The Man Known by Few") (Stockholm: Natur och Kultur, 1961) S.

Wedberg, A. *Filosofins historia* ("History of Philosophy"), 3 vols. (Stockholm: Bonnier, 1958–1966) S.

————. *Plato's Philosophy of Mathematics* (Stockholm: Almqvist and Wiksell, 1955) E.

Wennerberg, H. *Den cartesianska cirkeln* ("The Cartesian Circle") (Stockholm: Natur och Kultur, 1971) S.

Westerståhl, D. *Some Philosophical Aspects of Abstract Model Theory* (Göteborg: Institutionen för filosofi, Göteborgs universitet, 1976) E.

JOURNALS

Filosofi-och Psykologilärarnas Medlemsblad
Filosofiska Småtryck
Insikt och Handling
Studier I Praktisk Filosofi Utgivna Av Filosofiska Institutionen
Theoria

BIBLIOGRAPHICAL NOTE

For a very complete, though slightly outdated, work, see *Scandinavian Directory of Philosophy*, published by the Department of Philosophy, University of Uppsala, 1972.

Swedish philosophical books are listed in *Svensk Bokkatalog* (Catalog of Swedish Books), which is now published yearly. Unfortunately, no bibliography of papers exists.

West Germany and Austria

HANS M. BAUMGARTNER

The present situation of philosophy in the Federal Republic of Germany (West Germany) and Austria—its central problems, thematic focal points, and regional peculiarities—is quite obscure, and not just to the external observer. The reason is largely that West German institutions and universities have mushroomed since 1960. Whereas there were only eighteen institutions in 1962, there are now seventy-five, and the number of instructors in philosophy at these institutions has grown from approximately 90 (1962) to about 260. Austria has only six universities (Graz, Innsbruck, Klagenfurt, Linz, Salzburg, and Vienna); nonetheless the thematic development of philosophy runs rather parallel to West Germany's inasmuch as the institutions in the two countries have such close contacts.

A description of contemporary philosophy and its development must by its very nature limit itself to those problems and discussions that have attracted interest outside the academic realm. Moreover, this description can only be an ideal-typical sketch of the main currents in philosophy.

The main issues in philosophic thought then fall into three problem areas which themselves can be further broken down: (1) scientific theory and the history of science into which also enter the numerous contemporary assessments of language theory and linguistics; (2) a renewed practical philosophy which encompasses the entire horizon of the classical, idealistic, and postidealistic tradition up to the beginning of historico-philosophical and socio-theoretical assessments; and (3) philosophy's own understanding of its present function in the face of the highly complex state of development of industrial societies. In order to obtain a basic overview of the genesis of these problem areas, it is appropriate to differentiate four phases of development in the Federal Republic of Germany as well as in Austria.

The first phase, directly following World War II, can be viewed as the renewal of relations with the philosophies of the 1920s and the older traditions. The basic themes of phenomenology, ontology, metaphysics, theory of knowledge, and philosophical anthropology were taken up and developed further, with problems of existentialism accounting, not least as a result of the impact of World War II experiences, for the majority of the discussion.

English translation by Lewis W. Tusken, professor of German, University of Wisconsin-Oshkosh.

The second phase may be characterized by the label "internationalization of philosophical research." It was distinguished by the reception of Anglo-American philosophy and a resumption of the logical-empirical tradition of the Viennese Circle. Into this period also falls the consolidation of political and economic relations of the now democratically conceived societies in West Germany and Austria. At the same time, the first indications of differences between traditionally oriented (continental) and neopositivistic or pragmatic (Anglo-American) philosophy could be perceived.

The third phase, which encompasses the second half of the 1960s and the beginning of the 1970s, was essentially a phase of confrontation between analytic-scientistic and traditional philosophy. At the center stood the political philosophy which, with retrospective consideration of the entire spectrum of the political-theoretical tradition from Aristotle to Marx, Max Weber, and Carl Schmitt, turned to the structural problems of modern industrial societies. The argument "scientism versus dialectic" found its culmination not so much in scientific-theoretical questioning, which at first glance appeared to be dominant, but rather in the reciprocally imputed socio-political consequences.

During the fourth phase, partisan controversy has faded away because of a broadening of horizons. Features of a "great coalition" have appeared in which the great gestures of battle and defense have given way to a detailed critical argument and, in some cases, to discriminating mediation between points of view. The confrontation has changed into critical coexistence within the three great problem areas mentioned above. Negatively formulated, this phase is characterized by the turning away from two hypertrophic ideas: from the mania for science, which pronounced the supremacy of science and its corresponding scientistic philosophy; and from the utopia of democratization, which romantically put complete faith in the dialogue model of personal encounter. Positively formulated, this phase appears as the period of a new enlightening matter of factness, which has passed through its extreme stages.

1945 TO THE MID-1950s

Philosophical discussion during the first postwar years was dominated by the names Friedrich Georg Jünger, Romano Guardini, Hans Freyer, Theodor Litt, Erich Rothacker, Philipp Lersch, Nicolai Hartmann, Otto Friedrich Bollnow, Eduard Spranger, Heinz Heimsoeth, Josef Pieper, Caspar Nink, Gustav Siewerth, Aloys Wenzl, Karl Jaspers, and Martin Heidegger. Common to all of them is a critical position vis-à-vis recent philosophy and its consequences, such as the abandonment of the neo-Kantian tradition of German university philosophy of the first thirty years of the twentieth century. The most significant influences were the historicism of the Dilthey school, the beginnings of a philosophical anthropology (Arnold Gehlen, Helmut Plessner, and Max Scheler), Heidegger's existential analysis of *Sein und Zeit* ("Being and Time"), Nicolai Hartmann's reformulation of problems of ontological status, his philosophy of intrinsic values (*an-sich-seiende Werte*), and Karl Jaspers' sketch of an existential philosophy which divides itself into *Daseinserhellung* (Dasein clarification), world orientation, and metaphysics.

These new beginnings had a common ground in Germany's political collapse which called for general reflection, establishment of a position toward the present period, as well as a basic interpretation of the meaning of human existence. The decisive external influences were the French existentialism of Sartre and Camus as well as Ortega's existentially oriented *Lebensphilosophie*. By disregarding the multiple peripheral aspects of the central problems of self-interpretation of human existence in the past and the present, the advance of philosophical thought in this first postwar phase can be constructed in ideal-typical form as follows.

The phenomena of *Angst,* failure, loneliness, and the tragedy of human existence; the impossibility of being able to reach back to a stabilizing metaphysical interpretation of human being; the experience of sheer existence and the boundary situations of human death, guilt, and suffering—all made man appear as an existence without essence, as an absolute but simultaneously empty freedom. Nihilism, which is incorporated in this concept, could best be understood historically. It could not, however, be overcome by means of any of the familiar philosophical theories of man (Weischedel). The Christian existential philosophy of Gabriel, Marcel, Maritain, and Windischer as well as the phenomenologically oriented *Wertphilosophie* (axiology) seemed just as hopeless in the face of this experience as perhaps Pieper's renewal of Thomas Aquinas' thought or the neo-Scholastic tradition of classical metaphysics.

Only when Jaspers as well as Heidegger, even if in different ways, made Nihilism and its basic phenomena recognizable as structural moments of human experience, and thereby reformulated the question of the object-less "Nichts" as a question of the Being of beings, was the Nihilism problematic simultaneously opened up and conquered from within.

Whereas Jaspers, however, interpreted the relationships of existence-world-transcendence by returning to Kant's structure of reason (hence, in the manner of the classical and philosophical tradition), Heidegger held fast to the idea of the historicity of Being in such a way that Nihilism could at the same time appear historically as the culmination point of occidental metaphysics in general. Entitled "Kehre," this change in the fundamental ontological assessments of *Being and Time* (1927) became the crystallization point of philosophical discussions. This idea of the historicizing of Being was attractive because it appeared to bring all latent, and even pronounced, basic views of the time into consideration: the concept that the catastrophe had to have an intellectual-historical background; the historistic view that the nature of man is only to be understood from his history; the anthropological position, according to which man would have to be understood in the realm of the organic as a singular being; the classical metaphysical position that the central question of philosophy consists in the pursuit of Being; the antimetaphysical tradition, according to which it is no longer permitted to speak of an eternal nature of things or even of man.

Only the thinkers who persisted in maintaining the basic significance of the sciences for mankind, who, like Aloys Wenzl, counted themselves as belonging to the tradition of an inductive metaphysics, or, who, like Nicolai Hartmann, represented a scientifically taught new ontology, found no point of contact with Heidegger's theory of *Seinsgeschick* (Destiny of Being). From their rank, therefore, came the sharpest critical comments, even during this early period. Nevertheless, this criticism remained ineffective at first, even though it seemed to most that the sciences stemming from the spirit of the Renaissance and modern philosophy, especially the objectivification of natural science and the technical civilization deriving from it, together with the innate tendency for self-destruction, represented one of the basic causes of the European catastrophe.

A change in the situation outlined resulted first as an indirect consequence of the question initiated by Heidegger. The attempt at "overcoming metaphysics at its roots" by returning to the pre-Platonic philosophy (the attempt which, at the same time, was supported by the proposition that the metaphysical tradition since Plato was to be characterized as the forgetting of being and led necessarily to a metaphysics of the will to power and to the self-destruction of mankind in the technical age) likewise called for a systematic interpretation of all phases of classical philosophy, as if to test the course of historical development of European man. However, it also meant more precise research into the origin of the modern sciences and a discussion of the historico-philosophical premises posed by Heidegger.

Consequently, there followed a considerably broadened spectrum of philosophical as well as historically interpretive and systematic research, as a result of which the one-sided, although understandable, perspectives of human existence in its finiteness and historicity gradually sacrificed their central position. It is significant that Jaspers began to write his extensive work *The Great Philosophers* while Heidegger was awaiting the arrival of new thinking because of the demands of Being. Nonetheless, it was precisely Jaspers' universal-philosophical as well as his philosophical-historical claim that led to the reestablishment not only of the philosophical positions of the 1920s but also of a renewed, open metaphysics as opposed to the entire philosophical tradition (Coreth, Krings, Max Müller, Rahner, and Siewerth). In addition, it also gave occasion for a new philosophical question oriented toward language and hermeneutics. By freeing the range of vision from the strictures of existential philosophy, not only the phenomenological assertions of Husserl (Fink, Landgrebe, and Spiegelberg) returned to the fore, but also the various experiments of the Joachim Ritter school (Gründer, Lübbe, Marquard, Oeing-Hanhoff, Oelmüller, and Spaemann) which were oriented toward a theory of the intellectual sciences and political philosophy, and which, in conjunction with Ritter's interpretations of Aristotle and Hegel, turned the entire breadth of philosophical tradition toward a hermeneutical focus. Lost sight of were inductive metaphysics and the new ontology of Nicolai Hartmann. However, their theoretical-knowledge basis of critical realism and their positive evaluation of the individual sciences gained indirectly in significance through the above-described broadening of the historical, as well as the systematic, horizon.

INTERNATIONALIZATION OF PHILOSOPHICAL RESEARCH: THE REHABILITATION OF SCIENCE—NEW HERMENEUTIC

The incipient broadening of the philosophical horizon following the solution of the existential problematic encouraged the beginnings of editorial activity and, on the other hand, was tendentiously strengthened precisely because of the deeper involvement with classical philosophers. With the Löwen-Husserl edition (introduced and arranged by Van Breda), not only Husserl's idea of philosophy as a strict science was brought anew into the discussion, but also, at the same time, the general questions of a transcendental egology and *Konstitutionslehre*. The Munich Fichte edition (Hans Jacob and Reinhard Lauth) was a prelude to a large number of further undertakings of philosophical editions. It strengthened—just as the appearance of the Hegel edition did—the turn to the classical tradition of German idealism (Henrich, Pöggeler). It also rehabilitated the significance of transcendental philosophy from its beginnings with Kant beyond its reconstruction by Fichte, as a systematic possibility for philosophical thought. It was precisely transcendental philosophy in the tradition of Kant—less in the sense of the narrower neo-Kantianism—which opened a new evaluation of scientific knowledge, even if it was Kant himself who, in his transcendental logic, opposed philosophy as a pure science to an *a posteriori* science of experience in the sense of empirical knowledge of the special laws of nature. Otherwise, the whole of German idealism with its thoughts of a systematic philosophical science held fast to the positive significance of science. For this reason, inductive metaphysics with its intentions toward an empirically oriented nature-philosophy gained new impetus. Hence, thinkers like Heisenberg, Jordan, and Carl Friedrich von Weizsäcker could join straightaway in the discussion of the problems of quantum mechanics and its significance for the theory of knowledge. But as a consequence, not only the fundamental problematic of the natural sciences returned to the general philosophical consciousness, but also the discussion of its relevance for philosophy and its basic concepts of space, time, substance, and causality (Reichenbach, Weyl). This problematic had already caused the philosophers of the Vienna Circle (Mach, Avenarius, Schlick, Neurath, Carnap, Popper, and Pap), in its turn, to renounce a philosophy that strongly recommended more metaphysical and empirically independent evidence.

Even before the philosophy of the Vienna Circle (where Anglo-American philosophical thought had found a voice), had again made its way to the Federal Republic of Germany where Stegmüller achieved a reception (Stegmüller had now become the successor to the Wenzl chair of philosophy), the heated discussions concerning the philosophical significance of mathematical logic had also prepared the way for the international entrance of German philosophy. Bochenski's *Formal Logic* was nonetheless understood as an historical representation of the course of development of logic which culminated in a logistic characterized by formalization, axiomatization, and calculization. Just as Stegmüller, so, too, did Scholz and, later, Menne struggle in the sometimes sharp discussion (Freytag-Löringhoff) for a calculated understanding of progress made possible through the work of Frege, Whitehead, Russell, Wittgenstein I, and Lukasiewicz. The semiotic formulated by Morris also became important for this discussion, which helped to clarify basic problems of logic by means of an exact and effective differentiation between syntax, semantics, and pragmatics (compare, Tarski, Gödel, and others). At the time, the differentiation of the various logics of testimonial, predicational, and relational calculuses and their formulation permitted the breadth of problems of logic to be recognized. It was, however, much less of an impetus per se for violent discussion than perhaps was the issue concerning the possibility of a many-valued logic linking with the concepts of a modal logic (Lewis). Paul Lorenzen had already distinguished himself in dealing with the question of a founding of logic. In any case, only later did his constructive statement find a general echo in the discussion concerning final founding in philosophy.

Science and scientific knowledge together could only be regarded as fully rehabilitated after a long first phase of distrust vis-à-vis the consequences of a new rationality culminating in the sciences—not until the return of logical empiricism from the United States. Supported by the successes of the technically replaceable knowledge of natural science, philosophy now seemed forced to abdicate in favor of science. In the face of the empirical meaning-criterion for determining the truth of statements and the suspicion of the meaninglessness of every metaphysical concept, the role left to philosophy was simply the discussion of problems thrown up by science itself: perhaps the discussion of the possibilities of formulating and making precise scientific concepts; the discussion of relationships between the language of theory and the language of observation; the construction, or better, the more precise explication of the basic concept of experience; the question of the general structure of scientific explanation (Hempel, Oppenheim); the problem of whether scientific statements can be proved valid through verification or only through falsification (Carnap and Popper); and finally the question of the status of theoretical concepts and their relationship to experience. These discussions were introduced into the German discussion or were kept active by Victor Kraft as well as Stegmüller, and later by Kutschera, Frey, Patzig, Haller, Weingartner, and others. But already Stegmüller—again influenced by the American scene—had formulated the internal problems of the empirical theory of science. Today, he is still involved with clarification, precision, and continuity as evidenced by his great and significant work on the theory of science and analytical philosophy. It was precisely he who made possible an appropriate judgment of this philosophical aim after an early over-estimation of the theory of science and the sciences.

In the beginning, however—and this is the characteristic element of the second phase—philosophy seemed, insofar as it wanted to be more than a simple reconstruction of scientific knowledge, to be put to the basic test by scientism. Should it actually be so, that the metric, i.e., the quantifying concept, is the most precise instrument of the sciences; and should it in fact hold true that all sciences, their various subject matters notwithstanding, seek laws according to the manner of natural laws, that they are bound to one and the same pattern of scientific explanation, and finally produce a generally valid and methodically gained knowledge of law?

At this point, within the framework of the linguistic-philosophical tradition founded by Gadamer in *Truth and Methods,* the new hermeneutic begins. In its analysis of the historicity of understanding, it reaches back beyond the neo-Kantian and the hermeneutic tradition carried from Schleiermacher to Dilthey. In Herder's criticism of Kant, it finds the systematically meaningful beginnings of a linguistic theory of human existence and being, which established the knowledge of philosophy and intellectual sciences in a new manner and in differentiation from knowledge of nature. The universally oriented hermeneutic with its linguistic theory of understanding (compare, too, Erich Heintel and Liebrucks) permitted the sciences and their development itself to become understandable once again as historically alterable products. It also showed the superiority of understanding over the methodical proceedings of more objective science. Its success and acceptance by the intellectual sciences, from the literary sciences to theology, fulfilled the function of a counterweight, opposing analytical philosophy's claim of being the only possible philosophy. While the scope of research was becoming international, neopositivism, or logical empiricism, had been appropriately received. It had, however, immediately announced its claim to exclusive validity and had forced the remaining philosophical claims into the role of being able to legitimize themselves only as philosophical history. In this context, hermeneutics (which also set out to establish itself universally as the true philosophy) appears as an effective bulwark of the continental tradition. Its renunciation of method and concept did not remain uncontested within the framework of the classical tradition. Moreover, the alternative "Theory of Science Contra Hermeneutics" also emerged through the gradual further development of analytical philosophy from the analysis of scientific languages to ordinary language philosophy (Wittgenstein II). Further discussion, which already carries over into the next stages, at first crystallized in a new problem, which could not be sufficiently overcome by either of the two sides. The problem, that of a logic for the social sciences, was not only a question of social philosophy that had been brought about again by the return to a philosophical tradition, but also a question that concerned structural social conditions.

THE PHASE OF CONFRONTATION: SOCIOLOGY-METHODOLOGY-POLITICAL PHILOSOPHY

The third phase of Germany's postwar philosophy is characterized by an encompassing argument with the entire field of analytical philosophy which limits scientific as well as rational concepts. The background for this confrontation was formed by the democracies which were newly established after the war and in the meantime stabilized and consolidated their social, political, and economic relationships. These democracies are now beginning to reveal the first traces of weariness of expansion and symptoms of sobering. The central point of controversy is the determination of a rationally established society and the conception of a social science adequate for it.

Both viewpoints of the confrontation that is now emerging have their roots in discussions and publications of the late 1950s and the early 1960s. Both refer to controversies within the framework of sociology: to the problem of the technical-scientific civilization, a problem which has become a part of human life because of the dominance of technical categories (see Freyer, Gehlen, Schelsky, Ritter), as well as the problem centered around the "Positivism Battle" in sociology kindled by Adorno and Popper, which repeated on a sociological plane the criticism of Viennese traditional thought as reformulated by the new hermeneutic. In any case, the one-time opponent (new hermeneutics) of logical empiricism had meanwhile basically changed from empiricism to critical rationalism because of Popper's research logic and his socio-philosophical assertions—even if the change was not immediately noticed everywhere. Carnap's reproach of traditional metaphysics for senselessness was just as little to be expected from Popper as, on the other side, the reproach of Popper's positivism missed the actual point of contention. The new situation was understood as a controversy concerning the logic of the social sciences and, therefore, as an argument about "scientism" or "dialectic" as scientific-theoretical assertions. The central problem now was the question of whether social-scientific knowledge in the sense of the concept of a unified science *(Einheits-wissenschaft)* was identical in structure to the knowledge of the natural sciences, or whether its own structural methods would have to be claimed for the social sciences. The labels scientism, hermeneutic, and dialectic mark the various suggestions and positions in this respect.

Thus, two main perspectives—the problem of civilization ruled by science in democratic societies and the determination of the status of the social sciences—were becoming peculiarly entwined and virulent against the background of socioeconomic experiences.

The problem of the highly developed industrial societies and their structural consequences of availability, manipulability, and quantification of humanity came to the fore under the influence of Herbert Marcuse (who is also regaining significance in Europe) in a fundamental criticism of the quantitatively productive society and its social structures. In the face of the rule of technology, the

sciences that led to it, and its technocratic management, the technocracy critique
went beyond Marcuse's idea of the "great refusal" to a utopia, a new society
free of repression and directed by the principle of desire. The American functionalism in sociology (see Parsons and Merton), supported by Dahrendorf in
contrast to the careful analysis and evaluation on the part of Habermas, was
subjected to as much criticism as the behavioral and critically rationalist approaches to the theoretical conception of social action. That this criticism of
scientific civilization could gain such far-reaching significance in the period of
the student movement of the late 1960s was due to the fact that the sociological
analysis of the present time, with a view to a possible therapy of the diagnosed
conditions and structures, met up with—seen from the historical-philosophical
point of view—an old systematic problem of philosophy itself: the relationship
of theory and practice. This old, unsolved problem, existing since Aristotle's
time and ever formulated anew, pressingly demanded a solution. The early
reception of Ritter's and Hennis's achievements in the area of Aristotelean
philosophy, Ritter's interpretation of Hegel's *Rechtsphilosophie,* and the consequent reception within the circle of the Ritter school (Lübbe, Marquard,
Oelmüller, Rohrmoser, and Spaemann) gave the topical question an historical
depth-dimension. At the same time, the critical theory, founded by the reestab-
lished Frankfurt Institute for Social Research (Adorno, Horkheimer) and later
continued by Habermas, was able to connect the systematic problem of the
relationship between theory and practice with a philosophy of history for practical
purposes—to change society, as it were, by means of the *a priori* goal of
emancipation. This was accomplished by the systematic recovery of the Marxian
assertion of philosophy becoming political and politics becoming philosophical.
The interpretation of social change as "the Dialectic of Enlightenment" attempted by Horkheimer and Adorno was at the same time a denial of the naively
understood Enlightenment concept of progress, a "Critique of Instrumental
Reason," which called the appropriate sciences, along with their existing relationships, into question. Its far-reaching, basic concept was first dispelled by
Habermas. It was expanded, with practical intent, into a philosophy of history
which seemed to open a path upon which the power of technical availability
could theoretically and practically be combined with the idea of a "good life"
and with technology, science, and democracy under the conditions of an advanced industrial society.

The resulting confrontations are collectively arguments concerning structural
questions of a political philosophy. If one disregards the more internal argument
of the Frankfurt school with Marcuse, then it can be said that, of the various
facets of the thematized problem area, two of these, with modifications, have
determined the third phase.

On the one side, it is a matter of the controversy carried on in many publications and replies between critical theory and critical rationalism concerning
the concept of reason, whose protagonists, following the example of Adorno
and Popper, have now become Habermas and Wellmer, Albert, Topitsch, and

Spinner. On the one hand, the idea of a reason, in which objective cognition and interest, theory and practice are thought of as a unity, has remained in irreconcilable contradiction to a concept of reason, which, to be sure, understood itself in the same way as critical authority, yet believed itself able to prove that the postulated unity of objective cognition and decision was a speculative myth. From this time on, the understanding of the social sciences, the relative value of the concept of "understanding," the evauation of the possibilities of historical-philosophical analyses, and the judgment of possible and meaningful rules and strategies for changing society in general have also remained controversial.

On the other side a confrontation developed between the critical social theory now represented exclusively by Habermas and his followers, and the system theory of Niklas Luhmann, which is a continuation of functionalism. Unlike the first controversy, both opponents held fast to the universal claim of socio-philosophical analysis. Their differences lay especially in their understanding of the basic structural impulses of social systems. Whereas Habermas interpreted society as the manner of realizating rational subjects, and therefore holding fast to the idea of the free, rational, and autonomous subject, Luhmann interpreted society primarily as a functional joining together of self-regulating system-segments independent of subjective intentions. The ego identity of rational subjects claimed and affirmed by Habermas was seen by Luhmann as an element that had become functionless within the levels of complexity of a highly industrialized society, which, moreover, threatened the survival of the social system. No wonder that the critical theory had to resist decisively and held fast (contra Luhmann, reproached for his cynicism and feared destruction of practical reason) to the moral reality of society and to the concept of rational and free decisions of individuals in a self-realizing progressive democracy, which, incidentally, is theoretically supported by evolution. The question that became urgent for Habermas in this argument—how we can consider and justify the capability to ascertain what is true in practical testimony by means of which even the highly complex industrial societies could legitimize their structure—led him to the conception of a communicative ethic, the discussion of which is already overflowing into the last phase of postwar philosophy in Germany.

The experience with democracy and its dangers (especially the problem of turning everything into scientific and quantitative entities) had already prepared the ground for an extensive argument concerning an adequate understanding of democracy and of a concept of the social sciences—and of social theory—which was simply reproducing the structures of quantification and alienation of the individual. The investigation of this turbulent period in social-historical and intellectual-historical analyses, the open questions concerning the understanding of the sciences, the understanding of the system structures of societies, and the problem of interpreting the relationship between individual and society are already projecting themselves as resultant problems into the next phase. The utopia of democratic societies oriented toward the pleasure principle, but also (in the broader sense of an ethic of communicative discourse) of a self-formulating idea of democratization of all areas of life and all institutions (basically, however, a misconception and self-destructive assertion), proved theoretically invalid during the course of discussion. Without a conclusive solution, the decisive problem of the relationship between ethics and institutional theory remained but a concept of society. The search for an alternative to an ethic of communication oriented toward discourse and practical reason (Apel, Habermas) and to a plurality of ethics, which is being presented concerning the momentary "unburdening" function of the various institutions (Gehlen), became the driving motive of the practical philosophy which had meanwhile moved into the center of general philosophical discussion.

FROM CONFRONTATION TO CRITICAL COEXISTENCE: THE EXPLORATION OF NEW POSSIBILITIES

The final phase, which is only several years old, seems at first glance to be a phase of general exhaustion. In truth, it can be understood as a return to the critical discussion of detail, though now on a cooperative basis. It is characterized by the noticeable broadening of the horizon of the former opponents analytical philosophy or critical rationalism and dialectical philosophy or critical theory.

The research in the history of science produced by Thomas Kuhn, Lakatos, and Musgrave and the research in the Federal Republic, part of which is original and part an extension of the history of science (compare, the Hamburg Institute for History and Natural Sciences: Sticker, Scriba, Schütt, Weyer as well as the Starnberg Max Planck Institute for Research into the Living Conditions of Scientific-Technical World: C. F. von Weizsäcker, Habermas, Böhme, Van den Daele, and Krohn; compare also the investigations of Blumenberg, Diederich, Hübner, Krüger, Mittelstrass, Schäfer, Stegmüller, Ströker, and Weingart) have produced a dynamic understanding of the sciences and their advancement of knowledge which interrelates and mediates differentially the viewpoints of hermeneutics as well as of critical theory and critical rationalism. On the other hand, analytical philosophy, mediated by the linguistic propensity of Austin, Chomsky, Searle, Wittgenstein II, and others, and by its turn to the question of utilitarian principles of ethics, has found new access into linguistic-philosophical and moral-practical problems of the classical-philosophical tradition which have undergone especially heavy discussion in Germany and Austria. The criticism by Albert and Hans Lenk of the neutrality thesis of meta-ethics, the new formulation of the analytical ethic by Frankena, the consideration of the problem of universalization (Hare, Singer), Rawls' theory of justice which recalls that of Kant, and the critical reception of this turn of analytical ethics to questions of the principles of morality by Hoerster, Annemarie Pieper, Höffe, Patzig and Kaulbach have helped the "Rehabilitation of Practical Philosophy" (Riedel and many others) succeed in the necessary systematic differentiations. But even the critical theory of the Frankfurt school has been decisively changed by its expansion into linguistics and the speech act theory, as well as by its surrender to the pragmatic shift begun by Apel and the critical reception of his efforts. Apel showed an early interest in the analytical tradition of the philosophy of language and lingustics. He reconciled this philosophy with the hermeneutic philosophy of language which followed from Heidegger. The later reception of Apel's work on Kant and Peirce was thereby not only assured of the necessary universal horizon, but was also helped to become widely effective.

At the same time, the historical-philosophical problematic of genre history (and its critical discussion in connection with the analytical philosophy of history from Danto to Baumgartner, Rüsen and again Habermas, among others) was forced, if not to reinterpret, at least to make precise its basic historical-materialistic premise and to modify it in the direction of an evolutionary theory of history, which now interprets the formations of society as sociocultural standards of learning. It is, therefore, no wonder that the concept of dialectic, which originally stood at the center of the conflict, has more or less disappeared from the circle of vision. Even the strategical alternative "Reform versus Revolution" has sacrificed its ideological, confessional character, giving way to a differentiated investigation of the circumstances to determine how desirable societal changes are possible and achievable. To be sure, the basic problem of the relationship of the rational individual to social reality has by no means been satisfactorily settled. Particularly as a problem of institutions, it determines, now as before, down to the fundamental questions of practical philosophy, the discussion of the problem of justifying a normative ethic, be it transcendentally, pragmatically, or constructivistically interpreted. But it also determines the argument that has arisen recently concerning the role and function that can be assigned to philosophy in the face of technical-scientific civilization and its highly complex societal formations.

The above-described broadening of horizons, the critical exchange among the earlier feuding camps, has produced a matter-of-fact climate of critical cooperation which, in conclusion, may be clarified by means of three examples. It concerns three active discussion groups that have been established in recent years, meet semi-annually and/or annually, respectively, and bring philosophers and scientists of the most varied backgrounds and orientations together for the critical analysis of philosophical problems.

The theory of historical and social sciences, especially the themes of "The Objectivity of History and Partiality," "History as Process," and "Theory and Narration in the Science of History," have been continually treated since 1974 in a discussion group of the Werner-Reimers Foundation. (Participants include Acham, Baumgartner, Berding, Faber, Fleischer, Gründer, Habermas, Hedinger, Kocka, Koselleck, Lübbe, Marquard, W. J. Mommsen, Nipperdey, Patzig, and Rüsen.) The first results of the work are already available in the omnibus volume *Theorie der Geschichte. Beiträge zur Historik,* Vol. 1, Munich (1976). Another discussion group, called into existence by the Fritz-Thyssen Foundation (Gerd Brand), has also been treating, since 1974, the central problem of the "Role and Function of Philosophy" under representative participation of all those philosophical orientations which had been expressed in past years in publications and lectures concerning the question "Why Philosophy?" (Apel, Baumgartner, Bubner, Gethmann, Hermann, Hinske, Kambartel, Kockelmanns, Krings, Lenk, Lübbe, Marquard, Mittelstrass, Riedel, Alfred Schmidt, Spaemann, Zimmerli, et al.) Similar discussion groups concerned with the same theme have been established by the Thyssen Foundation in England and in the United States. They are in contact with one another via individual members.

A third discussion group, founded in 1976 in Paderborn by Oelmüller, is dedicated to the fundamental questions of practical philosophy, especially the themes "Difficulties of Transcendental-Philosophical Norm Establishment," "Is the Claim of Universality of Moral and Political Norms Justifiable?," and "Norms and History." This group has been convening all the schools and philosophers who have been determining the nature of discussion in recent years and who are concerned with the theme "Ethikbegründung" (justification in ethics) and with moral problems in general: the Erlangen-Constance school of philosophical constructivism, founded by Lorenzen, continued by Schwemmer and Kambartel, and represented by Kambartel; the universal-pragmatically oriented critical theory represented by Habermas; the transcendental-pragmatic represented by Apel; the transcendental-philosophically oriented ethic represented by Krings; the various orientations originating with the Ritter school and represented by Lübbe, Marquard, and Oelmüller; and the analytical ethic represented by Hoerster and others.

Beyond the focal issues described, contemporary philosophy in the Federal Republic of Germany and Austria is complex and discriminating. It has found realization in a climate of critical matter of factness far removed from any rapturous gesture. Its chance lies in the common exploration of new possibilities in the style of cooperative communication. Beyond that which has already been done in this regard, perhaps we should note the sounding out of perspectives of an encompassing theory of self-consciousness (Henrich), the regaining of a general *Naturphilosophie* linking with the physical sciences (Kanitscheider), and the philosophical clarification of the resurging problem of the evolution of life (Monod, Eigen, and Wickler), as well as structures of knowledge (Piaget, Konrad Lorenz, and Vollmer).

The present state of philosophy in the Federal Republic of Germany and Austria will be lamented solely by those who believe that philosophy only possesses sociocritical and public significance when it indulges in violent polemics, disputes among its various schools, and announces itself loudly in the daily battle of public opinion.

APPENDIX

I. Organizational Framework of Philosophy

    A. Philosophy can be studied in West Germany at Universities (U), Pedagogical Colleges (PC), Technical Universities (TU), General Colleges (GC), Technical Colleges (TC), Philosophical-Technical Colleges (PTC), Sports Colleges (SC), and Colleges of Scientific Education (CSE).

    Institutes of higher learning where philosophy is taught are found at the following locations in West Germany: Aachen (TC, PC); Augsburg (U); Bagreuth (U); Bamberg (GC); Berlin (U, TU); Bielefeld (U); Bochum (U); Bonn (U, PC); Braunschweig (TU); Bremen (U); Cologne (U,PC,SC); Darmstadt (TC), Dortmund (PC); Duisburg (GC, PC); Düsseldorf (U); Eichstätt (GC); Erlangen-Nuremberg (U); Essen (GC); Flensburg (PC); Frankfurt (U); Freiburg (U, PC); Giessen (U); Göttingen (U); Hamburg (U); Hanover (TU); Heidelberg (U); Karlsruhe (U); Kassel (GC); Kiel (U); Koblenz (CSE); Konstanz (U); Mainz (U); Mannheim (U); Marburg (U); Munich (U, PTC, TU); Münster (U); Neuss (PC); Oldenburg (U); Paderborn (GC); Regensburg (U); Reutlingen (PC); Saarbrücken (U, PC); Stuttgart (U); Trier (U); Tübingen (U); Worms (CSE); Wuppertal (GC); Würzburg (U).

    The organizational structure of the departments of philosophy is not always uniform at the institutes of higher learning. The traditional faculties of philosophy were for the most part separated into subject areas following the reorganization of the universities. At some institutions, the subject of philosophy falls under the jurisdiction of a single department; at others, it has become a consolidated field of study along with other subjects (usually psychology and pedogogy).

    Unique up to now is the establishment of a Center for Philosophy and Foundations of Science at the University of Giessen.

    In Austria, philosophy is offered at universities in the cities of Graz, Innsbruck, Klagenfurt, Linz, Salzburg, and Vienna.

    B. Philosophical research and editions of philosophical authors are promoted, as a rule, by the Deutsche Forschungsgemeinschaft (German Society for Research), as well as by the funds of the Verband der Wissenschaftlichen Gesellschaften Österreichs (Organization of the Scientific Societies of Austria), earlier *"Notring,"* and directed by the following academies: the Academy of Sciences in Göttingen, established in 1751; the Bavarian Academy of Sciences in Munich, established in 1759; the Austrian Academy of Sciences in Vienna, established in 1847; the Heidelberg Academy of Sciences, established in 1909; the Academy of Sciences and Literature in Mainz, established in 1949; and the Rhenish-Westphalian Academy of Sciences in Düsseldorf, established in 1969. Philosophical discussion groups have been established: the Fritz-Thyssen Foundation, the Werner-Reimers Foundation, and the Foundation Alliance for German Science (Stiftverband für die Deutsche Wissenschaft).

    C. Special research articles for individual editions have been provided by the following archives and institutes: the Albertus Magnus Institute (Cologne); the Grabmann Institute (Munich); the Hegel Archive (Bochum); the Husserl Archive (branches in Freiburg, Cologne, and Aachen); the Thomas Institute

(Cologne); the Leibniz Archive (Hanover/Munich); and the Leibniz Research Institute (Münster/Berlin).

Especially to be noted is the International Research Center for Basic Questions of Science, Salzburg, which includes various institutions, e.g., Institutes of Scientific Theory, of Politology, of Media Research, and, among others, an Institute of Religious Sciences.

D. Attention is being paid to the general interests of philosophy by the General Society for Philosophy in Germany (AGPD), founded in Bremen in 1950. This duly qualified professional organization for philosophy in the broadest sense attempts to interest the widest circles in philosophical work as well as to represent the interests of philosophy as an academic discipline to the public. The "inner circle" of the AGPD consists of teachers of philosophy at institutes of higher learning. It provides for the exchange of scientific results, the exchange of philosophical views, and the discussion of all affairs concerning philosophy.

Since 1977, a study group of philosophic publications has also existed within the AGPD. The interests of the subject of philosophy at the *Gymnasien* (secondary level II) are represented by the official National Society of Philosophy Teachers, whose national chairman is a member of the enlarged directorate of the AGPD.

II. Congresses and Meetings

The following congresses have been organized in West Germany since 1945. Since 1954, they have been held under the leadership of the AGPD.

1. Garmisch-Partenkirchen, 1947
2. Mainz, 1948
3. Bremen, 1950
4. Stuttgart, 1954
5. Marburg, 1958
6. Munich, 1960
   General topic: "The Problem of Order"
7. Münster, 1962
   General topic: "Philosophy and the Question of Progress"
8. Heidelberg, 1966
   General topic: "The Problem of Language"
9. Düsseldorf, 1969
   General topic: "Philosophy and Science"
10. Kiel, 1972
    General topic: "Nature and History"
11. Göttingen, 1975
    General topic: "Logic. Ethics. Theory of the Arts"

To be mentioned also are the meetings of the Inner Circle of the AGPD, which are dedicated to more special philosophical topics and which are held from time to time in the years between the large congresses.

By invitation of the AGPD, the Sixteenth World Congress for Philosophy of the International Federation of Philosophical Societies (FISP) was held in Düsseldorf in 1978. The general theme was "Philosophy and the World View of the Modern Sciences."

In addition, philosophical meetings are being organized within the framework of Catholic (Munich, Vienna, and elsewhere) and Protestant (Hofgeismar, Tutzing, and elsewhere) academies by the Catholic Academic Societies in Germany and Austria, as well as annual meetings of the Görres Society, and in Walberberg (OP). As concerns Austria, special mention should be made of the fact that the Salzburg and Alpach institutional celebrations as well as the Austrian Wittgenstein Society in Kirchberg am Wechsel (near Vienna) regularly treat philosophical themes.

SELECT BIBLIOGRAPHY

BOOKS AND ARTICLES

Acham, K. *Analytische Geschichtsphilosophie* (Freiburg: Alber, 1974).

Adorno, T. *Negative Dialektik* (Turin: G. Einaudi, 1970).

———. *Prismen. Kulturkritik und Gesellschaft* (Berlin: Suhrkamp, 1969).

———. *Zur Metakritik der Erkenntnistheorie* (Frankfurt: Suhrkamp, 1970).

———, et al. (eds.) *Der Positivismusstreit in der deutschen Soziologie* (Neuweid: Luchterhand, 1969).

——— and Horkheimer, M. *Dialektik der Aufklärung* (Frankfurt: Fischer, 1969).

Albert, H. "Der Kritische Rationalismus K. R. Poppers," *Archiv für Rechts-und Sozialphilosophie* 46 (1960).

———. *Konstruktion und Kritik* (Hamburg: Hoffmann, 1974).

———. *Traktat über die Kritische Vernunft*, 2d ed. (Frankfurt: Mohr, 1975).

Apel, K.-O. *Der Denkweg von Charles S. Peirce* (Frankfurt: Suhrkamp, 1975).

——— (ed.). *Sprachpragmatik und Philosophie* (Frankfurt: Suhrkamp, 1975).

———. *Toward a Transformation of Philosophy*, trans. D. Frisby and G. Adey (Boston: Routledge and Kegan Paul, 1979).

———. *Transformationen der Philosophie*, 2 vols. (Frankfurt: Suhrkamp, 1973).

Baumgartner, H. M. *Kontinuität und Geschichte. Zur Kritik und Metakritik der historischen Vernunft* (Frankfurt: Suhrkamp, 1972).

———, Höffe, O., and Wild, C. (eds.). *Philosophie-Gesellschaft-Planung* (Munich: Bayerische Staatsinstitut für Hachschulforschung und Hochschulplanung, 1974).

——— and Jacobs, W. G. *J. G. Fichte-Bibliographie* (Stuttgart: Frommann, 1968).

——— and Rüsen, J. (eds.). *Seminar: Geschichte und Theorie* (Frankfurt: Suhrkamp, 1975).

——— and Sass, H. M. *Philosophie in Deutschland 1945–1975, Standpunkte-Entwicklungen-Literatur* (Meisenheim: Hain, 1978).

Biser, E. *Theologische Sprachtheorie und Hermeneutik* (Munich: Kösel, 1970).

Bloch, E. *Das Prinzip Hoffnung*, 3 vols. (Frankfurt: Suhrkamp, 1954–1959).

———. *Naturrecht und menschliche Würde* (Frankfurt: Suhrkamp, 1969).

Blumenberg, H. *Die kopernikanische Wende* (Frankfurt: Suhrkamp, 1965).

———. *Die Legitimation der Neuzeit* (Frankfurt: Suhrkamp, 1966).

———. *Selbsterhaltung und Beharrung. Zur Konstitution der neuzeitlichen Rationalität* (Mainz: Akademie der Wissenschaften und der Literatur, and Wiesbaden: Kommission bei Steiner, 1970).

Bochenski, I. M. *Die zeitgenössischen Denkmethoden* (Munich: Francke, 1971).

———. *Europäische Philosophie der Gegenwart* (Munich: Francke, 1951).

———. *Formale Logik* (Freiburg: Alber, 1956).

Böhme, G., van den Daele, W., and Krohn, W. *Experimentelle Philosophie* (Frankfurt: Suhrkamp, 1977).

Bollnow, O. F. *Die Lebensphilosophie* (Berlin: Springer, 1958).

———. *Einfache Sittlichkeit* (Frankfurt: Klosterman, 1947).

———. *Existenzphilosophie*, 6th ed. (Stuttgart: Kohlhammer, 1965).

———. *Neue Geborgenheit. Das Problem einer Überwindung des Existenzialismus*, 3d ed. (Stuttgart: Kohlhammer, 1972).

Brand, G. *Der Lebenswelt. Eine Philosophie des konkreten Apriori* (Berlin: W. de Gruyter, 1971).

———. *Welt, Geschichte, Mythos und Politik* (Berlin: W. de Gruyter, 1978).

Camus, A. *Der Mensch in der Revolte.* (Hamburg: Rowohlt, 1963).

———. *Der Mythos von Sisyphos. Ein Versuch über das Absurde*, 2d ed. (Hamburg: Rowohlt, 1958).

Carnap, R. *Der Logische Aufbau der Welt*, 2d ed. (Hamburg: Meiner, 1961).

———. *Logische Syntax der Sprache*, 2d ed. (Vienna: Springer, 1968).

———. *Scheinprobleme in der Philosophie* (Frankfurt: Suhrkamp, 1966).

Coreth, E. *Metaphysik eine Methodischsystematische* (Innsbruck: Grundlegung, 1961).

Dahrendorf, R. *Die angewandte Aufklärung. Gesellschaft und Soziologie in Amerika* (Munich: Piper, 1963).

Diederich, W. (ed.). *Theorie der Wissenschaftsgeschichte: Beiträge zur diachronischen Wissenschaftstheorie* (Frankfurt: Suhrkamp, 1974).

Ebbinghaus, J. *Gesammelte Aufsätze, Vorträge und Reden* (Hildesheim: Olms, 1968).

Faber, K. G. *Theorie der Geschichtswissenschaft* (Munich: Beck, 1974).

Feyerabend, P. *Wider den Methodenzwang. Entwurf einer anarchistischen Erkenntnistheorie*, trans. H. Vetter (Frankfurt: Suhrkamp, 1975).

Fink, E. *Sein, Wahreit, Welt; Von-Fragen zum Problem des Phänomen-Begriffs* (The Hague: Nijhoff, 1958).

———. *Studien zur Phänomenologie, 1930–1939* (The Hague: Nijhoff, 1966).

Franzen, W. *Martin Heidegger* (Stuttgart: Metzler, 1976).

Freyer, H. *Theorie des gegenwärtigen Zeitalters* (Stuttgart: Deutsche Verlagsanstalt, 1956).

———. *Theorie des objektiven Geistes. Eine Einführung in die Kulturphilosophie* (Leipzig: Taubner, 1928).

———. *Über das Dominantwerden technischer Kategorien in der Lebenswelt der industriellen Gesellschaft* (Mainz: Abhandlungen Der Akademie, 1960).

Frisch, A. *Grossmacht Technokratie-Die Zukunft der Gesellschaft* (Frankfurt: Agenor, 1955).

Gadamer, H.-G. *Hermeneutik und Dialektik. Festschrift für H.-G. Gadamer*, eds. R. Bubner, K. Cramer and R. Wiehl, 2 vols. (Tübingen: Mohr, 1970).

———. *Kleine Schriften* (Tübingen: Mohr, 1967).

———. *Wahrheit und Methode* (Tübingen: Mohr, 1960).

Gehlen, A. *Der Mensch; Seine Natur und Seine Stellung in der Welt*, 10th ed. (Wiesbaden: Akademische Verlagsgesellschaft Athenaion, 1974).

———. *Die Seele im technischen Zeitalter* (Hamburg: Rowohlt, 1957).

———. *Urmensch und Spätkultur* (Bonn: Athenäum, 1956).

Geldsetzer, L. *Allgemeine Bücher-und Institutionenkunde für das Philosophiestudium* (Freiburg: Alber, 1971).

Gethmann, C. F. *Verstehen und Auslegung. Das Methodenproblem in der Philosophie Martin Heideggers* (Bonn: Bouvier, 1974).

Grewendorff, G. and Meggle, G. (eds.). *Linguistik und Philosophie* (Frankfurt: Athenäum, 1974).

———. (eds.). *Seminar. Sprache und Ethik* (Frankfurt: Suhrkamp, 1974).

Guardini, R. *Das Ende der Neuzeit. Ein Versuch zur Orientierung* (Würzburg: Werkbund, 1950).

———. *Freiheit, Gnade, Schicksal* (Munich: Kösel, 1948).

———. *Welt und Person, Versuche zur Christlichen Lehre vom Menschen* (Würzburg: Werkbund, 1955).

208 Western Europe, Australia, and Israel

Habermas, J. *Antworten auf Herbert Marcuse* (Frankfurt: Suhrkamp, 1969).

———. *Erkenntnis und Interesse mit einem neuen Nachwort* (Frankfurt: Suhrkamp, 1968).

———. *Technik und Wissenschaft als "Ideologie"* (Frankfurt: Suhrkamp, 1968).

———. *Theorie und Praxis* (Frankfurt: Suhrkamp, 1971).

———. *Zur Logic der Sozialwissenschaften* (Tübingen: Mohr, 1967).

———. *Zur Rekonstruktion des Historischen Materialismus* (Frankfurt: Suhrkamp, 1976).

——— and Luhmann, N. *Legitimationsprobleme im Spätkapitalismus* (Frankfurt: Suhrkamp, 1973).

———. *Theorie der Gesellschaft oder Sozialtechnologie—Was leistet die Systemforschung?* (Frankfurt: Suhrkamp, 1971).

Hartmann, N. *Der Aufbau der realen Welt,* 2d ed. (Meisenheim: Hain, 1949).

———. *Grundzüge einer Metaphysik der Erkenntis,* 4th ed. (Berlin and Leipzig: W. de Gruyter, 1949).

———. *Zur Grundlegung der Ontologie* (Berlin and Leipzig: W. de Gruyter, 1948).

Heidegger, M. *Einführung in die Metaphysik* (Tübingen: Niemeyer, 1953).

———. *Holzwege* (Frankfurt: Klostermann, 1950).

———. *Sein und Zeit* (Halle: Niemeyer, 1955).

———. *Über der Humanismus* (Frankfurt: Klostermann, 1949).

———. *Vom Wesen der Wahrheit* (Frankfurt: Klostermann, 1954).

———. *Was ist Metaphysik?,* 4th ed. (Bonn: Cohen, 1955).

Heintel, E. *Die beiden Labyrinthe der Philosophie* I (Vienna: Oldenburg, 1968).

———. *Einführung in die Sprachphilosophie* (Darmstadt: Wissenschaftliche Buchgesellschaft, 1972).

Heisenberg, W. *Wandlungen in den Grundlagen der Naturwissenschaft* (Leipzig: Hirzel, 1944).

Hennis, W. *Politik und Praktische Philosophie. Eine Studie zur Rekonstruktion der politischen Wissenschaft* (Nuewied: Luchterhand, 1963).

Henrich, D. *Fichtes ursprüngliche Einsicht* (Frankfurt: Klostermann, 1967).

———. *Hegel im Kontext* (Frankfurt: Klostermann, 1971).

———. *Identität und Objektivität* (Heidelberg: Winter, 1976).

———. "Über die Einheit der Subjektivität," *Philosophische Rundschau* 3 (1955).

Hinst, P. *Logische Propädeutik* (Munich: Fink, 1974).

Hoerster, N. *Utilitaristische Ethik und Verallgemeinerung* (Freiburg: Alber, 1971).

Höffe, O. *Strategien der Humanität. Zur Ethik öffentlicher Entscheidungsprozesse* (Freiburg and Munich: Alber, 1975).

——— (ed.). *Über John Rawls Theorie der Gerechtigkeit* (Freiburg and Munich: Alber, 1977).

———. "Zur Situation der zeitgenössischen Philosophie in der Bundesrepublik Deutschland" (in Japanese), *Riso* 10 No. 473 (1972) and 12 No. 511 (1975).

Holzhey, H. and Zimmerli, W. (eds.). *Esoterik und Exoterik der Philosophie. Beiträge zu Geschichte und Sinn philosophischer Selbstbestimmung Rudolf W. Meyer zum 60 Geburtstog* (Basel and Stuttgart: Schwabe, 1977).

Horkheimer, M. *Zur Kritik der Instrumentellen Vernunft,* ed. A. Schmidt (Frankfurt: Fischer, 1974).

Hübner, K. "Zur Frage des Relativismus und des Fortschritts in den Wissenschaften," *Zeitschrift für allgemeine Wissenschaftstheorie* 5 (1974).

Jacobs, W. G. "Bedeutung und Problematik philosophischer Editionen. Zur Lage dieser Editionen in der Bundesrepublik," *Philosophisches Jahrbuch* 79 (1972).

———. "Editionen im Bereich der Philosophie," *Philosophisches Jahrbuch* 80 (1973).

Jaspers, K. *Der Philosophische Glaube* (Munich: Piper, 1954).

———. *Die Grossen Philosophen* (Munich: Piper, 1957).

———. *Philosophie,* 3 vols. (Berlin: Springer, 1948).

———. *Vom Ursprung und Ziel der Geschichte* (Munich: Piper, 1952).

———. *Von der Wahrheit,* 2d ed. (Munich: Piper, 1958).

Jordan, P. *Die Physik und das Geheimnis des organischen Lebens* (Braunschweig: Vieweg, 1941).

Jünger, F. G. *Die Perfektion der Technik* (Frankfurt: Klostermann, 1953).

———. *Orient und Okzident* (Hamburg: Dulk, 1948).

Kambartel, F. *Erfahrung und Struktur* (Frankfurt: Suhrkamp, 1968).

——— (ed.). *Praktische Philosophie und konstruktive Wissenschaftstheorie* (Frankfurt: Suhrkamp, 1968).

———. *Was ist und soll Philosophie?* (Konstanz: Universitätsverlag, 1968).

Kanitscheider, B. *Philosophisch-historische Grundlagen der physikalischen Kosmologie* (Stuttgart and Berlin: Kohlhammer, 1974).

Kaulbauch, F. *Ethik und Metaethik* (Darmstadt: Wissenschaftliche Buchgesellschaft, 1974).

Klibansky, R. (ed.). *Contemporary Philosophy: A Survey* (Florence, Italy: Nuova Italia, 1968–1971).

——— (ed.). *Philosophy in the Mid-Century* (Florence, Italy: Nuova Italia, 1958).

Koselleck, R. *Kritik und Krise* (Freiburg: Alber, 1959).

——— and Stempel, W. D. (eds.). *Geschichte, Ereignis, und Erzählung* (Munich: Fink, 1973).

Kraft, V. *Der Wiener Kreis. Der Ursprung des Neopositivismus,* 2d rev. ed. (Vienna: Springer, 1968).

Krings, H. "Die Wandlung des Realismus in der Philosophie der Gegenwart," *Philosophisches Jahrbuch* 70 (1962–1963).

———. *Fragen und Aufgaben der Ontologie* (Tübingen: Niemeyer, 1954).

———. *Tranzendentale Logik* (Munich: Kösel, 1964).

———, Baumgartner, H. M. and Wild, C. (eds.). *Handbuch philosophischer Grundbegriffe* (Munich: Kösel, 1973–1974).

———. (eds.). *Philosophie. Zur Situation des Faches Philosophie an den Hochschulen der Bundesrepublik Deutschland* (Munich: Bayerisches Staatsinstitut für Hochschulforshung und Hochschulplanung, 1974).

Lakatos, I. and Musgrave, A. (eds.). *Kritik und Erkenntnisfortschritt* (Braunschweig: Vieweg, 1974).

Landgrebe, L. *Der Weg der Phänomenologie* (Gütersloh: Mohn, 1963).

———. "Husserls Abschied com Cartesianismus," *Philosophische Rundschau* 9 (1961).

———. "Metaphysik und Ontologie," in *Contemporary Philosophy. A Survey III Metaphysics, Phenomenology, Language and Structure,* ed. R. Klibansky (Florence, Italy: Nuova Italia, 1969).

———. *Phänomenologie und Geschichte* (Gütersloh: Mohn, 1963).

———. *Phänomenologie und Metaphysik* (Hamburg: M. von Schröder, 1949).

———. *Philosophie der Gegenwart* (Frankfurt: Athenäum, 1958).

———. *Was Bedeutet uns Heute Philosophie?* (Hamburg: M. von Schröder, 1954).

Lenk, H. "Der 'Ordinary Language Approach' und die Neutralitätsthese der Metaethik," in *Das Problem der Sprache,* ed. H.-G. Gadamer (Munich: Fink, 1967).

——— (ed.). *Handlungstheorie-interdiziplinär,* 4 vols. (Munich: Fink, 1977).

———. *Metalogik und Sprachanalyse* (Freiburg: Rombach, 1973).

——— (ed.). *Neue Aspekte der Wissenschaftstheorie* (Braunschweig: Vieweg, 1971).

———. *Philosophie im technologischen Zeitalter,* 2d ed. (Stuttgart, Berlin, Cologne and Mainz: Kohlhammer, 1972).

———. *Pragmatische Philosophie* (Hamburg: Hoffman and Campe, 1975).

———. *Wozu Philosophie?* (Munich: Piper, 1974).

Liebrucks, B. *Sprache und Bewusstsein,* 6 vols. (Frankfurt and Bern: Lang, 1964–1974).

Litt, T. *Wege und Irrwege geschichtlichen Denkens* (Munich: Piper, 1948).

Lorenz, Ko. *Die Rückseite des Spiegels,* 2d ed. (Munich: Piper, 1973).

Lorenz, Ku. *Elemente der Sprachkritik. Eine Alternative zum Dogmatismus und Skeptizismus in der Analytischen Philosophie* (Frankfurt: Suhrkamp, 1970).

Lorenzen, P. *Methodisches Denken* (Frankfurt: Suhrkamp, 1970).

———. *Normative Logic and Ethics* (Mannheim, Vienna, and Zürich: Bibliographisches Institut, 1969).

——— and Kamlah, W. *Logische Propädeutik* (Mannheim, Vienna, and Zürich: Bibliographisches Institut, 1973).

——— and Schwemmer, O. *Konstruktive Logik, Ethik, und Wissenschaftstheorie* (Mannheim, Vienna, and Zürich: Bibliographisches Institut, 1973).

Löwith, K. *Heidegger. Denker in dürftger Zeit* (Frankfurt: Fischer, 1953).

Lübbe, H. *Fortschritt als Orientierungsproblem* (Freiburg: Rombach, 1975).

———. *Theorie und Entscheidung Studien zum Primat der praktischen Vernunft* (Freiburg: Rombach, 1975).

———. *Unsere stille Kulturrevolution* (Zürich: Edition Interfrom, 1976).

Luhmann, N. *Zweckbegriff und Systemrationalität. Über die Funktion von Zwecken in sozialen Systemen* (Frankfurt: Suhrkamp, 1973).

Marcuse, H. *Der eindimensionale Mensch*, 7th ed. (Neuweid: Luchterhand, 1969).

———. *Triebstruktur und Gesellschaft*, trans. M. von Eckhardt-Jaffe (Frankfurt: Suhrkamp, 1970).

Marquard, O. *Schwierigkeiten mit der Geschichtsphilosophie* (Frankfurt: Suhrkamp, 1973).

Marx, W. *Heidegger und die Tradition* (Frankfurt: Fischer, 1961).

Meyer, H. *Geschichte der abendländischen Weltanschauung V Die Weltanschauung der Gegenwart* (Paderborn: Schöningh, 1966).

Mittelstrass, J. *Die Möglichkeit von Wissenschaft* (Frankfurt: Suhrkamp, 1974).

——— and Kambartel, F. *Zum Normative Fundament der Wissenschaft* (Frankfurt: Athenäum, 1973).

——— and Riedel, M. *Vernünftiges Denken: Studien zur praktischen Philosophie und Wissenschaftstheorie* (Berlin: W. de Gruyter, 1978).

Müller, M. *Existenzphilosophie im geistigen Leben der Gegenwart*, 3d ed. (Heidelberg: Kerle, 1964).

———. *Sein und Geist* (Tübingen: Mohr, 1940).

Nink, C. *Ontologie* (Freiburg: Herder, 1952).

———. *Philosophische Gotteslehre* (Munich: Kösel, 1948).

Noack, H. *Die Philosophie Westeuropas im zwangzigsten Jahrhundert*, 2d ed. (Basel and Stuttgart: Schwabe, 1976).

Nusser, K. H. "Sachliteratur zur Philosophie und Soziologie," in *Kindlers Literaturgeschichte der Gegenwart V Die deutschsprachige Sachliteratur*, ed. R. Radler (Munich: Kindler, 1977).

———. *Vademecum Deutscher Lehr-und Forschungstätten. Ein Hanbuch des Wissenschaftlichen Lebens* (Essen: Stiftverband für die Deutsche Wissenschaft, 1978).

Oelmüller, W. *Die unbefriedigte Aufklärung* (Frankfurt: Suhrkamp, 1969).

———. (ed.). *Materialien zur Normendiskussion I Tranzendental philosophische Normenbegründungen* (Paderborn: Schöningh, 1978–   ).

Ortega y Gasset, J. *Aufstand der Massen* (Stuttgart: Deutsche Verlagsanstalt, 1951).

———. *Die Aufgabe unserer Zeit* (Stuttgart: Deutsche Verlagsanstalt, 1930).

———. *Gesammelte Werke* (Stuttgart: Deutsche Verlagsanstalt, 1954–1956).

———. *Geschichte als System* (Stuttgart: Deutsche Verlagsanstalt, 1952).

Otto, S. "Die Kritik der historischen Vernunft innerhalb der Denkfigur des Hegelschen 'Vernunftschlusses'," *Phass* 81 (1974).

———. "Faktizität und Transzendentalität der Geschichte," *Zeitschrift für philosophische Forschung* 31 (1977).

Patzig, G. *Ethik ohne Metaphysik* (Göttingen: Vandenhoech and Ruprecht, 1971).

———. *Sprache und Logik* (Göttingen: Vandenhoech and Ruprecht, 1970).

Pieper, A. "Analytische Ethik. Ein Überblick über die seit 1900 in England und Amerika erschienene Ethik-Literatur," *Philosophisches Jahrbuch* 78 (1971).

———. *Sprachanalytische Ethik und praktische Freiheit* (Stuttgart: Kohlhammer, 1973).

Pieper, J. *Musse und Kult* (Munich: Kösel, 1948).

———. *Philosophia negativa* (Munich: Kösel, 1952).

———. *Wahrheit der Dinge*, 4th ed. (Munich: Kösel, 1966).

Pöggeler, O. *Der Denkweg Martin Heideggers* (Pfullingen: Neske, 1963).

——— (ed.). *Heidegger-Perspektiven zur Deutung seines Werks* (Cologne: Kiepenheuer and Witsch, 1969).

——— (ed.). *Hermeneutische Philosophie. Zehn Aufsätze* (Munich: Nymphenburger, 1972).

Popper, K. R. *Das Elend des Historizismus*, 2d ed. (Tübingen: Mohr, 1969).

————. *Die Offene Gesellschaft und ihre Feinde* (Munich: Francke, 1975).

————. *Logik der Forschung* (Tübingen: Mohr, 1974).

————. *Objektive Erkenntnis* (Hamburg: Hoffmann and Campe, 1974).

Rahner, K. *Geist in Welt* (Munich: Kösel, 1957).

Reichenbach, H. *Der Aufstieg der wissenschaftlichen Philosophie*, 2d ed. (Braunschweig: Vieweg, 1968).

Riedel, M. "Der Denker Herbert Marcuse. Die Philosophie der Weigerung," *Merkur Heft* 236 (1967).

———— (ed.). *Rehabilitierung der Praktischen Philosophie*, 2 vols. (Freiburg: Rombach, 1972–1974).

Ritter, J. *Hegel und die Französische Revolution* (Cologne: Westdeutscher, 1957).

————. *Metaphysik und Politik. Studien zu Aristoteles und Hegel*, 2d ed. (Frankfurt: Suhrkamp, 1977).

————. *Subjektivität* (Frankfurt: Suhrkamp, 1974).

————. "Zur Grundlegung der praktischen Philosophie bei Aristoteles," *Archiv für Rechts-und Sozialphilosophie* 46 (1960).

Rohrmoser, G. *Das Elend der Kritischen Theorie* (Freiburg: Rombach, 1970).

————. *Subjektivität und Verdinglichung* (Gütersloh: Gütersloher, 1961).

Rothacker, E. *Einleitung in die Geisteswissenschaften* (Darmstadt: Wissenschaftliche Buchgesellschaft, 1972).

————. *Mensch und Geschichte* (Bonn: Athenäum, 1950).

————. *Probleme der Kulturanthropologie* (Bonn: Bouvier, 1948).

Rüsen, J. *Für eine erneuerte Historik* (Stuttgart: Frommann-Holzboog, 1976).

———— (ed.). *Historische Objektivität* (Göttingen: Vandenhoeck and Ruprecht, 1975).

Sartre, J.-P. *Das Sein und das Nichts* (Hamburg: Rowohlt, 1952).

————. *Ist der Existenzialismus ein Humanismus?* (Zürich: Europa, 1947).

————. *Kritik der dialektischen Vernunft* I (Hamburg: Rowohlt, 1967).

Schäfer, L. *Erfahrung und Konvention. Zum Theoriebegriff der empirischen Wissenschaften* (Stuttgart: Frommann-Holzboog, 1974).

Schelsky, H. *Der Mensch in der wissenschaftlichen Zivilisation* (Cologne: Westdeutscher, 1961).

————. *Die sozialen Folgen der Automatisierung* (Düsseldorf: Diederich, 1957).

Schischkoff, G. "Deutsche Philosophie von Garmisch bis Kiel," *Zeitschrift für philososphische Forschung* 26 (1972).

Schmidt, A. *Geschichte und Struktur. Fragen einer marxistischen Historik* (Munich: Hanser, 1972).

———— (ed.). *Kritische Theorie. Eine Dokumentation*, 2 vols. (Frankfurt: Fischer, 1968).

Schneider, F. *Philosophie der Gegenwart* (Munich: Reinhardt. 1964).

Schulz, W. *Philosophie in der veränderten Welt* (Pfullingen: Neske, 1972).

Schwemmer, O. *Philosophie der Praxis* (Erlangen: Nürnberg, 1970).

————. *Theorie der rationalen Erklärung* (Munich: Beck, 1976).

Siewerth, G. *Das Schicksal der Metaphysik von Thomas zu Heidegger* (Einsiedeln: Johannes, 1959).

————. *Der Thomismus als Identitätssystem* (Frankfurt: Schulte-Bulmke, 1939).

Simon, J. (ed.). *Aspekte und Probleme der Spachphilosophie* (Freiburg: Alber, 1973).

———— (ed.). *Freiheit. Theoretische und praktische Aspekte des Problems* (Freiburg and Munich: Alber, 1977).

————. *Wahrheit als Freiheit* (Berlin and New York: W. de Gruyter, 1978).

Spaemann, R. "Courants philosophiques dans l'Allemagne d'Aujourdhui," *Archives des Philosophie* (1958).

————. "Philosophie," in *Der Grosse Herder* XII, Supplementary Volume XI: sections 1187–1308, especially 1283–1290 (Freiburg: Herder, 1962).

————. *Zur Kritik der politischen Utopie* (Stuttgart: Klett, 1977).

Specht, E. K. *Die sprachphilosophische und ontologische Grundlage im Spätwerk Wittgensteins* (Cologne: Kölner Universitäts-Verlag, 1963).

Spiegelberg, H. *The Phenomenological Movement. A Historical Introduction*, 2 vols. (The Hague: Nijhoff, 1960).

Spinner, H. *Pluralismus als Erkenntnismodell* (Frankfurt: Suhrkamp, 1974).

Stegmüller, W. *Collected Papers on Epistemology, Philosophy of Science and History of Philosophy*, 2 vols. (Dordrecht: Reidel, 1977).

————. *Hauptströmungen der Gegenwartsphilosophie*, 2 vols., 5th ed. (Stuttgart: Kröner, 1969–1975).

————. *Metaphysik-Wissenschaft-Skepsis*, 2d ed. (Berlin and New York: Springer, 1969).

————. *Probleme und Resultate der Wissenschaftstheorie und analytischen Philosophie*, 2 vols. (Berlin and New York: Springer, 1969–1970).

Ströker, E. *Einführung in die Wissenschaftstheorie* (Munich: Nymphenburger, 1973).

————. *"Geschichte als Herausforderung," Neue Hefte für Philosophie*, No. 6/7, (1974).

————. *Wissenschaftsgeschichte als Herausforderung* (Frankfurt: Klostermann, 1976).

Theunissen, M. *Gesellschaft und Geschichte. Zur Kritik der Kritischen Theorie* (Berlin: W. de Gruyter, 1969).

Topitsch, E. *Vom Ursprung und Ende der Metaphysik*, 2d ed. (Vienna: Springer, 1962).

————, et al. (eds.). *Logik der Sozialwissenschaften* (Cologne and Berlin: Kiepenheuer Witsch, 1965).

Tugendhat, E. *Der Wahrheitsbegriff bei Husserl und Heidegger* (Berlin: W. de Gruyter, 1967).

————. *Vorlesungen zur Einführung in die sprachanalytische Philosophie* (Frankfurt: Suhrkamp, 1976).

van Peursen, C. A. *Phänomenologie und analytische Philosophie* (Stuttgart: Kohlhammer, 1969).

Vollmer, G. *Evolutionäre Erkenntnistheorie* (Stuttgart: Hirzel, 1975).

von Kutschera, F. *Sprachphilosophie* (Munich: Fink, 1971).

von Rintelen, F.-J. *Contemporary German Philosophy and its Background* (Bonn: Bouvier, 1969).

————. *Philosophie des lehendigen Geistes in der Krise der Gegenwart* (Göttingen: Musterschmidt, 1977).

von Savigney, E. *Analytische Philosophie* (Munich: Alber, 1970).

————. *Die Philosophie der normalen Sprache* (Frankfurt: Suhrkamp, 1969).

von Weizsäcker, C. F. *Die Einheit den Natur* (Munich: Hanser, 1971).

————. *Die Geschichte der Natur* (Göttingen: Vanderhoeck and Ruprecht, 1970).

————. *Zum Weltbild der Physik* (Stuttgart: Hirzel, 1970).

Waldenfels, B. *Das Zwischenreich des Dialogs* (The Hague: Nijhoff, 1971).

Weingart, P. "Die Bedeutung der Wissenschaftsgeschichte für die Wissenschaftstheorie," *Studia Leibnitiana* Special Number 6 (1977).

————. *Wissenschaftssoziologie*, 2 vols. (Bonn: Athenäum, 1972–1974).

Weingartner, P. *Wissenschaftstheorie*, 3 vols. (Stuttgart: Frommann-Holzboog, 1971–1976).

Weischedel, W. *Der Gott der Philosophen. Grundlegung einer philosophischen Theologie im Zeitalter des Nihilismus*, 2 vols. (Munich: Nymphenburger, 1971–1972).

————. *Wirklichkeit und Wirklichkeiten* (Berlin: W. de Gruyter, 1960).

Wellmer, A. *Methodologie als Erkenntnistheorie* (Frankfurt: Suhrkamp, 1967).

Wenzl, A. *Materie und Leben* (Stuttgart: Schwab, 1949).

————. *Wissenschaft und Weltanschauung* (Leipzig: Meiner, 1936).

Wieland, W. *Die Aristotelische Physik* (Göttingen: Vandenhoeck and Ruprecht, 1970).

Wittgenstein, L. *Philosophische Untersuchungen* ("Philosophical Investigations") (Original German text with English translation) (Oxford: Blackwell, 1958).

Wohlgenannt, R. *Was ist Wissenschaft?* (Braunschweig: Vieweg, 1969).

JOURNALS

West Germany

The Journal for Philosophical Research, newly established by G. Schischkoff and published in conjunction with the AGPD, has had a major influence on the revival of philosophy since World War II, along with the continuing publication of the *Philosophisches Jahrbuch* of the Görres Society and the *Kant-Studien* which did not appear again until somewhat later. This new publication has been followed by a series of other journals, which since that time have been giving form to philosophical life in West Germany.

Archiv für Geschichte der Philosophie (formerly *Archiv fur Philosophie*), Berlin, 1887/1888– . Resumed publication in 1960– .

Philosophisches Jahrbuch, Freiburg/Munich, 1888– .

Kant Studien, Berlin, 1897– .

Archiv für Rechts- und Sozialphilosophie, Wiesbaden, 1907– .

Theologie und Philosophie (formerly *Scholastik*), Freiburg, 1926– .

Zeitschrift für philosophische Forschung, Meisenheim, 1945– .

Archiv für Philosophie, Meisenheim, 1947–1964.

Philosophischer Literaturanzeiger, Meisenheim, 1949– .

Philosophia Naturalis, Meisenheim, 1951– .

Philosophische Rundschau, Tübingen, 1953– .

Archiv für Begriffsgeschichte, Bonn, 1955– .

Ratio (German and English edition), Hamburg, 1957– .

Erkenntnis. An International Journal of Analytic Philosophy, Hamburg/Dordrecht, 1966– .

Philosophy and History. A Review of German-Language Research. Contributions on Philosophy, History, and Cultural Developments (German Studies, Section I). 1968– .

Philosophische Perspektiven, Frankfurt, 1969–1973.

Zeitschrift für allgemeine Wissenschaftstheorie, Wiesbaden, 1970– .

Neue Hefte für Philosophie, Göttingen, 1971– .

Phänomenologische Forschungen, Freiburg, 1975– .

Allgemeine Zeitschrift für Philosophie, Stuttgart, 1976– .

Austria

Zeitschrift für Katholische Theologie, Vienna, 1876– .

Wort und Wahrheit. Monatsschrift für Religion und Kultur, Vienna, 1946– .

Wiener Zeitschrift für Philosophie, Psychologie und Pädagogik, 1947– .

Wissenschaft und Weltbild, Vienna, 1948– .

Salzburger Jahrbuch für Philosophie, 1957– .

Conceptus. Zeitschrift für Philosophie, Innsbruck, 1967– .

Wiener Jahrbuch für Philosophie, 1968– .

Grazer Philosophische Studien. Internationale Zeitschrift für analytische Philosophie, 1975– .

EDITIONS

At the present time the following editions are being produced (continued or begun) in West Germany:

Albertus Magnus-Ausgabe, Bonn/Münster

Anselm von Canterbury-Ausgabe, Stuttgart

Bolzano-Ausgabe, Munich

Cusanus-Ausgabe, Heidelberg

Dilthey-Ausgabe, Stuttgart/Göttingen

Eckhart-Ausgabe, Stuttgart

Fichte-Ausgabe, Munich

von Freiberg-Ausgabe, Bochum

Hegel-Ausgabe, Bochum

Heidegger-Ausgabe, Frankfurt

von Hildebrand-Ausgabe, Stuttgart/Regensburg

Husserl-Ausgabe, Löwen (Branches in Freiburg, Cologne, and Aachen)

Jacobi-Briefe-Ausgabe, Munich

Kant-Ausgabe, Göttingen (formerly Berlin)
Kepler-Ausgabe, Munich
Kopernikus-Ausgabe, Munich/Berlin
Leibniz-Ausgabe, Münster/Hanover/Berlin
Nietzsche-Ausgabe, Berlin
Paracelsus-Ausgabe, Marburg
Scheler-Ausgabe, Bern/Munich
Schelling-Ausgabe, Munich
Friedr. Schlegel-Ausgabe, Paderborn/Zurich
Schopenhauer-Ausgabe, Darmstadt
Deutsche Thomas-Ausgabe, Salzburg/Walberberg
Also worthy of mention are the diligent undertakings for the publications of the *Historischen Wörterbuch der Philosophie,* Basel/Stuttgart, 1971–   , and the *Reallexikons für Antike und Christentum,* Stuttgart, 1950–

Australia

SELWYN A. GRAVE

The dominant figure in Australian philosophy in 1945 was John Anderson, Challis professor of philosophy at the University of Sydney. Various aspects of Anderson's philosophy are, more or less adequately, described by Anderson himself as "realist," "naturalist," "materialist," "pluralist," "determinist," "positivist," and "empiricist."

THE ANDERSONIAN PHILOSOPHY

Anderson contends that there is "only one way of being"—being in space and time—and, correspondingly, "only one way of knowing." Attempts to "divide reality into 'realms' " run up against "the impossibility of finding any *relation* between the different realms,"[1] between a God and the world, for instance, between the body and an immaterial mind, between a realm in which determinism holds and one in which indeterminism holds. That is one type of argument Anderson employs to illustrate the doctrine of a single way of being. He uses an infinite regress argument against the attempt to claim special status for some entity. He argues that the entity has no content or that, if describable, it lapses to the level it was supposed to transcend. He maintains that "conditions of discourse" have been violated.

The doctrine of a single way of being pronounces against all "ultimates and derivatives." There is no First Cause, no simple units out of which complexities are built, no Absolute, and, correspondingly, no degrees of truth. The doctrine rejects discontinuities generally. There are only truths, and no necessary truths; "good" is as naturalistic a predicate as "green"; there is no body-mind dualism.

Anderson's realism maintains the independence of everything that is known from its being known: there is nothing the nature of which is to be known. Equally, there is nothing the nature of which is to know. Knowing and being known are relations, and relations cannot constitute the terms they relate, which must have an existence of their own and qualities of their own.

In 1950, G. Ryle wrote an article for the *Australasian Journal of Philosophy* entitled "Logic and Professor Anderson." Ryle focuses on three of Anderson's

The writer of this survey wishes to acknowledge the assistance—at times essential—he has received in its composition.

doctrines: good, a "description of certain things, helping us to recognize them just as their being green might do";[2] geometry, an empirical science; and implication, a "sensible fact." "What has gone wrong?," Ryle asks. He sees at least part of the answer in the poverty of Anderson's "logical alphabet." "His regular touchstone is the question 'Quality or Relation?'. Is knowing (or willing) a quality? No; so it must be a relation. Is good a relation? No; so it must be a quality."[3]

J. L. Mackie, who was one of Anderson's students and who is now one of the best known contemporary philosophers from Australia, countered the charge that Anderson's logic is too exiguous.[4] Ryle, he begins, does not argue that Anderson's position as regards the nature of good, geometry, and implication is absurd; taking it to be absurd, he infers that Anderson's logic is too exiguous. Mackie, of course, agrees that if the "categories" are "the types of predication found in ordinary language," there will not be only two of them. "But if we ask how many sorts of facts there are, it is much less obvious that there are facts which consist neither in things having (or not having) a certain quality nor in relations between two or more things" (p. 110). Ryle's own procedure in *The Concept of Mind*, Mackie remarks (p. 113), brings to bear on the linguistic complexity of his material "a much simpler background logic, which recognizes two sorts of propositions, hypotheticals and those about events."

GASKING AND JACKSON

At Melbourne, the rival city to Sydney, the new force was Wittgensteinian, which around 1945 was especially associated with the names of Douglas Gasking and A. C. Jackson. Gasking's influence has been out of all proportion to the quantity of his writing. Of this writing, we shall barely mention his celebrated papers which were written before the beginning of the period covered by this survey, namely, "Mathematics and the World," "Causation and Recipes," and "Avowals." Here we will limit ourselves to a discussion of his paper "Clusters," which is less well known abroad.

Without an understanding of the logic of what he calls a "cluster," Gasking suggests, there can be no hope of satisfactorily handling many metaphysical questions. We shall have to leave unsummarized Gasking's careful building up of the notion of a cluster. The example he works with is that of the ship-cluster: twenty-six ships, named from A to Z, each in visual contact with at least one of the others, so that each is "serially in contact" with every other ship in the group, but with no ship outside the group. The situation is stable enough for the group to be regarded as a single enduring entity and given a proper name. The philosophical issues which Gasking discusses in connection with the notion of a cluster, and with this example of one, include the following: whether the meaning a person gives to a word coincides with his criterion for applying it; questions of implication as between different levels of language; and the concept of a "natural kind."

A. C. Jackson's great influence has been upon his students and upon philosophers who have known him personally. He gave the John Locke Lectures at the University of Oxford a number of years ago but has not published them.

PASSMORE

John Passmore occupies a special place as an Australian philosopher. His books on Cudworth (1951) and Hume (1952), his *A Hundred Years of British Philosophy*, and a number of his papers are written with accuracy and economy, and convey an insight into positions quite alien to his own. These works have made him one of the most distinguished living philosophical historians. No other Australian philosopher has his range: In addition to his work in the history of philosophy and in central areas of philosophy, his writings on aesthetics and the philosophy of science have also received attention.[5] Two recent books, *The Perfectibility of Man*, which is a history of, and prophylactic against, perfectibilist ideas, and *Man's Responsibility for Nature*, exemplify that concern with broad human issues which Passmore maintains to be part of the business of a philosopher.

Passmore has been an unremitting proponent of the "Sydney" conception of philosophy as concerned with the world and only incidentally with language. Acknowledging a debt to Anderson ("In part, what I am describing is what he practiced"), as well as to Ryle, Passmore sets out in *Philosophical Reasoning* to examine types of argument that are characteristically philosophical, such as the infinite regress arguments, which are not always fully understood by philosophers, Passmore maintains, and are liable to be found puzzling by nonphilosophers.

"THE IDENTITY THEORY OF MIND"

For about twenty years, a good deal of the best philosophical energy in Australia has gone into the discussion of what is sometimes referred to abroad as Australian materialism, the theory, according to which states of consciousness are identical with states of the brain or of the central nervous system. At Adelaide in 1955, U. T. Place propounded a version of the theory and defended it in argument with J.J.C. Smart, a convert two years later. In 1956, Place published his paper "Is Consciousness a Brain Process?"[6] in the *British Journal of Psychology*. In the interests of an account of the mind entirely in terms of concepts employed by the physical sciences, the paper attempts to deal with the problem presented by a class of mental concepts apparently recalcitrant to behaviorist analysis. The concepts are those "clustering around the notions of consciousness, experience, sensation, and mental imagery where some sort of inner process story is unavoidable."

It is essentially *not* Place's thesis that statements about sensations and mental images, for example, can be translated into statements about processes in the brain. The thesis is that events of consciousness happen to be brain processes, as lightning happens to be an electrical discharge. That lightning *is* an electrical discharge—and not caused by an electrical discharge—follows from the fact that technical observations made in the context of a scientific theory "provide an immediate explanation of the observations made by the man in the street." Similarly, to establish the identity of events of consciousness with certain brain processes, what is necessary is to show that "the introspective observations reported by the subject can be all accounted for in terms of processes which are known to have occurred in his brain" (p. 106).

Place does not directly explain the meaning of this "accounted for in terms of brain processes," but he goes on to deal with an objection to the possibility of any such account. The objection results from what he calls the "phenomenological fallacy," the mistake of supposing that when we describe our experience—how things look, sound, smell, taste, or feel to us—we are describing the "phenomenal properties" of internal objects. In fact, we describe an experience "by reference to the actual physical properties of the concrete physical objects, events, and processes" which normally give rise to that sort of experience (p. 108). When we "describe the after-image as green, we are not saying that there is something, the after-image, which is green; we are saying that we are having the sort of experience which we normally have when . . . looking at a green patch of light" (p. 108). There is nothing in the brain which is green, but that, Place contends, does not block the experience we report from being a brain process, for the after-image is not something which is green.

There is nothing in reports of sensations and other events of consciousness incompatible with its being brain processes whose occurrence is reported is what Smart's "topic-neutral" characterization of these reports is to show. Giving the same sort of account as Place does of the occurrence of an after-image—*There is something going on which is like what is going on when* I really see an object of a certain shape and color—Smart draws attention to the "quasilogical" character, the "topic-neutrality" of the italicized words.[7] Place holds that this abstractness of the introspective reports explains how some event of consciousness can be a brain process and yet the person reporting it knowing nothing of brain processes. So far from exhibiting any anxiety about the phenomenological adequacy of the introspective reports thus characterized, Smart sees as explained "the singular elusiveness of 'raw feels'—why no one seems to be able to pin any properties on them" (p. 167).

The line of argument in Smart's paper has two components. One is directed towards meeting objections to the possibility that states of consciousness are through and through identical with brain processes. Here, the most important consideration brought forward is the topic-neutrality thesis. The other component in Smart's line of argument is an application of "Occam's razor." The razor is not applied out of an abstract deference to economy, in order to remove the immateriality of states of consciousness merely as a needless supposition. A gross anomaly, as Smart sees it, has to be removed: "There does seem to be, so far as science is concerned, nothing in the world but increasingly complex arrangements of physical constitutents. All except for one place: in consciousness'' (p. 161).

In his contribution to *The Identity Theory of Mind*,[8] Peter Herbst accuses the identity theorists of a lack of enthusiasm for arguments of the form: the mental entity A has such and such a property; the physical entity B does not have this property, therefore A is not identical with B. They do not actually denounce ''the principle of the indiscernibility of identicals,'' but they seem to think they can get round it by way of ''the thesis that mental talk and physical talk have different 'logics' '' (p. 44). If A has some property which B lacks, A and B are not identical. Max Deutscher, in his contribution to *The Identity Theory of Mind*, contrasts that truth with the supposition that if anything can be predicated of a subject term ''A'' and not of a subject term ''B'', A and B are not identical. The supposition is false, he argues, and the source of spurious objections to the identification of mental states with brain states. Imagine, he says, a community whose language employs one primitive term ''cheacup'' to designate what we would call teacups on chairs and another term ''neacup'' to designate our teacups but only when these were not on chairs. With that vocabulary, it would be necessarily true to say that a cheacup was on a chair and self-contradictory to say that a neacup was. Imagine further that the people have never seen cups put onto or taken off chairs; then, quite likely, there will be philosophers in that community who would deride the theory that cheacups and neacups were, in fact, the very same thing.

Commenting in *The Identity Theory of Mind* on the preceding papers, Smart says that he should not have spoken of a difference in ''logic'' as between reports of sensations and reports of brain processes. Rather, he should have confined himself to the contention that the properties reported in reports of sensations are topic-neutral and therefore properties ''*compatible* with physicalism.'' He has now come to the opinion, however, that his topic-neutral analysis will not do. An argument of M. C. Bradley's (a summary of which we shall come to) has shown it to be circular, he thinks.

Although his own topic-neutral analysis of reports of sensations fails, Smart would still maintain that ''ordinary language is at least very nearly topic-neutral or compatible with physicalism'' (p. 91). But he admits that he may be wrong: perhaps the conceptual framework of our introspective reports is stubbornly dualistic. If so, then drawn to physicalism by its attractiveness ''from the point of view of Occam's razor and of the unity of science'' and ready to desist if a sufficiently powerful argument turned up, he would be for moving ''in the direction of simply *replacing* dualistic conceptions by physicalist ones,'' as the Newtonians replaced the Aristotelian conception of a falling body by the gravitational conception (pp. 91–93).

From Keith Campbell's paper ''Colours,''[9] we take a summary of arguments raised by two of Smart's former colleagues, C. B. Martin and M. C. Bradley, against his account of color:

Smart concedes that

(a) *S* sees *O* as red

cannot be analyzed as

(i) *S* has trouble distinguishing *O* among carnation petals (or other paradigm) but not among lettuce leaves (or other paradigm).

This analysis is vulnerable to C. B. Martin's objection that systematic color changes in things could make (a) false yet (i) true. It is also vulnerable to M. C. Bradley's objection that if *S* saw everything in shades of grey (a) would be false yet (i) could be true.[10]

So the analysis of (a) must be supplemented by

(ii) *S* is having impressions of red.

But now if (a)'s analysis is to be in solely physical terms, (ii) cannot be left as it is. It in turn gives way to

(iii) Something is going on in *S* like what has hitherto gone on in him when he looks at red surfaces.

As Bradley points out in his review,[11] this is circular in that it introduces red surfaces into part of the analysis of (a). For on Smart's account *O is* red surface only if *S* sees *O* as red. Now if (iii) is altered to avoid this, so that it becomes

(iv) Something is going on in *S* like what has hitherto gone on in him when he looks at ripe tomatoes (or other paradigm),

then the whole analysis of (a) as (i) and (iv) is once more vulnerable to the original objections of Martin and Bradley, that under color shift or vision in shades of grey (i) and (iv) could both be true, yet (a) be false.

Smart came to think that the charge of circularity against his topic-neutral thesis could be met on the basis of an account of color suggested to him by the American philosopher David Lewis.[12] This account breaks a *definitional* connection between color, on the one hand, and color behavior and color experiences, on the other.

That a person is "incorrigibly" aware of his sensations, that he cannot be mistaken about them—about whether or not he is in pain, for instance—has been argued to be incompatible with an identification of sensations with brain states, since there is always the logical possibility of a mistake about a brain state, as about any physical entity or process. Materialists have argued against incorrigibility. M. C. Bradley, who in his review of Smart's *Philosophy and Scientific Realism* had brought considerations of incorrigibility against the identity theory, in a later paper[13] rejects as invalid the argument from incorrigibility in any form known to him. He shows that it falls foul of standard difficulties involving modal and intentional properties.

In the same paper, Bradley proposes an argument against the identity theory based on the location of bodily sensations. He first gives reasons for regarding many bodily sensations as being spatially located "in just the sense in which physical bodies are so located." Then he concludes that there are many sensations which cannot be identified with states of the central nervous system, since they are located in parts of the body at a distance from the central nervous system.

David Armstrong's conception of philosophy as continuous with science came, along with much else in his thinking, from the teaching of John Anderson. One of "the great problems that must be solved in any attempt to work out a scientific, world-view," he writes in *A Materialist Theory of the Mind*, is that of "bringing the being who puts forward the world-view *within* the world-view." This is to be done by treating man, his mental processes included, as purely physical. This successfully done, "the knower differs from the world he knows only in the greater complexity of his physical organization. Man is one with nature" (p. 366).

The principal task undertaken in *A Materialist Theory of the Mind* is an elucidation of the concept of mind and of individual mental concepts, especially those that have been regarded as raising difficulties for materialism. Armstrong regards the results of this elucidation as still leaving the possibility of a dualist position open, but as rendering, if they stand, an identification of the mental with the physical "neither particularly paradoxical nor particularly bold" (p. 355). He thus sees more as coming from the philosophical investigation of mental concepts than the earlier identity theorists, who looked only for the removal of conceptual obstacles to physicalism. The identifying step itself is to be taken on the grounds of economy, scientific plausibility, and the many difficulties of a dualist position. As regards this step, Armstrong is rather more tentative than the earlier identity theorists and less confident that the physicalist explanations could ever be carried through. These explanations might be unable to deal with paranormal psychical phenomena.

Armstrong refers to the "monistic vision" of materialism, but elements that are traditional in dualist accounts of the mind are strongly present in the account he gives of the mind in general and of individual mental concepts as well. Mind, he argues, is within, as it was classically conceived to be, and again, as it was classically conceived, it is the cause of action. To see the will as an "inner cause" ("the will" labels all mental activities of a conative sort), to see these activities as inner causes, is to have before us an open door, Armstrong maintains, to the understanding of such concepts as that of intention. One notable characteristic of Armstrong's book is that it argues for propositions that have been widely discredited by philosophers but that to many people seem to have truth in them.

There are considerable similarities of a general kind between the account Armstrong gives of the mind and that given by B. H. Medlin in his paper "Ryle and the Mechanical Hypothesis" (Presley, op. cit.). Medlin argues that mental states are causes of behavior; being in pain, for example, is being "in that state—whatever it may be—which tends to produce pain-behaviour" (p. 96). If mental states are causes of behavior, they are physical, for "there is overwhelming evidence for the belief that all biological movement is explicable in physicochemical terms" (p. 96). (In the interests of the identity theory and, to some extent, of any account of the mind which wants to regard the mind in a traditional way as causally operative, Medlin's paper turns on *The Concept of Mind* some of the most important criticism it has ever received.)

Armstrong acknowledges his indebtedness to Medlin for a model for the identification of mental states with brain states. The model is the identification of the gene with the DNA molecule. Postulated as the factor "apt for the production of hereditary characteristics," Armstrong writes, the gene, which could have been all sorts of things, turned out to be the DNA molecule. Mental states are "states of the person apt for the bringing about of certain sorts of physical behaviour." They might be immaterial in nature. Armstrong will bet on it that their nature is physicochemical.

The theory of perception in *A Materialist Theory of Mind* is substantially the same one which Armstrong proposed in his earlier book, *Perception and the Physical World*. This is interesting because that book was written before Armstrong adopted the identity theory. Its motivation was epistemological—its is described as "a defence of Direct Realism"—but its theory of perception fits in very nicely with the materialism Armstrong was to adopt. It eliminated all nonphysical sensory items from a role in perception, anything of the sense-impression kind, whether conceived of as an object of perceptual experience or as a phenomenal property of that experience. Perception, Armstrong states in *A Materialist Theory of the Mind,* "is nothing but the acquiring of true or false beliefs concerning the current state of the organism's body and environment. . . .Veridical perception is the acquiring of true beliefs, sensory illusion the acquiring of false beliefs" (p. 209). Where we are not taken in by the illusory appearance, perception is the acquiring of "an inclination to believe," an inclination to believe being "a belief that is held in check by a stronger belief."

Armstrong goes into the difficulties of including a reference to the sense organs in his "definition" of perception. The omission of this reference in conjunction with the disappearance of anything of a sense-impression kind into the acquiring of beliefs or inclinations to believe requires the reader to keep reminding himself that it is sense perception that Armstrong is explicating. Critics have seen his account of bodily sensations in particular as too intellectualist, as turning the *feeling of pain,* for instance, into a merely cognitive awareness, into the feeling (which evokes a reaction of dislike) that a disturbance is going on in some part of the body.

Keith Campbell broadens this type of criticism *(Body and Mind)* into a general criticism of a theory of the mind of the sort put forward by Armstrong: it leaves out "what waking life is like to him who is living it." Rather than have the feeling/sensory features of everyone's experience left out, as he thinks they have to be, if they are identified with states of the brain or of the central nervous system having only physicochemical properties, Campbell is prepared to regard them as epiphenomenal—as nonmaterial, causally inefficacious—occurrences within the body. Since they are causally inefficacious, they present no threat to the causal explanation of behavior in physicochemical terms. Epiphenomenalism is a view which all parties to the dispute over the identity theory would once have repudiated. That a philosopher has come (gritting his teeth) to such a view is a forceful reminder that consciousness does indeed present a stubbornly anomalous appearance.

OTHER MINDS, FREE WILL, AND DETERMINISM

In "The Identity Theory and Other Minds," Alec Hyslop argues that the identity theory is no better off than a dualist position as regards the other minds problem. The mental states of others remain unobservable in the way that creates the problem. Observable, mental states must indeed be if they are brain states, but not, therefore, "observably mental." (An identity theorist, with a causal account of the mind, might see the problem of other minds as the very manageable one of establishing similar causes for similar behavioral effects, but this simplicity leaves unestablished that there is anything introspectible in the minds of others.) In "Other Minds as Theoretical Entities," Hyslop maintains that inference, of the best explanation type, to other minds as "theoretical entities" requires appeal to one's own case and, therefore, is not available as an alternative to the traditional analogical argument. With F. C. Jackson (in 1972 and 1975), Hyslop defends this argument against the traditional charge that it is a bad inductive argument.

A large number of Australian writings have focused on free will and determinism. To what is about to be mentioned should be added Robert Young's book *Freedom, Responsibility and God,* which fits under the heading philosophical theology.

Several philosophers in the 1960s argued as to whether choice has to be causally determined or random. J.J.C. Smart in *Mind* contends that there is no "third possibility." This issue and others connected with it are taken up in the *Australasian Journal of Philosophy* 41 (1963) and 42 (1964) in an exchange between R. D. Bradley and K. W. Rankin (both of whom have now left Australia), following Bradley's review of Rankin's *Choice and Chance.* Written before Rankin came to Australia, this book attempts to construct a metaphysics of libertarianism. Two antilibertarian papers written by Bradley, which should be mentioned, are "Free Will: Problem or Pseudo-Problem" and "Must the Future Be What It Is Going to Be?"

R. L. Franklin's *Freewill and Determinism* is a defense of libertarianism. The work makes a very moderate claim, namely, that there are "no adequate reasons" for rejecting its conception of freedom. How far his arguments tend to establish this conception and how far they reflect his acceptance of it is something, Franklin says, that he is unable to decide. The defense of libertarianism is set in the context of a study of the opposing conceptions of human nature and of man's place in nature, which Franklin sees as lying behind libertarian and determinist accounts of human action. What might well be seen as the most valuable thing in the book is the understanding it effects of what a libertarian position on free will needs to be. This understanding is effected in part by its criticism of the "moral libertarianism" associated with the name of C. A. Campbell.

PHILOSOPHICAL LOGIC

Some of the work which could have come under this heading is, for various reasons, mentioned elsewhere in this article. From all the rest, we pick out for mention—arbitrarily to a considerable degree, of course—discussion of one particular topic which has gone on intermittently over a period, papers in the volume *Contemporary Philosophy in Australia,* and a book of Armstrong's.

Work which has been done on the concept of identity since around 1960 includes C. B. Martin, *Religious Belief,* and G. Nerlich, "On Evidence for Identity" and " 'Continuity' Continued," more recent discussions by M. C. Bradley (1969), M. S. Candlish (1971), B. Langtry (1972 and 1975), and M. K. Rennie in *Some Uses of Type Theory in the Analysis of Language.* This research is of general interest because of its significance in areas of nontechnical concern, such as personal identity and survival after death. Of this work we shall mention two papers in particular. In "The Inexplicability of Identity," Candlish maintains that no sufficient condition for identity can be formulated without circularity and that the attempt to frame a necessary condition results either in incoherence or in the imposition of impossibly strong demands. Langtry, in his 1975 paper, with some reference to Martin and countering arguments put forward by Nerlich, maintains that an object might cease to exist and the same object begin to exist again.

In *Contemporary Philosophy in Australia,* Peter Herbst criticizes Strawson's theory of the nature of facts, as well as his own former view which he advanced in "The Nature of Facts." He now regards facts as being "events conceived as proper objects of reliance for thought or deed." Dealing in the same volume with a topic which is at present interesting some Australian philosophers, Brian Ellis argues in favor of à concept of truth as "a special concept of probability." Also dealing with a topic of some current interest, L. Goddard maintains that argument can establish an existence of universals, which is "independent of any particular thesis about their nature." Max Deutscher proposes a causal account of inferring which has been given a place in the edifice of a materialist theory of the mind.

David Armstrong's writings as they come out build up a system. *Belief, Truth and Knowledge* "is offered as a contribution to a naturalistic account of the nature of man." Belief is "a certain *continuing state*" of the mind ("contingently" identified with a state of the brain), the truth of a belief is its correspondence with reality, and knowledge is reliable true belief. A reader might find its "Thermometer" view of noninferential knowledge the most interesting thing in the book. Armstrong develops the following analogy: "When a true belief unsupported by reasons [for example, that there is something pressing on one's body] stands to the situation truly believed to exist as a thermometer reading in a good thermometer stands to the actual temperature, then we have noninferential knowledge'' (p. 166).

FORMAL LOGIC

There was no great interest in formal logic in Australia before the mid-1960s. The widespread interest that exists now can largely be traced to Leonard Goddard (now at the University of St. Andrews), Richard Routley, and David Londey. Despite the newness of this area, Australia has already produced a number of important contributions to logic. The first volume of Goddard and Routley's *The Logic of Significance and Context* is a mammoth work which explores the application of formal logical techniques to areas that many had previously thought to be beyond their scope. It is common for philosophers to claim that certain views are not plain false, but meaningless (Wittgenstein's "hidden nonsense," for example, and Ryle's "category mistakes"). Goddard and Routley set out to develop the theory of those formal systems which capture these ideas and in general to bring the context of sentences and their significance within the range of formal logic. They aim "eventually, to provide a logic not previously developed, for much of modern philosophy (p. 6)."

A standard criticism of classical (i.e., Frege-Russell) logic is that it maintains that anything is a logical consequence of a contradiction, and, conversely, a logical truth is a consequence of anything. In the late 1950s, the American logicians Alan Anderson and Nuel Belnap attempted to produce a new account of logical consequence not subject to these odd properties. Although they produced formal systems, they were unable to give any semantical account of their ideas. Robert Meyer and Richard Routley solved the problem of how to formulate the semantics, and their solution has led to a number of developments in the area of entailment. Their results are to appear in a monograph to be entitled *Relevant Logics and Their Rivals*.

Two other Australian contributions to formal logic which deserve mention are J. N. Crossley, *Constructive Order Types* and M. K. Rennie, *Some Uses of Type Theory in the Analysis of Language*.

The most significant developments from Australia in the near future will likely derive from the application of nonclassical logics, especially the relevance-type logics of Routley and Meyer. Until recently, the study of these logics has been somewhat introverted; only their internal properties had been studied. Now that these logics have established their credentials, logicians are beginning to look at the results of using them in wider areas.

The most important accomplishment to date in this direction was announced at the meeting of the Australasian Association of Logic held at the Australian National University in October 1976. In 1931, Gödel brought out his now famous consistency theorem, according to which a more advanced theory is required to prove the consistency of any nonelementary mathematical theory. This theorem was taken to have great significance in the foundations of mathematics. At the 1976 meeting of the association, it was announced that Robert Meyer had shown that if the mathematical theory is formulated with a nonclassical logic, the consistency theorem is false. If this has been shown, the theorem becomes an interesting fact about classical logic rather than a deeply significant theory for mathematics.

Another area that has opened up as a consequence of the use of nonclassical logics is the investigation of inconsistent theories. Many interesting theories appear to be inconsistent (for example, naive set theory and naive semantics). Yet, if classical logic is used, these theories are reduced to complete triviality since, classically, a contradiction entails everything. The use of a nonclassical logic allows such theories to be investigated seriously for the first time. The consequences of these investigations may go very deep, but it is as yet too early to predict. In 1930, Wittgenstein remarked: "Indeed, even at this stage, I predict a time when there will be mathematical investigations of calculi containing contradictions and people will actually be proud of having emancipated themselves from consistency." Wittgenstein could not have foreseen where his prediction would begin to come true.

PHILOSOPHY OF SCIENCE

Work in the philosophy of science has been considerably occupied with methodology and related matters. In *Method in the Physical Sciences,* George Schlesinger (now no longer in Australia) examines certain methodological principles that are implicit in the actual practice of scientists, guiding the choice of scientific strategies. He discusses four of these principles: the principle of simplicity; the principle of microreduction (according to which "the properties of level n + 1 will . . . be explained in terms of the properties of entities of level n"); the important, little discussed principle of connectivity ("Two physical systems never differ in a single aspect only"); and the principle of verification, which, Schlesinger shows, has an application within science. Schlesinger contends that the principle of microreduction "has no rational foundation," a contention that has an obvious relevance to the discussion of central-state materialism.

Brian Ellis's book, *Basic Concepts of Measurement,* is written with the intention of disturbing sleep over the logic of measurement. He maintains that more or less arbitrary conventions, whose rationale he discusses, have been concealed by metaphysical assumptions "made by positivists and non-positivists alike."

W. H. Leatherdale's book, *The Role of Analogy, Model and Metaphor in Science,* surveys a great amount of contemporary discussion of the topics assembled in its title. Its special interest is in the idea that metaphor is essential to science. Leatherdale's position on the place of metaphor in science requires him to contest the views advanced by Mary McCloskey in an important paper, "Metaphors." McCloskey maintains that truth or falsity is not to be ascribed to metaphors and that metaphors provide no basis for inference.

A number of writers have criticized the views of Karl Popper. Beginning with "Popperian Confirmation and the Paradox of the Ravens," there is an exchange (with a Canadian intervention, "On Not Being Gulled by Ravens") between D. C. Stove and J.W.N. Watkins. In "Popper's Problem of an Empirical Base," Max Deutscher argues that Popper "leaves no logical room for the role played by observation in science." In "Popper on Law and Natural Necessity," G. Nerlich and W. A. Suchting argue that Popper's definition of a law of nature fails to distinguish a law of nature from an accidental universal. Moreover they state that, of the revisions to which it is open, one renders the definition equivalent to a view which Popper rejects and the other renders it circular. Popper replies in the same volume of the journal (and is replied to by Suchting in Vol. 20). In an Addendum in the second English edition of *The Logic of Scientific Discovery,* Popper remarks that he does not now think his reply to Nerlich and Suchting was very good, and he goes on to stress the unimportance, in his opinion, of definitions.

Using premises taken from the theory of logical probability, D. C. Stove in *Probability and Hume's Inductive Scepticism* sets out a refutation of Hume's argument for inductive skepticism. He also brings refutatory arguments against the "deductivist" premise of Hume's argument, the premise according to which a deductively invalid argument cannot render its conclusion probable. Stove's claim to have refuted Hume's argument has naturally provoked sharp debate. "Hume, Induction, and the Irish," which is Stove's reply to three critics, concentrates the issues. (The Irish Question, according to *1066 and All That,* was never settled because when the English government was getting the answer, the Irish changed the question. Stove accuses some of his critics of objecting to his refutation of Hume's argument on the grounds that it does not do what they want to see done.)

SPACE AND TIME

J.J.C. Smart, in "Causal Theories of Time," attacks theories of time, such as Grünbaum's, which seek to explicate the concept of time in terms of causality. One consideration he adduces is that this type of analysis of the concept of time does not allow for theories, which do not seem to be inconsistent, in which events neither cause nor are caused by other events.

That time really does flow, that thinking this temporal flow does not require us to postulate a supertime in terms of which time can be thought of as flowing, are propositions maintained by George Schlesinger in "The Passage of Time" in *Contemporary Philosophy in Australia.* He identifies time with "the clock which emerges when the principle of the maximization of simplicity is applied to the laws of physics governing processes" (p. 213). In "What Does the Denial of Absolute Space Mean?," Schlesinger examines the contentions of Schlick and Grünbaum as to what bearing the supposition of an expansion in size of all bodies uniformly has on the concept of space. A rejoinder by Grünbaum appears in the same volume of the journal.

In *The Existence of Space and Time,* Ian Hinckfuss sets down "four basic paradoxes regarding space and time." The question he addresses is whether the truth in statements that "seem to refer to space and time" can be expressed in statements that do not have this reference, and the paradoxes be thus eliminated. He concludes that this can be done, but at a price. As contrasted with the relationalist leanings of Hinckfuss, Graham Nerlich in *The Shape of Space* defends a strong absolutist position claiming that space is a particular since it has a concrete property, namely, shape.

The Logic of Special Relativity by the mathematician S. J. Prokhovnik is dedicated to the memory of Geoffrey Builder, who established a school in Sydney for study of the interpretation of special relativity. His book deals with the logic of various interpretations. Prokhovnik argues the case for an "Aether," and in the last chapter he constructs "a physical model of the universe," according to which the various interpretations have "an exact and credible validity at different levels of description."

Though not a work in the philosophy of science, W. D. Joske's *Material Objects* might be mentioned here. Undeterred by the thought that his contention will lack "the excitement which always follows upon the evaporation of a category," Joske argues that the concept of a material object is irreducible.

THE SOCIAL SCIENCES

Studies in methodology have been predominant in the philosophy of the social sciences. In *The Logic of Social Enquiry,* Quentin Gibson maintains that, in general, no other procedures than those of the natural sciences are available in the social sciences. However, these procedures do have a special subject matter. Gibson deals particularly with the significance for the social sciences of the fact that their subject matter is the behavior of partly rational beings.

Robert Brown in *Explanation in Social Science* sorts out seven different kinds of explanation used in the social sciences, characterizes each, and adduces considerations to show that explanations in terms of the intentions and reasons of agents have only a minor place. He therefore concludes that explanation in the social sciences is, in principle, very similar to explanation in the physical sciences. In *Rules and Laws in Sociology,* Brown examines the practice of sociology. Where might sociologists find social laws instead of the social regularities they come up with? In "the causal conditions from which rules and rule-following arise."

MORAL PHILOSOPHY

In the area of moral philosophy, we will first concentrate on works dealing with the general nature of morality. One of the purposes of *The Moral Point of View* by Kurt Baier (who is no longer in Australia) is to show that value judgments, including moral judgments, are straightforwardly true or false and that some of them are indubitably true. The book reminds us of the obvious—as in the following passage—and defends it.

That Landy is a better miler than I, that Plato was a greater philosopher than Joad, that cars are better than they were fifty years ago, that *Hamlet* is a greater play than *A Streetcar Named Desire*, that Gandhi was a better man than Stalin, are not matters of opinion, but are quite indubitably true. Anyone who maintained the opposite would have to be said not to know what he was talking about (p. 65).

Baier's last chapter offers an answer to the question: Why ought one to treat moral reasons as superior to reasons of self-interest? Moral reasons are not to be invoked, nor reasons of self-interest. This is not the place to try to determine how Baier takes himself to have shown that the moral point of view is the rational point of view.

Moral Notions by Julius Kovesi is a many-sided attack on the traditional dichotomy between description and evaluation from which arises the problem of inference from fact to value. The problem is created, Kovesi remarked in a comment on his book, "by the terminology in which it is discussed." "Good" is not like "yellow," he argues, and the difference between those terms does not illuminate the difference between evaluative and descriptive terms. "Good" is a wholly untypical evaluative term, and "yellow" an untypical descriptive term. "Table" is the right sort of term to examine for an understanding of both descriptive and evaluative terms and for an understanding of the way in which description and evaluation are related.

Hume could not find in murder any "matter of fact or real existence" which was its viciousness. So he looked within himself and found a sentiment of disapprobation. Kovesi will not allow Hume his illustration: murder is not a perceivable and describable object, in Hume's sense of "description." "In an important sense, in the world there *is* no value"—and "there are no murders, tables, houses, accidents or inadvertent acts. But our language is not about *that* world" (p. 19). Murders are as real as tables, and wrongness is as integral to the notion of murder as killing is: anyone who did not think murder an object of "disapprobation" "would not understand the notion of murder."

D. H. Monro has had a special interest in eighteenth-century British philosophy. He is the author of *Godwin's Moral Philosophy* and *The Ambivalence of Bernard Mandeville*. Writing in the tradition of Hutcheson and Hume, he offers in *Empiricism and Ethics* a sophisticated defense of an old and simple view of what it is for something to be good or bad. It is for it to have characteristics which evoke approval or condemnation in anyone calling it good or bad. In the course of a "subjectivist" and "naturalist" account, as he calls it, of the nature of morality, Monro severely criticizes the "universalizability thesis."

According to R. M. Hare, a person thinking morally has universalization forced upon him as a matter of logic. If it is asserted as a moral proposition that such and such ought to be done by or to *X,* the speaker is committed in consistency to holding that the same thing ought to be done by or to anyone, including himself, in the same position as *X.* From this purely formal characteristic of moral concepts, "a middle way between subjectivism and objectivism" is supposed to result, Monro writes. The objectivist gets the impartial application of moral principles to everyone as a logical necessity. The subjectivist keeps his view that, "ultimately, moral principles are rules of conduct that a man accepts."

Monro distinguishes three different kinds of universalizability requirements, and then a fourth from these. He argues that the first three can be satisfied by the principle "Let everyone do what will make my interests prevail over everyone else's." It could not satisfy the fourth universalizability requirement—impartiality—but that requirement, Monro argues, is a moral, not a logical, one. No mediation between subjectivism and objectivism has been effected. The principle of impartiality, being a moral principle, is "exposed to all the traditional questions about the nature and justification of moral principles."

Arguing that naturalistic analyses of moral concepts and "noncognitivist" accounts of moral assertions "misdescribe morality and the logical properties of moral discourse," H. J. McCloskey in *Meta-Ethics and Normative Ethics* maintains that the terms "right," "good," and "obligatory" are *sui generis;* that whether something is right, good, obligatory, is intuitively determined; and that moral assertions are straightforwardly true or false—necessarily true or false.

UTILITARIANISM

An interest in utilitarianism has been a feature of Australian moral philosophy. In a paper entitled "But Suppose Everyone Did the Same," A. K. Stout distinguishes between two forms of utilitarian universalization: a "causal" form and a "hypothetical" form. In the causal form, the effect of one's breaking a rule on the tendency of others to keep it goes into the calculation of consequences which determine the rightness or wrongness of the action one is contemplating. Any such effect of one's action on others is irrelevant in hypothetical universalizations; no one, it can be supposed, knows of one's action. What is the force of my adverting to the consequences of everyone's doing the same when, say, there is water rationing, and "the little drop I need to save my prize azaleas won't make any difference and no one will know"? An answer is that I am bringing home to myself the unfairness of what I contemplate doing. But it is not an answer, Stout maintains, which a utilitarian could accept.

In a widely known paper[14] attacking rule-utilitarianism from an act-utilitarian standpoint, J.J.C. Smart makes use of Stout's distinction to characterize the two positions: "an extreme [act] utilitarian would apply the universalization principle in the causal form, while a restricted [rule] utilitarian would apply it in the hypothetical form" (p. 173). For the extreme utilitarian, moral rules, Smart says, are good "rules of thumb"; he will usually act according to them. He will do so "because he can argue that probably he will most often act in an extreme utilitarian way if he does not think as a utiliarian" (p. 174).

Smart emphasizes that, to his mind, ethics is concerned with the rational thing to do. To stick to a rule when you have taken into account the indirect as well as the direct consequences of breaking it, and have seen that the optimific thing to do is to break it, is irrational, is "superstitious rule-worship."

In "An Outline of a System of Utilitarian Ethics,"[15] Smart appeals to the sentiment of "generalized benevolence" in the hope that those in whom this sentiment is present will be won over to utilitarianism when they see clarifications made and objections answered, and when they see how much harder it is than is commonly supposed, to produce "clearheaded and acceptable" alternatives.

In this essay, Smart replies to an objection to utilitarianism raised by Baier. The requirement that the optimific act be always done has the absurd consequence, Baier remarked,[16] that a man relaxing after a hard day's work is doing wrong because he is not doing good. Smart does not attempt to show that it is not an implication of act-utilitarianism that the sky is the limit to what can be morally exacted of us. Easing up on good works today, he says, might increase our capacity for more tomorrow.

In the essay, Smart also takes up H. J. McCloskey's comment[17] that it is open to the utilitarian, faced with the possibility of an unjust system of punishment which has utilitarian justification, to argue that it would be superstitious rule-worship to adhere to the just system. Smart does not at all suggest that what meets the utilitarian standard cannot really be unjust. His retort is that "if a case really *did* arise in which injustice was the lesser of two evils (in terms of human happiness and misery), then the anti-utilitarian conclusion is a very unpalatable one too" (p. 72).

In a paper written subsequently to the comment which touched off these remarks, McCloskey allows that unjust punishment may be morally justified—if the good achieved is so great as to outweigh the injustice. His objection to utilitarianism is that "it does not take account of the relevance of the claims of justice. . . . For the utilitarian, the utility of punishment is the only morally relevant consideration."[18] Dealing in *Punishment and Desert* with the question of whether good consequences ever outweigh the evil of injustice, J. L. Kleinig draws our attention to the importance of the examples used in its discussion; executing an innocent man to prevent a riot, fining an innocent man £5 to prevent a riot, are not good examples. Partly with the intention of exhibiting its independence of any particular moral theory, Kleinig shows the concept of desert to be applicable outside moral contexts, to be applicable, indeed, beyond human agents and their artifacts. We can speak of "the Western Australian Coastline deserving to be well known as that of the East" (p. 53).

The relevance of the various "elements" of an act, such as its circumstances, intentions, and motive, to its moral evaluation—a topic which, since Bentham, has received little attention from philosophers—is carefully discussed by Eric D'Arcy in *Human Acts*.

ENVIRONMENTAL ETHICS

The most considerable piece of work done on environmental ethics is J. A. Passmore's *Man's Responsibility for Nature*. The book examines the "moral, political and metaphysical" assumptions underlying a great deal of the discussion of its subject. Passmore maintains that we shall owe our ecological survival, if it is to come about, to the intellectual, moral, and political resources of Western civilization. The advocacy of primitive, prescientific attitudes, and the mystical exaltation of nature over man are contributions to disaster. Discussing the book in the *Australasian Journal of Philosophy* (1975), Val Routley criticizes Passmore for taking man's responsibility for nature to be entirely a matter of man's obligations to other human beings. A nonanthropocentric ethic is needed, she maintains. This does not have to claim rights for nature, though "a right to habitat and independence," she remarks, may be as properly claimed for some wild species as for groups of human beings. In his presidential address to the Conference of the Australasian Association of Philosophy in 1974, Stanley Benn offered considerations for setting persons above all other valuable things and argued that the value of other things need not be anthropocentrally derived.

POLITICAL PHILOSOPHY

At a time when it was fashionable for philosophers to distinguish sharply between "first order" and "second order" statements in politics and to confine their professional attention to the second of these, P. H. Partridge and H. J. McCloskey were not thus aloof from substantive issues in their philosophical discussion of political topics. Commenting on the distinction when it was fashionable, Partridge wrote:

By and large, the political scientists have been sensible enough to see that the drawing of this sharp boundary is hopelessly disabling for the study of social theory, and have ignored it. . . .the philosophers who have imposed it have been left in occupation of only a wafer-thin slice of the territory of politics (p. 36).[19]

The paper from which this quotation is taken deals with a number of matters, particularly with the significance of the nonevaluative accounts of democracy that were being proposed.

H. J. McCloskey has worked over a long period on a conceptual and evaluative examination of the ideals of liberalism. In the course of this work, he has directed severe criticism, from what he would insist was a liberal standpoint, against claims for liberty standardly made by liberals. He considers these claims to be naive and inconsistent. In an early paper, "The State and Evil" (1958), McCloskey held that the liberals traditionally opposed to the views he is supporting "implicitly accept these views in a muddled way." He argues for the propositions that "error has no rights" and that the state should promote all the good it can, including moral goodness. In "Some Arguments for a Liberal Society," he distinguishes various notions of liberty which the liberals employ but do not always carefully sort out.

The extent to which ethical considerations lie at the foundations of Marxism, and the specific nature of these considerations, are the main themes of *The Ethical Foundations of Marxism* by Eugene Kamenka. In addition to concerning itself with the understanding of Marxism, the book discusses "the significance of Marxism for the theory of ethics." (The phrase comes from one of Kamenka's later books, *Marxism and Ethics.*)

From Stanley Benn's writing on a wide variety of topics, two papers are selected for mention here. In "Egalitarianism and the Equal Consideration of Interests," the principles of egalitarian thinking are sorted out, and "the limitations they face" are set against them. The task undertaken in "Freedom and Persuasion" is "to extend the application of the classical concepts of liberalism so that they can function coherently in the discussion of persuasive techniques," (p. 261) where there is no question of an authority and of a subject of that authority.

In *Democracy and Disobedience,* Peter Singer asks whether the fact that a system of government is democratic puts it in a special position as regards obedience to its laws. The answer reached is Yes: because in a democracy there is "a fair compromise between competing, otherwise irresolvable, claims to power" and because participation "in a decision-procedure, alongside others participating in good faith, gives rise to an obligation to act as if one had consented to be bound by the result of the decision-procedure." These reasons hold only if there has been no infringement of rights "essential to the functioning of a fair compromise decision-procedure" (pp. 133–134).

PHILOSOPHICAL THEOLOGY

There has been a dearth of attempts in Australia to construe religious belief nonpropositionally. In 1958, two formidable deterrents appeared in the *Australasian Journal of Philosophy:* Passmore's article reviewing *New Essays in Philosophical Theology* and "Modern Philosophers Consider Religion" by the late Professor A. Boyce Gibson.

Written with a feeling for religion, C. B. Martin's book, *Religious Belief,* contends that assertions essential to theistic religion are in deep "conceptual disorder.'' God is asserted to be perfectly good, for example, and, incoherently (Martin argues), to be so necessarily. The book contains a cold chapter on reductive substitutes for traditional theistic belief.

What is vaguely referred to as ''the problem of evil'' has been of special interest to philosophers in Australia. In ''Evil and Omnipotence,'' J. L. Mackie argues that if any two of the propositions ''God is omnipotent,'' ''God is wholly good,'' and ''Evil exists'' are true, the third is false. He saw himself as having to counter the move in theodicy which combines the proposition that a universe which contains some evil is better than one which is a painless paradise, with the proposition that the moral evil in the universe is due to the free agency of creatures.

When the existence of evil has been held to be incompatible with the existence of a God omnipotent and wholly good, direct contradiction has not been claimed; the need for a connecting link has been acknowledged, at least implicitly. M. B. Ahern in *The Problem of Evil* examines a number of principles that have been advanced to supply this link and finds them all wanting—Mackie's, for instance. Mackie's principle is that ''good is opposed to evil, in such a way that a good thing always eliminates evil as far as it can.''[20] It is not true, Ahern objects, that what is good eliminates or—to widen the principle—prevents evil as far as it can. ''The non-prevention of both moral and non-moral evil may be morally justified . . . the direct causing of non-moral evil may be justified'' (p. 35). There would be this justification if the not preventing or the direct causing of evil were necessary—logically necessary where omnipotence is involved—if some ''proportionate good'' were to come about. Mercy, forgiveness, and fortitude are examples of things that are good, to the existence of which the existence of evil is logically necessary.

H. J. McCloskey's book, *God and Evil*, brings together his views on topics he has been writing about for many years. Here we are concerned with two of these topics. The first is McCloskey's contention that on any ''subjectivist,'' ''noncognitivist'' account of what it is for something to be good, no problem of evil arises, for the goodness of God then becomes ''a purely contingent goodness, a response to him in us'' (p. 24). The second is McCloskey's reply, naming Ahern, to the argument that the existence of evil is compatible with the perfection of God, since there are good things—fortitude and sympathy, for example—logically dependent on evil, which their goodness outweighs. The ''value judgment involved is completely untenable,'' McCloskey writes (p. 75): what would we think of a human being who did evil in order to provide an opportunity for fortitude and sympathy?

George Schlesinger argues in ''The Problem of Evil and the Problem of Suffering'' that the problem of evil is incoherent. We have no grounds for supposing that the ''possibilities for happiness are finite.'' Of any universe, therefore, which God might have made, it could be asked why He did not make one containing more happiness, which He, being omnipotent, could have done. In posing the problem of evil, the assumption is made that ''the universe could be different from what it is now and that then the problem would disappear. But . . . alter the universe as you wish—it does not affect the problem. It therefore does not arise in the first place'' (p. 246).

In *Freedom, Responsibility and God,* Robert Young argues that there is no incompatibility with the human freedom presupposed by Christian theism in any of the following: in the implications of certain logical doctrines, in the supposition that determinism is true, in the supposition that there is an omniscient God, in the supposition that there is an omnipotent God. The logical doctrines (of which the law of excluded middle is one) and omniscience threaten all our actions with logical necessitation. The problems for human freedom raised by determinism and omnipotence have to do with causal necessitation. Young will have no less a freedom than one making possible "moral guilt."

A well-known contribution by Australia to the discussion of a topic which is still neglected by philosophers, even after some shift of interest towards questions of broad human concern, is Kurt Baier's lecture on "The Meaning of Life." Delivered in 1957 as Baier's inaugural lecture as professor of philosophy at Canberra University College, the lecture was reprinted in *Twentieth Century Philosophy,* ed. M. Weitz.

Finally, two books on the existence of God should be mentioned. *Theism and Empiricism* by A. Boyce Gibson seeks to show how a study of "the most general structures of the world" can yield a knowledge of God on the one hand, "as immediate as realists claim knowledge of the external world to be," and on the other, a knowledge which "is opaque and discontinuous."

From Belief to Understanding by Richard Campbell is not primarily an historical study, though a large part of it examines two chapters of St. Anselm's *Proslogion.* The result is a new interpretation of Anselm's argument for the existence of God, with an emphasis upon its unlikeness to the ontological argument of Descartes. The argument is discussed in detail, and it is also presented fully formalized. It is maintained to be formally valid. In a sense of "proof" (indeed, in Anselm's sense of it), Campbell claims that the argument is a proof of the existence of God. He likens (p. 213) Anselm's argument to the argument employed by Wittgenstein to show "how we cannot use our natural language to deny the existence of the 'external world'."

NOTES

1. *Studies in Empirical Philosophy,* pp. 122–123. This book, which is a collection of Anderson's principal philosophical papers (with an introductory essay by J. A. Passmore), was published in the year he died.

2. Anderson, p. 265.

3. G. Ryle, *Collected Papers,* I, p. 241.

4. "Logic and Professor Anderson," *Australasian Journal of Philosophy* [henceforth abbreviated as *A.J.P.*]

5. *"The Dreariness of Aesthetics," Mind;* "Can the Social Sciences Be Value-free?"

6. Quotations are taken from a revised form of the paper as contained in *The Philosophy of Mind*, ed. V. C. Chappell (Englewood Cliffs, N.J.: Prentice-Hall, 1962).

7. "Sensations and Brain Processes," in Chappell, p. 167. The paper was first published in the *Philosophical Review*.

8. *The Identity Theory of Mind*, ed. C. F. Presley (St. Lucia, Queensland: University of Queensland Press, 1967). This volume is based on papers read at the Conference of the Australasian Association of Philosophy, 1964.

9. *Contemporary Philosophy in Australia*, eds. R. Brown and C. D. Rollins. The quotations are from p. 153 of this volume.

10. These objections are discussed by Smart in *Philosophy and Scientific Realism*, pp. 81–83.

11. AJP 42 (1964). The review is of *Philosophy and Scientific Realism*.

12. See Smart's papers in *Synthese* 22 (1971) and *Philosophical Aspects of the Mind-Body Problem*, ed. C.-Y. Cheng (Honolulu: University of Hawaii Press, 1975).

13. "Two Arguments Against the Identity Thesis," in Brown and Rollins.

14. "Extreme and Restricted Utilitarianism." This paper first appeared in the *Philosophical Quarterly* 6 (1956). A revised version is printed in half a dozen or so collections, including *Theories of Ethics*, ed. P. Foot (Oxford: Oxford University Press, 1967), to which the page numbers refer.

15. First published at Melbourne in 1961 and reprinted in a revised version in *Utilitarianism For and Against*, to which page numbers refer.

16. *The Moral Point of View*, pp. 203–204.

17. "A Note on Utilitarian Punishment," *Mind* 72 (1963): 599.

18. "Utilitarian and Retributive Punishment," *Journal of Philosophy* 64 (1967): 91–92.

19. "Politics, Philosophy, Ideology," *Political Studies* and reprinted in *Political Philosophy*, ed. A. Quinton, to which the page number refers.

20. "Evil and Omnipotence," *Mind* 64 (1955): 201.

SELECT BIBLIOGRAPHY

BOOKS AND ARTICLES

Ahern, M. B. *The Problem of Evil* (London: Cambridge University Press, 1971).

Anderson, J. *Studies in Empirical Philosophy* (Sydney: Angus and Robertson Pub. Pty., Ltd., 1962).

Armstrong, D. *A Materialist Theory of the Mind* (London: Cambridge University Press, 1967).

——. *Belief, Truth and Knowledge* (London: Cambridge University Press, 1973).

——. *Perception and the Physical World* (London: Cambridge University Press, 1961).

——. "The Meaning of Life," in *Twentieth Century Philosophy*, ed. M. Weitz (New York: Free Press, and London: Collier-Macmillan, 1966).

Baier, K. *The Moral Point of View* (Ithaca, N.Y.: Cornell University Press, 1958).

Benn, S. "Egalitarianism and the Equal Consideration of Interests," in *Equality* (*Nomos* IX), eds. J. R. Pennock and W. J. Chapman (New York: Atherton Press, 1967).

——. "Freedom and Persuasion," *Australasian Journal of Philosophy* 45 (1967).

——. "Two Arguments Against the Identity Thesis," in *Contemporary Philosophy in Australia*, eds. R. Brown and C. D. Rollins (London: Allen and Unwin, 1969).

Bradley, M. C. "Critical Notice of *Identity and Spatio-Temporal Continuity*," *Australasian Journal of Philosophy* 47 (1969).

——. "Critical Notice of *Philosophy and Scientific Realism*," *Australasian Journal of Philosophy* 42 (1964).

——. "Two Arguments Against the Identity Thesis," in *Contemporary Philosophy in Australia*, eds. R. Brown and C. D. Rollins (London: Allen and Unwin, 1969).

Bradley, R. D. "Free Will: Problem or Pseudo-Problem," *Australasian Journal of Philosophy* 34 (1958).

———. "Must the Future Be What It Is Going to Be?" *Australasian Journal of Philosophy* 37 (1959).

———. "Quixotic Reasoning," *Australasian Journal of Philosophy* 41 (1963).

Brown, R. *Explanation in Social Science* (London: Routledge and Kegan Paul, 1963).

———. *Rules and Laws in Sociology* (London: Routledge and Kegan Paul, 1973).

——— and Rollins, C. D. (eds.). *Contemporary Philosophy in Australia* (London: Allen and Unwin, 1969).

Campbell, K. *Body and Mind* (London: Macmillan, 1971).

———. "Colours," in *Contemporary Philosophy in Australia*, eds. R. Brown and C. D. Rollins (London: Allen and Unwin, 1969).

Campbell, R. *From Belief to Understanding* (Canberra: Faculty of Arts, Australian National University, 1976).

Candlish, M. S. "The Inexplicability of Identity," *Australasian Journal of Philosophy* 49 (1971).

Crossley, J. N. *Constructive Order Types* (Amsterdam: North-Holland, 1969).

D'Arcy, E. *Human Acts* (Oxford: Clarendon Press, 1963).

Deutscher, M. "Mental and Physical Properties," in *The Identity Theory of Mind*, ed. C. F. Presley (St. Lucia, Queensland: University of Queensland Press, 1967).

———. "Popper's Problem of an Empirical Base," *Australasian Journal of Philosophy* 46 (1968).

Ellis, B. *Basic Concepts of Measurement* (London: Cambridge University Press, 1966).

Franklin, R. L. *Freewill and Determinism* (London: Cambridge University Press, 1967).

Gasking, D. "Avowals," in *Analytical Philosophy, 1st Series*, ed. R. J. Butler (Oxford: Barnes and Noble, 1962).

———. "Causation and Recipes," *Mind* 64 (1955).

———. "Clusters," *Australasian Journal of Philosophy* 38 (1960).

———. "Mathematics and the World," *Australasian Journal of Philosophy* 18 (1940).

Gibson, A. B. "Modern Philosophers Consider Religion," *Australasian Journal of Philosophy* 36 (1958).

———. *Theism and Empiricism* (London: S.C.M. Press, 1970).

Gibson, Q. *The Logic of Social Enquiry* (London: Routledge and Kegan Paul, 1960).

Goddard, L. and Routley, R. *The Logic of Significance and Context* (Edinburgh: Scottish Academic Press, 1973).

Grave, S. A. *The Scottish Philosophy of Common Sense* (Oxford: Clarendon Press, 1960).

Grünbaum, A. "The Denial of Absolute Space and the Hypothesis of a Universal Nocturnal Expansion, A Rejoinder to George Schlesinger," *Australasian Journal of Philosophy* 45 (1967).

Herbst, P. "A Critique of the Materialist Identity Theory," in *The Identity Theory of Mind*, ed. C. F. Presley (St. Lucia, Queensland: University of Queensland Press, 1967).

———. "The Nature of Facts," in *Essays in Conceptual Analysis*, ed. A. Flew (London: Macmillan, 1956).

Hinckfuss, I. *The Existence of Space and Time* (Oxford: Clarendon Press, 1975).

Hugget, W. J. "On Not Being Gulled By Ravens," *Australasian Journal of Philosophy* 38 (1960).

Hyslop, A. "Other Minds as Theoretical Entities," *Australasian Journal of Philosophy* 54 (1976).

———. "The Identity Theory and Other Minds," *Philosophical Forum* 2 (1970).

——— and Jackson, F. C. "A Reply to Don Locke," *Australasian Journal of Philosophy* 53 (1975).

———. "The Analogical Inference to Other Minds," *American Philosophical Quarterly* 9 (1972).

Joske, W. D. *Material Objects* (London: Macmillan, 1967).

Kamenka, E. *Marxism and Ethics* (London: Macmillan, and New York: St. Martin's Press, 1969).

———. *The Ethical Foundations of Marxism* (London: Cambridge University Press, 1962).

Kleinig, J. L. *Punishment and Desert* (The Hague: Nijhoff, 1973).

Kovesi, J. *Moral Notions* (London: Routledge and Kegan Paul, 1967).

Langtry, B. N. "Identity and Spatio-Temporal Continuity," *Australasian Journal of Philosophy* 50 (1972).

————. "Similarity, Continuity and Survival," *Australasian Journal of Philosophy* 53 (1975).

Leatherdale, W. H. *The Role of Analogy, Model and Metaphor in Science* (Amsterdam: North-Holland, 1974).

Mackie, J. L. "Evil and Omnipotence," *Mind* 64 (1955).

————. "Logic and Professor Anderson," *Australasian Journal of Philosophy* 39 (1951).

Martin, C. B. *Religious Belief* (Ithaca, N.Y.: Cornell University Press, 1959).

McCloskey, H. J. "A Note on Utilitarian Punishment," *Mind* 72 (1963).

————. *God and Evil* (The Hague: Nijhoff, 1974).

————. *Meta-Ethics and Normative Ethics* (The Hague: Nijhoff, 1969).

————. "Some Arguments for a Liberal Society," *Philosophy* 43 (1968).

————. "The State and Evil," *Ethics* 69 (1958).

————. "Utilitarian and Retributive Punishment," *Journal of Philosophy* 64 (1967).

McCloskey, M. "Metaphors," *Mind* 73 (1964).

Medlin, B. H. "Ryle and the Mechanical Hypothesis," in *The Identity Theory of Mind*, ed. C. F. Presley (St. Lucia, Queensland: University of Queensland Press, 1967).

Meyer, R. and Routley, R. *Relevant Logics and Their Rivals* (forthcoming).

Monro, D. H. *Empiricism and Ethics* (London: Cambridge University Press, 1967).

————. *Godwin's Moral Philosophy* (London: Oxford University Press, 1953).

————. *The Ambivalence of Bernard Mandeville* (Oxford: Clarendon Press, 1975).

Nerlich, G. " 'Continuity' Continued," *Analysis* 21 (1960–1961).

————. "On Evidence for Identity," *Australasian Journal of Philosophy* 37 (1959).

————. *The Shape of Space* (Cambridge: Cambridge University Press, 1976).

———— and Suchting, W. A. "Popper on Law and Natural Necessity," *British Journal for the Philosophy of Science* 18 (1967).

Partridge, P. H. "Politics, Philosophy, Ideology," *Political Studies* 9 (1961); rpt. in *Political Philosophy*, ed. A. Quinton (London: Oxford University Press, 1967).

Passmore, J. *A Hundred Years of British Philosophy* (London: Duckworth, 1957).

————. "Can the Social Sciences Be Value-free?" *Proceedings of the Xth International Congress of Philosophy* 2 (1948); rpt. in *Readings in the Philosophy of Science*, eds. H. Feigl and M. Brodbeck (New York: Appleton-Century-Crofts, 1953).

————. *Hume's Intentions*, rev. ed. (New York: Basic Books, 1968).

————. *Man's Responsibility for Nature* (London: Duckworth, 1974).

————. *Philosophical Reasoning* (London: Duckworth, 1961).

————. *Ralph Cudworth* (Cambridge: Cambridge University Press, 1951).

————. "The Dreariness of Aesthetics," *Mind* 60 (1951); rpt. in *Aesthetics and Language*, ed. W. Elton (Oxford: Blackwell, 1954).

————. *The Perfectibility of Man* (London: Duckworth, 1970).

Place, U. T. "Is Consciousness a Brain Process?" *British Journal of Psychology* 47 (1956); rpt. in *The Philosophy of Mind*, ed. V. C. Chappell (Englewood Cliffs, N.J.: Prentice-Hall, 1962).

Popper, K. *The Logic of Scientific Discovery*, 2d ed. (London: Hutchinson, 1968).

Prokhovnik, S. J. *The Logic of Special Relativity* (Melbourne: Melbourne University Press, 1971).

Quinton, A. (ed.). *Political Philosophy* (London: Oxford University Press, 1967).

Rankin, K. W. *Choice and Chance* (Oxford: Blackwell, 1961).

————. "More on the Deterministic Windmill," *Australasian Journal of Philosophy* 42 (1964).

Rennie, M. K. *Some Uses of Type Theory in the Analysis of Language* (Canberra: Australian National University, 1974).

Routley, V. "Critical Notice of *Man's Responsibility for Nature*," *Australasian Journal of Philosophy* 53 (1975).

Ryle, G. *Collected Papers*, 2 vols. (London: Hutchinson, 1971), I, *Critical Essays;* II, *Collected Essays 1929–1968.*

————. "Logic and Professor Anderson," *Australasian Journal of Philosophy* 29 (1950).

Schlesinger, G. *Method in the Physical Sciences* (London: Routledge and Kegan Paul, 1963).

——. "The Passage of Time," in *Contemporary Philosophy in Australia*, eds. R. Brown and C. D. Rollins (London: Allen and Unwin, 1969).

——. "The Problem of Evil and the Problem of Suffering," *American Philosophical Quarterly* 1 (1964).

——. "What Does the Denial of Absolute Space Mean?" *Australasian Journal of Philosophy* 45 (1967).

Singer, P. *Democracy and Disobedience* (London: Oxford University Press, 1973).

Smart, J.J.C. "An Outline of a System of Utilitarian Ethics," in *Utilitarianism For and Against*, eds. J.J.C. Smart and B. Williams (London: Cambridge University Press, 1973).

——. "Causal Theories of Time," *Monist* 53 (1969).

——. "Comments on Papers," in *The Identity Theory of Mind*, ed. C. F. Presley (St. Lucia, Queensland: University of Queensland Press, 1967).

——. "Extreme and Restricted Utilitarianism," *Philosophical Quarterly* 6 (1956); rpt. in *Theories of Ethics*, ed. P. Foot (London: Oxford University Press, 1967).

——. "Free Will, Praise and Blame," *Mind* 70 (1961).

——. "On Some Criticisms of a Physicalist Theory of Colors," in *Philosophical Aspects of the Mind-Body Problem*, ed. C.-Y. Cheng (Honolulu: University of Hawaii Press, 1975).

——. *Philosophy and Scientific Realism* (London: Cambridge University Press, 1963).

——. "Reports of Immediate Experiences," *Synthese* 22 (1971).

——. "Sensations and Brain Processes," *Philosophical Review* 68 (1959); rpt. in *The Philosophy of Mind*, ed. V. C. Chappell (Englewood Cliffs, N.J.: Prentice-Hall, 1962).

Stout, A. K. "But Suppose Everyone Did the Same," *Australasian Journal of Philosophy* 32 (1954).

Stove, D. C. "A Reply to Mr. Watkins," *Australasian Journal of Philosophy* 38 (1960).

——. "Hume, Induction, and the Irish," *Australasian Journal of Philosophy* 54 (1976).

——. "Popperian Confirmation and the Paradox of the Ravens," *Australasian Journal of Philosophy* 37 (1959).

——. *Probability and Hume's Inductive Scepticism* (London: Oxford University Press, 1973).

Watkins, J.W.N. "Mr. Stove's Blunders," *Australasian Journal of Philosophy* 37 (1959).

——. "Reply to Mr. Stove's Reply," *Australasian Journal of Philosophy* 38 (1960).

Young, R. *Freedom, Responsibility and God* (London: Macmillan, and New York: Barnes and Noble, 1975).

JOURNALS

Australasian Journal of Philosophy
The Australian Humanist
Sophia

ISRAEL

ELAZAR WEINRYB

I

The state of Israel was founded in 1948; it is thus reasonable to begin this survey at that point. In order to explain some features of the more recent situation, however, first something ought to be said of philosophical activities in Palestine.

The Department of Philosophy at the Hebrew University of Jerusalem was founded in 1928. In 1950, it had three members, while two philosophers were teaching in other departments of that university, which then was the only university in Israel. By 1977, Israel had six universities, with more than one hundred teachers of philosophy.

There is no Israeli philosophy in the sense in which it is possible to speak of a German or a French philosophy. This fact hardly needs an explanation. Israel (and Palestine, before 1948) is first of all a country of immigrants. The few scholars who established philosophical activities in this country brought with them the traditions and ways of thinking with which they had been previously familiar. These foreign philosophical bents have become more or less firmly rooted. Moreover, an important phase in the education of many Israeli-born philosophers (who were educated in Israel) has taken place in some foreign philosophical center such as Oxford, Boston, or Paris. Finally, the quick growth of Israeli higher education (not to mention the Zionist idea itself) has continued to attract a steady influx of philosophers, some of whom made considerable contributions before their immigration.

These facts make it quite difficult even to delimit precisely the reference group of this survey. More important is the following implication. Much of the style, interests, and achievements of the Israeli philosopher depends on the influence of the school or the trend with which he identifies himself.

The founding fathers, so to speak, of philosophy as an academic activity were Leon (Hayyim Yehudah) Roth (1896–1963),[1] Shmuel Hugo Bergman (1883–1975),[2] and Julius (Yitzhak) Guttmann (1880–1950).[3] Their approach to philosophy was primarily historical. Roth and Bergman aspired to create the possibility of philosophizing in Hebrew, which for them meant making available Hebrew translations of Western philosophical classics, as well as textbooks

This survey is based partially on personal accounts of the philosophers. I should like to acknowledge my debt to Professor Rotenstreich for reading an earlier draft of this paper.

describing and explaining the main systems and traditions. Theirs was not an easy job, since it was necessary to devise philosophical terminology for modern Hebrew. The task of translation still requires much energy.

Even today language raises some serious problems for the Israeli philosopher. On the one hand, he is always influenced by some foreign tradition or school. On the other hand, if he is a native speaker of Hebrew, then to some extent at least that tradition is alien to him: the language of his everyday thinking is not identical with the language he uses philosophically. The importance of one's sensitivity to language is nowadays universally acknowledged. Moreover, insofar as the philosophical contribution of the Israeli is not in Hebrew, there is a danger of estrangement between him and his natural audience.

Roth, Guttmann, and Bergman displayed a continental European interest in the history of philosophy. Though an Oxonian, Roth was not typically English. He devoted his energies to the study of rationalism, especially Spinoza's, and he tried to determine the extent to which Spinoza had been influenced by Descartes and Maimonides. Guttmann's major book, *Die Philosophie des Judentums,* deals with the history of Jewish philosophy. But the posthumously published *On the Philosophy of Religion* reveals influences of Kant and phenomenology. (See also his *Religion and Knowledge.*) One critic has remarked that when Guttmann went beyond Kant in the question of religion he utilized the ideas of Schleiermacher.[4] And in Bergman's teaching the influence of Brentano was combined with that of the neo-Kantianism of H. Cohen and E. Cassirer.

It is surprising how small the influence of Martin Buber (1878–1965) has been.[5] He was well known to the public, and his teaching was much discussed in youth circles and the Kibbutzim. Since 1948, about two hundred articles were written on him in Hebrew, most of them in the nonprofessional press. When I say that Buber has had almost no influence I mean, first of all, that no philosopher in Israel has ever tried to continue Buber's line of thought in any serious way. Perhaps Buber can hardly be imitated. Second, his doctrines are only rarely taught on the University level.

There is, perhaps, some explanation of this phenomenon. Buber's view of the nature of philosophy was rather ambivalent. Insofar as philosophy is science and not immediate life, it necessarily substitutes the subject-object for the authentic I-Thou relation, and thus distorts the essence of the human condition. On the other hand, Buber had no doubt that an adequate description—such as his own—of that condition is not only legitimate but also indispensable, though he preferred to call such an undertaking "philosophical anthropology." Now the point is that such an adverse attitude towards the larger part of the past of the philosophical enterprise seems quite inappropriate, if one aspires to establish philosophical activities in a newborn society and fluid culture. Considerations of this sort may have minimized Buber's influence on philosophical education. His philosophical writings appeared in Hebrew only in the late 1950s. A deep respect towards the past great systems with emphasis on Kantianism dominated.

II

PHILOSOPHY OF RELIGION AND JUDAISM

Those who expect Israeli philosophy to be a continuation of traditional Jewish philosophy will be surprised not to find any system-builders who bear comparison with F. Rosenzweig or H. Cohen. Most of the work done in Jewish philosophy is purely historical and hermeneutic.[6] This does not mean that problems of religious belief and Jewish identity and destiny do not engross attention. On the contrary. But only rarely are they systematically dealt with.

Guttmann's book has already been mentioned. By method of elimination, he tried to prove that the religious sphere has a uniqueness of its own and that, as there are various kinds of truths, the *sui generis* character of religious truth by no means makes it inferior or suspect. Its character is one of personal certitude, which is nevertheless absolute; for the object of religious belief is a supreme reality of infinite value. It therefore becomes apparent that revelation is no longer necessarily the only source of religious conviction. Guttmann believed that the relationship with God has many modes of realization. But even if there is a direct relation with God, observance of the religious commandments *(Mitzvoth)* is indispensable because no man is filled all the time with religious ecstasy. Bergman found it also necessary to justify belief in God, even though at times he followed Buber's dialogue approach, according to which any attempt to prove God's existence is an expression of the misleading subject-object relation, while God is truly the eternal Thou. It is possible to talk with Him but not to prove His existence. Recent developments in Western thought show, according to Bergman, that secular humanism is impossible. His argument for the existence of God runs as follows.[7] The existence of man, *qua* rational being, cannot be explained unless the individual human being is seen as a member of a community, but the unity of humanity is understood only as a correlate of the real unity of God. Buber described the relationship with God as the supreme exemplification of the I-Thou relationship. Bergman's qualification means that this relationship is of the We-Thou type. He speaks thus of "the humanism of the covenant."

Yeshayahu Leibowitz (1903–   ),[8] a chemist and neurophysiologist by profession, exhibits an Aristotelian approach to philosophy, according to which one should have knowledge in every branch of science and discipline in order to be able to form a systematic world-view. His ideas concerning religion, which show uncompromising coherence, as well as his position in Israeli politics, are quite heterodox. Professional philosophers will find many flaws in his arguments.

According to Leibowitz, Judaism is an institutional religion in the sense that the Jewish religion is identical with the commandments *(Mitzvoth)*. The identification rests first on historical reflection: all phenomena of Judaism, except the *Halachah* (the religious commandments), were but transitory episodes. Second, there are systematic considerations. The validity of the commandments is derived from a decision to fulfill them, for which no rational justification is conceivable. God is understood only as the source of the commandments. As one critic observed, in this system God is constituted by the constitutive rules[9] of institutional religion. Leibowitz denies that the Holy Scriptures and other religious sources say anything informative either about God's existence or about His relationship with the world and humanity. Neither did God create the universe, nor is there any sense in speaking of Providence; and the idea of messianic redemption has always been insignificant. Only science is informative. Leibowitz adheres intransigently to three well-known dualisms, two of which the reader may have already recognized. A doctrine of a twofold truth—religion versus science—is argued for by a religious version of the is-ought dichotomy rather similar to Hare's prescriptivism. Leibowitz's version of the body-soul dualism emphasizes the impossibility of a scientific approach with respect to psychic phenomena as well as the utter unintelligibility of mind-body correlations. In politics, Leibowitz constantly demands a total separation of religion from state and denies any intrinsic value to the state.

Finally, Gershom (Gerhard) Scholem's (1897–   )[10] ideas, which are diametrically opposed to those of Leibowitz, should be considered because of Scholem's highly influential position as the founder of, and the leading scholar in, the historical research of the *Kabbalah* and Jewish mysticism in general.

For Scholem (as it was for Rosenzweig), creation, revelation, and redemption were, are, and will be the basic elements of Judaism. Belief in God may be independent of any revelation and may not entail any specific theology. Yet, it is impossible to waive the idea of creation, which may be considered the only act of revelation, in favor of a naturalistic cosmogony because any explanation of that sort smuggles in teleology. Redemption is nowadays the most stable of the three elements. Its secular version particularly has the wilder threads of messianism. According to Scholem, a secular, rational atheistic morality is impossible. He does not, moreover, believe that secularization will ever be complete. Zionism for Scholem has a religious content and potential. The uniqueness of the people of Israel is meaningless in secular terms, and there is a "theocratic hope," even if this hope necessitates a totally secular phase. Belief in God cannot be extinguished, and the uniqueness of Judaism would have been destroyed had atheism prevailed. Scholem, however, does not commit himself to any specific form of religion. Belief has many forms, and the *Halachah* should not be considered its only expression. Scholem's prediction of religious revival does not include a reference to strict observance of the *Halachah,* and he himself has expressed his entire distaste for "kitchen Judaism." It seems that Scholem combines a sharp eye with wishful thinking in a manner reminiscent of Bergman's above-mentioned argument. Moreover, Scholem overestimates the significance of what he calls the "dialectical approach" to historical processes.

III

Guttmann died in 1950; Roth left Israel in 1951; Bergman's influential position remained intact until the 1970s. During the 1950s, however, two younger philosophers came to the foreground: Nathan Rotenstreich (1914–   )[11] and Yehoshua Bar-Hillel (1915–1975).[12] Quite as impressive was the contribution of Pepita Haezrahi. (1921–1963).[13] The second generation of Israeli philosophers—the first one to be educated here—comprised these three.

Although some of Rotenstreich's writings are historical, for him historical research is not an end in itself. In *Philosophy, the Concept* and *Its Manifestations,* he defines philosophy as the "deliberate knowledge of the nature of knowledge" (p. 169). The great systems of the past should be conceived as important data for inquiry into the foundations of knowledge because they themselves are expressions of knowledge. Moreover, man has a historical dimension. So philosophy cannot ignore the exemplification of man's historicity in the development of philosophy itself. Finally, the history of philosophy presents us with concepts and instruments that were created in an attempt to solve permanent problems. An understanding of these concepts may help us in our groping for solutions of the same philosophical problems.

It may be said that Rotenstreich's method in philosophy is that of conceptual analysis, the data of which are neither ordinary language nor the scientific one, but rather the philosophical systems of the past. This method is clearly exemplified in his *Theory and Practice,*[14] the first part of which describes the history of both ideas from Plato and Aristotle to the present, while its second part is an attempt to redefine these concepts in order to determine how they are mutually related. The classical distinction between theory as a detached contemplation of the world and practice as an intentional involvement in it is maintained. Besides, there is a sense in which theory has priority over action because, to begin with, action must be guided by understanding and, second, understanding is sometimes self-understanding. Finally, Aristotle's basic idea that *theoria* has priority because it has as its object the Supreme Being can be retained if man, world, and time, as irreducible spheres of existence, are considered as substitutes for that Being.

Rotenstreich's method in some of his other important books (*Spirit and Man; On the Human Subject*) is perhaps correctly described as phenomenological. In *On the Human Subject,* he himself uses the expression "phenomenological features" to denote the object of his inquiry. According to Rotenstreich, there is a sphere of meanings, concepts, or categories that the consciousness reveals in its self-reflective activity. Here "category" has both Aristotelian and Kantian connotations.

The basic category is that of the irreducible concrete human subject, an entity *sui generis* whose status is not exhausted even by the totality of its aspects. This is an experiencing subject, receptive on the one hand and spontaneous on the other. Spontaneity elevates the subject from its total submergence in the world around him to a position of "detached attachment" *vis à vis* the world. As consciousness recognizes the distance between subject and object, it is led to acknowledge the supreme principle—the principle of truth. Spontaneity also means the receptivity to principles and norms, which the subject in turn tries to realize in the world. Activity of the concrete subject thus has two basic directions: encountering the world and realizing principles. Rotenstreich acknowledges similarities between his approach and Whitehead's discussion of the "superject." Rotenstreich holds that "spirit" refers to the activity of categories and principles. In the realizing of principles by the human subject, not only is he active; the Spirit itself acts independently. Man's existence is thus a necessay condition for the existence of the Spirit, but there is no identity here. Against Hegel, Rotenstreich argues that, even though human beings are receptive of principles and continuously endeavor to realize Spirit, there is no guarantee that the realization will ever be complete and that the real and the spiritual will be identical.

The three basic categories—consciousness, experience, and Spirit—do not function only as philosophical notions, but also as explicit manifestations in human life. Detachment, for instance, reveals itself first in the creation of tools, such as language, which mediate between man and his environment, and, second, in man's historicity. Furthermore, certain basic positions concerning human freedom and dignity as well as other basic standpoints are implied by the analysis that takes the concrete subject as central. Thus, rationality is the ground of morality, and the human subject who realizes the principle of good which has but instrumental value becomes an end in itself. Here Rotenstreich acknowledges Kant's influence, although it is sufficiently clear from what has just been said that he disagrees with Kant's position concerning the priority of practical reason.

In her early essay "On Scepticism" (M. A. Thesis, 1945), Pepita Haezrahi argues that because of the hypothetical character of Kant's transcendental categories, the critical approach cannot appease the skeptic's qualms. She maintains that the essence of philosophy is its uncompromising urge towards the Absolute, the unattainability of which contributes a tragic dimension to the philosophical enterprise. Her book on morality *(The Price of Morality)* discloses the same skeptical mood. In the formulation of the moral law, the influence of Kant is conspicuous. "Never injure the dignity of any human being" rests on the assumption that all men *qua* men are endowed with dignity, which is, contrary to Kant's view, unjustifiable in principle. But as soon as one accepts this principle he is entitled to act on it. Nevertheless, no actual performance is ever in complete agreement with the moral law because man's value is infinite and every action has numerous nonmoral aspects.

Haezrahi's most important work is *The Contemplative Activity*, a study in aesthetics. Here a phenomenologically flavored analysis suggests that aesthetic experience is doomed to failure in its attempt to bridge the object-subject gap. When the character of this experience is emotional, the importance of the subject is enhanced. On the other hand, mystical experience focuses on the object. But in neither way is the intended complete union ever achieved. Haezrahi proposes, however, a definite answer to the question of criteria for aesthetic evaluation. Creation of a work of art consists of an elegant and brilliant problem-solving. Objective evaluation criteria should reflect the extent to which the artist was successful in solving his problem.

Yehoshua Bar-Hillel[15] was a close follower of R. Carnap. He describes his first reading of the initial volumes of *Erkenntnis* as nothing short of a revelation, and Carnap's *Logische Syntax der Sprache* as the most influential book he has ever read. In his contribution to the Schilpp volume on Carnap, Bar-Hillel observes that the most important philosophical thesis of logical empiricism has been "that many, if not most, philosophical controversies are not, as they are commonly regarded by participants and onlookers alike, theoretical disagreements on questions of fact . . . but rather disagreements . . . on the kind of linguistic framework to be preferably used in a certain context and for a certain purpose."[16] This is the gist of Carnap's insistence on translation from the material to the formal mode of speech. And even though Bar-Hillel confesses in the preface to *Language and Information* that his "utter disgust of metaphysics and speculative philosophy . . . has never wavered," he actually thinks that some traditional philosophical problems retain significance even under translation into the formal mode.

In details, however, Bar-Hillel is much less of a logical positivist than it might be thought. He criticizes the exclusive attention paid by logicians of that school to formalized languages on the one hand, and hasty applications of logical apparatus to natural languages on the other. The logicians' disregard of the Aristotelian tradition of ordinary language logical analysis he dubs "treason." He is much more a critic than a system-builder, and even when in a constructive mood, what he says is programmatic rather than systematic.

One of Bar-Hillel's most important suggestions is that logicians should devote their energies to the construction of a logic for natural languages in which full justice would be done to the pragmatic aspects. Indexicality of some expressions is but a symptom of the general feature of context-dependency of expressions in natural languages. Bar-Hillel proposes, therefore, the following threefold classification: a *sentence,* which is a linguistic entity, is used in an *utterance,* a spatio-temporal event, in order to make a *statement* (a command, a question), the meaning as well as the truth-value of which depends on the sentence-type and the context of the utterance. In order to test the validity of arguments in natural languages, we need (1) a system of normalization rules which will enable us to represent utterances (i.e., sentences coupled with contexts) as statements; and (2) rules for representing these statements as sentences of a formalized language, to which the rules of formal logic may be applied.

Bar-Hillel's interest in the logical features of natural languages brought him very early to assess favorably Chomsky's transformational grammar and see the promising prospects of close collaboration between linguists and logicians (as well as psychologists and so forth). In the recent history of linguistics, a special significance is attached to the Bar-Hillel-Chomsky 1954 exchange.[17] Bar-Hillel argued then that linguists should pay attention to the achievements of the logical semantics of Carnap and others. He distinguished between theory of meaning and theory of reference, and argued for the high relevancy of theory of meaning alone. Chomsky objected that the central concepts of semantics, such as synonymy and equivalence, are, in fact, void. It thus happened that until the early 1960s almost no attention was paid to Bar-Hillel's idea and linguists dealt almost exclusively with syntax. Then linguists began to study semantics, but only in the later 1960s did they become interested in questions of reference. By then, however, it was felt that Bar-Hillel's 1954 distinction between theory of meaning and theory of reference was becoming obsolete.

IV

Through Bar-Hillel, the analytical approach has become firmly established in Israel; this may be considered his most important contribution to Israeli philosophical life. But even though he adhered to logical positivism, his influence was not confined to it, and the atmosphere he created made possible all kinds of analytic philosophy. However, Bar-Hillel's expressed abhorrence of metaphysics, as well as his conviction that philosophical problems should be dealt with only after sufficient philosophical and logical understanding has been achieved, did not apparently encourage young philosophers to go deeply into problems of ontology or ethics. His immediate followers are interested almost exclusively in the philosophy of language. Besides, as everywhere, specialization is a characteristic tendency of those Israeli philosophers who identify themselves with the analytic tradition.

The growth of analytic philosophy was taking place side by side with continuation of the tradition established by Roth and Bergman. As was stated above, they were exceptional in taking the liberty of abandoning their historical and exegetical studies. Rotenstreich has been a follower of these thinkers to the extent that he has approached philosophy along the lines that may be called continental European, and historical research has been of considerable value for him. Even Haezrahi, who paid attention to the teaching of philosophers such as Ross and Moore, was preoccupied with Kant. But theirs was definitely the first serious attempt in Israeli philosophy to defend an original position concerning various philosophical questions. Unfortunately, insofar as it is possible to achieve a fair appreciation of the present situation, it can be said that those who may be considered Rotenstreich's followers retain only his interest in historical and hermeneutic research. Studies in Kant, Hegel, and others have been recently published.[18] Thus, not a few members of the present generation imitate the first generation.

V

LOGIC AND LANGUAGE

Some younger philosophers have taken seriously Bar-Hillel's challenge: the systematic treatment of the logic of natural languages. Asa Kasher[19] has developed a theory of language use according to which linguistic activity takes place within linguistic institutions governed by constitutive rules and is carried out by rational agents. Under these ideal conditions, an answer is given to the question, When is the linguistic act appropriate? Thus, it is possible, for instance, to derive conversational maxims, which have much in common with Grice's implicature rules, from the principle of rationality of action itself, as it is defined by David Richards in *A Theory of Reasons for Action* (p. 28), rather than from some ad hoc principle, such as Grice's. In this manner, the theory is intended to provide an explanatory framework for a variety of pragmatical aspects.

In a not dissimilar vein, Ruth Manor[20] explores the possibility of analyzing speech situations like monologues and dialogues, in a given context, in order to answer what seems to her the central question, To what proposition has the speaker committed himself by a given speech-act, and what conversational function has it served? Nathan Stemmer[21] proposes an empiricist theory of language acquisition. Avishai Margalit[22] suggests that if inductive reasoning is to play an essential role in semantics, then even metaphors could be adequately dealt with within the general framework.

METAPHYSICS AND EPISTEMOLOGY

In two books on Kantian themes, Yirmiahu Yovel[22] uses a confrontation with the Kantian heritage to present his own conception of what he has called "finite rationality" and its consequences for the aim and method of philosophy. There are many points of similarity between Yovel's approach and Rotenstreich's. According to Yovel, human rationality is inherently linked with the following characteristics of man: existential finitude, the activity of a concrete subject, a variety of "subrational" attitudes, a form of interest ("eros"), self-transcendence, openendedness, and historicality. As finite, it is particularly marked by a form of "metaphysical interestedness" which philosophy can neither "cure" (*pace* Wittgenstein) nor satisfy (*pace* Hegel), nor submerge in social action (*pace* Marx). Rather, by explicating the inherent tension between metaphysical queries and the impossibility of answering them, philosophy should illuminate man's finitude. Philosophy is thus a mode of self-consciousness which has a liberating as well as a disillusioning function. Jacob Joshua Ross, who has written the book *The Appeal to the Given*, defines himself as a neo-Wittgensteinian, but his actual approach seems traditionally Israeli, since what he has to say is presented as an interpretation of things other philosophers have said.

His book explores the various meanings philosophers have given to the concept of the given. These meanings, Ross maintains, reflect the different metaphysical world-views of the philosophers. Epistemology is thus a part of metaphysics, which Ross tries to distinguish both from common sense and from science.

In her many books (most of them written before her settlement in Israel), Elaine Amado Lévy-Valensi[24] is concerned primarily with the relationship between philosophy and psychoanalysis. Her purpose is to show that in the therapeutical dialogue of the psychoanalyst and his patient some basic epistemological presuppositions become illuminated. Jacques Schlanger[25] has developed the concept of metaphysical structure and has applied it to the history of philosophy. Ben-Ami Scharfstein[26] emphasizes the artificiality of divisions that separate philosophy from other fields of study and the necessity of taking into account Eastern philosophies in any overall synthesis. (For E. M. Zemach, see below.)

ETHICS

The recent increase of interest in ethical problems may lead to remarkable contributions in the future. For the time being, this is not the strongest side of Israeli philosophy. The awakening of interest reflects the growing doubts, typical of the younger generation, that the ideologies which guided the society since the beginnings of Jewish resettlement in Palestine have no answers to some basic ethical and social questions. Thus, Yehudah Melzer[27] has recently published a book on the problem of the just war—quite a problem for an Israeli. In the philosophical part of the book, Melzer analyzes various arguments for pacifism and explains to what extent pacifism depends on the rather spurious double-effect doctrine.

AESTHETICS

Eddy M. Zemach's[28] work in aesthetics exemplifies his general philosophical outlook, according to which the world is comprised of material objects that are directly perceived and known. He develops and defends this thesis from the ontological, epistemological, and logical points of view. As many arguments against the materialist view of aesthetic objects are based on the fact that a work of art is often regarded as a type, Zemach developed an ontology in which types are neither abstract entities nor universals, but rather particular material objects. (See his "Four Ontologies.") The type-token distinction is really such that, whereas a token can recur in entirety only in time (at the same place) but not in space (at the same time), a type can do both. In logic, this led Zemach to develop (with E. Walther)[29] a substitute for predicate calculus that uses no predicates. Every formula in the new calculus expresses identity between entities. The idealistic approach, Zemach argues, gains little from the fact that poems may be composed in one's head. For thinking is identical with having a series of mental (mostly acoustic) images. But images have no separate existence, and imagining is only one of many ways in which we directly perceive real material objects. (See "Seeing 'Seeing' and Feeling.") Aesthetic properties (such as beautiful or ugly) are objective and are open to public observation no less than colors. There are standard observation conditions for aesthetic properties—those under which objects of the kind examined look, on the whole, at their aesthetic best. Zemach describes his view as an interpretation of the Keatsian tenet "Truth is Beauty, Beauty Truth." His argument to the effect that pains are observable properties of objects such as hands and hearts is another attempt to eliminate mental, private entities. (See his "Pains and Pain Feelings.")

Finally, Zemach sees the interpretation of art works as something quite like a theoretical scientific hypothesis. The criteria for the plausibility of an aesthetic interpretation, however, differ remarkably from criteria for the acceptability of a scientific theory, notwithstanding the considerable similarity. For if performance is viewed as an interpretation, then interpretation and the interpreted object are tokens of the same type. Therefore, the greater aesthetic value of the interpreted object under certain interpretations contributes to the plausibility of that interpretation.

PHILOSOPHY OF SCIENCE

In the view of Joseph Agassi,[30] Faraday exemplifies a recurring pattern in the history of science according to which metaphysical theories, i.e., views about the nature of things, determine which scientific problems are chosen, while the scientific theories suggested as solutions to those problems serve as tests of the metaphysical view. History of science is not the history of success in information accumulation. The rationality of the dispute is the important thing. As a follower of Popper, Agassi identifies rationality with a critical approach, but he deprives testability of its unique status and argues for a plurality of criteria for being scientific. Rationality, however, is relative, and what was rational yesterday is not rational any more today. Agassi has recently developed a social and political theory in which his concept of rationality plays a major role.

Yehudah Elkana,[31] too, has emphasized the importance of metaphysical presuppositions in physics, but it seems that his approach is even more relativistic in that he strives to reduce epistemology to sociology of knowledge. He sees science as a cultural system. He believes that the intellectual history of Europe since the Renaissance should be interpreted as the evolution of the culture of science.

PHILOSOPHY OF HISTORY

Yirmiahu Yovel, in an unpublished manuscript, has recently paid increasing attention to problems of the philosophy of history. He thinks that the basic approach of the speculative as well as analytical philosophy of history is quite mistaken because it is essentially object-directed. The subject matter of history is thought of as an external and alien object, "out there in the world." The root of this mistake is the substitution of the historian's conception of himself as confronting history for his actual existential situation as belonging to it. Human historicality means that there is no "pure ego" existing beforehand which then is "thrust" into history. On the contrary. The ego constitutes itself and becomes a distinct self through a network of historical relations. From this point of view, understanding history is an expanded form of self-consciousness and self-interpretation. Although the object-directedness is thus rejected, history must not be considered a purely subjective affair. Regulative norms of objective research are valid.

Elazar Weinryb[32] has written on problems of causal attributions in history. By analyzing the controversies over causal theses such as those of Turner and Weber, he has come to the following conclusions: The disputes are generally about the right descriptions of the cause or the effect or about the (sometimes implicit) theory which justifies the claim of causal connection. The analysis clarifies the essential connection between description and explanation by showing that "colligatory" descriptions are always theoretical relative to lower level factual descriptions.

VI

INSTITUTIONS AND PERIODICALS

The Jerusalem Philosophical Society was founded in 1943 and comprised members from all over the country. It was one of the founding societies of the Institut International de Philosophie (in 1948). The Israel Philosophical Association was founded in 1973 by members of the philosophy departments of all Israeli universities. The association fosters all kinds of philosophical activities and cultivates connections with foreign philosophical associations. It organizes annual country-wide meetings on various philosophical issues. There are more than one hundred association members. In general, only those who have a degree in philosophy may join.

Iyyun, the Hebrew Philosophical Quarterly, has appeared since 1945. S. Ucko was its first editor, and E.I.J. Poznański was its editor for many years. Its present editor is Yehudah Melzer. *Iyyun* is the only philosophical periodical in Hebrew. It sometimes publishes contributions not originally written in Hebrew. *Iyyun* is published by the Jerusalem Philosophical Society and the Hebrew University.

Philosophia, the Philosophical Quarterly of Israel, is an international journal in English published by Bar-Ilan University. It was founded in 1971 by Alex Blum and Asa Kasher, and is now edited by Kasher. *Philosophia* is in the analytic tradition, in the broad sense of the term.

NOTES

1. Roth studied at Oxford, and lectured at Manchester University (1923–1927) and at the Hebrew University of Jerusalem (1928–1953).

2. Bergman studied at Prague and Berlin, was the chief librarian of the Jewish National Library (1920–1935), and taught philosophy at the Hebrew University from 1928 on.

3. Guttmann lectured at Breslau University (from 1910), at the Hochschule für die Wissenschaft des Judentum in Berlin (from 1919), and at the Hebrew University (1934–1950).

4. Fritz Bamberger, "Julius Guttmann—Philosopher of Judaism," in *Leo Baeck Institute Year Book*, pp. 16–17.

5. Buber came to Palestine in 1938, and from then until 1951 was professor for social philosophy in the sociology department, the Hebrew University.

6. For the works of Shlomo Pines, a leading scholar in this field, see the bibliography.

7. In a series of lectures, "God and Man in Modern Thought" (1956), reprinted in his *Men and Ways*.

8. Leibowitz was born in Riga, studied in Germany and Switzerland, and joined the Hebrew University in 1935. See his *Judaism, the Jewish People and the State of Israel*.

9. "Constitutive" in the sense of Rawls and Searle.

10. Scholem was born and educated in Germany, settled in Jerusalem in 1923, and lectured at the Hebrew University (1927–1965). See his *Explications and Implications* (in Hebrew) and *The Messianic Idea in Judaism and Other Essays on Jewish Spirituality*.

11. Rotenstreich was born in Poland and emigrated to Palestine in 1932. He studied at the Hebrew University and has taught at that university since 1949.

12. Bar-Hillel was born in Vienna and came to Palestine in 1933. He studied at the Hebrew University where he has lectured since 1953. He was a visiting professor and research scholar at many American universities, including MIT.

13. Pepita Haezrahi came to Palestine in 1934, was educated at Jerusalem and London, was a fellow of Newnham College, Cambridge (1950–1957), and has lectured at the Hebrew University since 1957.

14. An English translation to be published by Nijhoff, the Hague, will appear shortly.

15. See Bar-Hillel's three collections of essays: *Language and Information; Aspects of Language;* and *Logic, Language and Method*.

16. See "Carnap's *Logical Syntax of Language*," in *The Philosophy of Rudolf Carnap*, ed. P. A. Schilpp, p. 533.

17. Y. Bar-Hillel, "Logical Syntax and Semantics," *Language* 30 (1954):320–327; for Chomsky, "Logical Syntax and Semantics: Their Linguistic Relevance," see *Language* 31 (1955):36–45. In what follows, I draw heavily on J.M.E. Moravcsik, "Linguistics and Philosophy," *Current Trends in Linguistics* 12 (1974). For a discussion of Bar-Hillel's philosophy of language, see M. Kroy, "Bar-Hillel, Generative Semantics and Generative Pragmatics," *Logique et Analyse* 17 (1974):3–59.

18. See especially the works by Avineri, Bar-On, Fleischmann, Levy, Parush, Sigad, and Yovel in the bibliography.

19. Kasher teaches at Tel Aviv University and Bar-Ilan. See "Logical Forms in Context: Presuppositions and Other Preconditions," *The Monist* 57 (1973); "Mood Implicatures: A Logical Way of Doing Generative Pragmatics," *Theoretical Linguistics* 1 (1974); "Conversational Maxims and Rationality," in *Language in Focus*, ed. A. Kasher.

20. Ruth Manor teaches at Tel Aviv University. See her "On Propositional Commitment and Presuppositions," *American Philosophical Quarterly* 12 (1975).

21. Stemmer teaches at Bar-Ilan University. See his *An Empiricist Theory of Language Acquisition*.

22. Margalit teaches at the Hebrew University. See A. Margalit and L. J. Cohen, "The Role of Inductive Reasoning in the Interpretation of Metaphor," *Synthese* 21 (1970).

23. Yovel teaches at the Hebrew University. See his *Kant and the Rehabilitation of Metaphysics* and *Kant and History*.

24. Formerly at the Sorbonne and since 1969 at Bar-Ilan University. See her *Les niveaux de l'être, la connaissance et le mal; La dialogue Psychoanalytique; Le temps de la vie morale; La racine et la source, Essais sur le Judaisme; and Les voies et les pieges de la psychoanalyse.*

25. Schlanger teaches at the Hebrew University. See his *La structure metaphysique.*

26. Scharfstein teaches at Tel Aviv University. See his *Mystical Experience.*

27. Melzer teaches at the Hebrew University. See his *Concepts of Just War.*

28. Zemach teaches at the Hebrew University. See his *Analytical Aesthetics* and *Aesthetics.*

29. "Substance Logic" (with E. Walther), in *Language in Focus*, ed. A. Kasher.

30. Agassi teaches at Tel Aviv University and Boston University. See his *Faraday as a Natural Philosopher; Science in Flux;* and *Towards a Rational Philosophical Anthropology.*

31. Elkana teaches at the Hebrew University. See his "The Problem of Knowledge in Historical Perspective," *Proceedings of the Second International Humanistic Symposium;* "Rationality and Scientific Change," in *Boston Studies in the Philosophy of Science* (forthcoming).

32. Elazar Weinryb teaches at the Hebrew University. See his "The Justification of a Causal Thesis," *History and Theory* 14 (1975).

SELECT BIBLIOGRAPHY

*BOOKS AND ARTICLES**

Agassi, J. *Faraday as a Natural Philosopher* (Chicago: University of Chicago Press, 1971).
———. *Science in Flux* (Dordrecht: Reidel, 1975).
———. *Towards a Rational Philosophical Anthropology* (The Hague: Nijhoff, 1977).
Avineri, S. *Hegel's Theory of the Modern State* (London: Cambridge University Press, 1972).
———. *The Social and Political Thought of Karl Marx* (London: Cambridge University Press, 1968).
Bamberger, F. "Julius Guttmann—Philosopher of Judaism," in *Leo Baeck Institute Year Book* V (London and Jerusalem: East and West Library, 1960).
Bar-Hillel, Y. *Aspects of Language* (Jerusalem: Magnes Press, The Hebrew University, 1970).
———. "Carnap's *Logical Syntax of Language*," in *The Philosophy of Rudolf Carnap*, ed. P. A. Schilpp (La Salle, Ill.: Open Court, 1964).
———. *Language and Information* (Jerusalem: Academic Press, and Reading, Mass.: Addison-Wesley, 1964).
———. *Logic, Language and Method* (Tel Aviv: Sifriat Poalim, 1970). H
———. "Logical Syntax and Semantics," *Language* 30 (1954).
Bar-On, A. Z. *Principles of Being and Knowledge* (Jerusalem: Bialik Institute, 1967). H
Batscha, Z. *Gesellschaft und Staat in der politischen Philosophie Fichtes* (Frankfurt: Europäische Verlagsanstalt, 1970).
Bergman, S. H. *Faith and Reason* (Washington, D.C.: B'nai Brith Hillel Foundation, 1961).
———. *Men and Ways* (Jerusalem: Bialik Institute, 1967). H
———. *The Philosophy of Solomon Maimon* (Jerusalem: Magnes Press, The Hebrew University, 1967).
———. *Thinkers and Believers* (Tel Aviv: The Hebrew Writers Association and Dvir, 1959). H
Blum, A. "A Logic of Belief," *Notre Dame Journal of Formal Logic* 17 (1976).
Buber, M. *Der Jude und sein Judentum* (Cologne: Melzer, 1963).
———. *Werke* (Munich: Kösel, and Heidelberg: Schneider, 1962).
Chomsky, N. "Logical Syntax and Semantics: Their Linguistic Relevance," *Language* 31 (1955).
Elkana, Y. "Rationality and Scientific Change," in *Boston Studies in the Philosophy of Science* (forthcoming).

———. "The Problem of Knowledge in Historical Perspective," *Proceedings of the Second International Humanistic Symposium* (Greece, 1972).

Fleischmann, E. J. *La Philosophie politique de Hegel (Paris: Plon, 1964)*.

———. *La Science universelle ou la Logique de Hegel* (Paris: Plon, 1968).

———. *The Problem of Christianity in Modern Jewish Thought* (Jerusalem: Magnes Press, The Hebrew University, 1964). H

Glouberman, M. "Doctrine and Method in the Philosophy of P. F. Strawson," *Philosophy and Phenomenological Research* 36 (1976).

———. "Space and Analogy," *Mind* 84 (1975).

Groll, M. *Selected Writings* (Tel Aviv: Sifriat Poalim, 1966–1969). H

Guttmann, Y. J. *Die Philosophie des Judentums* (Munich: E. Reinhardt, 1933).

———. *On the Philosophy of Religion* (Jerusalem: Magnes Press, The Hebrew University, 1976; Hebrew ed., 1958).

———. *Religion and Knowledge* (Jerusalem: Magnes Press, The Hebrew University, 1955). H

Haezrahi, P. *On Perfect Reality: Studies in Plato and His Predecessors* (Jerusalem: Academon, 1964). H

———. *On Scepticism* (Jerusalem: Magnes Press, The Hebrew University, 1966). H

———. *The Contemplative Activity* (London: Allen and Unwin, 1954).

———. *The Price of Morality* (London: Allen and Unwin, 1961).

Horovitz, J. *Law and Logic* (Vienna: Springer, 1972).

Kasher, A. "Conversational Maxims and Rationality," in *Language in Focus*, ed. A. Kasher. (Dordrecht: Reidel, 1976).

——— (ed.) *Language in Focus* (Dordrecht: Reidel 1976).

———. "Logical Forms in Context: Presuppositions and Other Preconditions," *The Monist* 57 (1973).

———. "Mood Implicatures: A Logical Way of Doing Generative Pragmatics," *Theoretical Linguistics* 1 (1974).

Klein, Y. "La Philosophie et son Histoire," *Revue internationale de Philosophe* 117–118 (1976).

Kroy, M. "Bar-Hillel, Generative Semantics and Generative Pragmatics," *Logique et Analyse* 17 (1974).

Landau, Y. *The Desire of Matter Towards Form in Aristotle's Philosophy* (Tel Aviv: University Student Association, 1972). H

Leibowitz, Y. *Judaism, the Jewish People and the State of Israel* (Tel Aviv: Schocken, 1976). H

Levy, Z. *A Precursor of Jewish Existentialism: The Philosophy of F. Rosenzweig* (Tel Aviv: Sifriat Poalim, 1969). H

———. *Spinoza and the Concept of Judaism* (Tel Aviv: Sifriat Poalim, 1972). H

———. *Structuralism: Method and Theory* (Tel Aviv: Sifriat Poalim, 1976). H

Lévy-Valensi, E. A. *La dialogue Psychoanalytique* 2d ed. (Paris: Presses Universitaires de France, 1972).

———. *La nature de la pensée Inconsciente* (Paris: J-P. Delarge, 1978).

———. *La racine et la source, Essais sur le Judaisme* (Paris: Zikarone, 1968).

———. *Le temps de la vie morale* (Paris: Vrin, 1968).

———. *Les niveaux de l'être, la connaissance et le mal* (Paris: Presses Universitaires de France, 1963).

———. *Les voies et les pièges de la psychoanalyse* (Paris: Éditions universitaires, 1971).

Manor, R. "An Analysis of Speech," *Philosophical Linguistics* (forthcoming).

———. "On Propositional Commitment and Presuppositions," *American Philosophical Quarterly* 12 (1975).

Margalit, A. "Talking with Children, Piaget Style," in *Language in Focus*, ed. A. Kasher (Dordrecht: Reidel, 1976).

——— and Cohen, L. J. "The Role of Inductive Reasoning in the Interpretation of Metaphor," *Synthese* 21 (1970).

Melzer, Y. *Concepts of Just War* (Leyden: Sijthoff, 1975).

Moravcsik, J.M.E. "Linguistics and Philosophy," *Current Trends in Linguistics* 12 (1974).

Parush, A. *Trends in the History of Scepticism* (Jerusalem: Magnes Press, The Hebrew University, 1974). H

Pines, S. "Scholasticism after Thomas Aquinas and the Teachings of Hasdai Crescas," *Proceedings of the Israel Academy of Science and Humanities* I, No. 10 (Jerusalem: 1967).

———. "Spinoza's Tractatus Theologieo-Politicus, Maimonides and Kant," *Scripta Hierosolymitana* 20 (1968).

——— (ed. and trans.). *The Guide of the Perplexed by Moses Maimonides* (Chicago: University of Chicago Press, 1963).

Revière, S. *Studies in Greek Philosophy* (Jerusalem: Magnes Press, The Hebrew University, 1974). H.

Richards, D.A.J. *A Theory of Reasons for Action* (Oxford: Clarendon Press, 1971).

Ross, J. J. *The Appeal to the Given* (London: Allen and Unwin, 1970).

Rotenstreich, N. *Basic Problems of Marx's Philosophy* (Indianapolis, Ind.: Bobbs-Merrill, 1965).

———. *Between Past and Present* (New Haven, Conn.: Yale University Press, 1958; Hebrew ed., 1955).

———. *Experience and Its Systematization, Studies in Kant,* 2d ed. (The Hague: Nijhoff, 1972).

———. *On the Human Subject* (Springfield, Ill.: Thomas, 1966).

———. *Philosophy, History and Politics* (The Hague: Nijhoff, 1976).

———. *Philosophy, the Concept and Its Manifestations* (Dordrecht: Reidel, 1972).

———. *Power and its Mould* (Jerusalem: Bialik Institute, 1964). H

———. *Spirit and Man* (The Hague: Nijhoff, 1963; Hebrew ed., 1959).

———. *Theory and Practice* (Jerusalem: Bialik Institute, 1969). H (English ed. Boston: Kluwer, 1977).

Roth, L. *The Guide for the Perplexed by Moses Maimonides. An Exposition* (London and New York: Hutchinson, 1948).

Ruskin, V. *A Theory of Restricted Sublanguages* (Moscow: Moscow University Press, 1971; English ed. forthcoming).

Scharfstein, B.-A. *Mystical Experience* (Oxford: Blackwell, and New York: Bobbs-Merrill, 1973).

Schlanger, J. *La structure metaphysique* (Paris: Presses Universitaires de France, 1975).

Scholem, G. *Explications and Implications* (Tel Aviv: Am Oved, 1976). H

———. *The Messianic Idea in Judaism and Other Essays on Jewish Spirituality* (New York: Schocken, 1971).

Schweid, E. *Feeling and Speculation* (Ramat Gan: Massada, 1970). H

———. *Judaism and the Solitary Jew* (Tel Aviv: Am Oved, 1975). H

Scolnicov, S. "On the Epistemological Significance of Plato's Theory of Ideal Numbers," *Museum Helveticum* 28 (1971).

———. "Three Aspects of Plato's Philosophy of Learning and Instruction," *Paideia* 5 (1976).

Scwarcz, M. *From Myth to Revelation: The Later Teaching of Schelling and "The Star of Redemption" by F. Rosenzweig* (Tel Aviv: Hakkibutz Hameuchad, forthcoming). H

———. *Language, Myth, Art* (Tel Aviv: Schocken, 1966). H

Seliger, M. *The Liberal Politics of John Locke* (London: Allen and Unwin, 1968).

Sigad, R. *Studies in Existentialism* (Jerusalem: Bialik Institute, 1975). H

Stemmer, N. *An Empiricist Theory of Language Acquisition* (The Hague: Mouton, 1973).

Strauss, M. *Meaning and Meaning Bearers* (Tel Aviv: Sifriat Poalim, forthcoming). H

Ucko, S. *Philosophy of Education* (Jerusalem: Bialik Institute, 1974). H

Ullman-Margalit, E. *The Emergence of Norms* (Oxford: Oxford University Press, 1977).

Weiler, G. *Fritz Mauthner's Critique of Language* (Cambridge: University Press, 1970).

———. *Jewish Theocracy* (Tel Aviv: Am Oved, 1976). H

Weinryb, E. "The Justification of a Causal Thesis," *History and Theory* 14 (1975).

Yovel, Y. "Bible Interpretation as Philosophical Praxis: A Study of Spinoza and Kant," *Journal for the History of Philosophy* 11 (1973).

———. *Kant and the Philosophy of History* (Princeton, N.J.: Princeton University Press, 1979).

———. *Kant and the Rehabilitation of Metaphysics* (Jerusalem: Bialik Institute, 1973). H

———. "Metaphysique et propositions mathematiques chez Kant," *Archives de Philosophie* 36 (1973).

———. "The God of Kant," *Scripta Hierosolymitana* 20 (1968).

Zemach, E. M. *Aesthetics* (Tel Aviv: University Publications, 1976). H

———. *Analytical Aesthetics* (Tel Aviv: Daga Press, 1970). H

———. "Four Ontologies," *Journal of Philosophy* 67 (1970).

———. "Pains and Pain Feelings," *Ratio* 13 (1971).

———. "Personal Identity Without Criteria," *Australasian Journal of Philosophy* 47 (1969).

———. "Seeing 'Seeing' and Feeling," *Review of Metaphysics* 23 (1969).

——— and Walther, E. "Substance Logic," in *Language in Focus,* ed. A. Kasher (Dordrecht: Reidel, 1976).

JOURNALS

Iyyun
Philosophia

*Titles of books in Hebrew are translated into English. A capital "H" means that the book is available only in Hebrew.

Part II: Eastern Europe

CZECHOSLOVAKIA

JAROMIR DANĚK

HISTORICAL CONTEXT (1415–1945)

The philosophy of the Czech and Slovak nations grew out of concerns common to the European realistic and empirical tradition. Its earliest beginnings can be found in the moral rigorism of the Protestant reformer John Hus who was burned at the stake by ecclesiastical conservatives in 1415. In the work of Jan Amos Komenský-Comenius (1592–1670), that ethical realism acquired a distinctively pedagogic and sociocritical orientation. Ever since Comenius, Czech and Slovak philosophy confronted clerical and political dogmatism, monarchic oppression, and autocratic deformations of national growth with the challenge of a universal humanistic ideal.

The theme of humanistic critique emerged in the Czech lands in modern times in the work of Bernard Bolzano (1781–1848), one of the founders of modern mathematical logic as well as a forerunner of the phenomenological grounding of the realistic world-view with its universally human and ethical implications. It remained pronounced in the work of František Palacký (1798–1876), a romantic philosopher-historian who fused the vision of a historical ideal with a practical national policy, and it flared up brightly in Augustin Smetana (1814–1851), a neo-Hegelian revolutionary democrat echoing the integrative tendencies of early German idealism. It dominated the thought of Brentano's pupil and Husserl's classmate, Tomáš G. Masaryk (1850–1937). A pragmatic philosopher sharing Husserl's positivistic tendencies, Masaryk became the theoretician of metaphysically grounded democracy, a humanistic statesman, and a critic of Marxist theory from the 1890s to its consequences in practice after 1917. His critical spirit lived on in the work of Emanuel Rádl (1873–1942), a philosopher of history and an antiromantic metaphysician, a realist by conviction who gave the idealism of Czech philosophy a new pregnant form and opened up new prospects. The phenomenological fruition of contemporary Czech philosophy explores those prospects in a dialogue with positivism and one-sided pragmatism.

In the present phenomenological fruition, the concept of freedom plays a central role. In post-Kantian skepticism and socio-political critique, it functioned as a universal ideal. In its objective counterparts, it had the significance of the

---

English translation and editing by e.k.

principle of world history and its philosophy. In principle, freedom represents the *a priori* claim of every human to his own person; in history, it represents the reflexive spirituality of the human who can be neither owned nor manipulated by another.

That conception of the human, derived from Hegel's *Philosophy of Right,* underwent a double development in Czech and Slovak philosophical thought. In a humanistic interpretation, it passed over into the Czech critical idealism. As an abstract conception of the human as the maker of history, it passed into Marxism. There, stripped of its eternal significance, it came to be conceived as a universal and historical objectivity, displacing all recognition of concrete subjectivity and its individualized freedom. The critical focus of contemporary Czech and Slovak philosophy—especially once Marxism became the ideology of the dictatorship brought to power by the postwar crisis of the traditional Czech democracy—is one of uncovering that deformation of the concept of freedom both in principle and in all its theoretical and practical consequences.

PHILOSOPHICAL CRITIQUE AGAINST THE IDEOLOGY OF FORCE (1945–1967)

The brief *period of relative freedom* (1945–1948) after the war was a time of revival after the devastation of the German occupation. The multiplicity of Czech philosophy had not yet coalesced into an articulate critique. The period saw a revival of Hegelian scholarship and pragmatism (J. Kozák), as well as existential responses to postwar problems, and a revival of phenomenological research (J. Patočka). Arnošt Kolman, arriving in Prague from Moscow, represented orthodox Marxism, while several younger scholars attempted a reinterpretation of Marxism as a scientific methodology and a humanistic national program.

None of those trends was to survive (except in secret) the *period of repression* (approximately 1948–1953) which followed the communist seizure of power. Marxism, endowed by the coup with political power and a highly systematic repressive apparatus, quickly degenerated into an ideology of power, destroying both the dissenters and its own independent supporters. All non-Marxist philosophers were expelled from the universities; bookstores and libraries were purged of the works of modern thinkers, Czech and foreign alike; the works of Husserl, Heidegger, Carnap, Sartre, and even Patočka and others could no longer be published. Philosophical instruction was restricted to a simplified, schematic version of historical and dialectical materialism and to the classics, though in these an idiosyncratic historicism replaced historical scholarship. Some access to mathematical and logical scholarship abroad remained but was severely restricted by practical difficulties. In those dark days, classics like Komenský or Bolzano became a consolation from philosophy.

In the *period of stagnation* (approximately 1954–1960, and in some respects up to 1967), genuine philosophical work at the official Philosophical Institute of the Czechoslovak Academy of Science and in the universities was restricted to the history of philosophy (Popelová) and to logic (Zich, Berka). Philosophical anthropology, ethics, critical epistemology, and the ontology of being-human, all central philosophical disciplines, could develop only in private.

Yet, that privacy was not empty. Philosophy always represents a certain return to the resources of the subject, leading through them to a universal transcendental and historical conception of that subject, and so to a more profound grasp of practical and theoretical human activity. Such returns are hermeneutic and axiological. They are journeys of rediscovery of the perennial values which structure the everyday world as a significant one. All philosophy echoes the commitment to such perennial values. The growth of positive science confirms the mundane significance of the faith in the human as the subject of those values. Philosophical critique draws on them. In that sense, even history of philosophy is genuine philosophy, recovering universal significance in the temporal realizations of the concrete *a priori* of the human and his world.

Thumbing through the books of Czech and Slovak philosophy in the 1950s and the 1960s—as the collective work, *Filosofie v dějinách českého národa* ("Philosophy in the History of the Czech Nation"), in Ivan Sviták's *Voltaire,* in M. Sobotka's Hegelian studies (especially *Člověk, Práce a sebevědomí* ["Man, Labor and Self-Consciousness], in M. Machovec's descriptions of Augustine's "eternal paradox," in Cvekl's *Čas lidského života* ("The Time of Human Life"), and others—we discover a complex orientation of philosophical reflection which turns to the history of pure thought to grasp the truth of the world and of its time.

At the same time, new philosophical directions which were to emerge in public in the 1960s were taking shape in private in the thought of men like Daněk, Dubský, Hejdánek, Kosík, Tondl, Průcha,. and Zumr. A new Hegelianism, drawing on Lukács, Sartre, Kołakowski, and others, was beginning to crystallize. The work of Teilhard de Chardin, stimulating a return to the philosophy of freedom, attracted intense attention. As a counterweight to the officially sanctioned philosophical speculation, there emerged a new scientistic positivism (Tondl). Most of all, there grew a broadly based, multifaceted phenomenological search for the concrete models of the synthetic *a priori* of the period, seeking to recover the lived reality beneath the manipulated surface of the official "truth."

The works which began to appear in the *period of experimentation* (1960–1967) are the fruit of that silent effort. Jan Patočka's historical studies, *Aristoteles* and *Úvod do studio Husserlovy fenomenologie* ("Introduction to the Study of Husserl's Phenomenology"), Karel Kosík's *Dialektika konkrétního,* or Sviták's *Nevědecká antropologie* ("Unscientific Anthropology") point to a theoretical foundation of the inevitable revision of the ruling ideology. A new, and profoundly traditional, democracy constitutes the program of Sviták's philosophical initiative. (We shall deal with Jan Patočka and Karel Kosík in separate sections.) Together, they represent the rebirth of philosophical critique, the *raison d'être* of philosophy.

The period was also one of a reviving unity of philosophy, science, and religious faith. While a vulgar positivistic interpretation of science may point to a "scientific atheism," genuine philosophy does not preclude the hypothesis that the scientific schemata of the cosmos point towards a confirmation of God's presence rather than absence. For the mid-1960s, Teilhard's search for the whole human and his hope of an eternal horizon of the openness of life—together with Husserl's explorations of this openness—represented genuine social values. At that time, Teilhard and, on a different level, Husserl contributed more to the Czech philosophical program than Heidegger's fundamental ontology (whose critique of everydayness and alienation is, for obvious reasons, attracting greater interest in the present period of enforced "normalization"). Thus, on the eve of the Czechoslovak Spring of 1968, Czechoslovak philosophy poised itself as a critical reflection against the theory and practice of coercion whose *ancilla et debitor* was the official Marxist ideology.

THE CZECHOSLOVAK SPRING OF 1968 (1968 – 1970)

The Czechoslovak Spring of 1968, associated in the West with the name of Alexander Dubček, triggered a tremendous outburst of vitality. Banned classics reappeared (notably the works of T. G. Masaryk, together with M. Machovec's study, *Masaryk*), banished philosophers returned to the classrooms (Jan Patočka, Ivan Sviták), university seminars reflected student interests (focusing overwhelmingly on Husserl and Heidegger), and works of foreign scholars appeared in translation (notably Husserl's *Ideas I, Cartesian Meditations,* and *Crisis*).

The Spring came to an end with the Soviet occupation on August 21 of that year. Though vestiges of freedom lingered until 1970, the time was too brief to produce a distinctive philosophy. Rather, the Spring brought to the forefront the two outstanding Czech thinkers of our time, Jan Patočka and his younger colleague, Karel Kosík, each of whom deserves special notice.

Jan Patočka (1907–1977), one of the great thinkers of postwar Europe, both expresses and defines the genius of modern Czech philosophy. His Socratic dedication, destiny, and death—he died on March 13, 1977, after a prolonged police "interrogation," having affixed his signature to the human rights manifesto of the Czechoslovak opposition, *Charta 77*— challenge the conscience of his time.

Patočka studied philosophy in Prague during the transition between the positivist era (professor Krejčí) and antiromantic metaphysics (E. Rádl). During his stay in Paris, he attended Husserl's lectures later published as *Cartesian Meditations,* and, in 1932–1933, he continued his study in Germany. In Berlin, he studied under Hartmann and did work with Brock, Reichenbach, and Jacob Klein. After the eruption of Nazi violence, he followed Husserl to Freiburg. Husserl received him cordially. In his work with Husserl and Fink, Patočka received a critical introduction to the central problems of transcendental phenomenology which was to shape his life's work dedicated to a surpassing of positivism along phenomenological lines. His interest in ancient philosophy—and his work on

Heidegger with W. Brock—led him to the conclusion that transcendental phenomenology must follow a hermeneutic extension to history and the world. His Czech heritage, as well as his encounter with political violence, convinced him that that extension must be a hermeneutic circle, returning to the subject in his primordial primacy, though now also in his historical and existential fullness. This was the route indicated by Husserl in Section 43 of his *Crisis*. When Patočka earned his doctorate with a thesis on "The Concept of *Evidenz*," his path was set. Subjective reflection became, for Patočka, both a starting point and a program for embracing all the problems of our time.

In his first major work, *Přirozený svět jako filosofický problém* French trans., *Le Monde naturel comme un probleme philosophique*, trans. J. Daněk), the first Husserlian analysis of the world of ordinary experience, Patočka confronted the hitherto neglected problem of *objectification*—of the world of logical constructs and mathematical laws which has become a second nature to us. The modern human subject evolves in a double milieu: in the universe of conceptually ordered objects and in the pretheoretical sphere of common sense. Thus, the objectivist conception of the world is not primordial but derivative. Philosophy needs to press beyond it to the primordial world of human activity to see the derivative objectification in its terms.

The problem, starting with the objectification of movement in Greek philosophy, led Patočka along Husserlian lines beyond Heidegger's ontology of being to the historical process of the self-realization of human existence and to an objective teleology as a historical specification of the metaphysics of life as transcendental. In its transcendental (and so universal) dimension, that life is the self-awareness and self-formation of the human world, the object of transcendental sociology. It calls for elaboration in three stages: in the transcendental domain (descriptive phenomenological analysis), on the level of human dwelling and practice (existential analysis), and on the level of verbal communication (logico-semantic analysis). Patočka arrived at the programmatic recognition that all reality is correlative to the subjectivity of the human in the world and that the ground of that subjectivity needs to be methodically articulated in its transcendental—that is, universal—meaning. The aim of the method is to open the way to the component which constitutes both the point of departure and the telos, the human, dwelling in the world, his meaning and being.

That program constitutes only one chapter in the elaboration of the insight of the founder of phenomenology. Patočka pointed out as much in his second major work, *Úvod do studio Husserlovy fenomenologie* ("Introduction to the Study of Husserl's Phenomenology") in which, while faithfully presenting Husserl, he criticized the analytic conception of the phenomenological epoch as a reduction to pure immanence. Patočka is an heir to Husserl's and Masaryk's humanism; for him, the pure ego must be conceived not as an epistemological vanishing point but as a full human presence, a transcendental person. The world, however, while subject-related, surpasses the meaning of the world as created by subjects. Philosophical reflection can make the move from the logico-mathematical ideal to a historico-spiritual ideal of a scientific world-view only by an hermeneutic detour.

That detour must include a reexamination of classic thinkers which Patočka undertook in a series of studies marked by a profound familiarity with philosophical tradition and an intimate knowledge of classic culture and philology. Among these, four stand out as decisive—Aristotle *(Aristoteles)* Descartes, Comenius, and Hegel.

The Aristotelian scheme of *hyle-steresis-eidos* is the first attempt to resolve being into its essential moments, linked to a new conception of the *eidos* as immanent. Its application to movement, however, leads to a breakdown of the reductive ontology. *Archai* of the moving—i.e., becoming—being would call for an *episteme* correlative to such a being, but such a being can only be understood as temporal and so compatible only with a *doxa,* not an *episteme.* That posed the problem for the founders of the modern theory of science from Cusanus to Galileo who, however, lost sight of the ontological nature of movement and process. Mathematics of movement came to obscure the unity of becoming in the universe. The question which that poses for philosophy is one for the temporal and spatial unity of distance as human: for the subject as the ground of the unity of the natural world.

The Cartesian world is the world of mathematized science. The point of a return to Descartes, however, is not to confront him with the objections appropriate to an existential philosophy but rather to continue where he stopped short, at the certitude of the *ego cogito* which Descartes left behind in turning to construct his proof of divine existence. Descartes correctly poses the question for the ground of meaning, but, preoccupied with justifying God, the world, and the soul, he loses sight of his own discovery. For Patočka, who is profoundly Husserlian in thought and commitment, the return to Descartes leads to a different continuation: to a reaffirmation of the transcendental ego and its noematic correlate, the world as meaning. The phenomenology based on it is basically a theory of the constitution of the natural world.

In Comenius, that movement of thought acquires an ethical and existential density. The universality of the philosophical approach to the world here follows the lines of God's creation in which the ideal becomes actual in a process of concretization to which human labor, social organization, and the quest for spiritual purity restore its intrinsic unity.

Patočka's studies of Hegel (and his translation of Hegel's *Aesthetics* into Czech) led him to the conviction that Hegel does not seek the essence of truth in an adequation of the object and the subject but rather in the unveiling of hidden being. Approaching objects of the world as beautiful overcomes the finitude and unfree condition of the subject and his object. The possibility of truth lies in the surpassing of death, which sooner or later extinguishes the attributes of finitude. Patočka, the philosopher of the natural world, was in all his work aware that he could escape that fate only if he could recognize in the temporal the light which dwells in the Platonic world of eternal truth and value.

After this exploration of the classics, Patočka was ready for the transition from a mathematico-logical to a historico-spiritual conception of the world. This he did in a major study, *Kacířské eseje o filozofii dějin* ("Heretical Essays in the Philosophy of History," published so far only as *samizdat*), in which he examines the relation of transcendental history and the history of the world of ordinary experience. Phenomenology, as Patočka presents it, is a study not only of being but also of its historical appearance and of the why of that appearance. The discovery of the logos of history is nothing less than the continuous intentional movement of philosophy in the rational unveiling of being—of rational being, of being as Reason itself.

Husserl did insist on a genetic reconstitution more than on static analysis, on the role of passive genesis, and on the origins of all components in the immanent consciousness of time. All static elements point to their genesis and so to history. However, transcendental genesis can reach only those structures susceptible to being grasped in the reflection of an ahistorical disinterested observer. Patočka, while retaining Husserl's humanistic emphasis on the primacy and ultimate significance of the subject, here turns to Heidgger's conception which moves not only to genesis but also to the subject as an involved agent—the subject as *Dasein*. His examination of the logos of history, however, retains a Husserlian humanistic emphasis. Philosophy, by a reflection on the problems of humanity, prepares for participation in the elaboration of an ethical and political program for the human and for its realization. Its hermeneutic circle returns to the human with the recognition of the grounds of human rights and the sources of freedom and justice as the ideals which define the future.

In the last two years of his life and in his death, Patočka returned to the question of the dwelling place of the human, which he raised forty years earlier in his *The Natural World*. He now had a clear answer: the human as human dwells in the charter of human rights, in his participation in the resistance against the constraints of his time, against injustice, violence, lies, and manipulation.

Much of Patočka's work remains inaccessible, circulating only privately in manuscript. This is true of his last series of lectures, *Tělo, jazyk, společenství a svět* ("The Body, Language, Community, and World"), of several historical studies *(Smysl budoucnosti* ("The Meaning of Tomorrow"), *Princip vědeckého vědomí* ("The Principle of Scientific Consciousness"), *Dva eseje o Masarykovi* ("Two Essays on Masaryk"), *Inteligence a oposice* ("Intellectuals and the Opposition"), and perhaps others. Many of his older works, such as *Česká vzdělanost* ("The Autonomy of Czech Culture") and the highly important *Dvojí rozum v německém osvícení* ("Two Senses of Reason in the German Enlightenment," important for understanding the culture that gave us both Goethe and Hitler), lie buried in long-forgotten and long-banned journals.

Nonetheless, the essential outline and meaning of his work are clear. His work is an hermeneutic extension of Husserl's phenomenology in the spirit of Masaryk's humanism. His hermeneutic circle, moving from the subject as transcendental to the world of human experience to return to the subject as fully human, includes both the traditional quest of Czech philosophy for the eternal dimension of the temporal and its perennial return to the temporal in the name of the eternal as the normative ideal, challenging all the deformations and dogmatisms of the temporal.

Karel Kosík (1926–   ), the other major figure of postwar Czechoslovak philosophy, represents the other approach to philosophy under Marxist rule, that of seeking humanistic dimensions within Marxist theory itself. Kosík came to Marxism in the nondogmatic revolutionary guise which it adopted during the wartime resistance. Subsequently, confronted with the realities of Marxism in power, he turned first to the history of his own nation. In his book *Čeští radikální demokraté* ("The Czech Radical Democrats"), he was led to the speculative dialectics of the neo-Hegelians (A. Smetana) and to the question of the immanent sources of philosophy as against the objective sources stressed by the Marxists. Learning from Lukács, he undertook an intensive study of Husserl's and Heidegger's phenomenology before publishing his next book.

That book, *Dialektika konkrétního,* translated into numerous languages (including English as *Dialectics of the Concrete,* by Karel Kovavda), effectively broke the hegemony of the conception of Marxism as an uncritical and undialectical objectivist ideology of coercion. It opened out the self-imposed limits of Marxism with the radical question about the significance of the subject and the role of the idea in history.

The implicit question throughout Kosík's work is whether Marxist philosophy is still capable of being the arena of truth or whether it is necessarily a mystification, identifying the rational with whatever is real. Kosík treats the category of totality—traditionally "Being," the real totality correlated with actual praxis—as fundamental to materialist dialectics. He is concerned with the act of freedom which breaks through the false totality posited by dogma. Thus, his metaphysics of everyday existence is existential rather than materialistic (or idealistic), seeking the openness of the human rooted in the praxis which Kosík regards as the true sphere of human self-constitution.

Kosík's thesis of the totality as a horizon of indefinite reality, basic to both act and thought, points to a phenomenological overcoming of dogmatism. Even his more traditional opening chapter makes the point that the reproduction of the real in thought must be critical, not naive. For Kosík, reality is grasped concretely only in the relation of the particular phenomenon to the totality. Any hypostatization of the sum of particular phenomena as the totality leads to abstraction and apologetics. In his subsequent chapters, Kosík overcomes the opposition of being and knowing, traditional in dialectical materialist gnoseology, through his recognition of the human in his activity as a constitutive subject. Lived reality, constituted in the subject act (praxis) which unites the subject and the object, is the primordial *concretized whole* which cannot be explained away in terms of a hypostatized "material real basis."

In this thesis, Kosík moves significantly beyond the sterile opposition of mind and matter, idealism and materialism, to a recognition of the primacy of lived experience. In *Dialectics of the Concrete,* however, he still stops short of the recognition that such a dialectics is possible only on the basis of a fundamental ontology of being-human. Banned from teaching and print since 1970, Kosík has thus far been unable to publish his further investigations.

Kosík's search for humanism is the search for the human behind the pseudoreality of ideological rather than real relations. To uncover such real relations—the "things themselves," in Husserl's sense—means to make the human and his place in the cosmos the focus of philosophy. Kosík, starting from a nondogmatic Marxism, comes to the recognition that the twin focus of philosophy is the human existing with the full profundity of freedom in the totality of the world and the totality of the world which the human uncovers in history.

THE PRESENT AND THE FUTURE (1970–   )

After 1970, the stabilization of Soviet domination, officially called "normalization," brought with it a new wave of purges of thinkers, students, and books. A schematized Marxist ideology once again assumed a total monopoly of public expression, supported by an efficient repressive machinery. Philosophy in Czechoslovakia has once more become strictly a private endeavor.

As before in Czech history, some Czech philosophers continue their work abroad. Milic Čapek, (1913–   , exiled in the United States since 1948) brings the traditional Czech humanism to the philosophy of science, exploring in his books a nonpositivistic alternative along Bergsonian lines *(The Philosophical Impact of Contemporary Physics, Bergson and Modern Physics).* Jaromír Daněk (1925–   , exiled in Canada since 1968) emphasizes the continuity of Czech humanism with that of the West *(Weiterentwicklung der Leibnizschen Logik bei Bolzano).* Erazim Kohák (1933–   , exiled in the United States since 1948), a Husserl scholar who publishes both in Czech *(Národ v nás)* and in English *(Idea and Experience),* seeks a phenomenological foundation and a personalistic expression for a humanism in the spirit of T. G. Masaryk. With a number of other Czech philosophers who are currently living in the West, other works may well come forth.

Within Czechoslovakia itself, rigorous censorship has given the official Marxist ideology (represented by Ladislav Hrzal and Vladimír Ruml) a total monopoly on public expression. At the same time, by identifying it as the ideology of oppression, it has been discredited as a live philosophical option. What evidence is available—as manuscripts circulating as *samizdat,* works reaching the West, requests for books from abroad—suggests that the eight years of unrelenting repression have lent some credence to what is in effect a modern version of classical cynicism (as the Diogenes-like figure of Zbyněk Fišer, pseudonym Egon Bondy, *Útěcha z ontologie* ["Comfort From Ontology"]). The attempt to revise and redeem Marxism (Karel Kosík, Zdeněk Mlynář) appears to have retained some, albeit strictly limited, interest. The continued popularity of *samizdat* works like Patočka's *Heretical Essays* or Milan Machovec's *Jesus for*

Atheists, however, suggests that when the mainstream of Czechoslovak philosophical thought can once again express itself openly, it will prove consistent with the traditional humanistic critique.

SELECT BIBLIOGRAPHY

BOOKS AND ARTICLES

Bondy, E. (Fišer, Z.) *Útěcha z ontologie* ("Comfort From Ontology") (Prague: Academia, 1967).

Čapek, M. *Bergson and Modern Physics* (Dordrecht: Reidel, 1971).

———. *The Philosophical Impact of Contemporary Physics* (Princeton, N.J.: Van Nostrand, 1961).

Cvekl, J. *Čas lidského života* ("The Time of Human Life") (Prague: Svoboda, 1967).

Daněk, J. *Weiterentwicklung der Leibnizschen Logik bei Bolzano* (Weisenheim: Hain, 1970).

Filosofie v dějinách českého národa ("Philosophy in the History of the Czech Nation") Protokol Celostátné konference v Liblicích ve dnech 14.–17. dubna 1958 (Prague: 1958).

Husserl, E. *Cartesianische Meditationen und Pariser Vorträge* (The Hague: Nijhoff, 1973).

———. *Die Krisis der europäischen Wissenschaften und transzendentale Phänomenologie,* ed. Biemel (The Hague: Nijhoff, 1969).

Kohák, E. *Idea and Experience* (Chicago: University of Chicago Press, 1977).

———. *Národ v nás* (Toronto: '68 Publishers, 1977).

Kosík, K. (ed.). *Čeští radikální demokraté* ("The Czech Radical Democrats") (Prague: Státní nakl. politické literatury, 1953).

———. *Dialectics of the Concrete,* trans. K. Kovavda (Dordrecht: Reidel, 1977).

———. *Dialektika konkrétního* (Prague: CSAV, 1964).

Lobkowicz, N. *Marxismus-Leninismus in der ČSR; die tschechoslowakische Philosophie seit 1945* (Dordrecht: Reidel, 1962).

Machovec, M. *A Marxist Looks at Jesus* (London: Darton, Longman and Todd, 1976).

———. *T. G. Masaryk* (Prague: Melantrich, 1968).

Patočka, J. *Aristoteles* ("Aristotle") (Prague: Nakl. Československé Akademie věd, 1964).

———. *Charta 77: Documents* (n.p., 1977).

———. *Die Philosophie der Erziehung des J. A. Comenius* (Paderborn: Schöningh, 1971).

———. *Kacířské eseje o filozofii dějin* ("Heretical Essays in the Philosophy of History") (Samizdat, 1975).

———. *Le monde naturel comme probléme philosophique,* trans. J. Daněk, et al. (The Hague: Nijhoff, 1976).

———. *Princip vědeckého vědomí* ("The Principle of Scientific Consciousness"), Manuscript.

———. *Přirozený svět jako filosofický problém* ("The Natural World as a Philosophical Problem") (Prague: Laichter, 1939).

———. *Smysl budoucnosti* ("The Meaning of Tomorrow"), Manuscript.

———. *Tělo, jazyk, společenství a svet* ("The Body, Language, Community, and World"), Manuscript.

———. *Úvod do studio Husserlovy fenomenologie* ("Introduction to the Study of Husserl's Phenomenology") (Prague: Státní Pedagogické Nakl., 1966).

———, Kopecký, and Kyrášek, J. *Jan Amas Komensky* ("J. A. Comenius") (Prague: Státní Pedagogické Nakl., 1957).

Sobotka, M. *Člověk, Práce a sebevědomí* ("Man, Labor and Self-consciousness") (Prague: Svoboda, 1969).

Svitak, I. *Man and His World,* trans. J. Veltrusky (New York: Dell, 1970).

———. *Unwissenschaftliche Anthropologie,* trans. P. Kruntorad (Frankfurt: Fischer, 1972).

———. *Voltaire,* trans. J. Veltruská (Chico, Calif.: California State University, 1973).

JOURNALS

Estetika
Filosofia
Filosofický Casopis
Sbornik Prací Univerzity J E Purkyne Brne
Teorie A Metode
Teorie Rozvoje Vedy

East Germany

HAN S-MARTIN   SASS

Since 1945, philosophy in East Germany (the German Democratic Republic) has developed under two historical conditions: (1) the fascist contribution to the collapse of the intellectual tradition, and (2) the Soviet domination of Eastern Europe since the end of World War II. Consequently, the Leninists introduced Marxism-Leninism as an obligatory ideology for the newly created state as well as for the individual.

In West Germany, the open democratic society allowed the growth of a number of philosophical movements, such as existentialism, hermeneutics, critical theory, neopositivism, phenomenology, analytic philosophy, and different forms of Marxism. In East Germany, the state insisted that there be only one philosophy and gave that philosophy its full support in order to become the state ideology. Marxist-Leninist philosophy in its official form called itself the ideology of the working-class people, namely, the proletarians.

In view of the dominant position of the Leninist state in every sector of human life, philosophy's task was to serve socialist society. "Science continues increasingly to contribute to the regular improvement of production and to the development of the economic and intellectual-cultural life of all members of the working class. It promotes the prosperity, health and intellectual needs of man in socialism."[1]

The special contribution of Marxist-Leninist philosophy has been to establish "the theoretical foundation of practical activity of the revolutionary party of the working class, it serves as a prescription for activities in class struggle, in socialistic revolution, and in socialistic and communistic development."[2] According to Lenin, Marxism-Leninism is "the modern form of materialism and the modern form of scientific socialism." Intellectual theory and political society are so closely related that "the ancient conflict between philosophical theory and social reality is solved in communist practice."[3]

In an ideological-political system, philosophy has a higher responsibility than philosophy as an academic discipline in pluralistic democracies normally has. In such a system, there are different tasks for philosophy, such as the establishment and preservation of dogmatics in general, the making of definite decisions in contrasting ideological contexts of competitive or "revisionist" philosophical positions, the acquiring and evaluating of the cultural tradition, the standardizing of philosophical language, the prescription for the proper use of key words, the development of a theory of science which is efficient enough and at the same time acceptable to classical dogmatics, and, finally, the education of the individual and the masses.

The general dogmatics of Marxism-Leninism are perferably taught in systematic volumes as well as in hermeneutics of the classical texts. The very first patterns were disseminated in the translation of Stalin's *History of the Communist Party of the Soviet Union,* in the collected works of the Department of Philosophy of the Soviet Academy of Sciences, and later in the collected works of East German philosophers.[4] The classical Marxist texts—Marx, Engels, Lenin, and Stalin—are available in cheap editions. *The Marx-Engels-Werke,* including the supplemental volumes, are more complete than the Russian version. The new *Marx-Engels-Gesamt-Ausgabe* (MEGA), which is incomplete, serves as a basis for all further translations, textbooks, and popular editions. The basic patterns of textbooks are reproduced in different forms of publication, such as schoolbooks and correspondence courses. Education in Marxism-Leninism is an integral part of all academic studies and of vocational training.[5]

The general apologetic critique against "revisionist" and "bourgeois" philosophy was set forth by Engels, whose essay "Feuerbach and the End of Classical German Philosophy" is an example in content as well as in method.[6] The basic polemical approach against the revisionist (i.e., nondogmatical, which is identical to nonofficial) and the bourgeois (i.e., both irrational and connected with capitalism) philosophy is the concept of Marxism-Leninism as the final and fully developed form of scientific socialism. Therefore, the polemics claim to be scientific. The Leninist position sees no contradiction in its thesis that scientific socialism must always be partial. The elite of the party defines partiality as that which serves the interests of the working-class people. Partiality, according to the party, is a precondition of being scientific. In addition to the periodicals which either are more academic and technical or more cultural and bound to actual political and educational problems,[7] a series of critiques of bourgeois ideology[8] is most effective.

The historiography of philosophy serves several purposes: (1) the exclusive restriction of the cultural heritage to the "working class," which is the only legitimate heir of the history of ideas, (2) the hermeneutical transformation of the heritage for the purpose of its proper use, and (3) the dispossession of the bourgeois and revisionist of this heritage. The antagonism between materialism and idealism is the general pattern of the process of the history of philosophy. This interpretation contains the thesis that the materialistic position is a progressive one. Dialectical hermeneutic has developed a highly efficient technique of biased interpretation of its position.[9] The history of philosophy, in addition to its official purposes, serves as a special reservoir for teaching philosophy. As one example among others, the contributions made by the best educated East German philosophers at the biennial international Hegel congresses, which are dominated by communist ideas, serve as an indication of what they are doing in this regard. There are also a number of remarkable critical editions.[10]

The theory of science[11] in Marxism-Leninism deals not only with the problems of scientific methodology and the structures of its development, but also with the relation between ideology and science, the social premises for scientific progress, and the social consequences of scientific results. The theory of science is only one sector within the whole framework and system of scientific socialism. Science is a productive power *(Produktionskraft)* and a social force *(soziale Kraft)*. Because the theory of science in the modern sense was a very new discipline, ideological opposition to modern concepts of operationalism arose. The first step toward the reception of the theory of science and modern logic took place around the year 1960 when G. Klaus's books on cybernetics were published.[12] Since that time a lively discussion on science as a productive power in socialism and on the structures of the scientific revolution has been going on.[13] These studies demonstrate a genuine Marxist-Leninist response to the present discussions of Western philosophy and the theory of science, mixed with apologetics concerning the concept of the history of the class struggle. There is a growing tendency to strengthen philosophical theses by means of scientific analyses.

The theory of science and research in the historiography of philosophy, apologetic strategies, and Marxist-Leninist dogmatics culminate in the cultural activities of communist education. Education serves to develop the individual socialist understanding of the political and cultural programs of the party. Education is widely disseminated through the mass media. General prescriptions for a normal use of highly important ideological words are set forth in the *Philosophiches Wörterbuch*. This text serves both the academic purpose of giving definitions and apologetic critiques of improper use of philosophical words in revisionist and bourgeois philosophy, and the educational purpose of standardizing the socialistic vocabulary.[14] Revised versions of ideological phraseology are considered as progress in Marxist-Leninist hermeneutics, and the dispossession of the cultural heritage, as well, as progress in setting up new limits to other philosophical positions in bringing about the change of present political and cultural conflicts. Ritual exercises are a part of cultural activities which promote the process of communist education.[15]

The organization of philosophy and philosophical institutions and their influence on culture and society in East Germany are extremely complex. There are departments of philosophy at the universities at Leipzig, Berlin, Jena, Halle, and Greifswald. Jena seems to be the center for the history of philosophy; Leipzig specializes in epistemology; and Berlin in the philosophy of science and correspondence courses. East Germany's most important institution for research in philosophy, however, is the Department of Philosophy of the Academy of Sciences (Zentralinstitut für Philosophie der Akademie der Wissenschaften der DDR) in Berlin. Its most important specializations are in the history of philosophy, actual problems of bourgeois and revisionist positions, dialectical materialism, philosophical problems of the development of science, and editions of philosophical authors. More technical research in Marx and Engels is being done by the Institut für Marxismus-Leninismus (IML) which together with the IML in Moscow publishes the new MEGA. The IML is directly attached to the Central Committee of the Communist party (SED), as is the most important Academy for Social Sciences (Akademie für Gesellschaftswissenschaften beim Zentralkomitee der SED), which serves the purposes of interdisciplinary research, postgraduate studies, and counseling the top officials and authorities of political bodies. The Parteihochscule der SED educates the cadres of the Communist party. The conglomeration of these different institutions demonstrates the interdisciplinary and political functions of Marxism-Leninism. The departments of philosophy of the above-mentioned universities, the Zentralinstitut für Philosophie der Akademie der Wissenschaften der DDR, the Institut für Philosophie bei der Akademie für Gesellschaftswissenschaften, and the Lehrstuhl für Philosophie bei der Parteihochschule der SED form the Wissenschaftlicher Rat für philosophische Forschung der DDR (Council of Philosophy) which is headed by Erich Hahn in Berlin. This council is East Germany's most important discussion forum and the chief instrument for top-level coordination of different philosophical projects and of philosophical and political requirements.

Actual philosophical trends in East Germany more or less represent the communist answer to external and internal challenges. There seems to be a growing interest in the fields of history of science and theory of science, and a great deal of work has been expended in these areas. There might be more Western influence in the field of the logic of science, too. The human rights discussion, especially following the Helsinki conference in 1975, develops the thesis that human rights really are ethnic rights of the self-determination of nations. "A 'human' right of the individual which is opposed to the nation's right for self-determination is an obstacle to liberty and does not serve progress but reaction."[16]

In the future, conflicts might arise in East Germany with regard to the methodology and strategy of taking over more and more of the cultural heritage and of eliminating all other contemporary philosophical positions. The history of philosophy and of science are fields in which a more traditional philosophy might find a place.

The polemics will contribute to the preservation of the relatively conservative political system against liberating and reforming influences from external and internal factors. On the other hand, it seems to be inevitable for great nations, even Marxist-Leninist ones, to have internal commissions and teams which will study the results of philosophy and theory of science in the West in order to make practical use of these results without being prejudicial to apologetics.

Even if the very basic positions of Marxism-Leninism are treated in a fundamentalist manner in the future, there might be a change in details and more liberty for philosophical actions which are not exploitable by society and state authorities in a direct way. But that is a genuine political question. Spinoza in the *Tractatus Theologico-Politicus* and Locke in the *Letters Concerning Toleration* developed some ideas for treating these political problems in a philosophical manner.

NOTES

1. *Programm der sozialistischen Einheitspartei Deutschlands*, p. 45.

2. *Philosophisches Wörterbuch*, II, eds. G. Klaus and M. Buhr, 10th ed., p. 738, entry: "Marxism-Leninism."

3. Lenin, *Werke*, XXI (1961–   ), p. 38, quoted in the entry "Marxismus-Leninismus"; see note 2 above. O. Finger, "Philosophisches Erbe und ideologischer Klassenkampf," in *Marxistisch-Leninistische Philosophie in der DDR. Resultate, Standpunkte, Ziele*, eds. G. M. Klein, F. Richter and V. Wrona, p. 225.

4. Stalin, *Geschichte der KPDSU*, Chapter 4, 2, "On Dialectic and Historical Materialism," many editions. *Grundlagen der Marxistisch-Leninistischen Philosophie*, ed. Academy of science, Department of Philosophy, collective authorship, German version, Berlin, 1971, 4th ed., 1974. *Marxistische Philosophie* (textbook), ed. A. Kosing, Berlin, 1967. *Dialektischer und historischer Materialismus. Lehrbuch für das Marxistische Grundlagenstudium*, eds. F. Fielder, O. Finger, et al. (officially recognized textbook at universities and technical schools by the Minister für das Hochund Fachschulwesen, May 1974).

5. The most important correspondence courses in "History of Marxism-Leninism," "Introduction to the Study of the Classical Authors of Marxism-Leninism," and "Foundations of the Philosophy of Marxism-Leninism" are produced by a special section within the Department of Philosophy and the Division of Marxist-Leninist Philosophy at Humboldt University, Berlin.

6. F. Engels, *Ludwig Feuerbach und der Ausgang der klassischen deutschen Philosophie*, 15th ed., 1977.

7. *Deutsche Zeitschrift für Philosophie*, since 1953, the most important organ of academic research, teaching, and review. *Einheit. Zeitschrift für Theorie und Praxis des wissenschaftlichen Sozialismus*, ed. Zentralkomitee der Sozialistischen Einheitspartei Deutschlands, most important for ideological and political purposes since 1945.

8. *Zur Kritik der bürgerlichen Ideologie*, since 1971, ed. by Manfred Buhr, Head of Department of Philosophy in the Academy of Science of GDR, seventy-eight brochures until 1977, deals, e.g., with Garaudy and revisionist schools, critical theory, Marcuse, "bourgeois" Marx-interpretation, existentialism, and theories of science in the West.

9. Steps on this way are G. Lukács; *Die Zerstörung der Vernunft;* A. Abusch, *J. G. Fichte und die Zukunft der Nation; Wissen und Gewissen. Beiträge zum 200. Geburtstag J. G. Fichtes*, ed. M. Buhr; M. Buhr and G. Irrlitz, *Der Anspruch der Vernunft*, Vol. I: *Revolution der Denkart oder Denkart der Revolution. Beiträge zur Philosophie Kants*, eds. M. Buhr und T. I. Oiserman (in cooperation between the Departments of Philosophy of the Soviet and the East German Academies of Science); and M. Buhr, *Vernunft, Mensch, Geschichte. Studien zur Entwicklungsgeschichte der Klassischen bürgerlichen Philosophie* (excellent). As a general history of philosophy, the German translation of the still Stalinist, voluminous collective work of the Russian Academy of Science (5 vols., 1961–1963) yet serves, though with an antiquated view. The exclusive demand to be the only heir to the cultural tradition sometimes becomes a caricature. For example, at a Beethoven Congress in March 1977, a sentence of Hans Eisler of 1927 was reproduced: "He was not a composer of the proletariat, his music however belongs to us, and not to the bourgeoisie." For more details, see O. Finger: "Philosophisches Erbe und ideologischer Klassenkampf," in *Marxistisch-Leninistische Philosophie in der DDR. Resultate, Standpunkte, Ziele*, eds. G. M. Klein, F. Richter, and V. Wrona, pp. 253–293, especially 288–292.

10. In addition to the genuine classical authors Marx and Engels, editions of the works of Leibniz, Feuerbach, Dietzgen, and others have been continued or started.

11. As to the very early beginnings of a theory of science discussion in East Germany, compare H. Hoerz, "Die Beziehungen der Marxistisch-Leninistischen Philosophie zu den anderen Wissenschaften," in *Marxistisch-Leninistische Philosophie in der DDR*, l.c., p. 169–202, especially 175–181.

12. Compare H. Hoerz, l.c., pp. 208–225. G. Klaus, *Einführung in die formale Logik;* G. Klaus, *Kybernetik in philosophischer Sicht;* and G. Klaus, *Semiotik und Erkenntnistheorie.*

13. G. Kroeber and H. Laitko, *Sozialismus und Wissenschaft* (most important). *Wissenschaft und Gesellschaft*, Vol. I, ed. G. Kroeber, "Wissenschaft im Sozialismus. Probleme und Untersuchungen."

14. The widely spread out and very influential *Philosophisches Wörterbuch*, eds. G. Klaus and M. Buhr, was published in two volumes in its tenth revised version (326–400,000 exemplars); the first edition was in 1964 (1–30,000 exemplars).

15. D. M. Ugrinowitsch, "Das Wesen und die sozialen Funktionen von Brauchtum und Ritual in der sozialistischen Gesellschaft," *Deutsche Zeitschrift für Philosophie* 25 (1977):15-24, stresses the thesis that, by means of ritual exercises, cultural contents are transferred from one generation to the other. Ugrinowitsch differentiates between social-political rituals (e.g., demonstrations), childhood-rituals, rituals of labor, rituals in families, and mixed rituals (e.g., induction order of the army). The complex system of newly developed socialist rituals is valued positively.

16. H. Klenner, "Menschenrechte im Klassenkampf," *Einheit. Zeitschrift für Theorie und Praxis des Wissenschaftlichen Sozialismus,* 32 (1977):156-165, quoted p. 162. A Kosing, "Unser realer Humanismus und seine Grundlagen," *Einheit. Zeitschrift für Theorie und Praxis des Wissenschaftlichen Sozialismus* 32 (1977):139-148.

SELECT BIBLIOGRAPHY

BOOKS AND ARTICLES

Abusch, A. *J. G. Fichte und die Zukunft der Nation* (Berlin: Aufbau, 1962).

Buhr, M. *Vernunft, Mensch, Geschichte. Studien zur Entwicklungsgeschichte der Klassischen bürgerlichen Philosophie* (Berlin: Akademie, 1977).

———— (ed.). *Wissen und Gewissen. Beiträge zum 200. Geburtstag J. G. Fichtes* (Berlin: Akademie, 1962).

———— and Irrlitz, G. *Der Anspruch der Vernunft*, I (Berlin: Akademie, 1968).

———— and Oiserman, T. I. (eds.). *Revolution der Denkart oder Denkart der Revolution. Beiträge zur Philosophie Immanuel Kants* (Berlin: Academie, 1976).

Fiedler, F., Finger, O., et al. (eds.). *Dialektischer und historischer Materialismus. Lehrbuch für das Marxistische Grundlagenstudium* (Berlin: Dietz, 1974).

Finger, O. "Philosophisches Erbe und ideologischer Klassenkampf," in *Marxistisch-Leninistische Philosophie in der DDR. Resultate, Standpunkte, Ziele,* eds. G. M. Klein, F. Richter, and V. Wrona (Berlin: Deutscher Verlag der Wissenschaften, 1974).

Hoerz, H. "Die Beziehungen der Marxistisch-Leninistischen Philosophie zu den anderen Wissenschaften," in *Marxistisch-Leninistische Philosophie in der DDR. Resultate, Standpunkte, Ziele,* eds. M. Klein, F. Richter, and V. Wrona (Berlin: Deutscher Verlag der Wissenschaften, 1974).

Karl Marx, Friedrich Engels Gesamtausgabe (MEGA) (Berlin: Dietz, 1972–   ).

Klaus, G. *Einführung in die formale Logik* (Berlin: Deutscher Verlag der Wissenschaften, 1959).

————. *Kybernetik in philosophischer Sicht* (Berlin: Dietz, 1961).

————. *Semiotik und Erkenntnistheorie* (Berlin: Deutscher Verlag der Wissenschaften, 1963).

———— and Buhr, M. (eds.). *Philosophisches Wörterbuch*, 10th ed. (Leipzig: Bibliographisches Institut, 1974).

Klenner, H. "Menschenrechte im Klassenkampf," *Einheit. Zeitschrift für Theorie und Praxis des Wissenschaftlichen Sozialismus* 32 (1977).

Kosing, A. "Unser realer Humanismus und seine Grundlagen," *Einheit. Zeitschrift für Theorie und Praxis des Wissenschaftlichen Sozialismus* 32 (1977).

Kroeber, G. "Wissenschaft im Sozialismus. Probleme und Untersuchungen," in *Wissenschaft und Gesellschaft* I, ed. G. Kroeber (Cologne, Berlin, Bonn, and Munich: Heymann, 1972).
——— and Laitko, H. *Sozialismus und Wissenschaft* (Berlin: Deutscher Verlag der Wissenschaften, 1972).
Lukaćs, G. *Die Zerstörung der Vernunft* (Berlin: Aufau, 1954).
Marxs-Engels Werke (Berlin: Dietz, 1956–1968).
Ugrinowitsch, D. M. "Das Wesen und die sozialen Funktionen von Brauchtum und Ritual in der sozialistischen Gesellschaft," *Deutsche Zeitschrift für Philosophie* 25 (1977).

JOURNALS

Deutsche Literaturzeitung für Kritik der Internationalen Wissenschaft
Deutsche Zeitschrift für Philosophie
Einheit. Zeitschrift für Theorie und Praxis des Wissenschaftlichen Sozialismus
Zeitschrift für Mathematische Logik und Grundlagen der Mathematik

Poland

KLEMENS SZANIAWSKI

The reader is warned that this is not a systematic presentation of the development of philosophical thought in postwar Poland. There is no attempt to cover all the disciplines that come under the name of philosophy. For instance, ethics and aesthetics, areas in which such distinguished writers as Maria Ossowska and Wradysław Tatarkiewicz have been active, are omitted. Also omitted are the history of philosophy and some trends in systematic philosophical thought, e.g., phenomenology, where the name Roman Ingarden comes first.

There is no value judgment implied in these and other omissions. They are explained by the fact that the task I have set myself is simply to present some developments in my own field of research, the philosophy (or general methodology) of science. In addition, the selection is guided by the tradition established in Polish philosophical thought in the period between the wars (1918–1939), which found continuation in the years after 1945. A few words of comment on this trend in Polish philosophy will perhaps be useful as an introduction to the present essay.

No single appellation is used to denote this school of thought, which is connected primarily with the names of Kazimierz Ajdukiewicz (1890–1963) and Tadeusz Kotarbiński (1886–   ). Ajdukiewicz himself used to call it "logistical anti-irrationalism" in order to stress its association with the development of modern logic and also its polemical character directed against irrationalism of any kind. Sometimes the expression the Lwów-Warsaw school was used, after the two main academic centers where this style of philosophy originated. H. Skolimowski uses the term "analytic philosophy" in Poland, which has the disadvantage of overemphasizing the similarities with the British school known under the same name. For the purpose of the present exposition, I shall use—in a purely conventional way—the term "Polish positivism."

The principal characteristics of this school were (1) a critical attitude towards the traditional language of philosophy; and (2) the use of newly discovered logical tools in philosophical analysis.

The critical component constituted a similarity with the philosophy of the *Wiener Kreis*. At the same time, the Polish positivists differed from their Viennese colleagues as to the nature of this criticism. They did believe that the language of philosophy was in need of radical reform, aiming at eliminating ambiguity and vagueness from its basic vocabulary. In this way, it was hoped, a number of spurious problems would disappear, together with the misunderstandings they had been based on. On the other hand, and contrary to the *Wiener Kreis* doctrine, the Polish positivists did not believe philosophy's fundamental problems to be spurious. In trying to solve them, they adopted the realist attitude in ontology and the empiricist attitude in theory of knowledge.

The application of logical tools to the articulation and solution of philosophical problems, now a common enough procedure, was at the time relatively new. Modern logic itself was in an early stage of development; its potentialities were a matter of conjecture rather than of firm knowledge. Stimulation, therefore, was mutual since the demands of philosophy led to discoveries in logic. One striking example is the work of Ajdukiewicz who contributed as much to logic as to philosophy, while trying to reformulate classical problems in such a way as to render them capable of a strict solution. It is also well known that the discovery by Jan Łukasiewicz of many-valued logical systems (in 1920) was motivated by philosophical considerations concerning the indeterminacy of future events.

The combination of logical and philosophical inquiry in Polish positivism is the result of the above-mentioned tendency to reform the language of philosophy. It also stems from the fact that during the prewar years Warsaw was one of the most active centers of research in formal logic. It suffices to mention the names of Jan Łukasiewicz (1878–1956), Stanislaw Leśniewski (1886–1939), and Alfred Tarski (1901–   ). The first of them, one of the founders of contemporary logic, was also a philosopher par excellence. He wrote on such topics as determinism, causality, limits of science, and the concept of reasoning. Leśniewski expressed his nominalistic beliefs in the form of logical systems: "ontology" and "mereology." Tarski's contribution to the theory of truth is widely known, as well as his pioneering work, together with Łukasiewicz, on philosophical aspects of many-valued logical systems.

These facts are stressed here because the close ties that existed in Poland between logic and philosophy survived World War II and influenced at least some developments in postwar philosophical thought. Indeed, the dividing line between logic and the philosophy of science became blurred and, as a result, a lot of philosophical work went under the name of logic, conceived in such a way as to cover more than just the logical calculus.

The continuation of the prewar trend outlined above was assured by the fact that, in spite of heavy personal losses in the period 1939–1945, its principal representatives were active for several years after 1945. One such representative, T. Kotarbiński (1886–   ), is one of the best known Polish philosophers today. Until his retirement in 1960, he was a professor at Warsaw University and also occupied important positions in academic life. From 1957 until 1963, he was president of the Polish Academy of Sciences. During the postwar period, he was president of the Polish Philosophical Society until 1977, when he refused reelection for reasons of health.

Kotarbiński's epistemological and methodological views are expressed in

Gnosiology: The Scientific Approach to the Theory of Knowledge. Written as a handbook for philosophy students, the book is actually a systematic exposition of a *Weltanschauung* in which the doctrine of reism, or concretism, plays a prominent role. Reism, in its ontological version, asserts the existence of material objects ("things") and of such objects only. As a program for discursive language, it postulates reducibility (in principle) of all sentences containing names of properties, relations, processes, and the like, to sentences which contain only names of things. The postulate was intended to act as an extremely sharp version of Occam's razor, eliminating pseudo-entities which are the cause of fruitless philosophical argument.

The implementation of this program turned out to be more difficult than had been expected. Large parts of Kotarbiński's postwar writings have been devoted to overcoming those difficulties. Probably the most serious of them was that the standard concept of set, used in mathematics, cannot be interpreted in the postulated manner. Sets, in the mathematical sense of the word, are not "things," i.e., material aggregates of their elements. (An exposition of the reason for that is to be found in Quine's well-known book *From a Logical Point of View.*) Sets must be treated as abstract entities, a fact which contradicts the existential tenet of reism. Moreover, the language of microphysics does not lend itself easily to the postulated translation. The concept of "thing" is well adapted to the world of macro-objects but seems hardly adequate to deal with subatomic phenomena. Kotarbiński, being aware of these objections, devoted part of his efforts to outlining possible solutions.

The part of Kotarbiński's work which is most original and interesting in the present context is the philosophical discipline that he created called "praxiology" or "general methodology." Foundations for this discipline were laid as far back as 1913 when he published a series of articles under the title *Practical Essays*. But it was only in 1955 that the monograph *Praxiology. An Introduction to the Science of Efficient Action* appeared, in which the subject was treated exhaustively and systematically.

Briefly speaking, praxiology is the general study of human action, from the point of view of its efficiency. The term "action" is taken here in its broadest meaning, including mental activity. Praxiology's objective is first to analyze the meaning of basic terms used to describe goal-directed actions. Such concepts as "goal," "agent," "material," and "instrument" are analyzed and redefined to form a consistent framework for a general theory of efficient action. Classic philosophical problems arise in this connection, e.g., those concerning the nature of causal relation (presupposed in the statement that *X's* action brought about a certain state of things) or the responsibility of the agent for the results of what he did.

This conceptual framework makes it possible to formulate principles of efficient action. They are of a very general nature, and in this respect they differ from the results obtained by the numerous specific disciplines that came into existence during the last decades, such as the theory of games, operations research, and theory of decision-making. In addition, while those disciplines build up formal models of rational behavior, praxiology's results (with the exception of a very few attempts to formalize certain concepts) are expressed in natural language sharpened by a number of terminological conventions.

The difference in approach may be exemplified by the case of rational behavior in conflict. It is well known how the theory of games reduces the problem to the choice of strategy from a given set, all the valuations having been summarized by a single numerical function (so-called utility). Praxiology, on the other hand, looks for generalizations arising out of observation of human practice. For instance, one such guiding principle, obviously inspired by analysis of military battles, recommends concentrating the effort on disabling that part of the opponent's forces on which the behavior of other parts depends (such as the commanding unit or the nervous system).

The main interest of praxiology is in *homo faber* as such. The pioneering work of Kotarbiński, who created this branch of philosophical investigation, has been one of the major components in the development of philosophy in postwar Poland. It soon ceased to be an individual effort. A center for praxiological research has been created in the Polish Academy of Sciences, where the late J. Zieleniewski (as well as W. Kieżun, T. Pszczołowski, W. Gasparski, et al.) have been active. A quarterly, *Prakseologia* ("Praxiology"), has appeared regularly for several years.

Another philosophical school owes its origin to Ajdukiewicz. Ajdukiewicz became known internationally in the 1930s, mainly through a series of articles he published in *Erkenntnis*. In these articles, he expounded his views on the relation between language and cognition. Starting from an analysis of the concept of meaning, he obtained a system which he called "radical conventionalism." Its principal tenet was that all knowledge (not only some part of it, as Poincaré and Le Roy used to assert) depends in an essential way on the choice of language.

In his postwar publications, Ajdukiewicz repudiated radical conventionalism (because of its unrealistic conception of language) and expressed some skepticism as to the correctness of such sweeping generalizations. Instead, he concentrated on more specific problems in the philosophy of science. For this discipline he formulated a program of "methodology that aims at understanding."

The program is an attempt to solve the old dilemma concerning the interpretation of methodological statements. If, on the one hand, they are assumed to be nothing more than descriptions of general patterns of behavior, reflecting the actual practice in science, then the question *"quid juris?"* is left unanswered. In other words, the philosopher avoids the problem of justification. If, on the other hand, methodological statements have normative meaning, then the philosopher is open to the objection that he places himself "above science," since he tells scientists how they should do their job. The dangers in such a ruling on science are easy enough to see.

Ajdukiewicz's solution of the dilemma can be outlined as follows. Any method is a prescription for acting in a certain way, and the reason we comply with the prescription is that we thereby hope to achieve something. Hence, the fundamental characteristic of any method is its efficiency with respect to a given objective. The argument for adopting a method is thus relative to the purpose the method is intended to serve and consists in showing that the method is efficient enough with respect to this purpose, or that it is the most efficient in a class of methods available. Efficiency, in turn, may be defined in various ways, depending on the context, but the main ingredient of the concept is the probability of achieving the purpose by the application of the method.

If this argument is agreed upon, the adoption of a method in science may, in principle, be justified along these lines. Such a procedure presupposes that the objective is unequivocally defined. Quite often, however, the scientist himself is not clearly aware of the purpose the method is to serve. In such cases, a hypothetical justification is possible of the following type: if this is the purpose the scientist had in mind, then the method is good in terms of its efficiency with respect to the purpose. Science can then be understood as a rational pursuit of possibly hypothetical goals.

This was the task Ajdukiewicz and his followers set themselves. Out of the results obtained, only a few can be mentioned here. Ajdukiewicz himself remained faithful to his old interest in semantics. He continued to investigate the problem of meaning and the way the conceptual framework of an empirical theory is built up—hence, his work on definitions, on analyticity, and on interpreting axiomatic systems. He also wrote on the logical foundations of measurement (see his *Pragmatic Logic,* published posthumously) and was one of the first to justify rules of nondeductive inference in terms of a non-negative balance of losses and gains in the long run. (See his paper on fallible methods of inference, reprinted in *Twenty Five Years of Logical Methodology in Poland.)* His essay on contradiction and change (1948) played a decisive role in the discussion concerning the alleged conflict between dialectics and formal logic. The Eleatic paradox of the flying arrow had been used to argue that movement implies contradiction; on the other hand, formal logic condemns contradiction as an inexcusable fallacy. Ajdukiewicz has shown conclusively that the argument is not valid since it rests on an error (in the definition of "being at rest") eliminated in the nineteenth century thanks to the mathematical definition of continuity.

The program outlined by Ajdukiewicz was carried out by a number of people, including, first of all, the older generation of philosophers who had already been active before the war. One of these, S. Łuszczewska-Romahnowa, has studied the concept of classification, interpreting it in terms of distance function. (See *Twenty Five Years of Logical Methodology in Poland.)* I. Dąmbska analyzed the role of models in science, "Le concept de modèle et son role dans les sciences." T. Czeżowski defined in a new way the types of reasoning in science, modifying the well-known classification of reasonings by J. Łukasiewicz; he also wrote on testability in empirical sciences. (See *Twenty Five Years of Logical Methodology in Poland.)* J. Kotarbińska wrote on definitions (so-called deictic definitions in particular), on the concept of sign, and the falsificationist view of hypothesis testing. (See her papers in *Twenty Five Years of Logical Methodology in Poland*.) M. Kokoszyńska worked mainly on the problem of analyticity. Since considerable progress has been achieved in this field since World War II, it is described in more detail here.

It may be said that the initial stimulus came from Ajdukiewicz who forcefully presented the problem and showed its philosophical implications. (See his paper, "The Problem of Justifying Analytic Sentences," reprinted in *Twenty Five Years of Logical Methodology in Poland*.) He questioned the almost universally accepted view that definitions and other terminological postulates are "true by convention," i.e., in a way that does not depend on experience. As regards nondefinitional postulates, such as so-called reduction sentences introduced by Carnap, this had been noticed early enough. It had been shown, for instance, that two or more reduction sentences specifying the meaning of a term, say T, may logically imply a nontautological sentence in which the term T does not appear. We then have a paradoxical consequence: truth by convention would imply empirical truth, or, even worse, it would imply empirical falsehood, in which case truth by convention would be no truth at all.

A considerable amount of research was devoted to answering this question. One answer consisted in saying that analytic sentences depend upon experience as to their meaningfulness (but not truth-value), whereas synthetic sentences depend upon experience in both ways.

There have been attempts to "split up" meaning postulates of a given language into a synthetic (factual) component and an analytic (definitional) one. In order to do that, both the language and its semantic properties had to be specified. Explicit consideration of relations between language and the reality it is intended to describe (its "model") is characteristic of such an approach to the classical problem of analytic sentences. The tools used in this investigation therefore belong to the logical theory of models.

Since it is impossible to enumerate here all the results obtained in this field, only some of their authors are mentioned: M. Kokoszyńska, L. Borkowski, Z. Czerwiński, A. Nowaczyk, M. Przełęcki, and R. Wójcicki. The last two authors gave an excellent summary of this work, up to 1969, in "The Problem of Analyticity," reprinted in *Twenty Five Years of Logical Methodology in Poland*.

More generally, the conceptual structure of empirical theories has received considerable attention from the Polish philosophers of science. *The Logic of Empirical Theories* by M. Przełęcki, can be quoted as a typical example. This book analyzes theories, both in terms of their syntactic properties and of their empirical interpretation. In the monograph by R. Wójcicki, *Methodologia formalna nauk empirycznych* ("Formal Methodology of Empirical Sciences"), we also find an attempt to describe the semantic aspects of empirical theories. Wójcicki in particular tries to define the relations between the language of a theory and its scope in such a way as to make it possible to say that the theory is approximately true. Although the concept of approximate truth seems necessary for a realistic description of science, it was seldom investigated by means of modern logic. Wójcicki's book is largely devoted to that purpose.

Here it ought to be mentioned that a number of Polish philosophers and logicians were concerned with problems of semiotics. This is not surprising, if one remembers that emphasis on language was characteristic of the Lwów-Warsaw school in philosophy. Thus, for instance, Kotarbiński's reism was to a large extent a conception of language, and Ajdukiewicz obtained his famous results when he tried to define the concept of meaning.

The postwar continuation of semiotic studies is due to many people. Most active was J. Pelc, professor of logical semiotics at Warsaw University. His main interest is in the logical structure of natural language; see his *Studies in Functional Logical Semiotics of Natural Language*. Pelc has also studied the history of semiotics and, as a result, has published several review papers and edited the anthology *Semiotyka polska 1894–1969* ("Polish Semiotics 1894–1969"). He is the editor of a serial publication called *Studia Semiotyczne* ("Semiotic Studies"), eight volumes of which appeared in the years 1970–1977.

A large part of semiotic studies in Poland has been devoted to the analysis of natural language in terms of formal logic. Thus, B. Stanosz showed how to define the concept of property in set-theoretic terms (which is important if we want to eliminate intentionality from natural language). W. Marciszewski has investigated the semantic structure of a coherent text, and R. Suszko has analyzed semantic antinomies. L. Koj has published a monograph, *Semantyka a pragmatyka* ("Semantics and Pragmatics"), on the relations between semantics on the one hand and linguistics and psychology on the other. An approach to semantics from the Marxist point of view is represented by A. Schaff's book, *Introduction to Semantics*.

Let us now return to the description of how Ajdukiewicz's program worked in the philosophy of science. A group of problems concerns the validity of scientific generalizations. Under which conditions is it justified to accept them as true? Philosophically, this is, more or less, the age-old problem of induction.

Attempts to solve it in the spirit of Adjukiewicz's program take as their starting point an analysis of scientific practice. In this case, the paradigm is provided by the so-called statistical inference, where the relation between premise and conclusion is of a probablistic nature. The acceptance of a conclusion according to a method of this type is justifiable relative to a hypothetical goal, such as minimization of error, maximization of information, and some compromise between these two. Research along these lines has been conducted by Z. Czerwiński (e.g., "On the Relation of Statistical Inference to Traditional Induction and Deduction"), K. Szaniawski (e.g., "Types of Information and Their Role in the Methodology of Science" and the papers reprinted in *Twenty Five Years of Logical Methodology in Poland)*, and H. Mortimer who also studied probablistic aspects of the language of scientific theories (e.g., the article on probabilistic definition of genotype in *Twenty Five Years of Logical Methodology in Poland)*.

A different approach to the problem of induction is seen in H. Greniewski (1903–1972). Greniewski adopted a cybernetician's point of view, and he stated that the purpose of Mill's methods was to find out how a relatively isolated system (a "black box") works, i.e., what is the relation between the possible states of its inputs and those of its outputs, *Elementy logiki indukcji* ("Elements of the Logic of Induction"). Earlier, in 1947, J. Łoś provided a formal analysis of Mill's methods; his paper is reprinted in *Twenty Five Years of Logical Methodology in Poland.*

Before closing this account of how the program for the philosophy of science has been put into effect, one ought to mention the work that has been done on the concept of "problem" or "question." Here, again, the initiative goes back to an early (1934) paper by Ajdukiewicz, in which foundations were laid for the logic of questions and basic types of questions were distinguished. T. Kubiński published extensively on formal theory of questions (e.g., "An Essay in Logic of Questions" and "Logic of Questions"), while J. Giedymin in *Problemy, założenia, rozstrzygnięcia* ("Problems, Assumptions, Solutions") investigated the types of questions (also, their presuppositions, the existence of solutions, and the like) in the social sciences and history.

A number of results just described appeared in the philosophical journals published in Poland: *Studia Logica* (in foreign languages, since 1974 exclusively in English), *Studia Filozoficzne* ("Philosophical Studies"), and *Dialectics and Humanism* (in English).

A number of philosophically significant contributions in Poland have come from disciplines other than philosophy. Sociology provides one instance. S. Ossowski (1897–1963), himself a former student of Kotarbiński, is the author of a penetrating analysis of the way in which the study of social phenomena differs from that of natural ones: *O osobliwościach nauk społecznych* ("On the Peculiarities of the Social Sciences"). In his other works, Ossowski applied the exacting standards set by the Lwów-Warsaw school to analyzing the meaning of emotionally loaded concepts that express the state of social consciousness. Ossowski created a school in the philosophy of the social sciences. A typical example is the collection of essays *Understanding and Prediction* by S. Nowak, his pupil and collaborator.

Another example of philosophical inquiry into the foundations of a discipline is to be found in the writings of O. Lange, the eminent economist (1904–1965). Looking for general principles that would make it possible to justify normative statements made in economics, he found them in a philosophical doctrine, namely, Kotarbiński's praxiology. According to Lange, economic statements, if they are correct, should be derivable from the principles governing efficient action. Lange was one of the leading Marxist thinkers in the field of economic theory. However, he did not consider Kotarbiński's philosophy to be foreign to his convictions.

The appearance of Marxism was probably the most important factor shaping the development of philosophy in postwar Poland. The word "appearance" is used here because before 1939 very few academic philosophers in Poland professed to be Marxists. After the fundamental changes in the political and social structure of Poland, Marxism became the officially acknowledged ideology. This change was, of course, not without consequences for philosophy as one of the subjects taught at the Polish universities.

The process that assured Marxism its present position in Polish philosophy was neither short nor simple. It had its dramatic periods, and the arguments used were not always of a purely theoretical nature. Any fair account of that process in all its complexity would have to place it against a wider historical background. Since such an account is impossible within the limits of this exposition, a summary description of the present situation must suffice.

As a subject for teaching, Marxist philosophy belongs to practically all the curricula of higher education in Poland. The majority of publications in philosophy represent the Marxist school of thinking. The policy of appointments to academic positions is to give preference to candidates who have Marxist views. Philosophical journals are run on Marxist lines (although non-Marxist articles do appear in them). These are but a few examples of Marxism's dominant role in the philosophical life in Poland.

The principle applies to all domains of philosophy: ontology, theory of knowledge, ethics, aesthetics, but in varying degrees, depending on the importance of a commitment to a philosophical doctrine for solving problems of a given type. Philosophy of science, with the exception of its most general problems, is relatively neutral in this sense.

It can be said that in the philosophy of science there was an exchange of ideas between Marxist philosophers and those who drew inspiration from the Polish positivistic tradition. The Marxist thinkers, while retaining their ontological views, viz., those of dialectical materialism, took over from "classical" philosophy of science some of its concepts and methods. In particular, they used in their analysis of scientific cognition the logico-mathematical tools that had been created in a rather different philosophical context. At the same time, it must be stressed that a philosophy of science developed on Marxist principles was openly opposed to logical positivism and to similar views expressed by the Lwów-Warsaw school in philosophy.

A good example is provided by the writings of a group of philosophers from Poznań University. (J. Kmita, L. Nowak, J. Such, and J. Topolski are the most prominent representatives.) The theoretical position of the Poznań group can be outlined as follows. First, we have to reject the current interpretation of Marx's views on the nature of scientific knowledge. According to that interpretation, Marx maintained that abstract statements, constituting scientific theories, are obtained by means of inductive generalization. This, however, is inconsistent with the fact that Marx used to distinguish between essential and inessential factors in opposition to the positivist view which replaces the concept of essence by that of repeatability.

The genuine position of Marx will then have to be reconstructed from his scientific practice, i.e., from the method he used in building up his economic theory. A careful analysis of *Capital* shows that Marx proceeded in a much more complex way than by simple induction. He started by formulating a law (for instance, the law of value) in a highly idealized form, i.e., under assumptions which are patently untrue: that capitalists are directed by one goal only (maximizing the surplus value), that the commercial profit on the goods produced equals zero, and so forth. In this form, the law is simple and shows the essential relation between value and price.

The next stage consists in successive concretizations of the law. The simplifying assumptions are removed, one by one, which brings the law closer to the phenomena it intends to describe. The different factors, first eliminated by the simplifying assumptions and then reintroduced, have different degrees of significance. In its basic form, the law deals only with what is essential. However, this essential regularity is obscured by the intervention of less important factors. Hence, it is necessary to abstract essential connections from their real life context.

According to the Poznań group, the method of abstraction and concretization constitutes the central element of Marxist philosophy of science, as opposed both to positivism in its many variants and to the hypotheticism of Karl Popper. Its description and development are to be found in the numerous publications by L. Nowak, e.g., *Zasady marksistowskiej filozofii nauki* ("Principles of Marxist Philosophy of Science"), and his collaborators.

Another classical problem which the Poznań group took up concerns the foundations of the humanities. What is the nature of explanation in the social and historical sciences? The answer provided by J. Kmita—*Z metodologicznych problemów interpretacji humanistycznej* ("On Methodological Problems of Humanistic Interpretation")—is, to some extent, based on Ajdukiewicz's methodological ideas. In agreement with Ajdukiewicz, Kmita wants to make explanation depend on the hypothetical goal which the agent presumably wanted to achieve. But he goes further in trying to bring out the structure of reasoning that leads from the postulated goal to the act to be explained. Unless this reasoning is a correct deduction, we cannot speak of explanation in the strict sense of the word. In practice, the reasoning is usually enthymematic, so that its reconstruction must supply the missing premises which, of course, are a highly controversial matter.

According to Kmita, the assumption tacitly made in explanations of this type is that the agent is a rational being, in the sense that he so chooses his actions as to bring about the state of things which for him has the highest value. In spite of its almost tautological character, the assumption of rationality is not the only candidate to play the role of general principle in explanations of human behavior. Thus, Kmita argues against the positivistic tendency to link goals with acts by means of some special psychological laws. Humanistic interpretation of human acts (this is the name he gives to the procedure just outlined) is empirically testable in just the same way as are explanations offered by the sciences.

It ought to be clear from the above examples that the interpretation of Marxism by the philosophers from the Poznań group aims at retaining the spirit, rather than the letter, of the original sources. In an article defining their theoretical position ("Against the False Alternatives"), Kmita, Nowak, and Topolski express the belief that Marxist philosophy is "a coherent system rich enough to compete with the remaining systems and win the competition. Upon the condition of course, namely, that Marxism will be given a clear, precise form and thus enabled to solve contemporary problems." The article was published in the journal *Poznań Studies in the Philosophy of the Sciences and the Humanities,* which has appeared since 1975 and is edited by philosophers from the Poznań group. Chronologically, the Poznań group was formed relatively late.

Considerable work has been done in Poland on the philosophical and methodological problems of physics. Z. Augustynek specializes in analyzing the concept of time. For instance, in his "Three Studies in the Philosophy of Space and Time," he discusses the topology of time as well as the relation of symmetry properties to other space-time properties. I. Szumilewicz has published on the direction of the flow of time, *O kierunku upływu czasu* ("On the Direction of the Flow of Time"), and on the nature of our cognition of the universe. S. Amsterdamski has analyzed certain basic concepts of science, e.g., that of probability, in "O obiektywnych interpretacjach pojęcia prawdopodobieństwa" ("On the Objective Interpretations of the Concept of 'Probability"). H. Eilstein, in her important essay on the concept of matter, "Przyczynki do koncepcji materii jako bytu fizycznego" ("Towards the Concept of Matter as Physical Being"), discusses the possibility of reducing in a nonmechanistic way all natural sciences to physics. It ought to be said here that H. Eilstein, for several years the editor of the journal *Studia Filozoficzne,* initiated many studies in the philosophy of science from the Marxist point of view; this trend owes a great deal to her activity.

The work of W. Krajewski also concerns the philosophical foundations of physics. Out of his numerous publications, only his recent *Correspondence Principle and the Growth of Science,* published in English, will be mentioned here. The main problem taken up in this book is the development and application of Bohr's principle of correspondence to an analysis of development in science. The book is also an excellent source of information on the results obtained in Marxist philosophy of science. Krajewski describes his own philosophical position in the following words: "I associate basic ideas of dialectical materialism (liberated from dogmatism and Hegelian phraseology) with logico-methodological achievements of the analytical philosophy of our century (liberated from positivistic narrowness). And first of all, the methods used in the sciences and the history of knowledge must be seriously examined" (p. x). This attitude is characteristic of the relations between Marxist philosophy of science and the traditions of Polish philosophy.

Problems of the evolution of scientific knowledge occupy a prominent place in the philosophical thinking of the last decades. S. Amsterdamski takes them up in his recent book *Between Experience and Metaphysics: Philosophical Problems of the Evolution of Science*. One of the main assertions of this book is that Kuhn's representation of the growth of science ought to be modified. The change of paradigm does not, as a rule, affect those convictions which serve as the basis for overcoming the crisis. Therefore, "revolutions in science" are in most cases local rather than global.

An attempt to describe formally the process of development of science, in the spirit of Marxism, is found in R. Suszko ("Formal Logic and the Development of Knowledge"). For this purpose, he uses "diachronic logic", i.e., the logic that takes time expressly into account. According to Suszko, knowledge is an epistemological relation between the subject (the language he uses) and the object (the model of the language). Changes in knowledge affect either the set of sentences asserted by the subject (evolution) or the language and its model (revolution).

Here we are concerned with the philosophy of science proper. However, certain Marxist contributions on the borderline between the philosophy of science and epistemology or ontology are sufficiently important to mention here. B. Wolniewicz provides a new interpretation of Wittgenstein's early philosophy; he also tries to elucidate basic epistemological ideas of dialectical materialism. C. Nowiński attempts to show (in "Biologie, théories du développement et dialectique") that dialectical methods are used on an increasingly large scale in modern biology and in other sciences analyzing development. In particular, he interprets the work of Jean Piaget in terms of dialectics. According to Nowiński, the relation is reciprocal: progress in biology influences the elaboration of dialectical methods.

O. Lange, in "An Essay in Logic of Questions," has shown the application of cybernetical concepts to the elucidation and proof of certain Marxist tenets. He analyzes the way in which the functioning of any system, biological or technical, depends on the behavior of its subsystems ("parts") and on the network of relations between them, i.e., the structure of the whole. Lange considered this to be a refutation of mechanism since it proves that the behavior of the parts is not enough to account for the behavior of the whole. Moreover, the mathematical theory serves as an argument against finalism. It turns out that there is no need to postulate some mysterious "force" in order to explain the phenomenon of adaptation to changing environment. The theory of ergodic processes is enough for that purpose.

No account of Marxist philosophy in Poland would be complete without mention of the work of A. Schaff. He is one of the initiators and main representatives of this philosophical school in postwar Poland. His writings are rather widely known through many translations. Schaff is concerned with classical problems of philosophy rather than with the philosophy of science proper. However, in his epistemological works, like *Geschichte und Wahrheit* or *Theorie der Wahrheit. Versuch einer marxistischen Analyse,* he discusses problems of validation of assertions made in science and historiography. Schaff's writings are strongly polemical, directed against any brand of what he considers idealism, especially neopositivism. He has had considerable influence on the development of Marxism in Poland, particularly in the first two decades.

In summary, it must be stressed that the philosophy of science, together with logical semiotics, traditionally occupied a prominent place in Polish philosophical thought. The tradition had much in common with logical positivism, but it had its own distinctive features. I call this trend, for lack of a better word, Polish positivism or the Lwów-Warsaw school. After 1945, Marxism was another factor that began to influence methodological studies. Although Marxism was and is explicitly opposed to positivism in any form, its analysis of scientific knowledge has very often been conducted in a way closely parallel to the Lwów-Warsaw school style of thinking. This phenomenon is worth noting.

Contemporary philosophy of science is preoccupied with the formal structure of scientific methods and scientific theories—hence the use of logical and mathematical language, sometimes specially developed for the purpose. This tendency is in harmony with the Polish tradition of philosophizing. The last statement can be substantiated by referring the reader to the prewar publications of the Lwów-Warsaw school and to *Twenty Five Years of Logical Methodology in Poland,* an anthology of methodological writings in Poland covering the postwar period up to 1974. In 1974, an international conference was held in Warsaw devoted to formal methods in the methodology of the empirical sciences. Its recently published proceedings *Formal Methods in the Methodology of Empirical Sciences)* provide a source of information on the present state of the philosophy of science in Poland.

SELECT BIBLIOGRAPHY

BOOKS AND ARTICLES

Ajdukiewicz, K. *Pragmatic Logic,* trans. O. Wojtasiewicz (Boston and Dordrecht: Reidel, 1974).
———. *The Scientific World-Perspective And Other Essays, 1931–1963,* ed. and intro. J. Giedymin (Dordrecht: Reidel, 1978).
Amsterdamski, S. *Between Experience and Metaphysics: Philosophical Problems of the Evolution of Science,* trans. P. Michałowski (Boston and Dordrecht: Reidel, 1975).
———. "O obiektywnych interpretacjach pojęcia prawdopodobieństwa" ("On the Objective Interpretations of the Concept of Probability"), in *Prawo, konieczność, prawdopodobieństwo* ("Laws, Necessity and Probability") (Warsaw: Wyndawnectwo książka i Wiedza, 1964).
Augustynek, Z. "Three Studies in the Philosophy of Space and Time," in *Boston Studies in the Philosophy of Science,* III, eds. R. S. Cohen and M. W. Wartofsky (Dordrecht: Reidel, 1967).
Czerwiński, Z. "On the Relation of Statistical Inference to Traditional Induction and Deduction," *Studia Logica* 8 (1958).
Dambska, I. "Le concept de modèle et son role dans les sciences," *Revue de Synthèse* (1959).
Eilstein, H. "Laplace, Engels i nasi współcześni," ("Laplace, Engels and our Contemporaries") *Studia Filozoficzne* 1 No. 4 (1958).

294 Eastern Europe

——. "Przyczynki do koncepcji materii jako bytu fizycznego" ("Towards the Concept of Matter as Physical Being"), in *Jedność materialna świata* ("Material Unity of the World"), ed. H. Eilstein (Warsaw: Wyndawnictwo Książka i Wiedza, 1961).

Giedymin, J. *Problemy, założenia, rozstrzygnięcia* ("Problems, Assumptions, Solutions") (Poznań: Państwowe Wydawnictwo Naukowe, 1964).

Greniewski, H. *Elementy logiki indukcji* ("Elements of the Logic of Induction") (Warsaw: Państwowe Wydawnictwo Naukowe, 1955).

Kmita, J. *Z metodologicznych problemów interpretacji humanistycznej* ("On Methodological Problems of Humanistic Interpretation") (Warsaw: Państwowe Wydawnictwo Naukowe, 1971).

——, Nowak L., and Topolski, J., "Against the False Alternatives," *Poznań Studies in the Philosophy of the Sciences and the Humanities* 1, No. 2 (1975).

Koj, L. *Semantyka a pragmatyka* ("Semantics and Pragmatics") (Warsaw: Państwowe Wydawnictwo Naukowe, 1971).

Kotarbiński, T. *Gnosiology: The Scientific Approach to the Theory of Knowledge*, trans. O. Wojtasiewicz (Oxford and New York: Pergamon Press, 1966). First Polish edition (1955).

——. *Praxiology: An Introduction to the Sciences of Efficient Action*, trans. O. Wojtasiewicz (Oxford and New York: Pergamon Press, 1965). First Polish edition (1955).

Krajewski, W. *Correspondence Principle and the Growth of Science* (Boston and Dordrecht: Reidel, 1977).

Kubiński, T. "An Essay in the Logic of Questions," in *Atti del XII Congresso Internazionale di Filosofia* V (Florence, Italy: Sansoni, 1958).

——. "The Logic of Questions," in *Contemporary Philosophy. A Survey*, ed. R. Klibansky (Florence, Italy: La nuova Italia, 1968).

Lange, O. *Papers in Economics and Sociology 1930–1960*, trans. ed. P. F. Knightsfield (Warsaw: Państwowe Wyndawnictwo Naukowe, 1970). First English edition (Oxford and New York: Pergamon Press, 1970).

——. *Wholes and Parts. A General Theory of System Behavior* (Oxford and New York: Pergamon Press, 1965).

Nowak, L. *Zasady marksistowskiej filozofii nauki* ("Principles of Marxist Philosophy of Science") (Warsaw: Państwowe Wydawnictwo Naukowe, 1974).

Nowak, S. *Understanding and Prediction. Essays in the Methodology of Social and Behavioral Theories* (Boston and Dordrecht: Reidel, 1976).

Nowiński, C. "Biologie, théories du développement et dialectique," in *Logique et connaissance scientifique*, ed. J. Piaget. Encyclopédie de la Pleiade (Paris: Gallimard, 1967).

Ossowski, S. *O osobliwościach nauk społecznych* ("On the Pecularities of the Social Sciences") (Warsaw: Państwowe Wydawnictwo Naukowe, 1962).

Pelc, J. *Studies in Functional Logical Semiotics of Natural Language* (The Hague: Mouton, 1971).

—— (ed.) *Semiotyka polska 1894–1969* ("Polish Semiotics 1894–1969") (Warsaw: Państwowe Wydawnictwo Naukowe, 1971).

Przełęcki, M. *The Logic of Empirical Theories* (London: Routledge and Kegan Paul, and New York: Humanities Press, 1969).

——., Szaniawski, K., and Wójcicki, R. (eds.). *Formal Methods in the Methodology of Empirical Sciences. Proceedings of the Conference for Formal Methods in the Methodology of the Empirical Sciences, Warsaw, June 17–21, 1974*, (Synthese Library 103).

——, and Wójcicki, R. "The Problem of Analyticity," *Synthese* 19, No. 3/4 (1969).

——. (eds.). *Twenty Five Years of Logical Methodology in Poland* (Synthese Library 87) (Warsaw and Dordrecht: Reidel, 1977).

Schaff, A. *Geschichte und Wahrheit*, ed. E. M. Szarota (Frankfurt and Zurich: Europa, 1970).

——. *Introduction to Semantics*, trans. O. Wojtasiewicz (Warsaw: Pergamon, and New York: Macmillan, 1962).

——. *Theorie der Wahrheit. Versuch einer marxistischen Analyse* (Vienna: Europa, 1971).

Such, J. *Problemy weryfikacju wiedzy* ("Problems of Verification of Knowledge") (Warsaw: Państwowe Wydawnictwo Naukowe, 1975).

Suszko, R. "Formal Logic and the Development of Knowledge," *Problems in the Philosophy of Science*, III, eds. I. Lakatos and A. Musgrave, (Amsterdam: North-Holland, 1968).

Szaniawski, K. "Types of Information and Their Role in the Methodology of Science," *Formal Methods in the Methodology of Empirical Sciences. Proceedings of the Conference for Formal Methods in the Methodology of Empirical Sciences, Warsaw, June 17–21, 1974* (Synthese Library 103), eds. M. Przełęcki, K. Szaniawski, and R. Wójcicki (Dordrecht and Boston: Reidel, 1977).

Szumilewicz, I. *O kierunku upływy czasu* ("On the Direction of the Flow of Time") (Warsaw: 1972).

Wójcicki, R. *Metodologia formalna nauk empirycznych* ("Formal Methodology of Empirical Sciences") (Wroclaw: Zaklad Narodowy Im Ossolinskich, 1974).

Wolniewicz, B. "A Parallelism Between Wittgensteinian and Aristotelian Ontologies," in *Boston Studies in the Philosophy of Science*, IV, eds. R. S. Cohen and M. W. Wartofsky (Dordrecht: Reidel, 1969).

———. "The Notion of Fact as a Modal Operator," *Teorema* (Valencia, 1972).

JOURNALS

Dialectics and Humanism
Etyka
Poznań Studies in the Philosophy of the Sciences and the Humanities
Ruch Filozoficzny
Studia Filozoficzne
Studia Logica

Romania

ALEXANDRU TĀNASE AND OCTAVIAN CHEŢAN

An integral component of the spirituality of the Romanian people, Romanian philosophy has constantly developed along the lines of authentic progressive tradition. Permanencies of Romanian culture in the past such as rationalism and humanism, rejection of excess, dogmatism, and exclusivism of any kind, and a strong feeling of humaneness and national dignity have, in socialist contemporaneity, fully asserted themselves and reached a higher plane. The postwar years in Romania marked an epoch of deep revolutionary democratic transformation, the inception of a new history for the country, and the fulfilling of ideals of social and national justice.

Philosophy in Romania is no longer the appanage of a few thinkers isolated from the everyday social and political issues of the world. In the work of building socialism, a philosophical approach is always needed in choosing among options, making decisions, and translating them into facts and achievements. Thus, philosophical activity finds a strong stimulus in the dynamics of social life, in the development of the revolutionary process. Marxist philosophy today expresses the ideological option of the entire Romanian people who, under the leadership of the Romanian Communist party, are firmly engaged in establishing a multilaterally developed socialist society in the country's prospective advance to communism. In creating a value system and a life ideal, Marxist philosophy proceeds from the objective developmental trends of contemporary social life, from the basic interests of the broad masses of the people, thus becoming its asset and, implicitly, a powerful social force, a priority area of social action. Society as a whole is deeply interested in the directions this development is taking and in realizing this philosophical outlook in the framework of research in the area.

Within the past decade, new vistas have been opened for Romanian philosophical and sociopolitical thought. The decisive step forward was made on the basis of the documents that emerged from the congresses of the Romanian Communist party and the works by President Nicolae Ceauşescu. These provide a high theoretical and ideological approach to a wide range of problems of the socialist revolution and the building of the new system, invigorating and substantially enriching the subject matter of Marxist philosophy.

Today, philosophical research work in Romania is primarily an activity of debate as well as scientific and critical examination of the issues facing the contemporary world and Romanian socialist society. It is an activity open to innovation and to problem-solving in the spirit of a Marxist philosophy which is viewed not as a summation of precepts or of dogmas working forever and everywhere. Rather, it is a philosophy that stimulates people's creative thought, facilitates scientific investigation, and involves responsibility and social-political commitment to the great humanistic and revolutionary ideal of socialism and communism.

THE ACTIVE AND PROSPECTIVE SENSE OF SOCIAL PHILOSOPHY

The profound changes that have occurred in all areas of social and political life in Romania have broken new ground for theoretical approaches directed to the present and the future. In this sphere of philosophical thought more than any other, it is imperative that philosophy alight in the city, cease being disinterested, futile contemplation, and become the direct or intermediate reflection of social and political quests.

Today philosophical interests are focusing on new problems: for example, on social life structures in the light of systems theory; the development of a democratic system in Romania's socialist society; relationships between information, decision-making and participation; social determinism and freedom; the development of socialist individual and social conscience; the principle of social equity; the socialist ethos and its theoretical foundations, and new dimensions of progress.

The major source of development and innovation within philosophy is social practice, including competent and responsible participation of the broad masses in conscious historical creation, the close interrelation between theory and practice, and greater concern for analyzing and generalizing Romania's experience of socialist revolution and construction. The philosophical conscience has thus become a component of the critical and revolutionary awareness of a society. In this society, the technical rationalism of its forces of production is in full agreement with the humanism of its social relations, in which people's alienated social existence becomes the main element in modeling a human personality that aims at plenary realization.

In recent years, a wide debate has been in progress concerning, among other things, the relationship between the general and the particular in Romania's socialist revolution, the concept of the multilaterally developed socialist society, the specificity of social dialectics, and the relation between freedom and responsibility under the conditions of socialism. Special attention has been given to studying the role of the nation in social life dynamics and the national-international dialectical relation. As a human community, the nation represents a major force in international policy. It is not merely a framework for existence; on the contrary, it is a fertile, culture-generating soil, the inner spring of material and spiritual creation. As President Ceauşescu has pointed out, Romania is the product of a complex historical process, of an epoch of great progress of civilization which, in turn, is a factor in progress and civilization. "The development of contemporary society," he states, "proves that the nation preserves its complete validity also today. The struggle for the assertion of nations is one of the essential components of the social-political picture of our epoch. Only by respecting the interests of each nation shall propitious conditions exist for establishing actually free interstate relations, greater interstate approaches."

In President Nicolae Ceauşescu's works, one also finds relevant analyses of the concept of patriotism, which is a basic concept in the socio-political philosophy of the Romanian socialist state. Patriotism implies an organic blend between one's love for one's homeland and one's plenary contribution to increasing its national wealth, defending its freedom, independence, and integrity, fighting against any national discriminations, chauvinism, racial views and manifestations, attaining full equality of rights for all working people, maintaining friendship with all the peoples of the world in the cause of peace and collaboration, and having respect for the national feelings of other peoples and for their freedom and independence.

Progress, the quality of life, and the dimension of the future are other favorite topics of Romanian social thought today. The category of social formation is fundamental to the socio-historical analysis; its necessary methodological complement, however, is the development criterion. The idea of progress is opposed to vulgar evolutionistic simplications and to skeptical views alike.

An open, realistic, and rigorous approach to the complex problems of contradictions under socialism has been stimulated by President Ceauşescu's in-depth analyses. This approach has fostered the detection of the specific character of social determinism in Romania today and the special role of the conscious action of the subjective factor (the revolutionary party of the working class, the socialist state, mass and public organizations, individuals as creative personalities) in the advance to communism. From this dialectical-materialistic outlook on social life, investigations have been undertaken with a view to revealing the concrete historical conditions for social and human progress. At the same time, the aim has been to discover how to bypass both the idealistic conceptions that deemed social development a linear, quasi-automated process, and the views ignoring or minimizing the capacity of socialism to increase the rate of social development. In this context, the multilateral comprehension of the laws of social development and increased competence and responsibility in people's participation have exerted a strong positive influence on the progress of the forces of production, raising the material welfare of the whole population.

Romanian philosophers define the quality of life as the most pregnant and synthetic concomitant of social and cultural progress. It is primarily a concept of social ontology that bears on the existential mode of human individualities within the frame of a civilization uniting the social functions of art, science, and philosophy.

In recent years, futures studies in Romania have recorded major developments.

The *Bucharest Declaration* of the Congress of Futurology (1973) which marked the inception of the World Future Studies Federation, recommended that prospective studies be related to development strategies and that the connection between futures studies and ideogical and praxiolological premises be emphasized.

Futurology resorts to methods and suggestions ranging from numerous natural and human sciences to subtle procedures of mathematical analysis. But, at the same time, it assumes the philosophical meditation on desirable goals, the capacity of subjective factors and of the progressive forces to direct social evolution along a positive, rational route. From a philosophical perspective, the future appears to be an open field of opportunities, a matter of constructive action. Futures studies should be based on a unity among cognition, reevaluation, and action. Action, as a modality of building and of creating the future, presupposes (1) democratic participation of the people in building up their own future—a future of the people and for the people should be the work of the people, the complex product of their historically conscious creativeness, and (2) organization and leadership of conscious activity with a view to building up the optimum future. If the future is an open time, then the action developed to attain it, the active finalization of elaborated projects and decisions, is dominated time. If in the past successful action was almost exclusively dependent on the ability to apply former models based on empirical knowledge, today long-term success depends on prospective action and models based on scientific knowledge and motivation.

Society-democracy-personality has been another fertile subject matter for reflection in postwar Romanian social philosophy, the more so as democratism and humanism are fundamental principles of the domestic and foreign policy of the Romanian state. According to the theoretical outlook of Romanian authors, democracy is not a simple political question but a complex problem of civilization, i.e., institutionalization, objectivization, and improvement of a certain system of social relations, moral behavior, and philosophical attitude. A true democracy provides full scope for the development of the people's creative energies. The active subject of democracy is man in his twofold capacity as a user of formative opportunities and influences, and a creative subject of a democratic system.

True democracy, as proven by Romanian thinkers, is fertile ground for attaining and asserting the integrity of the human individual. The core of socialist democracy does not consist of "noncritical," nondifferentiated, amorphous "masses of people" but rather of human collectivities already formed or in the process of formation. Therefore, democracy means not only improving the organizational-institutional system but also asserting man's creativeness. Realization of the human essence presupposes changing possible, ideal conditions into real conditions, turning the human world into a world of freedom.

The Romanian state has consistently promoted a humanistic conception of international relations in the area of foreign policy and in the field of social thought, philosophy included. The reason is that the basic concept of contemporaneity—the new international economic and political system—involves a value circuit which is likely to increase the rationality of the world we live in. President Ceauşescu, whose consistent promotion of the new concept of international relations has been acknowledged all over the world, has often emphasized that the progress of civilization is based on the knowledge of everything valuable in world culture and on the extensive exchange of material and spiritual values among all peoples.

At the level of large human communities, just as at the individual level, actual freedom is inconceivable unless everyone has equal (or equalized) opportunities and unless available resources are distributed equitably. This notion also implies a new ethical system, the assertion of a new international ethos undergirded by such values as freedom, personality, independence, sovereignty, equality, equity, cooperation, mutual respect, work, education, and humanization.

The vast area of social philosophy also covers more recent developments in praxiology and the theory of human action. Based on a comprehensive understanding of the concept of social action, a social structure model has been devised comprising a complex system of cognitive and material relations between man and reality. This system organically correlates, in terms of the feedback principle, with a multitude of objective and subjective social factors.

PHILOSOPHY, CULTURE, AND HUMANISM

Romanian philosophical thought, cultural problems and humanistic sense of culture hold a central place as a fundamental dimension of theoretical activity. The contributions to this field cannot be understood outside that spiritual climate which has afforded a considerable widening of the horizon of Marxist thought and investigation into some new areas of experience and conscience long neglected by dogmatic myopia. In order to develop a multilateral outlook on the human condition, a systematic approach was needed to some problems of the philosophy of man, philosophy of values, and philosophy of culture in the light of Marxist theory and methodology. While this conception never claimed a monopoly on truth, it proved capable of overcoming many traditional difficulties.

The value and dignity of man as the focal concern of thought and practice is a fundamental principle of humanism. But man as interpreted by socialist revolutionary humanism no longer resembles the abstract, historically and socially isolated man of old philosophical anthropologies, or man devised by traditional classical humanism. He is a concrete man—a synthesis of individual-subjective and social-objective relations, of national and worldwide relations, of the characteristics of the individual and the features of social groups, of economic, political, ethical, and cultural relations.

Let us turn now to Romania's individual thinkers. Following World War II, they continued their work amid the new conditions in the country, making valuable contributions to the new cultural life of their country.

Mircea Florian (1888–1950), a rationalistic, gnoseological philosopher and a follower of "ontological realism," was a consistent critic of modern irrationalism and religious mysticism. His philosophy, which is essentially materialistic, is implicitly a plea for the defense of human reason and the scientific spirit, the perennial sources of culture and civilization.

A philosopher and exceptional poet was Lucian Blaga (1895–1961). During the interwar as well as postwar period, his speculative and metaphoric philosophical work reflected deeply humanistic traits. After World War II, his evolution was marked by a rationalistic and dialectical outlook on man and culture. It was during this period that he developed the premises and structure of a philosophical anthropology. His work *Aspecte antropologice* ("Anthropological Aspects") presents the idea of man's cultural vocation as permanent historical being, always superseding its creation but never his condition of creator. Blaga establishes a close relationship between the human and the historical individual. Concrete history imposes upon the human individual stylistic trends, and, in turn, the individual may intervene and modify the objective stylistic field. This process, this mutual exchange of stylistic trends, has a permenent character.

D. D. Roşca (1895–   ), the doyen of contemporary Romanian thinkers, gained wide attention in European philosophical circles in the late 1930s through his brilliant doctoral thesis delivered at the Sorbonne. This work, *Hegel's Influence on Taine,* effected radical changes in the traditional image of Taine as a positivist. Roşca's philosophy is an original synthesis of romanticism and scientific realism, with a certain emphasis on some romantic tendencies and existentialist traits. His widely appreciated work, *Existenţa tragică* ("Tragic Existence,") (1934, latest edition, 1968), highlights the contradictory and tragic character of human existence, the source of a tragic conscience, and the conscience of an existence that always tends to adaptation and equilibrium yet is always in a state of conflict with the world. It is the conscience of inner tension, always troubled and dissatisfied, denying the datum as inexorable destiny. Metaphysical disquietude and revolt are its real states, and becoming its way of being. Tragic existence saves itself from the pessimistic tragic insofar as it becomes cultural existence. Cultural action and creation represent a constructive mode of life for man's tragic existence.

Some of the outstanding contributions to the development of Marxist philosophy in postwar Romania were made by Lucreţiu Pătrăşcanu and Gaál Gabor, eminent thinkers and theorists who continued their activity under the new sociopolitical conditions. In his studies and books, notably *Probleme de bază ale României* ("Romania's Fundamental Problems"), *Sub trei dictaturi* ("Under Three Dictatorships"), *Un veac de frămîntări sociale* ("A Century of Social Unrest"), and *Curente şi tendinţe în filosofia românească* (Currents and Trends in Romanian Philosophy''), Pătrăşcanu (1900–1954), a many-sided original spirit, made an in-depth materialist dialectical analysis of the evolution of the Romanian society over one hundred years of dramatic history (1921–1946). His entire philosophical and political work emphasizes the active part philosophy is called on to play in social life. Highlighting the role of philosophy in defining the stands taken by the individual and the collectivity on life and its problems, Pătrăşcanu has asserted the theoretical, methodological, and political value of Marxist philosophy.

The theoretical activity of Gaál Gabor (1891–1954), a Magyar Marxist publicist and thinker from Romania, is closely related to his contribution, as editor-in-chief of the journal *Korunk* in the years 1931–1940, to popularizing this progressive Magyar publication. In his writings, Gaál has thoroughly debated such problems as the reevaluation of Romania's cultural heritage, realism in literature and the arts, and the philosophy of culture and humanism in open confrontation with other philosophical and politico-ideological trends.

In recent decades, Academy Professor C. Ionescu-Guliah has contributed to the analysis of the philosophy of culture, of man, and of the human condition. From a predominantly ethical perspective, his philosophical work makes an in-depth study of some topical problems of the value universe: the objective character of ethical values, the relationship between value and necessity, the normative and hierarchical character of values, the establishment of some ethical and axiological typologies, and the unity between cognition and valorization as well as between the ethic of the state and the ethic of realization. In his view, Marxist philosophical anthropology is opposed to the idealistic and moralizing images of spiritualistic humanists and also to the narrow mechanistic, biologizing, and vulgarizing images of certain materialist-metaphysical anthropologists. Man is conceived as the unity and totality of some contrary determinations. The situation and sense of the individual ensue from the combination and dynamics of these determinations of man as realized existence, as accomplished historical becoming, or as potential existence, a desiderative or imperative projection, a spiritual model.

Also notable in this same framework are the systematic conerns for elaborating a Marxist philosophy of culture. As constituent moments of culture, the following have been evidenced and detailed: (1) cognitive moment—culture as the cognitive result of practical activity involving rational order and organization in the flow of practical experience and subjective sensations; (2) axiological moment—aiming at the human finality of culture and involving a selective, critical, constructive, and prospective attitude; (3) demiurgic moment—expressing the qualitative leap from a natural, social, individual fact to a fact of culture; and (4) moment of communication—circulating and integrating values into the whole of the social praxis, transformation of values into assets of civilization. The moment of communication is a moment of interference, of transition from culture to civilization, which amounts to the totality of cultural values integrated in social human praxis and becoming component elements of the mode of life, of the style of thought and action. It is culture in action integrated into an organized system of work, life, and thought.

The humanistic horizon of Romanian culture is also highlighted by research in axiology on the grounds of newly elaborated theoretical-methodological foundations. In analyses of value, this concept is seen as a social relation expressing the appraisal by an individual or a human collectivity of some qualities or facts (natural, social, psychological) according to their capacity to meet necessities, desires, and human aspirations historically conditioned by social practice. At the same time, value involves an act of option, a preferential orientation in a given situation.

The ethical dimension of the human condition and of the new type of civilization has been the object of scientific interest and theoretical concern ever since the early postwar years. It has also been the main object of practical cultural-educational action. Socialism has been gradually developing a new elementary ethical situation mirroring the complex combination of the new dignity of man, who has assumed freedom as his own condition of life, and the high-quality social requirements that stimulate human activity and commitment under the conditions of the diversification and progress of social life on all planes.

Circumscribing and defining the object of Marxist ethics, the concrete investigation into the ethos of work has led to a theory of socialist ethos. The focal concern of this theory is the dynamics of socialist ethics with its own formation and developmental laws.

The international congresses of aesthetics held in Bucharest in 1972 and Darmstadt in 1976 revealed that aesthetic research in Romania is undergoing modernization and maturation. The legacy of Romanian and universal aesthetics is being reevaluated by means of modern methodologies and interdisciplinary researches. Among Romanian traditions that have attained international prestige are the pioneer studies and investigations by Pius Servian Coculescu or Matyla C. Ghica, which renewed the methodology of the theory of art. Following these traditions, studies are being carried out on introducing the theory of information, mathematical statistics, game theory, semiotics, and structuralism into the exploration of the new, exceptionally rich, and varied artistic reality.

In contemporary civilization, the beautiful is no longer a purely aesthetic category. It now penetrates into the people's lives, into all the compartments and articulations of existence, and has become a necessary dimension of life. Hence, Romanian aestheticians should make an approach to such problems as the relationship between the ideal and aesthetic taste, the aesthetics of consumer goods, kitsch and the problems of design, aesthetic landmarks of the Romanian village today, the authentic and the nonauthentic in the aesthetic organization of the environment and of the rural and the urban habitat, and the aesthetic as a dimension of social life.

LOGIC AND EPISTEMOLOGY

Among postwar philosophical interests, research in logic, epistemology, and philosophy of science achieved unprecedented scope.

Athanase Joja (1904–1972), a philosopher and logician, conceived of the humanistic paean to reason as his own reason for being. He developed a multilateral approach, from converging viewpoints, to classical logic, history of logic, and the relationship between logic and philosophy. His works provide new, unitary interpretations of Aristotelian logic, a humanistic cultural perspective of some significant moments in the history of reason's efforts to reach self-cognizance and awareness of its own procedural laws. Joja's aim was to elaborate a *Novum Organum Dialecticum,* a dialectical logic conceived as a philosophical meta-theory of logic. He studied the correlation between this dialectical logic and classical and symbolic logic. He suggested the formulation of concrete identity as a logical law which, unlike the principle of abstract identity, could explain the dynamism of dialectical thought.

In that same period, Professor Dan Bădărău (1893–1968), a rationalistic thinker, was concerned with problems of logic and the history of logic. His works discuss the close relationships between Aristotle's logical forms and the cognizance they structure. They also examine the distinction between what certain theorists designate as "pure" (subconscious) thinking and logical, discursive thinking, the only fundamental of science, philosophy, and man's gradual mastering of his natural and social environment.

The logician Florea Tuțugan (1908–1961) also concentrated on developing the traditional syllogistic. Tuțugan focused his research on the analysis of the syllogistic of prediction judgments, the syllogistic with negative terms, and the classical theory of modalities, especially possible and contingent modes.

Over the past decade in particular, researchers in logic have tackled a wide range of problems of classical logic, philosophy of logic, and symbolic logic.

Of special interest in Professor Petre Botezatu's works are his discussions of the value of education, the relationship between deduction and induction, and the foundation of a natural logic. According to Botezatu, the effort to construct a natural logic involves, among other considerations, understanding the operational character of thought, especially the operation of the transfer of properties and construction of objects associated with various inference schemes. He attempts to organize the system according to natural deduction without proceeding from modern propositional logic with its "unnatural" situations like those connected with the paradoxes of material implication.

Logical studies have been elaborated on the theory of propositional functions, the status of the principle of duality in logic, problems of mathematics, theory of logical systems, and philosophy of logic, with emphasis on the theory of truth and implication, as well as studies of deontic logic.

In accordance with using modern logico-mathematical methods in studying the syllogistic, alternative axiomatizations have been suggested for Aristotle's assertoric logic which are of interest for delimiting its various subsystems. Studies have been made of Aristotelian and Theophrastic modal syllogistic problems raised by modeling the assertoric syllogistic and modal syllogistic on modern predicative logic.

Studies of symbolic logic are also concerned with a series of practical applications. Academician Grigore C. Moisil (1906–1973), a humanist mathematician with a complex personality, was interested in a wide range of problems. Among his concerns were generalizing the idea of implication, constructing on this ground a calculus for the most general aspect of any propositional calculus; studying the applications of polyvalent logic to technology; and contributing to the development of the algebraic theory of automata. He introduced the "trivalent and polyvalent" Łukasiewicz algebras, as he designated them, and used them in logic and in the study of commulation circuits.

In recent decades in particular, research has been carried out on that area of the theory of cognition which studies the general conditions, sources, structure, mode of development, and validity of the process of cognition as knowledge-yielding process. This research has focused on the problem of the relationships between subject and object, theory of truth, the logic of scientific research, the active, constructive involvement of the subject in cognition, the dialectical correlation between the empirical and the theoretical moment, types of abstraction, informational modeling, and cognitive procedures.

Contributions to the problems of the philosophy of science have been made both in some traditional areas like the philosophy of physics and microphysics, chemistry, biology, medical sciences, and psychology, and, more recently, in the interdisciplinary directions of study—philosophy and logic of language, semiotics, general system theory, game theory, philosophical problems of today's revolution in science and technology.

THE PAST, PRESENT, AND FUTURE IN ROMANIAN PHILOSOPHY

If what makes a culture aware of itself is philosophy, then in its turn philosophy can develop self-awareness only as long as it never ceases to critically reassess its own historical becoming.

Research into the history of universal philosophy has gradually acquired wider scope and deeper insight in Romania. In recent decades, moreover, Romanian philosophical culture has benefited by translations of studies and monographs on the philosophy of antiquity, Greek and Latin philosophies, preclassical and classical, the philosophy of the Middle Ages, modern philosophy, and major currents and trends in contemporary thought. The Romanian translations of the basic works of the philosophers of antiquity up to modern times—above all, the philosophical writings of Aristotle, Hegel, and Marx—have given broader segments of the reading public a deeper insight into the cardinal problems of contemporary man and civilization. These translations have helped enrich, polish, and enhance the subtlety of the Romanian philosophical language, facilitate the progressive integration of Romanian philosophical culture into the circuit of contemporary philosophical thought, and confer on philosophical education greater scientific rigor.

The priority interest for contemporaneity and the creative approach to fundamental areas and problems largely draw on the perennial appeal of the great classics, provided they are studied and assimilated according to scientific criteria. Characteristic of the Romanian works of philosophy and philosophical historiography is their power of discernment and their openness to dialogue.

Romanian research and results in the history of philosophical thought can be summarized as follows:

1. The history of philosophy is both a process of cognition and an ideological process permanently enriched with new ideas, solutions, and resolutions.

2. Romanian philosophers have a comprehensive approach to non-Marxist philosophy today. They are receptive to all new trends and problems, open to the assimilation of valuable contributions, and have replaced simplistic and vulgarizing name-calling by serious, well-founded criticism.

3. The monographs and studies devoted to some personalities, philosophical schools, or whole periods in the history of philosophy discuss problems in a broader context of contingency and significations. The result has been an objective, fertile dialogue with non-Marxist, humanistic orientations and with the innovating tendencies of modern logic and epistemology, ethics, aesthetics, social philosophy, and the philosophy of science. At the same time, these writings have produced a well-founded scientific criticism of definite idealistic, irrational, and fideistic trends hostile to science and progress.

Another major trend of historical-philosophical research covers the history of Romanian philosophy in an attempt to effect a multilateral Marxist-dialectical approach to the Romanian philosophical phenomenon by relating it to universal philosophy.

If reevaluation of its own legacy is one of the major duties of any culture, a source of invigoration and renewal, then for Romanian socialist culture it is an imperative. It is required by the very essence of a higher quality synthesis of the most valuable productions of our ancestors, of all that is authentic and progressive in the creation of past generations.

Stimulated by the bold, creative spirit that stamps the whole of Romanian spiritual life, in keeping with the cultural policy promoted by the Romanian Communist party and the theoretical and practical activity developed by President Ceauşescu, certain schematic simplifications and sociologizing interpretations that dominated in former periods could be overcome. Never in the past did research in the history of Romanian philosophy and, implicitly the act of reevaluating the cultural legacy, attain such scope and scientific rigor as in recent years.

In fact, Marxist investigators into the history of Romanian philosophy treaded on almost virgin soil. Today, the Romanian socialist society shows great respect for and appreciation of past thinkers. Humanism and the Enlightenment, the incipient moments of modern Romanian philosophy, are brilliantly represented in Romania by Dimitrie Cantemir, a humanistic scholar who has gained European fame, by the spiritual movement called the Transylvanian school, as well as thinkers like G. Lazăr, I. Heliade-Rădulescu, G. Asachi, and Eufrosim Poteca. Humanism and the Enlightenment have been profoundly analyzed in the context of the European philosophy of those periods, and as a result, remarkable studies and monographs have been produced. Studies have also covered mid-nineteenth-century Romanian philosophical rationalism and the socio-political and philosophical outlook of the main theorists and leaders of the 1848 revolutionary movement—Nicolae Bălcescu, Mihail Kogălniceanu, Simion Bărnuțiu, George Bariț, C. A. Rosetti, and others. A vast number of monographs and studies have been devoted to analyzing the materialistic tradition in Romanian philosophy and its illustrious, European-famous representative Vasile Conta. More rigorous exegeses have been made concerning the dissemination and development of Marxist philosophy in Romania and the works of some thinkers and theorists of the workers' and revolutionary movement like C. Dobrogeanu-Gherea and Lucrețiu Pătrășcanu. A mulilateral approach has been made to the complex, sometimes contradictory work and activity of eminent past personalities whose development took place in a heterogeneous spiritual climate, influenced by various class ideologies. Examples are the studies of such thinkers as Titu Maiorescu, A. D. Xenopol, Dimitrie Gusti, P. P. Negulescu, D. Drăghicescu, Petre Andrei, and Tudor Vianu.

A new stage in Romania's study of philosophy in the past began with the preparation and elaboration of the multivolume work *Treatise of Romanian Philosophical History*. It was preceded by a series of volumes entitled *Din isotoria filozofiei românești* ("From the History of Romanian Philosophy") and anthology collections of texts. The first volume of this treatise appeared in 1972.

The works of critical reappraisal of Romanian thought published over the past decade generally reflect an emphasis on distinguishing the internal articulations of each philosophical conception, the basic outlines of its specific structure. This methodological outlook, paramount today in Romanian philosophical research, has led to complex interpretations which highlight, besides the social functions of various schools, the connections among systems of thought, the multiple mediations that occur in shaping different conceptions.

A theoretical field never much approached in the past and the object of detailed studies at present is philosophical historiography, the study of problems relating to the philosophy of philosophical history. This area of internal and international study and debate is likely to give the methodology of historiographical research in universal and domestic philosophy greater rigor. It will also contribute to a better understanding of the history of philosophy as a continuous process, as superstructure indissolubly linked with history, pinpointing both the intimate particularities of the historical-philosophical process and its formation which some authors believe are the laws of the history of philosophy.

In light of this discipline (developed in Romania by Professor Ion Banu), the universal history of philosophy appears as a unitary and continuous process. Yet, it also appears to be contradictory and discontinuous, a discrete progression of philosophical cognition connected with the progress of history and of science. One may suggest schemes of structural models by epochs, dynamic, historical, stage-by-stage determined structures, passing one into another.

The traditions of Romanian philosophical culture have stimulated today's researchers to make an approach to new, topical problems in close relation to the contemporary movement of ideas, to the revolutionary transformations experienced by the Romanian people in building up a higher civilization, i.e., the socialist civilization. The Eleventh Congress of the Romanian Communist party and the Congress of Political Education and Socialist Culture presented the force lines of a vast program whose fulfillment depends on tomorrow's image of Romanian society and the destiny of the nation. The major goal inscribed in this program, simply and concisely called the building up of the multilaterally developed socialist society, implies concentration and orientation of a huge amount of practical and theoretical work. In this vast, revolutionary-oriented action, philosophy is called on to perform quite an important task. Consequently, contemporary Romanian philosophical thought is directed primarily at the following objectives:

(1) The concrete treatment of the problems of today's civilization, chiefly Romania's own social and national realities in the process of becoming, i.e., grasping significant facts, states of conscience, and axiological dimensions specific to the new spiritual civilization the Romanian people are building; analysis of problems relating to the formation and development of a socialist conscience; scientific-materialistic education of the broad masses; analysis of contradictions in socialist society with a view to perfecting social life; investigation of the cultural methods under socialism; and the humanism and ethics of coinhabitation and management.

(2) Furthering research in epistemology and logic in close correlation with world research in the area and the demands of modern social practice.

(3) Elaborating some fundamental syntheses and reference works—treatises, dictionaries, encylcopedias—definitive of a certain stage of maturity in a culture.

Philosophy has always been the concise, synthetic image of the spirit of an epoch. It is, therefore, all the more expected to provide such an image today when we live in an era which, despite the manifestations of some spiritual states nonreceptive to the philosophical message, strongly feels the need for an ideal, for plenary social and political commitment to multilateral social progress. The evolution of social and political life today indicates that the process of democratizing philosophy is strongly under way and that it is being turned into a permanent, necessary component of thought, of experience and of praxis, of the whole spiritual life of tomorrow's community.

Man has considerably extended and increased his capacity for thinking and acting. His memory, broadened by the computer, has accumulated an amount of information exceeding all that previous centuries put together have produced. His movement in time and space has acquired disconcerting proportions and rates. His action in the social and natural space can determine the life or death of the species itself. What guarantee do we have that information is handled to the benefit of man and not to his detriment? What can direct decisions and actions to humanistic ends? What guarantees have we that out of all possible futures the optimum one will be chosen? We deem that such guarantees are offered by a juster and better civilization—the socialist civilization on the plane of factual life and the dialectical, materialistic philosophy on the plane of spiritual life. We do not minimize beneficial contacts, the fertile dialogue with other rationalistic and humanistic philosophies when dealing with the constructive goals of philosophy in the world today. On the contrary, we promote them. What are these goals? Some of them are as follows:

(1) Realization of a new cognitive synthesis, bearing in mind the unprecedented expansion of man in the external universe, his historical progress in conquering the objective world, the considerable widening of the area of cognition, and the informational volume that exceeds the storage capacity of the human brain. In addition, the development of the meta-theoretical instances of various sciences, their capacity to theoretically process and synthetize. Nevertheless, a mature, comprehensive outlook on this inexhaustible field, viewed as totality in motion, can be provided only by philosophy, both by its traditional creations (philosophy of existence and cognition) and its recent vocations (philosophy of information, philosophy of action, philosophy of culture and civilization, and philosophy of science). The analytical spirit has been and shall always remain a necessity for knowledge, but our epoch is, *par excellence,* one of synthesis. Never has the need for synthesis been more stringent than today. Otherwise, no guiding methodological principles could be elaborated, and the result would be empiricism with no epistemological foundations for new ideals of action. At the philosophical level, synthesis has not only a methodological and epistemological value but also an ethical value.

(2) Realization of a new aesthetic synthesis through a fertile dialogue with modern art, taking into account its most valuable achievements concerning the essentiality and constructiveness of the act of artistic modeling.

Philosophy and art meet and cooperate not only on the level of the ultimate crystallization of their efforts—the true and the beautiful—but also on the road leading to them.

(3) Realization of its mission of facilitating man's awareness of his own existence. We also need philosophy as an all-embracing human perspective in keeping with the new and dramatic dimensions of present civilization.

A social philosophy and an ethical philosophy expressing the self-consciousness of man and society today cannot be conceived outside the contact of philosophy with that huge laboratory which is the people's life of work and commitment, the great release of spiritual, rational, and effective energies of men who have set as their task to change the course of history and build a new spiritual civilization. Together with the other forms of culture, philosophy may help embellish everyone's daily life, so that people will be spared dullness, uniformity, and lack of scope, and their existence will acquire a profounder sense.

The intrinsic rationality of a system of civilization and humanistic philosophical consciousness help men increase the density not only of the technological environment, but also of the spiritual environment by creation of and aspiration to the ideal and by thought and action.

SELECT BIBLIOGRAPHY

BOOKS AND ARTICLES

Achim, I. *Introducere în estetica industrială* ("Introduction to Design") (Bucharest: Ştiinţifică i Enciclopedică, 1968).

Apostol, P. *Calitatea vieţii şi explorarea viitorului* ("Quality of Life and Exploration of the Future") (Bucharest: Politică, 1975).

————. *Probleme de logică dialectică în filosofia lui G. W. F. Hegel* ("Problems of Dialectical Logic in the Philosophy of G. W. F. Hegel"), 2 vols. (Bucharest: Academiei Republicii Socialiste Romania, 1957).

Bădărău, D. *G. W. Leibnitz* (Bucharest: Ştiinţifică i Enciclopedică, 1966).

Bălă, P. and Cheţan, O. *Mitul creştin. Filiaţii şi paralele* ("The Christian Myth. Origins and Parallels") (Bucharest: Enciclopedică Română, 1972).

Banu, I. *Filosofia orientului antic* ("The Philosophy of the Ancient East"), I (Bucharest: Ştiinţifică i Enciclopedică, 1967).

————. *Platon, heracliticul* ("Plato, the Heracletean") (Bucharest: Academiei Republicii Socialiste Romania, 1972).

Becleanu Iancu, A. *Geneza culturologiei româneşti* ("The Genesis of Romanian Culturology") (Jassy: Junimea, 1974).

Bellu, N. *Etica lui Kant* ("Kant's Ethic") (Bucharest: Ştiinţifică i Enciclopedică, 1973).

Berar, P. *Religia în lumea contemporană* ("Religion in the World Today") (Bucharest: Politică, 1976).

Bieltz, P. *Principiul dualităţii în logica formală* ("The Principle of Duality in Formal Logic") (Bucharest: Stiintifică i Enciclopedică, 1974).

Blaga, L. *Aspecte antropologice* ("Anthropological Aspects") (Timişoara: Facla, 1976).

————. *Despre conştiinţa filosofică* ("On the Philosophical Conscience") (Timişoara: Facla, 1974).

————. *Experimentul şi spiritul matematic* ("Experiment and the Mathematical Spirit") (Bucharest: Ştiinţifică i Enciclopedică, 1969).

Boboc, A. *Etică şi axiologie în opera lui Max Scheler* ("Ethics and Axiology in Max Scheler's Work") (Bucharest: Ştiinţifică i Enciclopedică, 1972).

————. *Kant şi neokantianismul* ("Kant and Neo-Kantianism") (Bucharest: Ştiinţifică i Enciclopedică, 1968).

————. *Nicolae Hartmann şi realismul contemporan* ("Nicolai Hartmann and Contemporary Realism") (Bucharest: Ştiinţifică i Enciclopedică, 1973).

Borgeanu, C. *Eseu despre progres* ("On Progress, an Essay") (Bucharest: Politică, 1969).

Botezatu, P. *Schiţa unei logici naturale. Logică operatorie* ("An Outline of a Natural Logic. Operational Logic") (Bucharest: Ştiinţifică i Enciclopedică, 1969).

———. *Valoarea deducţiei* ("On the Value of Deduction") (Bucharest: Stiinţifică i Enciclopedică, 1971).

Cazan, G. A. *Fundamentul filosofic la Mircea Florian* ("The Philosophical Foundation of Mircea Florian's Work") (Bucharest: Politică, 1971).

Dan, C. *Intuiţionismul lui Henri Bergsson în lumina contemporaneităţii* ("Henri Bergson's Intuitionism in the Light of Contemporaneity") (Bucharest: Stiinţifică i Enciclopedică, 1966).

———. *Neoraţionalismul* ("Neo-rationalism") (Bucharest: Stiinţifică i Enciclopedică, 1968).

Dumitriu, A. *A History of Logic*, 4 vols. (Forest Grove, Ore.: International Scholarly Book Services, 1977).

———. *Istoria logicii* ("A History of Logic"), 4 vols. (Bucharest: Stiinţifică i Enciclopedică, 1966).

———. *Philosophia mirabilis. Incercare asupra unei dimensiuni necunoscute a filosofiei greceşti* ("*Philosophia mirabilis*. An Attempt at an Unknown Dimension of Greek Philosophy") (Bucharest: Enciclopedică Română, 1974).

———. *Teoria logicii* ("The Theory of Logic") (Bucharest: Academiei Republicii Socialiste Romania, 1973).

Dumitru, N. S. *Sistem social. Praxis-Experiment* ("Social System. Praxis-Experiment") (Bucharest: Stiinţifică i Enciclopedică, 1975).

Duţu, A. *Sinteză şi originalitate în cultura română* ("Synthesis and Originality in Romanian Culture") (Bucharest: Minerva, 1974).

Enescu, G. *Introducere în logica matematică* ("Introduction to Mathematical Logic") (Bucharest: Stiinţifică i Enciclopedică, 1965).

———. *Logica simbolică* ("Symbolic Logic") (Bucharest: Stiinţifică i Enciclopedică, 1971).

Ernö, G. *Scrieri despre naţiune şi naţionalitate* ("Writings on the Nation and Nationality") [In Hungarian] (Bucharest: Kriterion, 1975).

Flonta, M. *Adevăruri necesare. Studiu monografic asupra analiticităţii* ("Necessary Truths. A Monographic Study of Analyticity") (Bucharest: Stiinţifică i Enciclopedică, 1975).

Florea, E. *Naţiunea română şi socialismul* ("The Romanian Nation and Socialism") (Bucharest: Academiei Republicii Socialiste Romania, 1974).

Florian, R. *Procese definitorii ale dezvoltării societăţii socialiste* ("Definitory Processes of the Development of Socialist Society") (Bucharest: Stiinţifică i Enciclopedică, 1975).

———. *Sensul istoriei. Insemnări pe marginea unei dezbateri filosofice contemporane* ("The Sense of History. Marginalia to a Contemporary Philosophical Debate") (Bucharest: Politică, 1968).

Frenkian, A. *Scepticismul grec şi filosofia indiană* ("Greek Scepticism and Indian Philosophy") (Bucharest: Academiei Republicii Socialiste Romania, 1957).

Ghişe, D. *Existenţialismul francez şi problemele eticii* ("French Existentialism and the Problems of Ethics") (Bucharest: Stiinţifică i Enciclopedică, 1967).

Ghiţă, S. *Filosofie şi ştiinţă in România (Problema ştiinţei în gîndirea filosofică, şi problema filosofice în gîndirea ştiinţifică)* ("Philosophy and Science in Romania. The Problem of Science in Philosophical Thought and Philosophical Problems in Scientific Thought") (Bucharest: Stiinţifică i Enciclopedică, 1970).

———. *Titu Maiorescu, filosof şi teoretician al culturii* ("Titu Maiorescu, a Philosopher and Theorist of Culture") (Bucharest: Stiinţifică i Enciclopedică, 1974).

Gogoneaţă, N. *Filosofia lui Vasile Conta* ("The Philosophy of Vasile Conta") (Bucharest: Stiinţifică i Enciclopedică, 1962).

——— and Ornea, Z. *A. D. Xenopol. Gîndirea socială şi filosofică* ("A. D. Xenopol. Social and Philosophical Thought") (Bucharest: Stiinţifică i Enciclopedică, 1965).

Grigoraş, I. *Principii de etică socialistă* ("Principles of Socialist Ethics") (Bucharest: Stiinţifică i Enciclopedică, 1974).

Grünberg, L. *Axiologia şi condiţia umană* ("Axiology and the Human Condition") (Bucharest: Politică, 1972).

Gulian, C. I. *Hegel and filosofia crizei* ("Hegel or the Philosophy of Crisis") (Bucharest: Academiei Republicii Socialiste Romania, 1970).

————. *Metodă sau sistem la Hegel* ("Method and System in Hegel's Work") (Bucharest: Academiei Republicii Socialiste Romania, 1957).

————. *Mit și cultură* ("Myth and Culture") (Bucharest: Politică, 1968).

Gulian, G. I. *Antropologie filosofică* ("Philosophical Anthropology") (Bucharest: Politică, 1972).

————. *Bazele istoriei și teoriei culturii* ("The Foundations of the History and Theory of Culture") (Bucharest: Academiei Republicii Socialiste Romania, 1975).

————. *Introducere în istoria filosofiei moderne* ("Introduction to the History of Modern Philosophy") (Bucharest: Enciclopedică Română, 1976).

Ianoși, I. *Dialectica și estetica* ("Dialectics and Aesthetics") (Bucharest: Stiințifică i Enciclopedică, 1971).

————. *Schița-pentru o estetică posibilă* ("An Outline of a Possible Aesthetics") (Bucharest: Mihai Eminescu, 1975).

Iliescu, I. *Geneza ideilor estitice în cultura românească* ("The Genesis of Aesthetic Ideas in Romanian Culture") (Timișoara: Facla, 1972).

Joja, A. *Studii de logică* ("Studies of Logic"), 4 vols. (Bucharest: Academiei Republicii Socialiste Romania, 1968–1976).

Joja, C. *Studii de filosofia științei* ("Studies of the Philosophy of Science") (Bucharest: Academiei Republicii Socialiste Romania, 1968).

Kallos, N. *Sociologie, politică, ideologie* ("Sociology, Politics, Ideology") (Timișoara: Facla, 1975).

———— and Roth, A. *Axiologie și etică* ("Axiology and Ethics") (Bucharest: Stiințifică i Enciclopedică, 1968).

Katz, A. *Dialectica în existență* ("Dialectics in Existence") (Bucharest: Stiințifică i Enciclopedică, 1972).

Mare, C. *Determinismul și fizica modernă* ("Determinism and Modern Physics") (Bucharest: Politică, 1966).

Mărgineanu, N. *Condiția umană. Aspectul bio-psiho-social și cultural* ("The Human Condition. The Bio-Psycho-Social and Cultural Aspect") (Bucharest: Stiințifică i Enciclopedică, 1973).

Mașek, V. E. *Artă și matematică* ("Art and Mathematics") (Bucharest: Politică, 1972).

————. *Mărturia artei. Eseu despre cunoașterea prin artă* ("The Testimony of Art. An Essay of Knowledge Through Art") (Bucharest: Academiei Republicii Socialiste Romania, 1972).

Matei, D. *Tradiție și inovație în artă* ("Tradition and Innovation in Art") (Bucharest: Academiei Republicii Socialiste Romania, 1971).

Micu, D. *Estetica lui Lucian Blaga* ("The Aesthetics of Lucian Blaga") (Bucharest: Stiințifică i Enciclopedică, 1970).

Miroș, L. *Etica neotomistă* ("Neo-Thomist Ethics") (Bucharest: Stiințifică i Enciclopedică, 1969).

————. *Intuiționismul etic—G. E. Moore* ("Ethical Intuitionism—G. E. Moore") (Bucharest: Stiințifică i Enciclopedică, 1973).

Mocanu, T. *Despre sublim* ("Concerning the Sublime") (Cluj: Dacia, 1970).

————. *Morfologia artei moderne* ("Morphology of Modern Art") (Bucharest: Meridiane, 1973).

Moisil, G. C. *Elemente de logică matematică și teoria mulțimilor* ("Elements of Mathematical Logic and Set Theory") (Bucharest: Stiințifică i Enciclopedică, 1968).

Nadin, M. *A trăi arta. Elemente de mataestetică* ("Living the Art. Elements of Meta-Aesthetics") (Bucharest: Mihai Eminescu, 1972).

Neagoe, F. *Arthur Schopenhauer—filosofia și etica* ("Arthur Schopenhauer—His Philosophy and Ethics") (Bucharest: Stiințifică i Enciclopedică, 1970).

Noica, C. *Rostirea filosofică românească* ("Romanian Philosophical Expression") (Bucharest: Stiințifică i Enciclopedică, 1970).

Onicescu, O. *Principes de logique et de philosophie methematique* ("Principles of Logic and the Philosophy of Mathematics") (Bucharest: Academiei Republicii Socialiste Romania, 1976).

Pantazi, R. *C. A. Rosetti, gînditorul, omul* ("C. A. Rosetti, the Thinker and the Man") (Bucharest: Politică, 1969).

314   Eastern Europe

————. *Filosofia marxistă în România* ("Marxist Philosophy in Romania") (Bucharest: Stiinţifică i Enciclopedică, 1965).

Pascadi, I. *Artă şi civilizaţie* ("Art and Civilization") (Bucharest: Meridiane, 1976).

————. *Destinul contemporan al artei* ("The Destiny of Art Today") (Bucharest: Meridiane, 1974).

Pătrăşcanu, L. *Curente şi tendinţe în filosofia românească* ("Currents and Trends in Romanian Philosophy") (Bucharest: Publicom, 1947).

Peatniţcki, I. *Determinismul în genetică şi fideismul contemporan* ("Determinism in Genetics and Fideism Today") (Bucharest: Politică, 1975).

Pîrvu, I. *Semantica şi logica ştiinţei* ("Semantics and the Logic of Science") (Bucharest: Socec, 1946).

Popa, C. *Teoria cunoaşterii. Perspectiva semioticopraxiologică asupra actului cunoaşterii* ("Theory of Knowledge. The Semiotic-Praxiological Outlook on the Act of Cognition") (Bucharest: Stiinţifică i Enciclopedică, 1972).

————. *Teoria definiţiei* ("Theory of Definition") (Bucharest: Stiinţifică i Enciclopedică, 1972).

Popescu, A. *Inceputuri ale filosofiei moderne. Bacon şi Descartes* ("The Beginnings of Modern Philosophy. Bacon and Descartes") (Bucharest: Stiinţifică i Enciclopedică, 1962).

————. *Platon. Filosofia dialogurilor* ("Plato. The Philosophy of Dialogues") (Bucharest: Stiinţifică i Enciclopedică, 1971).

Popescu, V. *Morala şi cunoaşterea ştiinţifică* ("Ethics and Scientific Knowledge") (Bucharest: Stiinţifică i Enciclopedică, 1974).

Răceanu, I. *Omul sub semnul posibilului* ("Man Under the Impact of the Possible") (Bucharest: Stiinţifică i Enciclopedică, 1974).

Ralea, M. *Explicarea omului* ("An Explanation of Man") (Bucharest: Cartea Românească, 1946).

Roşca, D. D. *Existenţa tragică* ("Tragic Existence") (Bucharest: Stiinţifică i Enciclopedică, 1968).

Rusu, L. *Logica frumosului* ("The Logic of the Beautiful") (Bucharest: Pentru Literatură Universală, 1968).

Smeu, G. *Relaţia social-autonom în artă* ("The Social-Autonomous Relationship in Art") (Bucharest: Academiei Republicii Socialiste Romania, 1976).

————. *Repere estetice în satul românesc contemporan* ("Aesthetic Landmarks in the Romanian Village Today") (Bucharest: Albatros, 1973).

Sommer, R. *Autonomia şi responsabilitatea în artă* ("Autonomy and Responsibility in Art") (Bucharest: Politică, 1969).

Stelian, S. *Etica durkheimistă* ("Durkheim's Ethics") (Bucharest: Stiinţifică i Enciclopedică, 1969).

Stere, E. *Din istoria doctrinelor morale* ("From the History of Ethical Doctrines") (Bucharest: Stiinţifică i Enciclopedică, 1975).

Stoichiţă, R. *Natura conceptului în logica lui Hegel* ("On the Nature of the Concept in Hegel's Logic") (Bucharest: Stiinţifică i Enciclopedică, 1972).

Tamas, S. *Cercetarea viitorului* ("Future Studies") (Bucharest: Politică, 1976).

————. *Progresul istoric şi contemporaneitatea* ("Historical Progress and Contemporaneity") (Bucharest: Politică, 1976).

Tănase, A. *Civilizaţia socialistă şi valorile ei* ("Socialist Civilization and Its Values") Coord. A. Tănase. (Bucharest: Stiinţifică i Enciclopedică, 1975).

————. *Confruntări despre om şi cultură* ("Confrontations on Man and Culture") (Bucharest: Academiei Republicii Socialiste Romania, 1972).

————. *Coordonate valorice ale civilizaţiei socialiste* ("Value Landmarks of Socialist Civilization"), Coords. A. Tănase and L. Miroş (Bucharest: Academiei Republicii Socialiste Romania, 1977).

————. *Cultură şi religie* ("Culture and Religion") (Bucharest: Politică, 1973).

————. *Cultura şi socialismul* ("Culture and Socialism"), Coord. A. Tănase (Bucharest: Stiinţifică i Enciclopedică, 1973).

————. *Cultura socialistă în România* ("Socialist Culture in Romania") Coords. A. Tănase and A. Becleanu Iancu (Bucharest: Politică, 1974).

————. *Introducere în filosofia culturii* ("Introduction to the Philosophy of Culture") (Bucharest: Stiinţifică i Enciclopedică, 1973).

Tertulian, N. *Artă şi comunicare* ("Art and Communication") (Bucharest: Meridiane, 1971).

————. *Artă şi realitate* ("Art and Reality") (Bucharest: Meridiane, 1971).

————. *Critică, estetică, filosofie* ("Criticism, Aesthetics, Philosophy") (Bucharest: Cartea Românească, 1972).

————. *Estetica filosofică şi ştiinţele artei* ("Philosophical Aesthetics and the Sciences of Art") (Bucharest: Stiinţifică i Enciclopedică, 1972).

————. *Esteticul în sfera culturii* ("The Aesthetic in the Realm of Culture") (Bucharest: Meridiane, 1976).

Tîrnoveanu, M. *Elemente de logică matematică* ("Elements of Mathematical Logic") (Bucharest: Didactică si Pedagogică, 1964).

Toma, G. *Xenopol despre logica istorei* ("Xenopol on the Logic of History") (Bucharest: Politică, 1971).

Tomoiagă, R. *Ion Heliade Rădulescu. Ideologia social-politică şi filosofia* ("Ion Heliade Rădulescu. Social-Political Ideology and Philosophy") (Bucharest: Stiinţifică i Enciclopedică, 1971).

Tonoiu, V. *Idoneismul, filosofie a deschiderii. Studiu asupra gîndirii lui Ferdinand Gonseth* ("Idoneism, a Philosophy of the Opening. A Study of Ferdinand Gonseth's Thought") (Bucharest: Politică, 1972).

————. *Spiritul ştiinţific modern în viziunea lui G. Bachelard* ("The Modern Scientific Spirit in G. Bachelard's Vision") (Bucharest: Stiinţifică i Enciclopedică, 1974).

Trandafoiu, N. *Aspecte din filosofia contemporană* ("Aspects of Contemporary Philosophy") (Bucharest: Academiei Republicii Socialiste Romania, 1970).

————. *Studii de istorie a filosofiei universale* ("Studies of the History of Universal Philosophy") (Bucharest: Academiei Republicii Socialiste Romania, 1969–1976).

————. *Substanţa şi cauzalitatea în interpretarea empirismului englez* ("Substance and Causality in the Interpretation of English Empiricism") (Cluj: Dacia, 1975).

Trăsnea, O. *Stiinţa politică. Studiu istorico-epistemologic* ("Political Science. A Historical Epistemological Study") (Bucharest: Politică, 1970).

Tudosescu, I. *Determinismul şi ştiinţa* ("Determinism and Science") (Bucharest: Stiinţifică i Enciclopedică, 1971).

————. *Structura acţiunii sociale. Schiţă a unei praxeologii materialist-dialectice* ("The Structure of Social Action. An Outline of a Dialectical-Materialistic Praxiology") (Bucharest: Politică, 1972).

Tuţugan, F. *Silogistica judecăţilor de predicaţie; contribuţii, adaosuri şi rectificări la silogistica clasică* ("The Syllogistic of Predication Judgments; Contributions, Addenda and Rectifications to Classical Syllogistic") (Bucharest: Academiei Republicii Socialiste Romania, 1957).

Vaida, P. *Curente şi orientări în istoria filosofiei româneşti* ("Currents and Trends in the History of Romanian Philosophy") (Bucharest: Academiei Republicii Socialiste Romania, 1967).

————. *Dimitrie Cantemir şi umanismul* ("Dimitrie Cantemir and Humanism") (Bucharest: Minerva, 1972).

————. *Din istoria filosofiei în România* ("From the History of Romanian Philosophy"), 3 vols. (Bucharest: Academiei Republicii Socialiste Romania, 1955–1960).

————. *Istoria filosofiei româneţi* ("The History of Romanian Philosophy," I, ed. Gogoneaţă (Bucharest: Academiei Republicii Socialiste Romania, 1972).

Vieru, S. *Axiomatizări şi modele ale sistemelor silogistice* ("Axiomatizations and Models of Syllogistic Systems") (Bucharest: Academiei Republicii Socialiste Romania, 1957).

————. *Probleme de logică* ("Problems of Logic"), 6 vols. (Bucharest: Academiei Republicii Socialiste Romania, 1968–1976).

Vlad, C. *Eseuri despre naţiune* ("Essays on the Nation") (Bucharest: Politică, 1971).

Vlăduţescu, G. *Ethos şi contemporaneitate* ("Ethos and Contemporaneity"), ed. Bellu (Bucharest: Stiinţifică i Enciclopedică, 1972).

————. *Etica lui Epicur* ("Epicurus' Ethics") (Bucharest: Stiinţifică i Enciclopedică, 1972).
————. *Introducere în istoria filosofiei medievale* ("Introduction to the History of Medieval Philosophy") (Bucharest: Enciclopedică Română, 1973).
————. *Tineretul şi idealul moral. Contribuţii la cercetarea problemei* ("Youth and the Ethical Ideal. Contributions to the Study of the Problem") (Bucharest: Academiei Republicii Socialiste Romania, 1969).
Wald, H. *Dialectica cunoaşterii ştiinţifice. Studii.* ("The Dialectic of Scientific Knowledge. Studies") (Bucharest: Academiei Republicii Socialiste Romania, 1962).
————. *Existenţă, cunoaştere, acţiune. Dialog şi confruntări în filosofia contemporană* ("Existence, Cognition and Action. Dialogue and Confrontations in Philosophy Today"), Coord. C. Popa (Bucharest: Stiinţifică i Enciclopedică, 1971).
————. *Materialismul dialectic şi ştiinţele moderne* ("Dialectical Materialism and the Modern Sciences"), 16 vols. (Bucharest: Politică, 1957–1975).
————. *Orientări contemporane în teoria cunoaşterii* ("Contemporary Orientations in the Theory of Cognition"), Coord. H. Wald (Bucharest: Academiei Republicii Socialiste Romania, 1976).
————. *Realitatea şi limbaj* ("Reality and Language") (Bucharest: Academiei Republicii Socialiste Romania, 1968).
————. *Teorie şi metodă în ştiinţele sociale* ("Theory and Method in the Social Sciences"), 10 vols. (Bucharest: Politică, 1965–1976).

JOURNALS

Annales de Philosophie
Noesis
Philosophic Studies and Scientific Socialism
Revue Romaine des Science Sociales, Serie de Philosophie et Logique
Revista de Filozofie
Revue des Sciences Sociales
Studia Universitatis "Babes-Bolyai," Series Philosphia
Studies of Philosophy and Scientific Socialism

Union of Soviet Socialist Republics

THOMAS J. BLAKELEY

Contemporary Soviet philosophy is unique in many respects, not the least of which is the fact that it can give an exact date of birth to itself—June 24, 1947. This was the day that Stalin's son-in-law, A. Zhdanov, passed down the word from on high that Soviet philosophers were to stop their scholastic discussions on ''safe'' topics, to emulate the ''Leninist style'' of philosophizing, and in general to be ''more creative.''[1]

To put this birthday in a proper perspective, we will first take a brief look at pre-1947 Soviet philosophy. Then we will deal in order with the following themes: the general traits of contemporary Soviet philosophy; its sources; how it views philosophy; the fate of individual philosophic disciplines in the Soviet Union, with particular focus on the historiography of philosophy; and finally, prospects for further evolution within contemporary Soviet philosophy.

PRE-1947 SOVIET PHILOSOPHY

Soviet philosophy was born in the turmoil of revolution; from the seizure of power (1917) to its consolidation (1921), little or no philosophizing was going on.

The first or ''creative'' period in Soviet philosophy runs from the establishment of the periodical *Under the Banner of Marxism*[2] in 1922 to the condemnation of the ''mensheviking idealists'' in 1931.[3] The two salient traits of this period are the gradual exclusion of all ''bourgeois'' philosophers and a great deal of creative infighting among the three leading interpretations of Marxism-Leninism: the ''mechanists'' (Bukharin, Axelrod et al.), the ''mensheviking idealists'' (Deborin, Trotsky et al.), and the ''orthodox'' (M. B. Mitin et al.).

The condemnation of 1931 issued in the so-called dead period—a time of increasing polarization of Soviet philosophy toward ever greater adultation of Stalin as *the* philosopher—which lasted through World War II and ended in the ''discussion'' of 1947.[4]

THE GENERAL TRAITS OF CONTEMPORARY SOVIET PHILOSOPHY[5]

The primary thrust of contemporary Soviet philosophy, as of Soviet philosophy in general, is the importance it has within the overall framework of Marxist ideology and communist politics. There is no contemporary philosophical attitude that is more highly valued by its proponents than Soviet philosophy is by communists the world over. This is due to a great extent to the famous Marxian principle of the "unity of theory and practice," but it is also due to the social cohesiveness that commitment to this theory provides.

Soviet philosophy is both dogmatic and theological, traits, which for many non-Marxist-Leninists constitute proof that it is not a philosophy in any acceptable meaning of the word. Contemporary Soviet philosophers are far less slavish in their use of the "classics" (Marx, Engels, Lenin, and, until his death, Stalin) than were their predecessors. However, the principle remains the same: namely, all the statements of Marx, Engels, and Lenin have axiomatic value, subject to interpretation only under very carefully controlled conditions.

Soviet philosophy is partisan and in two senses. First, partisanship means that what the non-Marxist-Leninist calls scientific objectivity is dysfunctional. Everything of importance (including, therefore, philosophy) is a matter of class war and consequently has to be viewed from the perspective of one's class. Even more concretely, however, partisanship here means direct control by the Communist party over the activity of contemporary Soviet philosophers. The party decides when meetings will be held and where; what will be discussed and for how long; and what the final outcome will be.

Contemporary Soviet philosophy is polemical and aggressive, especially as regards what they so affectionately call "foreign" philosophy. It is true that most contemporary Soviet philosophers no longer use the strong language that made them so infamous in their childhood—the West was referred to as the "cesspool of bourgeois decadence"; non-Marxist-Leninist philosophers were "running dogs of imperialism" and "toadies of the Vatican." However, they are still very aggressive, conceiving philosophy in terms of "militant stance" and "defensive posture," and of "philosophical class-enemies."[6]

THE SOURCES OF CONTEMPORARY SOVIET PHILOSOPHY

Marx, Engels, and Lenin all read Hegel, and all claimed to be "materialist" in some sense. Marx read widely in political economy, anthropology, and history. Engels attended the lectures of the very old Schelling, was fascinated by natural science, and had a somewhat populist version of socialism. Lenin stood consciously in the Russian revolutionary tradition, read some Aristotle, and was heavily indebted for his philosophical formation—such as it was—to Plekhanov.

Feuerbach and a series of French socialist theoreticians also contributed to the formation of the foundational heritage.

Contemporary Soviet philosophy, although it sometimes calls itself "Marxist," is Marxism-*Leninism* precisely because it is made up of the central ideas of Marx, reseen and domesticated for the Russian context by Lenin. Lenin performed this revision and domestication in his philosophical writings, the main ones being *Materialism and Empirio-Criticism* and the *Philosophical Notebooks.*[7] These two works are central to all Soviet philosophizing.

Next in order of importance are Engels' *Dialectics of Nature, Anti-Dühring,* and *Ludwig Feuerbach.*[8] Whereas the works of Lenin are important for dealing with problems of dialectics, materialism, knowledge, and the like, those of Engels serve to inspire contemporary Soviet philosophy in matters of science, anthropology, and the conflict with nineteenth-century idealism.

Finally and somewhat ironically, there are the works of Marx. From the outside, one could get the impression that the powers that be in the Soviet Union have done their best to keep "Marxist" philosophers away from Marx except as "sanitized" by Lenin. Until quite recently, the works of the "early Marx" were off-limits in the Soviet Union, and even *Capital* was discussed only in terms of carefully selected passages, passages which, of course, had been "treated" by Lenin. It is only since the early 1960s that the whole of Marx's literary production has become the object of research in the Soviet Union.[9]

THE NATURE OF PHILOSOPHY ACCORDING TO MARXISM-LENINISM

Because it is dogmatic and theological, contemporary Soviet philosophy can be easily expressed in catechetical form, i.e., in the form of apodictic theses which are derived either from the "classics" or from what the Marxist-Leninists call the "triumphal progress of modern science."

Marxism-Leninism is made up of theory and practice (the party). Marxist-Leninist theory is, in turn, made up of philosophy, political economy, and scientific socialism. Marxist-Leninist philosophy is defined as the study of the most general laws of nature, society, and human thought, and has as its parts dialectical and historical materialism.

For dialectical materialism all is matter; all matter is in motion; all matter in motion occurs in space and time (the "existential conditions" of all matter); and all motion is dialectical, meaning that it occurs in conformity with the three basic laws of the dialectic—the law of unity and conflict of contraries, the law of transition from quantitative change to qualitative change, and the law of negation of negation. Dialectical materialism's theory of knowledge is called the "Leninist theory of reflection," and sees consciousness as an attribute of highly organized matter, as function of the "dialectic of the absolute and relative," the "dialectic of the logical and the historical," and "practice as basis of knowledge and criterion of truth."[10]

Historical materialism is that part of contemporary Soviet philosophy which consists in the application of the laws and categories of dialectical materialism to the study of the most general laws of human society and history. The ground of human society and history is material production, which is intelligible through the dialectical relations between the forces of production (tools, raw materials, and the like) and the relations of production. It is the character of the forces of production that determines the character of the relations of production which constitute the "base" of society vis-à-vis its "superstructure." The superstructure is made up of legal and political theories, institutions, on the one hand, and philosophy, art, and religion, on the other. Just as, in dialectical materialism, thought is the reflection of matter, so in historical materialism social thought ("superstructure" or "ideology") reflects social being (forces and relations of production).

Following Engels, contemporary Soviet philosophy defines the basic question of philosophy as the question as to the relationship between thought and being between spirit and nature, i.e., which of the two is primary. There are only two answers to this question—that of the materialists and that of the idealists. The materialists make matter primary and thought secondary (or derivative); the idealists make thought primary and matter secondary; a dualistic compromise is contradictory and nonsensical.

RECENT DEVELOPMENTS IN PARTICULAR PHILOSOPHICAL DISCIPLINES

We will make no effort here at complete characterization of all the recent developments in contemporary Soviet philosophy. The reader will find such completeness in the works cited in the Notes and in the bibliography.[11] Instead, we will limit ourselves here to four areas of philosophic concern, where recent developments serve to illustrate the peculiar problems facing the contemporary Soviet philosopher. The four areas are logic, ethics, psychology, and historiography of philosophy. In each of these areas, we will open with a short description of the *status quo ante*, which will serve as background for understanding recent developments.

Logic, although it had been of importance to his mentor Hegel, did not occupy Marx to any great extent, nor did Engels or Lenin pay any great attention to it. As a matter of fact, logic was not at the forefront of anyone's philosophic concern during much of the nineteenth century and even well into the first third of the present century, until the emergence of the Vienna Circle and its sequels.

No wonder, then, that logical questions emerged for contemporary Soviet philosophy tardily and in a very peculiar fashion. Much of the advance in modern logic has been intimately tied up with technological progress and with the high-speed mathematical calculations it needs. However, since the "classics" had

had little to say on the subject, there was a need to proceed cautiously in the integration and definition of this new involvement. The first effort on the part of contemporary Soviet philosophers was to sanitize modern formal logic by pointing out that Engels had settled the matter by designating formal logic for "kitchen use," within the overall context of "dialectical logic." This effort issued in a discussion among three schools: dialectical and formal logic are distinct disciplines; dialectical logic dictates to formal logic; there is but formal logic and, if there is a dialectical logic, it can only be a subset within formal logic.

This discussion might have gone on forever were it not for an unforeseen and peculiar outcome of the very event that had given impetus to the whole discussion. Stalin's "Letters on the Linguistic Question"[12] had established that language did not belong to superstructure but to base. If language did not belong to superstructure, it did not fall under the party's ideological control, i.e., it was not subject to partisanship in the ordinary way. Stalin's philosophical minions hastened to point out that logic is a matter of language and, therefore, also to be "de-class-ified" in the same way, along with all the technological applications of logical devices.

The upshot was that formal logicians gradually gained the freedom to develop their subject as they saw fit, free of the interference of the dialecticians, and that dialectical logic came back to meaning what it did for Hegel; i.e., a species of ontology.

Ethics could not help being a major concern of Soviet philosophy, if only because Marxism began as a moral outrage against the evils of capitalism. Early Soviet philosophy paid attention to matters of morals and value almost exclusively from the pedagogical, Krupskajan viewpoint. An important component of this early ethical concern was opposition to religious morality in the form of a militant atheism.

World War II brought with it compromise with religion and, consequently, less emphasis on the contrast between religious morality and communist ethics. However, Marxist-Leninist ethics as such took shape only during the 1950s, in the form of a rather trite, anti-Kantian, conventional set of rules—rules for the behavior of the "good communist."

Several novelties have appeared in Soviet ethics as it is currently being developed. In the first place, contemporary Soviet philosophers have developed a commitment to providing for the "moral profile" of the "builder of communism." What is more, they are tending to lose their inferiority complex vis-à-vis religion and competing ethical systems in the West. Finally, there is a growing sense of being able to predict with some concreteness the value-structure of the coming communist society.

Psychology is a richly developed sector of Soviet philosophic concern, conditioned by the "Leninist theory of reflection" and by the early Soviet toleration of Pavlov.

As must be the case for any materialism, dialectical materialism has its hands full when it comes to explaining how there can be thinking when all is matter, or how the materiality of matter relates to the materiality of thinking, whatever that might mean. The resulting series of discussions around the problem of psychophysical parallelism has already been well documented.[13]

What has been happening most recently to psychological theory within the context of contemporary Soviet philosophy depends to a large extent on developments in other disciplines. Thus, progress in physiology in the Soviet Union has been spilling over into perception theory. Concrete sociological research—as problematic as it might be in and of itself—has been supplying data for attitudinal studies, although behavioral research still must be carefully camouflaged in the Soviet Union.

Historiography of philosophy has always been an integral part of Soviet philosophy, both because of its polemical and aggressive stance and because of the exclusivity that follows from its dogmatic and scholastic character.

The earliest technique to appear is Lenin's "quote and club." One takes a carefully groomed passage as the whole of the other's position and then one hammers away at the weakness of this position, using invective, irony, and the like. Of course, contemporary Soviet philosophers have an advantage over Lenin, in that they are able to use the works of the "classics" as absolute indictments of anyone who disagrees with them.

Another early technique is "guilt by association." Lenin uses this technique very effectively, associating his enemies with Mach, Avenarius, Kant, Hegel, and so on, after having established the obvious erroneousness of these thinkers' views. Again, the Soviet philosophers enjoy the distinct advantage of having a whole series of predesignated enemies—predesignated in the works of Marx, Engels, and Lenin. Thus, all one need do is show how a given philosopher's views are identical to those of someone already condemned by Lenin, and so on.

The most powerful weapon in the contemporary Soviet arsenal when it comes to the historiography of philosophy is the rigid classification of philosophers and philosophies according to materialism and idealism (with no middle road possible). Contemporary Soviet philosophers further specify idealists as "subjective" if they hold the spirit which has priority to exist solely in the mind, or "objective" if they hold that spirit to exist outside of the mind (e.g., God). They further specify materialists as "mechanist" if they are like Democritus, or "dialectical" if they have the truth. Further, philosophical methodology is either "metaphysical" or "dialectical."

Most recently, contemporary Soviet philosophers have devoted themselves to more extensive research on all pre-Marxist and non-Marxist philosophers. Instead of quoting just enough to club, they provide longer quotations and use these for sometimes quite sophisticated commentaries and interpretations. Thus, for example, there have recently arisen two schools of Hegelian interpretation—one at Alma-Ata, the other at Tiflis—which can hold their own with works on Hegel being published outside the Soviet Union.

There is also more attention to details in distinguishing the "philosophical class-enemies," so that Thomas Aquinas and Bertrand Russell are no longer lumped together as "objective idealists," and Husserl and Sartre are no longer seen as identical.

PROSPECTS

In addition to the elements of progress noted above, we might indicate the following as developments to watch over the next decade of philosophic activity in the Soviet Union:

—The "Prague Spring" with its "socialism with a human face" provided an impetus which has carried Soviet philosophy into the whole new field of the "scientific-technological revolution."

—More and more studies are devoted to "categories" in almost all philosophical domains; the resulting clarity will threaten many well-established Soviet positions.

—Discussions have become more and more institutionalized, so that the party tends to have less direct influence on the day-to-day carrying out of philosophical work.

—Many of the dominant figures in contemporary Soviet philosophy have died recently, making room for new faces.

—More and more serious philosophical works are coming out of the provinces, i.e., there is a centrifugal development of emphasis away from Moscow and toward places like Tiflis and Kiev.

—Finally, *samizdat* and the emigration of some of the best minds is not a simple matter of Soviet anti-Semitism; it has the net effect of intimidating anyone who might be tempted to come out with an original thought.

NOTES

1. For full details on the history of Soviet philosophy and on points of Marxist-Leninist doctrine, see G. Wetter, *Dialectical Materialism* and J. M. Bocheński, *Soviet Russian Dialectical Materialism*.
2. *Pod znamenem marksizma* (1922–1944), replaced by *Voprosy filosofii* (1947–   ).
3. Compare D. Joravsky, *Soviet Marxism and Natural Science 1917–1932*.
4. On the discussion, see the first issue of *Voprosy filosofii*, as well as Wetter and Bocheński above.
5. Compare Bocheński, *Soviet Russian Dialectical Materialism*, pp. 43–56.
6. Détente has in no way affected this state of affairs.
7. The former exists in English by International Publishers (1970); the latter, by the Foreign Languages Publishing House (1961).
8. The first and second in English by International Publishers, 1964 and 1959, respectively; the full title of the latter is *Herr Eugen Dühring's Revolution in Science*. The last was done in English in 1941 by the same publishing house, with the title *Ludwig Feuerbach and the Outcome of Classical German Philosophy*.
9. Soviet Marxologists have recently been concentrating on the "logic of *Capital*"; compare *Studies in Soviet Thought* 14, No. 1/2 (1974): 167–172. See also *Studies in Soviet Thought* 16, No. 3/4 (1976), devoted to *Capital*.

10. Compare T. Blakely, *Soviet Theory of Knowledge* and K. G. Ballestrem, *Die sowjetische Erkenntnismetaphysik und ihr Verhältnis zu Hegel.*

11. See the thirty-eight volumes of the *Soveitica* series (see the bibliography), the quarterly *Studies in Soviet Thought* (since 1961), and the *Bibliographie der sowjetsichen Philosophie* (seven volumes, plus current lists in *Studies in Soviet Thought*).

12. Compare *Marxism and Linguistics.*

13. Cf. T. R. Payne, *S. L. Rubinštejn and the Philosophical Foundations of Soviet Psychology.*

SELECT BIBLIOGRAPHY

BOOKS AND ARTICLES

Ballestrem, K. G. *Die sowjetische Erkenntnismetaphysik und ihr Verhältnis zu Hegel,* Sovietica Series 27 (Dordrecht and Boston: Reidel, 1968).

————. *Russian Philosophical Terminology,* Sovietica Series 19 (Dordrecht and Boston: Reidel, 1964).

Birjukov, B. V. *Two Soviet Studies on Frege,* trans. and ed. I. Angelelli, Sovietica Series 15 (Dordrecht and Boston: Reidel, 1964).

Blakeley, T. J. *Soviet Philosophy. A General Introduction to Contemporary Soviet Thought,* Sovietica Series 18 (Dordrecht and Boston: Reidel, 1964).

————. *Soviet Scholasticism,* Sovietica Series 6 (Dordrecht and Boston: Reidel, 1961).

————. *Soviet Theory of Knowledge,* Sovietica Series 16 (Dordrecht and Boston: Reidel, 1964).

———— (ed.). *Themes in Soviet Marxist Philosophy. Selected Articles from the "Filosofskaja Enciklopedija,"* Sovietica Series 37 (Dordrecht and Boston: Reidel, 1975).

Bocheński, J. M. *Die dogmatischen Grundlagen der sowjetischen Philosophie (Stand 1958) Zusammenfassung der "Osnovy Marksistskoj Filosofii" mit Register,* Sovietica Series 3 (Dordrecht and Boston: Reidel, 1959).

————. *Soviet Russian Dialectical Materialism (Diamat),* trans. N. Sollohub and rev. after 3d ed., T. J. Blakeley (Dordrecht and Boston: Reidel, 1963).

————. *The Dogmatic Principles of Soviet Philosophy (as of 1958),* Synopsis of the *Osnovy Marksistskoj Filosofii,* trans. T. J. Blakeley, Sovietica Series 14 (Dordrecht and Boston: Reidel, 1963).

———— and Blakeley, T. J. (eds.). *Bibliographie der sowjetischen Philosophie* ("Bibliography of Soviet Philosophy"), 7 vols., Sovietica Series 1, 2, 9, 10, 17, 28, 29 (Dordrecht and Boston: Reidel, 1959).

———— and Blakeley, T. J. (eds.). *Studies in Soviet Thought I,* Sovietica Series 7 (Dordrecht and Boston: Reidel, 1961).

———— et al. (eds.). *Guide to Marxist Philosophy. An Introductory Bibliography* (Chicago: Swallow Press, 1972).

Boeselager, W. F. *The Soviet Critique of Neopositivism. The History and Structure of the Critique of Logical Positivism and Related Doctrines by Soviet Philosophers in the Years 1947–1967,* trans. T. J. Blakeley, Sovietica Series 35 (Dordrecht and Boston: Reidel, 1975).

Dahm, H. *Vladimir Solovyev and Max Scheler: Attempt at a Comparative Interpretation. A Contribution to the History of Phenomenology,* trans. K. Wright, Sovietica Series 34 (Dordrecht and Boston: Reidel, 1975).

De George, R. T. and Scanlan, J. P. (eds.). *Marxism and Religion in Eastern Europe,* Sovietica Series 36 (Dordrecht and Boston: Reidel, 1976).

Engels, F. *Anti-Dühring: Herr Eugen Dühring's Revolution in Science* (New York: International Publishers, 1959).

————. *Dialectics of Nature* (New York: International Publishers, 1964).

————. *Ludwig Feuerbach and the Outcome of Classical German Philosophy* (New York: International Publishers, 1941).

Filosofskaja enciklopedija, 6 vols., ed. F. V. Konstantinov et al. (Moscow: "Soviet Excyclopedia" Publishing House, 1960–1970).

Fleischer, H. *Kleines Textbuch der kommunistischen Ideologie. Auszüge aus dem Lehrbuch "Osnovy marksizmaleninizma" mit Register*, Sovietica Series 11 (Dordrecht and Boston: Reidel, 1963).

————. *Short Handbook of Communist Ideology* Synopsis of the *Osnovy marksizma-leninizma*, trans. T. J. Blakeley, Sovietica Series 20 (Dordrecht and Boston: Reidel, 1965).

Gavin, W. J. and Blakeley, T. J. *Russia and America: A Philosophical Comparison*, Sovietica Series 38 (Dordrecht and Boston: Reidel, 1976).

Isotoria Filosofii, 6 vols. ed. M. A. Dynnik (Moscow: Akademii Nauk USSR Institut filosofi, 1957–1965).

Joravski, D. *Soviet Marxism and Natural Science 1917–1932* (London: Routledge and Kegan Paul, 1961).

Kirschenmann, P. K. *Information and Reflection on Some Problems of Cybernetics and how Contempoary Dialectical Materialism Copes with Them*, trans. T. J. Blakeley, Sovietica Series 31 (Dordrecht and Boston: Reidel, 1970).

Lachs, J. *Marxist Philosophy. A Bibliographical Guide* (Chapel Hill, N.C.: University of North Carolina Press, 1967).

Laszlo, E. *The Communist Ideology in Hungary. Handbook for Basic Research*, Sovietica Series 23 (Dordrecht and Boston: Reidel, 1966).

———— (ed.). *Philosophy in the Soviet Union. A Survey of the Mid-Sixties*, Sovietica Series 25 (Dordrecht and Boston: Reidel, 1967).

Lenin, N. *Materialism and Empirio-Criticism* (New York: International Publishers, 1970).

————. *Philosophical Notebooks* (Moscow: Foreign Languages Publishing House, 1961).

Lobkowicz, N. *Das Widerspruchsprinzip in der neueren sowjetischen Philosophie*, Sovietica Series 4 (Dordrecht and Boston: Reidel, 1960).

————. *Marxismus-Leninismus in der ČSR. Die tschechoslowakische Philosophie seit 1945*, Sovietica Series 8 (Dordrecht and Boston: Reidel, 1962).

Marx, K. *Capital*, 3 vols. (New York: International Publishers, 1967).

Müller-Markus, S. *Einstein und die Sowjetsphilosophie Krisis einer Lehre*, 2 vols., Sovietica Series 5 and 22 (Dordrecht and Boston: Reidel, 1960–1966), I *Die Grundlagen: Die Spezielle Relativitätstheorie; II Die allgemeine Relativitätstheorie.*

O'Rourke, J. J. *The Problem of Freedom in Marxist Thought. An Analysis of the Treatment of Human Freedom by Marx, Engels, Lenin and Contemporary Soviet Philosophy*, Sovietica Series 32 (Dordrecht and Boston: Reidel, 1974).

Payne, T. R. *S. L. Rubinštejn and the Philosophical Foundations of Soviet Psychology*, Sovietica Series 30 (Dordrecht and Boston: Reidel, 1968).

Planty-Bonjour, G. *Les catégories du matérialisme dialectique. L'ontologie soviétique contemporaine*, Sovietica Series 21 (Dordrecht and Boston: Reidel, 1965).

————. *The Categories of Dialectical Materialism. Contemporary Soviet Ontology*, trans. T. J. Blakeley, Sovietica Series 24 (Dordrecht and Boston: Reidel, 1967).

Rapp, F. *Gesetz und Determination in der Sowjetphilosophie. Zur Gesetzeskonzeption des dialektischen Materialismus unter besonderer Berücksichtigung der Diskussion über dynamische und statistiche Gesetzmäszigkeit in der zeitgenössischen Sowjetphilosophie*, Sovietica Series 26 (Dordrecht and Boston: Reidel, 1968).

Sarlemijn, A. *Hegel's Dialectic*, trans. P. Kirschenmann, Sovietica Series 33 (Dordrecht and Boston: Reidel, 1975).

Stalin, J. "Letters on the Linguistic Question," in *Marxism and Linguistics* (New York: International Publishers, 1951).

Vrtačič, L. *Einführung in den jugoslawischen Marxismus-Leninismus. Organisation/Bibliographie*, Sovietica Series 13 (Dordrecht and Boston: Reidel, 1963).

Wetter, G. *Dialectical Materialism: A Historical and Systematic Survey of Philosophy in the Soviet Union* (London: Routledge and Kegan Paul, 1958).

JOURNALS

Filosofskie nauki
Pod znamenem markiszma
Studies in Soviet Thought
Voprosy filosofii

Part III: The Americas

Canada

In 1945, Canada had few professional philosophers and very few programs for training more. Although a number of Canadian universities were empowered to grant the doctorate, only the University of Laval, the University of Montreal, and the University of Toronto awarded it regularly to students of philosophy. Most Canadians pursuing a higher degree in the field went to Great Britain, France, Belgium, Germany, or the United States. In matters of philosophy, many Canadian universities drew their syllabi, teachers, and ideas largely from a "mother country."

The end of World War II brought swelling enrollments and a new political concern for the universities which found systematic expression in the 1951 Report of the Massey Royal Commission. This document made clear the desire of a growing number of Canadian leaders for federal support of higher education. The commission also presented several specific proposals. One major recommendation, that the federal government provide grants to the provincial universities so that funds might be proportionate to the population of each province, was implemented in 1951. A second, that the federal government create a permanent national foundation which would support the arts and humanities, was implemented in 1957 when the death duties of Izaak Walton Killam and Sir James Dunn were combined with a parliamentary grant to finance the Canada Council. These two policies made possible not only the rapid growth of graduate programs in philosophy during the 1960s, but also the emergence of nationally accredited philosophical societies and journals.

In 1962, the Canadian Philosophical Associates (CPA) emerged as one of the federally subsidized learned societies. Its constitution provides that the president of the association will for one year be a scholar whose "first language" is French, the next year another whose "first language is English. (English and French are legally acknowledged as the two official languages of Canada.) Other officers and directors are chosen to provide linguistic, regional, and cultural balance. Such clear arrangements for sharing power and representation distinguish the CPA's policies from those of most philosophical groups in other countries. The association's official organ *Dialogue,* first edited by Venant Cauchy of the University of Montreal and Martyn Estall of Queen's University, offers equal space to French and English articles, discussions, and reviews. The association holds annual congresses in May or June of each year with sessions in each language and a number of bilingual sessions.

Greatly increased federal and provincial support as well as a buoyant Canadian economy made possible the very rapid expansion of undergraduate and graduate education during the 1960s. The number of universities in the country almost doubled. Whereas in 1945 only three Canadian universities regularly granted the doctorate in philosophy, active doctoral programs now exist in Quebec at Laval, the University of Montreal and McGill, in Ontario at the bilingual University of Ottawa, at Queen's University, the University of Western Ontario, Waterloo University, York University, and the University of Toronto. Ontario also offers a joint program operated by the University of Guelph and McMaster University. In western Canada, doctoral programs in philosophy are provided by the University of Alberta and the University of Calgary and by the University of British Columbia. A number of other departments of philosophy prepare students for the M.A.

This rapid growth of programs has been matched by an increase in the number of learned journals that carry philosophical material and are edited by Canadians. Besides *Dialogue,* now edited by François Duchesneau and John Woods, one finds the *Canadian Journal of Philosophy* (edited from the universities of Alberta and Calgary), *Philosophiques* (founded by Yvon Lafrance, now the organ of the Societé de Philosophie du Québec), the *Journal of Philosophical Logic* (edited by Bas van Fraassen at the University of Toronto), *Laval Théologique-Philosophique, Philosophy of the Social Sciences* (edited by I. C. Jarvie and several colleagues at York University), *Science et Esprit* (edited by the Society of Jesus in Montreal), and *Studies in Religion/Sciences Religeuses* (edited by William Nicholls at the University of British Columbia). The surge of philosophical publication has other Canadian outlets. *Phoenix,* which is the journal of the Canadian Classical Association and is edited by T. M. Robinson at the University of Toronto, publishes a good deal of work on ancient philosophy, and *Mediaeval Studies,* edited by J. Reginald O'Donnell at the Pontifical Institute of Mediaeval Studies, publishes much on medieval philosophy. Such periodicals as *Queen's Quarterly, University of Toronto Quarterly,* the *Dalhousie Review,* and *Revue de l'Université d'Ottawa* help to bring philosophy into the broader cultural life of Canada.

The expansion of the 1960s has been followed by a period of "retrenchment." Student enrollment has not risen as fast as had been predicted, and the expansion of Canadian doctoral programs no longer corresponds to a growing need for more professors. Because Canadian governments and industry do not regard doctoral training in philosophy as a valuable asset, and because many doctoral students are reluctant to abandon the dream of an academic career, the new economic climate has produced growing "underemployment" and some unemployment among recent Ph.D.s. This situation is exacerbated by Canada's policy of willingly granting work permits to foreign scholars, a policy that is not reciprocated by several of her major trading partners. The last few years have also been difficult ones for Canadian federalism and have raised serious questions about the very possibility of a bilingual and multicultural Canadian philosophical environment. Yet, cooperation among philosophers from different regions and language communities continues to increase.

Anglophone Philosophy

JOHN   KING-FARLOW
AND ·CALVIN   G.   NORMORE

As George Grant has emphasized (for example, in his article "Philosophy" in the *Encyclopedia Canadiana*), philosophy has never been central to creative intellectual and cultural life in anglophone Canada. Nineteenth-century pioneers were too busy with the questions of survival and economic expansion, and most of our twentieth-century intellectuals have focused their attention elsewhere. But anglophone philosophy in Canada does have a distinctive history. It began as a handmaiden to theology; it later became autonomous through careful study of the history of philosophy; later still, it turned to ethics and to social and political philosophy, to critical analyses of theism, and, most recently, to original work in the philosophy of science, logic, metaphysics, the philosophy of language, and the philosophy of mind.

The abundance and variety of recent anglophone Canadian philosophy necessitate a very selective treatment here both of scholars and of topics. Robert E. Butts' comprehensive essay on Canadian work in logic and the philosophy of science, "Philosophy of Science in Canada," discusses those fields more thoroughly than we can here. T. A. Goudge's "A Century of Philosophy in English-Speaking Canada" presents an excellent introduction to the historical background of the period considered in this essay.

The reader interested in the history of Canadian philosophy should also consult *Philosophy in Canada: A Symposium,* edited by John A. Erving, and T. A. Goudge's chapter "Philosophical Literature (1910–1960)" in *Literary History of Canada.* David Braybrooke's incisive review, "The Philosophical Scene in Canada," provides a short but excellent sketch of the current situation.

The emphasis here is on philosophers who are currently active and on work in the philosophy of religion, the history of philosophy, and social and political philosophy, all of which are traditional Canadian concerns. Very recent developments in other areas are also touched on briefly.

PHILOSOPHY OF RELIGION

Philosophy came to anglophone Canada in the service of theology and expressed a concern with the foundations of religion which has characterized its philosophers ever since.

Among currently active philosophers of religion, we may distinguish those who work with an Anglo-American analytical framework; the Roman Catholic philosopher-theologians centered at St. Michael's College in the University of Toronto, many—though not all—of whom work within a broadly Thomist framework; and those who draw their inspiration from neither of these traditions.

CRITICAL AND ANALYTICAL PHILOSOPHY OF RELIGION

Anglophone Canadian philosophy of religion has traditionally taken its direction from Britain. Since the most important British, American, and Australian discussions of the postwar period have concerned the meaningfulness and rationality of Judeo-Christian beliefs, it is not surprising that this debate has dominated the Canadian scene as well.

The most important center for the analytical philosophy of religion in Canada is undoubtedly the University of Calgary. Here Terence Penelhum, Kai Nielsen, and C. B. Martin are all currently working. Here, too, the leading British exponent of atheism, A.G.N. Flew, taught for several years. Both Martin (in his *Religious Beliefs*) and Nielsen (in a number of significant books and papers, including *Ethics Without God*, "Wittgensteinian Fideism," *Scepticism*, and *Contemporary Critiques of Religion*) offer theists the choice of construing their utterances as senseless or as obviously false. Both philosophers have been influenced by verificationism, but Martin works against a background of Australian materialism, while Nielsen employs certain weapons from a Marxist arsenal. Nielsen clarifies his views for undergraduates in his text *Reason and Practice*. Terence Penelhum is the doyen of philosophers of religion at Calgary. He is less concerned with attacking theists or atheists than with delimiting their legitimate claims in the interest of truth. Thus, in his *Survival and Disembodied Existence*, he rejects Platonist, Thomist, and Cartesian accounts of purely spiritual survival as senseless, while defending the possibility of a bodily resurrection, of God's being the only bodiless person, and of many theist beliefs being reasonable. Penelhum's impressively broad scope, as well as his varied attempts to establish a proper balance between believers and skeptics, can be studied with profit by laymen and scholars alike in his systematic work *Religion and Rationality*.

Outside Calgary, useful work on the question of the meaningfulness of religious language has been done by Alastair McKinnon at McGill and by D. D. Evans at the University of Toronto. Evans' work is exemplified by his book *The Logic of Self-Involvement* and by his essay "Differences Between Scientific and Religious Assertions," in *Science and Religion*. McKinnon argues for the necessary but factual character of religious claims in his *Falsification and Belief*. McKinnon's essays on Kierkegaard, "Miracle and Paradox," and related topics have appeared in the *American Philosophical Quarterly* and other noted journals.

The question of the rationality of religious belief has been discussed within context by C. G. Prado of Queen's University and John King-Farlow of the

University of Alberta. Of particular interest is King-Farlow's use of decision theory and related considerations from the theory of practical reason. His views are summarized in John King-Farlow and W. N. Christensen, *Faith and the Life of Reason,* and reviewed by Prado in *Dialogue* 13 (1974):745–799. Very recent studies in the philosophy of religion by Prado, Martin, King-Farlow, and McKinnon, as well as others by such specialists as F. E. Sparshott (Toronto), John Leslie (Guelph), Wayne Grennan (St. Mary's, Halifax), Richard Bosley (Alberta), Jay Newman (Guelph), and Francis Firth, C.S.B. (St. Joseph's, Edmonton) appear in *The Challenge of Religion Today,* edited by King-Farlow. A valuable and distinctly critical survey of works by McKinnon, Nielsen, King-Farlow, and Penelhum is B. Garceau's "La philosophie analytique de la religion; contribution canadienne (1970–75)" which appeared in *Philosophiques* II, 2 (1975): 301–340.

THOMISM AND NEO-THOMISM: THEOLOGICAL PHILOSOPHY

Theological philosophy as practiced in Canada since World War II has had three foci. One of these has been the working out of neo-Thomist natural theology under the stimulus of the papal encyclical *Aeterni Patris.* The leaders of this movement in Canada have been the scholars at St. Michael's College in the University of Toronto, and at the Pontifical Institute of Mediaeval Studies. Taking directions largely from Etienne Gilson (a co-founder of the institute) and Jacques Maritain, a group of distinguished scholars, including A. C. Pegis, Gerald Phelan, and Joseph Owens, have clarified both the Thomist doctrine of the relation between faith and reason and the philosophical underpinnings of Thomist theology. A particularly good example of the work of this school is Owens' *An Elementary Christian Metaphysics.*

A second and more innovative focus of theological philosophy has been the "transcendental Thomism" of Joseph Maréchal and Karl Rahner. The leading Canadian exponent of this approach is undoubtedly Bernard Lonergan whose monumental work *Insight* is a masterly blend of Kantian and Thomist themes.

A number of important Canadian Roman Catholic philosopher-theologians work outside the Thomist framework altogether. Perhaps the most interesting are Arthur Gibson and Leslie Dewart, both of St. Michael's College. Dewart's work in particular, as summarized in his *The Foundations of Belief,* has had considerable impact.

OTHER TRADITIONS

Outside Roman Catholic circles, the most important Canadian philosophical theologian is probably the University of Toronto's Emil L. Fackenheim. Fackenheim is a leading figure in the Jewish theological movement which seeks to interpret the religious significance of recent history, especially the Nazi holocaust and the founding of the state of Israel. A noted historian of continental thought, Fackenheim is much influenced by nineteenth-century German philosophy. His work is illustrated by his *Encounters Between Judaism and Modern Philosophy* and *God's Presence in History*.

The study of the philosophy of religion has gained new impetus in Canada through the founding of departments of comparative religion. It is hoped that a similar volume (on *Comparative Religion Since 1945*) will cover these scholars' contributions.

HISTORY OF PHILOSOPHY

Canadian philosophy emancipated itself from theology by turning to the intensive study of the history of philosophy under the leadership of G.B.S. Brett (who taught at the University of Toronto from 1908 to 1944). This change was accelerated between the wars by the founding in 1929 of the Institute (later the Pontifical Institute) of Mediaeval Studies in Toronto. The history of philosophy has since remained at the center of Canadian research.

The University of Toronto is the most important anglophone Canadian institution for the study of Greek philosophy. Notable among the Plato scholars working there are Reginald E. Allen *(Plato's Euthyphro and the Earlier Theory of Forms)*, Allen Bloom *(The Republic of Plato,* translated with notes and an interpretive essay), and T. M. Robinson *(Plato's Psychology)*. Aristotle scholarship is magnificently represented by Joseph Owens whose *The Doctrine of Being in the Metaphysics of Aristotle* has already become a classic. The study of Stoics and of Plotinus has been carried on most notably by J. M. Rist, whose research has appeared in a number of volumes, such as *Stoic Philosophy* and *Plotinus: The Road to Reality*.

Greek philosophy has also been intensively studied outside Toronto. Gregory Vlastos began his teaching career at Queen's University. David Gallop of Trent University has written a definitive introduction to Plato's *Phaedo,* while at the University of Alberta, Roger Shiner has recently published *Knowledge and Reality in Plato's Philebus* and Richard Bosley has developed a novel and interesting interpretation of Aristotle's logic in his *Aspects of Aristotle's Logic*.

Thanks largely to the Pontifical Institute of Mediaeval Studies and the impetus provided by Etienne Gilson, anglophone Canada has become a significant center of medieval philosophical scholarship. At the institute, Nikolaus Haring has worked extensively on the school of Chartres, Walter Principe has prepared excellent studies of early medieval theology, and J. F. Quinn has published a brilliant study of the philosophy of St. Bonaventure *(The Historical Constitution of St. Bonaventure's Philosophy)*. Joseph Owens, Armand Maurer, E. A. Synan, and Brian Stock have written on a number of medieval figures, and Maurer has prepared an excellent history of the period *(Mediaeval Philosophy)*. James A. Weisheipl's work on fourteenth-century physics, especially that of the Merton School, is a pioneering contribution. Pegis, Phelan, Owens, Maurer, and Weisheipl have also written extensively on Aquinas. An excellent introduction to the style and scope of the institute's scholarship can be found in *Nine Mediaeval*

Thinkers, edited by J. R. O'Donnell, and *Essays in Honour of Anton C. Pegis,* edited by J. R. O'Donnell.

Outside the Pontifical Institute, the study of medieval philosophy in anglophone Canada is represented by perhaps the most important twentieth-century scholar of medieval Platonism, McGill University's Raymond Klibansky *(The Continuity of the Platonic Tradition in the Middle Ages).* Klibansky has also worked extensively on Nicholas of Cusa. Late medieval logic has been illuminated by John Trentman of McGill and by E. J. Ashworth of the University of Waterloo. Ashworth's research to date has culminated in her *Language and Logic in the Post-Medieval Period.* A. E. Marmura of the University of Toronto and Nabil Shehaby of the Institute of Islamic Studies at McGill have worked extensively on Islamic philosophy during the medieval period, while B. K. Matilal of the University of Toronto has done pioneering research on medieval Indian logic and epistemology. An excellent and remarkably comprehensive bibliographical essay on Canadian contributions to the study of medieval philosophy is A. M. Landry's "La pensée philosophique médiévale: Contribution Candienne (1960–1973)", published in *Philosophiques* (1974).

Influenced, no doubt, by the strong British tradition in Canadian philosophy, anglophone scholars have tended to study the British empiricists rather than the continental rationalists. A noteworthy exception is R. F. McRae of the University of Toronto whose close study of Leibniz's philosophy of mind *(Leibniz: Perception, Apperception and Thought)* has recently appeared.

British philosophy, particularly the work of the British empiricists, has received very careful study in anglophone Canada. David Gauthier of the University of Toronto has worked on Hobbes' political theory in *The Logic of Leviathan.* John Yolton of York University has written extensively on Locke, and his *John Locke and the Way of Ideas* has become a classic of Lockean scholarship. Both Harry Bracken of McGill and John Davis of the University of Western Ontario have contributed to Berkeley scholarship. Bracken has helped place Berkeley's work in its historical context with his *The Early Reception of Berkeley's Immaterialism 1710–1733.* Terence Penelhum of the University of Calgary has written widely on Hume's philosophy and has done much to revive interest in Hume's theory of personal identity. His contributions are concisely integrated in his *Hume.* Stanley Tweyman of York University has also worked on Hume's ethics and theory of practical reason, and has helped to situate it historically in his *Reason and Conduct in Hume and His Predecessors.* Douglas Odegard (Guelph) has published valuable papers on all the empiricists. S. C. Patten (Lethbridge), Michael Stack (Manitoba), P. S. Ardal (Queen's), J. Noxon (McMaster), T. M. Lennon (Western Ontario), M. A. Neilsen (Windsor), D. F. Norton (McGill), and K. W. Rankin (Victoria) in his libertarian writings have all thrown useful light on Hume or his background assumptions.

Jonathan Bennett of the University of British Columbia has written on the British empiricists *(Locke, Berkeley and Hume)* but is better known for his incisive studies of Kant *(Kant's Analytic)* and *Kant's Dialectic.* Kant's philosophy has been much studied in Canada. Besides Bennett's work, we may mention D. P. Dryer's *Kant's Solution to the Problem of Verification in Metaphysics*, A.R.C. Duncan's *Practical Reason and Morality*, and T. C. Williams' *The Concept of the Categorical Imperative*.

Among nineteenth-century figures, Hegel has been most intensively studied by anglophone Canadian philosophers. Of special interest are Emil Fackenheim's *The Religious Dimension in Hegel's Development*, and Charles Taylor's recent *Hegel*. Important for Kierkegaard studies are Alastair McKinnon's *Indices* and his textual studies based on them. Noteworthy also is the University of Toronto Press edition of the *Collected Works of John Stuart Mill* with a substantial introduction by D. P. Dryer. Another leading Mill scholar is D. G. Brown of the University of British Columbia.

Collingwood, Russell, Whitehead, and Wittgenstein are the twentieth-century figures who have received most scholarly attention in anglophone Canada. Collingwood's work has been extensively studied by Lionel Rubinoff *(Collingwood and the Reform of Metaphysics)* and by A. Shalom at McMaster *(R. G. Collingwood: Philosophe et Historien)*. Russell scholarship in Canada has received a stimulus from the acquisition by McMaster University of the Russell Archives. Among those currently working on Russell are John Slater and Christine Cassin of the University of Toronto, and N. L. Wilson at McMaster. Whitehead's philosophy was brought to Canada by his students and has received careful study here. Especially notable is the work of A. H. Johnson at the University of Western Ontario. In *Whitehead's Theory of Reality*, he discusses Whitehead's metaphysics, and in *Whitehead's Philosophy of Civilization*, he extends his study to Whitehead's philosophy of history. Although Wittgenstein's influence on Canadian philosophy is extensive, there have been few book-length scholarly studies of his work. Of these, the most extensive are K. T. Fann's *Ludwig Wittgenstein* and J. C. Morrison's *Meaning and Truth in Wittgenstein's Tractatus*. Frege scholarship is also growing, as recent books by John Heintz (Calgary), E.-H. W. Kluge (Victoria), and J. D. B. Walker (McGill) can attest.

SOCIAL AND POLITICAL PHILOSOPHY

Much of the best philosophical work done in anglophone Canada since 1945 has been directed to what David Braybrooke has called the "Ethopolitical Intersection"—the intersection of ethical theory, and philosophy of history and of the social sciences, the theory of action, and political philosophy. Here the outstanding practitioners have been W. H. Dray of Trent University, P. H. Nowell-Smith of York University, and Charles Taylor of McGill. Dray and Nowell-Smith were among the chief architects of the "Oxford" attack on the view that explanation in history and the social sciences should always resemble explanation in the physical sciences. This attack is carefully formulated in Dray's *Laws and Explanation in History*. Taylor's work *The Explanation of Behavior* is a definitive defense of the role of teleological concepts in the explanation of human action. D. G. Brown's *Action* refines this approach, while Francis Spar-shott's *An Enquiry into Goodness and Related Concepts* applies the Oxford approach to ethical problems.

Working more explicitly within political theory (and outside departments of philosophy) are George P. Grant of McMaster University and C. B. Macpherson of the University of Toronto. Grant's work is radically conservative and em-phasizes the importance of tradition and continuity in social life. His books, particularly *Technology and Empire* and *Lament for a Nation*, have contributed much to the resurgence of Canadian nationalism. Macpherson works against a very different background. A democratic socialist deeply indebted to Marx, though critical of him, he has provided an analysis of the concept of power and an account of the philosophical underpinnings of liberal capitalism which have had great influence in Canada, especially among political economists. His major works include *The Political Theory of Possessive Individualism: Hobbes to Locke* and *Democratic Theory*.

Within departments of philosophy, the dominant ethical-political positions have been utilitarianism (represented especially by the University of Waterloo's Jan Narveson and the University of Toronto's J. H. Sobel), and various forms of social contract theory represented (with ever greater unease) by David Bray-brooke at Dalhousie and David Gauthier at the University of Toronto. Philo-sophical feminism is vigorously represented by Lorenne M. G. Clark (Toronto) and Christine Garside Allen (Sir George Williams, Concordia). A. Kawczak (Loyola, Concordia) philosophically interprets the moral themes of the Polish-Canadian psychiatrist K. Dabrowski.

BOUNDARY AREAS

Many of the most interesting recent developments within philosophy in Canada lie along a continuum between the boundary between linguistics and philosophy and that between philosophy and psychology. At the boundary with linguistics, Charles Travis of the University of Calgary has attempted to synthesize speech act theory with generative grammar in his *Saying and Understanding*. Hermann Tennessen of the University of Alberta worked closely with Arne Naess in the development of "empirical semantics" and has published extensively on the philosophy of language. At the intersection of linguistics, metaphysics, and the philosophy of language is the growing body of work by philosophers in Canada on the semantics of mass terms. Henry Laycock of Queen's University, F. J. Pelletier of the University of Alberta, and Robert Ware and Brian Chellas of the University of Calgary have all contributed to this area. Laycock in particular has argued persuasively for the need to posit eoncrete universals, "things" which are not particulars. At the boundary between logic and the philosophy of language is N. L. Wilson's *The Concept of Language*.

Some of Jonathan Bennett's most interesting and important work lies at the boundary between philosophy of language and philosophy of mind. His early book *Rationality* explores the relationship between intelligence and the capacity to communicate. His recent *Linguistic Behavior* critically evaluates his earlier standpoint. (Bennett's range of expertise is amazing.) This area has also been explored by John King-Farlow of the University of Alberta, notably in "Man, Beast and Philosophical Psychology" (with E. A. Hall) and "Two Dogmas of Linguistic Empiricism." The boundary between the philosophy of language and philosophy of mind is also the special interest of philosophers influenced by the later work of Wittgenstein. Notable among these are John Hunter and Jack Canfield of the University of Toronto, and Roger Shiner of the University of Alberta. Hunter's *Essays After Wittgenstein* includes provocative comments on Noam Chomsky.

Relatively little epistemology as such has been done recently in Canada but what there is, is of high quality. William Rozeboom of the University of Alberta has addressed himself to foundational problems in epistemology; Jack Stevenson of the University of Toronto has worked on the ethics of belief; and R. B. de Sousa, also of the University of Toronto, has studied the aims of rational inquiry, as well as its foe, self-deception.

The philosophy of mind has been discussed against a background of evolutionary theory and neurophysiology by Roland Puccetti of Dalhousie University. Puccetti has argued against epiphenomenalism and some versions of the identity theory on evolutionary grounds; he has explored the consequences of recent work on "split-brain" patients for our views about persons. For the latter, see his "Brain Bisection and Personal Identity" in *British Journal for the Philosophy of Science*.

The boundaries of the history of science and philosophy are admirably spanned by R. E. Butts (Western Ontario), a Kant and Whewell scholar, and by William R. Shea (McGill), author of *Galileo's Intellectual Revolution*. Michael Ruse (Guelph), T. A. Goudge (Toronto), and Hugh Lehman (Guelph), as well as E. Levy (British Columbia) and R. E. Tully (St. Michael's, Toronto), have made Canadian contributions to bridging the differences between philosophy and biology a matter for national pride.

The boundary between philosophy and psychology has been the special province of William Rozeboom, professor of psychology at the University of Alberta. Rozeboom has established an international reputation as an epistemologist (see, for example, his article "Why I Know So Much More Than You Do") and as a theoretical psychologist. His work at the intersection of these fields is exemplified by his "Problems in the Psychophilosophy of Knowledge" in *The Psychology of Knowing,* edited by Rozeboom and Joseph R. Royce.

The boundary between scientific methodology and metaphysics has become extremely porous of late. We will not discuss the philosophy of science in detail. (The interested reader should, we repeat, consult R. E. Butts' "Philosophy of Science in Canada.") It is appropriate to mention the work of York University's J. O. Wisdom on the relationship between scientific and metaphysical theories and the on-going "debate" between C. A. Hooker of the University of Western

Ontario and B. C. van Fraassen of the University of Toronto about the nature of theoretical entities. Van Fraassen has long defended the view that theories need not be understood to have ontological import, while Hooker has argued for a strict scientific realism. Professors P. S. and P. M. Churchland (Manitoba), Marcia Hanen (Calgary), and Roy Vincent (Manitoba) also deserve mention.

Interest in formal logic and in a formal approach to philosophy has been growing in Canada over the last twenty years largely under U.S. influence. The most important philosophical logician working in anglophone Canada is Bas C. van Fraassen of the University of Toronto whose development of the notion of logical space (for example, in "Meaning Relations and Modalities") and of the method of supervaluations (in, for example "Presupposition, Implication, and Self Reference") has had important consequences for philosophical logic. Logicians in Canada have also worked extensively on the Liar and related paradoxes. Van Fraassen has applied the method of supervaluations to these problems, while H. G. Herzberger, also of the University of Toronto, has developed an approach in which truth and correspondence are not coextensive concepts. Douglas Odegaard of the University of Guelph has also worked on this problem.

The study of logics that permit nondenoting terms was pioneered by Karel Lambert when he taught at the University of Alberta and has remained an interest of Canadian logicians. Van Fraassen has worked on free description theory and together with Lambert, his former teacher, has prepared an introductory textbook of free logic (*Derivation and Counterexample*. Charles Morgan of the University of Victoria has applied free logic techniques to the semantics of modal logic, and John Woods of the University of Calgary has worked extensively on the logic of fiction. Woods has argued against its identification with free logic *(The Logic of Fiction)*.

Mathematical logic was largely ignored in anglophone Canada until recently, but there is now a growing and active group in both philosophy and mathematics departments. Of interest to philosophers is the work of S. K. Thomason at Simon Fraser University on the semantics of modal and tense logics, Verena Huber-Dyson's work on proof theory, and Alasdair Urquhart's contributions to the semantics of relevance logics.

SELECT BIBLIOGRAPHY

BOOKS AND ARTICLES

Allen, R. E. *Plato's Euthyphro and the Earlier Theory of Forms* (London: Routledge and Kegan Paul, 1970).

Ashworth, E. J. *Language and Logic in the Post-Medieval Period* (Dordrecht: Reidel, 1974).

Bennett, J. *Kant's Analytic* (London: Cambridge University Press, 1966).

———. *Kant's Dialectic* (London: Cambridge University Press, 1974).

———. *Linguistic Behavior* (London: Cambridge University Press, 1976).

————. *Locke, Berkeley and Hume: Central Themes* (London: Oxford University Press, 1971).

————. *Rationality* (London: Routledge and Kegan Paul, 1964).

Bloom, A. (trans.). *The Republic of Plato* (New York: Basic Books, 1968).

Bosley, R. *Aspects of Aristotle's Logic* (Assen: Van Gorcum, 1975).

Bracken, H. *The Early Reception of Berkeley's Immaterialism 1710–1733* (The Hague: Nijhoff, 1956).

Braybrooke, D. "The Philosophical Scene in Canada," *The Canadian Forum* 53 (1974).

Brown, D. G. *Action* (London: Allen and Unwin, 1968).

Butts, R. E. "Philosophy of Science in Canada," *Zeitschrift für allgemeine Wissenschaftstheorie* 5 (1974).

Dewart, L. *The Foundations of Belief* (New York: Herder and Herder, 1969).

Dray, W. H. *Laws and Explanation in History* (London: Oxford University Press, 1957).

Dryer, D. P. *Kant's Solution to the Problem of Verification in Metaphysics* (Toronto: University of Toronto Press, 1966).

Duncan, A.R.C. *Practical Reason and Morality* (London: Nelson, 1957).

Erving, J. A. (ed.) *Philosophy in Canada: A Symposium* (Toronto: University of Toronto Press, 1952).

Evans, D. D. "Differences Between Scientific and Religious Assertions," in *Science and Religion*, ed. I. G. Barbour (New York: Harper and Row, 1968).

————. *The Logic of Self-Involvement* (New York: Herder and Herder, 1969).

Fackenheim, E. L. *Encounters Between Judaism and Modern Philosophy* (New York: Basic Books, 1973).

————. *God's Presence in History* (New York: New York University Press, 1967).

————. *The Religious Dimension in Hegel's Thought* (Bloomington, Ind.: Indiana University Press, 1967).

Fann, K. T. *Ludwig Wittgenstein* (New York: Dell, 1967).

Garceau, B. "La philosophie analytique de la religion; contribution canadienne (1970–75)," *Philosophiques* 2 (1975).

Gauthier, D. *The Logic of Leviathan* (Oxford: Clarendon Press, 1962).

Goudge, T. A. "A Century of Philosophy in English-Speaking Canada," *Dalhousie Review* 47 (1967).

————. "Philosophical Literature (1910–1960)," in *Literary History of Canada*, 2d ed., ed. C. F. Klinck (Toronto: University of Toronto Press, 1976).

Grant, G. *Lament for a Nation* (Toronto: McClelland and Stewart, 1970).

————. "Philosophy," in *Encyclopedia Canadiana* (Toronto: Grolier, 1968).

————. *Technology and Empire: Perspectives on North America* (Toronto: House of Anansi Press Ltd., 1969).

Harris, H. S. *Hegel's Development: Toward the Sunlight 1770–1801* (London: Oxford University Press, 1972).

Hunter, J. *Essays after Wittgenstein* (Toronto: University of Toronto Press, 1973).

Johnson, A. H. *Whitehead's Philosophy of Civilization* (Boston: Beacon Press, 1958).

————. *Whitehead's Theory of Reality* (Boston: Beacon Press, 1952).

King-Farlow, J. *Reason and Religion: Philosophy and Religion in a Scientific Age* (London: Darton, Longman and Todd, 1969).

————. *Self-Knowledge and Social Relations* (New York: Science History Publications, 1978).

———— (ed.). *The Challenge Of Religion Today: Essays on the Philosophy of Religion*, Canadian Contemporary Philosophy Series (New York: Science History Publications, 1976).

————. "Two Dogmas of Linguistic Empiricism," *Dialogue* 11 (1972).

———— and Christensen, W. N. *Faith and the Life of Reason* (Dordrecht: Reidel, 1972).

———— and Hall, E. A. "Man, Beast and Philosophical Psychology," *British Journal for the Philosophy of Science* 16, No. 62 (1965).

Klibansky, R. *The Continuity of the Platonic Tradition in the Middle Ages* (London: Warburg Institute, 1939).

Landry, A. M. "La pensée philosophique médiévale: Contribution Canadienne (1960–1973)," *Philosophiques* October (1974).

Lonergan, B. *Insight* (New York: Philosophical Library, 1957).

MacPherson, C. B. *Democratic Theory* (Oxford: Clarendon Press, 1973).

———. *The Political Theory of Possessive Individualism: Hobbes to Locke* (Oxford: Clarendon Press, 1962).

Martin, C. B. *Religious Beliefs* (Ithaca, N.Y.: Cornell University Press, 1959).

Maurer, A. *Mediaeval Philosophy* (New York: Random House, 1962).

McKinnon, A. *Falsification and Belief* (The Hague: Mouton, 1970).

———. *Indices* (Leiden: E. J. Brill, 1970–   ).

———. "Miracle and Paradox," *American Philosophical Quarterly* 4 (1967).

McRae, R. F. *Leibniz: Perception, Apperception and Thought* (Toronto: University of Toronto Press, 1976).

Mill, J.S. *Collected Works of John Stuart Mill* eds. F.E.L. Priestley, J.M. Robson et al. II-V, VII-XIX (Toronto and Buffalo: University of Toronto Press, and London: Routledge and Kegan Paul, 1963-). (Other volumes in preparation.)

Morrison, J.C. *Meaning and Truth in Wittgenstein's Tractatus* (The Hague: Mouton, 1967).

Nielsen, K. *Contemporary Critiques of Religion* (London: Macmillan, and Toronto: University of Toronto Press, 1971).

———. *Ethics Without God* (London: Pemberton, 1973).

———. *Reason and Practice* (New York: Harper and Row, 1971).

———. *Scepticism* (London: Macmillan, and New York: St. Martin's Press, 1973).

———. "Wittgensteinian Fideism," *Philosophy* 43 (1967).

O'Donnell, J. R. (ed.). *Essays in Honour of Anton C. Pegis* (Toronto: Pontifical Institute of Mediaeval Studies, 1975).

——— (ed.). *Nine Mediaeval Thinkers* (Toronto: Pontifical Institute of Mediaeval Studies, 1955).

Owens, J. *An Elementary Christian Metaphysics* (Milwaukee, Wis.: Bruce, 1964).

———. *The Doctrine of Being in the Metaphysics of Aristotle* (Toronto: Pontifical Institute of Mediaeval Studies, 1950).

Penelhum, T. *Hume* (London: Macmillan, and New York: St. Martin's Press, 1975).

———. *Religion and Rationality* (Toronto: University of Toronto Press, and New York: Random House, 1971).

———. *Survival and Disembodied Existence* (London: Routledge and Kegan Paul, 1970).

Puccetti, R. "Brain Bisection and Personal Identity," *British Journal for the Philosophy of Science* 24, No. 4 (1973).

Quinn, J. F. *The Historical Constitution of St. Bonaventure's Philosophy* (Toronto: Pontifical Institute of Mediaeval Studies, 1973).

Rist, J. M. *Plotinus: The Road to Reality* (London: Cambridge University Press, 1967).

———. *Stoic Philosophy* (London: Cambridge University Press, 1969).

Robinson, T. M. *Plato's Psychology* (Toronto: University of Toronto Press, 1970).

Rozeboom, W. "Problems in the Psychophilosophy of Knowledge," in *The Psychology of Knowing*, eds. W. Rozeboom and J. R. Royce (London: Gordon and Breach, 1972).

———. "Why I Know So Much More Than You Do," *American Philosophical Quarterly* 4 (1967).

Rubinoff, L. *Collingwood and the Reform of Metaphysics* (Toronto: University of Toronto Press, 1970).

Shalom, A. *R. G. Collingwood: Philosophe et Historien* (Paris: Presses Universitaires de France, 1967).

Shea, W. R. *Galileo's Intellectual Revolution* (New York: Science History Publications, 1972).

Shiner, R. *Knowledge and Reality in Plato's Philebus* (Assen: Van Gorcum, 1974).

Sparshott, F. *An Enquiry into Goodness and Related Concepts* (Toronto: University of Toronto Press, 1958).

Taylor, C. *Hegel* (London: Cambridge University Press, 1975).

———. *The Explanation of Behavior* (London: Routledge and Kegan Paul, 1964).

Travis, C. *Saying and Understanding: A Generative Theory of Illocutions* (New York: New York University Press, 1975).

Tweyman, S. *Reason and Conduct in Hume and His Predecessors* (The Hague: Nijhoff, 1974).

van Fraassen, B. C. "Meaning Relations and Modalities," *Noûs* 3 (1969).

————. "Presupposition, Implication, and Self Reference," *Journal of Philosophy* 65 (1968).

———— and Lambert, K. *Derivation and Counterexample: An Introduction to Philosophical Logic* (Encino, Calif.: Dickenson, 1972).

Williams, T. C. *The Concept of the Categorical Imperative* (Oxford: Clarendon Press, 1968).

Wilson, N. L. *The Concept of Language* (Toronto: University of Toronto Press, 1959).

Woods, J. *The Logic of Fiction* (The Hague: Mouton, 1974).

Yolton, J. *John Locke and the Way of Ideas* (London: Oxford University Press, 1956).

JOURNALS

Canadian Journal of Philosophy
Dalhousie Review
Dialogue
Journal of Indian Philosophy
Journal of Philosophical Logic
Mediaeval Studies
Philosophy of the Social Sciences
Phoenix
Queen's Quarterly
Russell: The Journal of the Bertrand Russell Archives
Social Praxis
Studies in Religion/Sciences Religeuses
University of Toronto Quarterly

Francophone Philosophy
JEAN-PAUL   BRODEUR

Although Canada is to some extent a bicultural country, it should not be concluded that the anglophone and the francophone philosophical communities are equal in size. The number of French Canadian philosophers deeply engaged in research has never at one time exceeded the rather optimistic figure of about forty people. In the early 1950s, when three of the presently existing eight faculties or departments of philosophy had not yet been created, this number was much smaller.

French Canadian philosophers have usually been torn between two conflicting demands. They might help to provide their community with a needed sense of collective identity by speaking to them about their own reality; or they might attain academic excellence in the pursuit of more scholarly goals. The first option eventually leads to a certain form of philosophical regionalism; the second to popular indifference and, often, to rejection by the larger community.

Although the number of people actively engaged in research has never been very high, the number of teachers in philosophy, particularly at the college level, is comparatively more important in French Canada than in some other countries. Up to 1963, the two last years of college were devoted mainly to philosophy. In the years following the reform of college-level education in Quebec, the teaching of philosophy became the target of mounting criticism, and philosophers were increasingly pressed to justify the need for this kind of teaching. Some of them devoted a great deal of time and energy to this task, thus reducing their time for research.

All francophone universities have been created within a religious (essentially Catholic) background. Hence, there is the statutory obligation, proclaimed at some time or other in most departments and faculties of philosophy, that staff commit themselves to the teaching of Christian (Catholic) philosophy, such as it may be represented in the works of Aquinas or his often less gifted modern commentators. At the present time, some departments are still struggling to free themselves from the remnants of this obligation. One consequence has been that French Canadian philosophers and their students have lacked training in the formal techniques required to gain access to the main trends of contemporary logic and philosophy of science.

The rest of this article presents some of the contributions of francophone philosophers to their discipline. Not all of these philosophers are Canadians, but all have spent a significant portion of their careers in Canadian universities.

HISTORY OF PHILOSOPHY

An important number of the books published by francophone philosophers belong to the history of philosophy. In the history of Greek philosophy, one must single out, apart from L. M. Régis' book on the theory of *doxa* in Aristotle, which was published earlier than 1945, the work of Décarie, Paquet, and Brisson. Vianney Décarie's main contribution to this subject was his *L'Objet de la métaphysique selon Aristote*, in which he stresses the continuity between Plato's dialectic and Aristotle's science of being. Léonce Paquet's book, *Platon: la médiation du regard*, is a detailed analysis of Plato's use of certain metaphorical expressions belonging to the vocabulary of sight. Paquet has also recently published *Les cyniques grecs: fragments et témoignages*. Luc Brisson is only in his early thirties, but he has already published *Le même et l'autre dans la structure ontologique de "Timée" de Platon* and *Le mythe de Tirésias*, as well as several articles on Greek thought and mythology. The first book is a systematic commentary on Plato's *Timaeus*, which also tries to substantiate its author's claim that the number of interpretations that can be given of a philosophical theory is both finite and relatively small. The second book is a structural analysis of different versions of the myth of Tiresias. As Brisson is still so young, much is to be expected of his future work.

It is impossible here to do justice to the extensive work of French Canadian medievalists. For a fuller picture, the reader should consult a survey of their work that was published in *Philosophiques* (October 1974) by A. M. Landry. Among French Canadian medievalists, the outstanding figure is Ephrem Longpré, a Franciscan who has devoted a life of immense labors to medieval and, particularly, Scotist studies. Having spent most of his life in different European institutes, Longpré is little known in Quebec except by a few specialists. (For a partial bibliography, see E. Parent's article in *Dialogue* [1967–1968]:481–496. French Canadian studies in medieval thought can be generally separated into two groups: those dealing mainly with Aquinas's philosophy and those dealing with other medieval thinkers. To the first group belong G. Jalbert's *Nécessité et contingence chez saint Thomas d'Aquin,* L. Lachance's *L'humanisme politique de saint Thomas d'Aquin,* G. Langevin's *Capax Dei,* and B. Garceau's *Judicium.* Apart from Longpré's work one should mention *La connaissance de l'individuel au Moyen-âge* by C. Bérubé and *Orose et ses idées* by B. Lacroix, which fall into the other group. Serge Lusignan is the editor of a periodical whose purpose is to present a survey of current research using computers in medieval studies. This periodical, *Computers and Mediaeval Data Processing,* is published, mainly in English, by the University of Montreal.

In the history of modern philosophy, French Canadian historians of philosophy have made two especially important contributions. The first is François Duchesneau's *L'empirisme de Locke;* the other is Pierre Laberge's *La théologie kantienne pré-critique.* Both books attempt to shed some light on the early formation of the thought of the philosophers with whom they are concerned. Duchesneau stresses the influence of Sydenham on Locke, and Laberge comments on less known material that Kant wrote before the *Critique of Pure Reason.* Also well worth mentioning is B. Carnois' *La cohérence de la doctrine kantienne de la liberté.* Carnois' book is a careful examination of the consistency of Kant's different notions of freedom in the contexts of pure and practical reason. German philosophy has been the object of further research in A. Klimov's book on Jacob Boehme *(Confessions. Précédé de le ''philosophe teutonique'' ou l'esprit d'aventure)* and in Y. Gauthier's reconstruction of Hegel's philosophy of language *(L'arc et le cercle).*

One last area in which there has been some concentrated work is that of phenomenology. Bertrand Rioux's *L'être et la vérité chez Heidegger et saint Thomas d'Aquin* is particularly noteworthy, for it reflects the transition that occurred in French Canadian philosophy in the late 1950s between Thomism and phenomenology. Fernand Couturier's book, *Monde et être chez Heidegger,* is an extensive and well-documented commentary on the philosophy of Heidegger. Perhaps the most remarkable of these books on phenomenology is T. Geraets' *Vers une nouvelle philosophie transcendantale.* Dealing mainly with Merleau-Ponty, the book also describes, in the words of Levinas, ''the springtime of phenomenology'' in France.

However briefly, we must mention, before leaving the history of philosophy, Jean Theau's monumental study of Bergson *(La critique bergsonnienne du con-*

cept), which is one of the most comprehensive studies of Bergson's theory of knowledge that has ever been published. Also teaching with Theau at the University of Ottawa is Guy Lafrance who has published a book on Bergson's political philosophy *(La philosophie sociale de Bergson).*

EPISTEMOLOGY AND THE PHILOSOPHY OF LANGUAGE

It is difficult to neatly classify the works dealing with different topics in contemporary philosophy. The reason is not that the material published is eccentric but that one would end up establishing well-known classes—like aesthetics—to which only one book might belong. Let it then be said that the heading chosen for this section should be understood in a wide sense.

Epistemology was first practiced within the conceptual framework of Aristotelianism and Thomism. The works of Charles de Koninck and of L. M. Régis are good examples of this way of doing epistemology. Father Régis's work has been translated into English *(Epistemology).* For a complete bibliography of de Koninck's works, see *Mélanges à la mémoire de Charles de Koninck,* pp. 9–22.

Outside the traditional Aristotelian framework, epistemology and the philosophy of language have been influenced both by the analytical and logical approach favored in the Anglo-Saxon world and by the more historical preoccupations that one finds in the work of French philosophers like Bachelard, Canguilhem, and Foucault.

Jacques Poulain's *Logique et religion* is a careful examination of the possibility of religious discourse from a Wittgensteinian standpoint. Apart from being the French translator of J. L. Austin's *How to Do Things with Words (Quand dire, c'est faire),* G. Lane has also published *Être et langage,* which is an inquiry into the possibility of objectivity, as defined by philosophical realism. Also influenced by analytical philosophy is the work of younger philosophers like Normand Lacharité, J.-P. Brodeur, and Claude Panaccio. Their work has been published in Canadian journals and in books edited by Alan Montefiore *(Philosophie et relations interpersonnelles)* and J.-P. Brodeur *(Culture et langage).*

If we set aside the well-known writings of Hugues LeBlanc, whose career thus far has been wholly spent in the United States, we must again stress the relative neglect of modern mathematical logic in French Canada. However, there is some indication that this situation might change. C. Castonguay has published his *Meaning and Existence in Mathematics* in English, and the book has been well received. Very recently, Y. Gauthier, who had written numerous articles for Canadian journals, also published *Fondements des mathématiques: Introduction à une philosophie constructiviste.* Finally, J. Danek's *Les projets de Leibniz et de Bolzano* is one of the few books in French dealing with the important work of Bolzano.

Closer to the continental historical tradition is Camille Limoges' *La sélection naturelle,* which deals with the formation of Darwin's concept of natural selection. In 1973, Limoges founded the Institut d'histoire et de sociologie politique des sciences at the University of Montreal. He is about to publish the results of two research projects undertaken with the help of collaborators. The first of these projects is devoted to a history of the French Museum of Natural Sciences in Paris and the second to the history of concept formation in ecology. In this area of philosophical history of sciences, one must also mention Réjane Bernier's *Aux sources de la biologie*.

Closer still to French contemporary philosophy are C. Lévesque's *L'étrangeté du texte* and Raymond Montpetit's *Comment parler de la littérature*. Both books belong to the theory of literature, the first one being strongly influenced by Blanchot and Derrida and the second one attempting to find an independent course beyond Ricoeur's hermeneutics and Barthes' semiology. G. Charron's *Du langage* compares Merleau-Ponty's philosophy of language and Martinet's linguistics. Two recently created journals, *Stratégie* and *Chroniques*, are at least partly devoted to the theory of literature. Both publications are influenced by Marxism.

"ESSAYS"

It was with some hesitation that the rather uninformative heading "Essays" was chosen for this section. Some of the books whose titles are quoted, like R. Miguelez's *Sujet et histoire* or P. Bertrand's *L'oubli: révolution ou mort de l'histoire*, both of which were very well received in France, would have easily fallen under the categories of political philosophy or philosophy of culture. But it would have been misleading to place under such a heading some of the books and articles we are most anxious to talk about in this section of our survey, because one might have expected a traditional academic approach to the questions they raise. Although they would not really belong to philosophy, understood as an academic discipline practiced mostly by university professors, these writings are among the ones that have had by far the most impact on French Canadian intellectual life.

The first of these writings is a manifesto published in 1948 in Montreal by a group of intellectuals. It bears the signature of Paul-Émile Borduas, perhaps the most famous of French Canadian painters, and its title is *Refus Global* (global refusal). In some of its passages, this is an extraordinary document, denouncing almost every aspect of French Canadian society. It produced an awakening and has had a lasting influence.

The restraint of Fernand Dumont is in sharp contrast to the wrath of Borduas. Dumont's activity has been threefold. In his books *(Pour la conversion de la pensée chrétienne* and *Le lieu de l'homme)*, Dumont has tried to give a Christian humanistic interpretation of the broad changes affecting society, most notably French Canadian society. In several articles published in the periodical *Maintenant*, Dumont assumes towards the French Canadian Catholic bourgeoisie a role not unlike that of the late François Mauriac in his *Bloc-notes* in the French daily *Le Figaro*. Finally, Dumont has been a moving force in the broad endeavor of French Canadian philosophers and sociologists to describe the ideological background of their own community.

Pierre Vallières has published, apart from several articles in *Cité Libre* (a periodical to which former Prime Minister Pierre Elliott Trudeau was once a frequent contributor), a book entitled *Nègres blancs d'Amérique (White Niggers of America)*. Blending autobiography with Marxist analysis, the book aroused passionate discussion at the time of its publication. Vallières was also involved with a group of intellectuals who founded *Parti-pris*, a periodical leaning towards Marxism that was published regularly in Quebec between 1963 and 1968. *Parti-pris*, which was also for some time the title of a political movement, has left a very deep mark on the generation of intellectuals and philosophers that contributed to it. Marxist studies are mostly undertaken in Quebec by philosophers and sociologists who were members of the editing staff of *Parti-pris* or in relation with them. One of the most productive theorists in the field of Marxist studies is Jean-Marc Piotte. He has published several books and articles on Gramsci *(La pensée politique de Gramsci)*, the struggles of the working class in Quebec *(Les travailleurs contre l'Etat)*, and on Lenin.

Pierre Vadeboncoeur has recently been awarded the highest literary honor in Quebec *(the Prix David)*. He has published several books, the best known consisting of essays in which Vadeboncoeur reflects on the past social and political impotence of French Canada and challenges the francophone community to overcome its traditional dread of asserting itself. Vadeboncoeur recently published *Un géonocide en douce*.

Perhaps the one single text that has exerted the most profound influence on French Canadian philosophers is Jacques Brault's "Pour une philosophie québécoise." This paper is reproduced in Yvan Lamonde's *Historiographie de la philosophie au Québec 1853–1970*. In this published lecture, Brault castigates French Canadian philosophy's "splendid uselessness." Brault summons francophone philosophers to the task of tagging and making explicit the different myths responsible for the partial alienation of their own society. His call has not remained unanswered. Quite a few younger philosophers, like Claude Savary, André Vidricaire, Normand Lacharité, Robert Nadeau, Louise Marcil-Lacoste, Claude Panaccio, and Jean-Paul Brodeur, now devote at least a part of their activity to fulfilling this task. Among these, Yvan Lamonde is the best known for his work in collecting material relevant to a description of French Canada's ideological background. There is admittedly a danger that these efforts may end in parochialism, but how much more deplorable for philosophy if it were to remain silent on the present *conjoncture* of French Canada.

This essay has dealt only with publications. It may be mentioned here that the different faculties and departments of philosophy in French Canada have devoted important efforts to making it a place where both the Anglo-Saxon and continental philosophical traditions could meet and communicate. While these efforts have not yet fully borne fruit, those who believe that such a dialogue is possible and would be beneficial to philosophy should not be deterred from striving to reach this goal.

SELECT BIBLIOGRAPHY

BOOKS AND ARTICLES

Bernier, R. *Aux sources de la biologie* (Montreal: Presses de l'Université du Québec, 1975).

Bertrand, P. *L'oubli: révolution ou mort de l'histoire* (Paris: Presses Universitaires de France, 1975).

Bérubé, C. *La connaissance de l'individuel au Moyen-âge* (Paris: Presses Universitaires de France, and Montreal: Presses de l'Université du Québec, 1964).

Borduas, P.-E. *Refus Global* (Montreal: Mithra-Mythe Editeur, 1948).

Brault, J. "Pour une philosophe québécoise," in *Historiographie de la philosophie au Québec 1853-1970*, ed. Y. Lamonde (Montreal: Hurtubise HMH, 1972).

Brisson, L. *Le même et l'autre dans la structure ontologique de "Timée" de Platon* (Paris: Klincksieck, 1974).

———. *Le mythe de Tirésias: essai d'analyse structurale* (Leiden: Brill, 1976).

Brodeur, J.-P. (ed.). *Culture et langage* (Montreal: Hurtubise HMH, 1973).

Carnois, B. *La cohérence de la doctrine kantienne de la liberté* (Paris: Seuil, 1973).

Castonguay, C. *Meaning and Existence in Mathematics* (New York: Springer, 1972).

Charron, G. *Du langage. André Martinet et Maurice Merleau-Ponty* (Ottawa: Editions de l'Université d'Ottawa, 1972).

Couturier, F. *Monde et être chez Heidegger* (Montreal: Les Presses de l'Université Montréal, 1971).

Danek, J. *Les projets de Leibniz et de Bolzano: Deux sources de la logique contemporaire* (Quebec: Les Presses de l'Université Laval, 1975).

Décarie, V. *L'Objet de la métaphysique selon Aristote* (Montreal: Institut d'études médiévales, 1961).

Duchesneau, F. *L'empirisme de Locke* (The Hague: Nijhoff, 1973).

Dumont, F. *Le lieu de l'homme; la culture comme distance et mémoire* (Montreal: Hurtubise HMH, 1968).

———. *Pour la conversion de la pensée chrétienne* (Montreal: Hurtubise HMH, 1964).

Garceau, B. *Judicium: vocabulaire, sources, doctrine de saint Thomas d'Aquin* (Montreal: Institut d'études médiévales, and Paris: Vrin, 1968).

Gauthier, Y. *Fondements des mathématiques. Introduction à une philosophie constructiviste* (Montreal: Presses de l'Université de Montréal, 1976).

———. *L'arc et le cercle. L'essence du langage chez Hegel et Hölderlin* (Montreal: Bellarmin, and Brussels: Desclée de Brouwer, 1969).

Geraets, T. *Vers une nouvelle philosophie transcendantale* (The Hague: Nijhoff, 1971).

Jalbert, G. *Nécessité et contingence chez saint Thomas d'Aquin* (Ottawa: Éditions de l'Université d'Ottawa, 1961).

Klimov, A. (ed.). *Confessions. Précédé de le "philosophie teutonique", ou L'esprit d'aventure* (Paris: Fayard, 1973).

Laberge, P. *La théologie kantienne pré-critique* (Ottawa: Éditions de l'Université d'Ottawa, 1973).

Lachance, L. *L'humanisme politique de saint Thomas d'Aquin* (Montreal: Éditions du Lévrier, and Paris: Sirey, 1965).

Lacroix, B. *Orose et ses idées* (Montreal: Institut d'études médiévales, 1965).

Lafrance, G. *La philosophie sociale de Bergson* (Ottawa: Éditions de l'Université d'Ottawa, 1974).

Lamonde, Y. (ed.). *Historiographie de la philosophie au Québec 1853-1970* (Montreal: Hurtubise HMH, 1972).

Landry, A. M. "La pensée philosophique médiévale: Contribution Canadienne (1960–1973)," *Philosophiques* (October 1974).

Lane, G. *Être et langage* (Paris: Aubier-Montaigne, 1970).

———— (trans.). *Quand dire, c'est faire* (Paris: Seuil, 1970).

Langevin, G. *Capax Dei* (Bruges: Desclée de Brouwer, 1966).

Lévesque, C. *L'étrangeté du texte. Essais sur Nietzsche, Freud, Blanchot et Derrida* (Montreal: V.L.B., 1976).

Limoges, C. *La sélection naturelle* (Paris: Presses Universitaires de France, 1970).

Miguelez, R. *Sujet et histoire* (Ottawa: Éditions de l'Université d'Ottawa, 1973).

Montefiore, A. *Philosophie et relations interpersonnelles* (Montreal: Presses de l'Université de Montréal, 1973).

Montpetit, R. *Comment parler de la littérature* (Montreal: Hurtubise HMH, 1976).

Paquet, L. *Les cyniques grecs. Fragments et témoignages* (Ottawa: Éditions de l'Université d'Ottawa, 1976).

————. *Platon: la médiation du regard* (Leiden: Brill, 1973).

Parent, E. "Un Medieviste Canadien-Français," *Dialogue* 6 (1967–1968).

Piotte, J.-M. *La pensée politique de Gramsci* (Paris: Anthropos, 1970.

————. *Les travailleurs contre l'Etat* (Montreal: L'Aurore, 1975).

Poulain, J. *Logique et religion* (The Hague: Mouton, 1973).

Régis, L. M. *Epistemology* (New York: Macmillan, 1959).

Rioux, B. *L'être et la vérité chez Heidegger et saint Thomas d'Aquin* (Montreal: Presses de l'Université de Montréal, 1963).

Theau, J. *La critique bergsonnienne du concept* (Toulouse: É Privat, 1968).

Université Laval. *Mélanges à la memoire de Charles de Koninck* (Quebec: Les Presses de l'Université Laval, 1968).

Vadeboncoeur, P. *Un génocide en douce* (Montreal: Parti Paris, 1976).

Vallières, P. *Nègres blancs d'Amérique* (Montreal: Parti Pris, 1968).

JOURNALS

Chroniques
Computers and Mediaeval Data Processing
Dialogue
Laval Theologique et Philosophique
Parti-pris
Philosophiques
Revue de l'Université d'Ottawa
Science et Esprit
Stratégie

Mexico and Latin America

ARTHUR BERNDTSON

Latin American philosophy since 1940 has been rooted in a movement which started in about 1910 in criticism of the positivism that had dominated Latin American thought during the last decades of the nineteenth century and the opening decade of the twentieth. The positivistic philosophy, led by Gabino Barreda under the influence of Comte, produced few texts and had results primarily in education and politics. The broadly idealistic philosophy which followed it was vigorous and creative for three decades. Its leaders, born between 1949 and 1883, were José Vasconcelos and Antonio Caso of Mexico, Alejandro Korn of Argentina, Alejandro Deustua of Peru, and Carlos Vaz Ferreira of Uruguay. The main sources of their thought were Bergson, Schopenhauer, and Kant. Several ideas dominated the movement. In methodology, it emphasized intuition as an alternative not to experience but to reason; it found reason inadequate because of the fixed concepts, external relations, and atomism that it associated with reason. These thinkers saw nature, especially man, as changing, dynamic, and creative; they were sympathetic to law but not to reductionism. Their approach to values was passionate as well as cognitive; they let pleasure and objects of desire defer to something more heroic or mystical, but not dogmatic. Uniting the real and the good was liberty, which had a promethean tone. Balancing these strenuous valuations was an interest in art and beauty: Vasconcelos, Caso, and Deustua wrote at length in aesthetics.

The recent period begins with Samuel Ramos in Mexico and Francisco Romero in Argentina, although it includes the late work of Caso and Vasconcelos. The principal influences are those of Husserl and Heidegger in phenomenology and existentialism; Scheler and Nicolai Hartmann in ethics and general theory of value; Ortega variously; Marxism in social thought; Anglo-American linguistic analysis; and philosophy of science from various places. Bergson has admirers but not devotees, and intuition with diminished import shifts from living and psychical processes to essences and values. The theses of change and novel levels are retained to a large extent. There are advocates alike of objective and subjective value, and liberty continues to be emphasized. There is less concern with art and beauty. The general tone is one of greater thoroughness and lesser commitment, except among philosophical thinkers whose principal conception is one of political revolution in places of poverty and oppression.

What is most striking and pervasive in the period is the concern with philo-

sophical anthropology and the destiny of man. Nature and God yield in importance to the conception of man in history, whose essence must be defined or
created in an ambitious pursuit of values. To this task come thinkers as diverse
as Ramos, an admirer of Scheler and Hartmann with residual influence from
Bergson; Romero, who provides a philosophy of nature as context for a phenomenology of man; Risieri Frondizi, who is influenced by Gestalt psychology;
Carlos Astrada, who left existentialism for Marxism; and Octavio Derisi, a neo-
Scholastic for whom "authentic humanism" is impossible without Christianity.

MEXICO

The most complex figure in Latin American philosophy is José Vasconcelos
(1882–1959), who has written prolifically in the fields of methodology, metaphysics, ethics, and aesthetics. He participated in the Mexican Revolution; led
the reform of Mexican education as secretary of education in the early 1920s;
lost a bid for the presidency in 1929; and was several times in political exile.
He was rector of the National University of Mexico and had a visiting appointment at the University of Chicago. In addition to many philosophical works
beginning in 1916, he wrote several books about the Indian contribution to
Mexican life and a three-volume autobiography. His sources in philosophy were
Bergson, Schopenhauer, Plotinus, and Pythagoras. A highly literate writer,
Vasconcelos has written, according to Aníbal Sánchez Reulet, some "perfect
pages." Works from the recent period which should be mentioned are *El realismo científico*, which also has metaphysical and aesthetic doctrines; *Logíca
orgánica*, which considers methodological as well as logical problems; and
Todología.

By "organic logic" Vasconcelos understands a method which uses deduction
and induction and the apparatus of scientific laws within a holistic framework
characterized by organic unities. By "scientific realism" he understands a philosophy which finds in modern science a corroboration of organic logic. Philosophy should not reduce the particular to the universal, but should relate it
to other particulars in an organic whole in which individuality is preserved.
Existence is irreducibly heterogeneous in its qualities, and this trait is also found
in the discontinuity of changes. Because of its emphasis on quantities, which
are homogeneous in their units, mathematics does not do full justice to existence.
The right method is aesthetic. The category of rhythm applies to discontinuous
changes which are repeated and so are coherent. The uniform sequences of
events have a melodic order, in which diverse characters have intimate unity.
The three levels of the physical, the living, and the spiritual, though irreducibly
distinct, have a coexistent unity which illustrates the category of harmony.
Reason thus has a limited place in the description of existence. It also has a
limited place in the creation of the world. The creator is a personal deity who
transcends the world. The biblical account of the divine Word signifies that God

created the world not by thought alone, but by an act of will symbolized by the act of speaking.

Art exemplifies these principles vividly and also sheds light on ethics. For example, a musical scale is constructed by the musician out of the apparent continuum of pitches in nature; its member tones are separated by fixed intervals. The discontinuity of the tones resembles the discontinuity of quantum phenomena in physics. In musical rhythm, melody, and harmony, diversity is maintained amid highly organic unity, and the arts instruct us about the highest values. Apollonian art is formalist and devoted to ideas. As it runs its course, it tends to decay in giganticism or in sensuality. It may be saved, however, by a shift to a dionysian emphasis on passion. Dionysian art does not decay: passion either destroys the human spirit or is transformed into religious intensity. The latter occurs in mystical art, in which emotion transcends human objects and focuses on God. Thus, passion is not doomed by fate but can be fulfilled in the divine. For Vasconcelos, Christianity provides the answer to the Greek fear of fate.

Less speculative than Vasconcelos is his early companion, Antonio Caso (1883–1946), who has written at length in ethics, aesthetics, the philosophy of history, and political philosophy. He was born in Mexico City and died there widely honored; he was a professor of philosophy at the National University of Mexico and an influential teacher; and he served as ambassador to several nations. His publications began about 1915; his complete works are being collected in thirteen volumes. His important earlier works include *La existencia como economía, como desinterés y como caridad* and *Principios de estética*. He was influenced mainly by Bergson, Schopenhauer, and Kant, and he published a book on Husserl in 1934.

In *La persona humana y el estado totalitario*, Caso develops a philosophy of freedom and human personality. There are three kinds of finite existents, he states: things, individuals, and persons. Things are physical; they can be divided without destroying their status as things; they may be objects of value but not subjects of value. Individuals are living existents; they cannot be divided without destroying their status as individuals, but they can be substituted for one another. They are subjects of economic value, which is egocentric and views other individuals as means. Persons are spiritual existents, which are unique and cannot be replaced. They are creators of values in the aesthetic domain, which transcends ego in the act of disinterested contemplation, and in the ethical domain, which transcends self in the acts of love and self-sacrifice. The development of personality requires a fine balance of inwardness and sociality. Personal depth and self-knowledge depend on inward awareness. But man is also a social being, a participant in human culture which reflects "the historical continuity of the generations and the moral solidarity of peoples."

Freedom has a generic character of spontaneity which may be found in all three levels of existence. Small bodies have irregularities of motion which elude law and prediction; the latter apply only to groups, in which the spontaneities of members are mutually compensated in statistical law. In the biological realm, and especially in the human domain, individuality of members increases and compensation decreases, with growth of spontaneity and freedom. In the human person, freedom adds the character of self-determination, which appears in my ability both to move my own body and to create values. The creation of values is the summit of human freedom. Self-determination may be blocked by communal pressure, especially in the modern form of the totalitarian state. According to Caso, both the German and Russian forms of totalitarian ideology involve the illegitimate transfer of the concept of the Absolute, as something perfect, necessary, and infinite, from a universal principle of existence to the state. The seed of totalitarian ideology is in Hobbes; it cannot be imputed to Hegel, who placed absolute spirit, i.e., art, religion, and philosophy, above the objective spirit of the state. The remedy for totalitarianism is not individualism, which shares with the former an egoistic attitude. Above individual selves are persons, who are organically related to one another in human culture. In this relation there is no compulsion.

A student of Caso's who subsequently diverged from him is Samuel Ramos (1897–1959), who has written on philosophy of man. He was born in Zitácuaro; spent an interval in France and Italy; and was a professor at the National University of Mexico. His *Historia de la filosofía en México* was a pioneer work. He was influenced by Bergson, Ortega y Gasset, Scheler, and Nicholai Hartmann.

In his *Hacia un nuevo humanismo,* Ramos sketches a philosophy which lodges man in nature but gives him the task of developing his humanity through liberal culture. Man is a synthesis of body and soul, of material forces which are blind, and of spirit which, of itself impotent, furnishes direction. He is distinguished by the psychical aspect of this partnership, which has three layers. Following Ortega, Ramos calls the levels vitality, soul, and spirit. Vitality is identified with the body as felt from within: internal sensations, instincts, and the like. Soul is composed of the emotions, which I recognize as mine but not as my self. Spirit is the essence of selfhood; it is composed of thought and volition. It proceeds by impersonal norms of logic for thought and of values for will. Because of this outward direction, spirit is objective, in contrast with the subjective character of soul.

The humanism of Ramos is concerned with the life of spirit as valuing and as free. Values have a being independent of acts of valuation. Judgments of value are influenced by emotions and by scarcity of objects; these facts attest not to subjectivism, but to error in judgments. It is possible to desire without esteeming and to esteem without desire. Values have the trait of oughtness. Since it is possible to judge that some reality is not as it ought to be, there must be "an ideal model with which to compare real facts." Values thus constitute, in their purity, an ideal world, as in Plato and Hartmann. The ought-to-be has an aspect of exigency or dynamism; Ramos seems to ascribe this aspect to ideal value itself, but he may instead locate it in man, who is the mediator between the worlds of ideal value and of reality. The spirit is not, however, determined automatically by the awareness of value and oughtness, as is shown by a decision against a given value. The spirit, or person in the axiological sense, has the ability to choose among values and so is free. "Man is a being of multiple possibilities with power of variable amplitude for choosing them; he can voluntarily propose to himself an end and fulfill it." Here freedom for Ramos appears to have a factor of indeterminateness. On the other hand, he accepts Hartmann's view that freedom must be positive and causal. Personality, consciousness, life, and physical nature constitute a series of levels in which the higher depends on the lower but has a defining novelty which cannot be reduced to the lower. Each level has a measure of freedom in relation to the lower by virtue of the novelty, but is fully determined internally. Hartmann did not reconcile the autonomy of the person with the general thesis of determination. It appears that Ramos did not do so either.

A kindred admirer of German axiologists in Eduardo García Máynez (1908–   ), a writer in the fields of ethics and philosophy of law. He was born in Mexico City; studied law and philosophy at the universities of Berlin and Vienna in 1932–1933; and was simultaneously a member of the faculties of law and of philosophy and letters at the National University of Mexico. Beginning in 1935 and continuing for three decades, he wrote many books in the philosophy of law, which deal with the ethical validation of law, the ontology of law, and the logic of law. In the area of ethics and general theory of values, García Máynez wrote *Etica,* published in 1944 with a nineteenth edition in 1972, and *El problema de la objetividad de los valores.* His ethics and axiology were influenced by Max Scheler, especially by Nicolai Hartmann's *Ethics,* "the best treatise on axiological questions written in this century."

García Máynez's account of the problems and schools of ethics involves several distinctions: absolute or objective and relative or subjective; *a priori* and empirical; material and formal; ends and means; and intentions and consequences of acts. He finds four schools of ethics: empirical ethics, ranging from anarchistic ethics to utilitarianism and social subjectivism; the ethics of final ends, for which pleasure, happiness, and virtue are candidates; formalist ethics, as in Kant; and the axiological ethics begun in Germany in the 1890s and culminating in the work of Scheler and Hartmann in the second and third decades of the twentieth century.

Empirical ethics is relativistic and leads to skepticism and nihilism. Utilitarianism is either a doctrine of pure utility, without discipline of means, or it becomes a theory of social happiness as the governing end and so an ethics of final ends. The advocates of social subjectivism, such as Durkheim, confuse generality of valuation in a society with objectivity of value. García Máynez finds the refutation of relativism in Husserl's arguments in the *Logical Investigations* for the objectivity of truth and of the logical contents of judgments. He believes that the ethics of ends has dominated ethical thought from Socrates to Kant, with eudemonism as its chief variety. But the desire for happiness is no proof that we ought to pursue happiness, and qualitative eudemonism implies that the true value lies in the distinctive quality and not in happiness itself. Kantian formalism has an emphasis on intention that brings moral value into its proper locus, the will and person. It errs, however, in its formalist preference for law, its intellecualist preference for reason, and its derivation of value from oughtness rather than the contrary position. These mistakes are corrected in the axiological ethics of Scheler and Hartmann. Following Hartmann especially, García Máynez holds that values are determinate or material essences, which are known by an emotional intuition, and which are the source rather than the derivative of oughtness. The intuition is itself *a priori*. Experience of facts does not settle what ought to be, and Socratic induction of the concept of a virtue from instances presupposes an idea of the value of the instances. In addition, values are objective in the mode of ideal being, or Platonic ideas.

For the moral value of an act and person, liberty is required. The most thorough part of García Máynez's *Etica* is a study of freedom of the will or, more profoundly, of the person. Following Hartmann, he asserts physical and psychological determinism, constituting a causal nexus, on which is built a teleological nexus which is not determined by the causal nexus. The values of the upper level oblige but do not necessitate: the individual person ought to enact them, but is free not to do so. This means that the person has a margin of freedom in regard to values. García Máynez does not take into account Hartmann's profound analysis of the conflict of values, which is involved in that freedom. He is aware, however, of the difficulty of establishing moral freedom, which is a freedom of choice and not simply of action. Freedom of the will is a metaphysical question, which can be discussed but is not subject to demonstration or refutation. But there are three indicators of freedom: the phenomenon of the consciousness of self-determination, the phenomenon of responsibility, and the phenomenon of guilt. These three phenomena have an ascending order of witness to the existence of a person, which, by definition, is a free actor in relation to values. This person is not free to create values in themselves, which have timeless being, but he is free to create in the realm of temporal being, where he can bring into being things and acts and volitions that realize values.

The *a priori* and absolute truths claimed by García Máynez stand in contrast to the analytic and critical approach of Fernando Salmerón (1925–   ), who wrote in ethics, philosophy of education, and history of philosophy. Salmerón was born in Córdoba, Veracruz; was educated through the licentiate in law in his native province; received the doctorate in philosophy from the National University of Mexico in 1965; and studied in Germany and France before that date. Since 1966, he has been director of the Institute for Philosophical Investigations at the National University and editor of *Diánoia*. He has written books on the young Ortega and on education in Mexico, and his dissertation was on Husserl, Hartmann, and Heidegger. His own views on method and on ethics are contained in *La filosofía y las actitudes morales,* in a comment on a lecture by

Augusto Salazar Bondy published in 1969, and in an inaugural lecture given at the Colegio Nacional in 1972. These views were influenced by Hare, Ryle, Popper, and others.

Salmerón distinguishes between philosophy in a wide sense of the term and philosophy in a strict sense. The first type consists of wisdom or a conception of the world; the philosopher deals "at the same time with his own destiny and the meaning of the world" and interweaves ideas about ultimate reality with principles of value. Such philosophy can neither be verified nor refuted; world conceptions cannot be tested by experience, and they arise out of value attitudes that are evaluative rather than cognitive. Salmerón discusses attitudes at some length, drawing on ordinary language and the findings of psychologists of several countries, but is more summary in the disclaimer of empirical relevance of world conceptions and in the claim that they are based on value attitudes. He does not, however, dismiss metaphysics as meaningless, but gives it a significant place in the life of values and a provisional function in the search for dependable knowledge. World conceptions give direction to moral action and provide justifications of a sort for it. Their influence on action lies between pure spontaneity on the one hand and rigorous knowledge on the other. They have endurance based on "a formidable power of adaptation which . . . reinterprets new results of scientific investigation to adjust them" to the conceptions. And they furnish materials for critical analysis by philosophy in the strict sense, which, according to a letter of 1977 from Salmerón, has the further task of giving them a "new articulation in a form better adjusted to contemporary moral changes and sensibility."

Philosophy in a strict sense is exemplified in logic, semantics, and epistemology; it is "dominated by an energy properly scientific" and uses "certain methods about which . . . there is general agreement." It leaves questions of fact and reality to the sciences, and assists the latter to clarification of theories and to understanding of the relation of the sciences to one another and to society. Such philosophy neither directs nor justifies actions and attitudes, but it can yield knowledge about the coherence of ideals and the validity of conceptions associated with those ideals. In regard to values, its relation to philosophy in the wide sense is that of meta-ethics to normative ethics. But whereas the sciences seek intersubjective agreement, ethics for Salmerón does not seek to "suppress the variety of attitudes or to unify the universe of moral ideals." Despite this breadth, Salmerón follows Hare in regard to the freedom, rationality, and universality of moral experience or discourse. Ethics must consider human nature and the interests of men, but offers no sanction for egoistic interest. Here also it appears that the difference between the two kinds of philosophy is not absolute.

Historicist, phenomenological, and existential ideas are dominant in several other writers of the recent period in Mexico. Leopoldo Zea, an historian of philosophy, favors an historical and relative conception of philosophy instead of a purely conceptual and universal view. In the Introduction to his *Positivism in Mexico*, a translation of his *El positivismo en México*, he declares that human problems originate in given circumstances of history, so that solutions are also circumstantial. Thus, "the truths of philosophy are dependent on a specific time and place." Philosophy changes with history, and the apparent contradictions in philosophy "are merely different solutions given in different situations." José Gaos, an influential historian of philosophy who left Spain at the time of the Civil War, has traced in phenomenological modes in his *Del hombre* the development of man from primitive sign functions to art and philosophy. Man developed from bare object-status to subjectivity, self-objectification, and intersubjectivity, a development which does not resolve the duality of the animal and human in man. Gaos earlier made a translation into Spanish of Heidegger's *Zein und Zeit*. Further existentialist activity appears in such writers as José Romano Muñoz, author of *Hacia una filosofía existencial*, and Augustín Basave Fernández del Valle, who wrote *Existencialistas y existencialismo* and *Metafísica de la muerte*.

ARGENTINA

The leading philosopher of the recent period in Latin America is Francisco Romero (1891–1962), a contributor to philosophical anthropology. He was born in Seville, Spain, but as a child moved to Argentina. His initial career was military, which ended in 1931. His academic appointments were at the universities of Buenos Aires and La Plata; he renounced them in 1946 and returned to them in 1955. Romero was a close friend of Alejandro Korn and was influenced by Scheler, Nicolai Hartmann, and Husserl. His major work is *Teoría del hombre*, translated as *Theory of Man;* it was preceded by *Papeles para una filosofía*. He also wrote several books in the history of philosophy.

The pervasive concept in Romero's thought is that of transcendence, whose opposite is immanence. Transcendence "is always a going out from oneself," or a passing beyond a given condition or boundary; immanence is "enclosure in one's own particular reality." The maximum of immanence is in the logical principle of identity; the maximum of transcendence is found in the spiritual acts of purely objective awareness and conduct. The two terms vary inversely. As the positive and creative principle, transcendence dominates Romero's methodology, account of reality, and axiology.

In methodology, reason is allied with immanence. Whether intuitive or discursive, reason seeks identity, homogeneity, and permanence. It favors atoms, which are similar and enduring, and causal laws, which assert uniformity of connections between events. It also seeks transparency as the condition of clarity, and so it ends with empty forms. Because of both ideals, reason favors space and geometry; it is therefore most applicable to physical objects. However, it has no datum of its own and thus no independent access to reality; it is a mere fabric of norms, which reality need not observe. Our knowledge of reality is based on experience, which supplies data to guide our knowing. Experience for Romero is not limited to sensation and introspection; it also includes direct awareness of essences and values. Apparently, it has no bias for either immanence or transcendence since it reveals a real world with both.

Romero divides phenomenal reality into four levels: the inorganic, the organic, the intentional, and the spiritual. Immanence declines with the ascent, and transcendence increases. In the dualities of thing and activity, of mechanical and organic wholes, and of quantities and qualities, the second of each pair is more evident with the advance, with a gain of transcendence since each of the three participates in transcendence in contrast with the immanence of its opposite. The inorganic and organic levels are spatiotemporal, while the intentional and spiritual levels are temporal alone; the temporal levels enjoy more freedom since they are not subject to the mathematical determination of the levels that include space. Transcendence thus is correlated with freedom. The four levels are so related that the later depend on the earlier but cannot be reduced to them. Phenomenal reality thus involves a pluralism of levels and a monism in regard to transcendence.

The inorganic level has some degree of transcendence in the internal nature of its particles since modern physics has replaced the inert corpuscle with a *foco activísimo*. In comparison with the physical time of mere bodies, the vital has true duration and so a gain in transcendence. Romero appears to ascribe a primitive, or preintentional, psyche to all living individuals; such a psyche is not properly conscious, has no distinction of subject and object, and is composed of an "undivided succession of states" of a subjective order. Perhaps he would grant transcendence in that qualitative interpenetration. The third level consists of the "superior or intentional psyche" whose "intentional activity transforms the states into objects." Here the distinction of subject and object arises, and with it consciousness as attribute of the subject intending an object. "The reiteration of subjective acts, the consolidation of the subject, and becoming accustomed to being a subject, make of the subject a 'self'." Corresponding to self is a world, which is an organization of objectifications. Intention is an objective and transcending act, but, at the merely intentional level, objects are subordinated to the "immediate goals of the percipient, who catalogues them under the earmark of interesting or indifferent, useful or useless." The return to the percipient indicates partial subjectivity, high particularity, and incomplete transcendence in the stage of merely intentional consciousness. These imperfections are removed in the fourth and spiritual level. Here the self intends an object and his attention remains with the object: "the subject yields himself to the object." The spiritual self is objective and universal, while retaining its separate individuality in relation to other spirits. The spiritual self is free in relation to the "propensities and attitudes" of the merely intentional self, but Romero does not decide whether spirit on its own level is necessitated or is contingent. Because of its objectivity, universality, and freedom, spirit enjoys absolute transcendence. It also enjoys absolute value.

For Romero, "value is the degree of transcendence." Value is the dignity that belongs to something because of the transcendence it embodies. Value is therefore objective, and its absolute or complete degree is found in spiritual acts. Cognitive value involves spirit contemplating what is, without taking sides. Ethical value is directed toward transcendence in what is. In ethical activity, the spirit gives special attention to transcendence and collaborates with it. The basic ethical precept is to act in such a way " 'that the direction of your act accords with the essential direction of reality.' "

The theory of transcendence ends with the question of a metaphysical or noumenal transcendence, which should course through the four levels as the increasingly complete creator of the phenomena described above. Knowledge of such a reality, if it is achieved, must be empirical, but metaphysical rather than sensible, and the required datum must be supplied by the transcending reality. Romero believes that such an experience is possible and that writers such as Schopenhauer and Bergson erred not in accepting such a datum, but in interpreting it. The will of the first and the *elán vital* of the second are modes of transcending but do not exhaust the latter, which begins with matter and ends with spirit. For Romero, the assertion of such a noumenal transcendence is an hypothesis which must pass various tests in order to be defensible. It appears that for Romero, transcendence in its basic nature is highly general and indeterminate. Given his apparent understanding of the successive phenomenal levels as forms and occasional references to activity and dynamism, his incomplete theory of noumenal transcendence may contain an implicit theory of power as such, which may be conceived as logically prior to matter and mind alike.

Risieri Frondizi (1910–   ), a friend and admirer of Romero, has contributed to philosophical anthropology and axiology. He was born in Posadas and educated in Buenos Aires; took graduate degress at the University of Michigan and the National University of Mexico and studied at Harvard under Whitehead and Perry; and was a professor at the University of Buenos Aires from 1956 to 1966, during part of which time he was president of the university. A man of exceptional courage, he went into exile for political reasons in 1946–1955 and again in 1966. He has been at Southern Illinois University since 1970. His principal writings are *El punto de partida del filosofar; Substancia y función en el problema del yo,* translated as *The Nature of the Self; Que son los valores?,* translated as *What Is Value?;* and recent articles on value in *Diánoia* (Mexico City) and *Journal of Value Inquiry,* both in 1972.

The starting point of philosophy for Frondizi is experience, which involves a self doing something with objects. We can be as sure of the independent existence of objects as of the existence of our awareness of them, due to the intentionality of conscious acts and to the resistance of objects. Knowledge of other selves is as primitive as knowledge of my self and the external world. Frondizi rejects the concept of substance by which he understands something simple, immutable, and independent, and whose vicissitudes he traces through a scholarly examination of the concept in Descartes, Locke, Berkeley, and Hume. He also rejects the atomistic empiricism of Hume, whose simples he shrewdly identifies with the criteria for substance. His preference is for the related concepts of function and Gestalt. The concept of function embraces the ideas of process, dynamic activity, and relation. Growing out of the last, and fully integrated with the concept of process, is the idea of Gestalt, as exemplified in psychology by leaders of that school. As treated by Frondizi, a Gestalt is an organic unity rather than a sum of parts. The whole has properties not to be found in any parts or their aggregate; the whole depends on the parts and the parts on the whole; the parts are not simple elements and differ in kind among each other; their difference even rises to opposition in a dialectical relation. Frondizi does not consider these concepts in material and living nature, but he applies them at length to problems of self and value.

The self has an endurance not to be found in its individual experiences or in their literal sum over a period of time. This enduring self is not an intuitive datum; it is implied by memory and anticipation, and by the fact that perception of changes requires an enduring perceiver. But the self is not an immutable substance unaffected by the individual experiences. Such a self would not grow from infancy to maturity and would not participate in the good and evil of its experiences. The latter in turn do not need a support beyond themselves. Neither a collection nor a detached substance, the self is a Gesalt which depends on its member experiences but has traits not found in them. It has permanence or constant presence to its experiences. While enduring, it changes by alteration through the deposit in it made by experiences which change by substitution or displacement. The experiences are not themselves simple and instantaneous; a moment of experience has its own past, present, and future, and successive experiences interpenetrate with a similar continuity to forge the continuity of the self. A cross-section of an experience is also complex and interweaving since in it intellectual, emotive, and volitional qualities blend with varying emphases. The self is not, however, merely passive to the organic traits of its member experiences; it is itself dynamic, creative, and free. The self therefore is immanent in its experiences, being dependent upon them, and is transcendent of them, having traits that cannot be reduced to its members or their mere aggregate.

Values are closely related to selves and also illustrate the principle of Gestalt. Frondizi criticizes the subjectivistic theories of value, which commonly identify value with pleasure or the object of desire or of interest. Neither pleasure, desire, nor interest is a guarantee of value, and value may occur apart from them. An added character, illustrated by "higher," is needed to secure a guarantee, and that character goes beyond the scope of the three criteria. None of the trio is able to resolve conflicts among persons in regard to values. Objectivism is also inadequate. Contrary to Scheler, values are not independent of man, they are not immutable, and they are not known *a priori*. The early G. E. Moore was correct in saying that values cannot be reduced to natural properties, but wrong in holding that they do not depend on such properties and that they are simple. Values depend jointly on subjective properties, including pleasure, desire, and interest, and on the characters of valued objects that influence our valuations.

The interplay of subjective and objective properties constitutes a Gestalt, whose novel quality is a value. Due to the dependence of the Gestalt on its members, a value is complex; due to the novelty of the Gestalt, a value is not reducible to the members and is not a natural quality. The concept of Gestalt is amplified by that of situation, which is physical, social, and personal. Moral values, like other values, depend on the situation, but the higher of two conflicting values in a situation is preferable. The denotative meaning of "higher" varies, however, with the situation. According to Frondizi, the hierarchical aspect of values preserves the situational ethics from relativism.

Humanism of a contrasting order is found in Carlos Astrada (1894–1970), an existentialist and Marxist. He was born in Córdoba; spent several years in the 1920s in Germany, where he studied under Husserl and Heidegger; had positions in philosophy at the universities of Buenos Aires and La Plata; and gave lectures in Moscow and Peking in 1956 and 1960. His many books reflect an early advocacy of Heideggerian thought and a subsequent shift to Marx, Hegel, and problems of the dialectic, with a survival of some basic concepts of the earlier phase in the later time. In his *Esitencialismo y crisis de la filosofía,* which is a revision of his *La revolución existencialista,* Astrada finds in Heidegger an existential ontology anchored in "irrationalist solipsism" and in Sartre a phenomenalist ontology "without any basis whatsoever." He contrasts these negative conditions with the vigor of dialectical materialism. But Astrada contributes to dialectical theory a literate humanism with an emphasis on what he conceives to be the essential liberty of man. This contribution appears in his *Humanismo y dialéctica de la libertad.*

According to Astrada, it is only by a universal humanism that man can achieve true liberty, and it is only through liberty that man can be redeemed from the condition of alienation and arrive at his humanity. Astrada traces the humanist ideal in Protagoras, the Renaissance, the Enlightenment, and Hegel, and he finds accompanying errors: slavery in Greece, a duality of noble and common men in the Renaissance, a generic and abstract conception of man in the Enlightenment, and emphasis on spirit and its ideas in Hegel. There are also virtues, which successively move toward the universal humanism sought after: man the measure; man and his earthly life as the end value; Pico de la Mirandola's notion that man can create himself, having no proper nature to constrain him; and Hegel's view of man as made concrete in history. Marx combined these insights with a doctrine of social praxis. In so doing, he achieved a universal humanism which liberates man from suprahuman bonds of eternal essences and truths, and from the subhuman bond of being a mere means to the production of material goods in the capitalist economy.

Astrada less readily defines the liberty at hand than the humanism which speaks for it. Liberty is the "reduction of the base of natural necessity," although it appears that liberty is not opposed to natural law but to contingent servitude in an unjust society. It depends on the malleability of man as fluid existence rather than static essence. Astrada, like Sartre, however, seems not to consider how such fluidity can be responsible or how it can be a foundation for the successive forms that define a person or a civilization. It is eminently dialectical, being a process of genesis of itself, in which oppositions are absorbed and transcended. Liberty so conceived is unlike Christian liberty as understood by Astrada, which is given instantly to man by Christ. Despite its dialectical nature, it was misconceived by Hegel, who reconciled liberty and necessity by saying that liberty is necessity understood by reason, so that liberty is restricted to cognitive acts whose object is the Idea. On the contrary, liberty is practical in the ordinary relations of men in society. Astrada perceives that spirit made objective in historical forms of its creating may become rigid in them, frustrating its own freedom. Here he cites Nicolai Hartmann as writing that the life of spirit in history is generally a combat with objectified spirit. He also warns, against some Marxists, that the dialectic is not automatic. History is fluid and subject to retrograde movements, so that it is necessary to have "full consciousness in action." Astrada is somewhat ambiguous about the value and role of the liberties associated with democratic liberalism: freedom of thought, of speech, and of suffrage. The classless society, however, is not the realization of the "total man" but only the starting point, from which a plurality of directions is open for the unfolding of the plenary being of man.

An orientation toward method and physical reality appears in Mario Bunge (1919–   ), a prolific writer in semantics and the philosophy of science. Bunge was born in Buenos Aires; received his doctorate in physico-mathematical sciences at the University of La Plata in 1952; was professor of theoretical physics at that university during 1956–1959, and of philosophy at the University of Buenos Aires during 1957–1962; and has been professor of philosophy at McGill University since 1966. Among his many books are *Causality,* which has been translated into several languages; *The Myth of Simplicity;* and *Scientific Research.* He is at work on a seven-volume series on "basic philosophy" dealing with semantics, ontology, epistemology, the philosophy of science, and value theory. The first two volumes, on semantics, appeared in 1974, and the third volume, on ontology, in 1977.

For Bunge, philosophy begins with analysis and ends with the creation of theories. The analysis in question is not directed to ordinary language and common sense; language often "harbors bad logic and superseded beliefs." The proper analysis does not construct "rigorous but utterly artificial 'languages'," which are "remote from living science" and thus from the understanding of the cognitive enterprise. It has its subject matter in the concepts and theories of mathematics and factual science. Although analysis often is thought to seek simple terms which are few in kind or one, Bunge warns against the "necessity of drastically reducing the number of basic concepts." Whatever the outcome of analysis, it can be improved if it is done with the help of mathematical logic and mathematics. Philosophy so fortified is "exact philosophy." Our immediate task is to build "well circumscribed theories in exact philosophy," ranging from semantics to metaphysics to value theory. Large systems may then emerge from the fusion of these limited theories. According to Bunge, his epistemology is a critical realism. His ontology is materialistic; it is pluralistic through emergence; it is deterministic, with a place for chance. Values are based on objective and subjective factors, and so are relational and functional. Ethics can be made scientific by formulating generalizations and justifiable value judgments.

OTHER COUNTRIES

In Peru, Francisco Miró Quesada (1918–   ) has written in logic and theory of knowledge. He was born in Lima; took doctorates in both philosophy and mathematics at the University of San Marcos, where he also taught; has lectured in many universities in Latin America and Europe; and has traveled at length in Russia and China. He has written books in mathematical logic, philosophy of law, and social philosophy.

In his *Apuntes para una teoría de la razón,* Miró Quesada examines the nature and validity of reason, which he identifies with logic and mathematics. The foundations of logical and mathematical knowledge lie in principles which, as prior to formalization, are known intuitively. There are three types of such intuited principles: logical principles; constructive principles, which involve numerical order; and principles other than these. The principle of noncontradiction is more radical than the constructive principles; it underlies all logical and mathematical deduction, which, in turn, underlies all explanation in the empirical sciences. The nature and validity of intellectual intuition therefore require examination. Intuition is a way of apprehending an object. It may contain an evidential character, which is "the quality, the tint which some of our intuitions acquire whereby they present an irresistible power of conviction." This character becomes the "criterion of truth of intuitive knowledge." It has generally, though not universally, been ascribed to intuition of the principle of excluded middle as well as to the principle of noncontradiction. But the Gödel theorem of undecidability leads to restriction of the application of the former law, while leaving the latter principle unchallenged since the argument leading to restriction "is based on the absolute necessity of respecting the principle of noncontradiction." Since intuitive evidentiality has failed in one case while being sustained in the other, it is necessary to look for a criterion of validity of such evidence. Miró Quesada finds this criterion within the "*dinámica* of evidences produced by an internal process of reason." Evidence is not authentic if the system which includes it leads to results which exceed it. Evidence is authentic if the same process which leads to such rejection presupposes that evidence constitutively. The principle of noncontradiction meets this test of authenticity.

Miró Quesada resumes the defense of this principle in his article "Dialéctica y recoplamiento," published in *Diánoia* in 1972. He shows that the dialectical method of thesis, antithesis, and transcending synthesis has not contributed to the solution of paradoxes in mathematics or to the discovery of truths in natural science. He argues that Marxist predictions of social change for the most part have not been fulfilled, to the disadvantage of the dialectical method used. The attempts of recent neo-Marxists to interpret the dialectical method as a theory of history "as the result of a system of reciprocal actions among individuals, groups and institutions" have merit in relation to history. But the revision illustrates not the dialectic, but the quite different concept of feedback. The feedback concept, applied to society, will not justify the classic theses of Marxism, such as the inevitable attainment of the classless society. But application of the relations of feedback to the analysis of social structures can be used in the future in planning the "just society."

A contrasting thinker in Peru is Augusto Salazar Bondy (1925–1974), an historian of philosophy. Salazar Bondy finished his undergraduate work at the University of San Marcos in 1950, studied in France and Germany in 1951–1953, and received his doctorate from San Marcos in 1953. He is the author of *Historia de las ideas en el Perú contemporáneo* and other works. In 1968, he gave a lecture at the University of Kansas, which was published the following year as *Sentido y problema del pensamiento filosófico hispanoamericano*. The lecture states his views on the nature of philosophy and the condition of Latin American philosophy.

According to Salazar Bondy, philosophy deals with reality as a whole and with the "vital commitment" of the whole man to that reality. It differs from science in its emphasis on totality, and from religion in its rationality. Philosophy does not arise in an historical vacuum; it expresses, or ought to express, the culture of the community in which it is located. Here "culture" is used in a "strong" sense to designate the "organic articulation of the original and differentiating manifestations of a community." A community is authentic when it has such a self-dependent and creative spirit, and a philosophy is authentic when it expresses such a community. Hispanic American philosophy is unauthentic. It imitates foreign models; it has no "characteristic, definitive tendency"; and it exists at a "great distance" from the "whole of the community." This condition of the philosophy is due to the absence of a true culture in the community; the unauthentic nature of the philosophy rests on the unauthentic nature of the community. The latter condition in turn stems from the widespread underdevelopment of nations under the political and economic domination of Spain, England, and the United States. Despite these pervasive and basic causes, Salazar Bondy thinks that philosophy can take the lead in improving itself and the community. Man can rise above his present condition, and philosophy, "the focus of man's total awareness," can "better than other spiritual creations, be that part of humanity that rises above itself." Only general formulas are stated for this redemption from alienation. Hispanic American philosophy must destroy prejudices and idols; it must search in the "historical substance of our community . . . for the qualities and values that could express it positively." It will be familiar with the concepts and methods of foreign philosophy, while keeping in mind "their provisional and instrumental character." Thus, Salazar Bondy made use of the concepts of authenticity, cultural relativism, and existential freedom, largely imported, to sketch a program for freeing Latin American philosophy from foreign bondage.

Uruguayan philosophy is represented by Juan Llambías de Azevedo (1907–1972), who has contributed to the philosophy of law and to axiology. In his article "La objetividad de los valores ante la filosofía de la existencia," Llambías de Azendo defends the objectivity of value and the value of the universe against the negations of Heidegger and Jaspers, while approving the Kierkegaardian interest in individual man as a unique existent concerned with his destiny. His defense is influenced by Scheler and Hartmann. For Llambías de Azevado, values are known by emotional acts, which, like intellectual acts, intend objects which they illuminate. The feeling of a value is at the same time a feeling of it as higher than some values and lower than others. There are subjective values, such as the agreeable and the useful, but spiritual values are objective. The being in itself of value results from the adequation between values and reality. A judgment of value of a person is not about the concept of the person or about our feeling toward the latter, but about the person himself. We cannot indifferently apply any value to any thing. The being in itself is epistemological, not ontological; a value is independent of the knower, but it is always the value of an entity. A value is something "more intimate and profound" in the entity than categorical traits, such as relation and quality. Value is "a moment of the being of the entity as such," to which are joined the other factors of the essence and the existence of that being. Changes of ideals in history come about because a given epoch discovers "a limited sector of the totality of the being of each value": the changes do not signify relatively of value. Because an entity is finite and contingent, Heidegger and Jaspers hold it to be without value. But a finite entity has a finite value. In conformity with his Catholic beliefs, Llambías de Azevado holds that there is a being which unites existence, essence, and value in themselves: God is absolute value.

Several other Hispanic countries have had philosophers of significance in the recent period. In Brazil, Alceu Amoroso Lima (1893–   ) has been influenced by the Thomistic philosophy of Jacques Maritain. His *O problema do trabalho* and *O existencialismo* state a Christian humanism as a reply to Marxism and existentialism. Vicente Ferreira da Silva (1916–1963) began with work in mathematical logic and moved on to interest in Heidegger and existentialism. His *Dialěctica das consciencias* and various journal articles set forth a philosophy of man for whose existence deity has an important role. Miguel Reale (1910–   ) has been active in Brazilian politics and has written many books in the philosophy of law. In his *Filosofía do direito,* he expounds a philosophy of values that emphasizes the person as source of values. Venezuelan philosophy is represented by Ernesto Mayz Vallenilla who was influenced by Heidegger and has written books on phenomenology and on Kant. In Chile, Jose Echeverria has written books on death and time, on Don Quixote, and on the philosophy of law; and Jorge Millas has written books that contain historical, social, and legal commentary, with criticism of dialectical and other forms of materialism.

SELECT BIBLIOGRAPHY

BOOKS AND ARTICLES

Amoroso Lima, A. *O existencialismo* (Rio de Janeiro: Agir, 1951).

———. *O problema do trabalho* (Rio de Janeiro: Agir, 1946).

Ardao, A. *La filosofía en el Uruguay en el siglo XX* (Mexico City: Fondo de Cultura Económica, 1956).

Astrada, C. *Existencialismo y crisis de la filosofía*, rev. ed. (Buenos Aires: Editorial Devenir, 1963).

———. *Humanismo y dialéctica de la libertad* (Buenos Aires: Editorial Dédalo, 1960).

Basave Fernández del Valle, A. *Existencialistas y existencialismo* (Buenos Aires: Editorial Atlántida, 1958).

———. *Metafísica de la muerte* (Madrid: Libreria Editorial Augustinus, 1965).

Berndtson, A. "Latin American Philosophy," in *Encyclopedia of Philosophy*, IV, ed. P. Edwards (New York: Macmillan, 1967).

Bunge, M. *Causality* (Cambridge, Mass.: Harvard University Press, 1959).

———. *Scientific Research*, 2 vols. (Berlin: Springer, 1967).

———. *The Myth of Simplicity* (Englewood Cliffs, N.J.: Prentice-Hall, 1963).

———. *Treatise on Basic Philosophy*, 3 vols. (Dordrecht and Boston: Reidel, 1974–1977). Four additional volumes are projected.

Caso, A. *La existencia como economía, como desinterés y como caridad* (Mexico City: Ediciones Mexico moderno, 1919).

———. *La persona humana y el estado totalitario* (Mexico City: Universidad nocional autónoma, 1941).

———. *Principios de estética* (Mexico City: Publicaciones de la Sria de edvcacion, 1925).

Caturelli, A. *La filosofía en la Argentina actual*, 2d ed. (Buenos Aires: Editorial Sudamericana, 1971).

Escobar, R. *La filosofía en Chile* (Santiago: Editorial Universidad Técnica del Estada, 1976).

Ferreira da Silva, V. *Obras Completas de Vicente Ferreira da Silva*, 2 vols. (São Paulo: Instituto Brasileira de Filosofia, 1964–1966).

Francovich, G. *Filósofos brasileños* (Buenos Aires: Editorial Losada, 1943).

Frondizi, R. *El punto de partida del filosofar*, 2d ed. (Buenos Aires: Editorial Losada, 1957).

———. *Introducción a los problemas fundamentales del hombre* (Mexico City: Fondo de Cultura Económica, 1977).

———. *Que son los valores?* (Mexico City: Fondo de Cultura Económica, 1958).

———. *Substancia y función en el problema del yo* (Buenos Aires: Editorial Losada, 1952).

———. *The Nature of the Self* (Carbondale, Ill.: Southern Illinois University Press, 1971).

———. *What is Value?* (La Salle, Ill: Open Court, 1971).

——— and Gracia, J.J.E. *El hombre y los valores en la Filosofía Latinoamericano del siglo XX* (Mexico City: Fondo de Cultura Económica, 1975).

Gaos, J. *Del hombre* (Mexico City: Fondo de Cultura Económica, 1970).

García Máynez, E. *El problema de la objetividad de los valores* (Mexico City: Editorial de el Colegio Nacional, 1969).

———. *Etica*, 19th ed. (Mexico City: Editorial Porrúa, 1972).

León-Portilla, M., et al. *Major Trends in Mexican Philosophy*, trans. A. R. Caponigri (Notre Dame, Ind.: University of Notre Dame Press, 1966).

Llambías de Azevedo, J. "La objetividad de los valores ante la filosofía de la existencia," *Revista de la Facultad de Humanidades y Ciencias*, No. 9 (1952).

Miró Quesada, F. *Apuntes para una teoría de la razón* (Lima: Universidad Mayor de San Marcos, 1963).

———. "Dialéctica y recoplamiento," *Diánoia*, No. 18 (1972).

Ramos, S. *Hacia un nuevo humanismo*, 2d ed. (Mexico City: Fondo de cultura Económica, 1962).

————. *Historia de la filosofía en México* (Mexico City: Imprenta Universitaria, 1943).

Reale, M. *Filosofía do direito*, 2d rev. ed. (São Paulo: Edicão Saraiva, 1957).

Romanell, P. *Making of the Mexican Mind* (Lincoln, Neb.: University of Nebraska Press, 1952).

Romano Muñoz, J. *Hacia una filosofía existencial* (Mexico City: Imprenta Universitaria, 1953).

Romero, F. *Papeles para una filosofía* (Buenos Aires: Editorial Losada, 1945).

————. *Teoría del hombre* (Buenos Aires: Editorial Losada, 1952).

————. *Theory of Man*, trans. W. P. Cooper (Berkeley, Calif.: University of California Press, 1964).

Salazar Bondy, A. *Historia de las ideas en el Perú contemporáneo*, 2 vols. (Lima: F. Moncloa, 1965).

————. *Sentido y problema del pensamiento filosófico hispanoamericano*, trans. D. L. Schmidt with comments by F. Salmerón and A. Berndtson (Lawrence, Kans.: University of Kansas Center of Latin American Studies, 1969).

Salmerón, F. *La filosofía y las actitudes morales* (Mexico City: Siglo Veintiuno Editores, 1971).

Sanchez Reulet, A. *Contemporary Latin-American Philosophy* (Albuquerque, N. Mex.: University of New Mexico Press, 1954).

Torchia Estrada, J. *La filosofía en la Argentina* (Washington, D.C.: Unión Panamericana, 1961).

Vasconcelos, J. *El realismo científico* (Mexico City: Centro de Estudios Filosóficas de la Facultad de Filosofía y Letras, 1943).

————. *Logíca orgánica* (Mexico City: Editorial del el Colegio Nacional, 1945).

————. *Obras completas de José Vasconcelos*, 4 vols. (Mexico City: Libreros Mexicanos Unidos, 1957–1961).

————. *Todología* (Mexico City: Ediciones Botas, 1952).

Vita, L. *Panorama da filosifía no Brasil* (Pôrto Alegre: Editôra Globo, 1969).

Zea, L. *El positivismo en México* (Mexico City: El Colegio de Mexico, 1943).

————. *Positivism in Mexico*, trans. J. H. Schulte (Austin, Tex.: University of Texas Press, 1974).

JOURNALS

Mexico

Crítica
Dianoia
Heraldo del Espiritismo
Logos
Renovación
Revisión Filosófica
Revista de Filosofía

Argentina

Cuadernos de Filosofía
Escritos de Filosofía
Philosophía
Revista de Filosofía
Revista Latinoamericana de Filosofía
Stromata

Brazil

Filosofar Cristiano
Ita-Humanidades
Kriterion
Presença Filosófica
Revista Brasileira de Filosofia

Chile

Atenea
Cuadernos de Filosofía
Revista de Filosofía

Colombia

Ideas y Valores
Razón y Fábula

Costa Rica

Praxis
Revista de Filosofía de la Universidad de Costa Rica

Cuba

Praxis

Ecuador

Bibliográfíca Básica de la Filosofía Ecuatoriana
Pucará
Puce

El Salvador

Tal

Peru

Tesque

Puerto Rico

Dialogos

Uruguay

Cuadernos de Filosofía

Venezuela

Episteme
Estudios Filosóficos
Revista Venezolana de Filosofía

United States

ANDREW J. RECK

At the end of World War II, philosophy in the United States was dominated by presences from an earlier age. Since then, traditional American philosophical tendencies have been transformed, and philosophical movements transplanted from abroad have flourished, with differing measures of yield, on American soil.

In 1945, John Dewey (1859–1952), then eighty-six years old, was widely esteemed as *the* philosopher of America. Heir to the pragmatism of C. S. Peirce (1839–1914) and William James (1842–1910), Dewey had pioneered progressive education. Perhaps more than any other educator, he had formulated the rationale which elevated the social sciences to a footing of parity with the humanities and the natural sciences. He had also invented a variety of pragmatism called instrumentalism, and he had recommended applying the problem-solving, experimental method of the natural sciences to the moral issues and value conflicts of contemporary society. In the 1940s, Dewey still contributed to the philosophical journals. With Arthur Bentley (1870–1957), he co-authored *Knowing and the Known,* a definitory work on experimentalist epistemology, transactional metaphysics, and the philosophical preliminaries to the social sciences. The work aroused considerable discussion when it appeared in 1949.

In 1945, the Englishman Alfred North Whitehead (1861–1947) was alive, if not well, in Cambridge, Massachusetts. Although he added little more to the articulation and explanation of his daringly speculative, systematic, and comprehensive philosophy of process, he was studied. His ideas, explored creatively as well as exegetically by students and associates like F.S.C. Northrop (1893–   ), Paul Weiss (1901–   ), and Charles Hartshorne (1897–   ), were communicated to later generations of philosophers. Furthermore, these ideas were advertised to a wider audience, as they had not been since the publication of his *Science and the Modern World* in 1925, through the sensitive preservation of his discussions and their popular posthumous publication by Lucien Price as *The Dialogues of Alfred North Whitehead).*

From abroad George Santayana (1863–1952), the Spaniard who quit these shores before World War I and who during World War II and for the remaining years of his life found sanctuary in a Catholic convent in Rome, continued to count as an American author as, indeed, he counted himself. His contributions to the development of realism and naturalism, along with his critical interpretations of American culture, had a profound and extensive impact on the American mind. His philosophical judgments on religion and on politics were welcomed, but with a degree of ambivalence. Some of his American followers were offended by his alleged flirtation with Italian fascism, and others by his preoccupation with essence and spirit in his later years.

Then there was the case of Charles S. Peirce, who, although he died before World War I, emerged only in the years following World War II as an American philosopher of the first rank. For Peirce, the obscure and eccentric father of pragmatism whose *Collected Papers* were edited and published in the 1930s, dealt with just those topics in logic, the theory of signs, and scientific method which fascinated the American student of philosophy a half century after his death. Whereas early commentators like James Feibleman (1904–   ) eagerly argued for a systematic and metaphysical interpretation of Peirce's thought, this interpretation, in consonance with the primary interests of his two editors, Charles Hartshorne and Paul Weiss, was slighted as less promising than the methodological, semiotic, and scientific aspects of his work. By 1960, the hitherto neglected Peirce, among academic American philosophers, came to eclipse his more famous contemporary, the philosopher-psychologist William James. In the 1970s, however, growing interest in philosophical psychology revived James' reputation and, in consequence of the rising concern with the principles of sociality, George Herbert Mead's (1863–1931) reputation as well.

From the late nineteenth century, when American philosophy came of age, four major philosophical tendencies emerged: naturalism, realism, idealism, and pragmatism. Each of these tendencies exhibited a distinctive stance with regard to knowledge, reality, and values. And although individual thinkers eclectically or syncretically exemplified more than one philosophical tendency, the four types prove pedagogically useful in organizing the multifarious philosophical activities and sentiments during the recent past. Still, it is undeniable that these tendencies, which have never in fact been pure types, have undergone radical transformation during the period. Affecting the traditional American philosophical tendencies are the main movements of European philosophy in the twentieth century: logical positivism, Marxism, neo-Thomism, linguistic analysis, existentialism, and phenomenology. The story of American philosophy since 1945 is, in large measure, the interplay of these movements and tendencies.

Naturalism is distinguished by its opposition to supernaturalism, its implacable exclusion of any appeal to supernatural agencies and principles to explain things, actions, and events. The scientific and the secular qualify the attitude of naturalism, its posture in regard to knowledge, reality, and values. Naturalism, moreover, is methodological or metaphysical. Methodological naturalism relies solely upon scientific methods to furnish knowledge and is skeptical about the possibility of metaphysics formulating a general theory of reality. Accepting the sciences and their methods, metaphysical naturalism, on the other hand, ventures further in contending that the categories, principles, laws, and hypotheses which these sciences reveal do indeed represent the constitutive and executive structures and elements of objective reality.

In 1945 and for nearly two decades thereafter, the headquarters for philosophical naturalism in America was New York City and, within New York City, Columbia University. In the prewar decade, John Dewey and F.J.E. Woodbridge (1867–1940) at Columbia, along with Morris Cohen (1880–1947) at City College, had been the leading figures in naturalism active on the American scene. At a distance, of course, was Santayana whose writings of his middle years, especially *The Life of Reason,* persisted as an influence. At Columbia in the immediate postwar period, the naturalist philosophers who commanded the most attention for their on-going contributions to the articulation of this tendency in American thought were John Herman Randall, Jr., (1899–   ), and Ernest Nagel (1901–   ). To be counted, too, although he eventually left New York City for California, is Herbert Schneider (1892–   ), whose *History of American Philosophy,* published in 1946 by Columbia University Press, established the study of American philosophy on a par with American literature or American history more than any work in the field published before or since. A somewhat younger exponent of naturalism who belonged to the Columbia group also worthy of mention is Justus Buchler (1914–   ). And in the neighborhood, at New York University, was the energetic self-confessed disciple of John Dewey, Sidney Hook (1902–   ). While these thinkers performed the tasks of philosophical research with different interests, they shared the common ground of naturalism: that in principle nature alone, accessible to the inquiring mind solely by means of the sciences, contains the laws and powers operative throughout experience and society.

It is primarily as an historian of philosophy that Randall has made his mark on the development of American thought in recent decades. In his youth, he published a sweeping and popular one-volume history of modern philosophy, *The Making of the Modern Mind.* In the 1960s, he published a multivolume history of modern philosophy which has no equal in the English language, *The Career of Philosophy.* Randall was not, however, exclusively an historian. No philosopher can be, for to study the history of philosophy properly is to engage in philosophical inquiry and critique. Thus, Randall's approach to the history of philosophy is to comprehend thinkers and ideas within major schools or traditions, each articulating and advancing common themes, in competition with the others. Nor did he approach history as a dead subject for archeological investigation. Rather, in line with the thinking of Dewey and Mead, Randall views the historical past as fundamentally a reconstruction in terms of the problems of the present. The past is, therefore, the background of the present; what it contains which merits consideration now is what is relevant to issues and topics of interest now. Randall's inquiries logically expanded into metaphysics. In his major contribution to the field, *Nature and Historical Experience,* he exhibits the influence of Woodbridge as much as that of Dewey. Showing a keen grasp of Aristotelian philosophy, in addition to an understanding of contemporary process metaphysics, Randall proposes a theory of substance as co-operative processes.

Ernest Nagel focuses on the philosophy of logic and science. A student of

Morris Cohen, Nagel abandoned his mentor's rationalism and realism for the pragmatic, experimental naturalism he found at Columbia. Later, he visited the logical positivist group in Vienna, and with Herbert Feigl (1902–   ) and Charles Morris (1901–1979), he was among the first to introduce logical positivism to America. Like Morris, he grafted Viennese positivism onto the indigenously American pragmatic movement. Nagel, who espouses a naturalism which is primarily methodological, argues for a logic without ontology. In numerous reviews and critical essays he promotes, almost without equal, the centrality of the philosophy of science in the development of American philosophical thought in recent decades. His book *The Structure of Science* is widely read and is often cited in studies of problems in the logic of scientific explanation.

Methodological naturalism, in alliance with pragmatic experimentalism stemming from Peirce and Dewey, proved fertile ground for the transplantation of logical positivism. In the 1940s, logical positivism, or logical empiricism, was the most exciting new philosophy on the American scene. From Central Europe, in flight from persecution and war, logical positivists sought refuge in America: Philip Frank (1884–1966) at Cambridge, Rudolf Carnap (1891–1970) at Chicago, Hans Reichenbach (1891–1953) at Los Angeles, and Carl Hempel (1905–   ) eventually at Princeton.

The logical positivists proposed three major theses which dominated philosophical discussion in the first decade after World War II. First, they held that all statements which are informative are empirical statements about facts that are, in principle, subject to verification. What such statements mean, moreover, is their mode of verification. An unverifiable statement is meaningless empirically. Second, the logical positivists, while agreeing with nineteenth-century positivism that all knowledge of the world is factual, nonetheless held that logic and mathematics express necessary truths. However, these truths are not informative of the facts; they are, to borrow a word from Wittgenstein's (1889–1951) *Tractatus Logico-Philosophicus,* tautologies. The *a priori*, as Carnap and Reichenbach stressed, is analytic; the necessity of logic and mathematics is purchased at the price of their saying nothing about the world. Such logically true statements represent the rules and structures of our language systems. Third, statements which are neither empirical nor logical are cognitively meaningless. This can be shown by exhibiting the logical structure of such statements and ascertaining the objective facts to which they allegedly refer. Upon examination, the class of cognitively meaningless statements proved to be quite large. It embraced traditional metaphysical statements, which the logical positivists condemned as violations of language rules and which they denounced as literal nonsense. It also included a large group of value statements in ethics and aesthetics. These statements the logical positivists deemed to be emotively meaningful. In a sophisticated and persuasive way, Charles Stevenson (1908–1979) elaborated the logical positivist position in his *Ethics and Language,* a book which was widely discussed, especially by British thinkers.

Because of its assault both upon metaphysics and upon the objectivity and cognitivity of value judgments, logical positivism encountered strong opposition from American philosophers. But this opposition alone did not determine its demise. Rather, the logical positivists themselves failed to formulate, in a plausible way, their criterion of empirical meaning. Such a criterion had at once to be broad enough to admit all the statements the sciences needed and narrow enough to exclude all the statements the sciences did not want. At the same time, the logical positivists and their heirs, the logical empiricists, began to question, as W. V. Quine (1908–   ) did, the validity of a sharp distinction between the analytic *a priori* and the synthetic, and they began to take another look at the structure of science, with a keener eye to its historical development. As Thomas S. Kuhn (1922–   ) contends in *The Structure of Scientific Revolutions,* facts are subordinate to the paradigms or models constructed by scientists, so that the advance of science is not linear and cumulative, but marked by revolutions. The positivist conception of science, the crux of its general philosophy, retreated before Kuhn's interpretation, which is attentive to history and sociology as well as to the ways theory dominates fact.

As logical positivism or logical empiricism flowed into the American philosophical currents of methodological naturalism and pragmatism, pragmatism, too, crossed with naturalism. John Dewey, for example, is both a naturalist and a pragmatist; this fact suggests that the distinction between pragmatism and naturalism in American philosophy is mainly a distinction of subcurrents within a broader stream. Unlike naturalism, which historically has centered on the concepts, laws, and principles of physics and mathematics, however, pragmatism has tended to focus on biology. Hence, pragmatism is intrinsically a form of *lebensphilosophie,* and biological categories, permeated with personal and social concerns, shape the pragmatist stance toward reality, knowledge, and values. The real, the true, the valuable are all defined and described by reference to the living organism, its needs and desires, its struggles and aspirations. Thus, pragmatism need not be naturalistic; it is often idealistic. Still, it has been for the most part naturalistic, perhaps because it was the outgrowth of the extension of the Darwinian theory of evolution to the philosophical problems of mind, knowledge, and valuation.

In 1946, the Harvard philosopher C. I. Lewis (1883–1964) published *Analysis of Knowledge and Valuation,* based on the Carus lectures he delivered before the annual meeting of the American Philosophical Association in December 1945, the first national assembly of philosophers held after America's entry into World War II. Upon its first appearance this work was heralded as a classic. Its author was already the acknowledged founder of a distinctive form of pragmatism called "conceptualistic pragmatism." For in *Mind and the World Order,* Lewis synthesizes a pragmatic conception of mind as an evolved natural instrument with a Kantian epistemology according to which concepts interpret and organize empirical materials. *Analysis of Knowledge and Valuation* sums up Lewis's thought in logic, epistemology, and value theory. Its target—logical positivism—is unmistakable. Rejecting the linguistic theories of the *a priori,* Lewis nevertheless proposes a purely analytic theory in which meanings rather than words are central. While he adheres to the verification theory for ascertaining the truth of empirical statements, he insists that verification presupposes meanings held in mind. He not only defines values naturalistically, but he also defends their objectivity. Furthermore, against the logical positivists, he stresses the cognitive nature of value judgments.

Like Lewis, Stephen Pepper (1891–1961) at the University of California in Berkeley presents a naturalistic theory of values, and against the logical positivists and others, he defends the cognitivity of value judgments. His book *The Sources of Value,* is the last major contribution by an American author to the field of axiology (general theory of value). During the first half of this century, this field was enriched by the works of W. M. Urban (1873–1952), R. B. Perry (1876–1957), DeWitt Parker (1885–1949), D. W. Prall (1886–1940), and John Dewey. Pepper also deserves credit for meeting frontally the logical positivists' rejection of metaphysics as non-sense. In *World Hypotheses,* Pepper presents the theory that there are four equally plausible types of metaphysical systems: formism, mechanism, organicism, and contextualism. Each ramifies a comprehensive categorical scheme from a root metaphor give in experience, each takes the world as the scope of its application, and each contains its own criteria of truth and meaning. Formism embraces the realisms of Plato and Aristotle; mechanism, the varieties of deterministic materialism; organicism, the objective or absolute idealisms; and contextualism, pragmatism, including process metaphysics. Although Pepper claimed neutrality with regard to the metaphysical types, it appears that his own approach to metaphysics stemmed from a deep-rooted contextualism. When, however, Pepper finally expounded his own type of metaphysical system in *Concept and Quality,* it was based on its own root metaphor of the selective act discovered in the formulation of his general theory of value, although it combined almost eclectically elements from both contextualism and mechanism.

Despite its emphasis on the practical, in the immediate post-1945 decade pragmatism seemed to turn to theoretical questions of knowledge and value. Nonetheless, some American philosophers did not neglect the practical. Certainly one of the most discussed books with practical bearings was *The Meeting of East and West* by the nonpragmatist Yale philosopher F.S.C. Northrop, who studied with Whitehead before the Englishman came to America. From a sound base in logic, epistemology, and the philosophy of science, Northrop turned to examine the conflicting ideologies which rent the twentieth century. He held that differing cultures and subcultures embody rival conceptions of knowledge, reality, and value, which explain their misunderstandings and clashes. He proposed to remedy the situation by means of an analysis of their philosophies, with the intention of establishing epistemic correlations requisite for reconciliation and synthesis through complementarity of their diversities. By means of philosophical anthropology as the investigation of contemporary cultures, Northrop sought to discover the conceptual foundations of a viable system of international law.

Whereas Northrop's approach to practical issues radiates an Olympian abstractness, the pragmatist Sidney Hook is the intensely engaged thinker, a moralist more than a philosopher, always in battle. A passionate and partisan polemicist long before the explosive 1960s, Hook has fought many skirmishes and wars during a long productive career stretching over half a century. Since 1945, he has spoken against pleading the Fifth Amendment during congressional investigations into communist activities, against card-carrying communists on college faculties, against the disarmament of the West in consonance with the slogan "Better Red than dead," against the New Left activists on the college campuses during the 1960s, and against the employment quotas for women and ethnic minorities proposed by affirmative action plans during the 1970s. Although the list of Hook's oppositions suggests he is a reactionary, he remains one of America's leading social philosophers, a rare democratic socialist within the academy. In such books as *Political Power and Personal Freedom,* Hook articulates a theory of social and political democracy which draws upon the historical materialism, economics, and sociology of Karl Marx, the pragmatic instrumentalism of John Dewey, and the political common sense of the American founding fathers. Whatever the final assessment of his behavior in practical affairs, Hook has earned a high place in the history of recent American thought for his pioneer work in the 1920s and 1930s interpreting Marxism and seeking to reconcile it with the pragmatic, naturalistic tendencies in American philosophy. His oppositions stem from his devotion to the ideals of a socialist democracy, ideals which he has not only ably expounded in nonpolemical theoretical studies but which he is also convinced have been betrayed by the Soviet Union, the Communist party, and those young American radicals who, to his eyes, have subverted and abused the basic rights of citizens and the legal and political procedures of a democratic society. For Hook, as for the American founding fathers, political liberty is the key to all other socio-political benefits.

Despite the prominence of Marxism as a worldwide philosophy, it has not attracted many adherents among academic philosophers in the United States. A group of able philosophical scholars, such as Robert Cohen (1923–   ) George Kline (1921–   ), and Richard De George (1933–   ) have subjected the ideology to critical scrutiny. Although grounded in a metaphysics of dialectical materialism, Marxism is primarily a program for revolutionary change, justified by means of a probing economic critique of capitalist society in terms of class warfare. To most American academic philosophers, the Marxist doctrines of reality and of knowledge are crude, its methodology of dialectics is unscientific, and its concepts of value are unsophisticated, and even downright immoral. Thus, the Marxism which has invaded philosophy in America is highly modified. Its leading representative is Herbert Marcuse (1898–1979). A German refugee of the Frankfurt school, Marcuse espouses a social philosophy that is rooted in Hegelianism and that owes as much to Freud as to Marx. His major work is *Eros and Civilization.* Viewing sexual repression as the source of societal deformations, Marcuse has proceeded to criticize the character of technological civilization, with the Soviet Union no less than the United States serving as his targets. As the Vietnam War heated the atmosphere on college campuses, Marcuse, who defined toleration as consistent with the denial of the exercises of the rights of speech and assembly to government officials, became a hero to student rioters and spokesmen of the New Left. Angela Davis (1944–   ) formerly a philosophy professor at the University of California in Los Angeles, has been his most notorious disciple. The vogue of Marcuse has passed, and all that remains as a result of the turbulent 1960s is the extension of philosophy to numerous applied fields: the philosophy of sexuality (including feminist studies), the critique of technology, the philosophy of law, and biomedical ethics. The cry for relevance, voiced by young militants in the age of the greening of America, is no longer a demand for revolutionary change, having succumbed to the vocationalism of the 1970s.

More successfully than Marxism, phenomenology and existentialism have been accepted into the fold of American philosophy. They began to invade America before World War II, entering by way of religion first. Phenomenology, founded by Edmund Husserl (1859–1938), is fundamentally a philosophical method. It prescribes investigating all experiences without reduction and without regard to their existential status; and it promises new access to the neglected qualities and hidden structures of human experience and social reality. Existentialism, harking back to Kierkegaard and popularized by the early Jean-Paul Sartre (1905–1980), posits concern with personal existence as primary. It faces and criticizes social institutions, political movements, historic forces, the natural causes uncovered by the special sciences, cultural principles, the faiths proclaimed by the particular religions, all from the standpoint of the single individual, responsible yet free. Numerous American philosophers have adopted the phenomenological method or have styled themselves existentialists, as the exegetes of thinkers like Martin Heidegger (1889–1976) multiply. Nevertheless, the major representatives of this complex philosophical style on the American scene have been European refugees.

Paul Tillich (1886–1965), invited to Union Theological Seminary by Reinhold Niebuhr (1892–1971) ranks as the only philosopher in recent times to formulate a systematic Christian theology. His greatest work, the three-volume *Systematic Theology*, recycles traditional concepts in the vocabulary of existentialism and depth psychology. Tillich construed theology as a response to the ultimate questions provoked by the human situation within a culture. The lectures which were published in *Courage To Be* conveyed deeply personal and challenging meanings to those Yale students who heard them during the first winter of the Korean War.

While Paul Tillich was prominent as a theologian of culture during the 1950s and 1960s, Hannah Arendt (1906–1975) led the field of cultural criticism from the vantage point of philosophy during the 1960s and 1970s. A refugee from Nazi Germany, she had studied under Karl Jaspers (1883–1969) and Martin Heidegger. Her first major publication, *The Human Condition*, explores the human triad of labor, work, and action. It displays a remarkable mastery of the categories of philosophical anthropology and sociology in a new style which revives ancient ideas and ideals. From this work, Arendt went on to apply her singular critical mind to the characteristic experiences and to the prominent figures and events of her times—*anomie*, terror, violence, revolution, civil disobedience, Auschwitz, Eichmann, Pope John, school integration, the Pentagon Papers, Watergate, and the Bicentennial.

As existentialism surfaced in the wake of the world wars which have shaken the foundations of European civilization during this century, idealism has submerged. Idealism locates the clues to the ultimate nature of reality within human experience by focusing on those traits which distinguish man as a spiritual being. On the American scene it has been manifest in two main types: one is absolute idealism, and the other, personalism. A symptom of the decline of philosophical idealism in America, the endeavor in the 1950s to resurrect the reputation of Josiah Royce (1855–1916) proved to be short-lived.

Nevertheless, the most distinguished American philosopher alive today, in view of the honors he has been awarded, is Brand Blanshard (1892–   ) of Yale, an exponent of idealism. Blanshard has erected his philosophy upon the Anglo-American Hegelianism of Bradley (1846–1924), Bosanquet (1848–1923), and Royce. He professes coherence as the nature and test of truth, the theory of the concrete universal, the doctrines of internal relations and of cosmic necessity. Transforming his inherited idealism into a cosmic rationalism, he has written a trilogy in defense of reason against its contemporary detractors. *Reason and Goodness* delineates the role of reason in morality and is particularly critical of those recent movements in moral philosophy—such as subjectivism, emotivism, and noncognitivism—which have sought to minimize or deny that role. *Reason and Analysis* takes the logical positivists and the linguistic analysts to task for undermining reason. *Reason and Belief* sharply criticizes the derogation of reason in the recent theology of the neo-orthodox, the neo-Thomist, and the existentialist varieties. Blanshard's impressive trilogy, unparalleled in recent American thought as a sustained systematic achievement, is also constructive. It projects the ideal of a rational system of necessary knowledge representing the world as an intelligible whole of internally related parts.

Whereas Blanshard's kind of idealism tends to reduce the finite individual person to a mere attribute of the absolute whole, personalism insists that the person is the ultimately real and valuable, and further, that the cosmos itself is personal. Personalism arose in the late nineteenth century in part as a reaction against absolutism.

During the twentieth century, it has been better able to assimilate the newer modes of thinking which stress change, temporality, existence, novelty, and creativity. Until his death in 1953, Edgar Sheffield Brightman (1884–1953), with his doctrine of the finite God, was the most original thinker among recent personalists. Since then, Peter Bertocci (1910–   ) has led the fold.

Perhaps a third species of idealism is panpsychism, which holds that mind pervades the universe, that indeed matter is alive. At least the most conspicuous living panpsychist, Charles Hartshorne, has chosen to call himself an idealist. *The Divine Relativity* is Hartshorne's most influential work. It depicts God as both personal and social, a being who changes, yet has absolute, eternal aspects. It upholds panentheism as well as panpsychism. Hartshorne's conception of God, which owes much to Alfred North Whitehead, is essential to the developing process theology. Though a self-confessed idealist, Hartshorne in his philosophical thinking better exemplifies the type known as process philosophy. Taking the flux of experience to be key to the nature of reality, process philosophy defines reality as whatever changes or is an element within change. It embraces a host of thinkers who, no matter how much they differ, concur on the primacy of change: Dewey, Randall, Pepper, and so on. The Whiteheadian school, which Hartshorne now heads, is distinguished for its concern with theology and speculative metaphysics.

Process philosophy is fundamentally, in the words of W. H. Sheldon (1875–1980), "America's progressive philosophy." Its emphases on change, creativity, novelty, sociality, and adventure underscore values characteristic of American culture and cherished by average Americans. A relative newcomer, process philosophy in midcentury confronted the ancient tradition of realism, so that for many the philosophical challenge of the times was to effectuate a higher synthesis.

The roots of realism in American philosophy are several and are intertwined. Realism is the theory that whatever is, is real. Epistemological realism affirms that the object of knowledge exists independently of the knower, and metaphysical realism asserts that conceptual objects, such as universals and relations, are as real as the physical objects of veridical perception. During the twentieth century, the career of realism in America has been exceptionally rich. In the beginning, new realism challenged idealism by utilizing the discoveries of symbolic logic and experimental psychology. Soon thereafter, critical realism rose in large measure to amend the alleged incapacity of new realism to account for error. The critical realists, among whom Santayana was the most famous, devised subtle theories of sense data and of essences to mediate between the knower and the external object.

Meanwhile, in Roman Catholic colleges and universities realistic philosophy was more than studied; it was advocated. The reputation of St. Thomas Aquinas was at its height in America after 1945. He was esteemed the greatest of philosophers for having achieved what was celebrated as the supreme synthesis. Reinterpreted to assimilate the arts, the sciences, and the humanities of modernity and to overcome the fragmentations, disunities, and disruptions which thronged a civilization wrecked by wars, economic depressions, cultural barbarisms, moral degeneration, and political dictatorships, his philosophy was metamorphosed into neo-Thomism. Born in France, neo-Thomism migrated to America, where it flourished best in Roman Catholic colleges and universities, but spread to affect many secular institutions. Indeed, Jacques Maritain (1882–1973), perhaps the most creative and preeminent neo-Thomist, taught at Princeton University from 1948 to 1956. At the University of Chicago, a band of Aristotelians, led by Mortimer Adler (1902–   ) and Richard McKeon (1900–   ), worked in unison. And at Harvard, John Wild (1902–1972) founded an association for realistic philosophy and called for a return to reason which had much in common with neo-Thomism. Eventually, Wild abandoned realism for existentialism, his defection signaling the fate of neo-Thomism. A vital movement with numerous adherents just two decades ago, neo-Thomism has since almost wholly disappeared from the American philosophical scene.

Realism persists nonetheless. It is manifest in the works of two of the most prolific systematic philosophers of the present: Paul Weiss of Yale and James Feibleman of Tulane.

Weiss began his career as a logician. A student of Whitehead, he undertook to expound his own metaphysics in *Reality*, where he revised process philosophy by restoring in modified form the Aristotelian category of substance. After World War II, Weiss endeavored to construct a moral philosophy on a naturalistic basis, but he discovered that his earlier ontology was inadequate. His new investigations came to fruition with the publication of his major work, *Modes of Being*. In this work, he unfolded a system of four equally real, independent, autonomous modes of being: actuality, ideality, existence, and God. Together, these modes constitute the cosmos. Next, Weiss applied his metaphysics to the systematic interpretation of all the concrete fields of human experience—law, politics, art, history, religion, science, education, and sport. Metaphysics, however, is at the heart of his inquiries. Finding defects in his modal ontology, he is now revising it, acknowledging additional finalities such as substance and unity in his latest books, *Beyond All Appearances* and *First Considerations*.

Feibleman came to academic philosophy from a career in business and an avocation in poetry. An interpreter of C. S. Peirce, he early became an advocate of philosophical realism in ontology, epistemology, and value theory. He has presented the basic categories of his system in *Ontology* and *The Foundations of Empiricism*. According to Feibleman, the universes of being are three: essence, existence, and destiny. Expounding his ontology in the face of scientific requirements during a period in which logical positivism has been influential, Feibleman has labeled his position "ontological positivism." He has indefatigably pursued the ramifications of realistic philosophy in all the arts, sciences, religions, cultures, and institutions, authoring more books and articles than any academic philosopher of his generation.

Weiss and Feibleman have undertaken to formulate speculative systems of metaphysical realism in an unfavorable climate of opinion. The dominant style has been analytic, appropriate to the professional with his narrow specialty.

No one surpasses Ludwig Wittgenstein as an agent influencing the climate of contemporary philosophy in America. In the summer of 1949, Wittgenstein, who had resigned his chair at Cambridge two years earlier, visited the United States to spend three months with his friend, Norman Malcolm, at Cornell. The visit presaged what might well be regarded as the Viennese thinker's conquest of American philosophers. His *Tractatus Logico-philosophicus* had inspired the logical positivists, and his method of ordinary language analysis, best represented in his posthumously published *Philosophical Investigations*, ushered in a new phase of analytic philosophy, abandoning earlier interests in formal structures for concentration on the actual usages of words. Throughout the 1950s and the 1960s, American philosophers, whose increasingly professionalized work was aptly suited to publication in succinct articles of a technical critical, and exegetical kind, succumbed to the promises of Wittgensteinian and post-Wittgensteinian analysis.

An index to the rule of Wittgenstein is a collection of fourteen young thinkers, bearing the title *Philosophy in America,* edited by Max Black (1909–   ) and published in 1965. The contributors seem to be unaware that much in contemporary philosophy has happened anywhere but in England. Whereas John L. Austin is cited six times, A. J. Ayer (1910–   ) five, Peter Geach (1916–   ) five, H.L.A. Hart (1907–   ) twelve, G. E. Moore (1878–1958) four, Bertrand Russell (1872–1970) seven, Gilbert Ryle (1900–1976) more than eight, and Wittgenstein more than nineteen, among American thinkers W. V. Quine is mentioned six times, John Dewey and Charles Peirce twice each, George Santayana once, and Josiah Royce and William James not at all.

But the end of the age of Wittgenstein is imminent. Its demise can partly be attributed to the resurgence of formal analysis now more cognizant of ontic commitment. It is also due to the emergence of analytic philosophers who after long decades of meticulous honing of the logical and the epistemological instruments are moving to the highground of systematic metaphysics. Finally, too, it is due to the philosophers who are mastering the interface of their discipline with empirical fields and social values.

Among thinkers who display the formal mode of analysis attentive to ontology, the most prominent are Nelson Goodman (1906–   ) and W. V. Quine. Goodman's *Structure of Appearance* advances beyond the logical constructionalism of Carnap. Along with Quine, who of all American philosophers alive today has been studied most, Goodman has been committed to a nominalistic ontology of individuals. On the other hand, Quine has waffled on the issues between realism and nominalism. Furthermore, besides attacking the distinction between the analytic *a priori* and the synthetic, central to earlier forms of logical empiricism, Quine has formulated the principle of the indeterminacy of translation, with implications which strike at foundationalism in epistemology. Nevertheless, against the later Wittgensteinians, he has upheld the regimentation of ordinary language in canonical form. Quine's major work is *Word and Object*.

The two philosophers Roderick Chisholm (1916–   ) and Wilfrid Sellars (1912–   ) have progressed from analytic epistemology toward constructive metaphysics. Chisholm's *Perceiving* is a remarkable essay on the topic which resolves the philosophical puzzles and problems that arise when we think and talk about perceiving. His latest investigations have been metaphysical, focusing on the theory of the self; they suggest that he is preparing a major work in Cartesian rational psychology. Meanwhile, Sellars has moved from the antimetaphysical position of logical empiricism to a kind of neo-Kantianism in which the self is crucial. His *Science and Metaphysics* offers, as the subtitle declares, "variations on Kantian themes."

In the 1960s, philosophy, like most academic disciplines in America, turned to face social problems of value in law, politics, economics, and so on. Among the countless thinkers who have written about such matters at the systematic theoretical level two stand out, John Rawls (1921–   ) and Robert Nozick (1938–   ). Rawls' *A Theory of Justice* is already a classic in the field. In terms of the quantity and the quality of the discussions it has stimulated, it surpasses even C. I. Lewis' *Analysis of Knowledge and Valuation*. Rawls systematically presents a contractarian theory of justice which, in recognition of basic human rights and equality, justifies the welfare state. In contrast, Rawls' younger Harvard colleague, Nozick, in *Anarchy, State, and Utopia*, has challenged the welfare state by resurrecting a libertarian conception of individual rights and considering the operative principles of the free market economy. Whereas Rawls' work encompasses the interface of philosophy and law, Nozick's masters the interface of philosophy and economics.

In sum, American philosophy since 1945 has been characterized by openness, pluralism, and change. Ideas from abroad have been welcome, as U.S. intellectual life is not only hospitable but also deferential. This openness has attracted to American shores thinkers who have proved more productive here than could have been anticipated in their native lands. The ideas themselves, engrafted upon indigenous growths, have fructified in amazing ways. Without an official philosophy enforced by a powerful institution, Americans and others resident in America have been free to think and publish whatever they deem to be true, their only censor being the critical judgment of their peers. The upshot has been that a greater number of philosophical views of high quality have been represented in America since 1945 than in any other country during an equal period of time. Pluralism is therefore the rule in American philosophy, as in American civilization at large. But more striking than openness and pluralism has been change. Schools and styles of philosophy, as well as the thinking of individuals, have changed at a startling rate. Within a few years, the implications of an idea or a doctrine are all worked out, and what was novel yesterday is faded and worn out today. In other times and nations, the same careers for ideas and doctrines have taken centuries. The acceleration of intellectual progress has been made possible by the large number of contributing thinkers, by the leisure and resources at their command, and by the professionalism of their performances. These qualities of openness, pluralism, and change may reasonably be expected to prevail in American philosophy in the future.

SELECT BIBLIOGRAPHY

BOOKS AND ARTICLES

Arendt, H. *The Human Condition* (Chicago: University of Chicago Press, 1969).
———. *The Life of the Mind,* 2 vols. (New York: Harcourt Brace Jovanovich, 1978).
Black, M. (ed.) *Philosophy in America* (Ithaca, N.Y.: Cornell University Press, 1965).

Blanshard, B. *Reason and Analysis* (LaSalle, Ill.: Open Court, 1962).

———. *Reason and Belief* (New Haven, Conn.: Yale University Press, 1975).

———. *Reason and Goodness* (New York: Macmillan, 1961).

Chisholm, R. *Perceiving: A Philosophical Study* (Ithaca, N.Y.: Cornell University Press, 1957).

Dewey, J. and Bentley, A. *Knowing and the Known* (Boston: Beacon Press, 1976).

Feibleman, J. *Ontology* (Baltimore: Johns Hopkins Press, 1951).

———. *The Foundations of Empiricism* (The Hague: Nijhoff, 1962).

Goodman, N. *Structure of Appearance* (Cambridge, Mass.: Harvard University Press, 1951).

Hartshorne, C. *The Divine Relativity* (New Haven, Conn.: Yale University Press, 1964).

Hook, Sidney. *Political Power and Personal Freedom* (New York: Macmillan, 1962).

Kuhn, T. S. *The Structure of Scientific Revolutions*, 2d ed. (Chicago: University of Chicago Press, 1970).

Lewis, C. I. *Analysis of Knowledge and Valuation* (LaSalle, Ill.: Open Court, 1971).

———. *Mind and the World Order* (New York: Dover, 1956).

Marcuse, H. *Eros and Civilization* (New York: Vintage Press, 1962).

Merrill, K. R. "From Edwards to Quine: Two Hundred Years of American Philosophy," in *Issues and Ideas in America*, eds. B. J. Taylor and T. J. White (Norman, Okla.: University of Oklahoma Press, 1976).

Nagel, E. *The Structure of Science: Problems in the Logic of Scientific Explanation* (London: Routledge and Kegan Paul, and New York: Harcourt Brace and World, 1961).

Northrop, F.S.C. *The Meeting of East and West: An Inquiry Concerning World Understanding* (New York: Macmillan, 1960).

Nozick, R. *Anarchy, State, and Utopia* (New York: Basic Books, 1974).

Peirce, C. S. *Collected Papers of Charles Sanders Peirce*, I–VI, eds. C. Hartshorne and P. Weiss; VII–VIII, ed. A. W. Burks (Cambridge, Mass.: Harvard University Press, 1931–1958).

Pepper, S. *Concept and Quality* (LaSalle, Ill: Open Court, 1967).

———. *The Sources of Value* (Berkeley, Calif.: University of California Press, 1958).

———. *World Hypotheses: A Study in Evidence* (Berkeley, Calif.: University of California Press, 1961).

Price, L. *The Dialogues of Alfred North Whitehead* (Boston: Little Brown, and London: M. Reinhardt, 1954).

Quine, W. V. *Word and Object* (Cambridge, Mass.: MIT, 1960).

Randall, J. H., Jr. *Nature and Historical Experience: Essays in Naturalism and the Theory of History* (New York: Columbia University Press, 1958).

———. *The Career of Philosophy: From the Middle Ages to the Enlightenment* (New York: Columbia University Press, 1962).

———. *The Making of the Modern Mind* (New York: Columbia University Press, 1976).

Rawls, J. *A Theory of Justice* (Cambridge, Mass.: Harvard University Press, 1971).

Reck, A. J. "Idealism in American Philosophy Since 1900," in *Contemporary Studies in Philosophical Idealism*, eds. T. O. Buford and J. Howie (Cape Cod, Mass.: Stark, 1976).

———. *Recent American Philosophy* (New York: Pantheon, 1964).

———. *Speculative Philosophy* (Albuquerque, N. Mex.: University of New Mexico Press, 1972).

———. *The New American Philosophers: An Exploration of Thought Since World War II* (Baton Rouge, La.: Louisiana State University Press, 1968).

Santayana, G. *The Life of Reason*, 5 vols. (New York: Collier, 1962).

Schneider, H. *History of American Philosophy*, 2d ed. (New York: Columbia University Press, 1963).

Sellars, W. *Science and Metaphysics: Variations on Kantian Themes* (London: Routledge and Kegan Paul, and New York: Humanities Press, 1968).

Stevenson, C. *Ethics and Language* (New York: AMS Press, 1976).

Tillich, P. *Courage To Be* (New Haven, Conn.: Yale University Press, 1952).

———. *Systematic Theology*, 3 vols. (Chicago: University of Chicago Press, 1951–1963).

Weiss, P. *Beyond All Appearances* (Carbondale, Ill.: Southern Illinois University Press, 1974).

———. *First Considerations: An Examination of Philosophical Evidence* (Carbondale, Ill.: Southern Illinois University Press, 1977).

———. *Modes of Being* (Carbondale, Ill.: Southern Illinois University Press, 1968).

———. *Reality* (Carbondale, Ill.: Southern Illinois University Press, 1967).

Whitehead, A. N. *Science and the Modern World* (New York: Free Press, 1967).

Wittgenstein, L. *Philosophical Investigations*, 3d ed. (Oxford: Blackwell, 1968).

———. *Tractatus Logico-philosophicus* (New York: Humanities Press, 1961).

JOURNALS

American Philosophical Quarterly
Ethics: An International Journal of Social, Political, and Legal Philosophy
History And Theory: Studies in the Philosophy of History
Idealistic Studies: An International Philosophical Quarterly
International Journal for Philosophy of Religion
International Philosophical Quarterly
International Studies in Philosophy
Journal of Philosophy
Journal of the History of Ideas
Journal of the History of Philosophy
Man and World: An International Philosophical Review
Metaphilosophy
Noûs
Philosophical Studies
Philosophy and Phenomenological Research
Philosophy and Public Affairs
Philosophy East and West
Philosophy of Science
Proceedings and Addresses of the American Philosophical Association
Proceedings of the American Catholic Philosophical Association
The Humanist
The Journal of Aesthetics and Art Criticism
The Monist
The Personalist: An International Review of Philosophy, Religion and Literature
The Philosophical Forum
The Philosophical Review
The Review of Metaphysics
The Southern Journal of Philosophy

Part IV: Africa and the Republic of South Africa

Africa

ANNA-LOUIZE CONRADIE

The expression "African philosophy" is, strictly speaking, a misnomer, for reasons which should become clear in the following pages. It is rather the problem of the *possibility* of African philosophy which interests the philosopher. This statement must not be seen to imply an inability on the part of African thinkers to practice philosophy. But one must bear in mind that there is a wide diversity of African peoples and cultures (J. S. Mbiti in his *African Religions and Philosophy* mentions more than a thousand); that life- and world-views do not yet constitute philosophy; and that Africa has but recently emancipated itself from colonialism or is still in the process of doing so. (The implications of colonialism for philosophy is a topic that will be treated later in this essay.)

What should be clearly understood from the outset is that the search for African philosophy is not an addendum to the work of the anthropologist. The anthropologist is concerned primarily with the systematic study of cultural patterns. He interprets these in terms of their mythologies and cosmologies, and in the wider parameters of material environment and social organization. Together, these involve the articulation of life- and world-views peculiar to such cultures. Research of this nature is invaluable. It reveals a rich diversity of experience which has almost totally atrophied in the dominant civilizations of today and in many respects has been eagerly appropriated by them. The influence of African art forms on European art in the early twentieth century is a case in point. The problem, however, is that the anthropologist, precisely in order to achieve his aim, fixes his subject matter, preserves it so to speak in aspic. The very activity which preserves and articulates these cultures at the same stroke immobilizes them as museum material. To many an anthropological analysis is added with regret the rider that with the inroads of "civilization" such a culture is losing ground. But it is precisely this historical process of change (I do not speak of progress, as this has pejorative nineteenth-century connotations,) which the philosopher has to take into account. His task is not to confine himself to a constellation of fixed world-views from which he will then attempt to extract a philosophy or philosophies, or at worst a common denominator. How could he possibly attempt such an undertaking with respect to even a few societies such as the Lele of Kasai, the Abaluyia of Kavirondo, the Lovedu of the Transvaal, the Mende of Sierre Leone, the Ashanti, the Fon people of the former kingdom of Dahomey or the Nuer? I do not even raise the question of the ancient influence of Christianity and Islam on many African cultures.

What, then, is the task of the African philosopher? There is no easy answer. It was primarily (but not exclusively) in French intellectual circles that an attempt was made in this century to interpret these world-views, rooted in myths and symbols, in a manner that would not turn them into philosophies but which would show their relevance for philosophy. The work of Lévi-Strauss cannot be dismissed without further comment. In his structuralist analysis of myth and social behavior patterns, he has shown interesting parallels between widely differing cultures, mainly in the Pacific and the Americas. His method, initially inspired by Roman Jakobson's phonemic oppositions, has contributed to a considerable body of literature ranging from folklore to mathematics, from psychology to art and sociology. In spite of his rejection of the term "structuralism," a philosopher of history like Foucault himself confirms the value of the method in his *Les Mots et les Choses*. However, even if we consider, as Piaget does, that structuralism provides the best method for interdisciplinary study, its transformation rules do not yet yield a philosophy. Furthermore, if we attempt to interpret phenomenology structurally, Mepham points out that the apparent similarity between Lévi-Strauss's *la pensée sauvage* and Merleau-Ponty's *l'être sauvage* is highly misleading. And if we were to subject African cultures solely to structuralist analysis, the resulting grids and slots, and the correspondences between such sets, would not bring us much beyond advanced comparative studies.

Among names such as van der Leeuw, Leenhardt, Eliade, Lévy-Bruhl, Gusdorf, and Bachelard (and these are only a few of many important scholars active in this field), it is C. van Peursen who, in papers and lecture courses, has perhaps made the most meaningful contribution with respect to the philosophical relevance of myth. It is not his originality which is at issue, for he leans heavily on Georges Gusdorf's *Mythe et Métaphysique*. It is rather in the interpretation of the themes provided by Gusdorf and others that van Peursen's value must be sought. He makes it quite clear that he is not dealing with an evolutionistic theory of knowledge but with a model that has no direct association with history or prehistory. In this respect, Comte's claims that his tier of theological, metaphysical, and positivist stages represents an actual historical progress is criticized as much as Lévy-Bruhl's interpretation of myth as prelogical. Van Peursen's own model substitutes for Gusdorf's mythological, intellectual, and existentialist phases three modes: mythical, ontological, and functionalist. Perforce leaving aside his prolonged and erudite analyses of the three modes, we may briefly say that the mythical mode is characterized primarily by participation (subject immersed in world); the ontological by dualism (subject opposed to object); and the functional as the synthesis of the mythical and ontological modes in a unique interrelation and interdependence between man and world. The notion of participation—the contribution of the mythical mode—is reinterpreted in such a manner that it becomes little more than an extended statement of the possibilities of the intentional arc already entrenched in existential phenomenology. The gain is the insight that myths are not only legitimate and illuminating exercises in meaning but that they also still function covertly in contemporary thinking. Van Peursen emphasizes that the reinterpretation of "participation" does not imply the discarding of myths as cultural detritus.

Such views are stimulating and helpful as attempts to clarify philosophy's understanding of itself at this time and age, but it does not help us to discover what an African philosophy may mean. Let us therefore turn to some actual attempts to formulate such a philosophy.

More than a century ago, G. Callaway collected and published the thoughts of several Zulu thinkers, but it was P. Radin who first made it clear that there was indeed an intellectual, critical, and reflective class in nonliterate societies. Their thinking was a genuine attempt to transcend current superstitions and static custom-dominated ways of life. Gutmann similarly drew attention to thinkers among the Chagga, as F. Boas did to leaders of prophetic and messianic movements who became the intellectual leaders of their peoples. M. Griaule, a Sorbonne professor, tells of one Ogotemmeli, a thinker of note in the Dogon, a tribe in the bend of the Niger, with whom he had thirty-three conversations concerning the ancient wisdom of Africa. These talks dealt with the origin and nature of things, the problem of unity and multiplicity, God, the end of man, good and evil, and so forth. He himself acted as scribe, writing down the thoughts of the blind sage.

When we turn to research published specifically as African philosophy, we first encounter the pioneer work of P. Tempels and A. Kagame.

Tempels' *Bantu Philosophy* is concerned primarily with the Luba of the Congo, but his generalizations have drawn considerable criticism from scholars dealing with different African cultures and traditions. Tempels attempts to adapt Aristotelian-Thomist concepts and terminology to a situation which in fact challenges such adaptation. "Being," he claims, is interpreted as "vital force," with the qualification that being *is* force rather than *has* force. At the apex is God, the source of that vital power which flows through the first founder of the clan (now in the mythical past which Mbiti terms Zamani), through the ancestors and thus to the families and individual members of the tribe. It may also flow through the juridical chiefs and elders. All forces or beings are created by God and can be destroyed by Him. Men can strengthen or weaken the vital force in themselves and in others in various magical ways. Lévy-Bruhl's phrase "to be is to participate" thus achieves a deeper dimension in the context of a notion of vital force, which is the very pulsation of tribal life. It is for this reason that here, as elsewhere in Africa, no choice is involved in the cultural situation. One is literally sustained in and through the tribe into which one is born and through which, by means of the hierarchy of powers, one participates in the source of vital force itself, namely, God. The "religious" nature of African thought and experience, which almost all scholars stress so strongly, means then the all-pervasiveness of vital force which infiltrates not only into every aspect of social life, but also into inanimate nature itself. Although at the time Tempels' work was rightly considered as a contribution of note, it is arguable whether the application of scholastic notions to Luba doctrines of vital force, without going into details of Luba custom, really gives us the right to call it a philosophy. Furthermore, the notion of vital force could perhaps with greater justice be linked to various explicit vitalist philosophies, unless the Aristotelian notion of act and potency is interpreted in an activist sense foreign to its original meaning.

Of a different order altogether is Kagame's philosophy of the Tussi people of the Ruanda. His method is to derive basic philosophical concepts from the classification of nouns. The four basic concepts are: *umuNtu* (being which has intelligence, that is, man, ancestor, god); *ikiNtu* (being devoid of intelligence and subject to *umuNtu*); *ahaNtu* (being ordering space and time); and *ukuNtu* modal being). C. M. Doke suggests that a fifth concept, *ubuNtu*, is required, which would deal with the qualities of being: the latter could then accommodate the remaining ten noun classes of Ruanda which account for the lexical equivalents of being. Deprived of its prefixes, only *Ntu* is left, a fact of considerable philosophical importance as it does not imply the unicity and independence of God. *Ntu* means being, but being which never occurs apart from the four forms. In spite of this static generic analysis, Kagame emphasizes that *Ntu* is not substance but universal cosmic force. However, *Ntu* as universal force is not an object of worship. It is not a creator and sustains no personal relationships. Man stands in a personal relationship only to the ancestors to whom he turns with his supplications and his problems. Kagame here diverges from a much more general acceptance in Africa of God as the heavenly *umuNtu*.

A student of the Ruanda would find it difficult to recognize in that rich world the barren linguistic abstractions of Kagame. But this also indicates his awareness of what a philosophical task might mean. He appears to be applying Aristotelian-type categories to linguistic material, specifically the nominal prefixes, in order to determine the categories of being and establish their metaphysical content. Both Tempels and Kagame turn to Aristotle in their attempts to articulate an African philosophy, although Kagame does so much more explicitly. The question remains to what extent the specific cultural worlds chosen by these thinkers for analysis would resist their reductionism and whether their philosophy indeed transcends the specificity of such worlds.

J. Jahn's *Muntu* gives evidence of wide reading, but only one section is devoted to religious and philosophic matters. He accepts from Kagame the four categories attributed to Ruanda culture. From Tempels, again, Jahn takes the idea of vital force or being which he relates to the linguistic stem *Ntu*. The latter, however, cannot be abstracted from its manifestations as Muntu, Kintu, Hantu, and Kuntu. Of less importance is J. V. Taylor's *The Primal Vision*, which on the one hand is overly concerned with Christian contact with Africa and on the other hand is insufficiently critical of the African traditional world. C. A. Diop's work, too, does not merit any extended discussion since he is concerned primarily with the superior role African values played in the historical destiny of the continent. He contrasts the positive morality of Africa with the pessimistic morality of Europe and even attempts to show that Egyptian civilization was a product of black Africa.

Many studies deal with African world-views, and an enumeration of them may elucidate the diversity of African cultures but not the problem of African philosophy. A great step forward was taken when the problem of *négritude*—a term first coined by the West Indian poet Césaire—was raised to a philosophic issue, initially in the context of French colonialism.

Négritude was an almost predictable reaction at a time when it was a fairly common colonial view that there was no African culture, civilization, or historical consciousness. The black man was in many instances considered a child, a savage, or a mentally deficient. In particular reaction against the "Prospero and Caliban complex," *négritude* tried to rehabilitate the African as an identity and a personality outside the Western framework. In emphasizing the value of African religion, tradition, culture, art, and experience, it emphasized the *us* as opposed to the *them*. The absolute necessity of the *other* ironically elevated colonialism to an evil genius, which at the same time conferred identity.

Leopold Sénghor, in line with his existentialist philosophical interest, attempted to develop *négritude* by introducing the notion of the "negro soul" versus the Western "essence." The racial mark branded by the colonizers becomes a symbol of identity and a confirmation of what was suppressed but is now liberated. Hence, Sénghor has a habit of contrasting the authentic African experience with the Western, a contrast which is by no means always correct.

As opposed to the "eye-reason" of the West, Sénghor posits "reason by embrace" (or, as it would be more generally termed, intuitive reason). This embrace means participation in the vital force which extends from God to the smallest grain of sand. Hence, "the African cannot imagine an object as different from man as its essence. He endows it with a sensibility, a will, a human soul." The law of participation means a direct spontaneous experience of the world, a life-surge and self-abandonment which effect a mystical sympathy with the universe. For this reason Sénghor can state: "Emotion is African, as reason is Hellenic." In accordance with Hellenic reason "the Western discursive method of reasoning merely stops at the surface of things, it does not penetrate their hidden resorts which escape the lucid consciousness. Only intuitive reason is alone capable of an understanding that goes beyond appearance, of taking in total reality. . . ."

In an article entitled "Négritude: A Humanism of the Twentieth Century," published in the second volume of *The Africa Reader: Independent Africa,* Sénghor stresses that these ideas do not express racialism but a confirmation of one's being, the rooting of oneself in the African experience. *Négritude* is "*the sum of the cultural values* of the black world; that is, a certain active presence in the world, or better, in the universe. . .'a way of relating oneself to the world and to others' " (p. 180). Sénghor allies himself with Teilhard de Chardin's rejection of traditional scientific and philosophical dichotomies in favor of a single reality, spirit-matter. In virtue of radical or psychic energy, man becomes a creative force who transcends himself by developing harmoniously the two complementary elements of the soul: the heart and the mind. Thus, for Sénghor *négritude* is more than a humanism; it is an exemplary humanism. For example, it is through *négritude* that decolonization has been accomplished without much bloodshed; that dialogue and reciprocity have been established between former colonizers and colonized; that a new spirit has been established in the United Nations where the "no" and bang of the fist on the table are no longer signs of strength. One reads between the lines that the humanism of *négritude* has a destiny beyond the African continent. It expresses a mode of life and a quality of experience which is Africa's peculiar gift to humanity.

These claims are somewhat exaggerated. Sénghor's thinking, in spite of the popularity it enjoyed at a certain stage, merits serious criticism. Perhaps the most hard-hitting criticism leveled at Sénghor is by his own mentor, Jean-Paul Sartre. He writes:

In fact, négritude appears as the minor term of a dialectical progression: the theoretical and practical assertion of the supremacy of the white man is the thesis; the position of négritude as an antithetical value is the moment of negativity. But this negative moment [of antiracist racism] is insufficient by itself, and the Negroes that employ it know it very well, they know that it is intended to propose the synthesis or realization of the human in a society without races. Thus negritude is the root of its own destruction, it is a transition and not a conclusion, a means and not an ultimate goal.

Further criticism has come from some of Sénghor's closest associates and colleagues. They see *négritude* as an idealistic construction—in fact, as the absolutization of an African "essence" which has little contact with existing, often execrable, social conditions. It is to Sénghor's credit that in his essay on humanism he explicitly recognizes this criticism and presents *négritude* as also implying practical social projects. In all fairness, it should be stated that Sénghor is correct in seeing that this historic task can only be realized on a proper socio-philosophical basis (which, for him, is *négritude*). However, his humanism does reveal a curious reluctance to come to terms with irreversible global phenomena such as technology and industrialism. Again, it is certainly an overstatement to present *negritude* as an historical incarnation of Teilhard de Chardin's ideal of integral personality on the rather slim evidence of Sénghor's interpretation of the law of participation. It is particularly striking that Sénghor shows little appreciation of non-African and non-Western conceptions of personality such as are to be found, for example, in Buddhism and Hinduism—conceptions which simply do not fit into the pattern of *négritude*. But he has certainly described, with rare sensibility and poetic vehemence, the experience of a cultural difference which he has transmuted not only into a gain but also into a prophetic program.

In reviewing Sénghor's position and some criticisms, we have mentioned that his assessment of the West is not always correct. Let us qualify this comment at once by stating that this does not imply criticism of the African mode of experience expressed by almost all scholars of Africa and abundantly exemplified in the rich diversity of African world-views. But we have also noted, as African scholars themselves insist, that Africa is undergoing an immense process of change and that its traditional values correspondingly need to be reinterpreted and integrated into socioeconomic factors which have become global. In searching for a meaning of the term "African philosophy," it is then not enough to echo Sénghor's sentiments. His own negative reaction to the West must be clarified, and an attempt must be made to establish a common universe of discourse within which philosophical questions may be framed.

In considering the possibility of an African philosophy or at least in attempting to clarify what such a concept may mean, two facts may be kept in mind.

The first is that Western-type philosophy is in fact taught at African universities. The African not only can but also does render his own contribution in this field. There is no question of a lack of understanding of Western philosophy or a lack of ability to conduct research at a very high level indeed. From this point of view, then, the African philosopher is simply a philosopher, one among others. As philosopher he has no particular bias, except that he may choose to pursue his investigations in this rather than that field, to feel attracted to this rather than that style of philosophizing.

The second is that the African philosopher, as a man, cannot avoid coming to terms with a historical fact, namely, decolonization. Here I think it is necessary to bracket aspects of this problem. Our concern is not with a historical account of this process; or with the political implications of decolonization and the body of literature it has produced; or with African poetry and fiction which deal with the transition from a centuries-old traumatic fixation of the black man as an "object" (in Sartre's sense) for the colonizer to a new and as yet not completely articulated self-determinism. We are concerned, rather, with the implications of decolonization in the philosophical field, that is, with the problem of how to assess a Western philosophy that has been historically associated with a Western world-view which produced colonization. This is important, not only for its own sake, but also for the light it throws on African efforts to "correct" Western philosophical attitudes.

The first fact requires no further elaboration. The second does, and it is in this area that we must search for a meaning of the term "African philosophy." It is by now clear that the African philosopher himself cannot interpret the manifold world- and life-views associated with mythologies and cosmologies as philosophy in any but an uncritical popular sense of the term. Our concern, then, is with what African philosophy may mean from an informed academic point of view.

At the start, we are confronted with a problem set by decolonization itself. Is this formulation of the problem not in fact a formulation from within the colonial context itself? Is the underlying assumption not exactly that Western philosophy is philosophy and that the problem of African philosophy is in advance geared to a specific Western problematic, a specific Western mode of questioning? In that case, there is little hope that the West will interpret African philosophy as much beyond a search for identity as exemplified in a philosophy of *négritude* (itself perhaps sketched in terms of Western existentialist questioning), or as a cluster of world-views loosely connected in a more or less vitalistic, intuitionist framework vaguely in line with the school of Bergson. A certain therapeutic value could then be attributed to African thought inasmuch as its central themes may revitalize a relatively impoverished Western world-view and life-style decimated by technology, dehumanized by the exploitation devices of the affluent society, and confused by its own child, ideological dialectical materialism. To formulate the problem more precisely: Africa considers that Western philosophy is analytical in a sense wholly arid, that it presupposes a subject-object dichotomy which breaks man's compact with the world, and that this same dichotomy leads to a frame of mind in which *domination of the object,* with its corollary, *alienation of the subject,* is the inevitable outcome. To accept Western philosophy as "philosophy" is thus to accept the epistemology of colonialism.

This criticism is interesting because it is partially true. It is true that, at least from the sixteenth to the nineteenth century, the Western world-view—to which philosophy contributed—did to a certain extent express these characteristics. For example, it is no accident that the Industrial Revolution in England coincided with Bentham's well-meaning but inhuman hedonistic calculus, or that the century of genius achieved its scientific successes against the background of Descartes' dualism of mind and matter. Descartes' famous dictum "Man is the master and controller of nature" further presupposed that this nature could be manipulated by mechanical means. And it has become a truism that the domination of nature is effected through the domination of man by man. Both the *Meditations* of Descartes and the *Leviathan* of Thomas Hobbes foreshadow the onslaught on Africa. But the socio-historical exploitation of philosophical ideas and the philosophical blindness of many early modern philosophers do not negate a tradition stretching from Plato to Kant in which various forms of dualism do not necessarily indicate a weakness but a constant struggle with the concepts at their disposal and which collectively achieve an immense leap forward in the exploration of the structure of knowledge. To say that Western philosophy is analytical and arid does not invalidate the achievements of a Locke or a Hume or the legitimacy of logic, and to say that reason is an embrace is not yet an intelligible criticism of aspects of, say, Kantian philosophy. It is understandable that in times of collective distress words should be used loosely, but the time has come that a proper dialogue should be conducted between African and European thinkers in terms of shared insights and agreed criteria. This alone makes philosophical communication and fruitful collaboration in a common enterprise possible.

Having said this, it may be added that the interpretation of Western philosophy to which the African objects is nothing new. It has been stated most strongly in the twentieth century by European philosophers themselves. Moreover—and this is a point of immense importance—Western philosophy has given birth to a type of philosophizing which is no longer specifically Western but global in the true sense of the term. It is here that we must look for contact with African philosophy and for its inevitable role.

Obviously, an in-depth discussion of what I have termed "global philosophy" would not only require an impracticable amount of time but would also divert us for too long from the thread of our argument. I shall therefore pick out at random certain statements and points of view, leaving aside the controversies surrounding them.

The first example comes from the introduction to Strawson's *Individuals*. Inasmuch as a paraphrase can only dull the clarity of the author's style, let us allow him to speak for himself in the form of two points:

(1) The inquiry with which he is concerned, says Strawson, aims "to lay bare the most general features of our conceptual structure." With respect to the continual changing face of philosophic tradition:

There is a massive central core of human thinking which has no history—or none recorded in histories of thought; there are categories and concepts which, in their most fundamental character, change not at all. Obviously, these are not the specialities of the most refined thinking; and yet the indispensable core of the conceptual equipment of the most sophisticated human beings. It is with these, their interconnections, and the structure that they form, that a descriptive metaphysics will be primarily concerned.

(2) Again:

For though the central subject-matter of descriptive metaphysics does not change, the critical and analytical idiom of philosophy changes constantly. Permanent relationships are described in an impermanent idiom, which reflects both the age's climate of thought and the individual philosopher's style of thinking.

These statements seem fairly obvious. He seems to be emphasizing merely the existence and necessity of a *philosophia perennis* subject to the exigencies of various contexts. However, if we realize that Strawson is not referring to a *philosophia perennis* in the traditional sense, that is, the slow unraveling of the relation of mind to being against the background of the double strain of empiricism and rationalism, then it becomes clear that he is referring to an entirely different problem. He is describing invariant structures which are not to be confused with the furniture of the Kantian ego.

The two basic categories with which Strawson deals are material objects and persons. For him, "person" is a primitive concept; notions such as a pure ego or pure individual consciousness are secondary, nonprimitive, derived—derived, that is, from a logically prior concept, "person." A person is a type of entity "such that *both* predicates ascribing states of consciousness *and* predicates ascribing corporeal characteristics, a physical situation, etc., are equally applicable to a single individual of that single type." A point of some importance should be noted briefly. Strawson attempts to move a certain class of P-predicates to a central position in the picture, namely, predicates involving action and intentionality. In his own work, the issues are not excessively problematical as it is fairly easy to distinguish between M- and P-predicates and to characterize them in terms of Strawson's criteria. When we turn to African thought, however, the first problem which arises is that, at least in many traditional African worldviews, this is exactly *not* the way we think about persons, *not* the way we think about material objects. A person is bound up not only with his ancestors and his clan but also with a whole universe through which vital power is deployed. Moreover, a man's soul may perch in a tree, his viscera may be an extension of the surrounding vegetation. Ordinary physical objects have human characteristics, and some are numinous, vibrant with power. Nothing can be separated out as "material" as opposed to "personal."

Does this constitute a criticism of Strawson? Have we here an African experience as against a European experience which will brand the distinction between M- and P-predicates a typically Western conceptualization? The answer is unequivocally *no*. There are "categories and concepts which, in their most fundamental character, change not at all"; but the description of the structure of these categories and concepts themselves is subject to the vicissitudes of idiom and style.

It cannot be denied that the grain of sand does not exhibit the ability to choose, act, or intend in the sense in which persons choose, act, or intend; hence, it is not a person. It is, in philosophical language, a material object *within a context agreed upon*. That it is filled with vital force is another matter altogether which does not fall within the philosophical universe of discourse, does not come into conflict with it, and is a perfectly acceptable item in a world-view. Again, it matters not a whit that my soul sits in the tree or that the vegetation invades my body. The man thus described still exercises his prerogative as a person. For the African philosopher, vast areas here lie fallow in which at least two immediately urgent tasks come to mind: (1) to establish the criteria in terms of which an ancestor may be described as a person, and (2) to establish the criteria by means of which the legitimate language usage of philosophy may be distinguished from the legitimate language usage of world-views. (I deliberately avoid the phrase "language games" as this involves issues not immediately relevant.) It should perhaps be emphasized that a philosophy is never in principle opposed to a world-view. One lives, acts, believes, and reasons in accordance with a world-view. The danger is that a world-view may become an ideology—a situation which easily arises when its fundamental presuppositions are uncritically accepted.

It is hardly necessary to add that Strawson's views have been introduced, not because they occupy any privileged position in contemporary philosophy, but simply because they are fairly well known and, at least in *Individuals,* deal with a topic which is both interesting and controversial. However, his views are by no means always satisfactory, and his conception of a person, even allowing for his own reservations regarding style and idiom, need to be filled out in terms of a philosophical anthropology which his own philosophy does not and indeed cannot produce. In many respects, Stuart Hampshire's *Thought and Action* would have been a better choice, but my selection was deliberately random.

The tracing of invariant structures is also the task of the phenomenologist. By means of the device of the epoché, the natural attitude is suspended, not only with respect to Western and African world-views but also with respect to the presuppositions and ideologies—scientific, philosophical, or magical—which may accompany them. It is important to note that the natural attitude is not destroyed but merely put aside in order that the *Lebenswelt* and its structures may become accessible to philosophic description. For Merleau-Ponty, at least, the most important structures to be described are perception, the body-subject, space, time, expression, and language—structures rooted in that "savage being" which sustains and nourishes the edifices of the abstractive, constructive, and constitutive consciousness. Such a reduction practiced on many African world-views could produce a picture astoundingly close to that drawn by Merleau-Ponty, a fact recognized by many philosophers and anthropologists. While his description of the experience of space in the *schéma corporel* has much in common with the African experience, much work remains to be done on temporal structures in an African phenomenology. Mbiti has given us a schematic account of *Sasa* and *Zamani* (see Appendix)—the time of the now and the great original time of the myths and cosmologies, as well as the backward-fading of *Sasa* into *Zamani*. But what is most urgently required is to work out the structure of a future—a task which is indispensable in a decolonized Africa. In addition, descriptions are required of the various forms of duration, protension, retension, stasis, and prolepsis, in a lived world in which the phenomenon of rhythm plays a predominating role. As these few suggestions have indicated, with the material at its disposal African philosophy may make an immense contribution to phenomenology by describing structures that at present are still too complicated and too obscure for the Western and, for that matter, Eastern mind to grasp. Here indeed is tremendous scope for creative contribution to a global enterprise.

Almost completely absorbed into the phenomenology of Merleau-Ponty is the philosophy of the Marx of the 1844 Manuscripts (as opposed to Marx-Engels, revisionist and ideological Marxism). The early Marx explores three aspects of man's being: his objective, species, and social being, showing them to be completely interdependent, as indeed man and world are interdependent. The body is shown as active and meaning-giving. Intersubjectivity is not a communion of pure consciousness but a meeting of enfleshed subjects in a common world. If we keep in mind that the black man conceives of himself not as primarily egocentric but as excentric, that he exists as an integral part of nature, a knot in far-flung social and cosmological structures, it becomes clear why a form of socialism is a natural and traditional expression of the African experience. The themes of the 1844 Manuscripts could thus be developed in an ambience foreign to both capitalism and communism in their present form.

A fourth philosophical movement which has moved beyond the traditional problematic of the West is the hermeneutics of Paul Ricoeur. Initially concerned with elaborating a phenomenology of freedom, he later turned to structuralism and finally to hermeneutics. Against the background of Russian formalism, Czech linguistics, and structuralism, the Parisian Tel Quel group, and specifically Lucien Goldmann's genetic structuralism, Ricoeur now devotes particular attention to the linguistic connections between structuralism and hermeneutics, with special emphasis on the dialectic of semiology and semantics. This undertaking implies a convergency of psychoanalysis, history of religions, anthropology, linguistics, sociology, and other disciplines. In spite of the fact that Ricoeur's most recent work is concerned with the semantics of Freud's *Traumdeutung*, our own immediate interest is in his attempt to establish what he terms a "global understanding of man" by means of the study of the language of myth and symbol.

The theme which initiates and sustains his research is the following: symbol invites thought. However, Ricoeur at once clarifies his position by insisting that the symbol is not demystified by thought through a process of reduction. It is a structure of meaning which has a literal sense juxtaposed to an indirect, secondary, figurative sense—in his own words "a logic of the double meaning" which involves advanced semiotic and semantic analysis. Interpretation decodes the latent sense, revealing the various layers of symbolic intentionality. Hence, the hermeneutics of symbol demands a threefold structure: (1) the primordial symbol itself, (2) the myth as first-degree hermeneutics, and (3) interpretation of the myth as second-degree hermeneutics.

There is, of course, a wide spectrum of primary symbols. Before moving on to the symbolism of psychoanalysis, Ricoeur confined himself almost exclusively to a few selected Hebrew and Hellenic myths concerned with the symbolism of evil. (Buber, with a similar purpose in mind, includes Iranian myths.) In Africa, there are a large number of myths concerned with evil as yet untouched by hermeneutical analysis. The Vugusu, the northernmost subtribe of the Abaluyia, have a creation myth which in many respects is similar to the Adam myth. The creation, comprising heaven, earth, and a first human pair, is completed in six days. Although the world is created good, man inherits mortality as a result of a curse by a chameleon to whom he has refused a share of his food. The Vugusu accept an evil god who is created an independent, though weaker, force. According to some views, God did not create evil and does man no evil; hence, societies like the Akamba and Herero feel no need to sacrifice to Him. The Ashanti hold that God created man with a knowledge of good and evil and that man may freely choose between the two without the intervention of God. In many African societies, spirits are originators or agents of evil, especially after they have become detached from links with the living after four or five generations. Most African peoples believe that God is the final source of moral codes, and transgressions by an individual usually involve the collective guilt of his household or kin. Some consider that man can directly offend God, and others that He is too remote from human affairs for them to feel guilty. There is also a widespread "establishment" view of evil which barely justifies the use of the term "evil." This simply means that the offense is "evil" if committed against a person superior or equal in the kinship hierarchy, but not if committed against somebody lower in the hierarchy.

The above examples are chosen to suggest that for Ricoeur hermeneutics bypasses the distinction between world-view and philosophy. To study the phenomenon of evil, for example, we need not move from mythic-symbolic language to a Western ethical vocabulary precisely because the latter in itself is insufficient. The symbolic "text," whether written or uttered or enacted, constitutes a semantic unity of univocal and equivocal symbols which may have many meanings. In the Adam myth, which Ricoeur discusses exhaustively in *The Symbolism of Evil*, he has uncovered under the overt univocal meaning at least three structures of evil: the tragic (anterior evil in the form of the serpent); the ethical (the moment of choice); and the Orphic (the notion of a "fall" of man). Similarly, the Vusugu myth has a tragic and an ethical aspect, but note the immense change when we turn to the evil effected by the living dead who have become spirits. Here we have a quasi-tragic symbolism combined with a kinship structure, which is further complicated by the fact that these evil spirits need to be activated by deeds on the part of the living which in some way or other insult or provoke them, such as lack of proper burial or disobedience of commands. These few examples do not even touch the surface of the deeper symbolic intentionality involved in such myths of evil. This is still very much work-in-progress.

Lack of progress in the field of hermeneutical exegesis of African myths is due both to the immensity of the undertaking itself as well as to lack of clarity in Ricoeur's own conception of what he terms the "hermeneutical circle." His research into myths as a clue to a global anthropology was seriously checked when he found that a hermeneutic developed to deal with symbols cannot be separated from semiology and semantics. While the first level of hermeneutics deals with exhaustive phenomenological studies of specific symbolic structures, Ricoeur has come to recognize that the ensuing comparative mythology endangers the very enterprise of a global anthropology. Moreover, he now feels that phenomenology itself cannot survive unless it can properly reply to the challenge of linguistics—a state of affairs which he contends has spread to all the human sciences. For this reason, the interpretation of equivocal meanings requires the interlocking of philosophy, linguistics, and cultural anthropology.

These remarks illustrate that philosophy does not need to sweep African world-views under the carpet. Indeed, it should set out to interpret them in accordance with the most sophisticated semiological methods available. This is really part of a larger problem which we have mentioned before: the relation between world-view and philosophy. From one point of view, then, the world-view must stand back in favor of global philosophy. From the point of view outlined above, the world-view has its own proper contribution to the global view, albeit in the circumscribed philosophical subdiscipline of hermeneutics.

CONCLUSIONS

Greek philosophy, by taking being *in view*, makes possible the distinction between the knower (subject) and the known (object). This philosophy is born as questioning, as wonder—but as a questioning and a wonder which are characterized by distance. Hence, it is no accident that the image of light and consequently of sight begins to orientate the philosopher's conception of his task. To stand off, to create a distance, is also to create the possibility of seeing, of taking something in view. The medieval philosophers used the term *lumen naturale*, that is, the natural light of reason which makes it possible to see what was before concealed. The Greek distinction received its classic expression in the High Middle Ages in the famous phrase of Aquinas: *veritas est adequatio rei et intellectus*. Already we have two entities: mind *(intellectus)* and things *(res)*, and almost imperceptibly metaphysics has become the science of that which is looked *at*. In this context, Sénghor's phrase "eye-reason" is particularly apposite.

This objectivity is the distinctive gift of Western man. He is able to fix his gaze on the object, regardless of the exigencies of the subject. That which is uncovered or illuminated in the act of knowing is in no way qualified by the situation of the thinker himself, for the properly intellectual vocation requires him to strip himself of his particularity brought about by his body, by history, and by the unruly inclinations of the will. This cognitive asceticism extends the meaning of objectivity to include universality: the notion of a truth which is true for all at all times exactly because man is able to renounce his particularity by identifying himself with that reason which he *is*.

Yet, it is often forgotten that the man who lives in cultures that are still related to living myths also knows objectivity. This objectivity certainly does not presuppose the distinction between subject and object, knower and known, for this distinction in the sense described above is as yet absent. But it makes its appearance in a different form of apperception, namely, participation—participation in the all-present vital power as well as in the exemplary mythical events of the great original time. He affirms his participation through the liturgy of repetition, which ensures both the constancy of his world and the success of his undertakings. For example, the appropriate ritual must be performed to guarantee the success of the crop, the hunt, or rainmaking.

Mythical interpretation is almost always verifiable by events which take place within the framework of a preestablished system of verification provided by the myth itself. (An unusual and uncharacteristic exception is to be found in the culture of the Lovedu of the Transvaal, where myths play an insignificant role.) We may thus legitimately speak here of objectivity, but of an objectivity which is totally incarnated in the praxis of everyday life. With Strasser we term this "objectifying praxis" the first objectivity. The magnitude of this achievement is even more evident if we consider that in the myth man confirms his humanity by articulating, for the first time, a meaningful model of the universe. In spite of the degradation of myth in allegory and gnosis, it still has the power to coerce us to perceive *according to it*, as even today we do not merely look *at* the cave painting but see *according to it*.

But this objectivity has a negative side. Africa, it is said, lacks the ability to think abstractly. This ability is the characteristic genius of Western culture, the genius of the second objectivity. To the question "What is it?" the Western philosopher replies by giving a definition which ignores whatever is accidental or irrelevant to the definiendum. Abstraction thus combines with the logic of classification to yield a kingdom of timeless essences which devaluates the everyday world to the status of appearance.

Here again a qualification is necessary which puts in question overzealous attempts to stress the African rejection of "abstract" and "arid" philosophical categories. Although Junod claims that there is no genera formation for animals in Tonga, the Tonga do correctly join species into genera. For example, *tsuna* is the name for all ferns. Function may also be the basis of classification: any parasite is *phakama*. This ability to classify, often in highly effective forms, occurs in many African cultures and makes nonsense of the idea that the notion of genus has been denied to Africans. An untutored Zulu herdboy can as a rule name hundreds of plant species. Furthermore, categorization in terms of cause and effect is also universal in Africa, although there are degrees of specificity. For example, while in Xhosa *ukuBanga* may denote historical, physical, or magical causation, in Swahili there are terms for ground, meaning, reason, and necessity, as well as for proximate, remote, efficient, material, and final causes. (Some scholars attribute this ability to Arabic influence.) While most Bantu verbs have causative forms, this does not, of course, imply that causality, as a philosophical problem in its Western guise, is an issue in African world-views. In this sense, then, it is true that abstraction is foreign to the African experience.

The dualism between subject and object, which made abstraction possible, was exacerbated in the seventeenth century by Descartes' distinction between thinking thing *(res cogitans)* and extended thing *(res extensa)*. It was scientism, however, which emerged triumphantly as the dominant ideology of the West. I deliberately speak of an ideology; for scientism, in claiming that the physico-mathematical sciences alone guarantee objective knowledge, has in fact practiced a speculative totalitarianism in no way permitted, or intended, by the universe of discourse of science itself. Following the pattern of the second objectivity, scientism, too, devaluates the lived world in relation to a world which it claims to be "real" and "objective," that is, the world discovered by the exact sciences. And it is now scientism which will present itself as mentor to a benighted humanity that nevertheless tenaciously clings to a certain habit of wisdom gleaned from its commerce with the world.

The achievement of the second objectivity is both the articulation of a universe of discourse expressed in univocal symbols and the rationalization of labor in technology. This achievement, too, has its negative side: an ignorance concerning the manner of its knowing and the nature of its evidences. It is thus necessary to develop a radical thinking which will expose the root of objective thinking and show how it is anchored in the pregiven world of everyday experience. This radical reflection is termed the third objectivity. In philosophy, the transition to the third objectivity is effected by a return to the primary evidences of the lived world. Its point of departure is the analysis of the conceptual confusions generated by the subject-object model in epistemology. According to this critique, there is no consciousness-in-itself which mirrors a "real," "objective" world-in-itself. Man is a multiple question, and every interrogation evokes a different answer, a different zone of meaning. In every academic discipline, a field of study is demarcated, certain models are chosen, and a certain appropriate vocabulary is selected. But every conceptualization refers back to that preabstractive, prereflective texture of meaning, that unity of experience which is man's being-in-the-world. It must be pointed out that this in no way implies an "archeology of reason" but rather a recognition of the irreducibility of man, the questioning being, to any of his own answers. Thus, W. Heisenberg writes: "Even in physical science. . .the object of research is no longer nature in itself but nature as exposed to man's questioning, and to this extent man here also encounters *himself* again."

And thus the problem of the third objectivity arises. If all disciplines are abstractive thematizations from the lived sociocultural world, how is it possible to know this world without abstraction? How, in the last analysis, is it possible to *be* man and to *think* man?

This aporia cannot be solved. In the very moment of recollection and self-reflection, the philosopher is checked. He discovers that he has to move from the antinomies of reason to the dialectics of his own being-in-the-world. He discovers that he has to formulate the problem of the contingency of his reason, which stubbornly resists formulation. He discovers that he has to think a new model of meaning itself: he has to think symbolically.

Here we are at the hub of an immense problem. The prereflective life, this everyday lived life, is transparent to itself. It knows, without instruction, the secrets of the body; it moves with prescience in the surrounding world; it anticipates the needs of others in daily encounter; and its vivid sense of contingency sharpens its awareness of a density of being which resists exploration. Yet, at the same time, this life is opaque. It is inaccessible to the abstractive analyses of the various sciences, precisely because it is the source of all abstractions only by disengaging itself from those abstract filaments and fragments of meaning which it leaves behind it as a residue in the discourse of the analytic disciplines.

If I say that it is the unenviable task of the third objectivity to articulate the immediate evidences of the lived world without abstractive conceptualization, you may consider that I am making things deliberately difficult. It is made even more difficult by the fact that man is living in a crisis situation. The magnitude of this crisis shows itself in numerous phenomena: in the rapid transition from primary to secondary systems in labor; in the equally rapid establishment of universal technological infrastructures which have profoundly altered the face of international politics; in the transvaluation of values; in the juxtaposition of extreme regimentation and maximum individualism; in terror and the balance of terror as concepts on which some kind of outraged intelligibility has to be conferred.

These are not isolated phenomena. They point back to the destruction of an old order, and they look forward to the emergence of a new order. In the fluid interim, man is subjected to continuous pressure to devise new models for understanding his situation and ordering his world. He is driven to find quick solutions for problems the magnitude of which far transcend our collective experience. But the philosopher, dedicated both to rigorous and responsible thinking, can only follow the tempo of his own mode of cognition. Let us return again to the notion of the third objectivity.

In a culture where the sun is worshipped as a god, it is seen differently. In a world of telephones and jet planes, proximity and absence are experienced differently. It is a common place in philosophy and psychology that a thing is always perceived in spatial, temporal, and cultural profiles or horizons. Architecture, for example, does not deal with an undifferentiated conceptual space but with lived space. It is not concerned with providing enough cubic feet per body but with dwellings for persons and families. The time of the physicist, again, is not that duration which we experience in the devising and maturing of our projects, nor does music or dancing obey the demands of a linearly constituted time. The medical doctor himself knows only too well that the body, too, has its reasons and in certain circumstances prescribes to the doctor. Man does not know only in the laboratory or in the study. Through his fingers, eyes, ears, his mobility, his gestures, a world is made present which, in its superabundance, invites without restraint a discourse which will be both rigorous and nourished by the enigma of the inexhaustible richness of its symbols: symbols which burgeon from an immeasurable ontological secrecy.

Thus, the third objectivity also raises the question of the horizon of meaning. We have stated that since its origin philosophy has always been concerned with such a horizon according to which the whole of knowledge could be interpreted and ordered. We have also shown that this horizon of meaning was conceived rationalistically in both the metaphysical and scientistic sense. We now need another notion to interpret the idea of a horizon of meaning, and this is the notion of symbol. For the horizon of meaning may no longer be conceived rationalistically and statically but as a dynamic contour of meaning ignited by symbols. Symbol, *symballein,* means throwing, gathering, binding together. It is the great symbols of mankind which have always gathered time together in that duration which we call a culture or a civilization. We may only refer in passing to those with which we are most familiar to realize that the symbol, unlike the essence, cannot be exhausted by theoria. In participating in them, man is related to a richness of signification which is already implied in the Greek word for truth, *aletheia.* This term originally meant not only the experience of the unhiddenness of that-which-is but also a recalling of a togetherness which has been forgotten. In this context, the first objectivity, that of participation, achieves a fuller meaning by becoming the dominant theme in the third objectivity.

At this moment an abyss opens before us, for we find ourselves in a decimated world where old symbols have effaced themselves and new symbols have not yet manifested themselves. The search for a new horizon of meaning is thus primarily an examination of the exigencies of contemporary culture which, in grappling with the crisis of certitudes, itself becomes the prototype of creative thinking. Far from pursuing its role as the abstract guardian of truth, philosophy has discovered itself as that very "fluid interim" which it must both articulate to the best of its ability and endure as its unavoidable condition.

Perhaps it is one of the functions of an African philosophy to step into this "fluid interim" to fulfill a task for which it is uniquely equipped: the articulation of the third objectivity in terms of the symbol, or rather, in terms of an experience of connaturality with symbolic structures. This task, assumed in conjunction with the other philosophical tasks briefly outlined here, could never, for Africa, be interpreted as merely a Western-type ethnic undertaking, unless the global village were seen as ethnic in relation to the featureless mystery of the galaxies. In this sense, then, Sénghor's *négritude* is perhaps a misapprehension of the true vocation of the African philosopher: his contribution to global philosophy.

SELECT BIBLIOGGRAPHY

BOOKS AND ARTICLES

DeWaelhens, A. *La philosophie et les expériences naturelles* (The Hague: Nijhoff, 1961).

Eliade, M. *Patterns in Comparative Religion* (Cleveland, Ohio: Meridian, 1963).

Esmail, A. *Themes for the Future: The Task of Philosophy in Africa* (Nairobi, Kenya: University of Nairobi, n.d.).

Fanon, F. *Black Skins, White Masks*, trans. L. Markmann (New York: Grove Press, 1968).

Forde, D. *African Worlds* (London: Oxford University Press, 1954).

Fortes, M. and Dieterlin, G. *African Systems of Thought* (London: International African Institute, 1965).

────── and Evans-Pritchard, E. E. *Introduction to African Political Systems* (London and New York: Oxford University Press, 1970).

Foucault, M. *Les Mots et les Choses* (Paris: Gallimard, 1966).

Gellner, E. *Thought and Change* (London: Weidenfeld and Nicolson, 1964).

Griaule, M. *Conversations with Ogotemmeli*, (London: Oxford University Press, 1966).

──────. *Dieu de l'Eau, Entretiens avec Ogotemmêli* (Paris: Éditions du Chene, 1948).

Gusdorf, G. *Mythe et Metaphysique* (Paris: Flammarion, 1953).

Hampshire, S. *Thought and Action* (London: Chatto and Windus, 1960).

Hermann, F. *Symbolik in den Religionen der Naturvölker* (Stuttgart: Hiersemann, 1961).

Irele, A. "Negritude: Literature and Ideology," in *Modern Black Novelists: A Collection of Critical Essays*, ed. M. G. Cooke (Englewood Cliffs, N.J.: Prentice-Hall, 1971).

Jahn, J. *Muntu* (London: Faber and Faber, 1958).

Junod, H. A. *The Life of a South African Tribe* (London: Macmillan, 1927).

Junod, H. P. *Bantu Heritage* (Johannesburg: Hortors, 1938).

Kagame, A. *La Philosophie Bantu-Rwandaise de l'Etre* (Brussels: Academie Royale des Sciences Coloniales, 1956).

Lévy-Bruhl, L. *Primitive Mentality* (London: Allen and Unwin, 1923).

Mannoni, O. *Prospero and Caliban: The Psychology of Colonization* (New York: Praeger, 1964).

Marcuse, H. *One-Dimensional Man* (London: Sphere Library, 1970).

Marx, K. *Economic and Philosophic Manuscripts of 1844*, trans. M. Milligan (Moscow: Foreign Languages Publishing House, 1961).

Mbiti, J. S. *African Religions and Philosophy* (London: Heinemann, 1969).

──────. *Concepts of God in Africa* (New York: Praeger, 1970).

Merleau-Ponty, M. *Phénoménologie de la Perception* (Paris: Gallimard, 1945).

Outlaw, L. "Language and Consciousness: Towards a Hermeneutic of Black Culture," *Cultural Hermeneutics* 1, No. 4 (1974).

Piaget, J. *Structuralism* (London: Routledge and Kegan Paul, 1971).

Radin, P. *Primitive Man as a Philosopher* (New York: Dover, 1957).

———. *Primitive Religion* (New York: Ligion, 1962).

Ricoeur, P. *Freud and Philosophy: An Essay on Interpretation*, trans. D. Savage (New Haven, Conn.: Yale University Press, 1970).

———. *The Symbolism of Evil* (Boston: Beacon Press, 1969).

Robey, D. (ed.). *Structuralism: An Introduction* (Oxford: Clarendon Press, 1973).

Sartre, J.-P. *Critique de la Raison Dialectique* (Paris: Gallimard, 1960).

Sénghor, L. S. *Die Wurzeln der Negritude in Afrika Heute—ein Jahrbuch* (1962); idem: *Pierre Teilhard de Chardin et la politique africaine* (Paris: Seuil, 1962).

———. "Eléments constructifs dúne Civilisation d'inspiration négro-africaine," *Présence Africaine* 24–25 (1959).

———. "Negritude: A Humanism of the Twentieth Century," in *The Africa Reader: Independent Africa*, II, eds. W. Cartey and M. Kilson (New York: Vintage Books, 1970).

Strasser, S. *Fenomenologie en empirische menskunde* (Arnhem: Van Loghum Slaterus, 1962).

Strawson, P. F. *Individuals* (London: Methuen, 1959).

Sundkler, B.G.M. *Bantu Prophets in South Africa*, 2d ed. (London: Oxford University Press, 1961).

Taylor, J. V. *The Primal Vision* (London: S.C.M. Press, 1963).

Temples, P. *Bantu Philosophy* (Paris: Présence Africaine, 1959).

Van der Leeuw, G. *De Primitieve mens en de religi* (Groningen: Wolters, 1952).

Werner, A. *Myths and Legends of the Bantu* (London: Harrap, 1933).

JOURNALS

African Thought and Practice
Cahiers Philosophiques Africains
Second Order
Uche

APPENDIX: *Analysis of African Concept of Time, as Illustrated by a Consideration of Verb Tenses Among the Akamba and Gikuyu of Kenya*

Tense	Kikamba	Gikuyu	English	Approximate Time
1. Far Future or Remote Future	Ningauka	Ningoka	I will come	About 2 to 6 months from now
2. Immediate or Near Future	Ninguka	Ninguka	I will come	Within the next short while
3. Indefinite Future or In-definite Near Future	Ngooka (ngauka)	Ningoka	I will come	Within a foreseeable while, after such and such an event
4. Present or Present Progressive	Ninukite	Nindiroka	I am coming	In the process of action, now
5. Immediate Past or Immediate Perfect	Ninauka (ninooka)	Nindoka	I came (I have just come)	In the last hour or so
6. Today's Past	Ninukie	Ninjukire	I came	From the time of rising up to about two hours ago
7. Recent Past or Yesterday's Past	Nininaukie (nininookie)	Nindirokire	I came	Yesterday
8. Far Past or Remote Past	Ninookie (ninaukie)	Nindokire	I came	Any day before yesterday
9. Unspecified Tene (Zamani)	Tene ninookie (Nookie tene)	Nindookire tene	I came	No specific time in the 'past'

SOURCE: John S. Mbiti, *African Religions and Philosophy* (London: Heinemann, 1969), p. 18.

Republic of South Africa
ANNA-LOUIZE CONRADIE

In South Africa, as elsewhere in the world, various philosophical trends are represented in departments of philosophy. There is this difference, however: in South Africa, these schools of thought to a certain extent follow linguistic and religious lines. Generally speaking, the English-medium universities follow Anglo-Saxon philosophical traditions, while the Afrikaans-medium universities tend to relate more closely to continental traditions. Hence, the student of philosophy at the English-medium university, if he wishes to pursue his studies overseas, will tend to do so at British or, occasionally, American universities, while the student at an Afrikaans-medium university will tend to proceed to the Netherlands, and sometimes to France and Germany. The student who has studied at a British university will sometimes return to South Africa to take up a post at an English-medium university, often via Australia, Tasmania, or New Zealand. An analogous situation holds in the case of the Afrikaans-speaking student.

Although English and Afrikaans are the two official languages of South Africa, the position sketched above does not imply fixed divisions and affiliations. Many Afrikaans-speaking students attend English-medium universities in South Africa and vice versa. At some Afrikaans-medium universities, attention is also devoted to analytical philosophy, while at English-medium universities, especially at a more advanced level, some attention is paid to trends such as phenomenology and Marxism. Interdisciplinary studies are becoming increasingly important in philosophical curricula. The Department of Philosophy of the University of Natal, Durban, is unique in the sense that both British and continental trends are equally represented in the form of analytical philosophy, on the one hand, and phenomenology in the tradition of Husserl, Sartre, Heidegger, Merleau-Ponty, and Ricoeur, on the other hand. In seminars and in lectures, attempts are made to promote a dialogue between these two traditions by applying both methods to the discussion of selected problems. It should perhaps be added that as far as is known no department of philosophy, either English or Afrikaans, will refuse to accept a dissertation presented in the other official language. Another area in which linguistic barriers and philosophical commitments are being overcome is at the annual Philosophical Congress, which is discussed later in this essay. The only university whose teaching is completely bilingual is the University of South Africa. Since it teaches by means of correspondence, all of its lecture material is offered in both official languages, and in view of its nature, it has by far the greatest number of students, which it draws from all sections of the community. For many years, the University of South Africa was also the mother institution governing various university colleges until they became independent.

The influence of religious affiliations on the choice of philosophical positions is a complex one and is better understood in relation to the position of particular philosophers. Suffice it to say here that, although neo-Thomism for many years played a role in the Department of Philosophy at the University of Cape Town, Catholicism has very little influence on South African philosophizing. Rather, Protestantism, specifically neo-Calvinism (taught exclusively at Bloemfontein and Potchefstroom), is the main example of a religiously oriented philosophy. Indirectly, however, the departments of philosophy at Stellenbosch and Pretoria are also involved as both have to service students attending the local theological seminaries. The seminary at Stellenbosch is exclusively Dutch Reformed, while that at Pretoria caters for two Afrikaans churches, Dutch Reformed and Hervormd (Reformed). At the Potchefstroom seminary, a different version of Reformed Protestantism ("Dopper") is accepted. The historical background, both theological and political, to these affiliations is extremely interesting. Its roots are in eighteenth- and nineteenth-century events as diverse as the importation of Scottish Presbyterian pastors into the Dutch Reformed church, and the theological battles in the Netherlands in the late nineteenth century, which involved a figure as important as the then Dutch prime minister and theologian, Abraham Kuyper. The English-medium philosophy departments have no specific religious commitments.

In discussing particular South African philosophers, we shall confine ourselves to those who have become known through their publications to a wider public, both in South Africa and overseas. As far as possible, they are discussed in accordance with the philosophical trends or schools they represent.

H. J. de Vleeschauwer (1899–   ) is considered a South African philosopher, although he achieved international fame as a world authority on Kant long before he settled in Pretoria after World War II. A student of Pirenne and Collé, he became professor of philosophy at the University of Ghent, Belgium, during which period his magnum opus, *La déduction transcendentale dans l'ouvre de Kant,* appeared in three volumes. It was also published in an abridged version as *L'Évolution de la pensée kantienne.* Heimsoeth's *Transzendentale Dialektik* was written over a period of ten years in collaboration with de Vleeschauwer. De Vleeschauwer also established himself as an authority on the Belgian philosopher Arnold Geulincx to whom he devoted about twenty works. His own journal, *Mousaion,* published by the University of South Africa, was devoted chiefly to studies in bibliography and librarianship, but it also contained interesting material on Luther, the Iberian Jesuits, Roger Bacon, Rousseau, and other philosophers. It is impossible to list here de Vleeschauwer's prodigious publications, but it may be stated that his forte is the historical development of philosophical movements from the Greeks to Eucken, at the beginning of this century.

Philosophy in South Africa has benefited immensely from the presence of this master during the past thirty years. He has presented papers at South African and overseas congresses. At the Leibniz Congress at Hannover, Germany, in November 1966, members were overwhelmed by his magnificent exegetical lecture, *Perennis quaedam philosophia.* He received many invitations to chairs at universities in other countries but chose to remain head of the Department of Philosophy at the University of South Africa. Since this university functions by means of correspondence courses, he retained enough leisure to devote himself entirely to scholarship. He is now retired. Much of his research on Kant has been continued by his former pupil, S.I.M. du Plessis, who at present is professor of philosophy at the University of Western Cape.

The idealist school of philosophy found its two most influential exponents in South Africa in R.F.A. Hoernlé (1880–1943) and A. H. Murray (1905–   ), the grandson of the famous nineteenth-century Scottish theologian and minister.

Professor A. H. Murray studied at the University of Stellenbosch and, as a Rhodes scholar, proceeded to Oxford, Geneva, and Paris. At Paris he studied under Henri Bergson, and at Oxford he obtained the degrees of D.Phil. and B.Litt. On his return to South Africa, he worked under Hoernlé for six years at the University of the Witwatersrand (Johannesburg), after which he was appointed head of the Department of Philosophy at the University of Cape Town. Apart from his academic duties, he has served on the Library Commission and the Commission of Native Education; as adviser to the Government on Communism and to the Hague International Court on South West African problems; and, since 1963, as a member of the Board of Censors. He is now retired. Apart from many articles, his major publications are *The Philosophy of James Ward, Die Volksraad,* and *The Political Philosophy of J. A. de Mist.* He also edited Gonin's translation of Beza's *De Jure Magistratum.*

Murray has always expounded a modified idealist point of view, notably that of Bradley and Bosanquet. As he is primarily a political philosopher, his main contribution to philosophy in South Africa has consisted in the application of a "synoptic liberalism," which he shared with Hoernlé, to problems that have arisen particularly in South African political thinking. This has taken the form of the development of a concept of liberalism which in many respects is opposed to that of Hoernlé.

According to Murray, true liberalism is to be tested in terms of the quality of the human life which it makes possible in a specific historical situation, in the maintenance of the sovereignty of law, and in the absence of stratification between the members of a society. The observance of the two historic devices of liberalism, rule of law and the internal autonomy of the historic community, shows us how to maintain liberalism in a racially plural state. When corporations are entrenched in their own legal rights, we may achieve liberalism without recourse to "techniques of domination." Murray contends that the liberal must not be afraid to admit the fact of diversities in the population and to maintain these historic diversities in the state. Their maintenance is one of the principles for which liberalism stands, as also devolution of sovereign power, decentralization of the administrative functions of the state, and a policy of separatism involving a diversity of internal autonomies for historical groups. Murray finds this conception of liberalism in the liberal tradition expounded by thinkers such as Grotius, Calvin, Beza, and especially in the *Vindiciae contra tyrannos,* which is now generally ascribed to du Plessis-Mornay and Hubert Languet. In his outstanding study of Commissioner-General J. A. de Mist, Murray shows how de Mist introduced the notion of political pluralism into South African political thinking during the Batavian period in order to maintain the rights of minorities.

An outstanding representative of the school of contemporary analytical philosophy was Professor D. J. Oosthuizen (1926–1969). Having completed his training at Stellenbosch, he studied linguistic philosophy in Amsterdam under Professor Pos and later in Britain. Oosthuizen was known primarily for his application of the analytical methods of British linguistic philosophy to political and religious problems. His most remarkable publication is *Analyses of Nationalism.* In these essays, he analyzes concepts such as "Afrikaans," "Afrikanerdom," "Christian," "Christendom," "National," and "the will of God," and explores the role of ideology and metaphor in current religious and political talk in South Africa.

Undoubtedly, two of the most gifted philosophers in South Africa today are Professor J. J. Degenaar of the University of Stellenbosch and Professor M. Versfeld of the University of Cape Town (now retired). Both are within the existentialist and phenomenological traditions, although Degenaar has of late made increasing use of analytical methods.

Professor J. J. Degenaar (1926–   ) studied at the University of Stellenbosch, thereafter at the University of Groningen in the Netherlands under Helmuth Plessner and Gerhard van der Leeuw, and at Leiden under C. A. van Peursen. His books are relatively short and consist mainly of essays dealing with aspects of a common theme. They are written in Afrikaans and are therefore inaccessible to a public not conversant with Afrikaans or Dutch. He has encountered considerable opposition from conservative Afrikaner intellectuals, but his influence at the University of Stellenbosch and at other Afrikaans universities is steadily increasing.

Degenaar's works fall into two categories. The first category deals more particularly with the interpretation and assessment of individual thinkers. *Evolusie en Christendom* is a sympathetic treatment of the French Jesuit and paleontologist Teilhard de Chardin. *Die Wereld van Albert Camus* is an introduction to the thought of Albert Camus, with emphasis on his treatment of absurdity, revolt, and solidarity. *Exsistensie en Gestalte* is devoted to an analysis of existentialist traits in the poetry of the greatest Afrikaans poet, N. P. van Wyk Louw, who was himself profoundly influenced by contemporary European philosophy.

The second category has a much wider scope. *Die Sterflikheid van die Siel* is an introduction to phenomenological anthropology. Here Degenaar rejects the traditional dichotomy between the mortal body and the immortal soul. His emphasis on the "mortality" of the soul in effect underlines the unity of man and his commitment to this world and to his fellow human beings.

Op Weg na 'n nuwe politieke lewenshouding consists of four essays in which Degenaar attempts to orientate man in the political realities of the twentieth century. The influence of Kierkegaard, Buber, Husserl, and Heidegger is clearly evident. The theme of the book, as presented by Degenaar, is as follows: *man is man through his relationship with men.* This involves a new humanism which rejects the Cartesian conception of man as a being enclosed within himself, a thing which manipulates other things and is in turn manipulated. This new humanism is not a fact but a task; it demands that one escape from self-created subjectivist and nationalist ghettos and stand open and receptive towards other men and other peoples. Only thus does man become whole and "at home" in the world.

In the important little book *Sekularisasie,* these ideas are further developed within the framework of the concepts of "secularization" and "solidarity." Degenaar argues that the secularization of Western culture either alienates men from one another and from their world, or leads to a growing solidarity and intersubjectivity among them. He is especially interested in the latter possibility, which involves a theology of encounter. Particular attention is paid to the contribution of political ideologies and theological dogmatism to the dehumanization of man. As in all his works, here Degenaar reveals his ability to present highly technical concepts of contemporary continental philosophy in an exceptionally clear and stimulating manner. This quality makes his thinking accessible to the nonphilosophic public as well.

Professor Martin Versfeld (1909–   ) is undoubtedly the most powerful philosophical personality in South Africa. He was educated at the universities of Cape Town and Glasgow, where he obtained a doctorate in philosophy under Professor A. A. Bowman. In spite of offers of chairs at other universities, he has chosen to remain in Cape Town.

Versfeld is fluent in both English and Afrikaans, and publishes in both languages. His most important works are *An Essay on the Metaphysics of Descartes; The Perennial Order; The Mirror of Philosophy; A Guide to the City of God,* a definitive work on St. Augustine; *Rondom die Middeleeue,* an excellent Afrikaans introduction to the philosophy of the Middle Ages; and *Persons,* a collection of essays. Professor Versfeld is the greatest medieval scholar in South Africa. However, his interest in medieval philosophy was always wedded to a personalist philosophy. Of late, his keen participation in ecumenical problems—he translated into English A. Husbosch's contentious theological work, *God's Creation*—and his growing interest in aspects of existentialism, phenomenology, and Eastern philosophy have caused him to break with many of the concepts, and the vocabulary, of official Thomism. His most recent publications express a situational philosophy which has caused him to write on many problems of acute topical interest in South Africa. His brilliant handling of the essay form, combined with his phenomenal erudition, has rightly earned him a reputation not only as a philosopher but also as a literary artist. This reputation is further confirmed by his translation into Afrikaans of Plato's *Symposium* and a commentary on *The Republic*.

Versfeld's publications in Afrikaans are *Oor Gode en Afgode*, and *Wat is Kontemporêr?*, both of which are collections of essays on morality and history; *Berge van die Boland* (with W. A. de Klerk), an account of his experiences as a mountaineer and amateur botanist (he has had a species of Cape wild flower named after him); and *Klip en Klei*. In *Klip en Klei*, he describes the building of a cottage for his large family on his farm in the Kouga in the Long Kloof. One of these essays, in which he relates his adventures and thoughts as an angler on the Cape coast, was written while he was visiting professor at Notre Dame University in the United States and reflects his nostalgia for his own country. The personal details are almost imperceptibly interwoven with philosophical reflections. The theme which he develops throughout the memoirs is that of "being at home," a theme which involves an analysis of one's relation to others, to nature, and to God. The last essay, *On Patriotism*, in which he also discusses General Smuts, the man and the thinker, achieves a scope and power which reveal the author's deep understanding of St. Augustine. In the last analysis, he states, the patriot is the man who can only be "at home" in his own country because he is a citizen of the City of God. A combined publication by Versfeld, Degenaar, Adam Small, and W. A. de Klerk, *Beweging Uitwaarts* has had a profound effect on a new generation of Afrikaans students who wish to change the existing status quo.

G. A. Rauche has published a number of books on existentialist themes based on the philosophy of Grisebach.

The northern provinces of South Africa boast only one outstanding and original philosopher, Professor H. G. Stoker (1899–   ), who some years ago retired from the chair of philosophy at the University of Potchefstroom in the Transvaal. He occupies a unique position in the philosophical life of South Africa as he was the first to develop an indigenous Calvinist philosophy. He has not only influenced the entire structure of studies at his university, but he has also inspired Calvinistic thinking in both Europe and America.

Stoker studied at the University of Potchefstroom. In 1922, he obtained his doctorate in Germany under one of the fathers of modern phenomenology, Max Scheler. His thesis, *Das Gewissen,* remains an authoritative work. In 1937, he was promoted to the chair of philosophy at the University of Potchefstroom. He has lectured at many international philosophical congresses, and he attended the Seventh International Congress at Oxford with Professor Hoernlé. He represented South Africa at the first Ecumenical Synod of the Reformed Churches at Grand Rapids, Michigan, in the United States. His lectures during this visit to America, as well as during former visits, has earned him a lasting reputation among American Calvinist philosophers.

During his long term of service at Potchefstroom University and as co-editor of *Philosophia Reformata,* the organ of the Dutch neo-Calvinist philosophy,

Stoker played an important role in the creation of a specifically Calvinist way of thinking and as the author of an original Calvinist school of philosophy. Calvin himself never developed a philosophy. The first signs of a "Calvinist" philosophy emerged in the thought of Abraham Kuyper. Kuyper believed that Calvinism was not only a theology but also a complete view of life that contained the principles of science and philosophy. These principles Kuyper found in the Scriptures. The school of Calvinist philosophy at the Free University of Amsterdam developed Kuyper's views by conceiving of philosophy as an account of the whole of reality. But such an account presupposes an "archimedean point," a standpoint outside the cosmos in terms of which the cosmic totality may be interpreted. For Bavinck, this archimedean point is Revelation, for Dooyeweerd it is the idea of God as Sovereign and supreme Lawgiver, and for Stoker it is God as Creator. Hence, his philosophic system is termed the philosophy of the Idea of Creation *(Wysbegeerte van die Skeppingsides)*.

Stoker differs from Dooyeweerd, the most influential exponent of neo-Calvinist philosophy in the Netherlands, in rejecting Dooyeweerd's philosophy of the cosmonomic ideal derived from the notion of God as Sovereign. Dooyeweerd's philosophy leads to a stratification of modal spheres, each revealing its own laws derived from God's universal law. For Stoker the idea of creation is more supple. It lacks the rigidity of Dooyeweerd's modal structures inasmuch as it emphasizes not only the lawfulness of the cosmos but also its spontaneity, freedom, and creative development. According to Stoker, the idea of creation permits of no single basic idea or archimedean point. He postulates a plurality of perspectives, all compatible with Calvinism, which has the advantage of encompassing a greater number and diversity of phenomena. Consequently, Stoker's philosophy is far less dogmatic than Dooyeweerd's. Nevertheless, Stoker agrees with Dooyeweerd that all philosophy is influenced by religious presuppositions which ultimately depend on the philosopher's commitment to an absolute, whether this absolute is the Christian God or some absolutization of a cosmic aspect. The analysis of the role of religious presuppositions in philosophy is one of the most important contributions of Calvinist philosophy.

Professor Stoker has applied his philosophy to various philosophical problems in many articles and publications, both in South Africa and overseas. His book *Beginsels en Motodes in die Wetenskap* shows its application especially in the field of university studies. In a much earlier work, *Die Stryd om die Ordes,* Stoker's conception of the unity and diversity of the cosmos leads to a theory of political pluralism. His philosophical position also explains his attitude to ecumenism. Ecumenism, interpreted as an attempt to eradicate bona fide religious commitments in favor of a common religious denominator, is a form of rationalism. For Stoker, a more acceptable interpretation of ecumenism is an open dialogue between the churches. The intention of this dialogue is not to obtain a consensus of opinion but to practice self-examination with respect to contradictions and antinomies in unacknowledged and in uncritically accepted theological assumptions.

Professor Stoker is not only one of the finest philosophical scholars in South

Africa but also one of the most open-minded of Calvinist philosophers. In 1969, Pro Rege-Pers published a volume of essays dedicated to Stoker on his seventieth birthday. Contributions in English and Afrikaans, as well as Dutch, were made by scholars from within and outside of South Africa. The publication fittingly coincided with the centenary celebrations of the University of Potchefstroom.

Most of the younger generation of philosophers are intimately concerned with philosophical issues involved in the wider South African context. Almost without exception they believe they have a role to play in the rethinking of traditionally ensconced political views. A remarkable fact is that in South Africa, a country of black and white Africans, there is no philosopher who has attempted to produce an "African" philosophy comparable to, for example, Leopold Senghor's work on *Négritude*.

A strong school of Eastern philosophy, both Hindu and Muslim, has developed at the University of Durban-Westville in its School of Oriental Studies. This development is particularly important as the Indian population of South Africa is largely centered in the province of Natal and especially in Durban itself. I myself have had the salutary experience of discovering in a small bookshop hidden in the predominantly Indian quarter of central Durban the works of Avicenna, Averrooës, and Gazali, in both Arabic and in English translation. The shopkeeper assured me that these works were bought and read, not by students, but by the Indian "man in the street." This experience should be related to the presence of the famous Grey Street Mosque just around the corner, the many shrines devoted to Hindu and Muslim saints both in Durban and the surrounding countryside, and to the still living intellectual pressure of the great "South African," Gandhi. In fact, in South Africa the growing influence of Gandhi's philosophy of passive resistance far exceeds the by now obsolete philosophical thinking of two South African prime ministers: J. C. Smuts' "holism and evolution" and D. F. Malan's Berkeley-inspired idealism.

The tension between different philosophical perspectives accentuates the need for communication among philosophers representing widely varying schools of thought. In South Africa, the result has been two important developments: attempts to create a representative philosophical journal and the institution of regular philosophical congresses.

The first development led to the publication of the *Bulletin* of the Department of Philosophy at the University of Cape Town (1953–1964), *Occasional Papers,* Rhodes University (1965–1967), and *Bulletin van die Suid-Afrikaanse Vereniging vir die Bevordering van Christelike Wetenskap* of the University of Potchefstroom (1965–   ). In 1964 appeared the more ambitious *South African Journal of Philosophy,* with an editorial committee consisting of Professors A. H. Murray, J. J. Degenaar, and S.I.M. du Plessis. The editorial board consisted of the heads of the departments of philosophy of all South African universities. South African philosophers from various universities were able to contribute to this journal, and it was also distributed overseas. Through lack of funds publication ceased in 1968. Since 1972, *Philosophical Papers* has been published under the wing of the Department of Philosophy of Rhodes University and has become the official organ of the South African Society of Philosophy.

In 1951, the first Congress for the Advancement of Philosophy was initiated and organized by the Department of Philosophy at the University of Cape Town. Thereafter every two years, and later every year, congresses have been held at all major universities in South Africa. At these congresses, usually at least one member of each department of philosophy in the country reads a paper. The discussions, both formal and informal, have contributed immensely to a better understanding among philosophers who are often separated by great distances both literally and figuratively. Congresses are conducted in both official languages in the sense that each participant may use the language of his choice, but the ensuing discussions flow easily in both languages. Of late, apart from plenary sessions, special workshops have been created where discussions have been channeled in accordance with specialized interests. A business meeting deals with all matters relating to the constitution, aims, and finances of the congress.

A most important date in the history of South African philosophical congresses was January 1972, when at the Rhodes Congress a new constitution was devised. At that meeting, it was decided that the name of the congress would be the Philosophical Society of Southern Africa. Its constitution was discussed at cabinet level (under the aegis of the la Grange-Schlebusch Committee), and its international and nonracial character was established once and for all. Special mention should be made of its elected chairman, Professor J. Taljaard of the University of Potchefstroom, who at great personal sacrifice succeeded in piloting the new constitution through many shoals. Since then, the congress has expanded into the most important philosophical body in South Africa.

It would be discourteous to conclude without mentioning the benefit derived from visiting philosophers to South African universities, for example, C. R. van Peursen, R. Kwant, H. van Riessen, S. U. Zuidema, and H. Dooyeweerd (the Netherlands); Karl Löwith (West Germany); G. Ardley (New Zealand); A.G.N. Flew, B. Farrell, D. Mitchell, A. Ryan, and P. Pettit (Great Britain); D. Armstrong (Australia); E. McMullan (United States); and others. These visits have been made possible by the Genootskap Nederland-Suid Afrika and by special visiting lecturer funds available at all universities.

In its turn, South Africa has contributed to the European philosophical scene D. O'Connor, J. N. Findlay, E. Harris, A. Meyer, V. Brümmer, and others, all of whom have assumed permanent positions at British and Dutch universities.

SELECT BIBLIOGRAPHY

BOOKS AND ARTICLES

Conradie, A. L. *Neo-Calvinist Philosophy* (Natal: University Press, 1960).
de Vleeschauwer, H. J. *La déduction transcendentale dans l'ouvre de Kant.* 3 vols. (Antwerp: De Sikkel, 1934–1937).

————. *L'Évolution de la pensée kantienne* (Paris: Alcan, 1939).

Degenaar, J. J. *Die Sterflikheid van die Siel* (Johannesburg: Simondium-Uitgewers, 1963).

————. *Die Wereld van Albert Camus* (Johannesburg: Afrikaanse Pers-Boekandel, 1966).

————. *Evolusie en Christendom* (Johannesburg: Simondium-Uitgewers, 1965).

————. *Exsistensie en Gestalte* (Johannesburg: Simondium-Uitgewers, 1962).

————. *Op Weg na 'n nuwe politieke lewenshouding* (Cape Town: Tafelberg-Uitgewers, 1963).

————. *Sekularisasie* (Pretoria: Academica, 1967).

Heimsoeth, R. and de Vleeschauwer, H. J. *Transzendentale Dialektik* (Berlin: de Gruyter, 1966).

Hulsbosch, A. *God's Creation*, trans. M. Versfeld (London: Sheed and Ward, 1965).

Murray, A. H. (ed.). *De Jure Magistratum*, auth. Benza, trans. Gonin (Cape Town-Pretoria: H.A.U.M., 1956).

————. *Die Volksraad* (Pretoria: Van Schaik, 1939).

————. *The Philosophy of James Ward* (Cambridge: The University Press, 1937).

————. *The Political Philosophy of J. A. de Mist* (Cape Town-Pretoria: H.A.U.M., 1958).

Oosthuizen, D. *Analyses of Nationalism* Occasional Papers I, No. 1 (Grahamstown: Rhodes University, Department of Philosophy, 1965).

Stoker, H. G. *Beginsels en Motodes in die Wetenskap* (Potchefstroom: Pro Rege-Pers, 1961).

————. *Das Gewissen* (Bonn: Cohen, 1925).

————. *Die Stryd om die Ordes* (Potchefstroom: Adm. Buro van die Gereformeerde Kerk, 1942).

Versfeld, M. *A Guide to the City of God* (London: Sheed and Ward, 1958).

————. *An Essay on the Metaphysics of Descartes* (London: Methuen, 1940).

————. *Die Simposium* (Kaapstad: Buren, 1970).

————. *Klip en Klei* (Cape Town: Human and Rousseau, 1968).

————. *'n Handleiding tot die Republiek van Plato* (Kaapstad: Buren, 1974).

————. *Oor Gode en Afgode* (Cape Town: Nasionale Pers, 1948).

————. *Persons* (Cape Town: Buren, 1972).

————. *Rondom die Middeleeue* (Cape Town: Nasionale Boekhandel, 1962).

————. *The Mirror of Philosophy* (London: Sheed and Ward, 1960).

————. *The Perennial Order* (London: Society of St. Paul, 1954).

————. *Wat is Kontemporêr?* (Johannesburg: Afrikaanse Pers-Boekhandel, 1966).

————, Degenaar, J. J., Small, A., and de Klerk, W. A. *Beweging Uitwaarts* (Cape Town: Malherbe, 1969).

————. and de Klerk, W. A. *Berge van die Boland* (Johannesburg: Afrikaanse, 1947).

JOURNALS

Bulletin
Bulletin van die Suid-Afrikaanse Vereniging vir die Bevordering van Christelike Wetenskap
Mousaion: Library Science Contributions
Occasional Papers
Philosophia Reformata
Philosophical Papers
South African Journal of Philosophy

Part V: Islamic Countries

Islamic Countries

SEYYED HOSSEIN NASR

To understand the development of philosophy in the Islamic world during the past few decades, it is necessary to mention, albeit briefly, the tradition of Islamic philosophy and the general intellectual background within whose bosom, or occasionally in opposition to which, philosophical activity has taken place and continues to take place in the Islamic world. However, because of the vastness of the Islamic world, stretching from the southern Philippines to the coast of the Atlantic, we are forced to concentrate in these preliminary remarks on the central lands of Islam, so that, although our vision has to be extended in time, it has to be somewhat contracted in space.

Islam was heir to the philosophical heritage of both the Mediterranean world and the Indian subcontinent. It transformed this heritage within the world-view of Islam and according to the spirit and letter of the Qurān, and brought into being a vast array of intellectual and philosophical schools, only some of which are technically called "philosophy" *(falsafah)*. But there are others, including several that did not bear the name of philosophy,[1] which have the greatest philosophical import according to the most genuine meaning of philosophy. This tradition produced such renowned intellectual figures as al-Fārābī, Ibn Sīnā, al-Ghazzālī, Suhrawardī, Ibn Rushd, Ibn ᶜArabī, Mīr Dāmād, and Mullā Ṣadrā, some of whom are well known in the West and others of whom are only now becoming known outside the Islamic world.[2] In the Arab world, philosophy as a distinct discipline disappeared after the sixth through twelfth centuries, and became drowned in the two seas of gnosis and theology. In Iran, the Turkish part of the Ottoman world, and the Indian subcontinent, in addition to theology and gnosis, philosophy as such also continued and in fact survived in many of those regions to our own day.[3] When the Islamic world first encountered the West in the nineteenth century in such countries as Egypt, Iran, Turkey, and the Indian subcontinent, the existing intellectual tradition reacted in each land according to the local conditions but within the general context of the universal intellectual tradition of Islam. Such figures as Sayyid Jamāl al-Dīn Astrābādī, known usually as al-Afghānī, Muhammad ᶜAbduh, Rashīd Ridā, Malkam Khān, Sir Ahmad Khān, Zia Gökalp, and Muhammad Iqbāl[4] set out to encounter Western thought and were influenced by it in varying degrees.

The influence of Western philosophy in each part of the Islamic world depended upon the form of colonialism which happened to dominate in a particular land.[5] The modernized circles in the Indian subcontinent became dominated by English philosophy of the Victorian period. The modernized groups in Iran, which were attracted to the French language and culture to escape British and Russian influences from the North and South, became infatuated with Descartes and later Cartesian philosophy, leading to the Comtian positivism of the nineteenth century. The modernized Turks were attracted to German philosophy, and the Westernized Egyptians to both the English and French schools, depending on the experience of various individual philosophers and thinkers. Likewise, North Africa and the French-speaking part of Islamic Africa became dominated by French modes of thought, and the English-speaking areas by the English.

With the end of World War II, most Muslim countries gained political independence, but the philosophical scene, especially at the university level, continued for the most part to be dominated by Western thought. Now, however, Marxism became a new element which attracted a number of thinkers, especially in lands where an intense struggle for independence had led certain people to join politically leftist causes. The sense of Islamic identity, however, continued to assert itself, and perhaps the most important philosophical concern of the most relevant intellectuals remained the tension between Islam and modern Western civilization. Such themes as the spread of Western thought, including its Marxist version, and the interaction between science and philosophies of a positivistic nature on the one hand and religion and religious philosophies on the other became the main concern of Muslims engaged in philosophical activity. During the past few decades, although the earlier schools of European philosophy, now out of fashion in the West, have continued to survive in a surprising fashion,[6] newer modes of Western thought such as logical positivism and analytical philosophy, existentialism, neo-Marxism, and even structuralism have begun to gain some attention.

But during this same period one can also observe another intellectual activity of the greatest importance, namely, the revival of traditional Islamic thought in its various forms such as Sufism, theology, and philosophy itself in its technical sense. A sense of disillusionment with modern Western civilization, uncertainty about the future, and the need to return to the heart of religion have turned many people, especially the educated, to a reexamination of Sufism and a rekindling of interest in its teaching. This change is seen in the larger number of younger people, including many from the professional classes, drawn to Sufi orders in such countries as Egypt and Iran[7] and the extensive spread of the teachings of such outstanding contemporary Sufi masters as Shaykh al-ᶜAlawī.[8] One can also observe the continuous spread of the earlier Wahhābī and Salafiyyah movements characterized by a moral puritanism, ''return'' to the norms of early Islam, and, to a large extent, disdain for philosophical discourse. Finally, these same forces have guided many people to a rediscovery of Islamic philosophy itself and its revival, especially in Iran.[9] Therefore, it can be said that at the same time that during the past three decades various forms of modern philosophy have penetrated further into the intellectual life of the Islamic world, a revival of traditional

Islamic thought in its various modes is also to be observed in most Islamic countries.

In this brief survey, one can refer only to the most salient features of philosophical activity in that vast stretch of earth called the Islamic world. It is only appropriate to begin with that heartland, namely, the Arabic-Persian-Turkish world which has nearly always provided the most widespread and enduring intelllectual and spiritual impulses for the Islamic community as a whole. Today, the peoples in this area remain a minority within the Islamic world, but this area must still be considered as the heart of that vaster world whose life and thought are determined by the Islamic revelation.

Let us begin with the Arab world and especially its eastern part. In this region, Egypt and Syria were the greatest centers of cultural and philosophical activity in the earlier decades of the twentieth century and continued to hold this position after World War II, although Lebanon also came into prominence after its independence. In Egypt, the important institutions of philosophical activity of earlier days, such as Al-Azhar, Cairo, Ain Shams, and Alexandria universities, and the Arab Academy of Cairo, have continued to be dominant. Moreover, many of the figures who had already gained prominence before and during World War II, such as ᶜUthmān Amīn, Ibrāhīm Madkour, A. A. Anawati, ᶜAbd al-Raḥmān Badawī, Aḥmad Fu'ād al-Ahwānī, Sulaymān Dunyā, Muḥammad Abū Rayyān, and Abu'l-ᶜAlā'al-ᶜafīfī, have continued to dominate the scene. Almost all of these figures have been interested in the revival of Islamic philosophy as well as its encounter with Western thought. Some of them, such as Badawī, have written on such modern Western schools as existentialism more as followers than as detached students. Some of the scholars and philosophers who have gained fame following these earlier figures, for example, Muḥammad Abū Rīdah and Abu'l-Wafā' al-Taftāzānī, have likewise combined training in Western thought with Islamic philosophy. They are best known for combining Western methods of philosophical analysis and scholarship with Islamic philosophical and mystical thought.

Since World War II, the aim of reviving Islamic thought has been combined with a major movement to translate Western philosophy into Arabic. There have also been major celebrations of the anniversaries of leading Islamic philosophers such as al-Kindī, al-Fārābī, Ibn Sīnā, al-Ghazzālī, Ibn Rushd, Suhrawardī, Ibn ᶜArabī, and Ibn Khaldūn in Egypt and often in many other countries of the Islamic world. These have led to the edition of texts, preparation of bibliographies, analytical monographs, and histories.[10] As for translations of European philosophy, they have included many of the best known works of post-Renaissance philosophy, especially those of French and German philosophers such as Descartes, Voltaire, Kant, and Hegel. There have also been histories of Western philosophy such as that of Luṭfī Jumᶜah. Unfortunately, many of these translations have been made by scholars not fully aware of the richness of classical philosophical Arabic and in quality fall far short of the earlier translations of Greek philosophical texts into Arabic.

Since the rise of the Palestinian problem, extreme Arab nationalism, and the spread of leftist ideologies in Egypt, there have also appeared many philosophical works concerned with political and economic themes rather than with theoretical philosophy. Some of the thinkers of Egypt, both Muslim and Christian, became followers of the fashionable Western leftist trends of the postwar era. But many of the more prominent, such as Anwār ʿAbd al-Malik, soon lost their infatuation with Marxism and other leftist ideologies and turned to either some form of cultural nationalism or Islam. This trend has thus joined the revival of Islamic thought within the traditional Islamic quarters in Egypt such as al-Azhar. This revival tends to be either of a puritanical vein following the Wahhābī-Salafī school of the earlier period[11] or concerned with Sufism, which has also been witness to an important revival over the past few years in Egypt. In this connection, it is of interest to mention the Muslim Brotherhood (Ikhwān al-Muslimīn) which, although intellectually akin to the Wahhābī school, was structured upon the model of the Sūfī orders. The leading intellectual figure of the Ihkwān, Sayyid Quṭb, although severely opposed to philosophy in its academic sense, himself produced a "philosophy" based upon the teachings of the Qurān, with which he sought to combat ideologies imported from the West.[12]

In Syria, a situation similar to that of Egypt is to be observed. Earlier figures such as Jamīl Ṣalībā and Khalīl Georr have remained active. The Arab Academy of Damascus has continued its concern with creating a terminology to express modern philosophical thought. More traditional scholars such as Sāmī al-Kiyālī and ʿĀrif Tāmir have been concerned with the revival of Islamic philosophy, while some of the Westernized intellectuals—mostly Christian but also some Muslim—have continued their earlier fascination with European philosophy, especially leftist politico-philosophical ideologies. Such men as Constantine Zurayk and Michele Aflaq who wrote theoretical works on Arab nationalism and socialism became fathers of political movements. Gradually, a form of Arab socialism became dominant in the name of the Baʿth party which still rules Syria as well as Iraq and which has caused many works of political philosophy to be written based on the idea of Arab socialism.

Parallel with this development has been the revival of interest in Sufism during the last few decades. Much of this revival is closely connected with the Shadhiliyyah Order and more specifically the great Algerian saint Shaykh al-ʿAlawī who had many disciples in Syria.[13] The revival has also produced works of intellectual quality as can be seen in the case of the Sufi master from Aleppo, Shaykh ʿAbd al-Qādir. In the field of Sufi metaphysics, it is also necessary to mention the extensive works of the Syrian scholar ʿUthmān Yaḥyā, who resides in Paris and also sometimes Cairo. Besides editing and studying the works of major figures of Sufism, especially Ibn ʿArabī, he has written as a philosopher living within the tradition of Islamic philosophy but concerned with contemporary problems, especially those of modern man in a secularized world.

Lebanon has been the focus of a more modernized form of philosophical activity than Syria or Egypt. In its universities, especially St. Joseph, most of the external philosophical influence has been French as is to be found also in

Syria. Only in the American University of Beirut has Anglo-Saxon philosophy been present. Until the recent civil war, Lebanon was the major center for the publication of Arabic books in the region, especially in the field of philosophy, vying with Cairo for the lead in the Arab world. Until recently, Lebanon tried to play the role of a bridge between the West and the Islamic world, although it was more of a bridgehead for the Western assault upon Islam than a bridge connecting two worlds.

In Lebanon, several eminent Christian Arab philosophers have been active. Perhaps the most famous is Charles Malik who, despite his immersion in the world of Western liberalism, remains deeply Christian. One can also mention Archbishop Khodr, who is one of the leading Orthodox theologians of our day. During the past few decades, there have been such Lebanese scholars, both Muslim and Christian, as ᶜUmar Farrukh, Ḥasan Ṣaᶜb, Kamāl al-Yāzijī, Farid Jabre, Albert Nader, Mājid Fakhrī, and ᶜAfīf 'Usayrān, who have been concerned with the study of Islamic philosophy, and Yūsuf Ibīsh, who is one of the foremost students today of Islamic political philosophy. Yūsuf Ibīsh is also devoted to a study of Sufism and is one of the leading exponents of the traditional point of view in the Arab world. As far as Sufism is concerned, it is also important to mention Sayyidah Fāṭimah Yashrūṭiyyah, who is perhaps the most eminent female figure in Sufism today and who has produced some of the most notable works on Sufism in Arabic in recent years.

With regard to Jordan and the Palestinian people, the traumatic events following the war of 1948 have turned the attention of the intellectual community of this region nearly completely to questions of a political nature, and the few Palestinians, such as ᶜAbd al-Laṭīf al-Ṭibāwī, who have been concerned with philosophy have been active in other countries. In Jordan, interest in philosophy is growing gradually as the University of Amman becomes interested in theological and philosophical studies, and slowly Amman becomes a center for the publication of works in Arabic dealing, among other subjects, with philosophy.

In Iraq, until World War II, the British style of education went hand in hand with the activity of major Islamic centers of learning, especially the Shiᶜite university in Najaf. The most notable activity during the past few decades has been the revival of scholarship in the field of Islamic philosophy, but tempered with discipline derived mostly from Anglo-Saxon but also from other European forms of scholarship. Iraq has produced several scholars of note who have combined both forms of discipline, namely, the Islamic and the European. These scholars include Kāmil al-Shaybī, Ḥusayn ᶜAlī Maḥfūẓ, and especially Muḥsin Mahdī, who has made noteworthy contributions to the study of al-Fārābī and Ibn Khaldūn. There has also been some effort to study the philosophy of Islamic education, especially by Fāḍil al-Jamālī. Moreover, in Iraq as in Syria, a number of philosophical works deal with various forms of Arab nationalism, socialism, and the like. Most of these works, however, are of a practical rather than a purely theoretical nature.

The western region of the Arab world was a much more conservative and "conserving" region than the Arab east until World War II. In this western area, embracing the region from Libya and Tunisia to the Atlantic, until the independence movements, traditional Islamic thought in both its metaphysical and theological aspects was very strong. Several outstanding Sufi masters dominated the spiritual and intellectual climate of the Maghrib. Disciples of Shaykh al-ᶜAlawī have kept his presence alive in many regions, although the heart of his spiritual teachings was to travel to the Occident where it has had a profound and incalculable effect. Other masters such as Shaykh Muḥammad al-Tādilī have also contributed to the preservation of the Sufi tradition.

Since World War II, at least two other notable tendencies have opposed Sufism in the Maghrib. The first is a crypto-Wahhābī puritanism inspired by movements of a similar nature in Egypt and other eastern lands of Islam, and modern antitraditional European philosophy. The puritanical rationalism of the Maghrib is little different from what is found among the Salafiyyah of Egypt and the Wahhābism of Arabia. It has been marked by an open opposition to Sufism, especially its popular form, which in the Maghrib is known as Maraboutism,[14] and a strong zeal for social reform as well as engagement in political action, with the aim of reestablishing the rule of Islamic sacred law (Sharīᶜah). In this connection, it is important to mention the Istiqlāl party of Morocco and its founder ᶜAllāl al-Fāsī who was one of the foremost thinkers of the Maghrib during the past few decades. He developed a political and social philosophy based upon certain traditional Islamic theses, with elements akin to certain Salafī and Wahhābī thinkers of the East but with a distinct Maghribī color.

The second tendency, namely, European philosophy, is of a rather peculiar character in the Maghrib. In Egypt, the European philosophy which became influential was not limited to a single school. In the Maghrib, because of the predominant French influence and the preponderance of Marxism and an agnostic existentialism in French university circles after the war, these schools have become nearly completely dominant as far as European philosophy is concerned. In no other region of the Islamic world have Marxism and existentialism of the French school had such influence within university circles as in the Maghrib. It is also here that over the past few years strange attempts have developed to wed leftist ideologies emanating from nineteenth-century European philosophy with Islam. The result is various forms of "Islamic socialism," and even "Islamic Marxism," which can be seen especially in Algeria and Libya. This type of thought, which is usually closely related to various political interests, is also to be found in other Muslim countries even outside the Arab world, although it is usually confined to limited circles.

The Maghrib has also produced a small number of well-known thinkers who have attempted to charter a more distinct course and not simply follow Western fashions. Among this group is the Moroccan philosopher Ḥabīb Lahbābī, who has developed what he calls "Islamic personalism" based on certain theses of Islamic thought and some of the predominant ideas of continental philosophy, especially existentialism. But he stands closer to modern thought than to the mainstream of Islamic philosophy. Another well-known figure from the Maghrib is the Algerian Muḥammad Arkoun who, after a serious study of Western thought including Marxism, has turned to Islamic philosophy as a living reality. He has written both on traditional Islamic schools of philosophy and the confrontation of Islamic thought with modernism. He is one of the first contemporary Sunni thinkers to interest himself in a dialogue with Shiʿism.

In Iran, Islamic philosophy did not cease to exist as a living tradition after the so-called Middle Ages, but has survived to the present day. In fact, there was a major revivial of Islamic philosophy during the Safavid period with the appearance of such figures as Mīr Dāmād and Mullā Ṣadrā.[15] A second revival took place during the thirteenth through nineteenth centuries led by Mullā ʿAlī Nurī, Ḥājjī Mullā Hādī Sabziwārī, and others.[16] This tradition continued strong in the Islamic universities *(madrasahs)*. From after World War I, European philosophy, especially of the French school identified with such figures as Descartes and more recently Bergson, became influential among the Western-educated classes, in particular at the modern universities and colleges. During the past few decades, the European influence has continued and in fact has been extended to include the existentialist school. At the same time, one can observe a major revival of traditional Islamic philosophy, even among the modern ed-ucated classes. This marks a unique phenomenon in the contemporary Islamic world inasmuch as this revival does not mean only interest in scholarship in the field of Islamic philosophy. It also signifies that the tradition of Islamic phi-losophy, especially the school of Mullā Ṣadrā, is being taken seriously as a living and viable intellectual perspective capable of meeting the challenge of various schools of European thought.[17]

Among the most active traditional figures in the revival of Islamic philosophy in Iran, one can mention ʿAllāmah Sayyid Muḥammad Ḥusayn Ṭabāṭabāʾī, himself an eminent philosopher and gnostic,[18] Murtaḍā Muṭahharī, Mahdī Ḥāʾirī,[19] Sayyid Jalāl al-Dīn Āshtiyānī, and Jawād Musliḥ. There are also those who have tried to deal with modern philosophical questions and the challenges of Western thought from the point of view of Islamic metaphysics and philos-ophy. Still others, although trained in modern universities, are concerned mostly with the edition and study of Islamic philosophical texts. This last-named group includes such scholars as M. Khwānsārī, M. Mohaghegh, J. Falāṭūrī, M. T. Danechepazhuh, M. Mo'in, and S. J. Sajjādī.

Those concerned mostly with European philosophy, its translation into Per-sian, and exposition for the Persian world include R. Shafaq, G. Ṣadīghī, Y. Mahdavī, and Sharaf Khurāsānī. During the past few decades, all of these scholars have made important studies and translations of European philosophy of the earlier period. Another group, including M. Bozorgmehr, N. Daryābandarī, and M. Raḥīmī, have been concerned more with contemporary European phi-losophy, the first two with Anglo-Saxon philosophy and the third with French existentialism. Recently, one can also see some interest in Heidegger, whose ideas have been expounded in comparison with traditional Islamic thought by

A. Fardīd and many of his colleagues and students. Likewise, some attention has been paid by a small group to various neo-Marxist modes of thought.

As in other Islamic countries, so in Iran, the last few decades have been witness to a major rise of interest in Sufism among the educated classes. Most of the important orders, such as the Niᶜmatallāhī and Dhahabī, are extremely active throughout the country and are also producing many mystical works of great philosophical significance. In this context, the voluminous writings of Javād Nourbakhsh, the spiritual leader of the Niᶜmatallāhī order, are of particular significance. Some of his shorter tracts on various aspects of Sufism have also been rendered into English and French.

Philosophical activity in Iran is so extensive that it is not possible to describe all of its facets in this short survey. Suffice it to say, both in traditional schools and in most modern universities, that philosophy is taught and studied, and numerous works appear on the subject every year. Iran is also the only Islamic country which has an active philosophical academy.[20]

Iran's neighboring country, Afghanistan, which shares the same philosophical tradition with it, has been distinguished during the past few decades mostly by activity in the domain of Sufism. Such scholars as G. Māyil Hirawī and M. I. Muballigh have made important contributions to the study of Jāmī and the metaphysical school of Ibn ᶜArabī in general. Scholars like A. G. Ravān Farhādī have delved into the teachings of Sufism, taking into consideration the works of such European orientalists as L. Massignon. Within university circles, the philosophical scene more or less resembles that of Iran, with somewhat less diversity as regards the influence of Western schools of thought.

In Turkey, the philosophical situation is similar to that in many other Islamic countries in that there has been a marked rise of interest during recent years in the study of Islamic thought and a definite Islamic revival. This revival, intellectually at least, is perhaps best exemplified by the renewal of interest in the works of Sayyid Saᶜīd Nūrsī. The more secular atmosphere of Turkey has also caused a wide range of philosophical works to be translated and studied in modern educational circles independent of Islamic considerations. In these circles, the influence of German schools of thought is more marked than in other Islamic countries.

The most notable contribution of Turkish scholars to philosophy over the past few decades has been in the domains of Sufism and the history of science rather than in the more narrowly defined philosophical disciplines. In the field of Sufism, such scholars as A. Gölpinarli, A. Ateş and T. Yazici have brought back the reality of the Sufi tradition to contemporary Turkish society, especially to the younger generation which is no longer familiar with the classical works of Sufism. As for the history of science, such figures as A. Sayili, E. Tekeli, and S. Ünver have made major contributions to the study of Islamic science and all that it implies philosophically. There have also been some notable Turkish contributions to the study of Islamic philosophy and theology themselves, as shown in the work of M. Türker, I. Choboqchi, H. Atay, and others. In contemporary Turkey, there is a polarization in the domain of philosophy between traditional Islamic thought and various forms of modern philosophy and ideology, including Marxism, which is more extreme than in other Islamic countries and which is reflected in the current political situation, especially within the universities.

In the Indian subcontinent, in addition to two Islamic countries, Pakistan and Bangladesh, there are tens of millions of Muslims in India, Sri Lanka, and Nepal. The philosophical situation in this part of the world is quite different from that of any other part of the Islamic world. As a result of British domination over the area, various schools of Anglo-Saxon philosophy became deeply entrenched in the philosophy departments of the major universities; they continue to be dominant today in the universities of all the above-mentioned countries. The earlier political and social "reformers" of the subcontinent, notably Sir Aḥmad Khān and Muḥammad Iqbāl, were also much more concerned with philosophy in its Western sense of the term than the "reformers" of the Arab world. Philosophical institutions, such as the All-India Philosophical Congress, were carried over into the era of independence, and both the Indian and Pakistan Philosophical Congresses have been active during past decades.[21] They have served as rallying points for philosophical activity, most of which is Western, specifically British and American philosophy. One can discern ever greater interest in Islamic thought, however, as in the monumental *A History of Muslim Philosophy*, edited by the late M. M. Sharīf, one of the leading intellectual figures of Pakistan.

In Pakistan, the older philosophers, including M. M. Aḥmad, M. M. Sharīf, A. C. Qādir, and K. 'Abd al-Ḥakīm, have focused on issues rising from European philosophy. They have also sought to find some of the answers in the Islamic tradition, particularly Sufism to which many of them, especially M. M. Aḥmad, have been devoted. Their most active students have pursued nearly the same interests but more developed in distinct directions. B. A. Dār has published numerous works on European philosophy, including Kant, while making comparisons with certain schools of Islamic thought. He thus exemplifies a trend which is strong among both Muslim and Hindu scholars in the subcontinent, namely, attempting to compare and often to synthesize Western and Eastern schools of thought.[22] Saeed Shaikh, another of the younger generation of philosophers, has been interested mostly in Islamic thought as has M.S.H. Maᶜṣūmī, while Manzoor Aḥmad has turned to the study of the philosophy of art and comparative religion. Pakistan has produced several thinkers of note concerned with philosophy and at the same time influential in the life of the nation. Perhaps foremost among them is A. K. Brohi, who after a long preoccupation with modern thought, has returned to the bosom of Sufism and through Sufi eyes has expounded some of the deepest aspects of Islamic thought. This group also includes M. Ajmal, a leading educationalist and psychologist. Ajmal is one of the first in the Islamic world who has sought to create a science of the soul based on the teachings of Sufism rather than on the imitation of Western psychoanalytical techniques and theories. A word must also be said about Fazlur Raḥmān, who has dealt with both with the revival of classical Islamic philosophy and a modernistic interpretation of Islam based on modern Western ideas. Finally, one must mention Maulānā Abu'l-ᶜAlā' Maudoodi, the founder of the *Jamāᶜ aῖī islāmī* who, although not strictly speaking a philosopher, is the most influential of all contemporary Pakistani thinkers and a major force in the revival of the social and economic philosophy of Islam as reflected in the *Sharīᶜah*.

In India, nearly the same tendencies have been observed over the past few decades. The major centers for intellectual Muslim activity during this period have been Delhi, Aligarh, Lucknow, and Hyderabad where some have devoted themselves to the revival of Islamic thought and others to the study of Western thought. In addition, there has been special interest in comparing the Islamic and Hindu traditions, an interest which is directly related to the particular situation of the Muslim community in modern India as a religious minority. This latter interest is reflected, for example, in the writings of H. 'Askarī and even M. Mujeeb. Such Muslim scholars as R. A. Rizvi, H. 'Abidī, H. S. Khān, A. Maᶜṣūmī, and M. Abdul Ḥaq Anṣārī have been concerned with the edition and analysis of classical works of Islamic philosophy, including the school of Mullā Ṣadrā. Men such as Mīr Valīuddīn have sought to reformulate and make better known the tradition of Sufism. Others like Mīr Vahīuddīn, Ābid Ḥusayn, and Sayidain have been involved in studies based on the confrontation between Western trends of philosophy and Islam.

Finally, in India as in Pakistan, there has been a great revival of interest in traditional Islamic medicine and its philosophy, as well as the ecological and philosophical issues involved in the confrontation between traditional and modern science. The Hamdard Institutes of Delhi and Karachi and the activities of their founders Ḥakīm 'Abd al-Ḥamīd and Ḥakīm Muḥammad Saeed, as well as the ancillary institutions established by them, especially the Institute of Islamic Studies at Delhi, represent centers whose activities are as important for philosophy as they are for science.

With regard to Bangladesh, its philosophical life until recently was completely wed to that of Pakistan. Since partition, the same trends have continued, with the remnants of the Anglo-Saxon schools of philosophy remaining strong in university circles. There is, however, a more marked interest in Islamic philosophy among younger scholars such as A. J. Mia and M. ᶜAbd al-Ḥaqq.

In the Malay-Indonesian world, comprising Malaysia, Singapore, and Indonesia, the last decades have been witness to an attempt to rediscover a half-lost cultural identity. In Indonesia, numerous Islamic revivalist movements have emerged, most of which have a Wahhābī color considering the close historical contact between that world and Arabia. There have also been attempts to revive Sufism and even certain modernistic movements claiming a traditional mystical background, such as Subud, which has gained many followers in the West thirsty for spiritual experience but often unable to distinguish between the wheat and the chaff. Malaysia, as part of the general intellectual scene, has experienced a revival of interest in Sufism, but here the more intellectual school of Ibn ᶜArabī and his followers as it developed in that region has received the greatest amount of attention. This particular slant in the study of Sufism is due most of all to Sayyid Naguib al-'Aṭṭās who has devoted numerous studies to this subject, especially the al-Rānirī. Another member of the same family, Sayyid Ḥusayn al-'Aṭṭās, who lives in Singapore, has charted a completely different course. He has tried to create an authentic school of social science based on philosophical principles derived from the traditions of Asia rather than nineteenth-century European philosophy.

Finally, a word must be said about various Muslim lands of Africa, which range from the Sudan in the east to Nigeria and Senegal in the west. In these lands, philosophical activity in the universities has for the most part followed English or French schools of thought, depending upon the colonial experience each land has undergone. But there are also active Sufi movements in many lands such as Senegal and Islamic revivalist movements based on a rigorous application of the *Sharīᶜah* in other areas. In Nigeria, the Islamic universities have shown some interest in the resuscitation of Islamic philosophy, while such thinkers as Aḥmadu Bo have sought to establish a form of Islamic wisdom which is at the same time profoundly African.

Since World War II, nearly all Islamic countries have gained their political freedom, but they are now struggling with another form of domination, one that is cultural and philosophical and that ranges from positivism to Marxism. Parallel with the spread of such forms of thinking is a revival of interest in all aspects of the Islamic tradition, comprising the *Sharīᶜah*, Sufism, theology, and traditional philosophy. Interest in these aspects is not the same everywhere, however. In this struggle between modern, Western patterns of thought, and the Islamic tradition, much remains to be done, including the achievement of a deeper understanding of the issues involved. Gradually, however, a few Muslim intellectuals have emerged who are at once profoundly Islamic and possess a truly intellectual perspective and who are seeking to provide an Islamic answer for the challenges posed by modern philosophy and science. They represent perhaps the most notable feature of recent philosophical activity in the Islamic world. In their hands lies the intellectual defense of the citadel of the Islamic faith at whose heart is to be found the purest form of *ḥikmah* or *sophia* with the appropriate means for its realization.

NOTES

1. We mean such schools as principles of jurisprudence *(uṣūl)*, theology *(kalām)*, and gnosis *(ᶜirfān* or *maᶜrifah)*.

2. On Islamic philosophy, see H. Corbin (in collaboration with S. H. Nasr and O. Yahya), *Historie de la philosophie islamique*, I; Corbin, *En Islam iranien aspects spirituels et philosophiques*, 4 vols.; S. H. Nasr, *Three Muslim Sages;* M. Fakhry, *A History of Islamic Philosophy;* and M. M. Sharif (ed.) *A History of Muslim Philosophy*.

3. See H. Corbin, "The Force of Traditional Philosophy in Iran Today," *Studies in Comparative Religion* (Winter 1968):12–26; also S. H. Nasr, *Islamic Studies,* Chapters 8 on.

4. On these so-called reformers, see A. Hourani, *Arabic Thought in the Liberal Ages,* and K. Cragg, *Counsels in Contemporary Islam.* A great deal of more genuine Islamic activity, mostly in the field of Sufism, took place, but it has received little attention until now. See S. H. Nasr, *Islam and the Plight of Modern Man.* See also M. Jameelah, *Islam and Modernism,* where the modernistic reformers have been criticized from the point of view of Orthodox Islamic teachings.

5. See S. H. Nasr, "The Pertinence of Studying Islamic Philosophy Today," in *Islamic Studies,* pp. 97–106.

6. We have often had occasion to mention that today late nineteenth-century British philosophy is taken more seriously in the universities of the Indian subcontinent than in British universities themselves.

7. See M. Berger, *Islam in Egypt Today,* and E. Bannerth, "Aspects de la Shadhiliyya," *Mélanges de l'Institut Dominicain des Etudes Orientales* (Cairo) 2 (1972): 248 ff.

8. See M. Lings, *A Sufi Saint of the Twentieth Century.*

9. See H. Corbin, "The Force of Traditional Philosophy in Iran Today," in *Studies in Comparative Religion.*

10. Perhaps the most extensive celebration was that held in 1952 and 1953 in Egypt, Iraq, Iran, India, and several other lands on the occasion of the millennium of Ibn Sīnā. It was responsible for hundreds of books and articles concerning the master of Muslim peripatetics. As far as Iran and Iraq are concerned, see *Millénaire d'Avicenne, Congrès de Bagdad;* Z. Safa (ed.), *Le livre du millénaire d'Avicenne,* 4 vols.

11. On the Wahhābī-Salafī line of thought and its background, see L. Gardet and M. M. Anawati, *Introduction à la théologie musulmane,* especially pp. 447 ff., which deals with the theological aspects of this movement.

12. On the Muslim Brethren, see I. M. Husaini, *The Muslim Brethren.*

13. On this remarkable figure, see M. Lings, *A Sufi Saint of the Twentieth Century.*

14. On Maraboutism in the Maghrib, see O. Dupont and X. Coypolani, *Les confrérie religieuses musulmanes,* and E. Dermenghen, *Le culte des saints dans l'Islam maghrébin.*

15. This school, now generally known as the School of Isfahan, is at last gaining recognition in the outside world. See H. Corbin, *En Islam iranien,* IV; S. H. Nasr, "The School of Isfahan" and "Mulla Ṣadrā," in *A History of Muslim Philosophy,* II, ed. M. M. Sharif; S. H. Nasr, *Ṣadr al-Dīn Shīrāzī and His Transcendent Theosophy.*

16. See M. Mohaghegh and T. Izutsu, *The Metaphysics of Sabzavari.*

17. See S. H. Nasr, *Islamic Philosophy in Contemporary Persia: A Survey of Activity During the Past Two Decades.*

18. See the introduction to M. Ṭabāṭabā'ī, *Shiʿite Islam,* trans. by S. H. Nasr.

19. He is perhaps the only master of Islamic philosophy trained originally in a traditional school who is also completely familiar with Western philosophy.

20. The Imperial Iranian Academy of Philosophy, besides publishing numerous works on Islamic thought, comparative philosophy, and the like, also publishes the biannual *Sophia Perennis* and an annual bibliography of works on philosophy published in Iran.

21. See R. V. De Smet, *Philosophical Activity in Pakistan.*

22. Some of these attempts have been, to put it mildly, far from successful. See Nasr, "Metaphysics and Philosophy East and West," in *Islam and the Plight of Modern Man,* pp. 27–36.

It is important to mention also the writings of Maryam Jameelah who, although of American origin, belongs to the Pakistani scene. Her writings are among the most rigorous criticisms of the West to come out of the contemporary Islamic world. They stand diametrically opposed to the facile comparisons and so-called syntheses of Eastern and Western thought which pollute the intellectual atmosphere of so much of the Islamic world.

SELECT BIBLIOGRAPHY

BOOKS AND ARTICLES

Bannerth, E. "Aspects de la Shadhiliyya," *Mélanges de l'Institut Dominicain des Etudes Orientales* (Cairo) 2 (1972).

Berger, M. *Islam in Egypt Today: Social and Political Aspects of Popular Religion* (Cambridge: Cambridge University Press, 1970).

Corbin, H. *En Islam iranien, aspects spirituels et philosophiques*, 4 vols. (Paris: Gallimard, 1971–1972).

————. "The Force of Traditional Philosophy in Iran Today," *Studies in Comparative Religion* (Winter, 1968).

————, Nasr, S. H., and Yahya, O. *Histoire de la philosophie islamique* (Paris: Gallimard, 1964).

Cragg, K. *Counsels in Contemporary Islam* (Edinburgh: Edinburgh University Press, 1965).

Dermenghen, E. *Le culte des saints dans l'Islam maghrébin* (Paris: Gallimard, 1954).

De Smet, R. V. *Philosophical Activity in Pakistan* (Lahore: Pakistan Philosophical Congress, 1961).

Dupont, O. and Coypolani, X. *Les confrérie religieuses musulmanes* (Algiers: 1897).

Fakhry, M. *A History of Islamic Philosophy* (New York: Columbia University Press, 1970).

Gardet, L. and Anawati, M. M. *Introduction à la théologie musulmane* (Paris: Vrin, 1948).

Hourani, A. *Arabic Thought in the Liberal Age, 1798–1939* (London: Oxford University Press, 1962).

Husaini, I. M. *The Muslim Brethren* (Beirut: Khayat's College Book Cooperative, 1956).

Jameelah, M. *Islam and Modernism* (Lahore: Mohammed Yusaf Khan, 1968).

Lings, M. *A Sufi Saint of the Twentieth Century: Shaik Ahmad al'Alawi*, 2d ed. (Berkeley, Calif.: University of California Press, 1961).

Millénaire d'Avicenne, Congrès de Bagdad (Cairo: Imprimerie Misr S.A.E., 1952).

Mohaghegh, M. and Izutsu, T. *The Metaphysics of Sabzavari* (Delmar, N.Y.: Caravan Books, 1977).

Nasr, S. H. *Islam and the Plight of Modern Man* (London: Longman, 1975).

————. *Islamic Philosophy in Contemporary Persia: A Survey During the Past Two Decades* (Salt Lake City, Utah: Middle East Center, University of Utah, 1972).

————. *Islamic Studies* (Beirut: Librairie du Liban, 1967).

————. *Ṣadr al-Dīn Shīrāzī and His Transcendent Theosophy* (Tehran: Imperial Iranian Academy of Philosophy, 1978).

————. *Three Muslim Sages: Avicenna, Suhrawardī, Ibn 'Arabī* (Delmar, N.Y.: Caravan Books, 1976).

Safa, Z. (ed.). *Le livre du millénaire d'Avicenne*, 4 vols. (Tehran: Societé iranienne pour la conservation des monuments nationaux, 1953).

Sharif, M. M. (ed.). *A History of Muslim Philosophy*, 2 vols. (Wiesbaden: O. Harrassowitz, 1963–1966).

Ṭabāṭābāī, M. *Shi 'ite Islam*, trans. S. H. Nasr (London: Allen and Unwin, 1975).

JOURNALS

Bangladesh

Darshan

Manan

Iran

Sophia Perennis

Morocco
Revue Philosophique

Pakistan
Al-Hikmat
Iqbal Review
Pakistan Philosophical Journal
Search
Wisdom

Turkey
Araştirma
Islâm Tetkikleri Enstitiisii Dergisi

United Arab Republic
Armant
Mélanges de L'Institut Dominicain d'Etudes Orientales

Part VI: Asia

India

B I M A L   K .   M A T I L A L

To write about the development of Indian philosophy in the last twenty-five or thirty years is by no means an easy task. The matter is complicated by numerous problems. "Philosophers often see problems where an ordinary man would not." To prove this charge true, I would say that even the meaning of the simple and innocent looking phrase "Indian philosophy" is far from clear and unambiguous in the present context. If it is contrasted with such phrases as "Greek philosophy" or "Islamic philosophy," it has one shade of meaning, but if contrasted with "Western philosophy," it inadvertently acquires a different meaning. In the first case, our task at hand would be to prepare an account of historical and philological research activities which modern scholars have done in the field of ancient and classical philosophies of India. In the second case, again, two different senses can be attached to the phrase. We may be asked to make a note of the recent philosophical activities in India. What have Indian professors, academics, and thinkers been doing recently vis-à-vis their Western compatriots? What contributions, if any, have they made recently to the field of philosophy in general? In both questions, one may assume that "philosophy" means what is known as philosophy in the Western tradition, and the questions will center around the creative continuation and critical evaluation of the tradition of Aristotle and Plato, Kant and Hegel, Russell and Carnap. The other way of looking at Indian philosophy would be to note the creative activities, sometimes through criticism, interpretation, and reinterpretation, and sometimes through comparison and contrast with similar thoughts and problems in Western philosophy, in the field of the traditional philosophy of India, i.e., the tradition of Nāgārjuna, Dinnāga, Śaṃkara, Udayana, and Gaṅgeśa.

Although three different senses of the phrase "Indian Philosophy" are distinguished above, this is not to say there is no overlap among them. In fact, philological scholarship is sometimes found along with critical examination of the ancient doctrine from a modern point of view. A modern exposition of an ancient doctrine is not always free from a novel interpretation and critical appraisal. Thus, the first and the third senses often overlap. Besides, even a creative paper by an Indian scholar on Western philosophy is sometimes seen to be tinged with an Indian outlook derived, consciously or unconsciously, from the traditional philosophies of India. In recent years, there have also been quite a few conscious and deliberate attempts at comparative-creative writings in India.

Although most of such writings have not been successful or philosophically productive, there are a few notable exceptions. In a relatively short survey, it is impossible to give equal importance to all these areas of philosophic activities in India today. Hence, the concentration is on a middle ground, on works that combine philological scholarship and exposition of traditional doctrines with philosophic creativity and critical appraisal. Of course, there are other areas as important as this one, and from time to time these areas will be referred to in this essay.

BUDDHISM: EARLY BUDDHISM

The philosophical doctrines of Buddhism form a major component of Indian philosophy. Modern interest in Buddhism is worldwide; thus, scholars and philosophers alike have been active in the field of Buddhist philosophy.

K. N. Jayatilleke, in his illuminating book *Early Buddhist Theory of Knowledge*, discusses many important problems connected with the earliest developments of Indian philosophy. In his foreword to the book, D. Friedman wrote:

the sphere of thought indicated by the collective name of "Indian philosophy" is extremely complex. Indeed, in terms of the history of ideas, its chief attraction must be sought, not only in its spiritual and cultural unity or in the perennial truths of its monistic-idealistic metaphysics, but rather in its rich diversity.

This warning was, indeed, timely. Jayatilleke, however, wanted to show that the Buddha was a verificationist and an empiricist. For him, the spirit of early Buddhism was close to that of modern logical positivism and analytical philosophy, with the exception that Buddhism admitted the validity of the data of extrasensory perception and of the experiential content of mysticism. This is a very big claim, and one feels that proper evidence has not been adduced in its favor. Nevertheless, one cannot ignore the merit of Jayatilleke's work. D. J. Kalupahana, a former student of Jayatilleke, follows the tradition of his teacher and argues, in his *Causality: The Central Philosophy of Buddhism*, that the doctrine of causality advocated by the early Buddhists (in addition to the Pali Canons, he used some Chinese Āgamas) was very similar to the phenomenalism of Hume.

E. Frauwallner (1956) gives a very illuminating interpretation of the philosophy of the Buddha and early Buddhism, although it is very different from the "comparative" approach mentioned above. Frauwallner's interpretation is enriched at every step by his historical scholarship. His view on the connection between the early Upanishadic ideas and the Buddha's own ideas is particularly interesting. In connection with Buddhism in general, E. Lamotte's several works (1944–1949, 1958, 1962, 1970) and E. Frauwallner's two books (1953, 1958) are undoubtedly landmarks in historical scholarship. Nevertheless, their importance for further research in Buddhist philosophy should be acknowledged. A.

K. Warder's *Indian Buddhism* is a survey in English of the history of Buddhism in India, and it contains some chapters that deal with different schools of Buddhist philosophy. Both Warder (in a 1963 article) and Jayatilleke (1963) have attempted to analyze the debates recorded in *Kathā vatthu* in terms of modern propositional logic in order to show that these early Indian debaters already presupposed some well-known rules of propositional logic. E. Conze's *Buddhist Thought in India* is philosophically more interesting, although it lays more stress on the Mahāyāna schools. Conze, however, is better known for his numerous publications on the Prajñāpāramitā philosophy and literature (1954, 1957, 1958, 1964, 1975, articles, 1951, 1953).

BUDDHISM: MĀDHYAMIKA

Publications in the field of Mādhyamika philosophy have been numerous, and only a few of them are mentioned here. Nāgārjuna (second-third centuries) was one of the most important Indian philosophers. Thus, his writings, like the writings of all great philosophers, admit of a number of interpretations and thereby sustain an ever increasing interest in philosophic circles. It is, therefore, no wonder that continuing in the line of T. Stcherbatsky, S. Schayer, and L. de La Vallée Poussin (of the 1930s), each of the monographs written by S. Mookerjee, T.R.V. Murti, K. Venkataramanan, R. Robinson, and F. Streng takes a different approach to interpret the philosophic position of the Mādhyamikas. Murti (2d ed. 1960), who was probably strongly influenced by Stcherbatsky's rather ambiguous translation of *pratītya-samutpāda* as "relativity," argues that the "emptiness" doctrine cannot mean pure negativity. As a result, other scholars have criticized him for showing a Vedāntic bias (see K. Inada, 1970) in his interpretation of the Mādhyamika. Murti describes "emptiness" as absolutism and compares it with the systems of Kant, Hegel, and Bradley. This section of the book is rather weak, however. For Murti simply shares with Stcherbatsky an abiding interest in analogies between Kant and Mādhyamika, a tendency which has been rightly criticized by Jacques May ("Kant et le Mādhyamika," 1959).

S. Mookerjee (1957) wrote an elaborate exposition on Nāgārjuna Vigrahavyārartanī (recently, K. Bhattacharya translated the entire text; see K. Bhattacharya, 1971) and compared it with Srīharṣa's method. Although Mookerjee is critical of Murti's interpretation, he himself characterizes the Mādhyamika position as the absolutist's standpoint in logic. R. Robinson (1967) uses Chinese source materials in his presentation of the Mādhyamika philosophy, but he believes that complete understanding of this school is an impossible task, for "the archaic mind abides like Schweitzer's Jesus in alien remoteness."

F. J. Streng searches for the religious meaning of the "emptiness" doctrine of Nāgārjuna in his *Emptiness: A Study in Religious Meaning*. Here he focuses on the soteriological significance of "emptiness" and argues that "emptiness" is used as "a means of ultimate transformation." This approach has apparently been influenced by the modern "death of God" theology. K. Inada (1970) has objected (quite rightly, I believe) to such descriptions of the Mādhyamika philosophy as "absolutism," "monism," "relativism," and "negativism." He calls Nāgārjuna's philosophy "the non-assertive type," although he admits that Nāgārjuna used dialectics with "an end in view," i.e., the search for the ultimate truth. He describes the middle path as the "supreme ontological principle" in Buddhism and Nāgārjuna as "the supreme Buddhist ontologist." This point is rather debatable, as is his further comment that "emptiness" or the middle path is to be understood "in the sense of inclusion or immanent transcendence."

K. Venkataramanan's (1961–1962, 1966) study of Nāgārjuna illustrates another interesting approach to the Mādhyamika school. The author bases his comments on his sound scholarship in Oriental languages. He argues that the Mādhyamika asks us to know the proper use of reason and concepts, not to negate them. Nāgārjuna studies have evoked great enthusiasm among some comparativists today, and numerous articles and several books have appeared in which Nāgārjuna's philosophy (along with Buddhism in general) has been brought to bear upon the interpretation of Ludwig Wittgenstein's thought and vice versa. Since most of these studies are based on speculations and second-hand materials, they merit no further comment.

Great interest has been generated in the logical interpretation of what may be the Buddhist tetralemma (*catuṣkoṭi*). C.T.K. Chari (1954, 1955) makes a rather provocative claim that just as the function of Brouwer's logic and Reichenbach's logic was to introduce into mathematics and mathematical physics, respectively, a domain of "restricted assertibility," the purpose of the "mystical" dialectics, presumably of Nāgārjuna and others, was to do the same thing, more or less, in the much larger field of human thinking. This is a very tall claim and hence requires little comment.

H. Nākāmura (1958) suggests that, although some of the arguments of Nāgārjuna appear to be erroneous from the point of view of "traditional Western logic," they could be shown to be in order "when viewed from the standpoint of the two-valued logical algebra of Schröder." R. Robinson (1967) claims instead that Nāgārjuna's principal form of inference is what he calls the hypothetical syllogism, and he is aware "to some degree of the principle of logical conversion." Using some Chinese Mādhyamika sources, Robinson argues that the tetralemma was understood by the Chinese as involving quantification. He also argues that the third and fourth alternatives of the four *Koṭis* are conjunctions of the Aristotelian I and O, and E and A forms. For this last point, he has been criticized by Jayatilleke (1963, 1967), who cites materials mainly from the *Pāli Nikāyas* to falsify Robinson's claim. Jayatilleke even observes that the problem of the tetralemma has baffled not only modern scholars but also Nāgārjuna himself.

B. K. Matilal (1971) suggests a simple solution of the problem by pointing out that the negation used by Nāgārjuna was not the ordinary negation of logic but that it was more akin to the *prasajya* negation used by the Indian logician-grammarians earlier than Nāgārjuna. Unlike ordinary negation, in this negation denial of a proposition *p* does amount to the commitment of the affirmation of NOT *p*. The Buddhist can say what is NOT the case, but thereby he is not committed to say what IS the case. Thus, Nāgārjuna's rejection of the first alternative does not make the formulation of the second alternative superfluous, nor does it make its rejection self-contradictory.

F. Staal (1966) offers a way to formalize the argument in the first verse of Nāgārjuna's *Mādhyamika-Kārikā* and gives a brief account of three varieties of negation. Staal (1975) also criticizes earlier interpretations of the tetralemma, and while he agrees with Matilal's point about the *prasajya* negation, he feels that Matilal's discussion, to the extent it does not distinguish between the law of noncontradiction and that of the excluded middle, is unsatisfactory. D. S. Ruegg in an elaborate article (1977) has reviewed the problem of the tetralemma in the context of various philosophic doctrines of Buddhism, viz., causation, existence, *svabhāva*, dependent origination, and nirvāṇa. As far as the logical aspect of the problem is concerned, he discusses the views of almost all the modern scholars and argues that the Mādhyamika reasoning is based on the twin pillars of the principles of noncontradiction and excluded middle, and that the negation of the four *Koṭis* serves to bring to a stop all discursive thinking. Ruegg concedes Matilal's point about the *prasajya* negation but disagrees with him on the ground that the soteriological significance of *catuṣkoṭi* would be lost if the rejection of alternative 1 could not be shown contradictorily opposed to the rejection of alternative 2. Ruegg also endorses Staal's point about the ''non-irrationalism'' of Buddhism but rejects his views about the excluded middle and his suggestion about a third truth-value (following Brouwer's intuitionistic logic) for the Mādhyamika.

YOGĀCĀRA AND A BHIDHARMA

Most of the Yogācāra texts (of Asaṅga, Vasubandhu, and Sthiramati) were edited and translated in the 1930s. The same is true of the important Mahāyāna sūtras such as *Sandhi* and *Laṅkā*. Recently, A. Wayman and H. Wayman published (1974) an English translation of the *Śrī-Mālā-Sūtra*, which mainly emphasizes the ''embryo'' theory (*Tathāgata-garbha*). The ''embryo'' theory states that the *Tathāgata-garbha*, which has the nature of pure and translucent consciousness, lies hidden in every man, and the purpose of man is to realize this Buddha-nature. A detailed analysis of this doctrine is to be found in the *Rat-nagotravibhāga*. J. Takasaki (1966) presents a very useful analysis of this text in his *A Study on the Ratnagotravibhāga*. He also speculates (following E. Lamotte) upon the possible connection between the *ālaya* theory and the *garbha* theory, as well as upon the possible influence of Yogācāra on later Advaita Vedānta. D. S. Ruegg (1969) presents to the scholarly world a very impressive and scholarly study of the theory of the *Tathāgata-garbha*. This book is indispensable for any future study on the soteriology of the *garbha* doctrine. G. M.

Nagao's translation of the *Madhyāntavibhāg(n)gasūtra* (1964) is another important addition to the study of Yogācāra idealism. But the most important translation of the Sūtras is that of *Vimalakīrtinirdeśa* by E. Lamotte (1962), which has already been mentioned.

S. Bagchi (1957) has given a free English rendition of Vasubandhu's *Viṃśatikā*, but, unfortunately, it has not been very successful. A. K. Chatterjée (1962) attempts to give a philosophical reconstruction of the Yogācāra idealism. Chatterjée depends solely on some Sanskrit texts and completely ignores the available translations in Western languages of some important Yogācāra texts (Chinese and Tibetan versions). Just as Kalupahana has followed Jayatilleke, Chatterjée has explicitly followed Murti in his approach to Buddhist philosophy, and thus he faces the same criticisms as Murti in his interpretation of the Mādhyamika. Chatterjée calls Yogācāra an "absolutism" and develops his own idea about "absolutism." While his frequent references to Kant, Hume, and Hegel are not very illuminating, his brief exposition of Advaita Vedānta and its contrast with the Yogācāra is helpful.

W. T. Chan (1963) has prepared a very useful annotated translation of selections from Hsüan-tsang's *Ch'eng wei-shih lun*, which contains Vasubandhu's *Triṃśika* and Hsüan-tsang's interpretation of the thirty verses based on, chiefly, Dharmapāla's commentary. Chan's presentation of the Yogācāra philosophy is lucid and brief, and his comments are helpful. B. K. Matilal (1974) gives a concise account of Vasabandhu's philosophical arguments for his "Consciousness-only" doctrine and shows their connection with Diṅnāga's *Ālambana-parīkṣā*. He also points out the distinction of the *sva-samvitti* doctrine of the Diṅnāga-Dharmakīrti school from Vasubandhu's *Vijñapti-mātratā*. Vasubandhu, Diṅnāga, and Dharmakīrti—all three—contributed to the most lively discussion of epistemological and ontological issues between the Buddhists on the one hand and the Nyāya-Vajśeṣika and Kumārila on the other. A summary of this controversy (to be found in Matilal, 1974) is philosophically interesting, and a study particularly of this period of the history of Indian philosophy should prove rewarding for a creative philosopher today. E. Sarachchandra (1976), in an interesting article, examines critically the Buddhist theory of the external world from the point of view of the British empiricism of Locke, Berkeley, and Hume.

On the *ālaya* problem, Frauwallner (1951) has written an important article showing the connection between *ālayavijñāna* and *amala-vijñāna*. L. Schmithausen (1969) has prepared a scholarly study and annotated translation (in German) of the Nirvāna chapter of the *Viniścayasaṃgrahaṇī* (from the Tibetan version). H. V. Guenther, a prolific writer on the Tibetan variety of Yogācāra Buddhism as well as Buddhist mysticism, has attempted to present Tibetan Buddhism as an independent system (1959) that can, and should, stand on its own. He challenges his readers to understand Tibetan Buddhism without their Sanskritic (or Indian) bias. The implicit premise is that the Tibetan ecclesiastics invented many terms and concepts (or, rather, added new shades of meaning to the Indian terms); therefore, we would falsify Tibetan Buddhism if we imposed the Indian Mahāyāna upon it. This point is very debatable, and Guenther has not helped the debate yet by showing, in clear and understandable terms, how original Tibetan Buddhism was. Guenther has received criticism not only for the above point, but also for deliberately making Tibetan Buddhism esoteric by choosing obscure English terms to translate the Tibetan terms. Moreover, he frequently refers to, and quotes from, C. D. Broad (especially his *Mind and Its Place in Nature*) to support his interpretation of Buddhism, a practice that is embarrassing, for it does very little to promote an understanding of Buddhism. However, two of Guenther's works are very important. In one (1959), he talks about the philosophy and psychology of the Abhidharma, and his exposition is based on Indian sources. The second is his paper on Buddhist mysticism (1974), which is a precise and succinct account of the subject.

Relatively little scholarly work has been done on the Abhidharma. However, besides Guenther's study of Abhidharma mentioned above, mention must be made of the annotated French translation of Asaṅga's *Abhidharmsamuccaya* by W. Rahula (1971). This work has enriched the study of Buddhist philosophy. K. Venkataramanan (1953) has done a service to scholars and philosophers by translating (into English) an Abhidharma text of the Sammitīya school (*Āśrayaprajñaptiśāstra*) from the extant Chinese version. P. S. Jaini (1959) published, for the first time, the *Abhidharmadīpa*, which is critical of the Abhidharmakośa. Jaini's elaborate introduction is also helpful. Śānti Bhikṣu has re-translated two Abhidharma texts, *Jñānaprasthāna* (1955) and *Abhidharmāmṛta* (1953), from the Chinese versions. Ñāṇamoli (1956) has translated the *Visuddhimagga* (The Path of Purification), which was edited in 1950 by H. Warren and D. Kosambi. N. Tatia (1957) discusses the theory of dependent origination as found in the *Visuddhi-magga*. Khemindra Thera and others have prepared an English translation of another important text, *Vimuttimagga* (The Path of Freedom, 1961).

On Tantric Buddhism, S. B. Dasgupta (1946, 1950) has written two very illuminating books based on sound scholarship. D. Snellgrove (1959) has translated the *Hevajra-Tantra* and also discusses the philosophical doctrine of the Tantrayāna. It is interesting to see how the Mahayānā "emptiness" and "wisdom" (*prajñā*) coincide with the goal of Tantra.

T. Ling (1973) proposes a different approach to Buddhism. He argues that Buddhism should be understood as a humanistic social philosophy, with political and economic dimensions, for that was the classical understanding of Buddhism. Thus, to call it "a personal religion" is to distort it. Ling's idea of Buddhism is fascinating and, perhaps, it is not without a touch of his personal philosophy.

DIŃNĀGA AND LATE BUDDHIST LOGIC

Diṅnāga (fourth century) was one of the most original thinkers in Indian philosophy, especially in epistemology and logic. Whether he was a Yogācāra or a Sautrāntika will probably never be known. Unfortunately, all of the original

Sanskrit texts he wrote have been lost. M. Hattori (1968) has thus done a great service to scholars and philosophers by reconstructing from the Tibetan version the chapter on perception of Diṅnāga's *Pramāṇasamuccaya*. He has prepared a very carefully annotated translation of Diṅnāga's text and discusses some important philosophic issues in his Notes.

E. Frauwallner has made several indispensable contributions to the study of logic in Diṅnāga and Vasubandhu. The logical texts of Vasubandhu are also lost. But Frauwallner (1957) shows that the entire *Vādavidhi* of Vasubandhu in all its essential points can be reconstructed from the available fragments as well as from a close study of the later developments in "dialectics" (*vāda*). According to Frauwallner, *Vādavidhi* is similar to the *Nyāyamukha* of Diṅnāga in many respects, but the genius of Diṅnāga lies in his addition of the *hetucakra* to Vasubandhu's system. In fact, Diṅnāga should be credited with the discovery of the *hetucakra* (a system of nine possible types of reasoning), which was a major step forward in the development of Indian logic. R.S.Y. Chi (1969) gives a formal representation of Diṅnāga's *hetucakra* ("wheel of reason"), as well as Uddyotakara's *hetucakra* (which was an extension of the former), by using Boolean algebra, Venn's diagrams, and some concepts of modern formal logic. His study is very interesting for creative philosophers today, and despite some debatable issues found in the book as a whole this kind of study offers some insight into the nature of the philosophy of logic today.

Frauwallner's best contribution to Diṅnāga study is his "Diṅnāga, sein Werk und seine Entwicklung" (1959). Here Frauwallner notes the transition in Diṅnāga's thought from the narrow confines of "eristic" logic to the general problems of epistemology, and how Diṅnāga's *Pramāṇasamuccaya* marked the great synthesis of logic and the theory of knowledge (*pramāṇa-śāstrâ*). In addition, he shows that Diṅnāga was much influenced, in his philosophical thoughts, by Bhartṛhari on the one hand and by the Sautrāntika Buddhists on the other. B. K. Matilal (1971) also notes the close affinity of Diṅnāga's idea of *Vikalpa* ("conceptual construction") with that of Bhartṛhari. Diṅnāga's theory of "construction" was supplemented by his most important innovation, the doctrine of *apoha* (by which one is roughly to understand universals or universal concepts as negations or exclusions). The *apoha* doctrine influenced the later Buddhist writers who were not always unanimous as to the exact interpretation of the doctrine. There is a puzzle about the notion of negation involved in the *apoha* doctrine. Matilal (1971) suggests that this negation is not the ordinary negation of the logicians but rather is tied to the general Buddhist conception of negation where the "commitment" aspect of negation is completely subordinated to the "denial" aspect. In fact, Diṅnāga's theory might have something to offer to the modern nominalists. H. Herzberger (1975) attempts a formal presentation of the "apohist" negation based on the theory of "detachability of presuppositions." The program envisages that a sentence could be factored into two components, presuppositions and manifest content, and that all Platonic commitments could be encompassed within the presuppositional ground. This is a useful exercise in creative study of comparative logic. In a recent article (1977), Hattori argues that the Sautrāntika theory of *prajñapti-sat* "nominal existence" provided the background for Diṅnāga's doctrine of universals as *apoha*.

Under the influence of Diṅnāga's logic, Bhāvaviveka developed the Svātantrika school in the Mādhyamika system. He argues that apart from the *reductio* (*prasanga*) argument, one can construct a "syllogistic" (in Diṅnāga's sense) proof for the "emptiness" doctrine. Scholars have generally paid little attention to Bhāvaviveka, but Y. Kajiyama (1957, 1964) has contributed two interesting articles on Bhāvaviveka's philosophy. Kajiyama (1966) also presents an annotated translation of an important text on late Buddhist logic (Mokṣākaragupta) and briefly discusses an important philosophic issue, consciousness with an *ākāra* (ascribed to Diṅnāga) versus consciousness without an *ākāra* (other Buddhists). In addition, he has written an article (1977) distinguishing the two senses of negation and the senses of affirmation in Buddhist and Indian writings.

H. Kitagawa's short article (1960) on Diṅnāga's logic shows its difference from the Scholastic version of Aristotelian logic. But his major work on the chapter of inference in the *Pramāṇasamuccaya* is written in Japanese. A. Kunst (1947, 1948, 1957) has written several articles on the Buddhist theory of inference, basing his study on Śāntarakṣita who belonged to the post-Diṅnāga period. He discusses such important topics of logic as the two-membered syllogism as well as the law of excluded middle. M. Nagatomi (1959) discusses the framework of Dharmakīrti's *Pramāṇavārttika*, but his translation of the *Pramāṇavārttika* still awaits publication in the Harvard Oriental series. S. Mookerjee and H. Nagasaki (1964), on the other hand, have translated the chapter on *Svārthānumāna* of the *Pramāṇavārttika*. Only the first fifty-one verses, along with Dharmakīrti's auto-commentary, have been translated, and the translators have added elaborate comments on each problem discussed. A. Malvania (1959) gives a brief analysis of the contents of the *Svārthānumāna* chapter of Dharmakīrti in his introduction.

E. Steinkellner (1967) has edited the Tibetan text and has carefully reconstructed the Sanskrit original of Dharmakīrti's *Hetubindu*, which is an improvement on the earlier reconstruction by S. Sanghavi. Steinkellner has also produced an annotated German translation (1967) of the text, which is helpful in understanding the abstruse points of Dharmakīrti. T. Vetter (1966) has worked on another important text of Dharmakīrti, *Pramāṇaviniścaya*. He has edited the Tibetan text, and has collected and identified the available Sanskrit fragments. In another study (1964), he gives a systematic account of Dharmakīrti's theory of knowledge, tracing its origin to Sautrāntika ontology and earlier Buddhist theory of *pramāṇas*. Another important addition to the Dharmakīrti studies is M. Gangopādhyaya's Sanskrit reconstruction (from the Tibetan version) and annotated translation of Vinītadeva's commentary on Dharmakīrti's *Nyāyabindu*. H. N. Ganguly (1963) has made an unconventional attempt to examine some doctrines of logical positivism in the light of the philosophic theories of Dharmakīrti, Prajñākara, and Bhartṛhari. The attempt is not very successful, mainly because he tried to cover too much material within a very short space. It was an ambitious project which the author tried to accomplish too quickly.

Ratnakīrti in the eleventh century A.D. wrote several short treatises summarizing the Buddhist position (in fact, the position of his teacher Jñānaśrīmitra) on several issues in logic and philosophy. Several modern scholars have turned their attention to Ratnakīrti. Y. Kajiyama (1966) gives a free translation of Ratnikīrti's treatise on causality, which is very useful. In another article (1965), he freely translates Ratnakīrti's refutation of solipsism from the Buddhist point of view. D. Sharma (1969) has translated the *apoha* section of Ratnakīrti, and A.C.S. McDermott (1969), the section on *vyāpti*. Both works suffer from some inaccuracies in translation. But the value of these books does not lie so much in the translation as in the creative thinking, in the context of modern philosophy, based upon the medieval Buddhist doctrines of logic and epistemology. McDermott, being particularly conversant with modern mathematical logic, has subjected the philosophical arguments of Ratnakīrti to Western analytic techniques and formalism of solutions. Sharma suggests that *apoha* is, in fact, a theory of meaning to be explained in terms of propositional attitudes.

Saṁkarasvāmin (500–600 acc. E. Frauwallner) was a disciple of Diṅnāga, and he apparently presented his teacher's system of logic quite faithfully in his *Nyāyapraveśa*. M. Tachikawa (1971) has prepared a useful translation of this text and has thus contributed to the study of Diṅnāga's logic.

CĀRVĀKA OR LOKĀYATA (MATERIALISM)

To counteract the popular belief that classical Indian philosophy was entirely spiritual in outlook and character, some scholars have drawn the attention of the philosophical world to the role of materialism in Indian thought. Daksinaranjan Shastri's *A Short History of Indian Materialism, Hedonism and Sensualism* (1957) brought this issue into focus. Shastri, on insufficient evidence, distinguishes four stages of development of Indian materialism and calls them Bārhaspatya, Lokāyata, Cārvāka, and Nāstika, respectively. Thus, he was rightly criticized by K. K. Mittal in his excellent work *Materialism in Indian Thought* (1974). Mittal analyzes the so-called antimaterialistic doctrines of such schools as Jainism, Nyāya-Vaiśesika, Sāṃkhya, and Buddhism, and shows how what he calls "materialistic traits" have crept into them. The book is a philosophical study, but Mittal does not wish to be called a "materialist" himself. Earlier, D. Riepe (1961) attempted an account of what he called "the naturalistic tradition" in Indian thought.

D. P. Chattopadhyaya's *Lokāyata: A Study of Ancient Indian Materialism* (1959) is provocative since the author has explicitly adopted the Marxist approach in analyzing the Indian materials on materialism. In this regard, he evidently follows the lead of Walter Ruben who has attempted a Marxist interpretation of Indian philosophy in several articles. Chattopadhyaya traces the origin of materialism in the sexual rites (body rituals) connected with primitive agriculture. Women were supposed to have discovered agriculture in primitive society, and they performed certain body-rituals which filtered through the Tantric rites and might have given rise to the identification of the body and soul (*dehātmavāda*).

The discovery and publication of Jayarāśi Bhaṭṭa's text by Sukhlalji Sanghavi created a new interest in the epistemological position of the Indian materialists. W. Ruben (1958) describes Jayarāśi as an "agnostic." A.K. Warder (1956) labels Jayarāśi a "positivist" according to modern ideas, but Jayatilleke takes exception to this comment. There is strong evidence, however, showing that the Indian materialists were also astute logicians. It can be argued, as Mittal and Chattopadhyaya have done, that they did not object to the inferential process as such but only rejected the claim of inference to be a means of establishing the reality of God, soul, and the afterlife. Mittal concludes that the Indian materialists upheld a "realistic and rationalistic empiricism" as their epistemological position. Even S. Radhakrishnan, who connects materialism with the freedom of speculation prevalent in ancient India, contends that its philosophy could not have been as coarse and unsophisticated as presented by Mādhavācārya and others, and he admits that it was upheld by many serious thinkers for centuries.

The ethical position of the Indian materialists has been a matter of great dispute. Chattopadhyaya rejects the general impression (created, inadvertently, by Mādhava's account) that these materialists endorsed not only hedonism but also egoistic sensualism and moral irresponsibility. D. Riepe (1955–1956), in a paper in *Philosophy and Phenomenological Research*, gives a fair and charitable account of the ethics of Indian materialism. Mittal argues that in the light of modern developments in philosophy, it is possible to defend the ethical hedonism of the Indian materialists and disassociate it from the doctrine of moral irresponsibility.

JAINISM

Jainism holds a unique position in the field of Indian philosophy, but modern scholars have not given sufficient attention to the philosophical doctrines of the Jainas. Thus, S. N. Dasgupta in his monumental history of Indian philosophy offers a very inadequate appraisal of Jainism. Even H. V. Glasenapp in his well-known book on Jainism ignores its philosophic importance. Fortunately, a few good scholars have recently done some work in this field. Thus, although Jainism has failed to create the same fervor and enthusiasm as Buddhism, it has now aroused some interest in philosophical circles.

Surprisingly, a long time ago, K. C. Bhattacharya, who is best known for his original and creative writings on Kant and Vedānta, did write on the Jaina theory of Anekānta-vāda. His paper, "The Place of the Indefinite in Logic" (published in his collected works, 1956), was also influenced, if only indirectly, by the Jaina philosophic theory. S. Mookerjee's *The Jaina Philosophy of Non-*

Absolutism (1944) is based on his detailed study of Hemacandra's *Pramāṇa-mīmāṃsa*. Although this expository work reflects the author's erudition and scholarship, his style is weighty, as a result of which his philosophic arguments often remain opaque to the non-Sanskritist philosophers today. N. Tatia's *Studies in Jaina Philosophy* (1951) is also a scholarly work in which philosophical doctrines have been studied with reference to the Jaina canonical texts. Tatia notes several peculiar views of the Jainas. Among other things, he shows that the early Jainas conceived of the soul as a quasi-material principle. In fact, for the Jainas the soul is not an eternal immutable substance in the ever-changing world of phenomena, but a substantial counterpart of the life-principle (they call it *jīva*) which is also conceived to be as mutable as the body itself.

Y. J. Padmarajiāh (1963) explicitly calls his book *A Comparative Study of the Jaina Theories of Reality and Knowledge*, and it is an excellent exercise in this direction. He combines scholarship with philosophical insight by choosing and explaining the important philosophical doctrines of Jainism and by comparing them with other Indian systems and similar phenomena of Western philosophy. Particularly interesting is the parallelism he draws between the metaphysical conclusion of A. N. Whitehead (*Process and Reality*) and the Jaina understanding of the problem of change and permanence. In his preface to the book, Frauwallner rightly points out that it will help to introduce certain "valuable ideas contained in Jainism to the philosophical discussion of today."

Pandit Sukhlalji Sanghavi is a modern Jaina thinker who is carrying on the classical tradition as well as adding to creative thinking in Indian philosophy. He has written many excellent pieces in Hindi, some of which have been translated into English and collected in the work called *Advanced Studies in Indian Logic and Metaphysics* (1961). Exhibiting the true spirit of Jainism, Sanghavi analyzes and comments on the philosophic problems of all the important schools of Indian philosophy. On the whole, Sanghavi argues that, unlike Nyāya-Vaiśesika and Pūrva-Mīmaṃsā, the realistic nature of the Jaina standpoint has remained "absolutely unaltered in essence." The English translation (K. K. Dixit) of Sanghavi's own original commentary on the *Tattvārtha sūtras* of Umāsvāti is another important contribution to creative philosophy in the traditional sense. (See L. D. Series No. 44, 1974.)

N. Shah (1967) presents Akalaṅka's criticism of Dharmakīrti's philosophy, and, in doing so, he discusses some main problems of metaphysics and epistemology, such as the criterion of reality, the problem of universals, and idealism versus realism. Although Shah makes frequent use of current Western philosophical terms, it is probably necessary to warn readers that these terms acquire slightly different meanings in the Indian context. K. K. Dixit's *Jaina Ontology* (1971) is another important contribution to the study of Jaina philosophy. Dixit, a powerful writer, presents a chronological discussion of the ontological theories of all the important Jaina authors.

D. Bhargava's *Jaina Ethics* (1968) presents a systematic study of the ethical principles of Jainism. Bhargava reveals that Jaina ethics implied the dignity of man, and the equality and independence of all individuals. He also shows the connection between the Jaina ethical doctrines and its philosophy on non-one-sidedness. Further, he argues, not without some cogency, that the Jaina ethical attitude has relevance to the problems of world peace and the survival of humanity. B. K. Matilal (1978) traces the origin of the Jaina doctrine of non-onesidedness to Mahāvīra's interpretation of what was called the *vibhayya-vāda* "analytic method" in the *āgamas*. After showing the difference between the approaches of the Buddha and the Mahāvīra, and the consequent difference between *śūnyatā* "emptiness" and *anekāntatā* "non-onesidedness," he points out the logical implication of the Jaina doctrine of sevenfold predication (*saptabhaṅgī*).

ĀJĪVIKA (FATALISM)

The Ājīvikas were fatalists. Thus, their philosophic position offered an interesting opportunity in Indian philosophy to introduce a discussion of the problem of free will and determinism. Unfortunately, their texts are lost, and fragments of their doctrine survive only in the citations in the Buddhist and the Jaina canons. A. L. Basham (1951) has collected and reconstructed their doctrine from these and other fragments. Jayatilleke (1963) also discusses their philosophy at some length but differs from Basham's version.

MĪMĀṂSĀ

Mīmāṃsā or Pūrva-mimāṃsā is another important school of Indian philosophy which believes in a realistic ontology and epistemology, but modern scholars and philosophers have given very little attention to this system. As G. Jha (1942) and C. Kunhan Rāja (1940) have pointed out, the explicit concern of this system is to explain the nature of *dharma* "moral law," the "duties of man" as well as the mechanism of *Karma*. Its realism derives from the fact that the very fulfillment of moral law requires the reality of this world as well as that men be real doers of actions with a full sense of responsibility. But both Kumārila and Prabhākara appeared in the prime period of Indian philosophy (between 400 A.D. and 1200 A.D.), and as such, at their hands, the system was transformed into a highly developed empirical, naturalistic, and pluralistic philosophy.

We should thus be thankful to G. P. Bhatta (1962) for presenting a comprehensive study of the realistic epistemology of the Bhāṭṭa school of Mīmāṃsā. Bhatta compares Kumārila with G. E. Moore as one who fought the idealistic trend in British philosophic thought. While it is true that Kumārila's common sense realism strongly resembles that of Moore, it is debatable whether Kumārila's main contribution lies, as Bhatta claims, in bringing about the end of the idealistic tradition in Indian philosophy. For idealism continued ever afterwards in its own glory.

Bhatta rightly points out that the Kumārila school recognizes perception only as sense perception and rejects all sorts of extrasensory perception such as Yogic intuition. In this regard, Kumārila agrees with the materialist and disagrees with all other Indian philosophers.

Prabhākara's views on the nature and function of knowledge, as discussed by Bhatta, Rāmasavami, and Mohanty (1966), are particularly interesting. The theory of *Triputi samvit* states that knowledge reveals not only the object but also the subject as well as itself. The realism of the Prābhākaras has led them to believe that there cannot be any proper error in knowledge, for "error" consists simply in our nonapprehension of the distinction between what is given and what is imagined or remembered. These two views were severely criticized by the Bhātta school on the one hand and the Nyāya-Vaiśesika on the other. In fact, the contribution of the Mīmāmsā school to the lively and philosophically fruitful discussion of Indian epistemology can hardly be ignored. Hattori (1968) has shown, for example, how a study of Mīmāmsā is helpful in understanding some problems in Diṅnāga and post-Diṅnāga Buddhism.

Since Mīmāmsā is concerned chiefly with *Dharma*, it is, as Mittal (1974) points out, overwhelmingly "this-worldly." Mittal further argues that the Mīmāmsā conception of soul is closer to materialism, but this contention is questionable. J. Sinha (1952–1956) describes the Mīmāmsā ethics as a blend of impersonal legalism, nonsecular egoistic hedonism, and eudaemonism. Further discussion of Mīmāmsā ethics is very much needed.

Mīmāmsā is sometimes called the *Vākyaśāstra* "study of sentences." G. V. Devasthali (1959) has written a comprehensive book on the Mīmāmsā theory of language based mainly on the earlier texts of Mīmāmsā, such as the sūtras of Jaimini and the *Bhāsya* of Sábara. He sets forth quite systematically the Mīmāmsā views on language, word, and sentence. He occasionally refers to the views of late Mīmāmsā writers on these topics. Since these topics are well-known problems of modern philosophy, Devasthali's study is a useful contribution to the modern discussion. As already stated, the Mīmāmsakas were realists, and the problem of language and meaning was a very significant part of their concern. For this reason alone, if not for anything else, the Mīmāmsā should be studied from a modern point of view.

Frauwallner (1968) has added another important piece of work to research into the philosophy of Mīmāmsā. He presents the earliest source material on the Mīmāmsā theory of knowledge by giving an annotated translation of the *Bhāsya* of Śabara on the *Mīmāmsa-sūtras* 1·1·1-5, as well as the polemical passages in Diṅnāga's *Pramānasamuccaya* that are related to the Mīmāmsā views. He also points out in the sequel the contribution of the Vṛttikāra to the development of Mīmāmsā epistemology. D. Venkataramiah's English translation of the *Śāstradīpikā* of Pārthasārathi Miśra is another useful addition to the study of Mīmāmsā philosophy (1940).

SĀMKHYA-YOGA

The Sāmkhya system, the earliest philosophical system of India, constitutes a fascinating phase in the history of Indian thought. F. Edgerton (1965) argues that all ancient Indian thought is "practical in its motive" and that the Sāmkhya is no exception. He rejects the idea of Sāmkhya as a metaphysical, speculative system and claims that it is simply a method of salvation through knowledge or "knowing." He also rejects the idea that Sāmkhya was atheistic or nonabsolutistic, and points out that the ancient texts on Sāmkhya frequently accept the Upanishadic doctrine of the self. D. Chattopadhyaya (1959), among others, claims that Sāmkhya was originally fully atheistic and materialistic, but it was submitted to a process of rigorous spiritualization and thus the original Sāmkhya passed into its opposite.

Long ago (1929), S. Radhakrishnan gave a general summary of the Sāmkhya doctrines and then argued (as against Jacobi and Garbe) that Sāmkhya at no stage of its development could be identified with materialism, for it insisted on the absolute reality and independence of spirit. C. D. Sharma (1962) provides another brief summary, and A. Sengupta (1959) gives a somewhat elaborate account of the system and then offers criticisms from the point of view of Advaita Vedānta. Criticism of Sāmkhya from the Advaita point of view is not at all new. For the *Vedānta-sūtras* of Bādarāyaṇa may be viewed as being written for the refutation of the Sāmkhya doctrines.

Frauwallner (1953, 1956, 1958) contends that a series of passages from the *Mokṣadharma* of the Mahābhārata represents an extremely old tradition of the Sāmkhya system. He argues for four successive stages of development of Sāmkhya. In the first few centuries A.D., according to Frauwallner, Sāmkhya was a leading system of thought in which the theory of knowledge was incorporated mainly by Vārṣagaṇya. In a separate article (1958), Frauwallner gives a brilliant analysis of the early Sāmkhya epistemology. M. Hiriyanna (1957) gives his interpretation of the theory of error in the classical Sāmkhya in the context of his description of other systems, and K. H. Potter (1963) draws our attention to this theory.

J.A.B. van Buitenen (1956) challenges Frauwallner's rather simple theory about the evolution of the Sāmkhya thought as a uniform or unified system and argues quite convincingly that the development of the Sāmkhya was incredibly complex. Van Buitenen's research is based on sound scholarship, and his final recommendation is that we would do better to allow for "the greatest diversity" in the evolution of Sāmkhya rather than "the greatest uniformity of doctrine." G. Oberhammer (1960) has deliberated on the authorship of the *Ṣaṣṭitantra*. Recently, E. Solomon (1973) published two hitherto unpublished (and presumably ancient) commentaries on the *Sāmkhya-kārikā*, one of which, she claims, has "the fairest claim to being the original of Paramārtha's Chinese version." She has also prepared a study (1974) of the commentaries of the *Sāmkhya-*

kārikā, where she compares and contrasts the interpretations found in different commentaries.

The comparativists in philosophy have tried various models to interpret the Sāṃkhya system. Long ago, J. Davies (1881, second edition, 1957) compared the notion of *prakṛti* with the notion of God or nature in Spinoza. He also brought the thought of Schopenhauer and that of von Hartmann to bear upon some notions of Sāṃkhya. However, these comparisons are too sketchy to require any comment. H. Zimmer (1951) tries to find similarities between Sāṃkhya psychology and Western psychoanalysis. A. Wayman (1962, 1974), on the other hand, finds a connection between Buddhist dependent origination and certain key concepts in Sāṃkhya.

G. J. Larson (1969), in his study of classical Sāṃkhya, summarizes the researches of previous scholars. As for his own interpretation, Larson tries to find "certain interesting parallels or similar concerns" in Sāṃkhya and the phenomenological ontology of Jean-Paul Sartre. Though undoubtedly there are some surface similarities between the two systems (e.g., their conception of universal suffering, their irrelevance to a conception of God), one cannot go too far in this direction. Thus, a timely warning comes from T. Gelblum (1970), who criticizes this creative section in Larson and argues, among other things, that the concept of *freedom-from* in Sāṃkhya should be distinguished from the concept of *freedom-to-choose* in Sartre.

It is sometimes argued that the ultimate cosmological position which is derivable from the Sāṃkhya conception of *prakṛti* renders the Puruṣa (spirit) superfluous. Thus, K. Bhattacharya (1965) comments that Sāṃkhya was "much in line with western thinkers" and claims "that natural processes are spontaneous and do not require any conscious agent." J. Sinha (1952) presents a useful account of Sāṃkhya, and then he asserts that its atheistic cosmology "will appeal to the modern realist, naturalist, positivist, humanist and agnostic." K. K. Mittal (1974) argues against the interpretation that makes the Puruṣa in Sāṃkhya superfluous. He thinks that if we approach the problem of Sāṃkhya dualism "from the side of epistemology rather than that of ontology," a more sympathetic and "truthful" understanding of the Sāṃkhya position is possible.

Of the numerous publications in Yoga, very few contain anything that is philosophically interesting. Patañjali's system of Yoga was, of course, a philosophic school which accepted the Sāṃkhya metaphysics with slight modification. M. Eliade (1958), whose research in the history of religions is well known, has written a book on Yoga as the philosophy of freedom. The original work in French has now been translated in English (1958). Eliade was highly influenced by S. Dasgupta's study of Yoga. He also discusses the connection (historical and doctrinal) between Yoga and Tantra (both Buddhist and non-Buddhist). He sees Yoga mainly as an exercise of *entasis*. A. Danielou's work on Yoga (1949) contains little that is philosophically significant. Recently, K. Werner (1977) has tried to deal with Yoga practices and theories from the point of view of one's personal philosophy.

LINGUISTIC PHILOSOPHIES

The Sanskrit grammarians share with the Mīmāṃsakas their interest in the problems of language and meaning. The Mīmāṃsakas were realists while the grammarians were anything but realists in their philosophical outlook. In any case, the philosophical and metaphysical views of the Sanskrit grammarians have been studied with great enthusiasm by many modern scholars; some of these scholars, as might be expected, have used the comparative method in this respect.

J. Brough (1951, 1952, 1953) has contributed three illuminating papers on the views of the Sanskrit grammarians on the problems of meaning and language. In the first article, he discusses the doctrine of *sphoṭa*, which he explains as "the linguistic sign in its aspect of meaning-bearer." He disagrees with those who wish to attach some mystical conception to the doctrine of *sphoṭa*. Among other things, Brough has demonstrated, by analyzing the *Pāṇini-sūtra* 1·1·68, that the Indian grammarians distinguished clearly between use and mention, or between what may be termed object-language and meta-language. F. Staal has emphasized this point in many cases (e.g., see Staal 1969). Recently, F. Staal (1975) has written an elaborate paper on the concept of meta-language in ancient Indian texts and has made some interesting observations on the difference between Indian and Western ideas.

D. S. Ruegg (1959) notes, almost impressionistically, the contributions of ancient Indian thinkers to the philosophy of language. At about the same time, G. N. Sastri (1959) published his important work in which he discussed some Indian approaches to the philosophy of word and meaning, with special reference to the philosophy of Bhartṛhari. Although Sastri's book contains some inaccuracies and errors (for example, he repeats the error of previous scholars by calling the Benares commentary on Kāṇḍa 1, *Vākyapadīnya*, that of Puṇyarāja), its discussion of the views of Bhartṛhari, Nyāya, and Mīmāṃsā about the nature and import of word and sentence is based on sound scholarship. The same is more or less true of the study by B. Bhattacharya (1962). Although his occasional references to Bertrand Russell and some other modern Western linguistic philosophers are not particularly illuminating, Bhattacharya's elucidation of the Indian theories of the connotation of words, elements of syntax, and nature of the sentence is based on reliable Sanskrit sources. In an earlier work (1958), Bhattacharya discusses the "science" of Sanskrit etymology as set forth in Yāska's *Nirukta*.

L. Renou has made numerous contributions to the study of Sanskrit grammar (1953, 1956, 1957, 1969). Although Renou approaches the subject from the point of view of linguistics, some of his writings also touch on the philosophical issues involved (e.g., "Philosophie grammaticale" in his *L'Inde Classique*, 1953). P. Thieme's study (1956) of Pāṇini and the Pāṇinīyās also belongs to the same class. Among other things, Thieme argues that the Sanskrit language, as described by Pāṇini, lacks the notion of the grammatical subject as a component of the sentence, a point which is of some interest to philosophers of language. E. Frauwallner (1960) has written an article that deals with the philosophy of speech in the *Mahābhāṣya*. H. Scharfe (1961) has prepared a monograph that deals with what he calls "logic" in the *Mahābhāṣya*.

B. Shefts (1961) has studied the grammatical method of Pāṇini with special reference to his treatment of the Sanskrit present tense. An annotated translation of the *Paspaśā* or introduction to the *Mahābhāṣya* (by Patañjali), prepared by K. C. Chatterji (1957), is useful for the succinct account of Patañjali's philosophy of grammar.

K. Kunjunni Raja (1963) presents a very interesting account of Indian theories of meaning in a lucid style. Starting with some general comments about the modern views of language and meaning, Raja presents a survey of different theories of meaning discussed by different schools of Indian philosophy. Following the scheme of J. Brough, Raja elaborates the theories of literal meaning (*abhidhā*), metaphorical meaning (*lakṣaṇā*), as well as the suggested meaning in poetry (*vyañjanā*). He covers a very wide field in a short book; hence, his account is somewhat impressionistic. R. C. Pandey (1963) takes a very different approach to the problem of meaning in Indian philosophy. He is more concerned with the search for what he calls the metaphysical basis of what we speak, and he claims that in Indian philosophy a harmony of language and reality is firmly maintained. He explains *sphoṭa* as "the ultimate principle of meaning."

Bhartṛhari (seventh-century) was obviously the most important philosopher-cum-grammarian in India. Recently, two scholars have concentrated on the philosophy of Bhartṛhari. M. Biardeau (1964a, 1964b) has done an annotated French translation of the *Brahmakāṇḍa* of *Vākyapadīya* along with the *Vṛtti* of Harivṛsabha, where she argues with some cogency that the author of the *Vṛtti* was not Bhartṛhari himself and that this might explain some doctrinal differences between the *Vṛtti* and the *Kārikās*. In her larger work (1964b), Biardeau deals with the theory of knowledge and the philosophy of language as set forth by Bhartṛhari and other Brahminical philosophers. She rightly emphasizes the idealistic metaphysics of Bhartṛhari and the mystical aspect of the *sphoṭa* doctrine. However, she is a bit critical of modern attempts (e.g., of Brough and K. K. Raja) to interpret Bhartṛhari in terms of linguistic philosophy, which underplays his metaphysical doctrine. K.A.S. Iyer (1965) has also prepared an annotated English translation of the *Brahmakāṇḍa* and the *Vṛtti* thereon. R. Pillai (1971) has translated Chapters 1 and 2 of *Vākyapadīya*. Iyer (1969) has produced a major work on Bhartṛhari, in which he discusses the historical as well as the philosophical problems connected with the study of this philosopher. His study is based on the ancient commentaries, and it strikes a balance between sound scholarship and philosophic sensitivity. In several chapters, Iyer has not only summarized Bhartṛhari's discussion of the nature of the sentence and the relation between the word and the meaning, but he has also expounded the philosophic and logical significance of various grammatical categories, such as *sādhana, karma, karaṇa,* and *guṇa, à la* Bhartṛhari.

S. D. Joshi (1967) has contributed to the study of the Indian philosophy of language, particularly the study of the *sphoṭa* doctrine, by preparing an annotated translation of the *Sphoṭa-nirṇaya* of Kauṇḍabhaṭṭa. Joshi argues, contrary to the general view of scholars, that Patañjali never used *sphoṭa* in the sense of the meaning-bearing unit and that, for Bhartṛhari, *sphoṭa* represents a class sound, sorted and extracted by the listener from the gross matter. Iyer (1969), however, challenges the second view of Joshi and gives his own interpretation of what Bhartṛhari meant by *sphoṭa*. Briefly, in this view, *sphoṭa* is the entity that is within us, and is manifested (*vyaṅgya*) by the sounds or noises (*dhvani, nāda*). It is also the expressor (*vācaka*) of the meaning.

J. F. Staal has written several interesting papers (1962a, 1962b, 1963, 1965, 1966, 1969) and a monograph (1967) dealing with the philosophy of language in India. He follows the Chomskian line and introduces the notion of deep structure in analyzing the notion of syntax and semantics of the Sanskrit grammarians. Particularly in their *Kāraka* theory, Staal argues, the Sanskrit grammarians were concerned "with sentence constructing, i.e., with syntax and semantics, or with what is nowadays called 'deep structure'.'' Commenting on the word order in Sanskrit, Staal offers a rather ambitious theory about generative grammar and linguistic universals.

P. Kiparsky and J. F. Staal (1969) approach Pāṇini's *Kāraka* rules from the point of view of generative grammar. R. Rocher (1964, 1966) argues that Pāṇini's *Kārakas* are purely notional, semantic, and extralinguistic categories. G. Cardona (1974) disagrees with this interpretation and gives an exposition of the *Kāraka* rules based on the study of the traditional commentaries. Cardona calls *Kāraka* concepts syntactico-semantic. Of Cardona's numerous publications on Pāṇini, some are philosophically relevant (Cardona, 1967, 1967–1968, 1974, 1975).

Analysis of the sentence and the resulting analysis of the proposition form an important part of the Sanskrit philosophy of language. B. K. Matilal (1966), while commenting on the definition of the sentence in Sanskrit, shows how the semantic contents of the cognition of meaning generated by a sentence are expressed by a paraphrase of the original sentence. This paraphrase is described in terms of the relation between a qualificand (*viśeṣya*) and a qualifier (*prakāra*). Matilal indicates how a complete semantic theory for at least declarative sentences could be constructed in terms of this relation. G. Cardona (1975) elaborately discusses the notion of paraphrase in the Indian context and its role in the sentence analysis. Cardona states that a consideration of this problem gives much insight into the nature of grammar as conceived by the Indian grammarians. He concludes that an Indian grammar deals with syntax, though a restricted one which involves sentences with derivational equivalents.

Although much has been written recently on the philosophy of language in India, it remains a virtually unexplored field. What is needed is probably a series of good translations of important texts as well as exploration of some crucial concepts. S. D. Joshi, for example, has embarked on a project of translating the entire *Mahābhāsya.* Five volumes have already appeared (1968, 1969, 1971, 1973, 1974). These are all welcome pieces of research and represent a move in the right direction.

NYĀYA-VAIŚEṢIKA

The joint school of Nyāya and Vaiśeṣika (later called Navya-nyāya) represents a dominant trend in Indian philosophy that has sometimes been described as realistic and commonsensical. In fact, its history has not been very saturated with spiritualism and religion. It presents a system that is dominated by logic, epistemology, and ontology. Accordingly, it has attracted the attention of many modern scholars who have been more exposed to the discipline of logical analysis in the West. Of numerous recent publications in this field of Nyāya-Vaiśeṣika, I shall mention only a few.

S. Bhaduri (1947) gives an analysis of the Nyāya-Vaiśeṣika metaphysics depending upon the original sources. Starting with the criteria of reality, he discusses the major problems such as the doctrine of substance, matter, time, space, whole and part, and causality. In spite of some misleading comments about Buddhist opponents (such as calling Nāgārjuna "the Buddhist nihilist"), the author's exposition of the Nyāya-Vaiśeṣika doctrines is generally sound. S. C. Chatterjee (1950) has prepared an account of the epistemology of the Nyāya school. His book is helpful, but sometimes the exposition is careless. Although J. Sinha (1958) proposes to deal with "Indian psychology" in general, his exposition is based mainly on the Nyāya-Vaiśeṣika and Mīmāṃsā.

D. N. Shastri (1964) gives an elaborate account of various ontological problems in the Nyāya-Vaiśeṣika, such as universals, inherence, and substance. This book is based primarily on three authors—Vācaspati, Śrīdhara, and Jayanta. J. V. Bhattacharya (1952–1957) has translated a major portion of the *Pramāṇa* section of Jayanta's *Nyayamañjarī,* which has been serialized and published in several issues of *The Calcutta Review.* The translation is not always literal, however. J. V. Bhattacharya (1966) has also prepared an excellent study of the problem of negation in Nyāya-Vaiśeṣika and Mīmāṃsā, offering comparisons with certain modern Western theories. G. Chemparathy (1972), in his study of Udayana's proofs for the existence of God, calls it rational theology.

M. K. Gangopadhyaya (1967, 1968, 1972) has done a service to the study of the Nyāya-Vaiśeṣika by producing not only an English translation of the *Nyāya-sūtras* and *Nyāya-bhāṣya* but also an elaborate Bengali commentary prepared by a great scholar-philosopher Mm. Phanibhusan Tarkavagisa in the 1930s. Tarkavagisa was a creative philosopher of India in the traditional sense. Thus, this work is a valuable addition to modern research. R. S. Dravid (1972) has written on a very interesting and important problem—the problem of universals in Indian philosophy. Dravid strongly presents the Nyāya-Vaiśeṣika and the Mīmāṃsā views and occasionally talks about comparisons with Western doctrines. The comparative part is sometimes careless with regard to modern philosophic terminology and theories.

K. H. Potter's book *Presuppositions of Indian Philosophies* (1963) is a good exercise in the creative classification of Indian philosophical doctrines. The chief strength of the work lies in the section on logic and epistemology, where basically Nyāya-Vaiśeṣika materials have been used. Potter's earlier work (1957) is actually an annotated translation (with some theoretical discussions) of a highly technical text on Navya-nyāya (see below), Raghunātha's *Padārthatattvanirūpaṇa*. Potter has also written several articles (1954–1955, 1961, 1970) dealing with the interpretation of such Vaiśeṣika categories as quality and relation. P. K. Mukhopadhyaya (1973), in his study of the concept of "cognitive act," mainly uses Jayanta from the Indian side and relates it to some modern discussions of the concept of consciousness. S. Bagchi (1953) has written about the role of *Tarka* or inductive reasoning in Indian logic. He utilizes both the early Nyāya and Navya-nyāya materials (as well as Jaina materials). The book deals with many technical points about Indian logic, but the presentation is not always clear.

G. Bhattacharya (1961), in an important study of the Nyāya-Vaiśeṣika theism, deals with the logical, ontological, and theological arguments of Udayana. Bhattacharya has also written several illuminating papers (1967, 1974, 1975, 1977) that cover such technical problems of Navya-nyāya as Raghunātha's concept of *vyāpti* (pervasion relation), the doctrine of *sāmānyalakṣaṇā, pakṣatā*, and *śābdabodha* (verbal cognition). N. Bandopadhyay (1977) has prepared a book on different types of *hetrābhāsa* (fallacious reasons) based primarily on Navya-nyāya texts.

B. K. Matilal (1971) discusses the Nyāya theory of perception as well as the doctrine of universals and relations showing Diṅnāga's critique of these notions and the defense that comes from Udayana and Gaṅgeśa. Matilal reconstructs Diṅnāga's theory of universals from the text of Uddyotakara and develops the principle of nesting to answer the Buddhist principle of "impenetrability" of real entities. He also discusses the implicit Nyāya semantic principle, which states that a simple, noncompound property can never be empty.

Swami Yogindrananda has recovered and edited two supposedly lost Nyāya works, *Nyāya-bhūṣaṇa* of Bhāsarvajña (1968) and *Mānā-mānchara* of Vādī Vāgīśvara (1973). These two publications should add fresh impetus to Nyāya research.

D.H.H. Ingalls (1951) has written an outstanding book which shows how some of the problems, discussed in such technical texts as *Vyāpti-pañcaka* of Gaṅgeśa and Mathurānātha, can be explained in terms of the modern concepts of formal logic and semantics. This book has inspired many other scholars and philosophers to study Navya-nyāya from the modern point of view. Both K. H. Potter (1957) and B. K. Matilal (1968) have followed Ingalls' lead with reasonable success. Potter examines the question of understanding the Vaiśeṣika categories. Matilal first explains some basic concepts of Navya-nyāya in the light of modern analytic philosophy and then examines the theory of negation as propounded by Vātsyāyaṇa, Gaṅgeśa, and Raghunātha. With regard to the study of Navya-nyāya, J. N. Mohanty (1966) presents an annotated translation of the *Pramāṇya* section of Gaṅgeśa. Mohanty analyzes the concepts of *jñāna* (cognition), knowledge, and truth. Both Mohanty and Matilal have shown how Brentano's problem of intentionality can be brought to bear upon the interpretation of the Nyāya concept of cognition. Matilal has also shown that the qualifier-qualificand analysis of cognition found in Nyāya is not very far removed from the modern logical analysis of propositions.

Sibajivan Bhattacharya (1968, 1974) also deals with some basic concepts of Navya-nyāya in the light of modern analysis, differing occasionally from Matilal's interpretation. Sibajivan, in a creative paper on modern philosophy of logic (1968), frequently draws insights from his study of Indian logic. Among other things, he argues that it is not necessary to specify a middle term in order to have a syllogism. J. F. Staal has written a number of papers (1960, 1962, 1968, 1961, 1973) in which he attempts symbolic interpretations of certain definitions of *vyāpti*, interprets the problem of definition in Indian logic in extensional terms, and studies the notion of contradiction in the Indian context. However, Sibajivan Bhattacharya presents a deeper analysis of the notion of "contradiction" (*pratibandhakatā*) as studied in Navya-nyāya (1974). Staal's contrast of the notion of *pakṣa* with the Aristotelian "minor term" is also very interesting (1973).

C. Geokoop (1967) has prepared an annotated translation of the entire *Vyāpti* section (different definitions of the "pervasion" relation) of Gaṅgeśa. In each case, he presents a symbolic rewriting of the definition, and in this matter he has followed Staal. T. Bhattacharya (1970) has made a study of the problem of evolution of the concept of *vyāpti* in Navya-nyāya (based mainly on the texts of Gaṅgeśa and Raghunātha). The problems Bhattacharya discusses are highly technical, and, unfortunately, his treatment of them is inadequate. D. C. Guha (1968) has studied several important concepts of Navya-nyāya (such as *paryāpti, anugama*) in some detail, but he leaves his exposition largely untranslated.

VEDĀNTA

Vedānta (both nondualism and dualism) has attracted the attention of scholars and laymen alike; as a result, we have numerous publications in this vast field. Even if we ignored the so-called popular or nonprofessional writings, the list of publications would be very big. Only a few of them are mentioned here. The Vedānta system is highly metaphysical and tends to be mystical. Because of the dominance of Vedānta in the writings of modern scholars and philosophers, Indian philosophy as a whole has been regarded as deeply metaphysical and mystical. But what has been said above about other systems of philosophy will show that such a belief is based on misconception.

V. Bhattacharya's (1943) excellent study (along with translation) of Gauḍapāda was met with severe criticism from the orthodox Vedantins, for he argued, quite justifiably, that Gauḍapāda was influenced by his deep study of Yogācāra and Mādhyamika Buddhism. Thus, it is that T.M.P. Mahadevan (1952, and many others followed him) expounded the philosophy of Gauḍapāda's Vedānta (the doctrine of nonorigination) showing its connection with earlier Upanisadic literature.

M. Hiriyanna, a scholar and philosopher of the Vedānta school, has written numerous essays, especially on the Advaita school. Several collections of his essays have been published (1952, 1957) and are available to scholars. He has reconstructed the philosophic view of the forgotten Vedantin, Bhartṛprapañca. His examination of the problem of truth and error is illuminating, and his note on the definition of Brahman shows a penetrating analysis. He has also written on Rāmānuja's theory of knowledge and the philosophy of *bhedābheda*. T.R.V. Murti (1958) has written an illuminating paper on the two definitions of Brahman based on the Vivarana text. Murti's interpretation of *avidyā* is also interesting. Both D.H.H. Ingalls (1953) and P. Hacker (1951, 1953) have commented on the question "Whose *avidyā* (ignorance?) is it?" They point out that Śaṃkara carefully avoids such a question. Ingalls (1954) also discusses how Śaṃkara refuted the Yogācāra idealism, and hence, Śaṃkara's philosophy can hardly be called idealism. J. F. Staal (1961) has prepared a very interesting comparative study of Advaita and Neoplatonism. Staal has given some evidence for the historical influence of Indian thought on Neoplatonism. In the introduction, he discusses the method and nature of comparative philosophy.

A. K. Ray Choudhury (1950, 1955) has written two important books on the concept of falsity and error in the Advaita system. Ray Choudhury's treatment is enriched by his sound Sanskrit scholarship and his philosophic insights. Both R. Das (1968) and E. Deutsch (1971) have written short treatises attempting a philosophic reconstruction of the Śaṃkara school from two different points of view. E. Deutsch and J.A.B. van Buitenen (1969) have prepared a sourcebook on Advaita Vedānta, making some earlier translations available for modern students. S. S. Ray's work (1965) is an echo of the usual modern Indian attempt to interpret Śaṃkara in terms of transcendentalism.

D. Venkataramìah (1948) has done an English translation of the *Pañcapādikā* of Padmapāda. B. K. Sengupta (1959) has studied some of the important and fundamental doctrines of the Advaita school in special relation to Vivaraṇa. S. S. Hasurkar (1958) appraises Vācaspati's contribution to the Advaita school. Together, these three works serve as a good introduction to the two subschools of Śaṃkara, *Bhamātī* and *Vivaraṇa*. T.M.P. Mahadevan (1958) has translated into English the *Sambandha-vārttika* of Sureśvara. K. Satchidananda Murty (1959) has prepared a study of the Advaita Vedānta by expouding the Advaita conception of scriptural revelation and the place of reason in the construction of Advaita metaphysics. He offers some critical reflections on the Advaita position.

T. Vetter (1969) has prepared a very scholarly and annoted German translation of Maṇḍanamiśra's *Brahmasiddhi* (Brahmakāṇḍa), and L. Schmithausen (1965) has studied the Indian theory of error based on Maṇḍanamiśra's *Vibhramaviveka*. Both works are important contributions to the study of Maṇḍana's theory of Advaita. K. Cammann (1965) continuing the tradition of P. Hacker, has contributed a scholarly study (in German) of Prakāśātman's doctrine (Vivaraṇa school) of Advaita. S.M.S. Chari (1961) discusses the doctrinal differences between Advaita and Viśiṣṭādvaita, based on the study of Vedāntadeśika's *Śatadūsaṇi*.

K. C. Varadachari (1943) deals with Rāmānuja's theory of knowledge as well as his metaphysics. A. Sengupta (1967) brings her expertise in Sāṁkhya thought to bear on Rāmānuja's Vedānta. Her comparative study of Sāṁkhya and Vedānta (1973) is also interesting. J.A.B. van Buitenen (1956) gives a synoptic view of Rāmānuja's philosophy in the introduction to his edition of *Vedārtha-saṁgraha*. J. B. Carman (1974) deals particularly with the theological aspect of Rāmānuja's thought. Although N. Smart (1969) covers the general field of Indian philosophy, he emphasizes the Vedantic (both Dvaita and Advaita) metaphysical doctrines and their implications for religious and theological thought in India. P. N. Srinivasachari (1934, 1946) has continued his study of Rāmānuja's philosophy; his new books are important contributions.

Of several publications and studies in Madhva's thought, some modern authors merit mention here. K. Narain (1962) has written an outline of Madhva's philosophy, introducing the usual questions that concern Vedānta thought in general: the problem of God and Brahman, the status of *jīva* (man), and the status of the world. Madhva among the Vedantins tends to be avowedly realistic. K. Narain (1964) has prepared another advanced study of Madhva's criticism of Śaṁkara's *advaita* view. B.N.K. Sharma (1962) presents a systematic account of Madhva's Vedānta, presenting his ontology, epistemology, doctrine of self and Brahman, and the general scheme of *sādhanas* ("practices") conducive to devotion and salvation. J. G. Shah (1969) has prepared a study of Vallabha's philosophy of religion and devotionalism.

On Kashmir Śaivism, the following may be mentioned. K. C. Pandey (1954) presents an outline of the history of Śaiva philosophy, a translation of *Iśvara-pratyabhijñā-vimarśinī*, and a short introductory article (1952) on Kashmir Śaivism. R. Gnoli (1957) has prepared an English translation of the *Śivadṛṣti* by Somānanda (Chapter 1). R. K. Kaw (1967) has written on the origin and development of Kashmir Śaivism, calling it the Pratyabhijñā philosophy or the doctrine of recognition. In this connection, we may mention two recent works on Abhinavagupta's philosophy of aesthetics: R. Gnoli (1968, enlarged second edition) and J. Masson and Patwardhan (1968). On Śaiva Siddhānta philosophy, a useful historical introduction has been prepared by K. A. Nilakantha Sastri (1956). S. Dasgupta's Volume 5 (1957) contains a good account of this school. Fortunately, the collected papers of Professor Suryanārāyana Sāstri have been published (1961), and this collection contains several illuminating papers on the different concepts of Śaiva Siddhānta. T.M.P. Mahadevan (1960) has written on the conception of God in Śaiva Siddhānta. The theological aspect of this school is very well developed. M. Dhavamony (1971) has prepared another study on the conception of God and the concept of love and devotion in Śaiva Siddhānta. A. Devasenápati (1958) presents an overall account of the Siddhānta philosophy, and H. J. Piet (1952) has prepared what he calls a logical presentation of Śaivism. K. Sivaraman (1972) emphasizes the philosophical aspects of Śaivism.

SOME MODERN THOUGHTS

Modern philosophic activity in India has not been negligible. Several anthologies of the philosophic writings of modern Indians are mostly by professors of Western philosophy in Indian universities. Some papers in these anthologies contain good philosophic insights and original thought. Only a few philosophers are mentioned here; for the rest, see an article by J. N. Mohanty (1974) in *The Review of Metaphysics*, where Mohanty discusses, in some detail, recent developments in philosophy in India.

Faced with the antimetaphysical thrust of contemporary philosophy, K. Bhattacharya (1972) has attempted to defend metaphysics in the traditional grand style by developing what he calls the concept of reflective awareness. Reflective intuition is distinct from unreflective awareness where the object is given as "fused." Bhattacharya confidently claims that reflective intuition is a better philosophic method than a dogmatic sensuous empiricism. J. N. Mohanty (1972) has done some creative work in the phenomenology of Husserl, noting the relevance of modern philosophic analysis to phenomenology. Mohanty also has concern for descriptive metaphysics. (See his recent *Phenomenology and Ontology*.) He expounds on the concept of intentionality and consciousness, bringing some Indian dimension to the problem. S. Ganguly (1972) criticizes the idea of descriptive metaphysics. He assumes the norm that a metaphysician's description should be unique, and he then argues that no such unique description in metaphysics can be achieved or is possible. He does admit, however, that a description of different conceptual frameworks (purportedly described by metaphysicians) is possible. This is what he calls "meta-description."

Krishna Daya (1966) challenges the historical veracity and validity of the oft-repeated cliché that Indian philosophy was always a means to spiritual salvation. He considers this to be one of the myths about Indian philosophy. Krishna Daya (1969) has also tried to develop a tradition of social philosophy in India, whereby a social philosopher should make his value commitments explicit. In the field of logic and philosophic analysis, Sibajivan Bhattacharya and P. Sen have contributed some interesting papers. While Sibajivan Bhattacharya derives his insight from his study of the problems of Indian logic, P. Sen explicitly concentrates on Western theories. C.T.K. Chari (1966, 1968, 1969) has made an extensive study of the modern philosophy of science. His interest ranges from the foundations of quantum mechanics, information theory, and cybernetics to neurophysiology and psychical research. In all his papers, he seeks to emphasize the importance of recognizing the value of human personality.

CONCLUSION

This essay has been prepared in order to present a comprehensive view of developments in Indian philosophy. For lack of space, this work contains little critical appraisal or assessment of the philosophical thoughts contained in the studies mentioned. In addition, numerous publications, some of which have considerable significance, have been passed over. Again, limitations of space dictated these omissions.

Finally, a few suggestions with regard to the future course of research seem in order here. If philological scholarship is somehow tempered with philosophical insight, we may expect better results in research into classical Indian philosophy. Reliable translations of important classical texts, with proper conceptual analysis, are greatly needed to stimulate further research activity and creative thinking.

SELECT BIBLIOGRAPHY

BOOKS AND ARTICLES

Bagchi, S. *Inductive Reasoning* (Calcutta: Sri M. Sinha, 1953).
———. (Eng. trans.) "Vasubandhu's *Vimśatika,*" *Nava-Nalanda-Research Publications* I (1957).
Baradachari, K. C. *Śrī Rāmānuja's Theory of Knowledge* (Tirupati: Tirumalai, 1943).
Basham, A. L. *History and Doctrines of the Ajivikas* (London: Luzac, 1951).
Bhaduri, S. *Studies in Nyāya-Vaiśeṣika Metaphysics* (Poona: B.O.R. Institute, 1947).
Bhargava, D. *Jaina Ethics* (Delhi: Motilal Banarsidaś, 1968).
Bhatta, G. P. *Epistemology of the Bhāṭṭa School of Purva-Mīmāṃsā* (Varanasi: Chowkhamba, 1962).
Bhattacharya, B. *A Study in Language and Meaning* (Calcutta: Progressive Publishers, 1962).
———. *Yāska's Nirukta and the Science of Etymology* (Calcutta: Mukhopadhyay, 1958).
Bhattacharya, G. "Raghunātha Śiromaṇi on Vyāptipañcaka," *Anvīkṣā* 2 (1967).
———. "Śābdabodha as a Separate Type of Pramāṇa," *Journal of Indian Philosophy* 5 (1977).
———. *Studies in Nyāya-Vaiśeṣika Theism* (Calcutta: Sanskrit College, 1961).
———. "The Concept of Pakṣatā in Navya-nyāya," in *Charvdeva Sastri Felicitation Volume*, 2 vols., eds. Satya Vrat, et al. (Varanasi: Chaukhambha Orientalia, 1974).
———. "Vyadhikaraṇābhāva—A Type of Negation," *Wiener Zeitschrift für die Kunde Süd-und Ostasiens* 19 (1975).
Bhattacharya, J. V. (trans.). "Nyāyamañjarī," serialized in *The Calcutta Review* (1952–1957).
———. *Negation* (Calcutta: Indian Studies Past and Present, 1966).
Bhattacharya, K. *Philosophy, Logic and Language* (Bombay: Allied Publishers, 1965).
———. "Place of the Indefinite in Logic," in *Search for the Absolute in Neo-Vedanta: K. C. Bhattacharya*, ed. G. B. Burch (Honolulu: University Press of Hawaii, 1976).

———. "The Dialectical Method of Nāgārjuna," (trans. of *Vigrahavyāvartani*) *Journal of Indian Philosophy* 1, No. 3 (1971).

———. "The Nature of Reflection in Metaphysics," in *Current Trends in Indian Philosophy*, eds. K. S. Murty, et al. (Waltair: Andhra University Press, 1972).

Bhattacharya, S. "Knowing That One Knows," in *Modern Logic: Its Relevance to Philosophy*, ed. K. Daya (Delhi: Impex India, 1969).

———. "Some Features of Navya-Nyāya Logic," *Philosophy East and West* 3 (1974).

———. "The Middle Term," *Notre Dame Journal of Formal Logic* 9 (1968).

Bhattacharya, T. *The Nature of Vyāpti* (Calcutta: Sanskrit College, 1970).

Bhattacharya, V. *The Agāmaśāstra of Gauḍapāda* (Calcutta: University of Calcutta, 1943).

Biardeau, M. *Theórie de la Connaissance et philosophie de la parole dans le brahmanisme classique* (Paris: Mouton, 1964).

———. (trans.). *Bhartṛhari, Vākyapadīya I* (Paris: Boccard, 1964).

Brough, J. "Audumbarāyaṇa's Theory of Language," *Bulletin of the School of Oriental and African Studies* 14 (1952).

———. "Some Indian Theories of Meanings," *Transactions of the Philological Society* (1953).

———. "Theories of General Linguistics in Sanskrit Grammarians," *Transactions of the Philological Society* (1951).

Cammann, K. *Das System des Advaita nach der Lehre Prakāśātmans* (Wiesbaden: O. Harrassowitz, 1965).

Cardona, G. "Anvaya and Vyatireka in Indian Grammar," *Adyar Library Bulletin* 31–32 (1967–1968).

———. "Cause and Causal Agent: The Pāṇinian View," *Journal of the Oriental Institute (Baroda)* 21 (1971).

———. "Negations in Pāṇinian Rules," *Language* 43 (March, 1967).

———. "Pāṇini's Kārakas: Agency, Animation and Identity," *Journal of Indian Philosophy* 2 (1974).

———. "Pāṇini's Syntactic Categories," *Journal of the Oriental Institute (Baroda)* 16 (1967).

———. "Paraphrase and Sentence Analysis: Some Indian Views," *Journal of Indian Philosophy* 3 (1975).

Carman, J. B. *The Theology of Rāmānuja* (New Haven, Conn.: Yale University Press, 1974).

Chan, W. T. (trans.). *The Platform Scripture* (New York: St. John's University, 1963).

Chari, C.T.K. "A Note on Some Computer Programs and Recursive Unsolvability," *Methodology and Science* (July 1968).

———. "Human Personality in East-West Perspectives," in *Philosophy, Religion and the Coming World Civilization. Essays in Honor of William Ernest Hocking*, ed. L. S. Rouner (The Hague: Nijhoff, 1966).

———. "Logical Issues About the Canonical Formalism in Classical and Quantum Mechanics," in *Modern Logic, Its Relevance to Philosophy*, ed. K. Daya, et al. (Delhi: Impex India, 1969).

———. "On the Dialectical Affinities Between East and West," *Philosophy East and West* 3–4 (1954).

———. "Quantum Physics and East-West Rapprochement," *Philosophy East and West* 5 (1955).

Chari, S.M.S. *Advaita and Viśiṣṭādvaita* (Delhi: Asia Publishing House, 1961).

Chatterjee, A. K. *Yogācāra Idealism* (Varanasi: Banaras Hindu University, 1962).

Chatterjee, S. C. *The Nyāya Theory of Knowledge* (Calcutta: University of Calcutta, 1950).

Chatterji, K. C. *Patañjali's Mahābhāṣya: Paspasāhnika* (Calcutta: Mukherjee, 1957).

Chattopadhyaya, D. *Lokāyāta: A Study of Ancient Indian Materialism* (New Delhi: People's Publishing, 1959).

Chemparathy, G. *An Indian Rational Theology* (Vienna: De Nobili Research Library, 1972).

Chi, R.S.Y. *Buddhist Formal Logic* (London: Royal Asiatic Society of Great Britain and Ireland, 1969).

Choudhury, A. K. Ray. *Self and Falsity in Advaita Vedānta* (Calcutta: Progressive Publishers, 1955).

464   Asia

. *The Doctrine of Māyā*, 2d ed. (Calcutta: Das Gupta, 1950).

Comman, K. *Das System des Advaita nach der Lehre Prakāśātnams* (Wiesbaden: Münchener Indologische Studien, 1965).

Conze, E. (trans.). *Abhisamayālankāra* Serie Orientale Rome, 6 (Rome: Instituto italiano per el Melio ed Estremo Oriente, 1954).

———. (trans.). *Aṣṭasāhasrikā prajñāpāramitā* (Calcutta: The Asiatic Society, 1958).

———. *Buddhism, Its Essence and Development* (New York: Philosophical Library, 1954).

———. *Buddhist Texts Through the Ages* (New York: Philosophical Library, 1954).

———. *Buddhist Thought in India* (London: Allen and Unwin, 1962).

———. *Buddhist Wisdom Books* (London: Allen and Unwin, 1958).

———. "The Iconography of the Prajñāpāramitā II," *Oriental Art* 3 (1951).

———. (trans.). *The Large Sutra on Perfect Wisdom* (London: Luzac, 1961-   ).

———. "The Ontology of the *Prajñāpāramitā*," *Philosophy East and West* 3 (1953).

———. *The Prajñāpāramitā Literature* ('S-Gravenhage: Mouton, 1960).

Danielou, A. *Yoga: The Method of Re-integration* (London: Johnson, 1949).

Das, R. *Introduction to Shankara* (Calcutta: K. L. Mukhopadhyay, 1968).

Dasgupta, S. B. *An Introduction to Tantric Buddhism* (Calcutta: University of Calcutta, 1950).

———. *Obscure Religious Cults of Bengal*, 2d ed. (Calcutta: K. L. Mukhopadhyay, 1962).

Dasgupta, S. *A History of Indian Philosophy*, 5 vols. (Cambridge: University Press, 1922–1957).

Davies, J. *The Sānkhya Kārikā of Iswara Krishna*, 2d ed. (Calcutta: Sushil Gupta, 1957).

Daya, K. "Active and Contemplative Values," *Philosophy and Phenomenological Research* 29 (1969).

———. *Social Philosophy: Past and Future* (Simla: I.I.A.S., 1969).

———. "Three Myths About Indian Philosophy," *Diogenes* 55 (1966).

———, et al. (eds.). *Modern Logic: Its Relevance to Philosophy* (Delhi: Impex India, 1969).

Deutsch, E. *Advaita Vedānta* (Honolulu: East-West Press, 1969).

——— and J.A.B. van Buitenen. *A Sourcebook of Advaita-Vedānta* (Honolulu: University of Hawaii Press, 1971).

Devasenapati, A. *Śaiva-Siddhānta* (Madras: University of Madras, 1958).

Devasthali, G. V. *Mīmāṃsā: The Vakya-śastra of Ancient India* (Bombay: Booksellers Publishing, 1959).

Dhavamony, M. *Love of God According to Śaiva-Siddhānta* (Oxford: Clarendon Press, 1971).

Dixit, K. K. *Jaina Ontology* (Ahmedabad: L. D. Institute of Indology, 1971).

Dravid, R. S. *The Problem of Universals in Indian Philosophy* (Delhi: Matilal Benarsidas, 1972).

Edgerton, F. *The Beginnings of Indian Philosophy* (Cambridge, Mass.: Harvard University Press, 1965).

Eliade, M. *Yoga: Immortality and Freedom*, trans. W. R. Trask (New York: Pantheon Books, 1958).

Frauwallner, E. "Amalavijñānam und Ālayavijñānam, Ein Beitrag zur Erkenntnislehre des Buddhisimus," in *Festschrift Walther Schubring: Beiträge zur indischen Philologie und Altertumskunde* (Hamburg: W. De Gruyter, 1951).

———. *Die Philosophie des Buddhismus* (Berlin: Akademie-Verlag, 1956).

———. "Diṅnāga, sein Werk und seine Entwicklung," *Wiener Zeitschrift für die Kunde Süd-und Ostasiens* 3 (1959).

———. *Geschichte der indischen Philosophie*, 2 vols. (Salzburg: O. Müller, 1956).

———. *Materialien zur Ältesten Erkenntnislehre der Karmamīmāṃsā* (Vienna: Herman Böhlaus, 1968).

———. "Sprechtheorie und Philosophie im Mahābhāṣya des Patañjali," *Wiener Zeitschrift für die Kunde Süd-und Ostasiens* 4 (1960).

———. "Vasubandhu's Vādavidhi," *Wiener Zeitschrift für die Kunde Süd-und Ostasiens* 1 (1957).

———. "Zur Erkenntnislehre des Klassischen Sāṃkhya-systems," *Wiener Zeitschrift für die Kunde Süd-und Ostasiens* 2 (1958).

Gangopadhyay, M. K. and Chattopadhyay, D. *Nyāya Philosophy Parts I, II, and III.* (Calcutta: Indian Studies Past and Present, 1967–1972).

Ganguly, H. N. *Philosophy of Logical Construction* (Calcutta: Sanskrit Pustak Bhander, 1963).

Ganguly, S. "Descriptive Metaphysics," in *Current Trends in Indian Philosophy*, ed. K. S. Murtz, et al. (Waltair: Andhra University Press, 1972).

Gelblum, T. "Sāṃkhya and Sartre," *Journal of Indian Philosophy* 1 (1970).

Geokoop, C. *The Logic of Invariable Concomitance in the Tattvacintāmaṇi* (Dordrecht: Reidel, 1967).

Gnoli, R. "*Sivadṛsti* by Somānanda, Chapter I," *East and West* 8 (1957).

————. *The Aesthetic Experience according to Abhinavagupta*, 2d ed. (Varanasi: Chow Khamba, 1968).

Guenther, H. V. "Buddhist Mysticism," in *Encyclopedia Britannica*, III (Chicago: Encyclopedia Britannica, 1974).

————. *Philosophy and Psychology in the Abhidharma* (Lucknow: Buddha Vihara, 1957), 2d rev. ed. (Boulder, Colo.: Shambhala Publications, 1974).

————. (trans.). *The Jewel Ornament of Liberation* (London: Rider, 1959).

————. *Tibetan Biddhism Without Mystification* (Leiden: Brill, 1966).

Guha, D. C. *Navya-nyāya System of Logic* (Varanasi: Bh. Vidya, 1968).

Hacker, P. "Eigentumlichkeiten der Lehre und Terminologie Śaṃkaras: Avidyā, Nāmarūpa, Māyā, Iśvara," *Zeitschrift der Deutschen Morgenlandische Gesellschaft* 100 (1951).

————. *Vivarta: Studien zur Geschichte der illustionistischen Kasmologie und Erkenntnistheorie der Inder* Abhandlungen der Geistes-und Sozialwiss-schaftlichen Klasse, No. 5 (Wiesbaden: Akademie der Wissenschaften und der Litteratur in Mainz, 1953).

Hasurkar, S. S. *Vācaspati Miśra on Advaita Vedānta* (Darbhanga: Mithila Institute, 1958).

Hattori, M. *Dignāga: On Perception*, Harvard Oriental Series (Cambridge, Mass.: Harvard University Press, 1968).

Herzberger, H. "Double Negation in Buddhist Logic," *Journal of Indian Philosophy* 3, Nos. 1–2 (1975).

Hiriyanna, M. *Hiriyanna Commemoration Volume*, eds. N. S. Sastry and G. H. Rao (Mysore: Kavyalaya, 1952).

————. *Indian Philosophical Studies* (Mysore: Kavyalaya, 1957).

Inada, K. *Nāgārjuna: A Translation of His Mūlamādhyamakakārikā* (Tokyo: Hokuseido Press, 1970).

Ingalls, D.H.H. *Materials for the Study of Navya-nyāya Logic* (Cambridge, Mass.: Harvard University Press, 1951).

————. "Śaṃkara on the Question: Whose Is Avidyā," *Philosophy East and West* 3, No. 7 (1953).

————. "Śaṃkara's Arguments Against the Buddhists," *Philosophy East and West* 3 (1954).

Iyer, K.A.S. *Bhartṛhari: A Study* (Poona: Deccan College, 1969).

———— (trans.). *The Vākyapadīya of Bhartṛhari with Vṛtti, Chapter I*, Eng. trans. (Poona: Deccan College, 1965).

———— (trans.). *The Vākyapadīya of Bhartṛhari with Vṛtti, Chapter III, Part ii*, Eng. trans. (Delhi: Motilal Banarsidas, 1974).

Jaini, P. S. (ed.) *Abhidharmapradīpa* Tibetan Sanskrit series 4 (Patna: n.p., 1959).

Jayatilleke, K. N. *Early Buddhist Theory of Knowledge* (London: Allen and Unwin, 1963).

Jha, J. *Pūrva-Mīmāṃsā and its Sources* (Benares: Benares Hindu University, 1942).

Joshi, S. D. (ed. and trans.). *Patañjali's Vyākaraṇa Mahabhāṣya*, I–V (Poona: University of Poona, 1968–1974).

————. (trans.). *The Sphoṭanirṇaya* (Poona: University of Poona, 1967).

Kajiyama, Y. *An Introduction to Buddhist Philosophy* (Kyoto: Kyoto University, 1966).

————. "Bhāvaviveka and the Prāsaṅgika School," *The Nava Nalanda-Mahāvihāra Research Publication* I (1957).

————. "Bhavaviveka's Prajñāpradīpah (1 Kapitel). Fortsetzung," *Wiener Zeitschrift für die Kunde Süd-und Ost-Asiens und Archiv für indische Philosophie* 8 (1964).

————. "Buddhist Solipsism; a free translation of Ratnakiri's *Saṃtanantaradūsana*," *Journal of Indian and Buddhist Studies* 13, No. 1 (1965).

————. "Three Kinds of Affirmation and Two Kinds of Negation in Buddhist Philosophy," *Wiener Zeitschrift für die Kunde Süd-und Ostasiens* 17 (1973).

————. *Trikapañcakacintā, Miscellanea Indologica Kiotiensia*, Nos. 4–5 (1963).

Kalupahana, D. J. *Causality: The Central Philosophy of Buddhism* (Honolulu: University Press of Hawaii, 1975).

Kaw, R. K. *The Doctrine of Recognition* (Hoshiarpar, India: V. Institute, 1967).

Kitagawa, H. "A Note on the Methodology in the Study of Indian Logic," *Journal of Indian and Buddhist Studies* 8, No. 1 (1960).

Kunst, A. "Kamalaśīla's Commentary on Śāntarakṣita's Amumānaparīkṣā," *Mélanges Chinois et Bouddhiques* 5 (1947).

————. "The Concept of the Principle of Excluded Middle in Buddhism," *Rocznik Orientalistyczny* 21 (1957).

————. "Two Membered Syllogism," *Rocznik Orientalistyczny* 15 (1948).

Lamotte, E. *Histoire du bouddhisme indien* (Louvain: Publications Universitaires, Institut Orientaliste, 1958).

————. *La traité de la grande vertu de sagesse de Nāgārjuna*, 3 vols. (Louvain: Bureaux du Muséon, 1944–1970).

————. *L'Enseignment de Vimalakīrtī* (Louvain: Publications Universitaires, Institut Orientaliste, 1962).

Larson, G. J. *Classical Sāṃkhya* (Delhi: Motilal Banarsidass, 1969).

Ling, T. *The Buddha: Buddhist Civilization in India and Ceylon* (London: Temple Smith, and New York: Scribner's, 1973).

Mahadevan, T.M.P. *Gauḍapāda: A Study in Early Advaita* (Madras: University of Madras, 1952).

————. "Religion and Philosophy of Saivism," in *The History and Culture of the Indian People* (Bombay: B. V. Bhavan, 1960).

————. (trans.). *The Saṃbandha-Vārttika of Sureśvarācārya* (Madras: University of Madras, 1958).

Malvania, D. (ed.). *Pramaṇavarttika by Dharmakīrti, Introduction* (Varanasi: Benares Hindu University, 1959).

Masson, J. and Patwardhan. *Abhinavagupta's Philosophy of Aesthetics* (Poona: B.O.R. Institute, 1968).

Matilal, B. K. "A Critique of Buddhist Idealism," in *Buddhist Studies in Honour of I. B. Horner*, eds. L. Cousins, K. R. Norman, and A. Kunst (Dordrecht and Boston: Reidel, 1974).

————. *Epistemology, Logic and Grammar in Indian Philosophical Analysis* (The Hague: Mouton, 1971).

————. "Gaṅgeśa on the Concept of Universal Property," in *Proceedings of the 3rd International Congress for Logic, Methodology, and Philosophy of Science*, ed. B. van Rootselaar (Amsterdam: North-Holland, 1968).

————. "Indian Theorists on the Nature of the Sentence," *Foundations of Language* 2 (1966).

————. "Jagadīśa's Classification of Grammatical Categories," in *Sanskrit and Indological Studies Dr. V. Raghavan Felicitation Volume*, eds. R. N. Dandakar, et al. (Delhi: Motilal Banarsidass, 1975).

————. "Mysticism and Reality: Ineffability," *Journal of Indian Philosophy* 3, Nos. 3–4 (1975).

————. "Nyāya-Vaiśesika" in *A History of Indian Literature*, VI, Fasc. 2, ed. J. Gonda (Wiesbaden: O. Harrassowitz, 1977).

————. "On Navya-nyāya Logic of Property and Location," *Proceedings of the 1975 International Symposium of Multiple-valued Logic* (Bloomington, Ind.: Indiana University, 1975).

————. "Ontological Problems in Nyāya, Buddhism and Jainism," *Journal of Indian Philosophy* 5, Nos. 1–2 (1977).

————. *The Central Philosophy of Jainism: Anekāntavāda* (Ahmedabad: L. D. Institute of Indology, 1978).

————. *The Logical Illumination of Indian Mysticism. An Inaugural Lecture* (Oxford: Clarendon Press, 1977).

————. *The Navya-nyāya Doctrine of Negation* (Cambridge, Mass.: Harvard University Press, 1968).

May, J. "Kant et le Madhyamika," *Indo-Iranian Journal* 3 (1959).

McDermott, A.C.S. *An Eleventh-Century Buddhist Logic of 'Exist'. Foundations of Language*, Supplementary Series (Dordrecht: Reidel, 1969).

Mittal, K. K. *Materialism in Indian Thought* (Delhi: Munsiram, 1974).

Mohanty, J. N. *Gaṅgeśa's Theory of Truth* (Santiniketan: Visva-Bharati, 1966).

————. *Phenomenology and Ontology* (Boston: Kluwer, 1970).

————. "Philosophy in India, 1967–1973," *Review of Metaphysics* 28 (1974).

————. *The Concept of Intentionality* (St. Louis, Mo.: Warren Green, 1972).

Mookerjee, S. "The Absolutist's Standpoint in Logic," *The Nava Nalanda-Mahāvihāra Research Publication* 1 (1957).

———— and Nagasaki, H. "The *Pramāṇavārttikam* of Dharmakīrti," *The Nava Nalanda-Mahāvihāra Research Publication* 4 (1964).

Mukhopadhyay, P. K. "Cognitive Act," *Journal of Indian Philosophy* 2 (1973).

Murti, T.R.V. *The Central Philosophy of Buddhism*, 2d ed. (London: Allen and Unwin, 1960).

————. *The Jaina Philosophy of Non-Absolutism* Jaina Series No. 2 (Calcutta: Bhāratī Mahāvidyālaya Publications, 1944).

————. "The Two Definitions of Brahman in the Advaita," in *K. C. Bhattacharya Memorial Volume* (Amalner: Indian Institute of Philosophy, 1958).

Murty, K. S. *Revelation and Reason in Advaita Vedanta* (London: Asian Publishing House, 1959).

Nagao, M. (ed.). *Madhyāntavibhā(ṅ) gasūtra* (Tokyo: Suzuki Research Foundation, 1964).

Nagatomi, M. "The Framework of the *Pramāṇa Varttika*," *Journal of the American Oriental Society* 78, No. 4 (1959).

Nakamura, H. "Buddhist Logic Expounded by Means of Symbolic Logic," *Indogaku-Bukkyōgāku Ken Kyū* 7, No. 1 (1958).

Nanamoli (trans.). *The Path of Purification* (Ceylon: Semage, 1956).

Narain, K. *A Critique of Mādhva Refutation of the Śaṁkara School of Vedānta* (Allahabad: Udayan Publishers, 1964).

————. *An Outline of Mādhva Philosophy* (Allahabad: Udayan Publishers, 1962).

Oberhammer, G. "The Authorship of the *Ṣaṣṭitantram*," *Wiener Zeitschrift für die Kunde Süd-und Ostasiens* 4 (1960).

Padmarajiāh, Y. J. *A Comparative Study of the Jaina Theories of Reality and Knowledge* (Bombay: Jaina Sahitya Vikas Mandal, 1963).

Pandey, K. C. (trans.). "Iśvara-Pratyabhijñā-Vimarśinī," in *Bhāskarī*, III, Eng. trans., The Princess of Wales Saraswati Bhavan Texts, No. 84 (Benares: Government Sanskrit Library, 1954).

————. "Kashmir Śaivism," in *History of Philosophy Eastern and Western*, ed. S. Radhakrishnan (London: Allen and Unwin, 1952).

Pandey, R. C. *The Problem of Meaning in Indian Philosophy* (Delhi: Motilal Banarsidass, 1963).

Piet, H. J. *A Logical Presentation of Śaiva Siddhanta Philosophy* (Madras: Christian Literature Society for India, 1952).

Pillai, R. *The Vākyapadīya Cantos I and II*, Eng. trans. (Delhi: Motilal Banarsidass, 1971).

Potter, K. H. "An Ontology of Concrete Connectors," *Journal of Philosophy* 58, No. 3 (1961).

————. "Are the Vaiśeṣika Guṇas Qualities?" *Philosophy East and West* 5 (1954–1955).

————. *Bibliography of Indian Philosophies* (Delhi: Motilal Banarsidass, 1970).

————. *Indian Metaphysics and Epistemology: The Tradition of Nyaya-Vaise-ṣika up to Gangesa* (Princeton, N.J.: Princeton University Press, 1977).

————. *Presuppositions of India's Philosophies* (Englewood Cliffs, N.J.: Prentice-Hall, 1963).

————. "Realism, Speech-Acts and Truth-Gaps in Indian and Western Philosophy," *Journal of Indian Philosophy* 1 (1970).

————. *The Padārthatattvanirūpanam of Raghunātha Śiromaṇi* (Cambridge, Mass.: Harvard-Yenching Institute, 1957).

Radhakrishnan, S. *Indian Philosophy*, 2 vols., 2d ed. (New York: Humanities Press, 1929).

Raja, C. K. *Introduction to Ślokavarttika-vyakhya*, ed. S.K.R. Sastri, Madras University Sanskrit Series 13 (Madras: University of Madras, 1940).

Raja, K. *Indian Theories of Meaning* (Madras: Adyar Library, 1963).

Ratnakirti. *Ratnakirti-nibandhāvalī*, ed. A. Thakur Tibetan Sanskrit Works Series, III (Patna: Kashi Prasad Jayaswal Research Institute, 1957).

Renou, L. *Études Vediques et Pāninnennes* (Paris: Boccard, 1956–).

———. "Les speculations sur le langage," in *L'Inde Classique*, II, eds. L. Renou and J. Filliozat (Paris and Hanoi: École Française d'Extrême-Orient, 1953).

———. "Pāṇini," in *Current Trends in Linguistics*, V, ed. T. A. Sebeok, et al. (The Hague: Mouton, 1969).

———. "Philosophie grammaticale," in *L'Inde Classique*, II, eds. L. Renou and J. Filliozat (Paris and Hanoi: École Française d'Extrême-Orient, 1953).

———. *Terminologie grammaticale du Sanskrit* (Paris: H. Champion, 1957).

Riepe, D. "Early Indian Hedonism," *Philosophy and Phenomenological Research* 16 (1956).

———. *The Naturalistic Tradition in Indian Thought* (Seattle: University of Washington Press, 1961).

Robinson, R. *Early Mādhyamika in India and China* (Madison, Wis.: University of Wisconsin Press, 1967).

Rocher, R. " 'Agent' et 'objet' chez Pāṇini," *Journal of the American Oriental Society* 84 (1964).

———. "Bhāva 'etat' et Kriyā 'action' chez Pāṇini," in *Recherche linguistiques en Belgique*, ed. Y. Lebou (Wetteren: Universa, 1966).

Roy, S. S. *The Heritage of Śankara* (Allahabad: Udayana Publishers, 1965).

Ruben, W. "Über den Tattvopaplavasimha des Jayarāśī Bhatta, eine agnostizistische Erkenntnis-kritik," *Wiener Zeitschrift für die Kunde Süd-und Ostasiens* 2 (1958).

Ruegg, D. S. "Ārya Bhadanta Vimuktisena on the gotra-theory of the Prajñāparamitā," *Wiener Zeitschrift für die Kunde Süd-und Ost-Asiens und Archiv für indische Philosophie* 12/13 (1968–1969).

———. *Contributions à l'histoire de la philosophie linguistique indienne* (Paris: Boccard, 1959).

———. *La théorie du tathāga thābha et du Gotra*. Publications de l'Ecole française d'extreme-Orient (Paris: Adrian-Maisonneuve, n.d.).

———. "The Uses of the Four Positions of the Catuskoti and the Problem of the Description of Reality in Mahāyāna Buddhism," *Journal of Indian Philosophy* 5 (1977).

Sanghavi, P. S. *Advanced Studies in Indian Logic and Metaphysics* (Calcutta: Indian Studies Past and Present, 1961).

Sarachchandra, F. *Buddhist Psychology of Perception* (Colombo: Ceylon University Press, 1958).

———. "From Vasubandhu to Śāntaraksita," *Journal of Indian Philosophy* 4, Nos. 1–2 (1976).

Sastri, G. N. *The Philosophy of Word and Meaning* (Calcutta: Sanskrit College, 1959).

Sastri, K.A.N. "A Historical Introduction to Śaivism," in *The Cultural Heritage of India*, IV (Calcutta: Ramakrishna Mission, Institute of Culture, 1956).

Sastri, S. *Collected Papers of Prof. Suryanārayan Sastri*, ed. T.M.P. Mahadevan (Madras: University of Madras, 1961).

Scharfe, H. *Die Logik im Mohabhāsya* (Berlin: Akademie Verlag, 1961).

———. *Māṇḍanamiśra's Vibhramavivekah* (Vienna: Osterreichische Akademie, 1965).

Schmithausen, L. *Der Nirvana-Abschnitt in der Viniscayasamgrahani der Yogacarabhumih* (Vienna: Herman Bohlaus, 1969).

———. *Máṇḍanamiśia's Vibhramavivekah* (Vienna; Österreichische Akademie, 1965).

Sen, P. "Entailment, Necessity and Formal Implication," *Journal of the Indian Academy of Philosophy* 6 (1967).

———. "The Problem of Entailment," in *Modern Logic: Its Relevance to Philosophy*, ed. K. Daya, et al. (Delhi: Impex India, 1969).

Sengupta, A. *A Critical Study of the Philosophy of Rāmānuja* (Varanasi: Chowkhamba, 1967).

———. *Śaṃkhya and Advaita Vedānta* (Lucknow: Monoranjan Sen, 1973).

————. *The Evolution of the Sāmkhya School of Thought* (Lucknow: Pioneer, 1959).

Sengupta, B. K. *A Critique on the Vivaraṇa School* (Calcutta: K. L. Mukhopadhyay, 1959).

Shah, J. G. *Srimad Vallabhācharya: His Philosophy and Religion* (Wadiad: Pusthimargiya, 1969).

Shah, N. *Akalaṅka's Criticism of Dharmakīrtī's Philosophy* (Ahmedabad: L. D. Institute of Indology, 1967).

Sharma, B.N.K. *Philosophy of Madhvācarya* (Bombay: Bhavan, 1962).

Sharma, C. D. *Indian Philosophy: A Critical Survey*, rev. ed. (New York: Barnes and Noble, 1962).

Sharma, D. *The Differentiation Theory of Meaning in Indian Logic* (The Hague: Mouton, 1969).

Shastri, D. N. *A Short History of Indian Materialism, Hedonism and Sensualism* (Calcutta: Bookland Private, 1957).

————. *Critique of Indian Realism* (New Delhi: Motilal Banarsidass, 1964).

Shefts, B. *Grammatical Method in Pāṇini: His Treatment of Sanskrit Present Stems* (New Haven, Conn.: American Oriental Society, 1961).

Sinha, J. *A History of Indian Philosophy*, 2 vols. (Calcutta: Sinha Publishing, 1952–1956).

————. *Indian Psychology: Cognition*, I (Calcutta: Mukhopadhyay, 1958).

Sivaraman, K. *Śaivism in Philosophical Perspective* (Delhi: Motilal Banarsidass, 1972).

Smart, N. *Doctrine and Argument in Indian Philosophy* (London: Allen and Unwin, 1969).

Snellgrove, D. L. (trans.). *The Hevajra Tantra. Part I* (London: Oxford University Press, 1959).

Solomon, E. *Sāmkhya-Vṛtti* (Ahmedabad: Gujarat University, 1973).

————. *The Commentaries of the Sāmkhya Kārikā—A Study* (Ahmedabad: Gujarat University, 1974).

Srinivasachari, P. N. *The Philosophy of Bhedābheda*, 2d ed. (Madras: Adyar Library, 1950).

————. *The Philosophy of Viśiṣṭādvaita* (Madras: Adyar Library, 1946).

Staal, F. *Exploring Mysticism* (Berkeley, Calif.: University of California Press, 1975).

Staal, J. F. *Advaita and Neoplatonism: A Critical Study in Comparative Philosophy* (Madras: University of Madras, 1961).

————. "Analyticity," *Foundations of Language* 2 (1966).

————. "Contraposition in Indian Logic," in *Logic, Methodology and Philosophy of Science: Proceedings of the 1960 International Congress*, eds. E. Nagel, P. Suppes, and A. Tarski (Stanford, Calif.: Stanford University Press, 1962).

————. "Euclid and Pāṇini," *Philosophy East and West* 15 (1965).

————. "Indian Semantics, I," *Journal of the American Oriental Society* 86 (1966).

————. "Negation and the Law of Contradiction in Indian Thought," *Bulletin of the School of Oriental and African Studies* 25 (1962).

————. "Review of Scharfe," *Journal of the American Oriental Society* 83 (1963).

————. "Review of Ruegg," *Philosophy East and West* 10 (1960).

————. "The Concept of 'Paksa' in Indian Logic," *Journal of Indian Philosophy* 2 (1973).

————. "The Theory of Definition in Indian Logic," *Journal of the American Oriental Society* 81 (1961).

————. *Word-Order in Sanskrit and Universal Grammar* (Dordrecht: Reidel, 1967).

———— and Kiparsky, P. "Syntactic and Semantic Relations in Pāṇini," *Foundations of Language: International Journal of Language and Philosophy* 5 (1969).

Steinkellner, E. *Dharmakīrti's Hetubinduḥ* (Vienna: Hermann Böhlaus, 1967).

————. *Dharmakīrti's Pramāṇaviniścaya II* (Vienna: Verlag der Österreichischen Akademie der Wissenschaften, 1973).

Streng, F. *Emptiness: A Study in Religious Meaning* (Nashville and New York: Abingdon Press, 1967).

Tachikawa, M. "A Sixth-Century Manual of Indian Logic," (trans. of the *Nyāyapraveśa*) *Journal of Indian Philosophy* 1, No. 2 (1971).

Takasaki, J. *A Study on the Ratnagotravibhāga (Uttaratantra)* (Rome: Istituto italiano per il Medio de Extremo Oriente, 1966).

Tatia, N. *Studies in Jaina Philosophy* (Banaras: Jain Cultural Research Society, 1951).

Thieme, P. "*Pāṇini and the Pāṇinīyas*," *Journal of the American Oriental Society* 76 (1956).

van Buitenen, J.A.B. "Studies in Sāṃkhya I," *Journal of the American Oriental Society* 76 (1956).

———. "Studies in Sāṃkhya II," *Journal of the American Oriental Society* 77 (1957).

——— (ed. and trans.). *Vedārthasaṃgraha of Rāmānuja* (Poona: Deccan College, 1956).

Varadachari, K. C. *Śrī Rāmanuja's Theory of Knowledge* (Tirupati: Tirumalai-Devasthanams Press, 1943).

Venkataramiah, D. *Śāstradīpikā of Pārthasārathi Miśra* (Baroda: Oriental Institute, 1940).

———. *The Pañcapādikā of Padmapāda* (Baroda: Oriental Institute, 1948).

Venkataramanan, K. "Āśrayaprajñaptiśāstra" *Visva-Bharati* Annals V (Sāntiniketan: Visvabharati, 1953).

———. *Nāgārjuna's Philosophy as Presented in the Maha-Prajñāpāramitā-śāstra* (Rutland, Vermont: Charles E. Tuttle, 1966; and Banaras: Bharatiya Vidya Prakashan, 1971).

———. (trans.). "Sammitīyanikayaśāstra (Abhedharma)," *Visva-Bharati Annals V* (Santiniketan: Visvabharati, 1953).

Vetter, T. *Dharmakīrti's Prāmaṇaviniścaya I* (Vienna: Akademie, 1966).

———. *Enkenntnisprobleme bei Dharmakīrti* (Vienna: Akademie, 1964).

———. *Maṇḍana Miśra's Brahmasiddhiḥ* (Vienna: Hermann Böhlaus, 1969).

von Glasenapp, H. V. *Der Jainismus, Eine indische Erlösungsreligion* (Berlin: Alf Häger, 1925).

Warder, A. K. *Indian Biddhism* (Delhi: Motilal Banarsidass, 1970).

———. "On the Relationship Between Early Buddhism and Other Contemporary Systems," *Bulletin of the School of Oriental and African Studies* 18 (1956).

———. "The Earliest Indian Logic," *Trudi Dvadtsat Pyatogo Mejdunarodnogo Kongressa Vostokovedov*, IV (1963).

Wayman, A. "Buddhist Dependent Origination and the Sāṃkhya *guṇas*," *Ethnos* 27 (1962).

———. "Buddhist Sanskrit and the Sāṃkhya Kārikā," *Journal of Indian Philosophy* 2 (1974).

——— and Wayman, H. *The Lion's Roar of Queen Srīmālā* English trans. of Śrī-Mala Sutra (New York: Columbia University Press, 1974).

Werner, K. *Yoga and Indian Philosophy* (Delhi: Motilal Banarsidass, 1977).

Zimmer, H. *Philosophies of India* (New York: Pantheon Books, 1951).

JOURNALS

Chintana
Darshana International
Indian Philosophical Journal
Indian Philosophical Quarterly (The Philosophical Quarterly)
Indian Philosophy and Culture
Indian Review of Philosophy
Journal of the American Oriental Society
Journal of Indian Philosophy
Journal of the Indian Institute of Philosophy
Journal of the Oriental Institute
Journal of the Philosophical Association
Mahajanmer Lagna
Philosophical Quarterly
Philosophy East and West
University Journal of Philosophy
Visva-Bharati Journal of Philosophy
Vivechana
Wiener Zeitschrift für die Kunde Süd-und Ost Asiens und Archiv für indische Philosophie

Japan

TOMIO ICHIYANAGI

I

This essay follows the development of philosophy in Japan since 1945 in the form of a general survey. It focuses on the phase that shows how philosophy in Japan concerns the Japanese tradition of mind and culture. Philosophy has only a one hundred year history in Japan amidst a Japanese tradition of over one thousand years. In this short paper, it has been necessary to limit the discussion to theoretical philosophy and to ignore religious ideas unique to Japan today, such as those of Buddhism, Shintoism, or Christianity.

The word *"tetsugaku,"* which means philosophy in Japanese, was finally coined as a Japanese equivalent by Nishi Amane (1829–1897) in 1874. Thus, the word that strictly indicates "philosophy" has been in existence only a little over a hundred years in Japan. While other sciences in Japan also have a short history, they have registered such remarkable achievements during this short one hundred-year history that some have attained worldwide stature. In the case of philosophy, however, circumstances were not so simple. Unlike the other sciences, philosophy cannot be confined within simplified principles and rules. Philosophy has built up its traditions of over two thousand years in Europe through transitions of societies and ages, namely, along with human history. Consequently, in Japan, which has not shared these traditions, the main thrust has been to gain experience in thinking about philosophical ideas through considering them in theory, accepting them as mere historical and ready-made results.

Yet, it seems impossible to master these philosophical thoughts apart from the historical experience in Europe. Because of this lack of historical experience, philosophy in Japan has developed in two different, though overlapping, ways. The first development originated in the attitude espoused by Tokyo University which sought to follow the historical experience in Europe from the beginning within a philosophical framework. The main stream of academic philosophy in Japan for the past one hundred years was composed of these minute historical studies of European philosophy. The second development stemmed from the attitude espoused by Kyoto University, under the guidance of Nishida Kitarō (1870–1945), which sought to build up philosophy in Japan to the European level by means of the Japanese, rather than the European, historical experience.

The first school accepted European philosophy as such and pursued the complete intellectual understanding of it as its primary task. The second school instead attempted to systematize those philosophical thoughts, which acceptance of European philosophy cultivated, through the Japanese historical experience. Of course it is this latter way that is proper to philosophy. In Japan where acquaintance with systematic knowledge in the form of "philosophy" had been made just one hundred years ago, it was extremely difficult to use such an imported cultural form to explicate the philosophical significance and generality implicit in the unique Japanese historical experience and cultural tradition. Those efforts by which Nishida and others undertook to overcome this difficulty left everlasting traces in the history of philosophy in Japan.

For Japan, philosophy presents an odd dual problem. On the one hand, the problem is to get rid of the traditional Buddhist and Confucianist ways of thinking through the acceptance of the philosophical tradition of Europe; on the other hand, the problem is to aim at a more comprehensive way of thinking. This dual problem was not peculiar to philosophy but rather characterized all other fields in modern Japan which sought to achieve Europeanization late in the nineteenth century. This has been a fatal problem during Japan's modern history.

Because of its acknowledgment of the power of European science and technology, Japan at last ended the isolation policy it had adopted in the first half of the seventeenth century. From then on, Japan's basic policy was *fukoku-kyohei* (national prosperity and defense), that is, to lose no time in possessing national power equal to that of the European nations by equipping itself with European science and technology. We hear the phrase "*wakon-yōsai*" (Japanese mind with European science), which expresses the basic character of modern education in Japan. The source of this phrase is "*wakon-kansai*" (Japanese mind with Chinese science) which originated in the ninth century when Japan was building up its constitution and culture through long assimilation of Chinese culture. Thus considered, these phrases can be said to symbolize the cultural destiny of Japan, the small islands in the Far East.

If philosophy is an indispensable factor in the achievements of a human culture, this cultural destiny is inevitably that of philosophy in Japan. So far as the building up of nation and culture in ancient Japan was carried out under the fundamental influences of Chinese culture, Chinese and Indian philosophy, which dominated religious thought in China, must have played an indispensable role in the development of ancient Japanese culture. Under the same conditions, European philosophy has played one and the same role in modern Japan. Nevertheless, Japanese culture is not Chinese, Indian, or European but just Japanese, and so realizes *wakon* (Japanese mind) at all times. Therefore, there must be a "Japanese philosophy" borne by *wakon*. In Japan, however, this name indicates only an ultranationalist philosophy that would criticize and refuse European citizenship dogmatically and display the Japanese one with fanaticism or fascination. It cannot be said to indicate the true philosophical mind anxious for a more general citizenship that critically transcends both. In other words, such an ultranationalist philosophy is only an immaturity. In the word "*tetsu-gaku*," born a hundred years ago, we must see these intricate and difficult conditions. This is nothing but the intricacy and difficulty of Japanese culture itself. In receiving foreign cultures, the Japanese tried to overcome these difficulties by means of a distinction between *kon* (mind) and *sai* (science).

But some sensitive Japanese, who had imbibed European philosophical ideas together with the science (*sai*) of the nineteenth century, became aware that such a distinction was impossible. As long as *wakon* is adhered to, *yosai* may never be truly acquired. Fukuzawa Yukichi (1834–1901) declared that the independence of a nation cannot be realized without the independence and self-reliance of each member of that nation. He believed that in order to build up a truly independent modern state, the pressing need of national education was to improve the character of the Japanese who are weak against the pressure of authority and community. Nakae Chōmin (1847–1901) argued that Japan had never yet had a philosophy, noting that the Japanese were deficient in the faculty of theoretical and systematic thinking based on principles. He also pointed out the unreality of a first-class national state without a philosophy carried out by such a faculty. In fact, the first side of the above-mentioned dual problem in philosophy was pursued just on the basis of this acknowledgment of the inseparability of *kon* and *sai*. Yet, however far this side may be pursued, the Japanese are Japanese, not European, and live with *wakon*, not with *yōkon* (European mind).

"*Sokuten-kyosi*" (resignation to the cosmic destiny in the sense of the ancient Chinese idea) was the ultimate ground of the thoughts of Natsume Sōseki (1867–1916), the famous novelist and scholar of English literature. Of course, *wakon* itself developed through Japanese modern history and research in European philosophy. Thus, it became capable of thinking more independently and systematically so as to be qualified for more general citizenship than ever before. It is natural that, borne by such a developing *wakon*, a philosophy should have begun to quicken. This may just have been Nakae's objective. This philosophy strove for a world citizenship that would transcend not only Japanese citizenship but the European one as well. Yet, for this philosophy world citizenship is inaccessible without European citizenship, and the latter without Japanese. This world citizenship demands from this philosophy not only completely acquiring both European and Japanese citizenship as the first step, but also critically transcending both of them as the next step. In Japan where "philosophy" was learned for the first time only one hundred years ago, philosophy would be unreal without fulfilling these two conditions. With a lack in either condition, the country would be either merely imitative or immature. It is not too much to say that Japan's history of philosophy is crowded with innumerable copies and immaturities. Nevertheless, as a result, a suggestion of what is worthy of the name of "philosophy" came to deeply affect the developing *wakon*.

It was Nishida, inspired by this suggestion, who first came to grips with this extremely formidable problem. In his young days, he wrote to one of his friends, Suzuki Daisetsu (1870–1966):

Ethical studies today in Europe are merely intellectual. Indeed they argue minutely but none of them has an eye to the profound *soul-experience* in the human bosom. They leave their foothold out of their minds. So to speak, some of them analyze and explain the components of bread or water, but none appreciates and clarifies the taste itself.

Here we have Suzuki Daisetsu's basic philosophical posture. Modern European rationalism since Francis Bacon, who intended to enlarge *regnum hominis* through the endless conquest of nature, led to the establishment of the minute procedures of the objective, analytical grasp of everything. No doubt that is the glory of modern Europe. In that light, Japan gave up her isolationist policy. But this rationalism could never objectify and analyze man himself, the subject so objectifying and analyzing everything else. The man thereby analyzed objectively was no longer the living man who does the analyzing. In this sense, this rationalism was subjectivism or an anthropocentrism. Reflection on this point must have been the first common problem of philosophy in twentieth-century Europe: namely, reconsideration, as far as possible, of the concrete figure of living man in his integrity or, in the widest sense, *"philosophy of man,"* as Cassirer said. One of the main disputations of twentieth-century philosophy has been about just this human integrity.

Nishida wrote the above in October 1902. The point at issue, he indicated, was that which John Dewey called *"a local 'subjective' phase of European philosophy."* Nishida had a rather good understanding of European philosophy: what sustained his understanding was *wakon* developed through the historical experience of modern Japan and research in European philosophy. Nishida devoted his life to acquire world citizenship for his philosophy based on this developed *wakon*. His endeavor was not successful, however, for his philosophy did not fulfill the two conditions noted above. In fact, this point is presumably *aporia* to every philosophy. Modern European philosophy could not objectify man himself who objectifies all. In the same way, while Nishida intended to reconsider basing them completely on the developed *wakon*, it is doubtful how far he succeeded in investigating in order to clarify the latter, *wakon* itself, as a philosophical object. And yet it belongs to the task of Japanese students of philosophy to clarify and develop *wakon* all the more just through this doubt. This belongs to the same context as the main philosophical problem of developing a *"philosophy of man"* in twentieth-century Europe. That task is evidently impossible to achieve without the development of *wakon* through the historical experience of modern Japan.

This developent requires above all the recognition that this historical experience is so related to world history that it is not unique to Japan. Only by experiencing history with this recognition could we expect philosophy in Japan to be truly worthy of the name of "philosophy." Only through this experience could Japan be set free from the cultural role it has had by being the small islands in the Far East. The historical direction of the twentieth century itself would support this expectation. Sooner or later not only Japan but also every region and country in the world will have the same historical experience. Only when all of them have lived through this same experience with all its presumed confusions and sacrifices will the world be a thoroughly new world. Then for the first time world citizenship will be common to all of us. Now is the time for all to meet together all over the world. It is evident that the history of mankind in the twentieth century is going inevitably in this direction. No other way is open for us but to progress in this direction. Together with all other human efforts, philosophy must take part in the work of developing this only way.

It is often said that the learned world of philosophy in Japan is the fairgrounds of world philosophy. These words are meant as a bitter criticism of the fact that various world philosophies are adopted in Japan and then discarded one by one, while little is done to cultivate a philosophy that systematically criticizes and goes beyond them. Indeed, because Japan's goal in its one hundred year history of philosophy was to acquire European citizenship as soon as possible and ultimately to become a world philosophy, it was natural that it imported various world philosophies. Yet, the fundamental principle to go beyond them, which is to be *wakon*, was still undeveloped and immature. Thus, Japan could not help but become the "fairgrounds of world philosophy."

The Pacific war was the final catastrophe in Japan's world experience beginning one hundred years ago. By that defeat Japan ought to have been brought into fruitful contact with the rest of the world. The future of philosophy in Japan, indeed, of Japanese culture itself, depends on, I believe, the Japanese recognizing the defeat as making their world experience more open. Now, what steps in this direction has Japan taken since her defeat thirty years ago?

II

Japan's defeat in World War II changed all. What had been deemed to be of value during the war was now completely rejected. So far as the war was the settlement of Japan's modern history, it seemed as if the history of modern Japan itself were being denied. In the world of philosophy, Nishida suddenly died on June 7, 1945, two months before the end of the war. He was seventy-five years old. In March of that same year, Tanabe Hajime (1885–1962) resigned his position at Kyoto University before the official retirement age. Hajime, though often an opponent of Nishida, was a central figure of the Kyoto school after Nishida resigned from Kyoto University, also before the official retirement age. Tosaka Jun (1900–1945), the most active and able Marxist philosopher, died a miserable death in prison six days prior to the defeat. Miki Kiyoshi (1897–1945), who had a more inclusive vision than Tosaka and was expected to become Japan's most prominent philosopher, was imprisoned as a communist sympathizer and died one month after his release of the illness from which he suffered while in prison.

After the war, all that had supported Japan disappeared, and it was then often said that the Japanese became thoroughly absent-minded. Before long, the Japanese who came out of this absent-mindedness sought mental life-support in philosophical ideas. Japan's connection with the learned world of philosophy in Europe had ceased with the outbreak of the war; Europe itself was as devastated as Japan. In such circumstances, one of Nishida's books was published. People stood in line overnight in front of the bookstores waiting for it to be sold. This story is remembered even today after thirty-five years. Tanabe also spoke frequently, earnestly, and actively on the political philosophy with which he would lead a defeated Japan. As information on the realm of ideas in Europe and the world's political state was gradually introduced, however, criticism and distrust began to develop on new theoretical bases against Nishida and Tanabe who had been Japan's philosophical leaders during the war. It may be said postwar philosophy in Japan began at this point.

There are many philosophical positions to be considered, but it is beyond the scope of this essay to include all of them here. The focus will be on several specific concepts and general trends. Generally there were three movements which reflected international affairs and the main current of world philosophy—Marxism, existentialism, and pragmatism. These movements were already accepted in Japan even before the war. The activities and progress of those movements after the war were incompatible with those of the prewar period, as was the case in the area of international communication.

Since the 1920s, Marxism had been gradually penetrating political and social movements. As a philosophical movement, the basic theoretical work was done mainly by the Study Group of Materialism founded in 1932. Tosaka was among the brightest and most energetic figures in the group. His destiny was tied up with that of Marxism in prewar Japan. After Japan surrendered, the chief role of Marxism was the radical criticism of Japan's historical experience, as well as direct criticism of Nishida's and Tanabe's philosophies, because they had been formed with *wakon* as their basis.

Existentialism became known before the 1920s when Watsuji Tetsurō (1889–1960) introduced Kierkegaard and Nietzsche to Japan. Among the existential ideas of the 1930s, when the militarists gained power with the economic crisis, the Shestov rage and the prominent works of Kuki Shuzō (1881–1941) should not be overlooked. Inasmuch as the Japanese mentality and intuition were richly innate in Watsuji and Kuki, in a sense the existentialist mood and receptivity matched the Japanese and corresponded well with *wakon*. With their defeat in the war, it was natural that the Japanese were attracted to existentialism, for they had to start all over again from the pure-self, which was all that was left to them.

Pragmatism also seems to be in harmony with the sensitivity of the Japanese. By 1910, many of James' and Dewey's ideas had already been introduced to Japan. Nishida, under the influence of James and others, assigned "pure experience" as the underlying principle and starting point of his philosophy.

Tanaka Ōdō (1867–1932), having studied under Dewey, was all his life actively engaged as a leading controversialist of pragmatism. Pragmatic thinking that focuses on the pattern of behavior aiming at the development of each unique situation rather than the principal systematic ways of thinking formulates some of the characteristics of *wakon*. Together with American democracy which had overthrown Japanese militarism, pragmatism became influential in postwar Japan.

In a comparison of these three movements in postwar and prewar Japan and with *wakon*, we find a common element—they are based on the denial or distrust of *wakon*. The development of Marxism, existentialism, and pragmatism is outlined in the following sections.

Marxism succeeded the struggle which had been initiated in the prewar period and inaugurated an attitude of completely negating the things of the prewar period. Existentialism grasped the war experience as its own problem and inaugurated an attitude of self-criticism and a search for a new possibility of the self. Pragmatism sought to develop a liberal personality and a rationalistic spirit, with the experience of democracy in the postwar period as its scaffold.

MARXISM

Marxism was suppressed during the war. Following the peace, "orthodox Marxism" radically negated all that related to its suppressors, but because of its angular dogmatism, it had lost the flexibility to meet the new postwar situation. Facing the gap realistically, Marxism in Japan met its first theoretical trial: the so-called controversy of subjectivity, a subject of great interest to journalists between 1947 and 1948.

Marxism rapidly extended its influence in various fields after World War II because it had exhaustively resisted the force that had carried out that reckless war. This growth in influence stimulated the theoretical extension of orthodox Marxism from the prewar period. At that time, existentialism was also extending its influence, and many people were affected by both positions. They thought that without "subjectivity," which existentialism emphasized, human liberation, which Marxism aimed at, would not be truly realized. According to the most energetic controversialist among them, Umemoto Katsumi (1912–1976), in order to realize human liberation, it is necessary to realize that self-sacrifice for the revolutionary class results in self-liberation. This self-liberation is possible when a practical subject realizes dialectically that only by a qualitative leap can the total and universal human liberation, which surpasses both social class and individuals, be the "absolute." The orthodox Marxists argued against this notion merely by telling them high-handedly that it was "modernism" from beginning to end. The logic of thinking with the "qualitative leap" must be regarded as not widely different from the dialectic of the Kyoto school during the war. The dialectical relationship among individuals, states, and the world shifted to the relationship among individuals, classes, and mankind. The pattern of the basic logic, which is characteristic of philosophical thinking in Japan, is shown here. The main characteristic of Japanese dialectic is that the wide gap between the ideal and the real, which in Japan comes to the question of "the individual and the whole," is filled with the "qualitative leap" = "nothingness" or "*soku*" (which means identity in *Zen*). This idea will undoubtedly be one of the cardinal themes of Japanese philosophy in the future. The issue raised by this argument represents the fundamental problem of Marxism today as it develops into the New Left.

One of the most remarkable Marxist theories of the early postwar era was the dialectic of Taketani Mitsuo (1911–   ). Taketani is a noted nuclear physicist who has contributed greatly to the development of the theory of the meson. Based on his experience in the field of nuclear physics, he presents his own dialectical grasp concerning the structure of nature through his criticism of Tanabe's interpretation of quantum mechanics using the theories of Marx and Lenin. He holds that cognition of nature is the reflection of its structure, and he looked for the one and only basis to substantiate the successful cognition of nature in its dialectical structure. He states that, based on this structure, cognition of nature develops through the following three stages: (1) the *an sich* phenomenalistic stage to describe phenomena; (2) the *für sich* realistic stage to pursue the structure of the object; and (3) the *an und für sich* essentialistic stage to clarify the movement principle of that object. Undoubtedly, however, real cognition will appear in a form with these three stages mixed together.

Indeed, this so-called Taketani dialectic has appeal since it is largely supported by his scientific contributions. But even though his theory has been confirmed in the field of physics, it seems too rough for application to the world of life, of consciousness, and of human beings. If one were to follow this theory and develop it, one would be required to energetically solve problems one by one in each field. For example, Taketani himself took Oparin's life theory and Lysenko's theory at their face value as suitable examples of the conscious application of this dialectic.

Among other Marxist theorists of the period was Matsumura Kazuto (1909–   ), who criticizes the idealist dialectic since Hegel, especially that in Japan as represented by Nishida and Tanabe since they resolve the confrontation into harmony rather than exhaustively overcoming it. Another Marxist, Saigusa Hiroto (1892–1963), was unique in trying to back up dialectical materialism with technological problems at its center and to explore the drift in the history of thought in Japan.

The Korean War produced a subtle change in Japanese Marxism. The recovery and reorganization movement of Japanese industry stimulated by this war, as well as Stalin's death, made that change gradually apparent. The Korean conflict forced the Japanese to meet the problem of "freedom and independence of a nation." It was Takeuchi Yoshimi (1910–1977), a researcher of Chinese revolutionary ideas, who investigated the matter of nationalism and bitterly criticized orthodox Marxism, which only handled class problems and neglected this matter. This criticism, compared with the above subjectivity theorists who emphasized individual existentialistic subjectivity, raised collective nationalistic subjectivity. Thus, it is perhaps a developed form of the controversy of subjectivity. In any case, postwar Marxism in Japan faced the second theoretical trial, unchanged since the prewar period. Both the first criticism from the existentialistic approach and the second from the nationalistic betrayed the same defect in orthodox Marxism. Moreover, this defect may be regarded as a defect common to all the ideas imported from Europe into modern Japan. As is discussed later, this same defect appears in different forms in different ideas as their characters differ. This defect can be overcome only through Japan's postwar historical experience, i.e., world experience. Most important is an open-minded attitude of grasping one's own experience as a world experience. Through this attitude only, Marxism and all other philosophical thought in Japan may become truly worthy of world citizenship.

As Japan's industry recovered and progressed rapidly in the late 1950s, popularization of the Japanese social structure was promoted and the amount of information increased rapidly. Keeping pace with that, Stalin was criticized and the thaw began. The Hungarian incident, however, shook the world. In 1960, the renewal year of the United States-Japan Security Treaty, all the forces that opposed the treaty were mobilized, with Marxism as the central force, and the movement burgeoned. Nevertheless, the treaty was renewed and the progressive leftists lost their self-confidence. As a result of this experience, Marxism came in for overall reappraisal. The chief element in this reappraisal was the so-called New Left. Apart from its vigorous sectarian struggles and propaganda, the New Left in Japan, as is in other countries, must still be labeled an unknown quantity philosophically. In Japan at least, it may be admitted that it keenly sensed the roots of the new distortion in human life which the highly industrialized, information-oriented, and controlled society had created in the 1960s, and it intended to surmount this distortion by amplifying existential intuition through action. It is not certain how much the New Left's intentions have been realized, but its radical critical mind is by no means as frivolous as its actions would indicate. The various problems the New Left raised seem to have stimulated, consciously or unconsciously, many fields of thought. They are brawlers who display the most unbridled license. By this disturbance, however, the development of philosophy is accelerated. Perhaps this negative moment may be the only philosophical merit of the New Left. Moreover, this confused struggle may be regarded as the Japanese reflection of the present state of society and civilization which is changing on a worldwide scale. Furthermore, in this reflection of the times, we notice that problems of thought intrinsic to Japan are still inherited unchanged. This is why the New Left's critical mind is never frivolous. Frankly speaking, we can see the New Left in Japan as the developed form of existentialistic and nationalistic subjectivity.

The seeds of today's New Left were already sown by existentialism. If one of the basic characteristics of existentialism in Japan lies in the matter of "body," it would not be unjust to regard this matter as the common keynote for these new interpretations of Marxism. At least from this epitome of the objective flow of thought, we may recognize an important philosophical problem. If we take the viewpoint that overcoming dualism, which modern European rationalism or subjectivism brought to the extreme, is the common theme of philosophical thought today, we find in this theme Marx's basic philosophical one, too.

This basic theme was written about intensively, though immaturely, in the "Ökonomisch-philosophische Manuskripte." By newly uncovering in this manuscript the anthropological moment that overcomes dualism, new ground was opened for various interpretations of Marx—"Western Marxism." In Japan at least, there emerges the matter of "body" among these interpretations. When dual confrontation between man and nature is overcome through labor, that labor is intrinsically an activity of "body," and through this activity, the concrete existence of man endowed with a body will become fully enriched. Without this bodily existential aspect, overcoming estrangement may not be accomplished. According to the traditional Japanese mind, man and nature should be one body in emotional and organic unity. Hence, the young Marx's ideas were rather familiar to the Japanese. But Marx's labor was rigidly social labor; therefore, nature was not merely emotional but social. The body is not merely limited to individuals but should be expanded to groups, which apparently exceeded the Japanese mentality. This point is an extremely important moment for the development of *wakon*. This "manuscript" was translated into Japanese in 1964—which may seem too late, but we may also say that objective and social conditions had finally ripened for this manuscript to be frankly accepted in Japan. In any case, today most college students have heard about this manuscript, and consequently so-called Marxism-Leninism no longer holds much attraction for them. With such a social and spiritual mood in the background, members of the New Left, by staking their individual bodies on practical activities, intended to seek solidarity with other bodies and obtain one collective body rather than merely acquiring ideologies and theories. We can follow them this far as a philosophical problem; whether they really succeed may be a matter beyond philosophy.

When observing Marxism in connection with the philosophical problems which Japan's New Left presents, we cannot overlook Hiromatsu Wataru (1933–   ) who boldly, and yet carefully, presents his own new interpretation in today's atmosphere of Marxism. According to Hiromatsu, Marx has overcome modern epistemology—dualism of subjectivity and objectivity—by emphasizing that the phenomena of consciousness, including sensation and emotion, are of a social nature. He tries to fully reinterpret Marx's philosophy, meeting today's philosophical themes by taking Marx's view mentioned above into his original doctrine of "theory of four members structure." This theory returns to epistemology and ontology in the stage of union before both were divided by the modern dualism of subjectivity and objectivity. Then, by inserting the ontological moment of form and matter into both members (subjectivity-objectivity) in the epistemological scheme, it clarifies the dual structure of both members. Objectivity is a material individual datum and yet is effectuated in the formal intersubjective sense; likewise, subjectivity is a material individual subjectivity and yet is effectuated in formal intersubjectivity. Hiromatsu's philosophical theme can be summarized as follows: he tries to clarify the *an sich* structure of the phenomenal world as a semiotical intersubjective structure in connection with such members' interrelationships. His critical doctrine presents various current problems for philosophy which cannot be dealt with in the framework of so-called Marxism. When we realize that the question of intersubjectivity lies at the center of his phenomenological method and semiotical approach and that this question cannot be developed without the matter of "body," we must then recognize that the historical experience in Japan is of necessity leading various philosophical movements to one common theme.

EXISTENTIALISM

As a result of Japan's defeat in the war, all that had preceded the defeat was denounced and the Japanese became the objects of much criticism among themselves. Such self-criticism occurred in the Kyoto school which had held the philosophical leadership during the war. At the beginning of 1944 when Japan's defeat seemed certain, this self-criticism had already happened in Tanabe's philosophy. His philosophy of *zange* (*metanoia*, contrition) is representative of this change.

Tanabe's philosophy as "philosophy of absolute mediation" may be called primarily a philosophy of faith in practical reason. It rejects any affirmative as immediate which can be grasped merely inferentially by speculative reason, and it is only based on practical reason which grasps all dialectically through negative mediation in practice. It is the self as a practical subject that bears practical reason. In this sense, Tanabe's philosophy was "the philosophy of the self," placing emphasis on *jiriki* (self-reliance in a Buddhist sense) rather than on *tariki* (other-reliance). According to Tanabe, the war should have been changed through the efforts of the practical reason of the "self." In reality, it was adverse. The reality was powerful enough to crush this conceit of the "self." In 1944, Tanabe began to speak about *zange*. *Zange* is throwing out the whole previous self when one's practical efforts are frustrated and utterly realizing the incapacity of the self. In fact, however, the self is thoroughly negated only by some other that surpasses the self. When we realize this point, we also realize that entrusting this other with all would make us reborn. Therefore, as *zange* itself is done by other-reliance, the philosophy of *zange* is the philosophy of other-reliance. As this is effectuated when surpassing the reason-philosophy of self-reliance, it negates all previous philosophies in Europe. In this sense, it is the "philosophy that is not philosophy." Tanabe calls this "*zange-do*" (the way to be reborn through contrition). This idea is unfolded using Shinran's (1173–1262) creed as an initiation. (Shinran was a great priest of virtue in the thirteenth century.) This idea leads the activity of the other, which gives a second birth to the self, to the matter of religious love: with the Christian Gospel and *bosatsu-do* (the way of *bodhi-sattva*, Buddha elect) of Mahayanist Buddhism as guidance, and by the medium of negation of limited self-death, it ultimately reaches the "philosophy of death" where one lives within absolute love. There opens the world of "existential communication through death and rebirth."

Toward the end of his life, Tanabe taught that the existential self beyond the self of practical reason communicates with the other in *bosatsu-do* and that one should live in existential love. In some sense, his philosophy may be said to be religious existentialism. Here we must bear in mind that the some other who supports what he calls existential communication is never God as transcendence but rather is an "absolute nothingness" which negates the self and brings death to it. Although the term "existential communication" reminds us of Jaspers and likewise the term "nothingness" of Heidegger, Tanabe's existentialism is fundamentally out of Japanese Buddhism and differs from the tradition of theism or ontology.

It may be said that Tanabe's self-criticism became criticism of the Kyoto school in the postwar period. After the defeat, the school promptly began to discuss Kierkegaard, Nietzsche, Dostoevsky, Heidegger, Jaspers, and others very shrewdly. It is undeniable that it was done out of their own inner necessity, but their shrewdness with these arguments of existentialism was so similar in tone to that of their nationalistic and totalitarian arguments in the war that it made their arguments the less persuasive. Their arguments lacked that tension which Tanabe's *zange* sustained in the exhaustive negation of the self. Accordingly, so little creativity is found in their arguments that they could not surpass Tanabe's existentialism and develop it further. Rather, Yamauchi Tokuryu (1890–) and Miyake Gōichi (1895–), both professors at Kyoto University but distant from the center of the Kyoto school, suggested some clues to the peculiar development of existential thought in Japan by their continuous studies. Yamauchi interpreted the concept of existence as man's concrete social being, which means to be *something* in a place possessed of a certain content and import. He posed and explained *detentio* (existence) as a concrete synthesis of *extentio* (matter) and *intentio* (mind), so that he might develop a new horizon surpassing both materialism and idealism. Miyake Gōichi grasped man's concrete actual being by his sensuous bodiliness, which means that man as the living subject is an *incarnate being* who lives the world *manifesting* through this body. He reexamined the question of mind and body anew, and gave a basic direction to the development of existential thought.

As previously stated, the existentialist mood and receptivity basically appeal to the Japanese mentality. The defeat in World War II has stimulated such a mood and receptivity, which consequently have spread through the manners, customs, and living attitudes of the postwar period. Literature, which keenly reflects such circumstances, was in vogue, and Sartre provided its chief philosophical buttresses. But it is doubtful how much Sartre's idea of freedom of consciousness, which is the core of his philosophy, affected the Japanese mentality. Certainly his leftism has influenced the existentialists in Japan, and it has been carried into the thoughts of the New Left. Nevertheless, its conclusion is not yet fixed; rather, it seems that it might drift away as time passes without getting firmly fixed. We may be able to say that Sartre's influence was in concrete and sensual forms rather than in brilliant arguments, and that the questions of "engagement" and "imagination" left marks on the Japanese. These questions present the problem of solidarity with others. Without fully facing this solidarity problem, especially in Japan, existentialism cannot be so persuasive. As mentioned earlier, the same was true for Marxism, i.e., the question of "the individual and the whole" was the core of the controversy of subjectivity. This fact shows that Japanese thinking is always ethically oriented, which is quite characteristic. This character seems to give a specific feature and limitation to the development of existentialism in Japan. This specific feature is found in Kaneko Takezō's (1905–) "philosophy of existential reason."

Kaneko was a professor of ethics at Tokyo University until he reached retirement age. Tokyo University, which traditionally undertook a positive study of the history of philosophy, was indifferent to existentialism as a general trend. But in ethics, whose main theme is seeking the ideal way of subjective practice, the idea of existentialism may intrinsically have significance. Through Confucianism, ethics in Japan had been developing in its own way long before modern times. It was first successfully systematized, at the same level as that of European philosophy, by Watsuji, who tried to clarify ethical phenomena by splendidly applying Dilthey—Heidegger's hermeneutical phenomenology, and by Kaneko, who tried to develop the system of *Sittlichkeit* using Hegel's dialectic. But the ethical situation in the postwar period causes us to question the conditions in which the ethical individual subject finds itself bogged down, which is more than mere hermeneutical elucidation or dialectical systematization. Kaneko discerned that existentialism had great significance for meeting the situation that provoked such a question. Moreover, in order to answer the question, he believed a new kind of rationalism was indispensable. "To truly exist in things," he said, is the only way for man to live, which is nothing but "existence." In order to perceive and then accept the truth of things—the holder of these things is nothing but oneself—without huddling over them at all, one needs to have a magnanimity which makes existence possible, i.e., reason. Kaneko calls this "existential reason." While he seems to embrace the dialectical unity of existence and reason as a Hegelian, he uses Jaspers' philosophy for guidance. He believes that by this existential reason Jaspers' "Kommunikation" becomes possible and that the very ground for this "Kommunikation" is the concrete ethical ground. Here his idea and Tanabe's theory of "existential communication" largely overlap. Furthermore, as an ethicist, Kaneko has his own idea of the "existential categories" as a new ethical theme to elucidate this ground's structure. By these categories, he maintains a new system of ethics will be formed that is appropriate to contemporary life.

Imamichi Tomonobu (1922–   ), a professor of aesthetics at Tokyo University, pursues the possibility of transcendence in mortal man in his unique style of phenomenology. He attempts to maintain this possibility by the identity of judgment, which is the basic structure of contemplation of transcendence. He also tries to demonstrate that the final cognition of identity is possible in "beauty" itself. Oshima Yasumasa (1917–   ), a professor of ethics at Tokyo University of Education, now Tsukuba University, has completed a bulky but precise study which elucidates the ethical significance of European existentialism. Other ethicists have produced various studies which reflect the existentialist position. Japan now has an association for the study of Kierkegaard and Jaspers. As in the case of Sartre, whether these studies will firmly establish existentialism as a new way of thought in Japan is not yet known. Originally, the Japanese mentality had a very strong existentialist bent, which in turn made it difficult for existentialism to become firmly fixed as a movement. Thus, it seems that a tendency that was increasingly becoming conspicuous as existentialism made a backward movement under the advancement of worldwide industrialization, information systems, and interdisciplinary fields in the 1960s. This tendency can be found in the studies of Merleau-Ponty (*corps*) and of Husserl in his later years (*Lebenswelt*).

When existentialism began to lose its novelty, studies were begun to probe what is behind existentialist thought. From Sartre to Merleau-Ponty, and then to Husserl in his later years, the line was followed in both journalistic and academic circles. The reason which caused them to follow this course is the matter of "body," which presents many intricate problems and can only be approached through interdisciplinary vision. In the study of German philosophy, much concern is also given to philosophical anthropology beyond Heidegger.

Merleau-Ponty's *Phénoménologie de la perception* was first translated into Japanese in 1967, and now we can read all of his works in Japanese. The works of Husserl, which are difficult to understand, are beginning to be translated. Studies in this area are still in an introductory stage and great achievements have not yet been made.

Scholars from Tohoku University are presently dominant in Japanese philosophy, and chief among them is Takiura Shizuo (1927–   ), a professor at Tohoku University. Takiura Shizuo has studied the question of "imagination" and "time." The reason we can entertain expectations, he says, is as follows. The central matter of "body" can be regarded as a fundamental problem in Japan's own long historical experiences, and not just as a philosophical problem newly created by existentialism. It may therefore be considered an element that forms the substance of *wakon*. This important theme elucidates Nishida's philosophy of the matter of "body," which started with the "question of life" as a basic motive. Certainly, Yamauchi's and Miyake's ideas mentioned above have also found each clue in Nishida's thought. It is no exaggeration to say that the dualism of mind and body, deeply rooted in European thought, against which existentialism has fought, is in stark contrast to *wakon*. Probably it is not a misjudgment to see the reason at this point why the Japanese mentality was originally harmonious with existentialism. It is doubtful how much the radical struggles of existentialism against traditional European thought have been understood, appealed to, and fixed among the Japanese. However, it can be concluded that the historical experiences of the Japanese have played a significant role in eliciting the new theme after these radical struggles. Positively executing this role seems to make *wakon* worthy of world citizenship in philosophy by acquiring more experience of the world. A study by Ichikawa Hiroshi (1931–   ), a professor at Meiji University, is a good example. Ichikawa develops his own theory of "body" using biological and ethological materials, while referring to the achievement of Merleau-Ponty and Tran Duc Thao. Indeed, existentialism itself has probably not left anything positive, but it must be highly rated since it has broken with certain set ideas, has raised questions from new angles, and has offered the ground for developing new views. The problem for *wakon* to cut a path to what is truly worthy of world experience has only been provided with a definite ground of development by existentialism in these last one hundred years.

PRAGMATISM

The democracy that came to Japan with the occupation forces caused a rebirth in the country. However, the success of this rebirth depended on how deeply democracy took root in the soil of Japan. And so, cultivation of the soil in Japan was necessary at the same time. Pragmatism should have been the central power in this cultivation. Democracy in postwar Japan, however, recognizes no other authority; and both the right and left criticize others and, except for the ultra right and left, justify themselves under the name of democracy. It is, so to speak, the flood-time of democracy. But a flood does not mean taking root. In such a circumstance, pragmatism encountered great difficulties in postwar Japan, where all views had to take an enlightening role in criticizing prewar thought. Immediately after the war, Japan entered its own period of enlightenment. Various groups formed around various philosophical views. The times were reminiscent of the Meiji restoration in Japan of one hundred years before. Among these views was pragmatism which had to reform the course of modernization in Japan, taking a role like that of the eighteenth-century European Enlightenment which the Japanese accepted one hundred years ago. Unlike the Marxist and the existentialist, the pragmatist needs a great deal of perseverance in his effort to effect the course of modernization in Japan. Without fully meeting the dual problem in philosophy in modern Japan, this job could not have been accomplished. Furthermore, it could not have been accomplished without appealing to the masses.

In accordance with this aim, a magazine entitled *Shiso no Kagaku* ("Science of Thoughts") was first published in May 1946 by Tsuru Shigeto (1914–   ), Tsurumi Kazuko (1918–   ), Tsurumi Shunsuke (1922–   ), and others. The first issue of the magazine opened with the Marxist physicist Taketani's essay "How Can Philosophy Restore Effectiveness?" In this essay, using as a model the approach of physics which examines theories by alternately repeating them and conducting experiments, Taketani emphasizes that philosophy also affects reality by cultivating its theories and systems through facts and actual experiences. He also points out how previous philosophies had been sluggish on this point. This conception is directly connected with pragmatism. In line with this emphasis, the magazine objectively analyzed not only former philosophies in Japan but also the patterns of all Japanese ideas and behavior. It tried to elucidate how they were effected and what reality they faced. This effort, made by applying various principles of pragmatism to reality, reflected the brilliant talent of the contributors. They maintained an approach unique for Japan. Nevertheless, the question that remains is how effective this approach is in reality. The Marxists and existentialists are not the only ones who are dissatisfied with these analyses, which touch merely the surface of Japanese consciousness. Of course, any approach from any standpoint may cause a gap between it and reality, but it is a fundamental characteristic of pragmatism that it does not provide a unifying principle or system to fill the gap. Thus, the gap it creates is very conspicuous in Japan.

Shimizu Ikutarō (1902–   ) was a prominent leader of the democratic enlightenment in postwar Japan. He tried to reach the masses by founding the Research Institute of the Twentieth Century.

As is the case with existentialism, it is not yet certain how much pragmatism appeals as a concept to the masses. And as in the case of existentialism, the same reason may apply. That is, the Japanese may be hidden pragmatists. Once pragmatism was turned into a theory by the American mentality, it began to be separated from the Japanese. In short, it is rigidly *Japanese* pragmatism; Ruth Benedict called this *"Situational realism"*. Because of this separation Nakae asserted, "There is no philosophy yet in Japan." Conversely, a true Japanese philosophy will never be born without developing this Japanese pragmatism as a theory in a Japanese way. As stated earlier, the problem of nationalistic subjectivity which Takeuchi raised is a problem not only in Marxism but also in existentialism and pragmatism—and there *wakon* casts her shadow.

As mentioned earlier, pragmatism had already left its traces in modern Japan's philosophical thinking before World War II, especially at Waseda University, where the most active pragmatist controversialist, Tanaka, taught. The tradition of pragmatism has been maintained by another professor, Ueda Seiji (1902–1963). Most of Seiji's work was in the collection of materials and the introduction of foreign philosophical literature, but his own theoretical scheme had not been formed. In time, his works were appreciated, and in his later years he became the editor of epoch-making cooperative studies which were the first in Japan on not only pragmatism but also logical positivism and analytical philosophy.

At Tokyo University, whose main concern had been the study of German philosophy, the analytical scholars were critical of both Marxism and existentialism, and thus gradually, in the postwar period, they became interested in English and American philosophies. Among these scholars was Professor Iwasaki Takeo (1918–1976). Through his analytical criticsm of the Kantian system of epistemology, he confirms that the cognition of man, who is only a finite being locked in empirical reality, is only possible through the experimental method. Furthermore, he states that this method forms a dialectic as the basic structure of how man, who lives consciously meeting reality, is. But he calls the dialectic which stems from Hegel the "dialectic of being" based on the standpoint of a suprahuman, infinite being. The genuine dialectic, he claims, is "the dialectic of self-consciousness" which is a logic of man's self-consciousness as a finite being. Man deepens the self-consciousness of himself, making approaches to reality by knowledge and conduct. Therefore, the dialectic of self-consciousness is a logic not only of cognition but also of practice. Both a scientific and an ethical principle is to be unfolded by continuously working on reality and by repeated trial and error using the dialectic of self-consciousness. A final principle must not be something supported by mere metaphysical or intuitive dogmatism. At this point, Iwasaki finds an error common to all former ethics. His view can be considered fundamentally pragmatic. His criticism, which dissolves even naturalism in the process of self-consciousness, is rather a trial to attain logical consistency for pragmatism. Yet, he has not developed more positively and concretely this "logic of self-consciousness," which is nothing but induction in a theoretical and systematic form. Even so, his logical and analytical study has formed the tendency of analytical philosophy at Tokyo University.

With Japan's intensive industrialization and information systematization in the 1960s, the country attained status as a major developed nation. As already noted, this experience brought a change to Marxism and existentialism in Japan. Pragmatism also left the enlightening stage through this experience, and it became possible and, in fact, necessary for it to face this historical reality. At the center of the problems pivoting around this reality was the matter of "language," which corresponds to that of "body" in existentialism and in the New Left, and requires analyses from a comprehensively interdisciplinary field of vision. Japanese pragmatism also entered the stage of neopragmatism, and parallel with that, attention has been paid to scientific philosophy and analytical philosophy, and Wittgenstein has often been discussed.

A logical and analytical study holding the matter of language at its center is different from the main current of the one hundred year history of philosophy in Japan. This study began only twenty years ago and is being carried out with severe criticism of former philosophies in Japan. One of the central figures, Sawada Nobushige (1916–   ), a professor at Keio University, thinks that it was because modern Japan was politically and socially distorted and immature that such a question as "how to live" was regarded as the intrinsic problem of philosophy. On the contrary, he stresses that normal philosophy in Europe originally started as a science. "Scientific philosophy," he states, is a means of organizing man's conduct as a whole by using the knowledge gained by scientific methods. This way can be possible, with a semiotical method in modern logic as its pivot, by placing thinking in the organic and total connection of man with the world and grasping it as the circular structure of hypothesis-verification-correction of hypothesis through sense-perception of "body."

Here we notice that the "effectiveness" Taketani spoke of and the "dialectic of self-consciousness" Iwasaki aimed at are being developed theoretically and systematically on a highly interdisciplinary scale, using modern semiotics as its key. In such a manner, Ichii Saburō (1922–   ), a professor at Seikei University who considers analytical philosophy in a wider sense than mere analysis, has tried to develop a theory of philosophical analysis in the fields of society and history, which consist of the sense of values and the conduct of individual or group. Yamamoto Ichirō (1910–1972), a professor at Ritsumeikan University, thought of "philosophy *as* language." According to Yamamoto, meaning-attaching is just the living state of philosophical cognition, and its function is to develop a circuit of meaning between the subject and the object. Therefore, philosophy is the possibility of the circulation of language and of information between the world and man, man and man. From this viewpoint, he tries to give a basis to the possibility and to unfold it theoretically and systematically. At Tokyo University, a distinct circle of analytical philosophy following Iwasake has been formed. This circle includes Professor Kuroda Wataru (1928–   ), who has attempted to strengthen the basis of empiricism by demonstrating, through the analysis of language-behavior, that language as a behavior is what intensively shows the structure of man's experience. Another is Professor Ōmori Shōzō (1912–   ), who as a phenomenalist perceives the world and man as a total *"appearance"* and tries to explain the state of all things, from the daily perceptual to the highly intellectual scientific, as variations of "how to apprehend" this one and same total *appearance*. He then attempts to "apprehend" that it is "language" and *"fancy"* which support the former that pile up variations connecting with each other and constantly form a total appearance. Professor Sueki Takehiro (1921–   ), also a member of the group, has done a serious study of Wittgenstein's *Tractatus*. The complete works of Wittgenstein are being translated into Japanese, and it is expected that there will be a vigorous development in this direction. As in the case of existentialism, what supports this development is the criticism of the dualism that is deeply rooted in European thought and also an effort to fill the gap between the other and the self, using as a guide the matter of "body" or of "language" rooted in it. We must recognize that the tradition of *wakon* fits in there. In such a context, the controversy between Russell and Dewey, for example, can hardly be at issue in Japan.

In this new situation, the enlightening effects of democracy on the Japanese mind have persisted. It is noteworthy that Tsurumi and others of the "Science of Thoughts" developed citizens' campaigns from the viewpoint that the citizens' sense of rights and freedom becomes their own only through the social practices of daily life. They were consistently active, especially in the citizens' campaign to seek freedom in Vietnam. We will have to pay attention to how Japanese pragmatism, through such democratic experiences, will produce future philosophical developments in *wakon*.

DEVELOPMENT OF WAKON—STRUGGLE AGAINST WAKON

Each of the three philosophical positions discussed above is now in flux and is intermingling with each other. Hence, we will need to revise our viewpoint and take another look at the whole so as to understand future developments. Everything is intermingled in today's world and previous distinctions are becoming invalid. Having been drawn into this global vortex, what direction is philosophy in Japan taking?

In order to answer this question, we only have to determine in which direction those three positions are moving. Judging from the intrinsic nature of philosophy, it was as a matter of course that *wakon* began to stand out in relief, as Japan came closer to the world level, or rather became involved in it by the global flow of the changing times.

As stated earlier, the destiny of Marxism, which had faced criticism from both sides, i.e., individual existentialistic and collective nationalistic subjectivity, was also the destiny of all European thought in modern Japan. Each movement of thought is gradually forming its subjectivity by struggling with this destiny. It is obvious that the element which comprises this subjectivity in Japan is nothing but *wakon*. Hence, it is quite natural that *wakon* should have become a common element of various movements of thought in this formative process. As if keeping pace with that, the distinctively European character of each movement of thought was eliminated and at the same time each movement began to intermingle with every other in a peculiar way. Here we may expect that new and original philosophical paths may be carved, which are not necessarily the same as those of Europe. Through the war, their defeat, and their historical experience since then, the Japanese have been thrown into the middle of the world. There is no way for them to live on in this world without developing their own philosophy and thought. Here there are no precedents. How does *wakon* meet this problem? It depends only on how well *wakon* can endure the experience of serious contact with the philosophizing occurring elsewhere in the world.

With regard to this point, let us examine the controversy surrounding Benedict's *The Chrysanthemum and the Sword*. This book was translated into Japanese for the first time in 1948 and received many book reviews. Among these reviews was one by Watsuji who denounced the book, stating that Benedict's characterization of the Japanese cultural pattern as "a shame culture" was unscientific. We must say, however, that Watsuji was himself not very scientific in his criticism. His *Nihon Rinri Shiso-shi (History of Ethical Thoughts in Japan)* (1952) might have been the best sample of shame cultures towards which Benedict directed her arguments. For Watsuji *wakon* must be said to be unexperienced and therefore undeveloped without "scientific" light thrown upon it. On the other hand, Benedict's account was scientifically quite productive. Using this scientific light cast by her as guidance, and by enlarging or supplementing her framework, many effective studies have been done. Without holding *wakon* "lonesomely" deep in mystery, as did Watsuji, efforts are being made to seek its world citizenship by throwing scientific light upon it and bringing it on to the world scene. It is quite noteworthy that the sense of "shame" and "other person" peculiar to the Japanese has been put under the light of the empirical sciences from various angles, not as a mere question of philosophy, but as a matter of positive materials and observations by Sakuta Keiich (1922–   ), a professor of sociology at Kyoto University, Doi Takeo (1922–   ), Kimura Bin (1931–   ), both of whom are psychiatrists, and others. One promising sign is that recently in various fields of ethnography, folklore, linguistics, and anthropology this question has been energetically raised from many novel and broad viewpoints, based on phenomenological or structuralistic methods. If these positive studies are carried out on a more interdisciplinary scale, they will raise philosophical issues. Undoubtedly, philosophy in Japan then will go into an epoch-making stage.

In considering future developments, we cannot forget Nishida's contributions. His fundamental motive, the "question of life," might be said to be the core of *wakon* and the source of all the works of philosophical thought in Japan. Of course, philosophical questions are not limited to the "question of life," and, as professor Sawada has already discerned, evidently that question is a characteristic rooted in the Japanese character. What lurks in the background of this question is probably the sense of "shame," "the world," and "here and now," as Benedict has indicated. In other words, as Nakae observed, the mental atmosphere in Japan may be the reason why philosophy has not developed there. Also due to this reason philosophy in Japan cannot be allowed to neglect this question or avoid it. It is quite doubtful whether a philosophy on a large scale or one that appeals to the depth of man's heart will be born from the "question of life." We may have to give a negative answer, judging from the history of the past one hundred years. As a rule, however, Nishida's philosophy, which directly faced this question, has been the most extensive and profound one among the various philosophies in Japan during these years. Philosophy in Japan may well surpass Nishida's philosophy and cut a path through "the question of life." Various philosophical positions in the postwar period, traced in the previous sections, have followed this direction on the whole. The word "life" gives the Japanese an image. We perceive this image, in the sound of Japanese, in the depth of *wakon*. This image is one of a bodily individual who is a transient human existence bearing a heavy burden. It may even be said to be the dominant image ever since the female authors' literature of the *Heian* period; "body" and "other person" are divided and related by the former through imagination, symbols, intersubjectivity, and so forth; and, above all, consciousness of un-controllably changing history serves as the scene including all of these. Nishida's philosophy is a potential garden where these factors can be developed. Unless we actualize this potential and completely develop each factor, we will not see the new horizon. Now we find that the postwar philosophical experience has followed such a path without its ever being noticed. We could feel here *"List der Vernunft,"* or rather, *"der wakon."*

With regard to the future of philosophy in Japan, we must consider what has caused Marxism, existentialism, and pragmatism to be in flux and to overlap each other since they were clearly separate from each other in 1945 when they negated all that had supported the previous state of things in Japan. Philosophy in Japan today is embracing what it negated thirty-five years ago, though the form is different. In fact, a process of negation in the true sense is underway, i.e., a process of hard and enduring self-negation. Thirty-five years ago, negation was extinguishing the self thrown out by the defeat as obsolete, as if in no relation to the present self; that was only object-negation—easy and abstract.

On the other hand, some conscious efforts have been made to tackle *wakon* and surpass Nishida, though these have been apart from the mainstream. As a rule, such conscious efforts have been made by Marxists. Of course, in the early period, there were only categorical, schematizing criticisms and negations, but from about 1960, such emotional or optimistic arguments disappeared. Affirming their own problems in those Nishida struggled with, they began to develop criticism of Nishida as a kind of self-criticism.

The Marxist Funayama Shinichi (1907–   ), a professor at Ritsumeikan University, tried to reconsider philosophy in modern Japan with a critical mind. He completed a laborious work on Japanese philosophical thought in the Meiji and Taisho eras. Although he believes that the fundamental character of Nishida's and others' philosophies in modern Japan is a kind of theodicy or realism in a political sense to protect the national establishment, he rates Nishida highly for his effort to elucidate Oriental philosophies, especially those in Japan which criticize Western philosophies and their logic at the European philosophical level. Although Nishida tried to maintain an Oriental or, rather, a Japanese viewpoint, he sought to lay the foundation of one philosophy at a universal level. Without stating whether Nishida succeeded, Funayama emphasizes Nishida's attitude in which he sought a basis for man to live in terms of the history and reality of Japanese life, confronting his way with the European way of questioning that basis. Funayama accepts as an important heritage the idea of *poiesis* (practice in the historical world) that Nishida perceived in this attitude.

Yamada Munemutsu (1925–   ), who probes the innermost mind of Nishida, traces Nishida's philosophical development in relation to the intellectual movements of the times. Yamada views his philosophy as an *"undeveloped* philosophy of bourgeois *citizens."* Unlike other Marxists, Yamada confirms its genuine nature in the "logic of the historical productive activity" reached in the peak of his career, and then he attempts to develop this genuine nature in "the future perfect tense" toward Marxism. Yanagida Kenjurō (1893–   ) confirms, with regard to Nishida's grasp of historical practice, what Marxist materialism must take in, though he labels Nishida's philosophical character as petit bourgeois. Yanagida praises Nishida highly. Nishida believed that creative development of the historical world could not be effected unless the individual self as a being unable to be a mere object itself became "a creative element."

Recently in Japan, there have been systematic reconsiderations of modern Japanese philosophy by Marxists and others who take a position close to Marxism. Most of them, including Funayama, Yamada, and Yanagida, are either Nishida's disciples or were introduced to philosophy by reading Nishida's works. All regard Nishida's philosophy in relation to themselves. Apparently, they are searching for their own philosophical possibilities by reconsidering Nishida in connection with modern Japan's historical experience through which they themselves have lived. Nevertheless, without a firm determination to break through old frameworks and to open up a new horizon to Marxism, their search for possibilities will probably be arduous beyond all expectations. It is regrettable that their studies rely on the scheme of Marxist formalism. Their basic scheme to grasp Japan's modern historical experience, which is their own destiny, is still poor. This situation probably explains why Japanese Marxism today is stagnant. This stagnation will end only when Marxism, by tackling Japan's historical experience more subjectively, composes its own framework, expands it, and opens up a new horizon—in short, when it confronts *wakon* more subjectively. Here we must remember the efforts of Yamazaki Masakazu (1912–   ), a former professor at Tokyo University, who, with various capable people besides Marxists around him, is carrying out cooperative studies in the history of philosophy. His stress is on the modern period of philosophy, including that of Japan.

Umehara Takeshi (1925–   ) and Ueyama Shunpei (1921–   ) figure prominently in the search for possibilities for philosophy in Japan and have evinced a desire to make up new schemes, in contrast with the poor basic schemata of Marxism. Both of them are associated with Kyoto University. Umehara thinks that the present age requires that the definition of philosophy be revised. According to Umehara, when one uses the definition of "new discovery of man and society" (which surpasses the framework of the traditional definition of European philosophy as self-consciousness of reason), even in the Japanese tradition of thought there lie philosophical principles that answer the question. Umehara believes that these principles consist in the ideas of life, mind, and the inferno, with Shintoism-Buddhism at their center, and he stresses these as clues in cultivating Japanese philosophy.

Ueyama, based on his own logical studies, views Marxism as a theory of social process and pragmatism as a theory of cognitive process, both of which are complementary, developed forms of dialectical logic from the viewpoint of the history of logical thought. At the same time, by making the most use of the methods of his original historical analysis, he tries to uncover traditional, native-born thought at the hub of modern thought in Japan. Furthermore, he searches for them in the overall context of the history of thought in Japan since antiquity. In his case, his logical study gives a theoretical basis to his historical one. From Ueyema's own viewpoint, which regards the dialectic as a unity of intuition and analysis, he positively evaluates Nishida's concepts of "practical intuition" or "contradictory identity" (Marxists usually deny these) as the development of Japanese native-born thought deriving from East Asian civilization. He also regards Nishida's "logic of nothingness" as holding significance for the future in thoroughly breaking away from all prejudices. Ueyama thinks that the bio-ecologist Imanishi Kinji's (1902–) influential contributions arise from "a kind of naturalistic intuitionism," which is the central characteristic of East Asian civilization according to Nishida's philosophy of life.

The ideas of Umehara and Ueyama are, among those who are tackling *wakon* in Japan today, theoretically most unbiased considering their intrepidity. There is no doubt that they focus on an indispensable element of philosophy in Japan. Yet, there are still too many questions concerning their ideas to use them to construct a philosophy truly open to the world, and their arguments are even more loosely knit than Nishida's without ever surpassing him. This problem can never be solved by a few students; it needs the continued endeavor of many in this field. It should become the mainstream of philosophy in Japan, if true philosophy is to take root and blossom there. The activities of Umehara and Ueyama should be viewed as stimuli.

Nakamura Yūjirō (1925–), a professor at Meiji University, contends that, among Japanese mental attitudes, the aesthetical ones have priority and that "emotional naturalism," in which they feel themselves related to all through emotion, dominates. But this attitude grasps all merely in itself and directly, and is weak in grasping that rational universality to be reached only by objectifying for its own sake. Therefore, he argues, this weak point becomes apparent when the Japanese talk about themselves, for they lack "self-objectification." Here lies the reason why the Japanese' own arguments on Japanese characteristics have been so inconsiderable. The historical and social reality of man cannot be effected without "institutions" which are "alienating objectivity." By self-objectification from this perspective, one can view man more rationally and universally. Nakamura warns that, while the starting point of philosophy for the Japanese must be such an "emotion" or "nature" as is peculiar to them, it must be the object of philosophy and not the principle of it. Since philosophy is a dialogue with heterogeneous things, he maintains that emotion and nature cannot be directly principles of philosophy in themselves. We must take this warning as a sharp criticism of *wakon*.

III

SUMMARY AND PROSPECT

When the Japanese became acquainted with philosophy one hundred years ago, they had to make up for their delayed modernization as soon as possible. Philosophy in modern Japan had developed through this historical experience of making up, of which World War II was the catastrophe. Accordingly, if the experience of the war and its defeat did not have any decisive significance for the philosophical development of these last one hundred years, it ought to be said that philosophical experiences in Japan are simply an intellectual pastime and a form of self-satisfaction too isolated from actual experiences to be nourished by them. How can that experience be assimilated? This problem confronts every kind of philosophical thought in Japan today. Where and how is *wakon* influenced by that experience, and how far has it opened to the world? From this perspective, we could appraise every philosophical endeavor in Japan for the last thirty years, regardless of its own intention. In short, the point is to open *wakon* into the world—namely, the dialectic between *wakon* and the world.

Karl Löwith, a German philosopher, wrote in *Shisō* ("Thoughts"), a leading magazine of philosophy in Japan, as early as November 1940, as follows: "The Japanese will not learn *für sich* what is *an sich* other than them. They don't realize themselves as the self, because they don't receive others as the other. And so, having no conversation with the other, the self remains ever as it is while the other does the same." According to his simile, the Japanese live in a two-story house: downstairs they think or feel in a Japanese way, while upstairs lives European learning from Plato to Heidegger. Yet, a European teacher wonders where is the ladder to climb up and down. Comparing such a Japanese attitude with the European critical mind, Löwith concludes: "In fact they love themselves as they are. They have never had the fruit of knowledge and never lost innocence. They have never suffered that loss which takes man out of within himself and makes him critical to himself."

If this evaluation is correct, it would be vain to speak of philosophy in Japan. At best, we could talk of a philosophy of Japanese narcissism referred to by many Europeans in addition to Löwith. But such a philosophy withers before long, because narcissism and philosophy do not mix with each other any more than water and oil do. This assumption might be illustrated by the fact that in Japan various philosophical ideas have become current and have faded one after another during the past one hundred years. Nevertheless, the historical experience of these years has never allowed the Japanese to indulge in narcissism on the whole, but it has gradually forced them to become aware of it at least and so has shoved them into the world by inches. It is obvious that the war and its defeat was the decisive step toward what Professor Löwith called "loss of innocence," though it will not be clear for some time if that experience has really brought about the loss. The next step then is to determine every characteristic of philosophical thought in Japan today.

On the whole, however, the situation is moving positively and steadily towards that next step. In every philosophical position, *wakon* is coming to the fore little by little, about to receive elucidation from many interdisciplinary directions, and about to be bound to and inlaid in the world willy-nilly. This process is merely one phase of that general process of philosophy today in which the concrete figure of living man is to be reconsidered in its integrity as fully as possible. This process is now beyond the clarifying capacity of the dualism or modern humanism that gave birth to scientific rationalism, the source of the power of modern Europe which swallowed Japan one hundred years ago. Apparently, *wakon* is at last ready to be included in this world process. Only by going on more actively in this direction and struggling with *wakon* in the context of world thought can we expect philosophy in Japan to attain world status. At this point, the problem remains unchanged from one hundred years ago, while method has been ever changing under the influence of the historical experiences of these years. Above all, the world upheaval of the last thirty-five years has decisively changed method.

Indeed, the development in methodology has been achieved only through steady accumulation during one hundred years of historical studies of philosophy. These studies must be pushed forward now as they were in the past. In Japan today, almost all of the classics of European philosophy can be read in Japanese. The complete works of Aristotle are already out (1918–1973), and those of Plato are available in two editions. A foreigner, Professor Löwith might have seen only some individual Japanese who seemed to him to live in a two-story house. As mentioned in his introduction, that house was necessary in starting philosophy in Japan. But that house did not remain unchanged throughout the last one hundred years. All discrete elements, whether willing or unwilling, are brought together sooner or later by history.

For example, a famous student of the history of modern European philosophy and a former professor at Tokyo University, Katsura Juichi (1902–), recently published a work tracing the historical development of that basic character of modern European philosophy which, based on the intellectual subject, saw the world as an external object. Katsura tries to elucidate the current philosophical problem of transcending that intellectual subject. He writes that what moved him to this investigation is a certain private interest in where the philosophizing self has its position in philosophy. Here we see a determination to no longer live peacefully in a two-story house. Moreover, we can never forget Mori Arimasa (1911–1976), who seems to have intended not only to leave the house but also to live among Europeans so completely that he might, by literally dwelling inside Europe bodily, realize the difference between them and the Japanese. He would thereby formulate anew the question as to what we are and refine it into a more developed and improved form. He intended to rebuild the house by himself. It is the most radical as well as the most pathetic intention among the Japanese who accepted Europe during these one hundred years. He died in Paris in the winter of 1976.

These two individuals are mentioned not because of their philosophical achievements but because of their attitudes. Katsura is a typical student in Japan of the history of modern European philosophy who strives for the objective acceptance of European philosophy. Mori Arimasa was one of the few in Japan who, because of birth and social position, lived in a European-style house. What led even these two to such attitudes suggests the basic problem Japanese philosophy ought to solve.

In conclusion, it may be said that philosophy in Japan is just emerging after one hundred years of preparation. What shaped this epoch were the war and the world fluctuation of the last thirty-five years. Above all, existentialism has played a major role in encouraging philosophy in Japan only now to meet *wakon*. To borrow Löwith's words, the Japanese have gotten to the stage of "learning *für sich.*" To become *für sich* means nothing but to be aware of one's own *an sich*: namely, the Japanese two-story house. Now the primary problem of philosophy in Japan is "struggle against *wakon.*" We may say that Japan has only just arrived at the real starting point. That nation's true worth and world citizenship rest utterly with the future.

SELECT BIBLIOGRAPHY

BOOKS AND ARTICLES

Aomi, J., et al. (eds.). *Kagaku-Jidai no Tetsugaku* ("Philosophy in the Age of Science"), 3 vols. (Tokyo: Baifū-kan, 1964).

Doi, T. *"Amae" no Kozo* ("Structure of 'Amae' ") (Tokyo: Kōbun-dō, 1971).

Funayama, S. *Meiji Tetsugaku-Shi Kenkyu* ("Researches into the History of Philosophy of the *Meiji* Era") (Kyoto: Mineruba-shobo, 1959).

———. *Nippon no Kannenronsha* ("Idealists in Japan") (Tokyo: Eihō-dō, 1956).

———. *Taisho Tetsugaku-Shi Kenkyu* ("Researches into the History of Philosophy of the *Taisho* Era") (Kyoto: Hōritsubunka-sha, 1965).

Hiromatsu, W. *Jiteki-Sekaikan e no Zenshō* ("The Outpost for a Factual View of the World") (Tokyo: Keisō-shōbō, 1975).

———. *Marukus-Shugi no Chihei* ("The Horizon of Marxism") (Tokyo: Keisō-shobō, 1969).

Ichii, S. *Tetsugakuteki-Bunseki* ("Philosophical Analysis") (Tokyo: Iwanami-shoten, 1963).

Ichikawa, H. *Seishin toshite no Shintai* ("Body as Mind") (Tokyo: Keisō-shobō, 1975).

Iijima, M., et al. (eds.). *Jitsuzon-Shugi* ("Existentialism"), 8 vols. (Tokyo: Risō-sha, 1968–1974).

Imamichi, T. *Dōitsusei no Jikososei* ("The Self-Formativeness in Identity") (Tokyo: Tokyo Daigaku Shuppan-kai, 1971).

Imanishi, K. *Imanishi Kinji Zenshū* ("The Complete Works of Imanishi Kinji") (Tokyo: Kōdan-sha, 1974–1975).

Iwasaki, T. *Benshōhō* ("Dialectic—Its Critique and Development") (Tokyo: Tokyo Daigaku Shuppan-kai, 1954).

———. *Gendai Eibei no Rinrigaku* ("Ethics in England and America Today") (Tokyo: Keisō-shobō, 1963).

————. *Rinrigaku* ("Ethics") (Tokyo: Yūhikaku, 1974).

————, et al. (eds.). *Gendai-Tetsugaku Nyūmon* ("Introduction into Philosophy Today"), 4 vols. (Tokyo: Yūshin-dō, 1968).

Kaneko, T. *Jitsuzon-Risei no Tetsugaku* ("Philosophy of Existential Reason") (Tokyo: Kōbun-dō, 1953).

————. *Rinrigaku Gairon* ("Ethics") (Tokyo: Iwanami-shoten, 1965).

Katsura, J. *Dekaruto-Tetsugaku to sono Hatten* ("Cartesian Philosophy and Its Development") (Tokyo: Tokyo Daigaku Shuppan-kai, 1966).

————. *Kinsei Shutai-Shugi no Hatten to Genkai* ("The Development and Limit of Modern Subjectivism") (Tokyo: Tokyo Daigaku Shuppan-kai, 1974).

Kimura, B. *Hito to Hito to no Aida* ("Between One and One: Psychopathological Essays on Japan") (Tokyo: Kōbun-dō, 1972).

Kuroda, W. *Keiken to Gengo* ("Experience and Language") (Tokyo: Tokyo Daigaku Shuppan-kai, 1975).

Miyake, G. *Ningen Sonzairon* ("Ontology of Man") (Tokyo: Keisō-shobō, 1973).

Mori, A. *Dekaruto to Pasukaru* ("Descartes and Pascal") (Tokyo: Chikuma-shobō, 1972).

————. *Kindai-Seishin to Kirisuto-Kyō* ("Modern Spirit and Christianity") (Tokyo: Kōdan-sha, 1972).

————. *Sabaku ni mukatte* ("Toward the Desert") (Tokyo: Chikuma-shobō, 1974).

Muramatsu, K. *Hegeru Ronrigaku Kenkyu* ("Researches for Hegel's Logic") (Tokyo: Hokuryū-kan, 1948).

Nakamura, H. *Hikaku-Shisō-Ron* ("Theory of Comparative Thoughts") (Tokyo: Iwanami-shoten, 1960).

Nakamura, Y. *Gendai Jōnen-Ron* ("On Sentiment Today: Between Aesthetics and Politics") (Tokyo: Keisō-shobō, 1972).

————. *Kansei no Kakusei* ("Awakening of Sensibility") (Tokyo: Iwanami-shoten, 1975).

————. *Nippon no Shiso-Kai* ("The Intellectual World in Japan: Before, Amid and After the War") (Tokyo: Keisō-shobō, 1967).

Ōmori, S. *Gengo, Chikaku, Sekai* ("Language, Perception and the World") (Tokyo: Iwanami-shoten, 1971).

————. *Mono to Kokoro* ("Thing and Mind") (Tokyo: Tokyo Daigaku Shuppan-kai, 1976).

Ōshima, Y. *Jitsuzon-Rinri no Rekishiteki-Kyōi* ("The Historical Situation of Existential Ethics") (Tokyo: Sōbun-sha, 1956).

————, et al. (eds.). *Gendai no Rinri* ("Ethics in Our Own Day"), 12 vols. (Tokyo: Chikuma-shobō, 1958–1959).

Saigusa, H. *Gijutsu no Tetsugaku* ("A Philosophy of Technics") (Tokyo: Iwanami-shoten, 1952).

————. *Nippon no Yuibutsuronsha* ("Materialists in Japan") (Tokyo: Eihō-dō, 1956).

Sakuda, K. *Haji no Bunka Saikō* ("Reconsideration of 'Shame-Culture' ") (Tokyo: Chikuma-shobō, 1967).

Sawada, Y. *Gendai ni okeru Tetsugaku to Ronri* ("Philosophy and Logic in Our Time") (Tokyo: Iwanami-shoten, 1964).

Shimizu, I. *Gendai-Shisō* ("Contemporary Thoughts"), 2 vols. (Tokyo: Iwanami-shoten, 1965).

Sueki, T. *Bitogenshutain Ronri-Tetsugaku Ronkō no Kenkyū* ("Researches in Wittgenstein's *Tractatus Logico-Philosophicus*"), 2 vols. (Tokyo: Kōron-sha, 1976–1977).

Taketani, M. *Benshōhō no Shomondai* ("The Problems of Dialectic") (Tokyo: Rigaku-sha, 1947).

————. *Benshōhō no Shomondai* and *Zoku Benshōhō no Shomondai* (Tokyo: Keisō-shobō, 1969).

————. *Gendai no Rironteki-Shomondai* ("Theoretical Problems Today") (Tokyo: Iwanami-shoten, 1968).

————. *Zoku Benshōhō no Shomondai* ("The Problems of Dialectic Continued") (Tokyo: Rigaku-sha, 1955).

Takeuchi, Y. *Takeuchi Yoshimi hyōron-shū* ("Collected Essays of Takeuchi Yoshimi") (Tokyo: Chikuma-shobō, 1966).

Tanabe, H. *Kirisuto-kyō no Benshō* ("Dialectic in Christianity") (Tokyo: Chikuma-shobō, 1948).

————. "Sie no Sonzaigaku ka Shi no Benshōhō ka," ("Either Ontology of Life or Dialectic of Death?"), *Tetsugaku-Kenkyu* 42, No. 483 (1962).

————. *Zange-Dō to shite no Tetsugaku* ("Philosophy as *Zange-Dō*") (Tokyo: Iwanami-shoten, 1946).

Tsurumi, S. *Tsurumi Shunsuke Chosaku-shū* ("Collected Papers of Tsurumi Shunsuke"), 5 vols. (Tokyo: Chikuma-shobō, 1975–1976).

Ueda, S. (ed.). *Bunseki-Tetsugaku Kenkyū Ronbun-shū* ("Papers of Inquiry into Analytical Philosophy"), 5 vols. (Tokyo: Waseda Daigaku Shuppan-bu, 1954–1960).

Ueyama, S. *Benshōhō no Keifu* ("A Genealogy of Dialectic—Marxism and Pragmatism") (Tokyo: Mirai-sha, 1963).

————. *Nippon no Shisō* ("Thoughts in Japan: A Genealogy of the Native-born and the Europeanized") (Tokyo: Saimal-Shuppan-kai, 1971).

———— and Umehara, T. *Nippongaku Kotohajime* ("The Beginning of Japanese Philosophy") (Tokyo: Shōgaku-kan, 1972).

Umehara, T. *Bi to Shūkyō no Hakken* ("A Discovery of Beauty and Religion: A Creative Essay on Japanese Culture") (Tokyo: Chikuma-shobō, 1972).

Umemoto, K. *Kakumei no Shisō to sono Jikken* ("The Revolutionary Thought and Its Experiment") (Tokyo: Sanichi-shobō, 1969).

————. *Marukus-Shugi ni okeru Shisō to Kagaku* ("Thought and Science in Marxism") (Tokyo: Sanichi-shobō, 1946).

Yamada, M. *Nippon-Gata Shisō no Genzō* ("The Original Figure of Typical Ideas in Japan") (Tokyo: Sanichi-shobō, 1961).

Yamamoto, I. *Kotoba no Tetsugaku* ("Philosophy of Language") (Tokyo: Iwanami-shoten, 1965).

Yamauchi, T. *Jitsuzon to Shoyū* ("Existence and Possession") (Tokyo: Iwanami-shoten, 1953).

Yamazaki, S., et al. (eds.). *Gendai no Tetsugaku* ("Philosophy in Our Time"), 6 vols. (Tokyo: Yūhi-kaku, 1958–1965).

Yanagida, K. *Nishida Tetsugaku to Yuibutsuron* ("Nishida's Philosophy and Materialism") (Tokyo: Aoki-shoten, 1972).

Yuasa, Y. *Kindai Nippon no Tetsugaku to Jitsuzon-Shiso* ("Philosophy in Modern Japan and Existential Thoughts") (Tokyo: Sōbun-sha, 1970).

JOURNALS

Bigaku
Indogaku Bukkyogaku Kenkyu
Journal of the Japan Association for Philosophy of Science
Nishi-Nihon Tetsugaku Kai Kaiha
Philosophy, Mito Philosophical Society
Philosophy, Philosophical Association of Japan
Philosophy East and West
Riso
Shisaku
Shīsō
Tetsugaku, Hiroshima Philosophical Society
Tetsugaku, Mita Philosophical Society
Tetsugaku Kenkyu
Tetsugaku Ronshu
Tetsugaku Zasshi

People's Republic of China

CHARLES WEI-HSUN FU

The philosophical scene in the People's Republic of China has been and is entirely dominated by Marxism-Leninism and particularly Mao Tsetung Thought. In his "Report on the Revision of the Party Constitution" delivered at the Seventh National Congress of the Communist Party of China on May 14, 1945, Liu Shao-ch'i, who became Mao's heir-apparent but was ousted from the party during the Cultural Revolution, announced for the first time the establishment of Mao Tsetung Thought as the guiding principle for all the party works in the general program of the party constitution. Mao Tsetung Thought was greatly praised as the highest expression of Chinese national wisdom and the ingenious Sinified Marxism unifying the universal truth of Marxism-Leninism and the concrete practice of the Chinese Revolution.[1] Despite the fact that Mao Tsetung Thought was deleted from the party constitution at the Eighth National Congress in 1956, partly resulting from the Chinese response to Khrushchev's shocking denunciation of Stalin and Stalinism, it has never lost its ideological prestige in China as the one and only correct guideline in both theory and practice. And it was rewritten, along with Marxism-Leninism, into the party constitution at the Ninth and the Tenth National Congresses (1969 and 1973) as the sole theoretical basis guiding the thinking of the whole party. In fact, Mao Tsetung Thought has become the ultimate theoretical basis for all philosophic, scientific, artistic, and politico-economic engagements throughout China. Indeed, it has become the ideological foundation of a new Chinese culture and way of life proletarianly severed from the traditional one.

Mao Tsetung Thought has been consistently developed, enriched, and deepened—along the apostolic line of Marxism-Leninism—in parallel to the various stages of Mao's revolutionary activity and experience from his early participation in the founding of the Chinese Communist party to the Cultural Revolution that was still continuing at the time of Mao's death. In the summer of 1964, Mao told his comrades of his long and thorny philosophical path as follows:

---

*This article was read as a visiting speech on "Maoism and Chinese Philosophy" at Fairfield University, sponsored by the Philosophy Honor Society, Phi Sigma Tau, the Philosophy Academy, and the Philosophy Department at Fairfield University, October 28, 1976.

I studied Confucius in the past, and spent six years on the *Four Books* and the *Five Classics*. . . . At that time, I believed deeply in Confucius, and even wrote essays [expounding the Confucian ideas]. Later I attended a bourgeois school for seven years. . . . This includes five years of normal school, two years of high school, and also the time spent in the library. . . . Originally I was a feudalist and an advocate of bourgeois democracy. Society impelled me to participate in the revolution.[2]

I once believed in idealism, in Confucius, and in Kantian dualism. Later the situation changed, and I participated in the organization of the Communist Party. . . . I should say that my own [intellectual] history consists of the change from slumber to awakening, from idealism to materialism, and from theism to atheism. It is not correct to say that I have been a Marxist-Leninist from the beginning. . . . I am now seventy-one years old but still ignorant of many things, and I study every day. . . . I am not a person already very perfect from the beginning; I have believed in idealism, in theism, and I have lost many battles and committed many mistakes. These lost battles as well as mistakes have educated myself. Other people's mistakes have also educated myself.[3]

Based on his exceptionally rich experience of revolutionary practice, Mao as a dedicated Marxist-Leninist expressed his proletarianly pragmatic conception of philosophy that

It is only when there is class struggle that there can be philosophy. It is a waste of time to discuss theory of knowledge separated from practice. . . . Those who engage in philosophical studies think that philosophy comes first. This is wrong. What comes first is class struggle. The oppressors oppress the oppressed, and the oppressed want to fight back and seek a way out, thus starting to look for philosophy. It is only when people make such a start that there is Marxism-Leninism and that they discover philosophy.[4]

In following the typical Marxist-Leninist approach to philosophy as an important part of the ideological superstructure and politically partisan in character, Mao pointed out two outstanding characteristics of dialectical materialism:

One is its class nature: it openly avows that dialectical materialism is in the service of the proletariat. The other is its practicality: it emphasizes the dependence of theory on practice, emphasizes that theory is based on practice and in turn serves practice. The truth of any knowledge or theory is determined not by subjective feelings, but by objective results in social practice. Only social practice can be the criterion of truth. The standpoint of practice is the primary and basic standpoint in the dialectical materialist theory of knowledge.[5]

I have argued elsewhere that "in Marxism-Leninism there is always an uneasy vacillation between the primacy of theory (a scientific-dialectical system of general and specific laws) and the primacy of practice (a working program of revolution)," and that "in his resolution of the dilemma between theory and practice in Marxist theory of knowledge, Mao is opting for the supremacy of practice: social practice is the ultimate test of all the truths (laws, theories, ideas, etc.) historically conditioned.''[6] In what sense and to what extent, then, has this Maoist principle of the primacy of practice over theory, the seminal idea of which comes from Lenin, affected Mao's own thinking on the essence of Marxism-Leninism? What are the basic characteristics of Mao Tsetung Thought, a body of thought which has reshaped the ultimate ground of historical materialism and its philosophical foundation dialectical materialism? And what justifies the view that Marxism-Leninism finally culminates in Mao Tsetung Thought, wherein is to be found the master key to uncovering the deep structure of Marxism-Leninism rooted in what I call *ethical proletarianism*?[7] The following pages deal first with Mao's unique reorientation of dialectical and historical materialism. To illustrate this point, the three major struggles of Mao Tsetung Thought with the revisionist line of China's philosophical front between 1949 and 1964 are discussed. Next follows an examination of the Maoist confrontation with traditional Chinese philosophy in regard to the problem of the history of Chinese philosophy, metaphysics, theory of knowledge, and practical philosophy that includes ethics, politico-social philosophy, and the philosophy of education. Finally, four dilemmas (philosophical, political, moral, and cultural) in Mao Tsetung Thought are pointed out and a philosophical way of resolving these dilemmas is suggested, thereby projecting the future course of the critico-creative inheritance of Chinese philosophical thought after Mao.

II

Mao Tsetung's theoretical contribution to materialist dialectics, in close line with Lenin's thinking, lies in his radical reduction of Engels' three fundamental laws to one, namely, the law of the unity of opposites reformulated Maoistically as "one divides into two." In his philosophical essay "On Contradiction," Mao asserted that "The law of contradiction in things, that is, the law of the unity of opposites, is the basic law of materialist dialectics."[8] He repeated and enriched this thesis twenty years later: "Marxist philosophy holds that the law of the unity of opposites is the fundamental law of the universe. This law operates universally, whether in the natural world, in human society, or in man's thinking. Between the opposites in a contradiction there is at once unity and struggle, and it is this that impels things to move and change."[9] Engels' law of the transition from quantity to quality is considered superfluous and undialectical, for the reason that partial qualitative change is necessarily involved in any process of quantitative change before the completion of qualitative change itself, which is final and abrupt. The mutual transformation of both quality and quantity thus constitutes a unity of opposites. The law of the negation of the negation is, Mao contended, also undialectical, for any moment or stage in any process of the change and development of things in nature and history is and must be simultaneously an affirmation and a negation. The mutual transformation of both the affirmation and the negation again constitutes a unity of opposites. From the

Maoist viewpoint of "one divides into two," the so-called negation of the negation, like the transition from quantity to quality, is a mere abstraction and is perfectly reducible to the law of the unity of opposites.

Mao said that "All contradictory things are interconnected; not only do they coexist in a single entity in given conditions, but in other given conditions they also transform themselves into each other. This is the full meaning of the identity [or unity] of opposites."[10] There are, then, two inseparable meanings here. The first meaning of the unity of opposites or identity of contradiction is that the two aspects opposite to each other in any given condition are and must be interdependent for their respective existence. In the unofficially circulated writings and sayings of Mao entitled *Long Live Mao Tsetung Thought*, Mao cited quite a number of examples to illustrate the mutual interdependence of the opposites, e.g., qualitative change and quantitative change, balance and imbalance, life and death, phenomenon and essence, matter and spirit, the finite and the infinite, content and form, possibility and actuality, necessity and freedom, analysis and synthesis, spring-summer and fall-winter, the nucleus and the electrons (within an atom), war and peace, unity and struggle, materialism and idealism, dialectics and metaphysics, socialism and capitalism, collective ownership (of the means of production) and ownership by the whole people, two politico-ideological lines (within the Communist party or the international communist movement), male and female, father and son, the party cadres and the masses, the worker and the peasant, the two mentalities (say, the proletarian and the petit bourgeois) within a single person such as an intellectual. The second meaning of the unity of opposites, which is far more important than the interdependence of the two contradictory aspects from the standpoint of revolutionary practice, is that each of the opposites transforms itself into its opposite, changes its position to that of its opposite, e.g., the transformation of the petit bourgeois nature (of an intellectual or a peasant) into the proletarian nature, the transformation of a semicolonial and semifeudal society into a socialist society, and so forth. Echoing Lenin's words, Mao insisted on the perpetual emerging and resolving of contradictions, that "the unity of opposites is conditional, temporary and relative, while the struggle of mutually exclusive opposites is absolute."[11] Hence, Mao's primary emphasis on the "negative" aspect of the identity of contradiction like abrupt (qualitative) change, imbalance, and the like.[12]

The full significance of Mao's "one divides into two" thesis cannot be understood well without noting its practical implications. According to Mao's revolutionary dialectics, the only correct way of proletarian revolutionary practice is, among other things, to discover and face courageously all the relevant contradictions existing at different revolutionary stages, to apply different methods of dialectical analysis to different kinds of contradiction in different revolutionary conditions, to recognize and set up the opposite that objectively exists, to actively search for and learn a valuable lesson from what Mao himself called "negative teachers" and "negative teaching materials" so as to discipline and strengthen the revolutionary force, and to take a precautionary means in anticipation of further contradictions to emerge at the next revolutionary stage. When different methods of dialectical analysis are applied to different kinds of contradiction, it is of utmost importance to distinguish the principal or decisive contradiction from the secondary or subordinate contradiction, the principal aspect of a contradiction from its secondary aspect, the antagonistic form of contradiction from the nonantagonistic form, to observe and analyze dialectically the possibility and actuality of the mutual transformation of the principal and the nonprincipal contradictions, of the antagonistic and the nonantagonistic contradictions, and to handle or resolve them correctly in accordance with the Marxist-Leninist principle of class struggle and proletarian dictatorship. These are the essentials of Mao's revolutionary dialectics of "one divides into two." In short, Mao's revolutionary dialectics attempts a perfect combination of "one divides into two" in principle and proletarian flexibility in application. This helps to explain Mao's ideological consistency and persistence, his political resoluteness and shrewdness, as well as his strategic and tactical artfulness and unpredictability—an extremely rare phenomenon of the human mind in the history of revolution.

Mao's revolutionary dialectics had not been successfully accepted and practiced without opposition before the Cultural Revolution was launched upon Mao's own initiative. According to the official account by the Chinese Communist party, three major struggles of principle took place on China's philosophical front between 1949 and 1964. The struggles centered around the question of China's economic base and superstructure, the question of whether there is identity between thinking and being, and the question of the dialectical nature of (the law of) the unity of opposites. These struggles were provoked one after another by Yang Hsien-chen, director of the Higher Party School, and some other theoreticians who supported the revisionist line of Liu Shao-ch'i and his associates, at crucial junctures in the conflict between the two classes (the proletariat and the bourgeoisie), the two politico-economic roads (socialism and capitalism), and the two ideological lines (Mao's proletarian revolutionary line and Liu's revisionist line). They were said to be a fierce battle between dialectical and historical materialism on the one hand and idealism and metaphysics on the other, and to reflect the philosophical front of the acute class struggle at home and abroad. The question of the dialectical nature of (the law of) the unity of opposites was the fundamental philosophical question. The two opposite solutions of this question help to reveal the essential nature of the mutually adversary approaches to the other two questions respectively taken by the two camps politically and ideologically clashing with each other.

According to the Maoist account of the philosophical debate on the question of materialist dialectics, Liu Shao-ch'i directed Yang Hsien-chen in 1964 to concoct the theory "combine two into one" in open opposition to Mao's revolutionary dialectics "one divides into two." The debate in question is not purely philosophical wordplay, for it reflects the deeply divided opinions concerning the Sino-Soviet dispute and China's economic policy, as well as its socialist education campaign renewed in 1963. The Maoists accused Yang, among other things, of misdescribing the interdependence of the two opposite aspects on each other for their existence as "links that cannot be separated," of denying completely the perpetual split and transformation of the opposite(s), of trying to harmonize the contradiction between the proletariat and the bourgeoisie that can only be resolved by socialist revolution, of abandoning struggle and opposing revolution, of "combining Marxism with revisionism," and of "combining socialism with capitalism and social-imperialism." In short, Yang's idealistic dialectics of "combine two into one" was attacked as setting up a counterrevolutionary philosophical basis for Liu's "theory of the dying out of class struggle," which followed in Khrushchev's revisionist steps.

The Maoist and the revisionist solutions of the question of the essential nature of the unity of opposites in materialist dialectics are philosophically linked—or better, philosophically determine—the two different answers to the question of the relationship between thinking and being in dialectical materialism. Again, Yang and his philosophical followers were accused of designing the theory that "there is no identity between thinking and being." Their alleged intent was to provide the theoretical basis for Liu's counterrevolutionary line aimed at overthrowing the dictatorship of the proletariat and restoring capitalism at the stage of socialist revolution.

Since Mao regarded the law of the unity of opposites in terms of "one divides into two" as the fundamental law of the universe, it must, of course, apply to the dialectical relationship between thinking and being. Although Mao never doubted the ontic primordiality of material being, he had gone beyond Engels and Lenin in stressing that "matter can be transformed into consciousness and consciousness into matter." From the Maoist standpoint of social practice, the active and revolutionary theory of reflection recognizes not only thinking as the reflection of being but also the reaction of thinking on being. Mao interpreted the dialectical materialist theory of knowledge to mean that "Often, correct knowledge can be arrived at only after many repetitions of the process leading from matter to consciousness and then back to matter, that is, leading from practice to knowledge and then back to practice."[13] Mao sometimes even emphasized the primacy of spirit over matter. He said:

A single word may rejuvenate a country; a single word may also bring disaster to a country. This is [what I mean by] spirit changing matter. Marx had one word, that is, the necessity of proletarian revolution and proletarian dictatorship. Isn't this a single word rejuvenating a country? Khrushchev also had one word, that is, no class struggle and no revolution. Isn't this a single word bringing disaster to a country?[14]

From the Maoist point of view, Yang Hsien-chen's theory originated the fallacy that "identity between thinking and being" and "dialectical identity" belonged to "two different categories," that "although the same in wording, they are different in meaning." It was said that Yang was attempting to set the theory of reflection against the identity between thinking and being, alleging that, with respect to the question of the relationship between thinking and being, "materialism uses the theory of reflection to solve it, while idealism solves it by means of identity." In denying the identity between thinking and being, Yang was thus accused of denying totally the great role of Mao's revolutionary theory, of negating the conscious and dynamic role of the masses, and of twisting the active and revolutionary theory of reflection into the mechanical theory of reflection.

The philosophical dispute between the Maoists and the revisionists did not end here. What was most crucial in the dispute concerns the question of the relationship between economic base and superstructure, that is, the question on the essence of historical materialism. Herein is found the most original thesis in the thought of Mao Tsetung.

III

Mao's interpretation of historical materialism during the pre-Liberation period mostly followed Lenin's voluntarist approach, with a strong emphasis on the remodeling of the superstructure. In "On Contradiction," Mao said:

True, the productive forces, practice and the economic base generally play the principal and decisive role; whoever denies this is not a materialist. But it must also be admitted that in certain conditions, such aspects as the relations of production, [revolutionary] theory and the superstructure in turn manifest themselves in the principal and decisive role. . . . When the superstructure (politics, culture, etc.) obstructs the development of the economic base, political and cultural changes become principal and decisive. Are we going against materialism when we say this? No. The reason is that while we recognize that in the general development of history the material determines the mental and social being determines social consciousness, we also—and indeed must—recognize the reaction of mental on material things, of social consciousness on social being and of the superstructure on the economic base.[15]

Mao also followed, somewhat naively, Lenin's line of reasoning that "antagonism and contradiction are not at all one and the same. Under socialism, the first will disappear, the second will remain."[16] Twenty years later, however, Mao was to coin a new term "antagonistic contradiction" and affirm its existence even in socialist societies like Russia and China. He was also to realize that, whereas Russia was ignoring the antagonistic contradiction and abandoning the class struggle, China would have to carry out the dictatorship of the proletariat advocated by Marx, Engels, and Lenin. Mao's discovery of Khrushchev's revisionist line, his struggle with the rightist intellectuals, rich peasants, industrial capitalists, and revisionist theoreticians within the party, as well as his struggle with Peng Te-huai and other party opponents regarding the Three Red Flags campaign, namely, General Line for Socialist Reconstruction, Great Leap Forward, and People's Commune, impelled him to reflect anew on the question of socialist revolution. Hence, the Maoist slogan "Never forget class struggle" (1962), the Socialist Education Movement (1963–1965), the Great Proletarian Cultural Revolution (1966–1969), the "criticism of Lin Piao and Confucius" campaign (1973–1975), the campaign to restrict bourgeois right and consolidate the proletarian dictatorship (1975), the criticism of "Water Margin" campaign (1975–1976), and the most recent campaign to "beat back the right deviationist attempt to reverse correct verdicts" until Mao's own death. All of these ideological campaigns have their theoretical ground in Mao's doctrine of uninterrupted or continuing revolution, wherein lies the essence of Mao Tsetung Thought and Mao's Copernican revolution in historical materialism.

Mao's unique reorientation of historical materialism was most radically presented in his long and unpublished "Reading Notes on the Third Edition of the Soviet Union's Textbook on Political Economy" (c. 1960), in which he said:

All the histories of revolution have proven that it is not the case that new productive forces are fully developed first before the old relations of production can be changed. Our revolution began with making propaganda for Marxism, and this was to create a new public opinion in order to push the revolution ahead. In the course of revolution, it is only after the old superstructure is overthrown that it becomes possible to put an end to the old relations of production. Once the old relations of production are destroyed and the new ones are set up, the way for the development of new social productive forces will be paved. Then, the technological revolution can be launched vigorously and the social productive forces can be greatly developed. Simultaneously with the development of productive forces, the remolding of the relations of production as well as the ideological remolding are to be carried on and out. [17]

From the viewpoint of world history, the bourgeois launched their revolution and founded the country of their kind not after the industrial revolution, but before it. They also brought about a change in the superstructure and seized the state apparatus first, and then made propaganda, gained strength, and pressed vigorously for a change in the relations of production. The smooth reorganization of the relations of production thus paved the way for the development of productive forces. The revolution in the relations of production is, of course, touched off by a certain development of productive forces, but the rapid development in productive forces generally takes place after the change of the relations of production. . . . First and foremost, create public opinion and seize political power, then resolve the question of ownership. And then develop productive forces on a grand scale: this is a general law. [18]

Here Mao is not only challenging the established Marxist view that the socialist revolution of the proletariat cannot be launched without undergoing the stage of capitalist production and exchange, but also disputing the traditional materialist conception of history that, in Engels' words, "the economic relations, however much they may be influenced by the other—the political and ideological relations, are still ultimately the decisive ones. . . ." [19] Lenin had to develop a new thesis, "imperialism is the highest stage of capitalism," still within the orthodox context of historical materialism, in order to justify his doctrine of socialist revolution in a single and less developed capitalist country such as Russia. At the same time, Mao was theoretically daring, based on his revolutionary experience and success in a semicolonial and semifeudal society, to assert that the revolution in the ideological superstructure can and does propel and determine positively the transformation of the relations of production and then of productive forces, especially in the case of poor and backward countries like China (and the Third World nations).

The philosophical contributions and moral implications of Mao's Copernican revolution in both theory and practice cannot be overemphasized. His reshaping of the foundation of historical materialism has posed an extremely important and hard-hitting question with respect to the line of demarcation between economic base (particularly the relations of production) and superstructure, as well as to the historical connection between productive forces and relations of production. In stressing the transformation of the (ideological) superstructure as serving the principal and decisive role in the development of history, it has also exposed the underlying structure of historical materialism as ultimately a revolutionary philosophy of practice deeply rooted in what can be called ethical proletarianism. This philosophy can now serve as a new justification for Marxism-Leninism, ethically and morally challenging all the nonproletarian moral theories and practices, past or present.

Mao's reorientation of historical materialism provoked a severe attack by the Russian Marxist-Leninists, who denounced Mao Tsetung Thought as anti-Marxist, antiscientific, chauvinistic, idealistic, and petit bourgeois. It also struggled hard with the revisionist theory of "synthesized economic base" at home, a variant of the "theory of productive forces," advocated by Yang Hsien-chen, Sun Yeh-fang, et al. This struggle, allegedly one of the three major struggles on China's philosophical front, again reflects the disagreement between two politico-ideological lines before the Cultural Revolution—the Maoist line, which emphasized "from the masses, to the masses," put politics in command, and held on unswervingly to the dictatorship of the proletariat and the uninterrupted revolution in the superstructure, *versus* the revisionist line, which stressed party bureaucracy, put economy in command, encouraged material incentives, and attempted to restore capitalism Russian-style. Yang asserted that "in the period of transition the economic base of the state power of the socialist type" was of a "synthesized nature" "embracing both the socialist sector and the capitalist sector, and the sector of individual peasant economy as well"; that "they can develop in a balanced and coordinated way"; that the socialist superstructure should "serve the entire economic base," including the capitalist economy and "also serve the bourgeoisie"; and that China, because of its backward productive forces, was destined to build a capitalist economic base first before it would be able to launch a socialist revolution. Yang's theory was attacked for making a fetish of economic spontaneity, for absurdly exaggerating the decisive role of productive forces reduced to productive means and techniques, and for completely negating the factor of man and denying the effect of revolution on the development of production, of production relations on productive forces, and of superstructure on economic base. In short, Yang's "synthesization" was said to constitute a clear case of attempting to "combine two into one," as well as to deny the contradiction and struggle between socialism and capitalism during the transition period, thus allowing capitalism to swallow up socialism.

No traditional Marxist prior to Mao had ever resolved the crucial issue over historical priority: which one exactly constitutes the ultimately determining element in history, economic base or superstructure, productive forces or production relations? Mao's unique resolution of the issue has at least two moral justifications. First, while the Soviet Union, which once produced and exported Marxism-Leninism, has abandoned at home the class struggle and the proletarian dictatorship leading toward the higher phase of communism, the oppressed people of the Third World are looking for a theoretically correct and workable and morally timely and inspiring guide for their revolutionary cause, the nature of which is basically different from that of the class struggle described in old-fashioned Marxist terms. The Maoist version of historical materialism does provide such a theoretical guide. As Mao experienced and reasoned, "The poorer they are, the more people want revolution. In Western capitalist countries, both the employment rate and the wage standard are relatively high, and bourgeois influence on the working people has been far-reaching. It looks as if it is not that easy to carry out socialist transformation in those countries. . . . The important question is the transformation of man."[20] And this point leads to a second one: the proletarian transformation of human nature.

Mao's discovery of and struggle with the revisionist tendency at home and abroad led him to the painful realization that "the question of which will win out, socialism or capitalism, is still not really settled. Marxists are still a minority among the entire population as well as among the intellectuals. Therefore, Marxism must still develop through struggle."[21] Until when? Mao's answer, in accord with his dialectics of "one divides into two," was that politico-ideological contradictions, struggles, and revolutions would still exist even after the stage of communism was reached. There would be new goals to be set, new tasks to be fulfilled, and many stages of the communist movement to be undergone. "Such struggles will never end. This is the law of development of truth and, naturally, of Marxism as well."[22] Hence, he developed a permanent attachment to uninterrupted revolution in the superstructure in primary terms of perpetual, moral transformation of man in the proletarian way. Mao's moral insight led him beyond Lenin to the conclusion that the ultimate question in Marxism-Leninism no longer concerns the attainment of the goal, but instead concerns the day-to-day proletarian transformation of human nature. In other words, Mao apparently reasoned that, since proletarian morality must be a matter of everyday habit and not of fixed rules, the ultimate way of realizing proletarian morality without any separation of theory and practice is to use an external coercive means to educate the masses at the initial stage of socialist reconstruction. In this way, the masses can and will eventually transform themselves internally and spontaneously into proletarian manhood, wherein is to be found the identity of proletarian moral integrity and supreme happiness of life. In this sense, Mao's Cultural Revolution is ultimately a matter of proletarian "ought," and not simply a matter of whether it will stimulate socialist production and construction.[23] It is in this sense, too, that Mao Tsetung Thought is the logical conclusion of Marxism-Leninism and that ethical proletarianism is the logical conclusion of Mao Tsetung Thought. The deep structure of dialectical and historical materialism thus turns out, by way of Maoist reorientation, to be the proletarian macroethical theory of perpetual revolution in the superstructure.

IV

Apart from the three major struggles with Marxist revisionism on China's philosophical front, Mao Tsetung Thought also confronted and struggled hard with traditional Chinese philosophy, which makes up the principal part of the old ideological superstructure to be critically inherited and transformed. Mao once said:

Our national history goes back several thousand years and has its own characteristics and innumerable treasures. But in these matters we are mere schoolboys. Contemporary China has grown out of the China of the past; we are Marxist in our historical approach and must not lop off our history. We should sum up our history from Confucius to Sun Yatsen and take over this valuable legacy.[24]

After the Liberation, however, most of the traditional Chinese legacy, especially the philosophical one, was found to be a "poisonous weed" rather than a "fragrant flower." We can only cite some of the most significant cases to illustrate the Maoist treatment of traditional Chinese philosophy.

First, let us examine the question of interpretation and inheritance of the history of Chinese philosophy. In January 1957, when the "let a hundred flowers blossom, let a hundred schools of thought contend" campaign was in full swing, more than one hundred eminent philosophers and philosophy teachers attended a forum on the problems of the history of Chinese philosophy taking place in the Department of Philosophy at Peking University. All the participants agreed that the history of Chinese philosophy was the history of the philosophical struggles between materialism and idealism representing two social forces, progressive and reactionary, at each particular period. Nonetheless, opinions were greatly divided between the hardliners and the halfway Marxists as to the question of how to inherit and evaluate each traditional philosopher and each school of philosophy. Fung Yu-lan, for instance, presented his "method of abstract inheritance," which was severely criticized by tough-minded Marxists like Ai Ssu-chi.[25] According to Fung's method, the philosophical proposition of abstract (universal) significance can be distinguished from that of concrete (particular) significance, and those universally true propositions in the idealistic tradition, if carefully sifted out and properly reinterpreted, can still be inherited and integrated into Marxist philosophy, one good example being Confucius's doctrine of *jên* (human-kindness) in its universal form. Fung was still using this method when he published the unfinished *New History of Chinese Philosophy* in 1962, which was supposed to replace his early *History of Chinese Philosophy* which he had already self-denounced as bourgeois and reactionary. Nonetheless, he was impelled to confess his bourgeois mistakes again during the Cultural Revolution. At the time he was revising his *New History*, the anti-Confucianism campaign began; he was once again impelled to make one more—probably the last—confession in strict line with Mao Tsetung Thought. In his most recent work, *On Confucius (Lun K'ung Tzu)*, Fung finally condemned Confucius as a counterrevolutionary attempting to restore slavery and its anachronistic (ideological) superstructure.

In contrast to Fung's repeated philosophical confessions and conversions, Maoist hardliners like Yang Jung-kuo have consistently and uncompromisingly repudiated Confucianism and all the traditional philosophical schools considered idealistic and reactionary from the Marxist-Leninist-Maoist point of view. Yang was the very Maoist philosopher who led off the anti-Confucianism campaign in 1973 by publishing an article "Confucius—A Thinker Who Stubbornly Upheld the Slave System" in *People's Daily*. In the revised edition of his *Concise History of Chinese Philosophy*, Yang intensified his early and relentless attack upon all the traditional philosophers and philosophical schools judged Maoistically as idealistic and counterrevolutionary. His *Concise History* represents the recent Maoist approach to the history of Chinese philosophy in primary terms of the constant struggle between two ideological lines, namely, the progressive legalist school and the reactionary Confucian school. Many philosophical thinkers traditionally regarded as Confucianists, such as Hsün Tzu, Liu Tsung-yüan, Ch'en Liang, and Wang Fu-chih, are now regarded as legalists.

Next, on the question of metaphysics, it is not difficult to see a striking resemblance, at least on the surface level, between Mao's thesis on the unity of opposites and traditional Chinese metaphysics of *Tao* and *Yin-Yang* variously presented in the *Lao-tzu*, the *Chuang-tzu*, the *Classic of Changes* and its *Great Commentaries*. Mao often liked to borrow the age-old metaphysical jargon *hsiang-fan hsiang-ch'êng* meaning "Things that oppose each other also complement each other," in order to illustrate the mutual transformation of the opposites in materialist dialectics. "Oppose each other," Mao said, refers to the mutual exclusion or the struggle of two contradictory aspects; and "complement each other" means that in given conditions the two contradictory aspects unite and achieve identity.[26] It should be noted, however, that in their respective deep structures Mao's dialectics of "one divides into two" and the traditional metaphysics of *Tao* and *Yin-Yang* are entirely different on at least two points: (1) The Maoist dialectics stresses the unconditional and absolute nature of contradiction and struggle, while traditional Chinese metaphysics tends to emphasize

the harmonious unity or identity as well as what is trans-metaphysically primordial in terms of *Tao, Yi, T'ai-chi* (the Supreme Ultimate), *Wu-chi* (the Trans-
Ultimate), *T'ien* (Heaven), and so forth; (2) whereas the Maoist dialectics sees
the development of things as their internal and necessary self-movement, the
fundamental cause of which lies in the internal contradiction of things themselves, traditional Chinese metaphysics generally takes an overall, external view
of the mutual reversion of the opposite things symbolized in terms of perpetual
Yin-Yang interaction. Although the Maoist philosophers are somewhat sympathetic to those metaphysical systems of thought containing naive or semidialec-
tical materialist elements, such as Wang Fu-chih's philosophy of vital force
(*ch'i*) or the metaphysics of changes (*Yi*), they would generally look down upon
nearly all the traditional metaphysical thoughts as undialectical, poisonous
weeds.

As to the question of theory of knowledge, none of the traditional Chinese
thoughts can pass the Maoist test demanding the dialectical unity of theory and
practice. Mao said:

Where do correct ideas come from? Do they drop from the skies? No. Are they innate
in the mind? No. They come from social practice, and from it alone; they come from
three kinds of social practice, the struggle for production, the class struggle and scientific
experiment. It is man's social being that determines his thinking. Once the correct ideas
characteristic of the advanced class are grasped by the masses, these ideas turn into a
material force which changes society and changes the world.[27]

From the viewpoint of Mao's revolutionary dialectics, Taoism and Buddhism,
both of which have never developed any theory of positive knowledge rooted
in social practice, are to be simply brushed off as a philosophical waste. Confucianism as a whole, unlike Taoism and Buddhism, has been consistently
engaged in the quest for the unity of knowledge and practice. Yet, it is moral
knowledge of a superclass and of a metaphysical nature, rather than scientific
knowledge, that has been the primary concern of the Confucian and neo-Con-
fucian doctrine of "investigation of things and acquirement of knowledge." In
short, no traditional philosophical school in China can be said to have developed
any theory of knowledge summing up and integrating the achievements of the
social practice of the toiling masses in traditional China. It is a generally known
fact that in traditional China theory of knowledge has never existed as an independent and important subject of philosophical inquiry.

Finally, let us explore the question of practical philosophy, including ethics,
politico-social philosophy, and the philosophy of education. Here we can see
quite a few interesting points of similarity between Maoism and Confucianism.
Mao's belief in and emphasis on the moral malleability and perfectibility of
human nature is comparable to the Confucian concern with "the transformation
of physical nature into moral nature"; the altruistic (other-concerned) and semi-
collectivistic (consanguinity-oriented) tendency in Confucianism is also com-

parable, though in a rather superficial sense, to the Maoist ethico-social collectivism with the proletarian motto "serve the people"; Mao's distaste for the bookish approach to education and learning, as well as his emphasis on the practical application of Marxism-Leninism, has been to some extent influenced by Confucian pedagogical pragmatism; the method of "criticism and self-criticism" in the Maoist ideological remolding strikingly resembles the Confucian way of moral education in terms of constant self-reflection and soul-searching, mutual advice, and encouragement with respect to the cultivation of personal life, as well as of the teacher-student relationship. Mao's moralistic perpetuation of the class struggle, despite its Marxist-Leninist tone, seems to have been strongly influenced by the Confucian emphasis on moral education for the purpose of transforming selfish man into unselfish man. Both the Confucian (morally) superior man (*chün-tzu*) and "Chairman Mao's good fighters" like Lei Fang or Wang Chieh share the identity of moral integrity and supreme happiness. The Confucian political utopia depicted as "the World of Grand Unity" is somewhat similar to the Marxist-Leninist-Maoist "higher phase of communism" on the surface level. Both the Confucianists and the Marxist-Leninist-Maoists agree that, upon the realization of their respective politico-social ideals, true morality in everyday life would become a matter of spontaneous habit, not of rules. Confucian humanism that advocates "Man makes the Way, not *vice versa*" coincides with Mao's proletarian insistence on the factor of man in the development of history.

A careful uncovering of their respective deep structures will reveal the fact that Maoism and Confucianism are ideologically and politically incompatible with each other. Confucian humanism can be basically characterized as a micro-ethical intuitionism grounded upon Confucian moral principle of *jên-yi* (human-kindness and its gradational extension) and Mencian intuitive belief in the potential goodness of man distinguishable from beastly instinct. Its political ideal and social practice, which can be expressed as the way of "inner sagehood and outer kingliness," is simply a natural extension or application of everyday micro-moral practice beginning with moral self-cultivation, parental care, brotherly affection, friendship, natural respect for elders and superiors, and so on. As against Confucianism, Marxism-Leninism-Maoism can be characterized as macro-ethical proletarianism, according to which ethics is part of politico-social philosophy rooted in revolutionary social practice under the dictatorship of the proletariat. From the Maoist point of view, the traditional Confucian debate over superclass, the inborn nature of man, good or evil, is idealistic and pointless, for "In class society there is only human nature of a class character; there is no human nature above classes."[28] By the same token, the Confucian doctrine of love of humanity (*jên*) and righteousness (*yi*) would have to be refuted Maoistically, for love of humanity as an idea must be considered a product of objective social practice. There cannot be, Mao held, any genuine love of humanity and righteousness until classes are eliminated all over the world.[29]

There is a basic disagreement between Maoism and Confucianism about ideal manhood and moral education. The Confucianists tended to justify the distinction between mental work and manual labor, and looked upon the intellectuals (*shih*), the most prestigious of the four classes (intellectual, peasant, worker, businessman) in traditional China, as most capable of becoming sages. Mao, however, as a true disciple of Marx totally rejected "the antithesis between mental and physical labour"[30] and demanded ideological remolding of the intellectuals by means of attending the May 7 Cadre School, by "going up to the mountain and down to the countryside" so as to learn from the masses, by transforming day to day their own petit bourgeois world outlook into the proletarian one, and so forth. Mao expected that, with the gradual transformation of the old ideological superstructure hampering the revolutionary social practice, a new type of intellectual would eventually be bred out of ordinary workers, peasants, and soldiers throughout China, in accordance with "the five requirements for successors to the revolutionary cause of the proletariat" stipulated in Article 3, Chapter II of the new constitution of the Communist party of China at its Tenth National Congress.[31] Thus, Mao's class struggle is none other than a proletarian moral education leading to the total transformation of each and every man's bourgeois or petit bourgeois class consciousness into that of workers and peasants, and this ultimately means the proletarian moral transformation of each individual himself. To Mao and the Maoists, Confucian moral doctrines are at best a negative teaching material and Confucian philosophers negative teachers. In short, instead of "taking this valuable legacy," Mao and the Maoists have finally reached the conclusion that there is almost nothing valuable and inheritable in traditional Chinese philosophy.

V

We now come to the problem of Mao Tsetung Thought itself, a careful analysis of which must expose four interrelated dilemmas yet to be resolved completely within or beyond the orthodoxy of Marxism-Leninism. The first dilemma is philosophical, that is, the dilemma between Mao's Copernican reorientation of dialectical and historical materialism, as we have seen, and his unyielding attachment to the orthodox position of Marxism-Leninism that it has discovered the universal truth of some necessary, dialectical, and fundamental laws of nature and history. If Mao would have consistently applied his principle of the primacy of practice over theory to dialectical and historical materialism, he could not have maintained the absolute truth-claim that abrupt change, contradiction, class struggle, the dictatorship of the proletariat, the final victory of revolutionary socialism, and the like, all constitute inexorable, dialectical laws *independent of man's will*. Furthermore, Mao's insistence on the perpetual development and enrichment of Marxism-Leninism by way of its ideological struggles with all the non-Marxist doctrines clearly indicates the priority of the proletarian moral "ought" to the dialectical necessity beyond human will. With regard to the complete resolution of the dilemma in question, dialectical materialism must be looked at again as the proletarian world outlook projected into nature on the basis of historical materialism, which in turn must be *ultimately* justified on the Maoist ground of revolutionary social practice in the light of the proletarian moral judgment about what man and society *ought* to be. Ethical proletarianism as the new foundation of historical and dialectical materialism does not and should not deprive the latter of its heuristic function in our future scientific research on nature and society. On the contrary, it will liberate all the Marxist-Leninist-Maoists from their doctrinaire slumber, and strengthen the philosophical self-consistency and moral superiority of Mao Tsetung Thought as the final culmination of Marxism-Leninism challenging any human doctrine that tends to separate theoretical speculation from social practice involving the necessary transformation of man and society.

Next, we consider the political dilemma embedded in the Leninist principle of democratic centralism which Mao had tried to observe faithfully. The dilemma here concerns the mutual struggle for supremacy between democratic autonomy (''the minority always ought to subordinate itself unconditionally to the decision of the majority'') and centralized authority (''the lower organization always ought to subordinate itself unconditionally to the decision of the higher''). It is extremely difficult to resolve such a dilemma even by the Maoist way that takes the mass line, the intraparty struggle on the highest level immediately after Mao's death being a very conspicuous instance. Another political dilemma is that between the dictatorship of the proletariat and individual freedom guaranteed in the *Constitution of the People's Republic of China*.[32] The complete resolution of the dilemma is practically impossible. What is to be expected is a rapid increase in the number of revolutionary successors coming out of the great masses of workers, peasants, and soldiers, so as to realize freedom as proletarian freedom, people's democracy as democracy under proletarian guidance, the unity of the party through peaceful and not physical struggles, and so forth.

Strictly related to the above dilemma is the moral dilemma between what can be called act-proletarian morality and rule-proletarian morality.[33] Although both act-proletarianism and rule-proletarianism would abide by the proletarian categorical imperative ''You ought to act in such a way that you always treat *proletarian* humanity as the one and only end'' as the highest governing principle of proletarian morality, they would have to disagree with each other respecting the way the proletarian action is to be taken in each and every revolutionary situation. While rule-proletarianism opts for strict observance of the party rules and the constitution of the state, act-proletarianism subscribes to the supremacy of the proletarian categorical imperative embodied by the correct politico-ideological line taken under the centralized leadership of, say, Stalin or Mao. Rule-proletarianism not only has collapsed into act-proletarianism as a matter of fact in both Russia and China, but also, as an ethical theory, would have to collapse into act-proletarianism. The reason for this collapse lies in *who* is supposed to consistently and persistently carry on and through the revolutionary dictatorship of the proletariat exhibiting the essential spirit of proletarian morality. Mao himself was certainly the champion of act-proletarian morality since he openly vindicated "the revolutionary spirit of daring to go against the tide" manifesting the principle "It is justified to rebel [against the reactionaries]."[34] Thus, the moral dilemma here, like the political dilemma, can hardly be resolved practically and completely. The only way to resolve it, if not completely, necessitates a successful transformation of the great majority of the people into well-disciplined act-proletarians as soon as possible. This is exactly what Mao and the Maoists have in mind in their radical attachment to continuing revolution in the super-structure. Of course, whether the Cultural Revolution will be an everlasting success remains to be seen.

Finally, there is the cultural dilemma between the Maoist determination to create a totally new proletarian culture and the practical necessity—as a matter of national pride, which even Mao could not afford to ignore—of taking over the valuable traditional legacy in Chinese philosophy, art, literature, and culture in general. The principal reason for the Maoist failure to "take over this valuable legacy" consists in the rigid employment of the oversimplified criterion already set in strictly Marxist-Leninist-Maoist terms of the oftentimes arbitrary distinction between materialism and idealism, when the Maoists interpret, evaluate, and decide how to inherit or reject the traditional cultural legacy critically and creatively for the sake of "serving the present needs." The arbitrariness and oversimplification in question are most serious in the case of the Maoist interpretation and evaluation of traditional Chinese philosophy as previously discussed. Hsün Tzu, for instance, is now praised highly as a great legalist, but his vindication of Confucian rules of propriety (*li*) as well as his method of personal cultivation can be considered to be as idealistic and counterrevolutionary as any other Confucian philosophical position.

Another instance is Chang Tsai's as well as Wang Fu-chih's philosophy of vital force (*ch'i*), which is Maoistically misrepresented as a kind of naive materialism. The fact is that in the metaphysical philosophy of both Chang and Wang the vital force, the original substance of which is called the "grand vacuity" (*t'ai-hsü*), is not simply matter or matter-energy; it is what constitutes the integrated whole of both matter and spirit metaphysically prior to their individuated differentiation. One can ask the Maoists: if you have no intention at all of letting the traditional philosophers speak for themselves first, then why bother yourself by wasting such time in studying the traditional philosophy? And, since Marxism-Leninism-Maoism is already accepted as the one and only absolute or universal truth, why do you have to concern yourself with such innumerable negative teachers and teaching materials in traditional Chinese philosophy? The cultural dilemma here is again hardly resolvable, unless the Maoist philosophers themselves are willing to regard Marxism-Leninism-Maoism, in the light of the primacy of the proletarian socio-moral practice over theory, as fundamentally ethical proletarianism. On this basis, dialectical and historical materialism serves for the proletarian revolutionaries as a heuristic methodological principle governing the scientific-dialectic investigation into nature and history. But the unnecessary and dogmatic claim for the absolute and universal truth of dialectical and historical materialism must be abandoned.

It is in this new proletarianly moral way that Marxism-Leninism and particularly Mao Tsetung Thought will be able to exert an enormously profound and everlasting influence on the future development of Chinese philosophy. Indeed, the historical development of Chinese philosophy likened to an ever-widening, ever-expanding, and open-ended great river of human thought cannot enter into a new and creative epoch without absorbing and integrating some Marxist-Leninist-Maoist elements in the fields of philosophy of science, epistemology, philosophy or dialectics of nature, ethics, philosophy of education, as well as of political, social, and economic philosophy. In particular, Mao Tsetung Thought as ethical proletarianism will certainly remain a great ideological and moral challenge for a long time to come. (I attempt a more elaborate and complete treatment of the above problems in my forthcoming book *Marxism-Leninism-Maoism as Ethical Proletarianism.*)

According to Edgar Snow, the late American journalist, Mao once described himself as "not a complicated man, but really very simple. He was," he said, "a lone monk walking the world with a leaky umbrella."[35] A lone monk, indeed, for none of his longtime and closest comrades has ever understood him correctly and thoroughly.

AFTERWORD

The above article was written immediately after the sudden fall of Chiang Ch'ing and her Shanghai group, the so-called "gang of four." All of them were arrested and ousted from the Politbureau of the Chinese Communist party as a tragic result of the intense political struggle on the highest level of the party in post-Mao China. Although it will take at least several years for us to unravel the entire mystery of the struggle and its aftermath, since then there have been some new signs suggestive of the post-Mao regime's determination to relax, if not totally abandon, the proletarian dictatorship in scientific, cultural, economic, and politico-idealogical engagements. The regime instead favors speeding up economic production and national defense, so as to "accomplish the comprehensive modernization of agriculture, industry, national defense and science and technology before the end of the century," as was proposed by the late Premier Chou En-lai at the Fourth National Congress of the People's Republic of China on January 13, 1975.[36] The publication of the fifth volume of the *Selected Works of Mao Tsetung* which includes Mao's major speeches and writings from 1949 to 1957, the "miraculous" rehabilitation of the twice-purged Teng Hsiao-p'ing, supposedly Chou's hand-picked successor to the premiership, and other important political decisions in recent months seem to indicate the post-Mao regime's drastic reversion of the "radical" aspect of Maoist ideology and strategy, as fully demonstrated during the ten-year long Cultural Revolution, to the "moderate" aspect exemplified in Mao's speech "On the Ten Major Relationships" delivered on April 25, 1956. This speech characterizes China's less adventurous economic-social policy prior to the risky and abortive "Three Red Flags" campaign which Mao himself initiated in 1958. It was published for the first time on New Year's Day of 1977, with an apparent intention to resume the moderate approach of the 1956–1957 period.

As far as the philosophico-ideological shift of priority or emphasis is concerned, we have noted a most crucial change, and that is that a new attempt has been gradually made to "correct" Mao's Copernican reorientation of historical materialism. For instance, in his recent article "Why Did the 'Gang of Four' Wield the Big Stick of the 'Theory of Productive Forces'?," Chin Yen, the author apparently representing the ideological position of the new regime, accused the "gang of four" of "tampering with the fundamental principles of historical materialism." Chin Yen stated:

Marxism holds that man's activity in production is the most fundamental practical activity. . . . The decisive factor in the development of history is, in the last analysis, the production and reproduction of material values. . . . The "gang of four" completely denied the aforesaid basic principles of historical materialism; they denied the fact that the productive forces are the most revolutionary factor and denied the decisive bearing the productive forces have on the relations of production. They confused people's thinking by talking glibly about "revolution" without referring to the need to develop the productive forces. . . . Therefore, one of the fundamental tasks of the dictatorship of the proletariat is to strive to develop the socialist economy. With the development of the productive forces, it will provide our country with a powerful material basis for strengthening the dictatorship of the proletariat and consolidating the socialist system; it will also create favourable conditions for pushing ahead the cause of socialist revolution, for the future transition of collective ownership to ownership by the whole people and finally the transition from socialism to communism.[37]

A careful reader of this article can clearly discern that the real target of Chin Yen's accusation was Mao himself. For one thing, he cited quotations from Marx and Lenin, but none from Mao, to support his point that the "gang of four" tampered with the fundamental principles of historical materialism. Furthermore, there is no mention of the proletarian necessity to carry on the continuing revolution in the superstructure, no talk about Mao's insistence that the Cultural Revolution must be repeated periodically, and no statement about the proletarian transformation of man prior to the attainment of the higher phase of communism. The recent announcement of the Albanian Communist party, that it would part company with China, seems to show the Albanian suspicion that China has been gradually deviating from Maoist theory and practice.

An extremely important question, then, arises: Will China completely abandon Mao's thought in both theory and practice in the foreseeable future, as was the case when Russia denounced Stalin and Stalinism? The Eleventh National Congress of the Communist Party of China, which took place in Peking from August 12 to August 18, 1977, officially confirmed Hua Kuo-feng as the new party chairman. He reassured the congress in his political report that "We must hold high the great banner of Chairman Mao and resolutely defend it. This is the sacred duty of the whole Party, the whole army and the people of all nationalities in our country, . . ."[38] But will the next national congress attempt any criticism of Mao and Maoism? I do not pretend to foresee any such possibility; all that can be said is that, unlike the case of the Russian denunciation of Stalin and Stalinism, the Chinese Communist party can hardly afford to damage Mao's prestige in any way, politically or ideologically, for the simple reason that Mao is the combination of Marx-Engels, Lenin, and Stalin in the entire history of the Chinese Communist party.

The October incident in Peking undoubtedly exposes the many serious economic, political, and ideological problems China has been facing in recent years. How shall China resolve the dialectical contradiction between the development of productive forces and the continuing revolution in the superstructure, the political dilemma between socialist democracy and the proletarian dictatorship, the communist dilemma between national autonomy and international proletarianism, the moral dilemma between act-proletarian morality and rule-proletarian morality, the cultural dilemma between Marxism-Leninism-Maoism and the traditional legacy, the artistic dilemma between individual creativity and collective work, the scientific dilemma between scientific research and its party control, the ideological dilemma between the primacy of theory and the primacy of practice? All the above questions can only be raised here, but I will come to grips with them in my forthcoming book. In any case, Mao was correct when he said that "the question of which will win out, socialism or capitalism, is still not really settled. Marxists are still a minority among the entire population as well as among the intellectuals. Therefore, Marxists must still develop through struggle."[39] Whether China can sustain its socialist line without retreating to the revisionist road remains to be seen.

NOTES

1. See Fang Chun-kuei (ed.), *Liu Shao-ch'i wên-t'i tzu-liao hsüan-chi* (A Special Collection of Materials on Liu Shao-ch'i) (Taipei, Taiwan: Institute for the Study of Chinese Communist Problems, 1970), p. 152.

2. "Talk on Questions of Philosophy" (August 18, 1964), in *Mao Tsetung ssu-hsiang wan-sui* ("Long Live Mao Tsetung Thought") (August 1969) [hereafter cited as *Wan-sui*]. See also its English translation *Miscellany of Mao Tsetung Thought* (1949–1968), 1974, p. 385 [hereafter cited as *Miscellany*].

3. See "Talks with Members of the Japanese Socialist Party" (July 10, 1964), in *Wan-sui*, pp. 541–543.

4. *Wan-sui*, pp. 548–549. See also *Miscellany*, p. 384.

5. See "On Practice," *Selected Works of Mao Tsetung*, I, p. 297, [hereafter cited as *Selected Works*].

6. "Confucianism, Marxism-Leninism and Mao: A Critical Study," *Journal of Chinese Philosophy* 1, Nos. 3/4 (June/September 1974):341–342.

7. "Rejoinder to Professor Howard Parsons' Critical Remarks," *Journal of Chinese Philosophy* 2, No. 4 (1975):453.

8. *Selected Works* I, p. 311.

9. *Selected Readings from the Works of Mao Tsetung*, pp. 442–443 [hereafter cited as *Selected Readings*].

10. *Selected Works*, I, p. 340.

11. Ibid., p. 342.

12. *Wan-sui*, pp. 213, 168–169, and 359–360.

13. *Selected Readings*, p. 503.

14. *Wan-sui*, p. 442. See also *Miscellany*, p. 319.

15. *Selected Works*, I, p. 336.

16. V. I. Lenin, "Remarks on N. I. Bukharin's *Economics of the Transition Period*," quoted in *Selected Works* (of Mao) I, p. 345.

17. *Wan-sui*, p. 334. See also *Miscellany*, p. 259.

18. *Wan-sui*, pp. 346–347. See also *Miscellany*, p. 269.

19. "Engels to W. Borgius in Breslau" (January 25, 1894), in Karl Marx and Frederick Engels, *Selected Works*, III, p. 503.

20. *Wan-sui*, pp. 333–334. See also *Miscellany*, p. 259.

21. *Selected Readings*, p. 464.

22. Ibid.

23. "Rejoinder," p. 449.

24. *Selected Works*, II, p. 209.

25. See *Chung-kuo chêh-hsüeh-shih wên-t'i t'ao-lun chuan-chi* (Collected Essays in the Problems of the History of Chinese Philosophy) (Peking: Science Press, 1957).

26. *Selected Works*, I, p. 343.

27. *Selected Readings*, p. 502.

28. *Selected Works*, III, 90.

29. Ibid., p. 91.

30. Marx, "Critique of the Gotha Programme," in *Selected Works* (of Marx and Engels), III, 19.

31. See *Peking Review* (September 7, 1973):27.

32. The new constitution states: "Citizens enjoy freedom of speech, correspondence, the press, assembly, association, procession, demonstration and the freedom to strike, and enjoy freedom to believe in religion and freedom not to believe in religion and to propagate atheism. The citizens' freedom of person and their homes shall be inviolable. No citizen may be arrested except by decision of a people's court or with the sanction of a public security organ," *Peking Review* (January 24, 1975):17.

33. See my "Marxism-Leninism-Maoism as an Ethical Theory," forthcoming in the special issue on the concept of justice East and West, *Journal of Chinese Philosophy*.

34. The following words of Wang Hung-wen, the second vice-chairman of the Central Committee of the Communist party of China until his fall one month after Mao's death, were probably written by Mao himself: "We must have the revolutionary spirit of daring to go against the tide. Chairman Mao pointed out: Going against the tide is a Marxist-Leninist principle. . . . When confronted with issues that concern the line and the overall situation, a true Communist must act without any selfish considerations and dare to go against the tide, fearing neither removal from his post, expulsion from the Party, imprisonment, divorce nor guillotine," in "Report on the Revision of the Party Constitution," the English translation of which appeared in *Peking Review* (September 7, 1973):31.

35. See Edgar Snow, *The Long Revolution*, p. 175.

36. See Chou's "Report on the Work of the Government," in *Peking Review* (January 24, 1975):23.

37. *Peking Review* (June 24, 1977):28.

38. *Peking Review* (August 26, 1977):24.

39. See note 21.

SELECT BIBLIOGRAPHY

BOOKS AND ARTICLES

Altaisky, M. and Georgiyev, V. *The Philosophical Views of Mao Tse-tung: A Critical Analysis* (Moscow: Progress Publishers, 1971).

Baum, R. *Prelude to Revolution: Mao, the Party, and the Peasant Question 1962–66* (New York: Columbia University Press, 1975).

—— and Bonnett, L. B. (eds.). *China in Ferment: Perspectives on the Cultural Revolution* (Englewood Cliffs, N.J.: Prentice-Hall, 1971).

Bettelheim, C. *Class Struggles in the USSR: First Period (1917–1923)* (New York: Monthly Review Press, 1976).

——. *Cultural Revolution and Industrial Organization in China* (New York: Monthly Review Press, 1974).

—— and Sweezy, P. *On the Transition to Socialism* (New York: Monthly Review Press, 1971).

Ch'en, J. (ed.). *Mao Papers: Anthology and Bibliography* (London: Oxford University Press, 1970).

Compton, B. (trans.). *Mao's China: Party Reform Documents, 1942–44* (Seattle, Wash.: University of Washington Press, 1952).

Dallin, A., et al. (eds.). *Diversity in International Communism: A Documentary Record, 1961–1963* (New York: Columbia University Press, 1963).

Devillers, P. *What Mao Really Said*, trans. To White (New York: Schocken Books, 1969).

Dittmer, L. *Liu Shao-ch'i and the Chinese Cultural Revolution: The Politics of Mass Criticism* (Berkeley, Calif.: University of California Press, 1974).

Engels, F. *Anti-Dühring* (Moscow: Progress Publishers, 1969).

——. *Dialectics of Nature* (Moscow: Progress Publishers, 1972).

——. "Materialism and Empirico-Criticism," in *Collected Works*, XIV (Moscow: Progress Publishers, 1962).

——. "Philosophical Notebooks," in *Collected Works*, XXXVIII (Moscow: Progress Publishers, 1961).

Esmein, J. *The Chinese Cultural Revolution*, trans. (from the French) W.J.F. Jenner (New York: Anchor Books, 1973).

Fan, K. (ed.). *Mao Tse-tung and Lin Piao: Post-Revolutionary Writings* (New York: Doubleday, 1972).

Foreign Language Press (ed.). *Philosophy Is No Mystery: Peasants Put Their Study to Work* (Peking: Foreign Language Press, 1972).

——. *Selected Articles Criticizing Lin Piao and Confucius*, 2 vols. (Peking: Foreign Language Press, 1974–1975).

——. *Three Struggles on China's Philosophical Front (1949–64)* (Peking: Foreign Language Press, 1973).

Franklin, B. (ed.). *The Essential Stalin* (New York: Doubleday, 1972). (See in particular "The Foundations of Leninism," "Dialectical and Historical Materialism," "Marxism and Linguistics," and "Economic Problems of Socialism in the USSR.")

Fu, C. W. "Confucianism, Marxism-Leninism and Mao: A Critical Study," *Journal of Chinese Philosophy* 1, Nos. 3–4 (June/September 1974).

——. "Marxism-Leninism-Maoism As an Ethical Theory," *Journal of Chinese Philosophy* (forthcoming).

——. *Marxism-Leninism-Maoism As Ethical Proletarianism: A Critical Inquiry* (forthcoming).

——. "Rejoinder to Professor Howard Parsons' Critical Remarks," *Journal of Chinese Philosophy* 2, No. 4 (1975).

Georgiyev, V. G., et al. *A Critique of Mao Tse-tung's Theoretical Conception* (Moscow: Progress Publishers, 1972).

Griffith, W. E. *The Sino-Soviet Relations, 1964–1965* (Cambridge, Mass.: MIT Press, 1967).

———. *The Sino-Soviet Rift, Analyzed and Documented* (Cambridge, Mass.: MIT Press, 1964).

Gurley, J. G. *Challenges to Capitalism: Marx, Lenin, and Mao* (San Francisco: San Francisco Book Co., 1976).

———. *China's Economy and the Maoist Strategy* (New York: Monthly Review Press, 1977).

Hinton, W. *Turning Point in China: An Essay on the Cultural Revolution* (New York: Monthly Review Press, 1972).

Important Documents on the Great Proletarian Cultural Revolution in China (Peking: Foreign Language Press, 1970).

Joint Publications Research Service (trans.). *Miscellany of Mao Tse-tung Thought (1948–1968) Part I and Part II* (Springfield, Va.: National Technical Information Service, U.S. Department of Commerce, 1974). [This is an incomplete translation of *Mao Tsetung ssu-hsiang wan-sui* ("Long Live Mao Tsetung Thought"), in three volumes (1967–1969) unofficially circulated among the Red Guards during the Cultural Revolution and now available in pirated edition published in both Japan and Hong Kong.]

Kuo-feng, H. "Political Report to the 11th National Congress of the Communist Party of China," *Peking Review* (August 26, 1977):23–57.

Lenin, V. I. *Selected Works*, 3 vols. (Moscow: Progress Publishers, 1963–1964).

MacFarquhar, R. *The Origins of the Cultural Revolution, 1: Contradictions Among the People 1956–1957* (New York: Columbia University Press, 1974).

Maitan, L. *Party, Army and Masses in China: A Marxist Interpretation of the Cultural Revolution and Its Aftermath*, trans. G. Benton and M. Colliti (London: NLB, 1976).

Mao Tsetung. *A Critique of Soviet Economics*, trans. M. Roberts (New York: Monthly Review Press, 1977).

Mao Tsetung Poems (Peking: Foreign Language Press, 1976).

Marx, K. and Engels, F. *Selected Works*, 3 vols. (Moscow: Progress Publishers, 1969–1970).

Marx, K.., Engels, F., and Lenin, N. *On Communist Society* (Moscow: Progress Publishers, 1974).

———. *On Historical Materialism: A Collection* (Moscow: Progress Publishers, 1972).

———. *On Scientific Communism* (Moscow: Progress Publishers, 1967).

Marx, Engels and Lenin on the Dictatorship of the Proletariat: Questions and Answers; rpt. *Peking Review* (October 3 to December 19, 1975) (New York: New China Books, 1976).

Myrdal, J. *China: The Revolution Continued*, rev. Swedish ed., trans. P. Austin (New York: Vintage Books, 1972).

———. *Report from a Chinese Village*, trans. (into Swedish) M. Michael (New York: New American Library, 1966).

Nee, V. and Peck, J. (eds.). *China's Uninterrupted Revolution* (New York: Pantheon Books, 1973).

Norman Bethune Institute (trans.). *A Basic Understanding of the Communist Party of China* (Shanghai: n.p., 1974, and Toronto: National Publications Centre, 1976).

Quotations from Chairman Mao Tsetung (Peking: Foreign Language Press, 1966).

Robinson, J. *The Cultural Revolution in China* (Baltimore: Penguin Books, 1970).

Schram, S. (ed.). *Authority Participation and Cultural Change in China* (London: Cambridge University Press, 1973).

——— (ed.). *Chairman Mao Talks to the People: Talks and Letters, 1956–71* (New York: Pantheon Books, 1974).

———. *Mao Tse-tung*, rev. ed. (Baltimore: Penguin Books, 1967).

———. *The Political Thought of Mao Tse-Tung* rev. and enl. ed. (New York: Praeger Publishers, 1969).

Schurmann, F., et al. (eds.). *Communist China* (New York: Vintage Books, 1966).

——— (eds.). *People's China* (New York: Vintage Books, 1974).

Selected Readings from the Works of Mao Tsetung (Peking: Foreign Language Press, 1971).

Selected Works of Mao Tsetung, 5 vols. (Peking: Foreign Language Press, 1965 and 1977).

Snow, E. *Red China Today* (New York: Vintage Books, 1971).

522   Asia

————. *The Long Revolution* (New York: Vintage Books, 1973).
Wakeman, Jr., F. *History and Will: Philosophical Perspectives of Mao Tse-Tung's Thought* (Berkeley, Calif.: University of California Press, 1973).

JOURNALS

Journal of Chinese Philosophy
Peking Review

South Korea

MIN-HONG CHOI

Since 1945, Korean philosophy has developed extensively. This development, far from the result of chance, came about from a variety of factors, two of which stand out as the most important: (1) the substantial reform in Korean thought, and (2) the widespread establishment of Korea's identity consciousness. These two factors, of course, arose from extremely difficult circumstances in the history of the development of Korean philosophy. Of note is the conflict between native Korean conservative ideas and the very different, progressive ideas introduced from the West. Faced with such a conflict and its attendant ills, Korean philosophy was forced to seek a remedy. The result is that today Korean philosophy has a new value system, a new view of truth and the world.

Following World War II, Korean philosophy underwent substantial changes. The primary cause was the shift from a semifeudalistic form of government in 1945 to a system of democracy. Traditional Korean philosophy was called upon at the time to support and develop the new political order of existence. In the process, many antiquated views and ideas came to the fore, and there was felt a need for a completely new ideological basis for the newly formed political order. Just as new material must be wrapped in new coverings so that everyone will notice, so the political system of Korea needed a fundamental change in Korean ideas in order to be effective.

Traditional Korean thought, influenced as it was by a Confucian sense of hierarchy, had to be changed into a form of thought in which a democratic society could take firm root. What developed at the time was Han philosophy. "Han" means one large totality or whole. Han philosophy was not a system of ideas introduced from the West, but was strictly a Korean development that reached maturity in 1960. Scholars from all areas began to reexamine Korean history, language, and culture in an effort to find a truly Korean and, at the same time, flexible, developing mode of thinking. At this juncture, Korean philosophy established a new identity, one that could develop with the changing situation of the modern world. In other words, Korean philosophy was reborn as Han philosophy. Let us now examine its epistemology.

In Han philosophy, the standard of truth is firmly based in nondualism. That is, it does not look at partial reality, but always tries to look at and grasp the whole. It does not distinguish as two separate realities the front and back of a thing—for example, the two sides of a coin, the beginning and ending of an event. Only by looking at the two as a whole, a unity, can we hope to discover the truth. Let's take the example of a movie theater. When we go into a theater to watch a movie, we cannot just look at the scene on the screen before us, its lightness, darkness, and say what it is that is there. We must also be aware of the projector behind us if we want to know the real situation of what is going on.

As seen above, looking on the front and back of a thing, not as two separate realities, but as a unified whole, is the view expressed in Han philosophy. If we concentrate on the front of a thing and forget its back, or if we concentrate on the back of a thing and ignore its front, we can never obtain the truth of the thing. This is what is expressed in the example of the movie theater. If we say that we have seen the mountains, we cannot say that we have not seen the trees. If we say that we have seen the ocean, we cannot say that we have not seen the water. To do so would be to miss the truth. In order to avoid this one-sided error, Han epistemology does not allow for the splintering of reality, the polarization of things.

This view of truth is not new to Korea. It can be seen in the view of life and death held by Koreans in ancient society. They did not look upon life and death as two separate, opposing realities. Living was a deferment from or extension of death. This view is without doubt the same one expressed in Han philosophy.

If we examine the tomb murals from the fifth and sixth century Koguryo Dynasty, we can see pictured this view of life and death as a complete whole. A man may live and die, but he does not cease to be; he continues to live in the earth. Life on the surface continues below. A few examples follow.

In Tong Gu, North Korea, there is a tomb painting dating from the early sixth century. A man and wife are depicted in the painting. The painting is drawn on the north wall of the master's room in the tomb. (Korean tombs had several rooms patterned along the arrangement of Korean houses.) The man and wife are seated side by side. The scene is not meant as a memorial portrait to be used for ancestor worship, but is taken directly from the life of the couple when they were alive. Here we see that the ancient Koreans viewed life and death as a unified whole.

There is also a tomb mural in Yong Gang, North Korea. Living accommodations are drawn on the wall for the dead. In the center of the mural, the man and his wife are again depicted. This time servants are depicted around the couple, the same servants that they had in life. Life and death are united. This spirit and way of thinking form the core of Han epistemology.

Long ago, even before Confucian rites were introduced, Koreans practiced ancestor worship. It is something that arises from this view of life and death as a unified whole. If someone dies, he does not completely cease to exist, but continues to live beneath the earth and communicate with the living. This way of thinking is the key element in a view of truth that avoids the polarization of things.

As an example of what we mean when we say that a man may die but never cease to be and that he continues to communicate with the living, let us look at an event from the Silla Dynasty.

In the reign of the fourteenth king of Silla, King Yuyae Isakeum, there was an attack on Keum Sung (Keum Fortress) by the people of Yi Soh. Many troops were mobilized to fight, but they were completely surrounded, and though they fought long and hard, they were not able to repel the enemy. Suddenly, some very strange looking soldiers appeared. They had bamboo leaves stuffed into their ears, and, joining the soldiers of Silla, they defeated the enemy. After the soldiers of Yi Soh retreated, these strange soldiers disappeared. The bamboo leaves they had worn were found piled at the tomb of Kin Michu. The people of Silla knew immediately that the dead king had quietly helped them to win the battle. They acclaimed his contribution to the nation and named his tomb *The Tomb Where Bamboo Appears*. The continuity of life and death is evident here.

According to Han philosophy, what people say exists or does not exist is to some extent based on their relative position and point of view. Take the example of a flower. If we are intent only on the beautiful flower that is blooming before our eyes, then the reality of a withered flower holds no meaning for us. On the other hand, if we free ourselves from this one-sided attachment to the flower in bloom and casually reflect on the flower withered in our mind, then we will not think that the flower we see blooms forever. Rather, we will feel to the same degree the meaningful appearance of the withered flower as we do for the blooming one. In this sense, the withered flower or the one in bloom can never be absolutized. This is because a flower, though withered, is not so forever, and a blooming flower does not do so forever.

The nature of a flower is that once it blooms it must wither; once withered it must bloom again. If we look on a withered flower as one that has ceased to be or on a blooming flower as one that will last forever, we have already polarized reality and adopted an absolutistic epistemology. A relativistic epistemology, on the other hand, though it may lead us to the awareness of the nonreality or nothingness of a flower, also makes us aware of the permanence of transient flowers. Here is where we discover the truth of things. What we say exists today exists because of the possibility for its existence. What we say does not exist does not exist because of our given circumstance. Therefore, what we say exists does not do so absolutely, and what we say has ceased to exist does not do so forever. This relative view of what exists and does not exist, taken from the position of unity or totality, forms the core of Han epistemology.

Han axiology is also firmly rooted in this total view of things. Through it, the hierarchic ethics of the semifeudalistic class society of Korea changed substantially, and Koreans were given ethical self-autonomy. The hierarchic ethics of the time were fundamentally ordered to securing unconditional obedience to a class hierarchy. In such an ethical system, there was no need to ask what was good or bad, right or wrong. All that was demanded was unconditional obedience to superiors. Han ethics could not sanction such a way of behavior.

The foreign ethical ideas that entered Korea in the 1950s were equally unacceptable to Koreans. The idea of individual freedom as absolute was not considered to be the true meaning of freedom. Taken in a bad sense, it meant license and lawlessness. Being absolutistic, it was hardly compatible with the view of ethics expressed in Han thought.

Finally, Han ethics sought to improve and raise to a higher dimension the ethics of native Korean individualism, which often tried to deprive men of their basic human rights. At the same time, it tried to resolve the conflicts arising from a sterile individualism, the product of Western mechanism.

As we have pointed out above, Han philosophy places the standard of the good in a unified, totalistic point of view. It does not look upon the ruler of a country and the people he rules as two separate realities. It does not allow for that kind of logic that condones the people being economically well off while the ruler is not, or the ruler being well off while the people are not. True ethics will not allow the ruler to be happy while the people are not, or the people to be happy while the ruler is not. The ruler and the people are not realities that can be polarized.

The main ideology at the time of the foundation of Korea was the idea of the *Hongik Ingan* ("Magnanimous Man"). The magnanimous man is one who always benefits and helps others. As mentioned above, the people cannot be separated from the ruler, so here in the idea of the magnanimous man people cannot be separated and live in isolation from each other. To be a man means that one gives and receives help from others. Giving and receiving do not mean that one gives once in order to receive twice or three times. To do so would mean a distinction between and separation of the individuals, that the self and others are not viewed as one whole. The concrete expression of helping others is to give once and receive once, or to give once and demand nothing in return. This same spirit is contained in Han ethics, the spirit that does not separate the self from others.

This kind of value system in Han thought appeared very early in ancient Korean society. An example of its political application can be seen in the *Meeting of the District Elders* in the Koguryo Dynasty. This meeting was a form of republicanism in which important matters of the country's welfare were decided. Matters of state were not left to the caprice of one man, but were decided upon by the representatives of each district. The king, though ruler of the country, could not decide by himself what to do in important matters. He had to submit to the opinions of the district heads. The value of the total, the whole, in Han thought was championed over that of the individual.

In the *Samguk Sagi* ("History of the Three Kingdoms"), we can read the story of Myongim Dapku, who killed King Cha Tae. Upon assuming the duties of king, Cha Tae began to rule as he pleased, without regard to the needs of the people. He was atrocious and ill mannered. When Myongim Dapku killed the king, the prime minister, Eoh Ji Ryu, immediately called a meeting of the district heads. At the meeting, the younger brother of the very respected and virtuous King Tae Jo was raised to the throne. Here we see plainly a rejection of dictatorship and an attempt to get back to some form of democratic government. Its basis is to be found in Han thought.

The same book records an event in the reign of the fourteenth king of the Koguryo Dynasty, Pongsan. At the time, the people were in great difficulty and had nothing to eat. Pongsan, however, seemed not to notice. He even went so far as to order alterations in the palace courtyards. Although the prime minister, Chang Jori, protested, the king remained adamant. The premier quit the court and met with the district head to discuss exiling the king. When Pongsan saw that there was no escape, he hanged himself. His suicide came from his fear of the totality, the completeness of public consensus. In electing a new king, the elders gathered together and, after much discussion, raised Ulbu to the throne. This was still another example of Han ethics.

We can also see this spirit in the Silla political institution called *Whabaek*. The meeting of the *Whabaek* was derived from a form of democratic government used by the early tribes of Korea. In the *Samguk Sagi*, we can read how the Koreans in the south lived in the mountain valleys and were organized into tribes. At the time of Jinhan (the older name for Silla and the period that preceded it), there were six main villages. These villages were later to become the center of the new Silla Dynasty. In each village several clans lived side by side. Each village was united to the others through a confederation of mutual help. When there were any important matters to discuss, the elders from each village would gather in one place and decide what to do. This early meeting of elders was later called *Whabaek* ("Clear Harmony," literally "Harmony White"). The *Whabaek* was governed by the rule of unanimous assent.

A reference to this form of government appears in the old Chinese book *Sui Shu* ("History of the Sui Dynasty"). It records that when the country had serious matters to be decided on, the head tribesmen would gather for frank, open discussion and then decide the matter according to the opinion of all. In the *Wen Hsien Tung Koh* ("Miscellaneous Essays on Political And Social Systems"), we read that when the country was faced with difficult problems, resolutions were only decided upon after everyone's opinion was asked. If even one person disagreed, the plan of action was dropped. This practice is just like our own modern-day veto.

In the meeting of the *Whabaek*, the king would listen to all the opinions of the elders, and if what he decided was not approved unanimously, it was immediately voided. An example occurred during the reign of the seventh king of the Silla Dynasty, Ilsong Nasakeum. Ilsong Nasakeum opened the meeting of the *Whabaek* and proposed that Silla attack the country of Malkal. The delegates rejected the idea, and the king was forced to give up his plan for an invasion. This short story illustrates that the spirit of Han thought runs counter to any form of bureaucratic dictatorship that would not allow for a totality of opinion.

Yet another Silla institution embodied this spirit—the *Wharang Do* ("the Way of the Flower Youths," an order of knights taken from the nobility). The purpose of the *Wharang Do* was to take gifted, intelligent young men from good families, put them into a separate community, and educate and train them to this spirit of unity and single-mindedness. When they put what they had learned into practice, it was without regard for any individual consideration, but only for the sake of the country and the race. Their standard of value went far beyond the individual to include the nation and all men.

Chae Chi Won (857–?) a poet, writer, and scholar of the Silla Dynasty and the first great Korean scholar of Chinese, commented on the basic beliefs of the *Wharang Do*. He said that Korean thought is an ideology of refinement and taste. The origin of this ideology is explained in detail in the *Sun Sa* ("History of Taoism"). Actually, it contains the teachings of the *San Chiao* ("three teachings of Confucianism, Taoism, and Buddhism"). The teaching that when at home one should be filial towards parents and that in society one should be loyal to the king is Confucian. The teaching that one should reside in *wu wei* ("nonactivity") and *tzu jan* ("naturalness") and act in quiet comes from Lao Tzu. Putting aside all evil thoughts and actions and doing only what is right is what the Buddha taught. This ideology of refinement contains Confucian, Taoist, and Buddhist ideas. It forms the special thought of Korea. Chae Chi Won said that the core of the *Wharang Do*'s spiritual life was to look at the total picture of life. They studied and cultivated a fine moral character. Through military skills and training, they developed their bodies, and through traveling to view mountains and streams, they established and refined their emotions. This kind of knowledge and training was apparent in their practical love of their country and the courage they displayed, as well as the friendship and trust they shared with one another. They always earned the trust and respect of the people and became the driving force in the development of the country and society of their time. The basis of their contribution is to be found in the values of Han philosophy. These same values have also come down to modern Koreans and form the basis of their spiritual life.

Han philosophy, the axis along which Korean philosophy has developed, is in step with the progress of world ideas. In all areas of life today, the modern world seeks harmony, the harmonization of a splintered and divided reality. Politics, economics, culture, and art are all moving in the direction of harmony. The very word "hamorny" holds great attraction for us. Han philosophy, as a philosophy of totality or unity, contains within itself the principle of harmony because harmony means the collection and integration of various ideas into a complete whole. In this sense, once philosophy gets beyond the borders of provincialism, race, history, and tradition, it can be united and it can become a philosophy of harmony.

In Korean philosophy, we can see British empiricism. The writings of Chae Han Gi (1803–1879) emphasize the distinct difference between the title or name of a thing and the real thing itself. He said that in ordinary daily living we use the words "miracle" and "luck," but if we think that such things really exist, we are mistaken. In the first volume of his *Chu Chuk Nok* ("Recorded Conjectures''), he also gives the example of the eye and the ear, the words we use and the practical contents of these words, to explain the difference between the object and its name.

If we change the names of the eye and ear and call the eye an ear and the ear an eye, we do not change the practical content of what we want to say. The eye, whether we call it an eye or an ear, is the same. The ear, though we call it an eye, is still an ear. What is more, if we don't even have a name for the eye or the ear, it does not affect our seeing or hearing. Even in ancient times, when there were no letters to indicate the eye or the ear, men could still see and hear. In our own times, we have names for them and letters to write down those names, but still we do not hear better or see better than the ancients. Therefore, the thing that really is, is more important than the name we give it. In European philosophy this kind of reasoning is called nominalism.

The *Novum Organum* of Francis Bacon (1561–1626) presents four idolatrous notions, one of which is the idolatry of the marketplace. This notion coincides with that of Chae Han Gi. Bacon pointed out that it was illusory for people to think that what they spoke of as a matter of convenience really existed. Here we see two notions, one Bacon's, the other Chae Han Gi's, that seem to transcend the gap between Oriental and Occidental ways of thinking, Korean and English traditions, and racial history. They form a harmonized empirical philosophy. From the point of view of Han thought, English philosophy and Korean philosophy are not polarized but are combined into one harmonious whole. In this sense, Han philosophy is a philosophy of harmonization.

We can also see concurrent ideas in Korean Tonghak philosophy and German existentialism. The statement in Tonghak that the mind of God is also the mind of man concurs philosophically with key ideas in existentialism. The reason they correspond is that they both demand self-reflection and a deep, personal self-awakening. In Tonghak, man's mind is not able to become the mind of heaven, or rather become what heaven's mind is, by itself. It does not do so naturally, but only through the deep personal awareness or enlightenment that one can maintain one's original pure mind and act and behave according to it. This kind of deep personal awareness or self-enlightenment is in no way different from what Martin Heidegger says when he states that man needs a personal awakening and awareness to recover his lost humanity. The degradation or loss of humanity according to Heidegger, *Verfallen*, corresponds to the Tonghak principle of *kakja wieshim* (''each man doing what he pleases''). *Kakja weishim* is not based on truth or some higher standard, but merely on man's desire to do and think what he pleases. This itself is moral degradation and corresponds to Heidegger's *Verfallen*.

Of course, these two expressions are different phonologically, but they represent the same state from which man must free himself by deep personal examination and reflection. They describe the same condition of man's having lost his original mind.

We can also point to a unique religious phenomenon in Korea, *shinkyo* (a type of monotheistic animism). The central point of this belief was internal enlightenment. The object of faith was called *haullim* (etymologically related to the word for sky and the word "han," meaning "great," "one," "whole"). *Haullim* was the highest, eternal, greatest arbiter of man's fortune and misfortune. The ancients knew that this heavenly spirit had mysterious power and wisdom, and that man could gain salvation from it if he would only follow his mind. This spirit hated disordered, evil things. Thus, the main purpose of *shinkyo* was to help man always to feel a heavy sense of responsibility about his actions and thoughts, and constantly seek to keep himself clean and upright. Man was not to think bad thoughts or do bad things because they were evil. This awareness of sin, or evil, in man is his fate; it is the condition of man. *Shinkyo* was concerned mainly with the clean and bright. As a result of this teaching, the ancients would always gaze to the east and practice cleaning their minds of evil thoughts.

Jaspers' existentialism contains something like this attitude concerning man's fate in *shinkyo*. In explaining guilt consciousness, Jaspers said that the very fact of man's being born into this world carries with it the basic meaning of guilt. His concept, however, goes beyond that of the ancient *shinkyo*. He said that it is man's fate and destiny, that even in walking and breathing he must be careful lest he kill even the smallest of microbes. Nevertheless, the two concepts are concurrent.

If we do comparative studies from the point of view of Han thought of these two, existentialism and Tonghak, we will arrive at a new philosophy of harmonization. This is especially important for the meeting of Eastern and Western philosophies. Han thought provides a seedbed for this harmony.

This problem of harmony is not limited to philosophy; it is also true of other areas. In the economic sphere, especially, we note that many nations are moving towards a unified commercial law. One of the fortunate results of World War II was the development of the European Common Market. People from member nations can now travel freely back and forth without visas and export products without tariffs. The harmonization of commercial laws in these countries is a *fait accompli*.

In Stockholm, the production of the York-Antwerp Agreement by the International Law Association is also a good example of this trend towards harmony. Han philosophy provides the ideological support for this kind of harmonization. As we have shown, the reason is the basic view of reality as a complete whole, without the absolutization or polarization of objects. As a result, Han philosophy not only provides a way for the development of Korean philosophy, but also contributes to mainstream world thought.

SELECT BIBLIOGRAPHY

BOOKS AND ARTICLES

Chae, H. *Chu Chuk Nok* ("Recorded Conjecture") (Peking: n.p., 1836).
Choi, M. *A History of Korean Ethical Thought* (Seoul: n.p., 1971).
————. *A History of Korean Philosophy* (Seoul: n.p., 1974).
————. *A Modern History of Korean Philosophy* (in English) (Seoul: n.p., 1978).
————. *Korean Philosophy* (Seoul: n.p., 1969).
Illyon. *Samguk Yusa* ("Tales from the Three Kingdoms") Original not extant. Republished 1512.
Kim, P. *Samguk Sagi* ("History of the Three Kingdoms") Original not extant. Republished 1145.
Kudangsoh Yaejon ("Tang History on Various Subjects")

JOURNALS

Chul Hak Yun Ku
Journal of Korean Philosophy

Appendix I: DIRECTORY OF PHILOSOPHICAL ASSOCIATIONS

Each entry gives the name of the association and, where available, the date of founding within parentheses, and publications. It should be noted that most of the philosophical associations listed were founded after 1945. This appendix testifies to the great proliferation of philosophical associations and publications internationally since that pivotal year. More detailed information may be found in the *International Directory of Philosophy and Philosophers* and the *Directory of American Philosophers* published by the Philosophy Documentation Center, Bowling Green State University, Bowling Green, Ohio, in 1978. Much of the material in this appendix is drawn from the latest editions of these two volumes.

UNIONS AFFILIATED WITH UNESCO

SCIENCE IN GENERAL

International Council of Scientific Unions (1931)
 51, Boulevard de Montmorency, 75 Paris 16

International Union of the History and Philosophy of Science (1956)
 12, Rue Colbert, Paris 11
Publ.: *Archives internationales d'Histoire des Sciences, Journal of Symbolic Logic*

DIVISION OF THE HISTORY OF SCIENCE

National Committees

Argentina: Grupo Argentino de la Union Internacional de Historia de las Ciencias
Austria: Austrian Committee for the History of Science
Belgium: Comité Belge d'Histoire des Sciences
Brazil: Academia Brasileira de Historia das Ciências
Czechoslovakia: Komise pro Dejiny Prirodnich ved a Techniky
France: Comité National d'Histoire et de Philosophie des Sciences
Great Britain: British National Committee for the History of Science
Hungary: National Committee for the History of Science
India: National Committee for the History of Science
Israel: Israeli Committee for the History of Science
Italy: Gruppo Italiano di Storia delle Scienze
Japan: Japanese Committee for the History and Philosophy of Science
Luxembourg: Section des Sciences de l'Institut Grand-Ducal de Luxembourg

Netherlands: Genootschap voor Geschiedenis der Geneeskunde, Wiskunde en Natuurwetenschappen
Poland: National Polish Committee for the History and Philosophy of Science
Portugal: Committee for the History of Sciences
Republic of China: Committee for the History of Natural Science of the Academy of Science of China
Romania: National Romanian Committee for the History and Philosophy of Sciences
Spain: Asociación para la Historia de la Ciencia Española
Sweden: Lärdomshistoriska Samfundet
Switzerland: Schweizerische Gesellschaft für Geschichte der Medizin und der Naturwissenschaften
Union of Soviet Socialist Republics: Soviet National Committee for the History of Science
Yugoslavia: Nacionalni Komitet Fnrj za Historiju Nauka
West Germany: Deutsche Vereinigung für die Geschichte der Medizin, Naturwissenschaften und Technik

International Committees

Académie Internationale d'Histoire des Sciences (1928)
    12, Rue Colbert, F 75002, Paris

DIVISION OF LOGIC, METHODOLOGY AND PHILOSOPHY OF SCIENCE

National Members

Argentina: Agrupación Rioplatense de Lógica y Filosofía Científica
Austria: Osterreichische Akademie der Wissenschaften
Belgium: Comité National Belge de Logique et de Philosophie des Sciences
Chile: Sociedad Chilena de Lógica, Metodología y Filosofía de las Ciencias
Finland: Gesellschaft für Logik und Ihre Anwendungen
France: Comité National pour la Division de Logique, Méthodologie et Philosophie des Sciences, Académie des Sciences
Great Britain: British National Committee for Logic, Methodology and Philosophy of Science
Hungary: National Committee for the Philosophy of Science
Israel: Israel Society for Logic and Philosophy of Science
Italy: Unione Italiana di Metodologia, Logica e Filosofia delle Scienze
Japan: Japan Association for Philosophy of Science
Mexico: Asociación Mexicana de Epistemología
Netherlands: Nederlandse Vereniging voor Logica en Wijsbegeerte der Exacte Wetenschappen
Poland: National Committee of the Division of Logic, Methodology, and Philosophy of the Sciences
Republic of China: Academia Sinica
Romania: Academy of the Romanian People's Republic
Spain: Spanish Society for the History and Philosophy of Sciences
Switzerland: Schweizerische Gesellschaft zur Pflege der Logik und Philosophie der Wissenschaft

West Germany: Deutsche Vereinigung für Mathematische Logik und Grundlagenforschung

International Members

Académie Internationale de Philosophie des Sciences
Association for Symbolic Logic
C. S. Peirce Society
Institute for the Unity of Science
Philosophy of Science Association

PHILOSOPHY AND HUMANISTIC STUDIES

International Council for Philosophy and Humanistic Studies (1949)
    UNESCO, 1, Rue Miollis, Paris XV
Publ.: *Diogenes*

International Academic Union (1919)
    1, Rue Ducale, 1000 Brussels

International Federation of Societies of Philosophy (1948)
    Institut dès Sciences Exactes, Sidlerstrasse 5, CH–3012 Berne

NATIONAL SOCIETIES

Australia: Australasian Association of Philosophy
Austria: Philosophical Society, Vienna
Bangladesh: Bangladesh Philosophical Association
Belgium: Société Belge de Philosophie
    Société Philosophique de Louvain
Brazil: Istituto Brasileiro de Filosofia
    Sociedade Brasileira de Filosofos Catolicos
    Sociedade de Estudios Filosoficos
Bulgaria: Institut de Philosophie de l'Académie des Sciences
    Philosophical Society of Bulgaria
Canada: Canadian Philosophical Association
    Société de Philosophie de Montréal
    Société de Philosophie de Québec
Czechoslovakia: Filosofica Jednota
    Société Philosophique Slovaque
Denmark: Selskabet for Filosofi og Psykologi
East Germany: Vereiningung der Philosophischen Institutionen
    der Deutschen Demokratischen Republik
Finland: Societas Philosophica Fennica
France: Cercle Philosophique Lorrain
    Société Alpine de Philosophie
    Société Azuréenne de Philosophie
    Société Bourgignonne de Philosophie
    Société de Philosophie de Bordeaux

Société de Philosophie de Strasbourg
Société d'Etudes Philosophiques
Société d'Etudes Philosophiques d'Aix-en-Provence
Société Française de Philosophie
Société Languedocienne de Philosophie
Société Lilloise de Philosophie
Société Lyonnaise de Philosophie
Société Méditéranéenne d'Etudes Philosophiques et Psychologiques
Société Poiterine de Philosophie
Société Toulousaine de Philosophie
Great Britain: British Academy, Section 2
    British Society for Phenomenology
    Royal Institute of Philosophy
Hungary: Comité National Hongrois de Philosophie
India: Indian Philosophical Congress
Indonesia: Indonesian Philosophical Association
Iran: Department of Philosophy of the University of Teheran
    Imperial Iranian Academy of Philosophy
Ireland: Irish National Committee for Philosophy
    Irish Philosophical Club
    Irish Philosophical Society
Israel: Israel Philosophical Association
    Philosophical Society of Jerusalem
Italy: Centro Filosofico di Gallarate
    Istituto di Studi Filosofici di Roma
    Società Italiana per gli Studi Filosofici e Religiosi
    Société Ligure de Philosophie
    Société Philosophique de Calabre
    Société Philosophique Italienne
Japan: Comité National pour les Etudes Philosophiques
Korea: Korean Philosophical Association
Mexico: Association Philosophique du Mexique
    Seminario de Problemas Científicos y Filosóficos
    Sociedad Mexicana de Filosofía
Netherlands: Algemene Vereniging voor Wijsbegeerte
    Vereniging voor Calvinistische Wijsbegeerte
Pakistan: Pakistan Philosophical Congress
Poland: Polskie Towarzystwo Filozoficzne
Sweden: Filosofiska Föreningen i Lund
Switzerland: Société Suisse de Philosophie
Turkey: Felsefe Kurumu, Ankara
Union of Soviet Socialist Republics: Institute of Philosophy of the Academy of Sciences
United States of America: American Catholic Philosophical Association
    American Philosophical Association
    American Society for Aesthetics
    American Society of Political and Legal Philosophy
    Association for Symbolic Logic
    Charles S. Peirce Society

Foundation for Creative Philosophy
Metaphysical Society of America
Mountain-Plains Conference
New Mexico and West Texas Philosophical Society
Society for Asian and Comparative Philosophy
Society for the Advancement of American Philosophy
Society for the Philosophical Study of Marxism
Uruguay: Philosophical Society of Uruguay
Venezuela: Centro de Estudios de Filosofía del Derecho
West Germany: Allgemeine Gesellschaft für Philosophie in Deutschland
   Deutsche Gesellschaft für Phanomenologische Forschung
   Kantgesellschaft

INTERNATIONAL SOCIETIES

Academia Romana di S. Tommaso d'Aquino di Rel Cattolica
Asociación Latino—Americana de Filósofos Católicos
Association of Philosophy Journal Editors
Association Internationale de Philosophie du Droit et de Philosophie Sociale
Cercle International de Recherches Philosophiques par Ordinateur
International Husserl and Phenomenological Research Society
International Institute of Philosophy
International Phenomenological Society, USA
Internationale Hegel—Vereinging
Philosophical Society of Southern Africa
Sociedad Iberoamericana de Filosofía
Société Internationale Gottfried—Wilhelm Leibniz
World Union of Catholic Societies of Philosophy, Austria

Société Internationale pour l'Etude de la Philosophie Médiévale

ASSOCIATE MEMBERS

Argentina: Centro de Estudios de Filosofía Medieval, Facultad de Filosofía y Letras,
   Universidad de Buenos Aires, Calle 25 de Mayo 217, Buenos Aires
Austria: Institut für Christliche Philosophie an der Theologischen Facultät der Universität
   Innsbruck, Universitätsstrasse 4B, A–6020 Innsbruck
Belgium: Centre de Wulf-Mansion: Recherches de Philosophie Ancienne et Médiévale,
   Institut Supérieur de Philosophie, Kardinaal Mercierplein 2, B–3000 Louvain
   Corpus Christianorum Continuatio Mediaevalis, St. Pietersabdij OSB, B–8320
   Steenbrugge Assebroek
   Ruusbroek-Genootschap, Prinsstraat 17, B–2000 Antwerpen I
Canada: Bibliothèque de l'Institut d'Etudes Médiévales, 2715 Chemin de la Côte Ste.
   Catherine, Montréal 250
   Institut d'Etudes Médiévales, Université de Montréal, 2715 Chemin de la Côte Ste.
   Catherine, C P 6128 Montréal 101
France: Abbaye de la Pierre-Qui-Vire, F–89830 St. Leger, Vauban
   Société Thomiste de Caen, 36, Avenue du 6 Juin, F–14000 Caen

Israel: Société Israelienne pour l'Etude de la Pensée Médiévale, Université Hébraïque, Jerusalem
Italy: Biblioteca Istituto Universitario di Magistero, Via Fabio Filzi, I–95100 Cantania
Centro per Ricerche di Filosofia Medioevale, Palazzo del Capitaniato 5, I–35100 Padova
Japan: Japanese Society of Medieval Philosophy, Sophia University, 7 Kiocho, Chiyoda-ku, Tokyo
Netherlands: Bibliotheek Meddeleeuwse Afdeling van Het Philosophisch Instituut der Katholieke Universiteit Nijmegen, Erasmuslaan 3, NL Nijmegen
Instituut voor Antieke en Middeleeuwse Wijsbegeerte der Rijksuniversiteit, 27a Maliesingel, NL Utrecht
Spain: Maioricensis Schola Lullistica, Apartado 17, E-Palma de Mallorca
West Germany: Deutsche Thomas-Ausgabe, D–5301 Walberberg-Bei-Bonn

RELATED ORGANIZATIONS

Argentina: Asociación Argentina para el Estudio de la Filosofía Medieval, Pontificia Universidad Católica Argentina
Austria: Institut für Christliche Philosophie an der Theologischen Fakultät, Salzburg
Belgium: Centre de Wulf-Mansion
Centre d'Etudes Médiévales
Centre National de Recherches d'Histoire de la Pensée Médiévale
Corpus Christianorum Continuatio Mediaevalis
Editions de la Bibliothèque S J
Faculteiten Sint Ingatius
Institut Historique Augustinien
Institut Interfacultaire d'Etudes Médiévales
Ruusbroec-Genootschap
Société Des Bollandistes
Union Académique Internationale
Colombia: Colegio Mayor de San Bonaventura
Pontificia Universidad Javeriana
France: Association Internationale d'Etudes Patristiques
Centre de Recherches d'Histoire des Religions
Centre de Recherches et de Confrontation sur la Pensée Médiévale
Centre d'Etudes Supérieures de Civilisation Médiévale
Cercle Thomiste Saint-Nicolas de Caen
Ecole des Chartes
Institut de Recherches et d'Histoire des Textes
Institut d'Etudes Augustiniennes
La Saulchoir
Great Britain: Warburg Institute
Greece: Academy of Athens
Italy: Centro di Studi Medievali
Centro Italiano di Studi sull'Alto Medioevo
Collegio Internazionale di S. Bonaventura
Edition Critique des Oeuvres de S. Tomas d'Aquin, Commission Léonini
Facoltà Teologica Marianum dell'Ordine dei Servi di Maris

Facoltà Teologica S. Bonaventura
Institut de Patristique Médiévale "Jean XXIII"
Istituto di Filosofia dell'Università di Roma
Istituto di Paleografia dell'Università di Roma
Istituto di Storia della Filosofia
Istituto Storico dei Fratri Minori Cappucini
Pontificio Ateneo Antoniano
Japan: Center of Medieval Studies of the Institute Saint-Thomas Aquinas
Lebanon: Institut des Lettres Orientales
Netherlands: Instituut voor Antieke en Middeleeuwse Wijsbegeerte der Rijksuniversiteit
  te Utrecht
  Instituut voor Laat Latijn
  Middeleewse Afdiling van het Filosofisch Instituut der Katholieke Universiteit te
  Nijmegen
Peru: Instituto Peruano de Altos Estudios Islámicos
Poland: Academia Teologii Katolieckiej w Warszawa
  Biblioteka Jagiellonska
  Instytut Badan Literackich Polskiej Akademii Nauk
  Instytut Filozofii i Sociologii Polskiej Akademii Nauk
  Zaklad Historii Filozofii
  Zaklad Historii Filozofii Sredniowiecznej
Portugal: Institute of Philosophy, Braga, Coimbra, Lisboa, Porto
Spain: Centro de Estudios e Investigación San Isodoro
  Centro de Estudios Históricos Internacionales
  Facultad de Filosofía de la Universidad Pontifícia de Comillas
  Facultad Pontifícia Complutense de Filosofía
  Facultad Teológica de San Estaban
  Instituto "Arias Montano" de Estudios Hebraicos y Oriente Próximo
  Instituto "Augustinus"
  Instituto Egipcio de Estudios Islámicos en Madrid
  Instituto Enrique Florez
  Instituto Hispano-Arabe de Cultura
  Instituto "Miguel Asin"
  Maioricensis Schola Lullistica
Turkey: Islam Arastirmalari Enstitüsü
Union of Soviet Socialist Republics: Institute of the Middle Ages of the Academy of
  Sciences of the USSR
West Germany: Albertus-Magnus-Akademie
  Albertus-Magnus-Institut
  Bayerische Akademie der Wissenschaften
  Grabman-Institut zur Erforschung der Theologie und Philosophie des Mittelalters
  Institut der Cusanus-Gesellschaft
  Katholisch-Theologische Fakultät der Universität Bonn
  Mittellateinisches-Theologisches Seminar, Bochum
  Monumenta Germaniae Historica
  Raimundus-Lullus-Institut
  Thomas-Institut an der Universität Kölm

OTHER INTERNATIONAL SOCIETIES AND ASSOCIATIONS

Association Internationale de Cybernétique (1957)
   Palais des Expositions, Place a Rijckmans B–5000 Namur, Belgium
Publ.: *Cybernetica, Actes des Congrès Internationaux de Cybernétique, Documents de Travail, Principes de Cybernétique, Sciences de l'Invariant*

Comité International des Professeurs de Philosophie (Enseignement du Second Degré)
   44 Münster, Gerhart Hauptmannstrasse 1, West Germany

Internationaal Constantin Brunner Instituut (1947)
   Batjanstraat 8, Den Haag

International Association for Philosophy of Law and Social Philosophy (1959)
   Box 1120, Washington University, St. Louis, Mo. 63130
Publ.: *Archiv für Rechts und Sozial Philosophie* (ARSP)

International Association for the History of Religions (1950)
   Department of Comparative Religion, University of Manchester, Manchester M13 9PL, Great Britain
Publ.: *Numen, Supplements to Numen, Proceedings of International Congresses, International Bibliography of the History of Religions*

International Association of Universities (1950)
   75732 Paris, Cedex 15
Publ.: *Bulletin*

International Committee for Aesthetics (1956)
   Instituut voor Esthetica, Nieuwe Achtergracht 170 IV, Amsterdam C
Publ.: *Bulletin International d'Esthétique*

Internationale Hegel Gesellschaft (1953)
   A 5020 Salzburg, Richard Strele Str. 16, Salzburg
Publ.: *Hegel Jahrbuch*

International Federation of the Societies of Classical Studies (1948)
   26 Rue de Vermont, 1202 Genève

International Humanist and Ethical Union (1952)
   Oudegracht 152, Utrecht
Publ.: *International Humanism, Bibliography of Humanism*

International Research Institute for Philosophy, Psychology and Physical Research (1964)
   Kuthal Gate, Mussoorie Road, P O Rajpur, Dehradum, U P, India
Publ.: *Darshana International, Psychics International, Gaveshana*

International Society for Oriental Research
   Orientalisches Seminar, J. W. Goethe-University, D–6000 Frankfurt/Main 1
Publ.: *Oriens*

WESTERN EUROPE, AUSTRALIA, AND ISRAEL

DENMARK

Institutes

Dansk Selskab for Videnskabsforskning (1977)
Aalborg Universitetscenter, Institute 3, P.O. Box 159, DK 9000 Aalborg
Publ.: *Videnskabsforskning, Skriftraekke for Videnskabsteori ved AUC*

Kierkegaard Akademiet
Sofievej 23, 2900 Hellerup, DK
Publ.: *Kierkegaardiana*

Kongelige Danske Videnskabers Selskab (1742)
Dantes Plads 5, 1556, Kobenhavn V

Societies

Filosofisk Forening i Aarhus (1961)
Filosofisk Institut, Aarhus Universitet, DK–8000 Aarhus C
Publ.: *Philosophia*, formerly *Philosophia Arhusiensis*

Selskabet for Filosofi og Psykologi (1926)
Filosofisk Institut, Kobmagergade 50, 1150, Kobenhavn K
Publ.: *Danish Yearbook of Philosophy*

Soren Kierkegaard Society (1948)
Sofievej 23, 2900 Hell, Kobenhavn
Publ.: *Populaere Skrifter, Kierkegaardiana*

Symposion
Filosofisk Institut, Ordense Universitet, Odense
Publ.: *Symposiom*

FINLAND

Institutes

Academy of Finland (1948)
Ruoholahdenkatu 4, Helsinki 18

Finnish Research Council for the Humanities (1950)
The Academy of Finland, Ratamestarinkatu 12, 00520 Helsinki 52

Societies

Academia Scientiarum Fennica
Snellmanink 9–11, 00170 Helsinki 17
Publ.: *Annales Academiae Scientiarum Fennicae*

Finnish Society for Philosophy and Phenomenology (1961)
    Hämeenkatu 30 C 28, Turku 10
Publ.: *Studia Philosophica Turkuensia*

Logiikan Seura (1942)
    Kuusitie 14 A 42, 00270 Helsinki 27

Philosophical Society of Finland (1873)
    Institute of Philosophy, University of Helsinki, Unioninkatu 40 B, 00170 Helsinki
    17
Publ.: *Acta Philosophica Fennica*

Societas Scientiarum Fennica (1838)
    Snellmaninkatu 11–13, Helsinki 17
Publ.: *Acta Societatis Scientiarum Fennicae—Opera Humanarum Litterarum*

FRANCE

Institutes

Académie des Sciences Morales et Politiques (1795–1803, 1832)
    Institut de France, 23, Quai de Conti 75006 Paris
Publ.: *Revue des Travaux de l'Academie des Sciences Morales et Politiques et Comptes Rendus de Ses Séances*

Centre d'Etudes du Dix-huitième Siècle
    Université de Paris-Sorbonne, 1, Rue Victor-Cousin, 75005 Paris
Publ.: *Dix-Huitième Siècle*

Centre d'Etudes Supérieures de Civilisation Médiévale (1954)
    24, Rue de la Chaîne 86022 Poitiers
Publ.: *Cahiers de Civilisation Médiévale*: 5 números par an dont un fascicule de bibliographie des travaux portant sur les Xe-XIIe siècles

Centre d'Etudes Supérieures de la Renaissance (1956)
    59, Rue Néricault-Destouches, B P 320, 37013 Tours Cedex
Publ.: *De Petrarque à Descartes*

Centre de Documentation et de Bibliographie Philosophiques (1958)
    Faculté des Lettres, Université de Besançon, 2, Rue Mégevand, 25030 Besançon-Cedex
Publ.: *Bibliographie Spinoziste*

Centre de Documentation Sciences Humaines (1950)
    54, Boulevard Raspail, 75260 Paris VI
Publ.: *Bulletin Signalétique*

Centre de Philosophie de Droit
    Université Paris II, 12, Place du Panthéon
Publ.: *Archives de Philosophie du Droit*

Centre de Recherche et de Documentation sur Hegel et sur Marx (1969)
    8, Rue René Descartes, F 86022 Poitiers
Publ.: *Recherches Hégéliennes*

Centre de Recherche Iconographique
22, Rue Descartes, 67000 Strasbourg

Centre de Recherches d'Histoire des Idées
U E R Civilisations, 06000 Nice
Publ.: Participation à 2 numéros de la revue belge "Réseaux," projet d'une revue specifique (cahiers annuels)

Centre de Recherches et de Confrontations sur la Pensée Médiévale
17, Rue de la Sorbonne, 75231 Paris V
Publ.: *Textes Philosophiques du Moyen Age*

Centre de Recherches sur la Logique Ancienne (1972)
Ecole Pratique des Hautes Etudes, Sorbonne, 45–47, Rue des Ecoles, 75005 Paris

Centre de Recherches sur la Pensée Antique (1947)
1, Rue Victor-Cousin, 75005 Paris

Centre International de Synthèse (1930)
12, Rue Colbert, 75002 Paris
Publ.: *Revue de Synthèse, Revue d'Histoire des Sciences, Semaines de Synthèse*

Centre National de la Recherche Scientifique (CNRS) (1939)
15, Quai Anatole France, 75007 Paris

Centre National de la Recherche Scientifique (CNRS), Section 41
15, Quai Anatole France, 75007 Paris

Centre Universitaire International de la Chancellerie des Universités de Paris (1955)
173, Boulevard Saint-Germain, 75272 Paris Cedex 06

Cercle Philosophique Lorrain (1966)
12, Rue Mozart, 57000 Metz
Publ.: Articles dans la presse régionale

Comité National pour la Division de Logique, Methodologie et Philosophie des Sciences (1948)
4, Rue Thénard, Paris V

Commission Nationale de Philosophie du CNRS (1938)
15, Quai Anatole France, 75007 Paris
Publ.: *Bulletin Analytique, Bibliographie de la Philosophie*

Ecole de Théologie des Frères Prêcheurs (1865)
1, Avenue Lacordaire, F 31078 Toulouse, Cedex
Publ.: *Revue Thomiste*

Equipe de Recherches (1966)
Université de Toulouse-Le-Mirail, 4, Rue Albert-Lautman, 31 Toulouse

Institut Catholique de Lyon (1932)
Faculté de Philosophie, 25, Rue du Plat, 69002 Lyon

Institut Catholique de Toulouse—Faculté Libre de Philosophie (1877)
31, Rue de la Fonderie, 31068 Toulouse Cedex

Institut d'Esthétique et des Sciences de l'Art (1959)
   19, Rue Chaptal, Paris IX

Institut d'Etudes Hispaniques (1959)
   56, Chemin de Mirail, 31 Toulouse
   Publ.: *Cahiers du Monde Hispanique*

Institut de Philosophie (1965)
   3, Rue des Tanneurs, 37041 Tours, Cedex
   Publ.: *Bulletins de la Société Ligérienne de Philosophie*

Institut de Recherche en Sciences de la Communication et de l'Education (1975)
   Faculté Pluridisciplinaire des Sciences Humaines et Sociales, Centre Universitaire,
   F66025 Perpignan Cedex
   Publ.: *Semiosis, Cahiers de l'Institut de Recherche en Sciences de la Communication et
   de l'Education*
   .

Institut de Recherche Universitaire d'Histoire de la Connaissance (1976)
   Université de Paris XII—Val de Marne, Avenue du Général de Gaulle, 94010 Créteil
   Cedex

Institut des Etudes Augustiniennes (1956)
   8, Rue François-ler, 75008 Paris

Institut Henri Poincaré (1931)
   11, Rue Pierre et Marie Curie, 75231 Paris Cedex 05
   Publ.: *Annales de l'Institut Henri Poincaré, Astérisque, Bulletin de la Société Mathématique
   de France, Bulletin des Sciences Mathématiques, Séminaires, Circulaire
   d'Informations de la Société Mathématique de France*

Institut International de Philosophie (1937)
   173, Boulevard Saint-Germain, 75006 Paris
   Publ.: *Bibliography of Philosophy, Philosophy and World Community, Philosophy in the
   Mid-Century, Contemporary Philosophy*

Institut Protestant de Théologie
   13, Rue Louis-Perrier, 34000 Montpellier
   Publ.: *Etudes Théologiques et Religieuses*

Séminaire d'Epistémologie Comparative
   Université de Provence, 29, Rue Robert Schuman, 13 Aix en Provence
   Publ.: *Travaux du S E C, Systèmes Symboliques, Science et Philosophie*

Service de Physique Théorique (1976)
   Université de Paris VI, 4, Place Jussieu, 75005 Paris V

UNESCO, Philosophy Division (1946)
   Philosophy Division, Sector of Social Sciences and Their Applications, UNESCO
   Place de Fontenoy, 75007 Paris

Societies
Amis de l'Homme (1919)
   22, Rue David d'Angers, 75019 Paris
   Publ.: *Le Moniteur du Regne de la Justice, Journal pour Tous*

Association d'Etudes Biologiques (1956)
 Facultés Catholiques, 25, Rue du Plat, Lyon 69002
Publ.: *Cahiers d'Etudes Biologiques*

Association des Amis d'Emmanuel Mounier (1953)
 19, Rue d'Antony, 92290 Chatenay-Malabry
Publ.: *Bulletin des Amis d'Emmanuel Mounier*

Association des Amis de Pontigny-Cerisy (1952)
 27, Rue de Boulainvilliers, 75016 Paris

Association des Professeurs de Philosophie de l'Enseignement Public (1945)
 1, Rue des Petits Carreaux, 75002 Paris
Publ.: *Revue de l'Enseignement Philosophique*

Association des Professeurs de Philosophie des Facultés Catholiques de France (1949)
 21, Rue d'Assas, 75270 Paris Cedex 06
Publ.: *Recherches de Philosophie*

Association des Sociétés de Philosophie de Langue Française (1937)
 12, Rue Colbert, 75002 Paris
Publ.: *Actes des Congrès*

Cymbalum Pataphysicum (1948)
 30, Boulevard de l'Organon, Vrigny 51140 Jonchery-sur-Vesle
Publ.: *Organographes du Cymbalum Pataphysicum*

Fédération des Sociétés Françaises de Philosophie (1963)
 Centre International de Synthèse, 12, Rue Colbert, Paris II

Maison d'Auguste Comte (1954)
 10, Rue Monsieur le Prince, 75006 Paris

Société Alpine de Philosophie (1952)
 Institut de Philosophie et de Sociologie, Université des Sciences Sociales de Grenoble, B P 47, 38040 Grenoble
Publ.: *Les Etudes Philosophiques*

Société Asiatique (1822)
 3, Rue Mazarine, 75006 Paris
Publ.: *Journal Asiatique, Cahiers de la Société Asiatique, Manuscrits de Haute Asie, Collection de Textes Orientaux*

Société Bourguignonne de Philosophie (1962)
 Faculté des Lettres, 2, Boulevard Gabriel, F 21000 Dijon
Publ.: *Rattachées aux Etudes Philosophiques*

Société Champenoise de Philosophie (1970)
 57, Rue Pierre Taittinger, 51 Reims
Publ.: *Médiations*

Société d'Esthétique (1932)
 162, Rue St. Charles, 75740 Paris Cedex 15
Publ.: *Revue d'Esthétique*

Société des Amis de Montaigne
  6, Villa Chanez 75016 Paris
Publ.: *Bulletin de la Société des Amis de Montaigne*

Société des Etudes Juives (1880)
  17, Rue Saint Georges, 75009 Paris
Publ.: *Oeuvres Complètes de Flavius Josèphe, Revue des Etudes Juives*

Société Française de Philosophie
  12, Rue Colbert 75002 Paris
Publ.: *Bulletin de la Société Française de Philosophie, Vocabulaire Technique et Critique de la Philosophie, Actes du Congrès Bergson, Revue de Métaphysique et de Morale*

Société Internationale pour l'Etude de la Philosophie Médiévale (1958)
  Institut Supérieur de Philosophie, Collège·Thomas More, Rue Montesquieu, B–1348 Louvain-la-Neuve, Belgique
Publ.: *Bulletin de Philosophie Médiévale*

Société Languedocienne de Philosophie (1945)
  Faculté des Lettres et Sciences Humaines de Montpellier

Société Ligérienne de Philosophie (1966)
  U E R des Sciences de l'Homme, 3, Rue des Tanneurs, F 37000 Tours
Publ.: *Bulletin de la Société Ligérienne de Philosophie*

Société Nietzsche (1969)
  27, Rue Lacépède, Paris 5e
Publ.: *Engadine*

Société pour l'Etude de la Philosophie Allemande (1966)
  22, Rue Descartes, 67000 Strasbourg

Société Strasbourgeoise de Philosophie (1945)
  1, Rue de Rome, 67000 Strasbourg
Publ.: *Actes de Colloques*

Société Théosophique de France (1887)
  4, Square Rapp, 75007 Paris
Publ.: *Le Lotus Bleu*, Nombreux Ouvrages Théosophiques

Société Toulousaine de Philosophie (1935)
  Université de Toulouse-Le-Mirail, 31076 Toulouse

Sociétés de Philosophie Provinciales
  c/o Pierre Aubenque, 5, Rue Berteaux-Dumas, F 92200 Neuilly S/Seine
Publ.: *Les Etudes Philosophiques*

GREAT BRITAIN

Institutes

British Academy (1901)
  Burlington House, Piccadilly, London, WLV ONS
Publ.: *Proceedings of the British Academy*

Royal Institute of Philosophy (1925)
    14 Gordon Square, London, WC1H OAG
    Publ.: *Philosophy*, annual edited volume of lectures; biennial edited volume of conference
        proceedings

Teilhard Centre for the Future of Man (1966)
    81 Cromwell Rd., London SW7 5BW
    Publ.: *The Teilhard Review, Teilhard Study Library*

Verulam Institute (1971)
    Shopwyke Park, Chichester, West Sussex

Victoria Institute (1865)
    130 Wood St., London EC2V 6DN
    Publ.: *Faith and Thought*

Societies

Alexander Society (1947)
    Department of Philosophy, The University, Oxford Road, Manchester

Aristotelian Society (1880)
    31 West Heath Dr., London, NW11 7QG
    Publ.: *Proceedings of the Aristotelian Society* and *Supplementary Volume*

Atlanteans (1957)
    42 St. George's St., Cheltenham, GL50 4AF
    Publ.: *The Atlantean, Atlanteanews*

Belfast Natural History and Philosophical Society (1821)
    Linenhall Library, Donegall S N, Belfast

Birkbeck College Philosophy Society (1957)
    Birkbeck College, University of London

British Society for the Philosophy of Science (1960)
    Hon. Secretary, Philosophy Department, London School of Economics, Houghton
        St., London, WC1A 2AE
    Publ.: *British Journal for the Philosophy of Science*

British Society of Aesthetics (1960)
    Department of Philosophy, Birkbeck College, Malet St., London WC1
    Publ.: *British Journal of Aesthetics*

British Society of Phenomenology (1967)
    Extra-Mural Department, University of Manchester, Manchester ML3 9PL
    Publ.: *Journal of the British Society for Phenomenology*

Leeds Philosophical and Literary Society (1820)
    Central Museum Calvarley St., Leeds 1, UK
    Publ.: *Proceedings of the Leeds Philosophical and Literary Society*

Manchester Literary and Philosophical Society (1781)
    36, George St., Manchester
    Publ.: *Memoirs and Proceedings*

Mind Association (1900)
   Department of Philosophy, The University, Southampton
Publ.: *Mind*

National Secular Society
   702 Holloway Rd., London N19 3NL
Publ.: *Freethinker*

Northern Association for Ancient Philosophy (1953)
   Department of Classics, University of Durham

Philosophical Society of England (1913)
   7 Cholmley Gardens, Alfred Rd., London NW6
Publ.: *The Philosopher, The Quest*

Philosophy of Education Society of Great Britain (1964)
   University of Reading, School of Education, London Rd., Reading, RGI 5AQ
Publ.: *Proceedings of the Philosophy of Education Society of Great Britain* Became
   Journal of the Philosophy of Education in 1978 with Vol. 12.

Radical Philosophical Society
   Philosophy Department, Prince of Wales Rd., Kentish Town, London NW5

Rationalist Press Association
   88 Islington High St., London N1 8EW
Publ.: *Question*

Royal Philosophical Society of Glasgow (1802)
   6 Hughenden Terrace, Glasgow W2
Publ.: *The Philosophical Journal*

Scots Philosophical Club (1900)
   Department of Philosophy, University of Stirling, Stirling, FK9 4LA
Publ.: *The Philosophical Quarterly*

Shanti Sadan (1932)
   29, Chepstow Villas, London W11 3DR
Publ.: *Self-Knowledge*

Social Morality Council
   c/o 17 York House, London, D8 4EY
Publ.: *Journal of Moral Education*

Société Britannique de Philosophie de Langue Française (1954)
   Philosophy Department, University of Hull HU6 7RX
Publ.: *Actes des Colloques*

Society for the Promotion of Hellenic Studies
   31–34 Gordon Square, London WC1H OPY
Publ.: *Journal of Hellenic Studies*

South Place Ethical Society (1793)
   Conway Hall, Red Lion Square, London WC1

Swedenborg Society (1810)
 20 Bloomsbury Way, London WC1A 2th
Publ.: *The Writings of Emanuel Swedenborg*, Catalogue and Annual Report

Theosophical Society in Europe
 Tekels Park, Camberley, Surrey GU15 2LF
Publ.: *Adyar*

GREECE

Institutes

Philosophical Research Center (1972)
 3 Haritos St., Athens 139
Publ.: *Deucalion*

Research Center for Greek Philosophy (1970)
 Academy of Athens, 14 Anagnostopoulou St., Athens 136
Publ.: *Philosophia*

Societies

Hellenic Society for Philosophical Studies
 40 Hypsilantou St., Athens 140
Publ.: *Diotima*

ITALY

Institutes

Accademia de Humanismo Cristiano
 Ismael Vergara 348–of, 102 Stgo
Publ.: *Escritos de Teoría*

Accademia della Scienze, Lettere ed Arti (1781)
 Piazza Indipendenza, Palermo 90129
Publ.: *Atti della Accademia*

Accademia di Scienze Iniziatiche e Tradizionali (1964)
 Via S. Zanobi 89, 50129 Firenze
Publ.: *Conoscenza*

Accademia Nazionale dei Lincei (1603)
 Palazzo Corsini, Via della Lungara 10, Roma

Accademia Virgiliana (1563)
 Via Accademia 47, 46100 Mantova

Aloisianum (1936)
 Via Gonzaga 8, 21013 Gallarate
Publ.: *Archivum Philosophicum Aloisianum*

Centro di Cibernetica (1956)
Via Festa del Perdono 3, 20122 Milano
Publ.: *Pensiero e Linguaggio in Operazioni*

Centro di Studi Filosofici di Gallarate (1945)
Via Donatello 16, 35100 Padova

Centro di Studi per il Lèssico Intellettuale Europeo (1964)
Instituto di Filosofia, Facoltà di Lettere, Università di Roma, Piazzale delle Scienze 5

Centro di Studi Vichiani (1968)
1 84100 Salerno, v dei Principati 42; 1 80133 Napoli, v S Aspreno 13
Publ.: *Studi Vichiani, Bollettino del Centro di Studi Vichiani*

Centro Internazionale di Studi Rosminiani
28049 Stresa
Publ.: *Rivista Rosminiana di Filosofia e di Cultura*

Centro Internazionale di Studi Umanistici (1949)
Faculté des Lettres, Université de Rome

Centro per i Problemi del Pensiero Filosofico e Religioso (1964)
Istituto di Filosofia, Università di Genova

Centro per la Storia della Tradizione Aristotelica nel Veneto (1956)
Istituto di Filologia Greca, Università degli Studi di Padova, Via Accademia 11, 35100 Padova

Centro Superiore di Logica e Scienze Comparate (1969)
Via Belmeloro 3, 40126 Bologna
Publ.: *Rassegna Internazionale di Logica*

Collegio S. Bonaventura di Quaracchi (1877)
I–00046 Grottaferrata, Roma
Publ.: *Bibliotheca Franciscana Scholastica, Spicilegium Bonaventurianum, Archivum Franciscanum Historicum*

Comissio Leonina (1880)
Collegio San Bonaventura, Via Vecchia di Marino, 24 I 00046
Publ.: *Sancti Thomae de Aquino Opera Omnia*

Facoltà Filosofica Aloisianum (1936)
V Gonzaga 8, 21013 Gallarate (Varese)
Publ. of Centro di Studi Filosofici di Gallarate: *Atti dei Convegni Annuali, Atti dei Conveghi degli Assistenti, Bibliografia Filosofica Italiana, Enciclopedia Filosofica, Collane Filosofiche*

Fondazione Giorgio Cini
Isola S. Giorgio Maggiore, Venezia

Fondazione Giorgio Ronchi (1946)
Largo e Fermi 1, 50125 Firenze
Publ.: *Atti della Fondazione Giorgio Ronchi*

Gruppo di Ricerca del Consiglio Nazionale delle Ricerche (1970)
Istituto di Filosofia, Via dell'Aquilone, 7 Perugia
Publ.: *Ricerche sul Trascendentale Kantiano, Ricerche sul Sommo Bene*

Index Thomisticus
Fondamenta Nuove 4885, 30121 Venezia

Institut International "Jacques Maritain" (1974)
Via dei Coronari 181, 00186 Roma
Publ.: *Notes et Documents de l'Institut International "Jacques Maritain"*

Istituto di Estetica
Università di Torino, Via S Ottavio 20, 10138 Torino
Publ.: *Rivista di Estetica*

Istituto di Filosofia (1921)
Facoltà di Lettere e Filosofia, Largo A Gemelli, 1 20123 Milano
Publ.: *Rivista di Filosofia Neo-scolastica*

Istituto di Filosofia (1774)
Viale delle Scienze, Facoltà di Lettere Filosofia e Lingue, 90128 Palermo
Publ.: *A journal of philosophy, in prospect*

Istituto di Studi Filosofici (1939)
Università di Roma, Facoltà di Lettere e Filosofia, Roma
Publ.: *Archivio di Filosofia*

Istituto Euro-Mediterraneo di Scienze Umane (1965)
Via dei Monti Parioli 44, Roma
Publ.: *Il Dialogo, Cooperazione Sociale*

Istituto Nazionale di Studi sul Rinascimento (1938)
Palazzo Strozzi, 50123 Firenze
Publ.: *La Rinascita, Rinascimento, Bibliographie Internationale de l'Humanisme et de la Renaissance* (in collaboration with the Fédération Internationale des Sociétés et Institutes pour l'Etude de la Renaissance)

Istituto Superiore Europeo di Scienze Umane (1968)
Via Bramante 54, Urbino

Societies

Associazione Biosofica Universale (1945)
00147 Roma, Piazza dei Navigatori 8, sc i/17
Publ.: *Metafisica Sperimentale*

Associazione Filosofia Arti e Scienze (1958)
Via Oberdan 15, 40126 Bologna

Associazione Filosofica Ligure (1955)
Via Balbi 4, Istituto di Filosofia, Genova

Biblioteca Filosofica dell' Università di Torino (1961)
18 Via Po, 10123 Torino
Publ.: *Quaderni della Biblioteca Filosofica di Torino*

Gnosis
    Via S. Zanobi 89, 50129 Firenze
Publ.: *Conoscenza*

Sezione Pisana della SFI (1960)
    Università degli Studi di Pisa

Società Dantesca Italiana (1888)
    Via Arte della Lana 1, Firenze
Publ.: *Studi Danteschi*

Società Filosofica Calabrese (1948)
    Via C. Battisti 12, 89015 Palmi
Publ.: *Studi Graviniani, Ricerche Filosofiche*

Società Filosofica Italiana (1935)
    Via Torino 98, Roma
Publ.: *Bollettino della Società Filosofica Italiana*

Società Filosofica Rosminiana (1958)
    Centro Internazionale Studi Rosminiani, 28049 Stresa (Novara)
Publ.: *Rivista Rosminiana, Quaderni della Cattedra Rosmini*, Opere di A. Rosmini

Società Italiana di Filosofia Giuridica e Politica (1936)
    Istituto di Filosofia del Diritto, Università di Roma
Publ.: *Rivista Internazionale di Filosofia del Diritto*

Società Italiana di Lògica e Filosofia delle Scienze (1950)
    Presso Cattedra di Filosofia della Scienza, Istituto di Filosofia, Via Balbi, 4, Genova

Società Italiana di Parapsicologia
    00186 Roma, Via dei Montecatini 7
Publ.: *Rassegna Italiana di Ricerca Psichica*

Union Mondiale des Sociétés Catholiques de Philosophie (1947)
    16 Via Donatello, 35000 Padova

NETHERLANDS

Institutes

Filosofisch Instituut (1964)
    Witte Singel 71, Leiden

Filosofisch Instituut (1969)
    Rijksuniversiteit te Utrecht, Heidelberglaan 2, Utrecht
Publ.: *Philosophical Texts and Studies*

Hoeven (Jan Van Der) Foundation for Theoretical Biology (1935)
    Institute for Theoretical Biology, Stationsweg 25, Leiden
Publ.: *Acta Biotheoretica* and special supplemental issues

Institute for Theoretical Biology (1957)
    Leiden University, Stationsweg 25, Leiden
Publ.: *Acta Biotheoretica*

Institute of Aesthetics (1967)
    Department of Philosophy, Amsterdam University, Roetersstraat 15, Amsterdam C
Publ.: *Bulletin International d'Esthétique, Lier en Boog*

Instituut voor Grondslagenonderzoek
    Roetersstraat 15, Amsterdam
Publ.: University of Amsterdam, Department of Mathematics Reports

International Humanist and Ethical Union (1952)
    Oudegracht 152, Utrecht
Publ.: *International Humanism, Bibliography of Humanism*, congress proceedings

Internationale School voor Wijsbegeerte
    Dodeweg 8, 3832 RD Leusden
Publ.: *Amersfoortse Stemmen*

Koninklijke Nederlandse Akademie van Wetenschappen
    Kloveniersburgwal 29, Amsterdam
Publ.: Publications in *Mededelingen* and *Verhandelingen*

Stichting Internationale School voor Wijsbegeerte (1916)
    Dodeweg 8, 3832 RD Leusden
Publ.: *Amersfoortse Stemmen*

Societies

Algemene Nederlandse Vereniging voor Wijsbegeerte (1933)
    Lorentzplein 4, Haarlem
Publ.: *Algemeen Nederlands Tijdschrift voor Wijsbegeerte*

Dutch Society of Aesthetics
    Institute of Aesthetics, University of Amsterdam, Roetersstraat 15, Amsterdam
Publ.: *Lier en Boog*

Genootschap voor Wetenschappelyke Filosofie (1923)
    Filosofisch Instituut, Heidelberglaan 2, Utrecht

Nederlands Filosofisch Genootschap (1922)
    52 Dever, Amsterdam-Buitenveldert
Publ.: *Handelingen*

Nederlands Klages-Genootschap (1968)
    Beethovenstraat 145, Amsterdam Z

Nederlandse Vereniging voor Logica en Wijsbegeerte der Exacte Wetenschappen (1947)
    Mathematical Institute, Budapestlaan 6, Utrecht

Stichting Bijzondere Leerstoelen voor Calvinistische Wijsbegeerte (1947)
    Everlaan 16, Wageningen

Theosophical Society
    Kruisstraat 7, Utrecht
Publ.: *Theosofia*

Vereniging voor Calvinistische Wijsbegeerte (1936)
p/a PB149, Maarssen
Publ.: *Beweging Philosophia Reformata*

Vereniging voor Filosofie Onderwijs (1971)
Pernambucodreef 41, Utrecht
Publ.: *Vereniging voor Filosofie Onderwijs Informatie en Communicatie*

Vereniging voor Wijsbegeerte des Rechts (1918)
Vÿverweg 7, Rotterdam
Publ.: *Wijsbegeerte des Rechts en Rechtstheorie*

Vereniging voor Wijsbegeerte te 'S-Gravenhage (1907)
Laan van Meerdervoort 567, Den Haag
Publ.: Syllabi of speeches

Wijsgerige Vereniging "Thomas van Aquino" (1933)
Centrale Interfaculteit, Katholieke Universiteit, Erasmuslaan, Nijmegen
Publ.: Lectures in the existing philosophical journals

SWEDEN

Societies

Filosofi- Och Psykologilärarnas Förening (1943)
Hammarkroken 130, 424 36 Angered
Publ.: *Filosofi- Och Psykologilärarnas Förenings Skriftserie*

Filosofiska Föreningen i Lund (1922)
University of Lund, Lund

Filosofiska Föreningen i Stockholm (1928)
Filosofiska Institutionen, Stockholms Universitet, 106 91 Stockholm

Filosofiska Föreningen i Uppsala (1870)
Department of Philosophy, Villavägen 5, S–752 36 Uppsala
Publ.: *Philosophical Studies*

Hans Larsson Samfundet (1953)
Tornaplatsen 2, S–223 63 Lund
Publ.: *Insikt och Handling*

WEST GERMANY

Institutes

Akademie der Wissenschaften in Göttingen (1751)
34 Göttingen, Prinzenstrasse 1
Publ.: *Göttingische Gelehrte Anzeigen, Nachrichten, Abhandlungen, Jahrbuch*

Akademie der Wissenschaften und der Literatur (1949)
65 Mainz, Geschwister Schollstrasse 2, Postfach 1220
Publ.: *Archiv für Begriffsgeschichte, Abhandlungen*

Albertus-Magnus Institut (1931)
Adenauerallee 17–19, D–5300 Bonn 1
Publ.: *Opera Omnia Alberti Magni*

Albertus-Magnus-Kolleg EV
Bischof-Kaller-Str 3, D–6240 Königstein
Publ.: *Königsteiner Studien*

Arbeitsgruppe Umwelt, Gesellschaft, Energie (1972)
Universität Essen Gesamthochschule, Forschungsbereich Umwelt und Gesellschaft,
4300 Essen 1, Postfach 6843
Publ.: Essays by the members

Bayerische Akademie der Wissenschaften (1759)
Marstallplatz 8, D 8000 München 22
Publ.: *J G Fichte, Gesamtaüsgabe der Bayerischen Akademie der Wissenschaften, Friedrich Wilhelm Joseph Schelling Historische-Kritische Ausgabe*

Deutscher Akademischer Austauschdienst (1950)
53 Bonn-Bad Godesberg 1, Kennedy-Allee 50
Publ.: Annual reports and study guides for foreign and German students

Europäische Nietzsche-Gesellschaft
Geschäftsstelle: D–8700 Würzburg, Residenzplatz 2
Publ.: *Perspektiven der Philosophie*

Existenzanalytisches Forschungsinstitut (1971)
Präsidium, D–7140 Ludwigsburg, Denkendorfer Str. 16
Publ.: *Anthropologica Universalia*

Grabman Institut
München

Hegel Archiv
Bochum

Heidelberger Akademie der Wissenschaft (1909)
Friedrich-Ebert Anlage 24, Heidelberg

Hönigswald-Archiv (1956)
Philosophisches Seminar A der Universität Bonn, D–53 Bonn, Am Hof 1
Publ.: *Richard Hönigswald, Schriften aus dem Nachlass*

Humanistische Union (1961)
8 München 2, Bräuhausstr 2

Husserl-Archiv (1950)
Werthmann-Platz, 7800 Freiburg i Br BRD
Publ.: *Edmund Husserl, Aufsätze und Rezensionen*

Institut für Gesellschaftspolitik
8000 München 22, Kaulbachstrasse 33
Publ.: *Civitas, Kirche und Dritte Welt, Freiheit und Ordnung*

Institut für Weltanschauungsfragen
8000 München 22, Kaulbachstrasse 33

Kant Gesellschaft
Philosophisches Seminar Universität, Saarstr 21, 6500 Mainz
Publ.: *Kant-Studien*

Kant-Index (1965)
Philosophisches Seminar A, Universität Bonn, D 53 Bonn, Am Hof 1
Publ.: *Allgemeiner Kantindex*

Kommission für die Herausgabe des Fichte-Nachlasses (1957)
Bayerische Akademie der Wissenschaften, 8 München 22, Marstallplatz 8

Leibniz-Archiv
München

Leibniz-Forschungsstelle (1956)
Universität Münster, Rothenburg 32, D–4400 Münster

Pfortebund für Wertidealismus EV (1947)
D–7300 Esslingen, Dulkweg 9
Publ.: *Die Pforte*

Philosophical Information Center (1967)
4000 Düsseldorf, Horionplatz 10
Publ.: *Zeitschriften-Bibliographien* (Gesamtregister zur Zeitschrift für philosophische Forschung), *Autoren-Bibliographien* (Primärliteratur, Sekundärliteratur), *Problem-Bibliographien*

Rechtsphilosophisches Seminar
Bonn, Adenauerallee 24–42 Westturm

Rothacker-Archiv (1969)
Rheinische Freidrich-Wilhelms-Universität, Philosophisches Seminar A, D–5300 Bonn, Am Hof 1
Publ.: *Gedanken über Martin Heidegger*

Schelling-Kommission der Bayerischen Akademie der Wissenschaften (1968)
Marstall-Platz 8, D–8000 München 22
Publ.: *Friedrich Wilhelm Joseph Schelling Historisch-Kritische Ausgabe*

Schopenhauer-Archiv (1860)
Bockenheimer Landstr 134–138, III, Stade und Universitätsbibliothek Frankfurt am main

Siminar für Scholastische Philosophie (1946)
6500 Mainz, Jakob Welder-Weg 18
Publ.: *Mainzer Philosophische Forschungen, Conscientia, Studien und Materialien zur Geschichte der Philosophie*

Thomas Institut der Universität zu Köln (1948)
5 Köln 41, Universitätsstrasse 22
Publ.: *Miscellanea Mediaevalia*

Verein Deutscher Ingenieure, Ausschuss Technikbewertung (1973)
D–4000 Düsseldorf 1, Postfach 1139, Graf-Recke-Strasse 84

Verzeichnis der Veröffentlichungen, Projektgruppe "Wissenschaftsforschung" (1974)
Universität Essen Gesamthochschule, Fachbereich 1, 43 Essen

Societies

Allgemeine Gesellschaft für Philosophie in Deutschland (1950)
Institut für Philosophie der Ruhr-Universität Bochum, Postfach 102148, D–4630 Bochum 1
Publ.: *Allgemeine Zeitschrift für Philosophie, Zeitschrift für Philosophische Forschung*

Deutsche Forschungsgemeinschaft (1949)
Kennedyallee 40, 5300 Bonn-Bad Godesberg

Deutsche Vereinigung für Mathematische Logik (1962)
Math Institute, University of Heidelberg

Gorres-Gesellschaft zur Pflege der Wissenschaft EV (1876)
D–5000 Köln 1, Postfach 100905
Publ.: *Philosophisches Jahrbuch*

Gottfried-Wilhelm-Leibniz-Gesellschaft
Niedersächsische Landesbibliothek, D 3000 Hannover, Waterloostr 8
Publ.: *Studia Leibnitiana*

Hegel-Kommission der Deutshcen Forschungsgemeinschaft (1961)
Bonn 5320 Bad Godesberg, Kennedyallee 40
Publ.: *Hegel-Studien*

International Hegel Association (1962)
Marsiliusplatz 1, 69 Heidelberg, Philosophisches Seminar der Universität
Publ.: *Hegel-Studien,* Supplementary Volumes

Jungius-Gesellschaft (1947)
2 Hamburg 13, Edmund-Siemers-Allee 1
Publ.: *Veröffentlichungen der Joachim Jungius Gesellschaft der Wissenschaften eV*

Klages-Gesellschaft Marbach (1963)
Schatten 6 Gewant, D 7000 Stuttgart-Büsnau
Publ.: *Hestia*

Leibniz (Gottfried Wilhelm) Gesellschaft (1966)
Niedersächsische Landesbibliothek, D 3000 Hannover 1, Waterloostr 8
Publ.: *Studia Leibnitiana, Zeitschrift für Geschichte der Philosophie und der Wissenschaften*

Schopenhauer-Gesellschaft (1911)
Beethovenstr 48, D–6000 Frankfurt am Main 1
Publ.: *Schopenhauer Jahrbuch, Manuscript Remains, Schopenhauer-Bildnisse*

Wissenschaftlicher Beirat der Cusanus-Gesellschaft (1960)
Institut für Cusanus-Forschung an der Universität Mainz
Publ.: *Mitteilungen und Forschungsbeiträge der Cusanus-Gesellschaft, Buchreihe der Cusanus-Gesellschaft, Nicolai de Cusa Sermones: Opera Omnia*

AUSTRIA

Institutes

Indologisches Institut der Universität Wien
Universitätsstr 7, A–1010 Wien
Publ.: *Wiener Zeitschrift für die Kunde Südasiens, Archiv für Indische Philosophie*

Institut für Christliche Philosophie (1924)
Katholische Theologische Fakultät, Universitätsstrasse 4 b, A–6020 Innsbruck
Publ.: *Philosophie und Grenzwissenschaften*

Institut für Christliche Philosophie (1950)
Katholisch-Theologischen Fakultät-Universität Wien, A–1010 Wien, Schottenring 21
Publ.: *Atheismusproblem, Grenzfragen Philosophie-Theologie*

Institut für Rechtsphilosophie
Universität Graz, A–8010 Graz 3

Institut für Wissenschaftstheorie (1961)
Internationales Forschungszentrum, A–5020 Salzburg, Mönchsberg 2a

Österreichische Akademie der Wissenshaften, Philosophisch-Historische Klasse (1847)
Dr. Ignaz Seipel-Platz 2, A–1010 Wien
Publ.: *Anzeiger, Sitzungsberichte*, Denkschriften

Philosophisches Institut (1927)
Katholisch-Theologische Fakultät, Universität Salzburg, Salzburg, Franziskanergasse 1/IV
Publ.: *Salzburger Jahrbuch für Philosophie, Salzburger Studien zur Philosophie*

Seminar für Philosophie an der Gesamthochschule (1972)
Teil-Universität, Feldkirchenstr 21, 8600 Bamberg/BRD

Societies

Gesellschaft für Ganzheitsforschung (1956)
Franz-Klein-Gasse 1, A–1190 Vienna
Publ.: *Zeitschrift für Ganzheitsforschung, Schrifttumsspiegel*

Philosophische Gesellschaft an der Universität Graz (1920)
Heinrichstrasse 26, 8010 Graz
Publ.: *Jenseits von Sein und Nichtsein*

Philosophische Gesellschaft in Salzburg (1967)
Franziskanergasse 1, A–5020 Salzburg

Philosophische Gesellschaft Wien (1945)
I Philosophisches Institut der Universität Wien, Universitätsstrasse 7, 1010 Wien

Rudolf Kassner Gesellschaft (1961)
Gumpendorferstrasse 15, 1060 Wien
Publ.: *Rudolf Kassner Sämtliche Werke Volume I–III*

Vereinigung für Wissenschaftliche Grundlagenforschung (1951)
Heinrichstrasse 26/VI, A–8010 Graz

Wittgenstein Gesellschaft
Kirchberg am Wechsel (near Vienna) A–2880
Kirchberg/Wechsel, Markt 234 Austria

AUSTRALIA

Institutes

Australian Academy of the Humanities (1969)
Second Floor, National Library Building, G. P. O. Box 93, Canberra 2600, Australian Capital Territory
Publ.: Annual *Proceedings*, monographs, occasional papers

Centre for Foundational Studies in Moral and Political Theory (1977)
Department of Philosophy, University of Wollongong, Northfields Ave., Wollongong NSW 2500

Societies

Australasian Association for Logic (1975)
Department of Philosophy, Research School of Science, The Australian National University, Canberra, A C T 2600

Australasian Association of Philosophy (1923)
Department of Philosophy, La Trobe University, Bundoora, Melbourne, Vic 3083
Publ.: *Australasian Journal of Philosophy*

Australian Fellowship of Evangelical Students Inc.
2d Floor, 129 York Street, Sydney 2000
Publ.: *Interchange*

Philosophy of Education Society of Australasia (1970)
University of New South Wales, P.O. Box 1, Kensington 2033

ISRAEL

Institutes

Bergman (S. H.) Centre
Department of Philosophy, The Hebrew University, Jerusalem
Publ.: *Iyyun*

Israel Academy of Sciences and Humanities (1961)
P.O. Box 4040, Jerusalem
Publ.: *Proceedings of the Israel Academy of Sciences and Humanities, Sources of Jewish Thought*

Societies

Israel Philosophical Association (1974)
    c/o Asa Kasher, Tel-Aviv University, Tel-Aviv
    Publ.: *Philosophia*

Israeli Branch of the International Union of History and Philosophy of Science (1969)
    Division of Logic and Philosophy of Science, Hebrew University Campus, Jerusalem

Jerusalem Philosophical Society (1941)
    The Hebrew University Campus, Jerusalem
    Publ.: *Iyyun* in collaboration with the S. H. Bergman Centre for Philosophical Studies

Van Leer Jerusalem Foundation (1956)
    Jabotinsky St. 43, P.O. Box 4070, Jerusalem

EASTERN EUROPE

CZECHOSLOVAKIA

Institutes

Czechoslovak Academy of Sciences
    Jilská 1, 110 00 Praha 1, Staré Mesto
    Publ.: *Filosofický Casopis*

Institute for Philosophy and Sociology of the Czechoslovak Academy of Sciences (1970)
    Jilská 1, 110 00 Prague 1
    Publ.: *Filosofický Casopis*

Institute of Philosophy of the Slovak Academy of Sciences (1946)
    Klemensova 27, Bratislava
    Publ.: *Filozofia*

Oriental Institute of the Czechoslovak Academy of Sciences (1928)
    Lázenská 4, Praha 1, Malá Strana
    Publ.: *Archiv Orientálni*

Societies

Czech Society for Aesthetics
    Czechoslovak Academy of Sciences, Praha 1, Hastalkská 6
    Publ.: *Estetika*

Jednota Filozofická (1881)
    Prague 1, Valdstejnská 14

EAST GERMANY

Institutes

Institut für Gesellschaftswissenschaften (1951)
    Einheitspartei Deutschlands, Lehrstuhl für Philosophie, 108 Berlin, Taubenstrasse
    19–23

Sächsische Akademie der Wissenschaften (1846)
DDR 701 Leipzig, Goethestr 3–5
Publ.: *Abhandlungen, Jahrbuch*

Societies

Vereinigung der Philosophischen Institutionen der DDR (1961)
701 Leipzig, Peterssteinweg 2

POLAND

Institutes

Instytut Filozofii i Socjologii PAN Zespól Historii Religii
Polska, Warszawa, Palac Staszica, Nowy Swiat 72
Publ.: *Studie Religioznawcze*

Instytut Nauk Spolecznych (1969)
Gdańsk-Wrzeszcz, ul Majakowskiego 11/12

Polska Akademia Nauk (1952)
Instytut Filozofii i Socjologii, Warszawa, Nowy Swiat 72, Palac Staszica
Publ.: *Studia Logica, Etyka, Materialy do Historii Filozofii Sredniowiecznej w Polsce,
Studia Filozoficzne, Archiwum Historii Filozofii i Mysli Spolecznej, Studia Me-
diewistyczni, Studia Estetyczne, Studia Religioznawcze, Mediaevalia Philosophica
Polonorum*

Spolteczny Instytut Wydawniczy "Znak"
Krakow, Ul Wiślna 12
Publ.: *Znak*

Societies

Association "Pax"
Warszawa, Ul Mokotowska 43
Publ.: *Zycie i Myśl*

*National Committee of the Division of Logic, Methodology and Philosophy of Science
(1957)*
Polish Academy of Sciences, Biuro Wspólpracy z Zagranica, Warszawa, Palac
Kultury i Nauki

National Polish Committee for the History and Philosophy of Science
Polska Akademia Nauk, Palac Kultury i Nauki, XVI Pietro, Pokoj 1621, Varsovie

Polskie Towarzystwo Filozoficzne-Toruń (1955)
Uniwersytet, Zaklad Logiki, Fosa Staromiejska 3, 87–100 Toruń

Polskie Towarzystwo Filozoficzne-Warszawa (1904)
00–901 Warszawa, Palac Kultury i Nauki
Publ.: *Ruch Filozoficzny*

Polskie Towarzystwo Semiotyczne (1968)
Palac Kultury i Nauki, 00–901 Warsaw
Publ.: *Studia Semiotyczne*

Towarzystwo Naukowe Katolickiego Uniwersytetu Lubelskiego (1934)
   Al Raclawickie 14, 20 059 Lublin
   Publ.: *Roczniki Filozoficzne*

ROMANIA

Institutes

Academia de Stiinţe Sociale si Politice a Republicii Socialiste România
   Str Oneşti No. 11, Bucureşti
   Publ.: *Revue des Sciences Sociales*

Institute of Philosophy (1953)
   Bd Ilie Pintilie 6, Bucharest
   Publ.: *Journal of Philosophy, Revue Roumaine des Sciences Sociales*

Romanian Committee for the History and Philosophy of Sciences (1958)
   Calea Victoriei 125, Bucharest
   Publ.: *Noesis*

UNION OF SOVIET SOCIALIST REPUBLICS

Institutes

Institute of History, Philology, and Philosophy (1965)
   Siberian Division of USSR Academy of Science, Prospekt Nauki 17, Novosibirsk
   630090 USSR

Institute of Philosophy of the Academy of Sciences of the USSR (1931)
   Leninskii Prospekt 66, Minsk 72

Mouminov's Institute of Philosophy and Law (1958)
   Suleimanova Str., 33 Tashkent 700017

*Scientific Council for the Philosophical Problems of Contemporary Natural Sciences
   (1959)*
   Volkhonka 14, Moscow

Societies

Ministry of Higher and Secondary Special Education of the USSR
   c/o Alley Khrustalnyi, 1–96, Moscow 103012
   Publ.: *Filosofskie Nauki*

Soviet National Association for History and Philosophy of Science and Technology (1965)
   Academy of Sciences of the USSR, Division of Logic, Methodology and Philosophy
   of Science, Staropansky per 1/5, Moscow K 12
   Publ.: *Voprosy Historii Estestvoznania i Techniki*

THE AMERICAS

CANADA

Societies

Canadian Philosophical Association, l'Association Canadienne de Philosophie (1957)
1390 Sherbrooke St. West, Suite 46, Montréal, Que H3G 1K2
Publ.: *Dialogue*

Canadian Society for History and Philosophy of Science (1956)
6220 Godfrey Ave., Montréal, Que H4B 1K2, 514–392–5839

MEXICO

Institutes

Instituto de Investigaciones de la Facultad de Filosifía y Letras (1975)
Apartado Postal 3024, Monterey, NL
Publ.: *Cuadernos de Metodología, Cuadernos de Filosofía*

Instituto de Investigaciones Filosóficas (1940)
Torre de Humanidades, 4 Piso, Ciudad Universitaria 20, DF
Publ.: *Dianoia, Colección Dianoia, Filosofía Contemporánea, Crítica*

Instituto de Investigaciones Humanísticas (1970)
Av Cerro de las Torres 395, 21, DF
Publ.: *Humanidades*

Seminario de Problemas Científicos y Filosóficos (1955)
Torre de Humanidades 4 Piso, Ciudad Universitaria, México 20 DF
Publ.: *Problemas Científicos y Filosóficos*

Societies

EMECU-Catedra Regional Mexicana
Apartado Postal No. 29–006, México 1, DF
Publ.: *Renovación*

Sociedad Fray Alonso de la Veracruz
Universidad Iberoamericana, Cerro de las Torres 395, México 21, DF
Publ.: *Revista de Filosofía*

ARGENTINA

Institutes

Centro de Estudios Filosóficos
Academia Nacional de Ciencias, Junín 1278, 1113 Buenos Aires
Publ.: *Escritos de Filosofía*

564   Appendix I

Centro de Estudios Filosóficos del Sur (1971)
Departamento de Humanidades, 12 de Octubre y Perú, Bahia Blanca

Centro de Investigaciones Filosóficas (1965)
Cangallo 1479, Piso 4, Of 6(1037) Capital Federal, Buenos Aires
Publ.: *Revista Laninoamericana de Filosofía*

Instituto de Bibliografía (1960)
Ministerio de Educación, 7–538, La Plata
Publ.: *Bibliografía Argentina de Filosofía*

Instituto de Filosofía
25 de Mayo 217, 2 Piso, 1002 Buenos Aires
Publ.: *Cuadernos de Filosofía*

Instituto de Filosofía (1943)
Facultad de Filosofía y Letras, Casilla de Correo 345, Centro Universitario, Mendoza
Publ.: *Philosophía, Cuyo*

Instituto de Filosofía
Machado 951, Morón
Publ.: *Revista de la Facultad de Filosofía y Letras*

Societies

Grupo Argentino de la Unión Internacional de Historia de la Ciencia (1933)
Las Heras 2954, 3 "F," Buenos Aires
Publ.: *Ciclos de Disertaciones*

BOLIVIA

Institutes

Instituto de Filosofía Jurídica y Social (1963)
Universidad Mayor de San Francisco Xavier de Chuquisaca, Sucre

BRAZIL

Institutes

Centro de Estudos Filosóficos (1970)
Pontificia Universidade Católica do Rio Grande do Sul
Publ.: *Revista Veritas*

Instituto Brasileiro de Filosofia (1951)
Avenida Joana Angélica 37, Salvador

Instituto Brasileiro de Filosofia (1969)
Department of Philosophy, University of Brasilia, Brasilia

Instituto Brasileiro de Filosofia (1954)
Rua Felipe Schmidt 58, Edificio Florencio Costa, App 1306, C P 998, Florianópolis

Instituto Brasileiro de Filosofia (1949)
   Rua Barao de Itapetininga 88, 7 Andar, S/701–5, São Paulo
   Publ.: *Revista Brasileira de Filosofia*

Instituto Neo-Pitagórico (1909)
   Caixa Postal 1047, 80000 Curitiba, Paraná
   Publ.: *A Lâmpada*

Instituto Tecnologico de Aeronautica
   Centro Tecnico Aeroespacial, 12 200 S José dos Campos, São Paulo
   Publ.: *Ita-Humanidades*

Seminário de Pesquisa Filosófica (1969)
   Departamento de Filosofia, 7 Andar, Prédio do Centro de Filosofia e Ciências
   Humanas, UFPE, Cidade Universitária, 50,000 Recife PE

Societies

Associação Latino-Americana de Filósofos Católicos (1972)
   Caixa Postal 11 587, 05000 São Paulo, S P
   Publ.: *Filosofar Cristiano*

Sociedade Brasileira de Filósofos Católicos (1970)
   Rua Manoel Vitorino 626, Departamento de Filosofia, Universidade Gama Filho,
   Ed Murta Ribeiro, 6 Andar, Piedade 20,000 Rio de Janeiro
   Publ.: *Presença Filosofica*

Sociedade Visconde de São Leopoldo
   Rua Euclides da Cunha 241, São Paulo
   Publ.: *Leopoldianum*

CHILE

Institutes

Instituto Central de Filosofía (1958)
   Casilla 2090, Calle Ed Larenas 240, Concepción
   Publ.: *Atenea*

Societies

Sociedad Chilena de Filosofía
   Instituto Chilena de Filosofía, Universidad de Concepción, Concepción
   Publ.: *Cuadernos de Filosofía*

COLOMBIA

Institutes

Seminario Mayor de Nuestra Señora Del Rosario (1902)
   Apartado 286, Manizales

Societies

Asociación Colombiana para la Investigación Filosófica *(1975)*
    Apartado Aéreo 53072, Medellín

COSTA RICA

Societies

Asociación Costarricense de Filosofía *(1958)*
    Departamento de Filosofía, Universidad de Costa Rica
    Publ.: The Philosophical Club ''Symposion''

Teori and Praksis (1973)
    Publ.: *GMT*

DOMINICAN REPUBLIC

Societies

Asociación de Jóvenes Amantes de la Filosofía *(1957)*
    Restauración 32 Altos, Santo Domingo

HONDURAS

Societies

Sociedad Hondureña de Filosofía *(1967)*
    Universidad Nacional Autónoma de Honduras

PERU

Institutes

Instituto Peruano de Estudios Islámicos
    Pasaje Caribe 170, Jesús María, Lima 11

Instituto Riva Agüero *(1947)*
    Camana 459, Apartados 1761–5729, Lima
    Publ.: *Boletín del Instituto Riva Agüero*

URUGUAY

Societies

Sociedad de Filosofía Uruguaya *(1956)*
    Instituto de Filosofía, Facultad de Humanidades y Ciencias, Cerrito 7–3, Montevideo
    Publ.: *Boletín de Filosofía*

VENEZUELA

Institutes

Instituto de Filosofía (1957)
Facultad de Humanidades, Universidad Central, Ciudad Universitaria, Caracas
Publ.: *Episteme*

Societies

Sociedad Venezolana de Filosofía (1972)
Apartado Postal 50371, Sabana Grande, Caracas
Publ.: *Estudios Filosóficos, Revista Venezolana de Filosofía* en colaboración con el
Departamento de Filosofía de la Universidad Simón Bolívar

UNITED STATES

Institutes

Center for Integrative Education (1947)
12 Church St., New Rochelle, N.Y. 10805
Publ.: *Main Currents in Modern Thought*

Center for Philosophic Exchange (1969)
Department of Philosophy, State University of New York, Brockport, N.Y. 14420
Publ.: Annual Proceedings of the Center for Philosophic Exchange

Center for Philosophic Linguistic Research
Chapel Hill, N.C.

Center for Philosophy, Law and Citizenship, Inc. (1974)
635 Washington Dr., Centerport, N.Y. 11721 or Knapp Hall, SUNY, Farmingdale,
N.Y. 11735
Publ.: *Aitia*

Center for Process Studies (1973)
1325 North College, Claremont, Calif. 91711
Publ.: *Process Studies* published quarterly since 1971, *Newsletter of the Center for
Process Studies* published quarterly since Spring 1975

Council for Philosophical Studies (1965)
Skinner Hall 1131, University of Maryland, College Park, Md. 20742

Franciscan Institute (1940)
Saint Bonaventure University, Saint Bonaventure, N.Y. 14778

Hegeler Institute
P.O. Box 1908, Los Gatos, Calif. 95030
Publ.: *The Monist*

Institute for Advanced Studies in Philosophy (1971)
227 Haven Ave., Room 1b–40, New York, N.Y. 10033

Institute for Philosophical Research and Development (1973)
1915 Las Lomas Road, NE, Albuquerque, N. Mex. 87106

Institute of Empirical and Philosophical Science (1972)
P.O. Box 4332, Berkeley, Calif. 94704
Publ.: *Philosophy Surlog, Technical Surlog, Empirical Surlog, Concordances Semiotica, Formation Analysis Records.*

International Association for Philosophy of Law and Social Philosophy (1909)
P.O. Box 1120, Washington University, Saint Louis, Mo. 63130
Publ.: *Archiv für Rechts und Sozialphilosophie*

National Council for Critical Analysis (1968)
Department of Philosophy, Jersey City State College, Jersey City, N.J. 07305
Publ.: *Journal of Critical Analysis* and *Journal of Pre-College Philosophy*

Philosophy Documentation Center (1966)
Bowling Green State University, Bowling Green, Ohio 43403
Publ.: *The Philosopher's Index, Philosophy Research Archives, Directory of American Philosophers, International Directory of Philosophy and Philosophers, Directory of Women in Philosophy*

Translation Center (1967)
School of Humanities, Southern Illinois University, Edwardsville, Edwardsville, Ill. 62025

World Institute for Advanced Phenomenological Research and Learning
348 Payson Rd., Belmont, Mass. 02178

Societies

Alabama Philosophical Society (1963)
Department of Philosophy, Spring Hill College, Mobile, Ala. 36608

American Academy of Religion (1909)
Department of Religion, Florida State University, Tallahassee, Fla. 32306
Publ.: *Journal of the American Academy of Religion, Bulletin of the Council on the Study of Religion,* the series "AAR Monograph Series," "AAR Dissertation Series," "AAR and SBL Religion in Art Series"

American Catholic Philosophical Association (1926)
Catholic University, Washington, D.C. 20064
Publ.: *The New Scholasticism, Proceedings of the ACPA*

American Catholic Philosophical Association, Florida Chapter
11300 NE Second Ave., Miami Shores, Fla. 33161

American Catholic Philosophical Association, New England Regional Conference
The Catholic University of America, Washington, D.C. 20017

American Catholic Philosophical Association, Northwest Regional Conference (1924)
Mount Angel Seminary, Saint Benedict, Ore. 97373

American Philosophical Association (1900)
University of Delaware, Newark, Del. 19711
Publ.: *Proceedings and Addresses of the American Philosophical Association, Jobs in Philosophy*

American Section of International Association for Philosophy of Law and Social Philosophy (1963)
c/o Michael D. Bayles, Executive Director, AMINTAPHIL, Department of Philosophy, University of Kentucky, Lexington, Ky. 40506
Publ.: *Human Rights: AMINTAPHIL I, 1971, Law and the Ecological Challenge, AMINTAPHIL II, 1978*

American Society for Aesthetics (1942)
The Cleveland Museum of Art, 11150 East Blvd., Cleveland, Ohio 44106
Publ.: *Journal of Aesthetics & Art Criticism*

American Society for Political and Legal Philosophy (1955)
c/o M. P. Golding, Department of Philosophy, Duke University, Durham, N.C. 27708
Publ.: Eighteen volumes of *NOMOS*, the society's yearbook, have appeared to date.

American Society for Value Inquiry (1970)
Department of Philosophy, Memphis State University, Memphis, Tenn. 38152

Association for Philosophy of the Unconscious (1971)
Department of Philosophy, Georgetown University, Washington, D.C. 20007
Publ.: Newsletter

Association for Symbolic Logic (1936)
P.O. Box 6248, Providence, R.I. 02940
Publ.: *Journal of Symbolic Logic*

Association of Philosophy Journal Editors (1971)
Department of Philosophy, Clark University, Worcester, Mass. 01610

Central Pennsylvania Philosophical Association (1969)
Department of Philosophy, Wilkes College, Wilkes-Barre, Penn. 18703

Chicago Society for Process Thought (1971)
Department of Philosophy, DePaul University, Chicago, Ill. 60614

Colloquium for Social Philosophy (1972)
Pennsylvania State University, Delaware County Campus, Media, Penn. 19063

Creighton Club-New York State Philosophical Association (1924)
Department of Philosophy, State University of New York, Fredonia, N.Y. 14063
Publ.: *Proceedings of the Creighton Club*

Division of Philosophical Psychology (1963)
1200 17th St., NW, Washington, D.C. 20036
Publ.: *Philosophical Psychologist* (newsletter)

Far Western Philosophy of Education Society (1952)
c/o Dr. Nicholas Appleton, Arizona State University, Tempe, Ariz. 85281
Publ.: *Proceedings*

Fellowship of Religious Humanists (1967)
Humanist Center, Yellow Springs, Ohio 45387
Publ.: *Religious Humanism*

Florida Philosophical Association (1955)
c/o Bryan Norton, New College, Sarasota, Fla. 33578

Fullerton Club (1925)
Bryn Mawr College, Bryn Mawr, Penn. 19010

Georgia Philosophical Society (1950)
Department of Philosophy, Oglethorpe College, Atlanta, Ga. 30319

Hegel Society of America (1969)
Department of Philosophy, Marquette University, Milwaukee, Wis. 53233
Publ.: *The Owl of Minerva*

Hume Society (1974)
Department of Philosophy, Northern Illinois University, DeKalb, Ill. 60115
Publ.: The *Bulletin* of the Hume Society

Illinois Philosophical Association (1955)
c/o William Rainly, Harper College, Palatine, Ill. 60067

Indiana Philosophical Association (1936)
Department of Philosophy, Indiana University-Purdue University at Indianapolis,
925 West Michigan St., Indianapolis, Ind. 46202

International Phenomenological Society (1939)
Department of Philosophy, State University of New York at Buffalo, Buffalo, N.Y.
14260
Publ.: *Philosophy and Phenomenological Research*

International Society for Chinese Philosophy (1975)
Department of Philosophy, University of Hawaii, Honolulu, Haw. 96822
Publ.: *Journal of Chinese Philosophy*

International Society for Neoplatonic Studies (1973)
Old Dominion University, Department of Philosophy, Norfolk, Va. 23508
Publ.: Annual Newsletter, *Neoplatonism: Ancient and Modern*, Volume 1, *The Signif-
icance of Neoplatonism*, SUNY Press at Albany, N.Y., 1976

International Society for the History of Ideas (1959)
Department of Philosophy, Temple University, Philadelphia, Penn. 19122
Publ.: *Journal of the History of Ideas*

John Dewey Society for the Study of Education and Culture (1935)
c/o Robert R. Sherman, Secretary-Treasurer, 314 Norman Hall, University of Florida, Gainesville, Fla. 32611
Publ.: *Insights, Current Issues in Education*, subsidy to *Educational Theory*

Kentucky Philosophical Association (1960)
Department of Philosophy, Eastern Kentucky University, Richmond, Ky. 40475

Long Island Philosophical Society (1964)
c/o Luis E. Navia, New York Institute of Technology, Old Westbury, N.Y. 11568
Publ.: Yearly newsletter and program notes for each meeting

Maine Philosophical Institute (1943)
Department of Philosophy, Bates College, Lewiston, Me. 04240

Metaphysical Society of America (1950)
Department of Philosophy, University of South Carolina, Columbia, S.C. 29208

Metropolitan Regional Conference, aCPA
Saint John's University, Jamaica, N.Y. 11439

Middle Atlantic States Philosophy of Education Society (1956)
Department of Foundations of Education, Hofstra University, Hempstead, N.Y. 11550

Minnesota Philosophical Society (1957)
Saint Cloud State University, Saint Cloud, Minn. 56301
Publ.: *Newsletter: Minnesota Philosophical Society* in Fall and Spring. Mailed to members.

Mississippi Philosophy Association (1948)
Millsaps College, Jackson, Miss. 39210

Mountain-Plains Philosophical Conference (1947)
c/o Paul Gery, Division of Social Studies, Western State College of Colorado, Gunnison, Colo. 81230

National Forum for Philosophical Reasoning in the Schools (1975)
Washburn University, Topeka, Kan. 66621
Publ.: *Newsletter*

New Mexico and West Texas Philosophical Society (1949)
c/o C. R. Stern, Department of Philosophy, University of New Mexico, Albuquerque, N. Mex. 87131
Publ.: *Southwest Philosophical Studies*

North Carolina Philosophical Society
c/o Michael D. Resnik, Department of Philosophy, University of North Carolina at Chapel Hill, N.C. 27514

North Central Philosophy of Education Society
c/o Robert Beck, Burton Hall, University of Minnesota, Minneapolis, Minn. 55455

Northern Illinois Philosophical Society (1960)
Omega College of College of DuPage, Glen Ellyn, Ill. 60137
Publ.: Recently, the society has begun sending a copy of its proceedings in abstract form to philosophers in the state.

Northern New England Philosophy Association (1972)
Plymouth State College, University of New Hampshire, Plymouth, N.H. 03264

Northwest Conference on Philosophy (1947)
    Seattle Pacific University, Seattle, Wash. 98119

Ohio Philosophical Association (1931)
    Department of Philosophy, Ohio State University, Columbus, Ohio 43210
    Publ.: Proceedings of annual meeting

Ohio Valley Philosophy of Education Society (1948)
    c/o David Engel, Department of Educational Foundations, University of Pittsburgh,
    Pittsburgh, Penn. 15213
    Publ.: *Annual Proceedings of the Ohio Valley Philosophy of Education Society*

Personalistic Discussion Group (1938)
    Boston University, 745 Commonwealth Ave., Department of Philosophy, Boston,
    Mass. 02215

Personalistic Discussion Group, Western Division (1950)
    Xavier University, Cincinnati, Ohio 45207

Phi Sigma Tau (1931)
    National Headquarters, Department of Philosophy, Marquette University, Milwau-
    kee, Wis. 53233
    Publ.: *Dialogue*, journal of Phi Sigma Tau, published two times yearly; *Phi Sigma Tau
    Newsletter*, published once yearly

Philosophic Society for the Study of Sport (1972)
    R. Scott Kertchmar, Faculty of Physical Education, SUC Brockport, Brockport,
    N.Y. 14420
    Publ.: *Journal of the Philosophy of Sport*

Philosophy of Education Society (1941)
    c/o Richard Pratte, 145 Ramseyer Hall, Ohio State University, 29 West Woodruff
    Ave., Columbus, Ohio 43210
    Publ.: *Proceedings of the Annual Meetings of the Philosophy of Education Society,
    Educational Theory*

Philosophy of Science Association (1934)
    13 Morrill Hall, Department of Philosophy, Michigan State University, East Lan-
    sing, Mich. 48824
    Publ.: *Philosophy of Science, Association Newsletter, Proceedings of Biennial Meetings*

Society for Ancient Greek Philosophy (1953)
    Department of Philosophy, Emory University, Atlanta, Ga. 30322

Society for Asian and Comparative Philosophy (1967)
    University of Hawaii, 2530 Dole Street, Honolulu, Haw. 96822
    Publ.: Sponsors monograph series

Society for Chinese Philosophy (1975)
    Department of Philosophy, University of Hawaii, Honolulu, Haw. 96822
    Publ.: *Journal of Chinese Philosophy*

Society for Comparative Philosophy (1962)
    P.O. Box 857, Sausalito, Calif. 94965
    Publ.: *Bulletin, The Alan Watts Journal*

Society for Exact Philosophy (1971)
c/o N. D. Belnap, Jr., Department of Philosophy, University of Pittsburgh, Pittsburgh, Penn. 15260

Society for Phenomenology and Existential Philosophy (1961)
University College, Rutgers University, New Brunswick, N.J. 08903
Publ.: Martinus Nijhoff, The Hague, *The Selected Shades in Phenomenology and Existential Philosophy*, six volumes already published

Society for Philosophy and Psychology (1974)
Department of Philosophy, The College of Charleston, Charleston, S.C. 29401

Society for Philosophy and Public Affairs (1969)
c/o James Rachels, Department of Philosophy, University of Miami, P.O. Box 8054, Coral Gables, Fla. 33124
Publ.: Occasional newsletter

Society for Philosophy of Creativity (1957)
303 South Tower Rd., Carbondale, Ill. 62901
Publ.: *Philosophy of Creativity Monograph Series*, SPC Newsletters

Society for Philosophy of Religion (1938)
c/o Frank R. Harrison, III, Department of Philosophy, University of Georgia, Athens, Ga. 30602
Publ.: *International Journal for Philosophy of Religion*

Society for Study of the History of Philosophy (1974)
c/o Craig Walton, Executive Director, Department of Philosophy, University of Nevada, Las Vegas, Nev. 89154

Society for the Advancement of American Philosophy (1972)
Fairfield University, Fairfield, Conn. 06430

Society for the History of Technology (1958)
Department of History, University of California at Santa Barbara, Santa Barbara, Calif. 93106
Publ.: *Technology and Culture*, monograph series irregularly

Society for the Philosophical Study of Marxism (1962)
1426 Merritt Dr., El Cajon, Calif. 92020
Publ.: *SPSM Newsletter; Dialogues on the Philosophy of Marxism, 1974; Marxism, Revolution, and Peace, 1975*

Society for the Scientific Study of Religion (1949)
P.O. Box U68A, University of Connecticut, Storrs, Conn. 06268
Publ.: *Journal for the Scientific Study of Religion*

Society for the Study of Process Philosophies (1963)
Dickinson College, Carlisle, Penn. 17013

Society for Women in Philosophy
Department of Philosophy, Western Illinois University, Macomb, Ill. 61455

Society of Philosophy and Social Science (1976)
P.O. Box 401, Kingston, Ontario, Canada

South Carolina Society for Philosophy
P.O. Box 2700, Charleston, S.C. 29403

Southeastern Philosophy of Education Society (1948)
c/o C.J.B. Macmillan, College of Education, Florida State University, Tallahassee,
Fla. 32306

Southern Society for Philosophy and Psychology (1904)
Department of Philosophy, University of Tennessee, Knoxville, Tenn. 37916
Publ.: Newsletters and copies of the program for the annual meeting

Southwestern Philosophical Society (1935)
c/o N.R. Luebke, 225 Hanner Hall, Oklahoma State University, Stillwater, Okla.
74074
Publ.: Presentations before the annual meeting are published in one issue of the *Southwestern Journal of Philosophy*. Minutes and announcements are published in the
Southwestern Philosophical Society Newsletter, issued two or three times yearly.

Southwestern Philosophy of Education Society (1950)
1905 Hardy Dr., Edmond, Okla. 73034
Publ.: *Proceedings of the Southwestern Philosophy of Education Society*

Swedenborg Scientific Association (1898)
Bryn Athyn, Penn. 19009
Publ.: *The New Philosophy*

Tri-State Philosophical Association (1967)
State University College, Fredonia, N.Y. 14063

Virginia Philosophical Association (1939)
c/o Department of Philosophy, Virginia Polytechnic Institute and State University,
Blacksburg, Va. 24061

Washington Philosophy Club (1956)
7018 Braeburn Place, Bethesda, Md. 20034
Publ.: Annual Newsletter (published in the summer)

West Virginia Philosophical Society (1947)
c/o W. Wallace Cayard, West Liberty State College, West Liberty, W. Va. 26074
Publ.: *Journal of the West Virginia Philosophical Society*

Western Conference on the Teaching of Philosophy (1948)
Department of Philosophy, University of Georgia, Athens, Ga. 30602

AFRICA

KENYA

Institutes

Archives of the Department of Philosophy and Religious Studies (1974)
P.O. Box 30197, Nairobi

Societies

Philosophical Association of Kenya
P.O. Box 30197, Nairobi
Publ.: *African Thought and Practice*

REPUBLIC OF SOUTH AFRICA

Institutes

Institute for the Advancement of Calvinism (1966)
Potchefstroom University for Christian Higher Education, Potchefstroom 2520

Societies

Radha Soami Association
PO Dera Baba Jaimal Singh, Via Beas Dist Amritsar, Punjab
Publ.: *Science of the Soul*

Royal Society of South Africa (1877)
University of Cape Town, Rondebosch, 7700
Publ.: *Transactions of the South African Philosophical Society, Transactions of the Royal Society of South Africa.* Exchanges of periodicals for the *Transactions* are welcomed for the society's library.

Vereniging Vir Christelike Hoër Onderwys
Posbus 1824, Bloemfontein, 9300
Publ.: *Roeping en Riglyne*

ISLAMIC COUNTRIES

INDONESIA

Institutes

Institute of Philosophy Driyarkara (1969)
JI Percetakan Negara, Jambatan Serong, Tromolpos 387, Jakarta
Publ.: *Seri Driyarkara*

IRAN

Societies

Société Iranienne de Philosophie et Sciences Humaines (1958)
Avenue Roosevelt 22, Rue Namdjou, Téhéran

LEBANON

Institutes

International Documentary Center (1965)
Maqdissi Street-Ras Beirut, Hanna Building, 2d Floor, P.O. Box 2668–7302, Beirut

John F. Kennedy American Center (1964)
    Abdul Aziz Street, P.O. Box 301, Beirut

MOROCCO

Societies

Société de Philosophie du Maroc (1962)
    Université Mohammed V, Rabat
    Publ.: Etudes Philosophiques et Littéraires

PAKISTAN

Institutes

Iqbal Academy (1951)
    90/B–2, Gulbert III, Lahore
    Publ.: Iqbal Review

Societies

Pakistan Philosophical Society (1954)
    Department of Philosophy, University of the Punjab, New Campus, Lahore

SUDAN

Societies

Philosophical Society of the Sudan (1946)
    P.O. Box 526, Khartoum
    Publ.: Sudan Notes and Records, Proceedings of annual conferences

TURKEY

Institutes

Institute for Research in Philosophy (1963)
    Faculty of Letters, Ankara University, Ankara
    Publ.: Araştirma Dergisi, Journal of the Institute

Institute of Islamic Studies (1954)
    Faculty of Letters, Istanbul University, Edebiyat Fakültese, Beyazit, Istanbul
    Publ.: Islam Tetkikleri Enstitüsü Dergisi

Societies

Felsefe Kurumu (1974)
    Institute of Humanities, Hacettepe University, Ankara

UNITED ARAB REPUBLIC

Institutes

Institut Dominicain d'Etudes Orientales (1953)
1 Rue Masnaa al-Tarabich, Abbassiah, Le Caire
Publ.: *Mélanges de l'Institut Dominicain d'Etudes Orientales*

ASIA

INDIA

Institutes

Academy of Comparative Philosophy and Religion (1952)
Gurudev Ranade Colony: Tilakwadi, Belgum 590011
Publ.: A quarterly journal, seminar proceedings

Centre for the Study of World Religions (1971)
Dharmaram College PO, Bangalore 560029
Publ.: *Journal of Dharma* in collaboration with other national and international centres

Centre of Advanced Study in Philosophy (1964)
Visva-Bharati University, PO Santiniketan, West Bengal
Publ.: *Visva-Bharati Journal of Philosophy*

East-West Research Centre (1973)
Department of Philosophy, Osmania University, Hyderabad

Indian Institute of World Culture (1945)
P.O. Box 402, No. 6, Sri B. P. Wadia Road, Basavanagudi, Bangalore 560 004

Pratap Centre of Philosophy (1916)
Amalner, Dist Jalgaon

Sikh Cultural Centre
116 Karnani Mansion, Park St., Calcutta 16
Publ.: *Sikh Review*

Sri Aurobindo Research Institute (1976)
Archana Civil Lines, Meerut (U P), Pin–250001

Sri Ramakrishna Math (1897)
Mylapore, P.O. Box No. 635, Madras 600 004
Publ.: Books and periodicals

Sri Ramanasramam
Tiruvannamalai 606 603
Publ.: *Mountain Path*

Yoga Institute
Santacruz, Bombay
Publ.: *Journal of the Yoga Institute*

Societies

All Orissa Philosophy Association (1969)
   Postgraduate Department of Philosophy, Utkal University, Bhubaneswar 4, Orissa
   Publ.: *Proceedings*

Bangiya Darsan Parishad
   20/2 A Halder Bagan Lane, Calcutta 4
   Publ.: *Darṣan*

Indian Philosophical Association (1949)
   PO Vidarbha Mahavidyalaya, Amravati 444604, Maharashtra
   Publ.: *Journal of the Philosophical Association*

Kaivalyadhama SMYM Samiti
   Lonavla, 410 403
   Publ.: *Yoga-Mīmāṃsā*

Maha Bodhi Society (1892)
   4–A, Bankim Chatterjee St., Calcutta 12, West Bengal
   Publ.: *Maha Bodhi Journal, Dharmaduta*

Moradabad Philosophy Association (1973)
   Bazar Diwan, Moradabad

Philosophical Society Andhra Pradesh
   Department of Philosophy, Osmania University, Hyderabad
   Publ.: *Indian Philosophical Journal*

Pratap Centre of Philosophy
   Department of Philosophy, Poona University, Poona
   Publ.: *Indian Philosophical Quarterly*

Ramakrishna Math and Mission
   PO Belur Math, Dist Howrah, W B 711202
   Publ.: *Awakened India*

Saiva Siddhanta Maha Samajam (1905)
   12 East Mada St., Mylapore, Madras 600004
   Publ.: *Siddhantam, Śaiva Siddhanta*

Sri Aurobindo Society
   Indian Administrative Service, 39 Udyanmarg, Bhubaneswar, Orissa
   Publ.: *Oriya-Aurovilian*

Theosophical Society (1875)
   Adyar, Madras 600 020
   Publ.: *The Theosophist, Adyar Newsletter, Adyar Library Bulletin*

World Jnana Sadhak Society (1956)
   36–B Bosepara Lane, Calcutta 700 003
   Publ.: *Universalist*

SRI LANKA

Institutes

Buddhist Academy of Ceylon (1952)
29 Rosmead Place, Colombo 7

Societies

Ceylon Humanist Society
35 Guilford Crescent, Colombo 7

Maha Bodhi Society of Ceylon (1891)
130 Maligakande Road, Colombo 10
Publ.: *Sinhala Bauddhaya, Maha Bodhi Journal, Buddhist Quarterly*

Royal Asiatic Society (1845)
Ceylon Branch, 1st Floor Grandstand Building, Race Course, Reid Ave., Colombo 7
Publ.: *Journal of the Ceylon Branch of the Royal Asiatic Society*

Theosophical Society in Ceylon (1926)
49 Peterson Lane, Colombo 6

JAPAN

Institutes

Chusei Tetsugaku Kenkyo-Jo (1945)
461 Kajii-chô, Hirokoji, Kawaramachi, Kamikyô-ku, Kyoto 602

Doshisha Daigaku Bunkagakkai (1946)
Karasuma-Imadegawa, Kamikyoku, Kyoto
Publ.: *Bunkagaku-Nempo*

Institute for the Study of Christianity and Culture (1963)
International Christian University, 10–2, 3–chome, Osawa, Mitaka, Tokyo 181
Publ.: *Humanities-Christianity and Culture*

Institute of Educational Research and Service (1953)
International Christian University, 10–2, 3-chome, Osawa, Mitaka, Tokyo 181
Publ.: *Educational Studies*

Institute of Medieval Thought (1954)
Sophia University, 7 Kioicho, Chiyoda-ku, 102 Tokyo

Niigata Daigaku Jinbungakubu Tetsugaku Kenkyukai (1950)
Nishiôhata 5215, Niigatashi

Research Institute for Humanistic Studies (1949)
Kyoto University, Ushinomiyacho, Yoshida, Sakyo-ku, Kyoto 606
Publ.: *Tôhô Gakuhô, zinbun Gakuhô, zinbun*

Sei Thomas Gakuin (1945)
    461 Kajii-chô, Hirokoji Kawaramachi, Kamigyô-ku, 602 Kyoto
Publ.: *Summa Theologiae* of Saint Thomas Aquinas in Japanese, *Prima Pars*

Tohoku Tetsugaku Kai (1950)
    Philosophical Seminar, Department of Literature, Tohoku University, Kawauchi,
    Sendai

Societies

Association de Recherches de Philosophie Française (1954)
    Faculté des Lettres de l'Université d'Osaka, 1–1, Machikaneyamacho Toyonakashi
    560
Publ.: *Etudes Bergsonniennes, Philosophies Françaises d'Aujourd'hui, La Philosophie
    Française*

Bigaku-Kai (1939)
    Bunkyo-ku Hongo 7–3–1, Institute of Aesthetics, Faculty of Letters, University of
    Tokyo, Tokyo 113
Publ.: *Bigaku*

Hiroshima Tetsugaku-Kai (1949)
    Hiroshima University, Hiroshima
Publ.: *Tetsugaku*

Japan Association for Philosophy of Science (1954)
    Institute of Statistical Mathematics, 4–6–7 Minami-Azabu, Minato-ku, Tokyo

Japanese Association of Indian and Buddhist Studies (1951)
    Department of Indian Philosophy and Sanskrit Philology, Faculty of Letters, Uni-
    versity of Tokyo, Tokyo
Publ.: *Journal of Indian and Buddhist Studies*

Japanese Society of Medieval Philosophy (1952)
    Institute of Medieval Studies, Kyoto University Yoshida-Honmachi Sakyoku, Kyoto
Publ.: *Chuseishiso-Kenkyu, Chusei Tetsugakkai Kaiho*

Jochi Daigaku Tetsugakkai
    Institute of Philosophy, Sophia University, 7 Kioicho, Chiyoda-ku, 102 Tokyo
Publ.: *Tetsugaku Ronshu*

Kansai Tetsugaku Kai (1951)
    Department of Philosophy, Osaka University

Kyoto Tetsugaku-kai
    Faculty of Letters, Kyoto University, Kyoto 606
Publ.: *Tetsugaku Kenkyu*

Mita Philosophical Society
    Keio University, Mita, Minato-ku, Tokyo 108
Publ.: *Philosophy*

Nihon Tetsugaku-Kai (1949)
    Department of Philosophy, Tokyo University
Publ.: *The Philosophy*

Nishi-Nihon Tetsugaku Kai (1950)
Department of Philosophy, University of Kyushu
Publ.: *Nishi-Nihon Tetsugaku Kai Kaiho*

Société Franco Japonaise de Philosophie (1974)
Maison Franco Japonaise, 2–3 Surugadai Kanda Chiyodaku, Tokyo 101

Tetsugaku-kai (1886)
Tokyo University, 7–3–1, Hongo, Bunkyo-ku, Tokyo
Publ.: *Tetsugaku-Zashi*

Toritsu-Daigaku-Tetsugaku-Kai (1957)
Tokyo Metropolitan University, Tokyo
Publ.: *Tetsugaku-Shi*

SOUTH KOREA

Societies

Han Kuk Chul Hak Yun Ku Hoe (1963)
Kyungpook National University, 1370 Sankyuck-Dong, Taegu
Publ.: *Chul Hak Yun Ku*

Society of Korean Philosophy (1969)
Chung-ang, P.O. Box 5724 Seoul
Publ.: *Journal of Korean Philosophy*

Society of Philosophical Studies (1963)
Department of Philosophy, College of Liberal Arts and Sciences, Seoul National
University, Seoul
Publ.: *Philosophical Studies*

Appendix II: CONGRESSES AND MEETINGS

There is no known complete, composite roster of particular international, national, and regional philosophic congresses, meetings, conferences, and colloquia, together with their respective locations, dates, and themes, if any, held from 1945 to the present. Announcements of some of these individual congresses, meetings, and colloquia are to be found in philosophic journals and the publications of philosophic institutes and societies. These announcements have become more international in coverage in recent years, although the primary focus remains national. Such compilations in English as the two-year registry *World Meetings: United States and Canada* (New York: Macmillan) and the two-year registry *World Meetings: Outside United States and Canada* (New York: Macmillan) lack an annual index and also are incomplete listings. The *World List of Future International Meetings*, published by the Reference Department of the U.S. Library of Congress, began in June 1959 but ceased publication several years ago. The listing in Appendix II mainly follows that in Varet, G., Cormier, R., Lineback, R., and Kurtz, P. (eds.), *International Directory of Philosophy and Philosophers, 1978–81* (Bowling Green, Ohio: Philosophy Documentation Center, Bowling Green State University, 1978) and Bahm, A. (ed.). *Directory of American Philosophers, 1978–79* (Bowling Green, Ohio: Philosophy Documentation Center, Bowling Green State University, 1978). The proceedings of many congresses and meetings since 1945 have been published as books, which can be found catalogued under the title of the congress or meeting, the name of the organization(s) sponsoring it, and/or the editor(s).

UNIONS AFFILIATED WITH UNESCO

Académie Internationale d'Histoire des Sciences
> Triennial assemblies in conjunction with the International Congress of the History of Science

Association Internationale de Cybernétique
> Organizes the International Congress of Cybernetics

Comité International des Professeurs de Philosophie (Enseignement du Second Degré)
> Organizes international congresses

International Association for Philosophy of Law and Social Philosophy
> Quadrennial plenary world congress, occasionally an Extraordinary World Congress

International Association for the History of Religions
> Quinquennial international congresses, periodical study conferences and local conferences

International Committee for Aesthetics
> Quadrennial meetings in a different center of studies in the philosophy of art

International Council for Philosophy and Humanistic Studies
    Biennial meetings

Internationale Hegel Gesellschaft
    Biennial international congress

International Federation of Societies of Philosophy
    The International Congress of Philosophy. The most recent congress was the XVI
    World Congress of Philosophy, Dusseldorf, West Germany, August 27-September
    2, 1978. General Theme: Philosophy and the World-Views of the Modern Sci-
    ences. Other international Congresses of philosophy have been held since 1945
    at Amsterdam (1948), Brussels (1953), Venice (1958), Mexico City (1963),
    Vienna (1968), and Varna (1973).

International Federation of the Societies of Classical Studies
    Quinquennial meetings

WESTERN EUROPE, AUSTRALIA, AND ISRAEL

DENMARK

Institutes
Dansk Selskab for Vidensabsforskning
    Annual meeting, symposia

Societies
Filosofisk Forening i Aarhus
    Meetings, seminars

Selskabet for Filosofi og Psykologi
    Monthly and annual meetings

Soren Kierkegaard Society
    Six to eight meetings a year

FINLAND

Societies
Philosophical Society of Finland
    Congresses, meetings

FRANCE

Institutes
Centre International de Synthèse
    Conferences

Cercle Philosophique Lorrain
Public conferences

Institut Catholique de Toulouse-Faculté Libre de Philosophie
Conferences

Institut d'Etudes Hispaniques
Conferences, international colloquia

Institut de Philosophie
Conferences

Institut International de Philosophie
Participation at congresses only upon invitation

Societies

Association d'Etudes Biologiques
Colloquia

Association des Amis d'Emmanuel Mounier
Conferences

Association des Amis de Pontigny-Cerisy
Colloquia, symposia

Association des Professeurs de Philosophie de l'Enseignment Public
Colloquia

Association des Sociétés de Philosophie de Langue Française
Biennial congresses

Fédération des Sociétés Française's de Philosophie
Official representative of French philosophy at international congresses and organizations

Maison d'Auguste Comte
University colloquia

Société Alpine de Philosophie
Four to six meetings a year

Société Asiatique
Monthly meetings

Société Bourguignonne de Philosophie
Conferences and colloquia

Société Champenoise de Philosophie
Conferences

Société d'Esthétique
International congress of aesthetics, monthly conferences

Société des Etudes Juives
Monthly meetings, annual general assembly

Société Française de Philosophie
  Descartes Congress, Bergson Congress, participation in international congresses and congresses of French philosophical societies

Société Internationale pour l'Etude de la Philosophie Médiévale
  Quinquennial international congresses

Société Ligérienne de Philosophie
  Four annual conferences, one annual three-day colloquium

Société Nietzsche
  Conferences, discussions

Société pour l'Etude de la Philosophie Allemande
  Meetings with German universities

Société Strasbourgeoise de Philosophie
  Conferences, colloquia

Société Théosophique de France
  Annual national convention, public conferences

Société Toulousaine de Philosophie
  French philosophical congresses and world congresses

GREAT BRITAIN

Institutes

British Academy
  Lectures, exchanges

Royal Institute of Philosophy
  Biennial conferences, annual lecture program

Teilhard Centre for the Future of Man
  Conferences

Verulam Institute
  Public lectures, monthly discussion groups

Societies

Alexander Society
  Weekly meetings

Aristotelian Society
  Annual joint session with the Mind Association, Fortnightly meetings

Atlanteans
  Lectures

Belfast Natural History and Philosophical Society
  Six meetings a year

Birkbeck College Philosophy Society
Six to eight meetings an academic year

British Society for the Philosophy of Science
Monthly meetings during the academic year

British Society of Aesthetics
Annual conference, colloquia

British Society of Phenomenology
Occasional international congresses, annual conferences

Leeds Philosophical and Literary Society
Irregular meetings

Manchester Literary and Philosophical Society
Six to seven formal lectures a year, informal meetings

Mind Association
Annual joint session with the Aristotelian Society

Northern Association for Ancient Philosophy
Annual conference

Philosophy of Education Society of Great Britain
Annual three-day conference, five meetings a year

Royal Philosophical Society of Glasgow
Fortnightly lectures October to March

Scots Philosophical Club
Occasional conferences, two meetings a year

Shanti Sadan
Annual convention, lectures

Société Britannique de Philosophie de Langue Française
International conferences of French philosophical societies, four colloquia a year

South Place Ethical Society
Meetings, lectures, forums, and discussions

Swedenborg Society
Annual meeting, lectures

GREECE

Societies

Hellenic Society for Philosophical Studies
International meetings

ITALY

Institutes

Accademia della Scienze, Lettre ed Arti
  Public lectures

Accademia Virgiliana
  Conferences

Centro di Studi Filosofici di Gallarate
  Annual meetings of university professors and assistants

Centro di Studi per il Lèssico Intellettuale Europeo
  International colloquia

Centro Internazionale di Studi Umanistici
  Congresses

Fondazione Giorgio Ronchi
  Congresses, symposia, conferences

Grupp di Ricerca del Consiglio Nazionale delle Ricerche
  Symposia

Institut International "Jacques Maritain"
  Meetings

Istituto di Studi Filosofici
  International congresses

Istituto Euro-Mediterraneo di Scienza Umane
  Conferences

Istituto Nazionale di Studi sul Rinascimento
  Congresses, meetings

Societies

Associazione Filosofia Arti e Scienze
  Annual meeting

Associazione Filosofica Ligure
  Conferences

Biblioteca Filosofica dell' Università di Torino
  Conferences

Sezione Pisana della SFI
  Congresses, conferences, discussions

Società Filosofica Calabrese
  Congress of the philosophical societies of southern Italy

Società Filosofica Italiana
  Meetings, conferences, national congresses, international congresses

Società Filosofica Rosminiana
Biannual meetings

Società Italiana di Filosofica Guiridica e Politica
Congresses and meetings

Società Italiana di Lògica e Filosofia delle Scienze
Conferences and meetings

Union Mondiale des Sociétés Catholiques de Philosophie
General meetings at the International Congress of Philosophy

NETHERLANDS

Institutes

Hoeven (Jan Van Der) Foundation for Theoretical Biology
Symposia on the philosophy of biology

Institute of Aesthetics
Meetings

Instituut voor Grondslagenonderzoek
Meetings

International Humanist and Ethical Union
Conferences

Societies

Algemene Nederlandse Vereniging voor Wijsbegeerte
Triennial meetings

Genootschap voor Welenschappelyke Filosofie
Three sessions a year

Nederlands Filosofisch Genootschap
Annual general meeting

Nederlands Klages-Genootschap
Conferences, meetings

Nederlandse Vereniging voor Logica en Wijsbegeerte der Exacte Wetenschappen
Annual meeting

Vereniging voor Calvinistische Wijsbegeerte
Triennial international philosophical symposia, annual national meeting, and several
local meetings

Vereniging voor Wijsbegeerte des Rechts
Biannual meetings

Vereniging voor Wijsbegeerte te 'S-Gravenhage
Six to seven meetings a year

Wijsgerige Vereniging "Thomas van Aquino"
Biannual meetings

SWEDEN

Societies

Filosofi-Och Psykologilärarnas Förening
Annual conference, lectures, regional meetings

Filosofiska Föreningen i Lund
Joint annual meeting with the Philosophical Society in Copenhagen, monthly meetings, lectures

Filosofiska Föreningen i Stockholm
Five to ten meetings a year

Filosofiska Föreningen i Uppsala
Ten meetings each academic year

Hans Larsson Samfundet
Annual meeting

WEST GERMANY

Institutes

Akademie der Wissenschaften in Göttingen
Several meetings a year

Societies

Allgemeine Gesellschaft für Philosophie in Deutschland
Biannual plenary meetings, congresses of philosophy, annual meetings of full professors and associate professors of philosophy. Congresses under the leadership of the AGPD have been at Stuttgart (1954); Marburg (1958); Munich (1960), General Topic: The Problem of Order; Münster (1962), General Topic: Philosophy and the Question of Progress; Heidelberg (1966), General Topic: The Problem of Language; Düsseldorf (1969), General Topic: Philosophy and Science; Kiel (1972), General Topic: Nature and History; Göttingen (1975), General Topic: Logic. Ethics. Theory of the Arts; Innsbruck (1979), General Topic: Man.

Deutsche Vereinigung für Mathematische Logik
Annual meeting

Gorres-Gesellschaft zur Pflege der Wissenschaft EV
Annual meeting

International Hegel Association
International congress every sixth year, biennial colloquium

Jungius-Gesellschaft
Biennial meetings

Klages-Gesellschaft Marbach
Annual meeting of members, biennial meetings

Leibniz (Gottfried Wilhelm) Gesellschaft
Quinquennial congresses (International Leibniz Congress, 1977)

Schopenhauer-Gesellschaft
Irregular international meetings, monthly local meetings

Wissenschaftlicher Beirat der Cusanus-Gesellschaft
International symposia, membership meetings

AUSTRIA

Societies

Gesellschaft für Ganzheitsforschung
Annual meeting

Philosophische Gesellschaft an der Universität Graz
International Philosophical Colloquium in Memory of A. Meinong (1970), lectures,
discussions

Philosophische Gesellschaft in Salzburg
Lectures, study groups

Philosophische Gesellschaft Wien
About ten lectures annually

Vereinigung für Wissenschaftliche Grundlagenforschung
Congresses, lectures, discussions

Wittgenstein Gesellschaft
Symposia

AUSTRALIA

Institutes

Centre for Foundational Studies in Moral and Political Theory
Public lectures

Societies

Australasian Association for Logic
Annual conference

Australasian Association of Philosophy
Annual conference, local meetings

Philosophy of Education Society of Australasia
Annual conference

ISRAEL

Societies

Israel Philosophical Association
Annual national conferences

Jerusalem Philosophical Society
Monthly meetings during the academic year

Van Leer Jerusalem Foundation
Discussions, seminars, lectures

EASTERN EUROPE

CZECHOSLOVAKIA

Societies
Jednota Filozofická
Conferences, lectures, annual meeting

EAST GERMANY

Societies
Vereinigung der Philosophischen Institutionen der DDR
Congresses, conferences, international discussions

POLAND

Societies
National Committee of the Division of Logic, Methodology and Philosophy of Science
International meetings

Polskie Towarzystwo Filozoficzne-Toruń
Annual general meeting, monthly meetings, conferences, symposia

Polskie Towarzystwo Filozoficzne-Warszawa
Annual general assembly, monthly branch scientific meetings

Polskie Towarzystwo Semiotyczne
Scientific meetings with lectures and discussions every other week

ROMANIA

Institutes
Romanian Committee for the History and Philosophy of Sciences
Scientific congresses and symposia

UNION OF SOVIET SOCIALIST REPUBLICS

Societies
Soviet National Association for History and Philosophy of Science and Technology
  Biannual meetings

THE AMERICAS

CANADA

Societies
Canadian Philosophical Association, l'Association Canadienne de Philosophie
  Annual congress

Canadian Society for History and Philosophy of Science
  Annual conference, annual general meeting

MEXICO

Institutes
Instituto de Investigaciones Filosóficas
  Conferences, symposia

ARGENTINA

Institutes
Centro de Estudios Filosóficos del Sur
  Regular and special meetings

Centro de Investigaciones Filosóficos
  Symposia, seminars

Societies
Grupo Argentino de la Unión Internacional de Historia de la Ciencia
  Conferences, public sessions, regular meetings

BOLIVIA

Institutes
Instituto de Filosofía Jurídica y Social
  Conferences

BRAZIL

Institutes

Instituto Brasileiro de Filosofia (Salvador)
Conferences

Instituto Brasileiro de Filosofia (Brasilia)
Regular meetings

Instituto Brasileiro de Filosofia (Florianópolis)
Conferences, meetings

Instituto Brasileiro de Filosofia (Sao Paulo)
Congresses, conferences, symposia

Instituto Neo-Pitagórica
International and national meetings, congresses, conferences, regular and special meetings

Societies

Associação Latino-Americana de Filósofos Católicos
Latin American Congress of Philosophy (1979)

Sociedade Brasileira de Filósofos Católicos
Biennial International Philosophy Week

COLOMBIA

Societies

Asociación Colombiana para la Investigación Filosófica
Monthly meetings

COSTA RICA

Societies

Asociación Costarricense de Filosofía
Congresses, conferences, seminars, annual meeting

HONDURAS

Societies

Sociedad Hondureña de Filosofía
Conferences, meetings

PERU

Institutes
Instituto Riva Agüero
   Periodic meetings, seminars

VENEZUELA

Societies
Sociedad Venezolana de Filosofía
   IX Inter-American Congress of Philosophy (1977), annual series of conferences, colloquia

UNITED STATES

Institutes
Center for Integrative Education
   Symposia

Center for Philosophic Exchange
   Conferences and seminars

Center for Philosophy, Law and Citizenship, Inc.
   Meetings several times a year

Center for Process Studies
   Conferences, seminars, lectureships

Council for Philosophical Studies
   Summer institutes for teachers of philosophy, working conferences, and a visiting philosopher program

Franciscan Institute
   Monthly staff meetings supplements daily collaboration

Institute for Advanced Studies in Philosophy
   Weekly meetings, philosophy seminars

International Association for Philosophy of Law and Social Philosophy
   Quadrennial world congresses

Societies
Alabama Philosophical Society
   Annual meeting

American Academy of Religion
   Annual meeting

American Catholic Philosophical Association
Annual national convention, quarterly regional meetings

American Catholic Philosophical Association, Florida Chapter
Biannual meetings

American Catholic Philosophical Association, New England Regional Conference
Biannual meetings

American Catholic Philosophical Association, Northwest Regional Conference
Irregular meetings

American Philosophical Association
One annual meeting of each of its three divisions: Eastern, Western, and Pacific

American Section of International Association for Philosophy of Law and Social Philosophy
Quadrennial international congresses, special congresses, plenary conferences every eighteen to twenty-four months

American Society for Aesthetics
Annual meeting

American Society for Political and Legal Philosophy
Annual meeting

American Society for Value Inquiry
Meetings held in conjunction with each of the annual meetings of the three divisions of the American Philosophical Association

Association for Philosophy of the Unconscious
Annual meeting held in conjunction with the annual meeting of the Eastern Division of the American Philosophical Association

Association for Symbolic Logic
Annual meeting in December or January in the United States, Summer meeting in Europe

Association of Philosophy Journal Editors
Annual meeting held in conjunction with the annual meeting of the Eastern Division of the American Philosophical Association, meetings frequently held in conjunction with the annual Western Division meeting of the same association

Central Pennsylvania Philosophical Association
Fall and Spring meetings

Chicago Society for Process Thought
Bimonthly meetings

Colloquium for Social Philosophy
Annual Spring conference

Creighton Club-New York State Philosophical Association
Fall and Spring meetings

Division of Philosophical Psychology
Annual meeting held in conjunction with the convention of the American Psychological Association

Far Western Philosophy of Education Society
Annual meeting

Fellowship of Religious Humanists
Annual meeting and discussion seminars

Florida Philosophical Association
Annual meeting

Fullerton Club
Monthly meetings

Georgia Philosophical Society
Two or three meetings a year

Hegel Society of America
Biennial meetings, symposia

Hume Society
Annual meetings called ''Hume Conferences''

Illinois Philosophical Association
Annual conference

Indiana Philosophical Association
Biannual meetings

International Society for Chinese Philosophy
International conferences, panel meetings in conjunction with the annual Eastern Division meeting of the American Philosophical Association

International Society for Neoplatonic Studies
Triennial international congresses, annual national and regional meetings

International Society for the History of Ideas
International conferences

John Dewey Society for the Study of Education and Culture
Annual meeting

Kentucky Philosophical Association
Fall and Spring meetings

Long Island Philosophical Society
Biannual meetings

Maine Philosophical Institute
Annual meeting

Metaphysical Society of America
Annual meeting

Metropolitan Regional Conference, aCPA
   Biannual meetings

Middle Atlantic States Philosophy of Education Society
   Fall and Spring meetings

Minnesota Philosophical Society
   Annual meeting

Mississippi Philosophy Association
   Annual meeting

Mountain-Plains Philosophical Conference
   Annual meeting

New Mexico and West Texas Philosophical Society
   Annual meeting

North Carolina Philosophical Society
   Annual meeting

North Central Philosophy of Education Society
   Annual Spring meeting

Northern Illinois Philosophical Society
   Fall and Spring meetings

Northern New England Philosophy Association
   Annual meeting

Northwest Conference on Philosophy
   Annual Fall meeting

Ohio Philosophical Association
   Annual meeting

Ohio Valley Philosophy of Education Society
   Annual meeting

Personalistic Discussion Group
   Annual meeting held in conjunction with the Eastern Division of the American
      Philosophical Association

Personalistic Discussion Group, Western Division
   Annual meeting

Philosophic Society for the Study of Sport
   Annual meeting

Philosophy of Education Society
   Annual Spring meeting

Philosophy of Science Association
   Biennial meetings

Society for Asian and Comparative Philosophy
   Annual meeting

Society for Chinese Philosophy
Conferences, seminars, workshops

Society for Comparative Philosophy
Seminars, lectures, workshops

Society for Exact Philosophy
Annual meeting

Society for Phenomenology and Existential Philosophy
Annual convention

Society for Philosophy and Psychology
Annual meeting

Society for Philosophy and Public Affairs
Symposia at American Philosophical Association divisional meetings, regular local
group meetings

Society for Philosophy of Creativity
Eastern, Western, and Pacific divisions each meet annually in conjunction with the
respective American Philosophical Association divisions

Society for Philosophy of Religion
Annual meetings

Society for Study of the History of Philosophy
Hobbes Tercentenary (1979), other occasional meetings, regional meetings in conjunction with other learned societies

Society for the Advancement of American Philosophy
Annual meeting, meetings in conjunction with divisional meetings of the American
Philosophical Association

Society for the History of Technology
Annual meeting

Society for the Philosophical Study of Marxism
Colloquia in conjunction with meetings of international and world congresses,
American regional and binational conferences, symposia in conjunction with annual meetings of the American Philosophical Association, quadrennial national
meetings, three regional meetings

Society for the Scientific Study of Religion
Annual meeting

Society for Women in Philosophy
Sessions at annual divisional meetings of the American Philosophical Association,
as well as independently organized programs

Society of Philosophy and Social Science
Monthly meetings

South Carolina Society for Philosophy
Annual Spring meeting

Southeastern Philosophy of Education Society
Annual meeting

Southern Society for Philosophy and Psychology
Annual meeting

Southwestern Philosophical Society
Annual meeting

Southwestern Philosophy of Education Society
Annual meeting

Swedenborg Scientific Association
Annual meeting

Tri-State Philosophical Association (New York, Pennsylvania, and Ohio)
Semiannual meetings

Virginia Philosophical Association
Annual meeting

Washington Philosophy Club
Annual program of six meetings

Western Conference on the Teaching of Philosophy
Sessions in conjuction with Western Division meetings of the American Philosophical Association

AFRICA

SOUTH AFRICA

Societies
Philosophical Society of Southern Africa
Annual congress held at all major universities in South Africa

Royal Society of South Africa
Eight meetings a year

ISLAMIC COUNTRIES

INDONESIA

Institutes
Institute of Philosophy Driyarkara
Lectures

IRAN

Societies

Société Iranienne de Philosophie et Sciences Humaines
  Monthly meetings

MOROCCO

Societies

Société de Philosophie du Maroc
  Colloquia, monthly conferences

PAKISTAN

Societies

Pakistan Philosophical Society
  Annual congress

SUDAN

Societies

Philosophical Society of the Sudan
  Annual conference

TURKEY

Institutes

Institute of Islamic Studies
  Colloquia, seminars

Societies

Felsefe Kurumu
  Seminars

ASIA

INDIA

Institutes

Academy of Comparative Philosophy and Religion
  Seminars, special lectures

Centre for the Study of World Religions
  Regular seminars

Centre of Advanced Study in Philosophy
  Seminars

Pratap Centre of Philosophy
  Seminars

Societies

All Orissa Philosophy Association
  Annual meeting

Indian Philosophical Association
  Annual meeting, seminars, lectures for the general public

Maha Bodhi Society
  Monthly meetings

Moradabad Philosophy Association
  Lectures, debates, discussions

Saiva Siddhanta Maha Samajam
  Annual conferences in Madras, Sri Lanka, and Malaysia; monthly meetings in
    Madras

Theosophical Society
  Annual international convention, periodic world congresses outside of India, various
    national annual conventions

SRI LANKA

Institutes
Buddhist Academy of Ceylon
  Schools, seminars

Societies
Maha Bodhi Society of Ceylon
  Monthly meetings

Royal Asiatic Society
  Public meetings and lectures

Theosophical Society in Ceylon
  Monthly meetings

JAPAN

Institutes

Doshisha Daigoku Bunkagakkai
  Seminars, lectures

Institute for the Study of Christianity and Culture
  Symposia, lectures

Institute of Educational Research and Service
  Symposia, seminars, lectures

Niigata Daigaku Jinbungakubu Tetsugaku Kenkyukai
  Monthly meetings

Tohoku Tetsugaku-Kai
  General meetings, meetings for reading papers

Societies

Association de Recherches de Philosophie Française
  Six meetings a year

Bigaku-Kai
  Annual national congress, regular congress five times a year

Hiroshima Tetsugaku-Kai
  Annual Fall convention, occasional public lectures

Japan Association for Philosophy of Science
  Annual congress

Japanese Association of Indian and Buddhist Studies
  Annual meeting

Japanese Society of Medieval Philosophy
  Annual meeting

Kansai Tetsugaku-Kai
  Annual meeting

Nihon Tetsugaku-Kai
  General meeting in May and regular meetings

Nishi-Nihon Tetsugaku-Kai
  Annual general meeting

Société Franco Japonaise de Philosophie
  Conferences, colloquia, two or three meetings a year

Tetsugaku-Kai
  Biannual meetings

Toritsu-Daigaku-Tetsugaku-Kai
  General meeting in May, several other meetings for reading papers

SOUTH KOREA

Societies

Han Kuk Chul Yun Hoe
Biannual general assembly

Society of Korean Philosophy
Biannual seminars

Society of Philosophical Studies
Symposia

Index of Philosophers

Subject Index

About the Contributors

HANS M. BAUMGARTNER was born in Munich on April 5, 1933. He is professor of philosophy at the Zentrum für Philosophie und Grundlagen der Wissenschaft der Justus Liebig-Universität Giessen and a member of the Schelling-Kommission der Bayerischen Akademie der Wissenschaften. He is co-editor of the *Historisch-Kritischen Schelling-Ausgabe der J. G. Fichte-Bibliographie*, the *Handbuchs Philosophischer Grundbegriffe*, and the *Zeitschrift für philosophische Forschung*. He is the author of *Die Unbedingtheit des Sittlichen. Eine Auseinandersetzung mit Nicolai Hartmann* and *Kontinuität und Geschichte. Zur Kritik und Metakritik der Historischen Vernunft* (1972). His more recent publications include "Wozu Philosophie?" in *Sammelband W. de Gruyter* (1978). He has also co-edited and contributed to *Philosophie in Deutschland 1945–1975* (1978).

ARTHUR BERNDTSON, born 1913, is professor of philosophy at the University of Missouri at Columbia. He is the author of *Art, Expression, and Beauty* (1969) and a contributor to the *Encyclopedia of Philosophy*, Vols. II, IV, VII, VIII; *History of Philosophical Systems* (1950), edited by V. Ferm; and *Process and Divinity* (1964), edited by W. Reese and E. Freeman. His articles have appeared in *Philosophy and Phenomenological Research, Journal of Aesthetics, Revue internationale de Philosophie*, and other journals. A new book, *Power, Form, and Mind*, will be published by Bucknell University Press in 1980.

THOMAS J. BLAKELEY, born 1931, is professor of philosophy at Boston College. He obtained his Ph.D. from the University of Fribourg (Switzerland) in 1960 with a work entitled *Soviet Scholasticism* and has subsequently written other books and articles on contemporary Soviet philosophy. Professor Blakeley is one of the editors of *Studies in Soviet Thought*, a member of the board of *Asian Thought and Society*, and a regular reviewer for the "Review of Books" of the African Studies Association.

JEAN-PAUL BRODEUR is professor of philosophy at the University of Quebec at Montreal, Canada. He is the author of numerous scholarly articles in professional journals. He is the editor of and contributor to *Culture et langage* (1973).

OCTAVIAN CHEȚAN was born on June 7, 1930, in Luduş, Romania. He is the principal scientific researcher in the Institute of Philosophy, and, since 1971, he has been the editor (*rédacteur-en-chef*) of *Revista de filozofie* of the Academy of Social and Political Sciences. He has published many studies in the fields of philosophical anthropology, history of philosophy, and philosophy and history of religion.

MIN-HONG CHOI is professor of philosophy at Chung-Ang University in Seoul and guest professor at Myong-Ji University. Professor Choi has been chairman of the Society of Korean Philosophy since 1969. He is the editor of the *Journal of Korean Philosophy*. Among his more recent publications are *History of Korean Philosophy* (1974), *A Modern History of Korean Philosophy* (1978) (in English), and *Comparative Philosophy of East and West* (1979).

L. JONATHAN COHEN, born in London, England, in 1923, was educated at St. Paul's School, London, and at Balliol College, Oxford. Since 1957, he has been a fellow, praelector, and tutor at Queen's College, Oxford University. Professor Cohen was elected a fellow of the British Academy in 1973 and president of the British Society for Philosophy of Science for 1977–1979. He was secretary of the International Union for History and Philosophy of Science (Division of Logic, Methodology and Philosophy of Science), 1975–1979. His principal publications include *The Principles of World Citizenship* (1954), *The Diversity of Meaning* (1962), *The Implications of Induction* (1972), and *The Probable and the Provable* (1977).

ANNA-LOUIZE CONRADIE organized the first philosophical congress ever held in South Africa in 1951. Since 1959, she has been attached to the University of Natal, Durban. Of her philosophical works, the best known is her *Neo-Calvinist Philosophy* (1960). She is also a novelist of distinction. At present, she is endeavoring to organize a philosophical congress in South Africa specifically devoted to bringing together philosophers from the continent of Africa.

JAROMIR DANĔK, born in 1925, was professor of philosophy in Czechoslovakia until 1967, and since 1967, he has taught in Austria and Canada. He is now a member of the Faculty of Philosophy, Laval University, Quebec. His main specializations are mathematical logic, ontology, and transcendental phenomenology. He has published numerous studies on Leibniz and Bolzano and on the philosophical problem of man and humanism in the contemporary world. His writings include *Les projets de Leibniz et de Balzano: deux sources de la logique contemporaine* (1973).

JOHN KING-FARLOW, born in London, England, on July 9, 1932, is professor of philosophy at the University of Alberta, Edmonton, Alberta, Canada. The author of articles in many areas of philosophy, he is particularly interested in metaphysics and the philosophy of language and religion. He is a published poet as well as a philosopher. Among his more recent philosophical books are *Reason and Religion* (1969); with William Niels Christenson, *Faith and the Life of Reason* (1972); editor of *The Challenge of Religion Today* (1976); and *Self-Knowledge and Social Relations* (1978).

CHARLES WEI-HSUN FU, born in Hsinchu, Taiwan, is professor of Buddhism and far eastern philosophy and religion in the Department of Religion, Temple University. He studied at National Taiwan University, University of Hawaii, University of California at Berkeley (on an East-West Center Fellowship), and University of Illinois. He taught at National Taiwan University, University of Illinois, and Ohio University. His publications include *A Critical History of Western Philosophy* (3rd ed., 1970). *Guide to Chinese Philosophy* (with Wing-tsit Chan, 1978), and articles in *Philosophy East and West, Journal of Chinese Philosophy, Inquiry,* and other journals and anthologies. His forthcoming books include *The Chinese Way* and *Fundamentals of Chinese Philosophy.*

EUGENIO GARIN, born in Rieti, Italy, on May 9, 1909, is a professor at the Scuola Normale Superiore in Pisa. He is a Doctor *Honoris Causa* of the University of Brussels, a corresponding fellow of the British Academy, a foreign member of the American Philosophical Society, the American Academy of Arts and Sciences, and the Polish Academy of Sciences, an honorary member of the .Institut International de Philosophie, and vice-president of the National Institute for Renaissance Studies. Since 1945, Professor Garin has been in charge of the Ancient and Medieval Philosophers and the Classics of Modern Philosophy series for the publishing house of Laterza. His many works include *Storia della filosofia italiana* 3 vols. (1966).

SELWYN A. GRAVE was born February 17, 1916, in Oamaru, New Zealand. He is professor of philosophy at the University of Western Australia. In addition to articles in professional journals, he is the author of *The Scottish Philosophy of Common Sense* (1960).

JUSTUS HARTNACK was born in Denmark on May 29, 1912, and received his formal education at Copenhagen University. He is Professor Emeritus at Aarhus University and the State University of New York College at Brockport. The author of numerous articles in philosophical journals, he wrote the article "Scandinavian Philosophy" as well as "Performative Utterances" for the *Encyclopedia of Philosophy* edited by Paul Edwards. Among the more recent of his many books are *Wittgenstein and Modern Philosophy* (1965); *Language and Philosophy* (1972); and *History of Philosophy* (1973).

JON HELLESNES, born in Norway in 1939 and educated in Bergen, is associate professor ("First Lektor") of philosophy at the University of Tromsø. He has published two books (in Norwegian)—*Self-knowledge and Other Minds* (1968) and *Socialization and Technocracy* (1975)—and a number of articles, mostly in Norwegian.

JAAKKO HINTIKKA (Kaarlo Jaakko Juhani Hintikka) was born in 1929 and educated in Finland and the United States. After a sojourn at Harvard as junior fellow (1956–1959), he served as professor of philosophy at the University of Helsinki in 1959–1970. Since 1965, he has also been connected with Stanford University. In 1970, he was appointed research professor at the Academy of Finland. He has held many offices in international, scientific, and scholarly organizations. In 1976, he received the Wihuri International Prize for his contribution to philosophical logic. Hintikka has authored eleven books and over one hundred papers in logic, the philosophy of language, epistemology, the philosophy of science, aesthetics, and the history of philosophy, especially Aristotle and Kant. He has co-authored one book and edited or co-edited eight volumes. In 1965–1976, he was editor-in-chief of the international journal *Synthese* (Dordrecht). Included among his more recent works are *The Intentions of Intentionality and Other New Models for Modalities* (1975) and *The Semantics of Questions and the Questions of Semantics* (1976).

TOMIO ICHIYANAGI was born in Yamagata-Shi in April 1929 and graduated from the Faculty of Literature, Tokyo University. His Master's thesis was on Nishida's philosophy compared with that of Kant. Tomio Ichiyanagi was professor of philosophy at Senshu University from April 1974 to 1978. During this time, he wrote major papers on Kant, Peirce, Dewey, and Russell in addition to Nishida, Watsuji, and others. His latest interests were in *die philosophische Anthropologie* and the theory of symbol. Professor Ichiyanagi died unexpectedly on December 3, 1978.

BIMAL K. MATILAL was born in Joynagar, India, on June 1, 1935, was educated at the University of Calcutta, and received his Ph.D. in Indian logic from Harvard University in 1965. He is currently Spalding Professor of Eastern Religions and Ethics, All Souls College, Oxford University, occupying the chair previously held by the late Professor R. C. Zaehner. Professor Matilal edits the *Journal of Indian Philosophy*. He has published numerous articles in professional journals, and his recent books include *Epistemology, Logic and Grammar in Indian Philosophical Analysis* (1971); *The Logical Illumination of Indian Mysticism. An Inaugural Lecture* (1977); and *The Central Philosophy of Jainism: Anekāntavāda* (1978).

EVANGHELOS MOUTSOPOULOS was born in Athens, Greece, on January 25, 1930. He studied at the University of Athens and received the D.Litt. from the University of Paris. He is now professor of philosophy at the University of Athens and has been rector since 1977. He is the editor of *Diotima* and *Corpus Philosophorum Graecorum Recentiorum*, and he has published many articles in professional journals. His more recent books include *Pleasures, A Phenomenological Study* (1977) and *Presocratic Thought* (1978).

ARNE NAESS is Professor Emeritus of philosophy, University of Oslo. He has lectured widely in the United States, particularly at the University of California at Berkeley. Professor Naess is the founding editor of *Inquiry*, a journal of philosophy and the social sciences. Along with Paul Hofseth, he is an editor of the series *Filosofiske Problemer*. In 1948–1949, he led the UNESCO investigation into democratic ideology, which resulted in his book *Democracy, Ideology and Objectivity* (1956). He has published many articles in philosophical journals. His numerous books include *Communication and Argument. Elements of Applied Semantics* (1966); *Gandhi and Group Conflict* (1974); and *Four Modern Philosophers. Carnap, Wittgenstein, Heidegger, Sartre* (1968).

SEYYED HOSSEIN NASR was born in Teheran in 1933. He received his early education in Teheran and then went to the United States where, upon completing his secondary education, he studied physics and mathematics at MIT. He received his Ph.D. in 1958 from Harvard in the history of science and philosophy. He is presently a member of the Supreme Council for Culture and the Arts and the National Council of Higher Education and was the chairman of the governing board of the Iran-Pakistan-Turkey (RCE) Cultural Institute. He has written twenty books and over two hundred articles in English, French, Persian, and Arabic. His works have been translated into several languages, including French, Italian, German, Yugoslav, Arabic, Turkish, Urdu, Bengali, and Japanese. Among his more recent books are *Islam and the Plight of Modern Man* (1975) and *Three Muslim Sages: Avicenna, Suhrawadī, Ibn 'Arabī* (1976).

CALVIN G. NORMORE was born June 25, 1948, in Corner Brook, Newfoundland, Canada. He was Killam Post-Doctoral Fellow at the University of Alberta and lecturer at York University. He is now assistant professor of philosophy at Princeton University. His more recent writings include a chapter entitled "Future Contingents" in *The Cambridge History of Later Medieval Philosophy* (1980); "Burley on Continuity" in *Continuity and Atomism in Antiquity and the Middle Ages* (forthcoming); and "The Limits of God's Power" in a special issue of *Paideia* devoted to the Middle Ages (forthcoming).

ANDREW J. RECK, born in 1927, is professor and chairman of the Department of Philosophy at Tulane University. Recently president of the Southern Society for Philosophy and Psychology, he is past president of the Southwestern Philosophical Society and of the Metaphysical Society of America. He is the author of nearly a hundred articles and numerous books. His more recent books include *Speculative Philosophy* (1972).

ROBERT B. ROSTHAL, born on October 16, 1923, is professor of philosophy at the University of North Carolina at Greensboro. His main research interests lie in the areas of contemporary European philosophy, philosophy of mind, and aesthetics. The author of numerous articles in philosophical journals, Professor Rosthal also is the translator of Garbriel Marcel's *Creative Fidelity* (1964).

HANS-MARTIN SASS, born in 1935, has been professor of philosophy at Ruhr-Universität Bochum since 1974, and he has served as general secretary and member of the board of the Allgemeine Gesellschaft für Philosophie in Deutschland since 1975. He was vice-president of the Sixteenth World Congress of Philosophy in 1978. His areas of specialization are Hegelianism, Marxism, existentialism, and the philosophy of technology. He is the author of fifteen books (including bibliographies and editions) and more than forty articles and fifty reviews in professional journals. His more recent publications include "Hegel's Concept of Dialectics" in *Proceedings of the 1976 Hegel Congress* (1978), "Bruno Bauer's Critical Theory" in the *Philosophical Forum* (1978), and *Ludwig Feuerbach* (1978).

KLEMENS SZANIAWSKI, born in Warsaw in 1925, is professor of logic at Warsaw University. His publications range from nondeductive forms of inference, decision theory, and the philosophy of science, to ethics. The major offices he has held include president of the Polish Philosophical Society and president of the Polish National Committee, International Union of History and Philosophy of Science. He is a member of the editorial board of *Synthese, Theory and Decision, Erkenntnis, Philosophy of Science, Studia Logica, Dialectics and Humanism*, and *Poznań Studies in the Philosophy of the Sciences and the Humanities*. He has co-edited *Formal Methods in the Methodology of the Empirical Sciences* (1977).

ALEXANDRU TĂNASE, born in Romania November 16, 1923, has held various academic positions. Since 1955, he has served as head of the research department of the Institute of Philosophy, Academy of the Socialist Republic of Romania. Since 1968, he has held the head chair of philosophy at Ciprian Porumbescu Conservatory, Bucharest. Professor Tănase is the author of numerous works, including

Culture and Religion (Romanian, 1973), *Culture. Civilization. Humanism* (French, 1974), and other publications on the problems of epistemology, sociology, the philosophy of values, the philosophy of culture and civilization, and the philosophy of history and art.

CORNELIS A. VAN PEURSEN was born at Rotterdam on July 8, 1920. He studied law and philosophy at the University of Leiden, with short study periods in Great Britain and Belgium. Since 1960 he has been professor of philosophy at the University of Leiden and since 1963 extraordinary professor in epistemology at the Free University at Amsterdam. He has given many guest lectures at universities abroad, including the United States, Great Britain, Belgium, South Africa, Indonesia, the Philippines, and Korea. His books have been translated into English, Spanish, German, French, Polish, and Indonesian. (Translations into Japanese and Korean are in preparation.) In addition, he has published some introductory works and some works in collaboration with other philosophers. Now in preparation in English are *Creative Capitulations; An Approach to Human Thought*; and *Sciences: Between Heuristics and Ethics*.

ANDERS WEDBERG was born in Stockholm in 1913. He was professor of theoretical philosophy at the University of Stockholm from 1949 to 1976. He has written *Plato's Philosophy of Mathematics* (English, 1955); and *A History of Philosophy*, 3 volumes (Swedish, 1958–1966).

ELAZAR WEINRYB, born in Jerusalem in 1937, has contributed to *Iyyun* (a Hebrew philosophical quarterly), *Inquiry*, and *History and Theory* on ethics, philosophy of history and philosophy of action. He is a lecturer at the Hebrew University, and he edits the philosophy section of the *Encyclopaedia Hebraica*.

About the Editor

JOHN R. BURR is Professor of Philosophy at the University of Wisconsin —Oshkosh. He coedited *Philosophy and Contemporary Issues* 3rd. rev. ed. (1980) and has contributed to scholarly journals.